FERGAL KEANE

Road of Bones

THE EPIC SIEGE OF KOHIMA

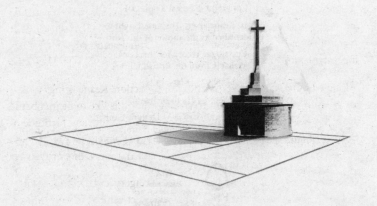

Harper
Press

Harper*Press*
An imprint of HarperCollins*Publishers*
1 London Bridge Street
London SE1 9GF
www.harpercollins.co.uk

HarperCollins*Publishers*
1st Floor, Watermarque Building, Ringsend Road
Dublin 4, Ireland

Visit our authors' blog: www.fifthestate.co.uk
Love this book? www.bookarmy.com

This HarperPress paperback edition published 2011

First published in Great Britain by Harper*Press* in 2010

Copyright © Fergal Keane 2010

Fergal Keane asserts the moral right to
be identified as the author of this work

A catalogue record for this book
is available from the British Library

ISBN 978-0-00-713241-6

Maps by Hugh Bicheno

Typeset in Minion by G&M Designs Limited,
Raunds, Northamptonshire
Printed and bound by CPI Group (UK) Ltd, Croydon, CR0 4YY

FERGAL KEANE was born in London and educated in Ireland. He is one of the [BBC's] most distinguished correspondents and an award-winning broadcaste[r] [and] author. He has reported for the BBC from Northern Ireland, Sou[th] Africa, Asia and the Balkans. He has been awarded a BAFTA, and [ha]s been named reporter of the year on television and radio, winni[n]g both honours from the Royal Television Society and the Sony Radio [A]wards, most recently for his BBC Radio 4 series *Taking a Stand*. Kean[e] has won the George Orwell Prize for literature and the James Came[r]on Prize. He is the author of a number of bestselling books, including *L[ett]er to Daniel* and his memoir, *All of These People*. He lives in London wit[h] his wife and two children.

From the r[ev]iews of *Road of Bones*:

'A brilliant [st]ory of human endeavour and suffering from both sides ... British inf[a]ntry performed a remarkable feat of arms, and Keane's masterly n[a]rrative does full justice to their achievement'

MAX HASTINGS

'A magnifi[c]ent and important book. Fergal Keane's strength is his ability to penetra[t]e the mentality of both sides in this extraordinary conflict. As a consequ[e]nce he has created a work of humanity, compassion and understan[d]ing out of one of the most terrible battles of the Second World War'

LAURENCE REES

'The strength of Keane's book is in the many human stories he has included, not just from the allied side but also the Japanese. While rightly deploring the atrocities carried out by the Japanese, Keane shows us that the men of Nippon all had human stories too ... Keane has produced a first-rate account of an epic of endurance on both sides that deserves a very wide audience ... Outstanding'   *Mail on Sunday*

'An epic story of the unfamiliar ... Vivid, compelling and terrifying. The evidence is meticulously gathered and the writing so powerful that it turns a book about a battle into a book about human beings, their existen[ce]   *Guardian*

05459749

'Humane, moving and brilliantly written, this is a classic of Second World War history. Fergal Keane's masterly new book shines light on one of the most savage and least remembered battles of that great conflict. The equal of Beevor's *Stalingrad* in scope and compassion, *Road of Bones* gives a terrifyingly intimate sense of what it feels like to fight a war, and a deeply compassionate account from all sides of a brutal conflict'
GENERAL SIR DAVID RICHARDS, *Chief of the General Staff*

'A profoundly tragic book by an eminent humanitarian [and] a passionate elegy for all battles, all empires and the very notion of war itself ... It is a noble book ... Its grandeur lies in its essential vision – decent, forgiving, pitying and always regretful'
The Times

'Along with his war correspondent's feel for action, Keane brings to task an eye for detail and a gift for describing what it is like to be in a battle at the lowest level ... the courage, motivation, training, and fortitude of ordinary men. *Road of Bones* captures this superlatively'
MAJOR GENERAL JULIAN THOMPSON, *Literary Review*

'The themes of *Road of Bones* are extreme savagery and extreme heroism in the last great stand of empire ... The perfect vehicle, in other words, for a man of Keane's empathic skills'
Daily Telegraph

'In his sweeping account of the Battle of Kohima in 1944, Fergal Keane does justice to the memory of the men who fell and who survived ... Keane's is a vivid account, which brings to life the brutality of that war'
Independent

By the same author

All of These People: A Memoir
Letter to Daniel: Despatches from the Heart
Season of Blood: Into the Heart of Rwanda
A Stranger's Eye: A Foreign Correspondent's View of Britain
Letters Home

In memory of John Shipster, soldier.

CONTENTS

LIST OF MAPS

LIST OF ILLUSTRATIONS

While every effort has been made to trace the owners of copyright material reproduced herein, the publishers would like to apologise for any omissions and will be pleased to incorporate missing acknowledgements in any future editions.

The Commanding Officer of the 1st Assam, Lieutenant Colonel
W.F. 'Bruno' Brown. *Taken from C. E. Lucas Phillips,* Springboard
to Victory *(Heinemann, London, 1966)*
Major Albert Calistan, 1st battalion Assam Regiment. *Taken from C. E.
Lucas Phillips,* Springboard to Victory *(Heinemann, London, 1966)*
John Young. *Courtesy of the former Hillhead High School Pupils
Organisation*
John Pennington Harman. *Courtesy of Diana Keast*
John Harman on Lundy Island before the war. *Courtesy of Diana Keast*
An artist's impression of the action for which Lance Corporal
Harman was awarded the Victoria Cross. *Courtesy of Diana
Keast/Painting by Charles Stadden*
Havildar Sohevu Angami. *Courtesy of the author/© Toby Sinclair*
Sepoy Wellington Massar. *Courtesy of the Council of the National
Army Museum, London. Taken from Captain Pieter Steyn,* A
History of the Assam Regiment *(Longman Orient, Calcutta, 1959)*
Ray Street. *Courtesy of Bob Street*
Lance Corporal Dennis Wykes. *Courtesy of Neil Hobday*
John Douglas Slim, 2nd Viscount Slim and son of the Field Marshal,
Bert Harwood and Dennis Wykes. *Courtesy of Kenneth Harwood*
Major Donald Easten. *Courtesy of Donald Easten*
Donald Easten with young officers of the Assam Regiment. *Courtesy
of Donald Easten*
Major John Shipster DSO. *Courtesy of the Shipster family*
Lieutenant General William 'Bill' Slim. *Imperial War Museum IND 3595*
Mountbatten with Slim (and General Oliver Leese). *Imperial War
Museum IND 4691*
Lieutenant General Montagu North Stopford. *Imperial War
Museum SEI 800A*
Major General John Grover. *Courtesy of The Kohima Museum,
Imphal Barracks*
Lieutenant General Renya Mutaguchi. *Taken from A. J. Barker,
March on Delhi (Faber, London, 1963)*
General Kotuku Sato with his wife Fumiko on the day of their
wedding. *Courtesy of Goro Sato*

General Sato between the wars. *Courtesy of Goro Sato*

General Sato with his officers before 31st Division crossed the
    Chindwin. *Courtesy of Goro Sato*

Lieutenant General Renya Mutaguchi salutes a British officer in
    Changi Jail. *Popperfoto/Getty Images*

General Sato with his family after the war. *Courtesy of Goro Sato*

The funeral of General Sato. *Courtesy of Goro Sato*

Lieutenant Masao Hirakubo. *Courtesy of Masao Hirakubo*

Masao Hirakubo after receiving his OBE for promoting
    reconciliation with British veterans. *Courtesy of Masao Hirakubo*

Lieutenant Takahide Kuwaki. *Courtesy of Takahide Kuwaki*

Dr Takahide Kuwaki in old age. *Courtesy of the author*

Lieutenant Hiroshi Yamagami. *Courtesy of Hiroshi Yamagami*

Hiroshi Yamagami at home in Tokyo in 2009. *Courtesy of the author*

The deputy commissioner's bungalow. *Taken from C. E. Lucas
    Phillips, Springboard to Victory (Heinemann, London, 1966)*

West Kent officers on Summerhouse Hill. *Unknown source. Courtesy
    of Bob Street*

The desolation of Garrison Hill. *Imperial War Museum IND 3698*

The terraces of the tennis court after the battle. *Imperial War
    Museum IND 3483*

The ruins of Kohima. *Unknown source. Courtesy of Bob Street*

Searching for the sniper. © *2004 Topfoto*

A Japanese soldier captured on the retreat is given tea and a
    cigarette by a Sikh soldier. © *Topfoto*

At a ceremony of remembrance on the Kohima tennis court.
    Courtesy of the author/© Toby Sinclair

The tennis court today. *Courtesy of the author/© Toby Sinclair*

We were soldiers once and young: Donald Easten at the memorial
    to the fallen in Kohima. *Courtesy of Donald Easten*

'The dreams of empire lure the hearts of kings – and so men die'

CORPORAL G. W. DRISCOLL,
BURMA, 1944

PROLOGUE

In the morning the general left his house after breakfast and walked into the country. He did this for two years. In the heat of summer the old soldier found the going harder. He sweated heavily and his bones hurt in the evenings. When the winter came he wore an old army greatcoat and walked along the ridges of the frozen rice paddies. He did not stop when the snows came and might amuse himself by trying to count the white geese in the fields. It was hard to tell where the snow ended and the birds began. The general was born here in Yamagata, among fishermen and farmers on the north-east coast of Japan. Here, in the town that lay between the mountains and the sea, he would atone for the great disaster. Every time a soldier's bones came home from the front he would set out on his travels. 'I will finish this before I die,' he told his son.

Kohima. It lived with him every day of his life. All of the men who had followed him lying in unmarked graves, lost along the mountain tracks, or drowned in the Chindwin river. At every house he bowed and introduced himself and having been invited in he would remove his shoes and sit with the family. Sometimes it would be a woman with young children, at other times a widow alone, or elderly parents. But all of them were linked to the general by the most immutable of bonds. He had taken their sons, husbands, fathers, over the mountains to India and they had not come back. At times they showed him photographs and letters. Many expressed surprise at his visit. The generals of the Imperial Japanese Army were not usually to be found calling on the homes of ordinary soldiers. The general carried a candle in his pocket and he would light this and read a poem for the dead. Its exact words have been lost with time, but he spoke of the soldiers' courage and how sorry he felt that they had lost their lives. His son, Goro, believed Lieutenant General Kotuku Sato wished he had died with them. 'I had the impression that he had very strong feelings of loss over what happened to his men on the battlefield,' he said. The general knew there were many officers who believed he should have killed himself. How could he live with the shame of such a defeat?

I listen to the story in Goro Sato's home in Ibaraki. He produces photo albums, a whole bundle of them, devoted to his father's memory. There are pictures of Kotuku Sato in cadet's uniform which date from the beginning of his career in the early 1920s. Later, in the 1930s, he is photographed standing next to Emperor Hirohito at a military exercise. There are images of the rising young officer dressed in furs and heavy boots on the Chinese border, and one of him relaxing in a kimono with a glass of sake and a broad smile on his face. There is one intriguing image. The general is dressed in a white linen suit, standing next to an American-made car. The photograph was taken outside a pagoda somewhere in South-East Asia. The general looks much older. There is a wariness in his expression that was not present in the earlier images.

'Where is that?' I ask.

'That is in Java, after he was relieved of his command,' Goro responds. He then tells me that a more senior general tried to have his father declared insane. He sent a medical team to Java to examine him. 'The rumour was that he was crazy. How else could they explain what he had done?' he says. But the doctors found that Sato was entirely sane. It is easy to see how his superiors might have thought him mad. A Japanese commander did not disobey orders to stand firm, he fought to the death. 'You must never forget that the men who survived loved him,' said Goro. 'They were only alive because of him.'

* * *

By the Japanese account nearly half of the 84,000 men of the 15th Army who marched into India were killed or died of starvation and disease. It was a disaster without parallel in the history of the Imperial Army. General Sato's 31st was one of three divisions of the 15th Army which crossed the Chindwin river in March 1944. Of his 15,000 strong force, almost half would never return, and those who did were emaciated fever-ridden ghosts. Yet Sato's march into India had started with victory. The 31st Division had annihilated every outpost in their way until they came to the small town of Kohima in the Naga Hills. Over two weeks of savage fighting they were held off by a British and Indian garrison which they outnumbered by ten to one.* The defenders were a mix of battle-hardened veterans and novices, thrown together in the last hours before the Japanese arrived. By the end, the defenders' perimeter was down to a circumference of just three hundred yards, into which the Japanese fired shell after shell, blasting the wounded as they lay in open pits. In the trenches men fought with guns, knives, spades, anything they could lay their hands on. A British infantryman, Mark Lambert of 4th battalion, Queen's Own Royal West Kent Regiment, recalled, 'We were being shot at and shooting, we were kicking, using our rifles as hammers, using the butts of our rifles if they got close. From both sides we were animals.' In one action a British subaltern sent his Indian troops to safety and faced the Japanese alone, a pile of grenades by his side and a gun in each hand. Another strangled a Japanese soldier, having woken next to him in a trench. Japanese officers charged with swords drawn into the teeth of British machine-gun fire.

Much of the fighting centred on a tennis court where men pitched grenades back and forth. Above all, the defenders were determined not to be taken alive by an enemy with a well-deserved reputation for cruelty. There were legion well-documented stories of prisoners being cruelly mutilated while still alive, or tied to trees for bayonet

---

* Sato's estimated strength of around 15,000 men in 31st Division was set against a garrison force of around 2,500. But of this number only 1,500 were fighting troops. (Japanese Monograph 134, p. 164. US Army Dept. of History.)

practice. 'They had murdered people in the dressing stations and we just thought they were animals. We thought they had forfeited their right to be treated as humans because they didn't behave like humans,' recalled Major John Winstanley of 4th battalion, the Royal West Kents.

Both sides fought and died among the rotting corpses of their comrades. For Sepoy Mukom Khiamniungan of the Assam Regiment the battlefield remains a haunted place to this day. 'I find Kohima appalling. By that I mean it's a place where airplanes and bombs had mixed flesh and earth. That's why I don't like staying there. I don't even have tea when I pass there.'

The defeat at Kohima precipitated the collapse of Japanese power in Burma and destroyed forever the Japanese soldier's belief in his invincibility. A song written by a survivor from the Japanese 58th Regiment described how their positions were bombed by allied aircraft:

> In the jungle, covered with green
> Afternoon showers of bombing
> Vegetation scattered, turning to empty field
> Not a bird song to be heard.

To the Japanese the retreat was 'the road of the bones'. Starving men begged their comrades to shoot them or blew themselves up with grenades. Lieutenant Yoshiteru Hirayama, a machine-gunner with 58th Regiment, saw dead soldiers lying along the river bank and others pleaded with him for scraps. 'Most were too weak even to do that,' he recalled, 'I didn't have food to give them.'

For the British it was a close affair. The defenders of Kohima and its smaller outposts bought vital time to bring in reinforcements. Even so it took another six weeks of bitter fighting for British and Indian troops to drive the Japanese from their well entrenched positions at Kohima. The story of the two week siege provides the core of this narrative not only because it describes an extraordinary struggle against great odds but because it offers a vivid portrait of a defining moment in the fortunes of two imperial powers. Both were in decline, and both desperately needed victory. It was the stand of the Kohima garrison which denied the Japanese a swift triumph and gave General William Slim's 14th Army the platform on which to launch his campaign to rout a battle hardened enemy. Kohima is a story of empires colliding in a world where high imperialism was already an anachronism, and where defeat might have profoundly altered the story of the end of the British Raj. The India that the men of 14th Army fought to defend was struggling to free itself from British control. As the battle of Kohima was taking place the country's main political leaders languished in colonial jails. Britain had brought India into the war without any reference to her people. The Viceroy, Lord Linlithgow, declared the war a fight for freedom and democracy, prompting the Congress leader Jawaharlal Nehru to ask, 'Whose freedom?' But Nehru also knew that the war represented the last stand of British rule in India, and that defeat by Japan could change the political dynamic in ways that neither he nor any other Indian leader could predict or be certain of controlling.

As for the Japanese, they had crossed into India proclaiming their desire to free the oppressed peoples of the Raj, yet they ruled over an empire brutalised by massacre and enslavement. They brought with them Indian rebels who, they hoped, would raise the population against the British, but were defeated by an army whose component parts reflected the greatest empire the world had ever seen. The battle was fought on the territory of a tribal people loyal to the Raj, but whose fate is one of the most haunting strands of this narrative.

There was a third power in this great struggle and its influence would be decisive. American aircraft would help ensure the survival and ultimate victory of the British and Indian forces, but beyond a shared desire to defeat Japan the war aims and strategies of the United States and Britain diverged sharply. President Roosevelt was determined that victory in the Far East would not lead to a reimposition of the colonial status quo. The influential American commentator Walter Lipmann wrote that 'there is a strong feeling that Britain east of Suez is quite different from Britain at home, that the war in Europe is a war of liberation and the war in Asia is for the defence of archaic privilege ... the Asiatic war has revived the profound anti-imperialism of the American tradition.' The American view was reflected in prolonged arguments over war strategy: Roosevelt believed the Burma campaign should be fought to aid his Chinese allies in the north and not as a battle of territorial redemption for the empire. The divisions over strategy were not a purely Anglo-American affair. The conduct of the campaign also produced the greatest rupture in Churchill's cabinet of the entire war, with the Chief of the Imperial General Staff (CIGS), General Sir Alan Brooke, and his colleagues threatening mass resignation over the prime minister's plans for ambitious, and logistically impossible, sea-borne operations. These high-level arguments form an insistent drum beat in the narrative of Kohima.

This book does not attempt to tell the story of every unit that fought at Kohima, nor does it describe in any detail the parallel battles fought ninety miles away at Imphal. The Imphal struggle, the adventures of Wingate's Chindits and General 'Vinegar Joe' Stilwell's Chinese divisions, and the interventions of Subhas Chandra Bose's rebel Indian National Army are discussed only as they relate directly to events at Kohima. In telling the story of the British 2nd Division, which led the ousting of the Japanese from Kohima in the second phase of the battle, I have concentrated my particular attention on the remorseless politics of war. The division's popular commander, Major General John Grover, was sacked from his job at the very moment of his triumph. A recommendation for a detailed account of the fighting exploits of the division is found at the end of chapter twenty-three.

In a story where epic courage and remorseless savagery are constant companions the narrative cannot avoid becoming, at least in part, a meditation on the nature of man. As a war correspondent of nearly thirty years' experience, and an ardent reader of history, I came to the story of Kohima believing I knew the extremes of human behaviour in war. But, for me, Kohima belonged in new territory entirely. It was not just the exceptional nature of the hand-to-hand fighting, but the other story that emerged, the long human aftermath of Kohima, an unlikely narrative of reconciliation between old enemies, but also of bitter enmity between men who once fought side by side, a story that reached its extraordinary denouement, in one case, at the funeral of a Japanese general.

I came to Kohima entirely by accident. Several years ago a good friend telephoned and asked if I would interview his father for a private memoir. 'We think he might open up more to somebody outside the family,' he said. Over several weekends I interviewed Colonel John Shipster at his son Michael's home in Hampshire. John had joined the Indian Army directly from public school at the age of eighteen and was commissioned into the Punjab Regiment. He arrived in Kohima after the siege but while the battle to retake the ridge from the Japanese was still at its height. At the outset I asked him what had been his proudest achievement of the war, a naive question in retrospect. 'My proudest achievement of the war?' he asked, a little bewildered. 'The fact that I survived it!' Only after he had detailed what had happened in the jungles and mountains could I say that I understood his answer. Towards the end of his life, memories of the war came back to haunt him, and he would frequently be woken by dreams of night fighting in the jungle.

This book is my account of the siege and relief of Kohima and is necessarily subject to one author's idea of what was compelling and significant. There may be those who disagree with my emphasis on this or that event, or my judgements of different characters, but I hope they will recognise in this work a sense of awe at what men endured on that forgotten Asian battlefield.

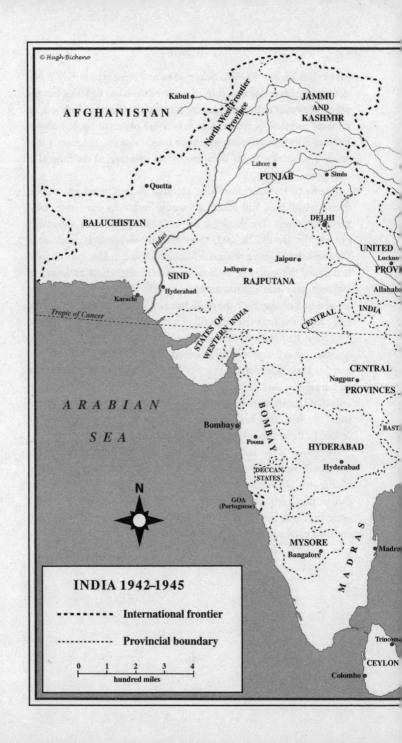

© Hugh Bicheno

AFGHANISTAN

Kabul

North-West Frontier Province

JAMMU AND KASHMIR

Quetta

BALUCHISTAN

Lahore

PUNJAB

Simla

DELHI

Indus

SIND

Hyderabad

Karachi

Tropic of Cancer

Jaipur

Jodhpur

RAJPUTANA

UNITED PROV

Luckno

Allahaba

CENTRAL INDIA

STATES OF WESTERN INDIA

CENTRAL

ARABIAN

SEA

BOMBAY

Bombay

Poona

DECCAN STATES

GOA (Portuguese)

N

CENTRAL PROVINCES

Nagpur

BAST

HYDERABAD

Hyderabad

MYSORE

Bangalore

M A D R A S

Madra

INDIA 1942–1945

- - - - - - - - International frontier

- - - - - - - - Provincial boundary

Trincoma

CEYLON

Colombo

0   1   2   3   4
hundred miles

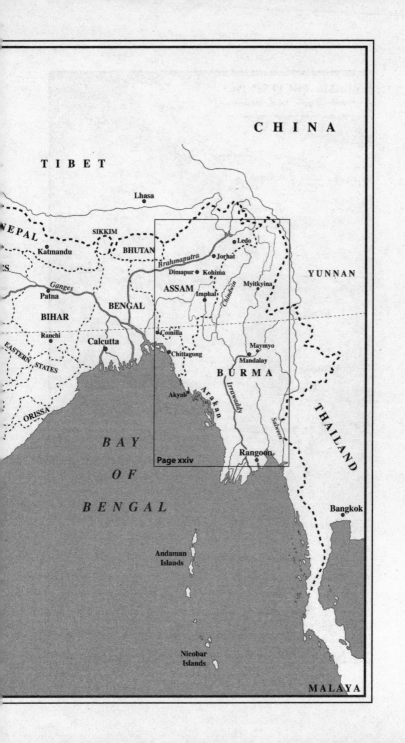

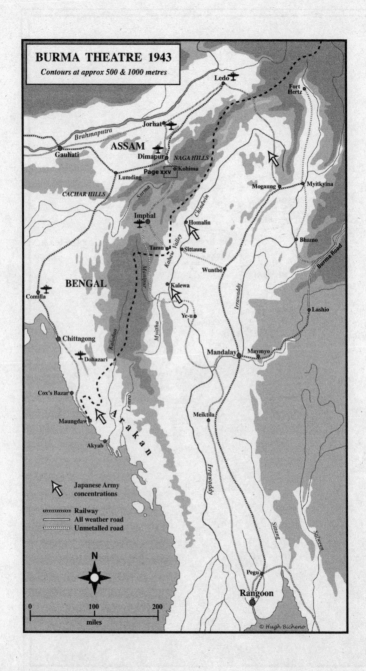

BURMA THEATRE 1943

Contours at approx 500 & 1000 metres

Brahmaputra

Ledo

Fort
Hertz

Jorhat

Gauhati

ASSAM

Dimapur

NAGA HILLS

Page xxv   Kohima

Lumding

Mogaung   Myitkyina

CACHAR HILLS

Surma

Imphal

Homalin

Chindwin

Bhamo

Tamu   Sittaung

Kabaw Valley

Wuntho

Burma Road

BENGAL

Kalewa

Irrawaddy

Comilla

Ye-u

Lashio

Myittha

Chittagong

Mandalay   Maymyo

Dohazari

Cox's Bazar

Kaladan

Lemro

Meiktila

Maungdaw

Arakan

Akyab

Irrawaddy

Japanese Army
concentrations

xxxxxx Railway
——— All weather road
········· Unmetalled road

Sittaung

Salween

N

Pegu

Rangoon

0   100   200
miles

© Hugh Bicheno

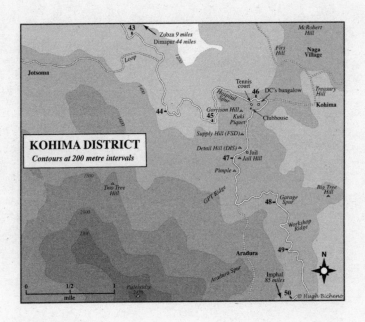

KOHIMA DISTRICT

Contours at 200 metre intervals

Zubza *9 miles*
Dimapur *44 miles*

43

Loop

1200

Jotsoma

1400

1600

McRobert
Hill

Firs
Hill

Naga
Village

Tennis
court

Hospital
Spur

Garrison Hill

Kuki
Piquet

46 DC's bungalow

Treasury
Hill

Kohima

Clubhouse

44

45

Supply Hill (FSD)

Detail Hill (DIS)

47 Jail
Jail Hill

Pimple

GPT Ridge

48 Garage
Spur

Big Tree
Hill

Workshop
Ridge

1800

Two Tree
Hill

2000

2200

Aradura

49

Aradura Spur

Imphal
85 miles

N

0   1/2   1
mile

Rifle Lodge
2321

50

© Hugh Bicheno

ONE

An Empire at Bay

Stepping inside from the breathless slump of the afternoon, Captain Thomas Pardoe found the grand lobby of the Strand Hotel a sanctuary of unimagined proportions. Gone, suddenly, the noise of the Burmese street, the call of the shoeshine boys and the rickshaw wallahs, and the air heavy with the smell of damp and river water. Rangoon in those days was a city aspiring to stature, made prosperous as the port through which Burma's vast rice crop was exported, but still only a minor eminence on the fringes of the eastern empire. Visitors from India found Rangoon lush with gardens that 'bloomed with tropical profusion – bougainvillea, poinsettas, laburnum and tall delphiniums of piercing blue. The Golden Mohur trees flamed like candles against the green foliage …' They might stop to admire the great pagodas of Sule and Shwedagon whose golden domes rose above the city, or enjoy a night at an English-language theatre and dinner at the Strand, before moving on to Singapore and Malaya or westward to India. With its high ceilings, roomy corridors and floors of teak, the Strand was built for an age before air conditioning. Its founders, the four Sarkies brothers, were Armenians who had emigrated to the Far East from Persia and established a chain of luxury hotels which included the Strand's more famous relation, Raffles Hotel in Singapore. The white-jacketed porters at the Strand would have taken Captain Pardoe's bags without fuss while he signed his name in the guests' register, a book that had in times past recorded the signatures of Somerset Maugham, Rudyard Kipling and the future king of England, Edward VIII, who had stopped there in

1922 while on a royal tour with his cousin, 'Dickie' Mountbatten. On that occasion a sumptuous barge, decorated with the Burmese symbol of royalty, four golden peacocks' heads, and topped by three model pagodas, was provided for the prince. Oarsmen in long, flowing robes steered the royal barge while the future king relaxed in the pavilion, sheltered from prying eyes by shimmering white curtains which billowed gently as the boat moved across the royal lake near the centre of the city. Later on his journey the prince played polo at Mandalay, the former home of the Burmese kings, and 'was entertained by dancing girls at a lavish reception'.

The city encountered by Captain Pardoe nearly twenty years later had grown outwards to accommodate the Indian migrant labourers working in the city's docks and factories. Daily they unloaded tons of supplies destined for the Chinese Nationalist armies fighting the Japanese across the border far to the north. A correspondent for the *Manchester Guardian* reported on 2 February 1942 that 5,000 lorries carrying 30,000 tons were using the 712 mile route every day.* As Pardoe settled into his airy room at the Strand he must have relished the prospect of some time, no matter how brief, in Rangoon, an altogether different prospect from the central Chinese city of Chungking to which he was normally confined. That overcrowded, filthy city served as the temporary capital of Generalissimo Chiang Kai-shek's Nationalist government. As a liaison officer to the Chinese military headquarters, Pardoe was obliged to live there among hundreds of thousands of refugees, soldiers and a vast assortment of carpetbaggers and chancers. The American newspaper correspondent Theodore White described the streets as 'full of squealing pigs, bawling babies, yelling men and the singsong chant of coolies carrying loads from up the river'. The generalissimo's court was riven by relentless intrigue, spurred by the insatiable ambition of Chiang's relatives to enrich themselves and by regional warlords who pleaded and menaced for favour.

---

* *Manchester Guardian*, 2 February 1942. Up to quarter of a million Chinese worked to build the road between 1937 and 1938, an epic feat of engineering and labour.

Pardoe arrived in Rangoon on 8 February 1941, but was given just a day to refresh himself before embarking on a mission to tour the country's borders with Thailand and China. It was to be a journey by road, rail, boat and air, to investigate the local defences and to coordinate possible future action with the Chinese. Pardoe met up with a Chinese military delegation a week into his tour at the town of Kyukok on the border of the Chinese province of Yunnan. With an air suggesting a weary familiarity with the ways of his allies, he noted that while the visit was 'supposed to have been strictly confidential, I am told its formation and proposed tour had already been announced over the TOKYO wireless'. Chiang's court was riddled with informers.

At this time, February 1941, the Japanese had not yet occupied Thailand, although there were numerous reports of fifth-column activities. Pardoe recorded the activities of suspected spies and Japanese attempts to subvert the local population in Burma.

At Lilem, on the border with Thailand, he reported a rumour that eight hundred Japanese wearing Thai uniforms had been spotted just across the frontier; while a postmaster at Tachilek, who was being paid ten rupees a month to spy for the British, gave news that as many as 5,000 Japanese had arrived in Bangkok. The information seems to have been exaggerated, possibly by a spy anxious to please his paymasters. Further north, Pardoe worried over the role of Italian priests in the Shan states bordering China, whose influence 'over some of their Asiatic converts is so strong, fifth column activities would be a possibility'. At Maungmagan on the Tenasserim coast he heard suspicions about a Mrs Leal, the Austrian wife of an Irish tin-mine owner. 'She also owns a mine in the Thai frontier area. She set off to visit this mine in early April, taking with her a portable wireless set. Up till the war she was admittedly strongly pro-Nazi. I saw a copy of her dossier … She is being watched. Mr Ruddy [Burma Auxiliary Force], who has known her a long time, considers she is either extremely clever or else entirely innocent.' Some official reader of this document in Rangoon has scribbled the words 'A remarkable statement!' next to this assessment of the curious Mrs Leal.

Another foreigner to arouse suspicion was a Mr G. R. Powell of the Watchtower Society of Australia. This representative of the Jehovah's Witnesses was placed under surveillance by the Burma police in a classic case of mistaken priorities. Mr Powell represented a religious faith that customarily excited the suspicion of colonial officials, yet the Jehovah's Witnesses were among the groups enthusiastically persecuted by Hitler's Reich and would have offered little threat to the security of Burma.*

The captain made detailed notes on roads and beaches that would make suitable invasion points. But for all the impressive detail on local military dispositions and possible enemy spies, Pardoe's report did not contain a single line about possible evacuation routes for a retreating army or for tens of thousands of refugees. In those becalmed days before Japan entered the war, he could hardly have foreseen such a necessity. At the end of the report an unnamed intelligence officer wrote, 'A very good report – may be very useful if fighting breaks out in Burma'. If – the conditional that masked a vast failure of intelligence, planning and, perhaps above all, imagination. The defence of Burma was left to a small garrison consisting of two British battalions and the eight battalions of local troops and military police that comprised the Burma Rifles and the Burma Frontier Force, as well as the part-timers of the Burma Auxiliary Force, all dispersed throughout the country's three military regions – upper, middle and lower Burma. It was a force useful for colonial missions of chastisement but utterly unfit for defending a country larger than France against invasion by a modern army supported by armour and aircraft.

From Churchill and the Chiefs of Staff in London to the GOC Burma, Major General D. K. McLeod, and the Governor, Sir Reginald Dorman Smith, nobody had allocated the resources needed to defend Burma against an invasion from Thailand. They simply had not visualised Japan occupying Thailand and then sweeping Britain aside. Forget the evidence of Japan's victory over the Russians four decades before, the abundant intelligence on Tokyo's new ships,

---

* The Jehovah's Witnesses' opposition to conscription may have been a factor.

aircraft and artillery, or the defeats inflicted on the Chinese over the past decade. The Japanese were still little yellow men, myopic and bandy-legged, and could never pose a mortal threat to the greatest empire the world had ever seen. As Corporal Fred Millem of the Burma Auxiliary Force, the local equivalent of the Territorial Army, ruefully put it after the disaster: 'China had exhausted Japan – she could not last more than three months. Japan's air force was no good, her pilots all had bad eyesight and could not fly by night … Etc, etc, etc, oh yeah, oh yeah, oh yeah!' When war came, the Japanese 15th Army would deploy four divisions against one and a half divisions of British, Burmese and Indians.

The overall responsibility for the defence of Burma was given to the Commander-in-Chief Far East, Air Chief Marshal Sir Robert Brooke-Popham, who spent a year pleading in vain for more resources. Four days before Pearl Harbor, the prime minister described the threat of Japanese action as a 'remote contingency'. Fighting alone in the years before America joined the war, he had understandably avoided confrontation with the Japanese. At one point the great enemy of appeasement was forced to kowtow in the face of Japanese insistence that he close the Burma Road, along which America shipped its war materiel north from Rangoon to the Chinese Nationalists. Shutting this lifeline would strangle the Chinese war effort and allow Japan to redeploy thousands of troops for use against America in the event of war. The closure of the road in July 1940 amounted, according to the old Burma hand George Orwell, to 'a semi-surrender to Japan'. From July to October 1940 Churchill closed the road, until American pressure forced him to change his mind. However limited Churchill's choices, the episode should have illustrated to the British just how much Burma mattered to the Japanese.

It is not known what ultimately happened to the report submitted by Captain Pardoe. It was certainly seen by the intelligence department in Rangoon, but whether it went higher than that we will never know. As for Pardoe, he would not survive the war. He was killed eight months later, fighting the Japanese in Hong Kong.

* * *

For Emile Charles Foucar, barrister-at-law, Saturday, 6 December 1941, was one of the most important days in the social calendar. He was not alone in waking with great excitement. That afternoon the finest ponies in Burma would race for the Governor's Cup at the Rangoon Turf Club. It was an event that would draw virtually the entire European population and, as the only club that allowed non-white members, it would also attract Burmese and Indians of good social standing. Sadly for Foucar, he would be without his wife Mollie. She and the couple's two children, a boy and a girl, had been shipped to England as a precautionary measure a few weeks before. Official Burma might play down the danger of invasion, but to Foucar the evacuation made good sense in view of the threatening noises coming from Japan. Emile Foucar was, above all, a man of common sense. He had been born in Burma, the son of a businessman who had come out from Britain in the late nineteenth century, a man swept eastward by the imperial dream at the very moment it was approaching its zenith. In the language of the colonial guidebooks, the Burma he found was wreathed in the exotic: 'Should Burma be visited after a tour in India, the traveller cannot fail to be struck with the great difference in the people and the scenery of the two countries. The merry, indolent, brightly-clothed Burmese have no counterpart in Hindustan, and the richness of the soil and exuberance of the vegetation will be at once remarked.'

Emile Foucar's father and uncle began a timber business, exporting Burmese teak all over the world from their mills in the coastal city of Moulmein. Here Foucar senior did his patriotic duty by joining the Moulmein Volunteer Artillery. Like most of the white community, he sent his son Emile to England to be educated. There the young Foucar left school just in time to fight as an officer in Flanders. After the war he studied law in London but, finding the pickings slim, decided to return home and set up in practice in the country of his birth. Foucar gathered a substantial clientele from across the country's racial mix. He could find himself representing a monk demanding the right to succeed to a monastery, investigating an insurance fraud by Chinese businessmen, or acting as counsel for a British plantation owner involved in a legal wrangle with the government.

When Emile Foucar arrived at the races on that humid December day he heard the band of 1st battalion, Gloucestershire Regiment (the 1st Glosters), playing and saw green lawns 'ablaze with flowers and brilliant costumes'. The Governor, Sir Reginald Dorman Smith, made a grand entrance, driven down the course to the members' enclosure, acknowledging the applause of the crowd with a gracious wave. It was, Foucar remembered, a golden afternoon.

He moved easily among the crowds, European and Asian, nodding to clients as he went. As an observer of his own society Foucar was sharp-witted and fair-minded, pushing at the limitations of his age and background. In a memoir published a decade after the war, he recalled how the Burmese were systematically excluded from British, and therefore influential, social circles, denied control over their country's resources, and encouraged in subservience and servility. They were barred from European strongholds such as the Pegu Club and the Rangoon Gymkhana Club, where much of the real business of money and politics was conducted. On the trains European passengers like Foucar's friend Bellows could make a scene if asked to share a carriage with a non-white. Bellows, who had been forty years in Burma, 'insisted to the stationmaster that his fellow traveller be removed … so the merchant was put elsewhere'. Foucar also had an eye for the hypocrisies of late imperial life. It was well known, he wrote, that Bellows had a Burmese wife.

On the journey back east from England after the First World War, Foucar heard his travelling companions agree that the old days were gone. 'Things aren't what they were,' an anonymous passenger told him. 'The young Burman considers himself as good as his master.' But this was still the colonial Burma of George Orwell's *Burmese Days*, torpid, self-satisfied, a haven for mediocrities who would have struggled in a more dynamic or egalitarian setting. Although Burmese politicians sat in a legislative assembly and there was a Burmese prime minister, real power remained in the hands of the Governor, who controlled foreign affairs and security.

The C-in-C Far East, Sir Robert Brooke-Popham, offered an acerbic view of the colonial Englishman in Burma, all the more surprising because Brooke-Popham had been a stout defender of the rights of white settlers in Kenya when he was Governor there in the late 1930s. There was, he wrote, 'a tendency among Englishmen to regard themselves as naturally superior in every way to any coloured race, without taking steps to ensure that this is always a fact … a failure to develop a sympathetic understanding with the Burmese … the majority of non-official Englishmen in Burma were more concerned making money and getting high dividends from their investments than of benefiting the native population.'

At the start of the 1930s an uprising led by the rustic monk and necromancer, Saya San, shook British rule. But it was the Indian minority rather than the British who suffered most. A colonial report noted that the Indians had 'driven the more apathetic Burman out of the more profitable means of employment'. When violence erupted the Indians were the first to be attacked. A prominent nationalist leader denounced them as 'birds of passage who have come to this land to exploit by fair means or foul in the fields of labour, industry or commerce'. Despite superior British firepower it took eighteen months to subdue a revolt that shook the British and inspired young nationalists to escalate their agitation against colonial rule. As Emile Foucar noted, 'The indications were plain to those who would read them; yet when manifested amongst students and the educated classes they were brushed aside as the complaints of disappointed office-seekers envious of the white man. This attitude of self-complacency was comforting to those of us who saw a long continuance of British domination.'

At the same time, Burmese intellectuals were absorbing ideas and theories spreading from Britain. One Rangoon writer observed that 'in the 1930s, so many of our students read the books which came out to us from Victor Gollancz's Left Book Club in London. The ideas of Marx reached Burma not from Russia but by way of England.' The generation of urban Burmese that came of age in the 1930s was educated and politically aware, and some of its leading figures were already in contact with the intelligence officers of a new imperial force.

The Japanese dressed their intervention in the clothes of Asian brotherhood. By the late 1930s Japanese spies were busy recruiting agents and attempting to create a pro-Tokyo army which would act as a fifth column on the outbreak of war. Several of the nationalist leaders went to Japan for military training, among them Aung San, the father of future pro-democracy leader Aung San Suu Kyi. This was the simmering Burma that lay beyond the European clubs and garden parties of Rangoon on the eve of war with Japan, and which thousands of British, Indian and Burmese troops would be asked to give their lives to defend.

The weekend of the Governor's Cup race meeting in December 1941 was the last great gala of imperial Burma, although few, if any, of those who were there would have sensed the imminence of its demise. The dancers who packed into the ballroom of the Strand Hotel on race night were confident that Britannia still ruled the East and would continue to do so for a long time to come. For Emile Foucar the highlight of the evening was when a 'stout lady, popular with local audiences … sang a comic song, concluding it by throwing up her skirt to show us the seat of her panties emblazoned with the Union Jack. How we cheered!' The only irritant was the absence of fresh air, brought about by a practice blackout ordered by the military authorities. Not that most people in that cheery crowd believed a blackout was necessary. As the racegoers made their way home in the muggy early hours, the Japanese seemed a very long way away.

Twenty-four hours later, on 8 December 1941, Emile Foucar woke up to the news of the Japanese attack on the Americans at Pearl Harbor and the landings in Malaya, some five hundred kilometres from Burma. More worrying still, Japanese troops were also moving into Thailand. An agreement had been reached with the Thai government to allow Japanese forces free passage to the Burmese border. There was fierce fighting with some Thai troops, unaware of the agreement, who opposed the Japanese landings in the south. Yet Rangoon was quiet that morning. To Corporal Fred Millem the news came as a relief. Rumours of war had been incessant. 'The suspense had been snapped and we knew where we stood. To me it was no surprise ... when it came we were almost joyful, for it seemed certain suicide for Japan – her last desperate throw ... Singapore, utterly and completely impregnable, still stood between the Japs and Burma.'

Emile Foucar immediately joined up to do his bit for the defence of the empire. As a former officer he was given the temporary rank of lieutenant colonel, working on intelligence and propaganda. On 10 December he went into the radio room at headquarters and found an operator anxiously trying to restore a connection. The man had heard something about the ships HMS *Prince of Wales* and HMS *Repulse*, which had been dispatched east the previous autumn to deter the Japanese, but he could gather no details apart from the fact that the voice on the wireless was referring to them in the past tense. It was only the following day that Foucar learned that more than eight hundred men had been killed, and British naval power humbled, when Japanese bombers sank the ships off the coast of Malaya.

By the middle of December a Japanese force had crossed from Thailand and seized the strategically important Victoria Point airfield, vital to the RAF if it was to bring in reinforcements. Two days before Christmas 1941,with Hong Kong about to fall and Singapore threatened, Foucar was entering his office when somebody shouted out to look in the direction of Mingaladon airfield, to the north of the city. He saw bombers approaching, flying in a V-shaped formation – twenty-seven of them, pursued by a few British fighters.

The streets of Rangoon filled with crowds who cheered and clapped when they saw a bomber burst into flames and fall from the sky. But then the explosions began and thick smoke floated up from the centre of the city and the docks area. Shocked silence followed and then the sounds of terror, the screams of the dying and the noise of hundreds of feet stampeding along narrow streets. When the dead were counted there were more than 1,600 bodies, while many more were badly wounded.* The city began to empty.

Seventeen-year-old Donald Mellican was manning a Burma Auxiliary Force anti-aircraft position at Mingaladon airfield when it was attacked. Not a man among his crew knew the feeling of utter vulnerability that comes with being caught in the open by air attack, the sense of being like an insect racing for protection as giant boots come down to crush it, nor did they know the blinding panic of the sudden arrival of shells. A man under shellfire for the first time learns the ruthless capriciousness of shrapnel, how the tiniest sliver of scorching metal can bring death, and will come to dread the extravagant mutilations of flesh caused by close proximity to the shock waves of a blast. Mellican's only experience of violence up until then had been the canings meted out at his school in Moulmein when boys were caught whistling at the girls playing hockey in the neighbouring academy. When the alarm was sounded at the airfield he assumed it was an exercise. Then, as the silver shapes in the sky came closer, he heard an officer shout to him to take cover. Bombs began to fall. After a few minutes of confusion Mellican climbed on to the anti-aircraft gun to shouts of 'Traverse right' and 'Traverse left', followed by 'Fire!'. His fear left him as he blasted at the Japanese.

The drama lasted for an hour and when the Japanese had gone Mellican looked around at a scene of carnage. There were fires and delayed explosions. Wounded men were crying out for help. One Bofors gun had taken a direct hit. Mellican was called out later that night to help remove the dead. 'The bodies were mangled, heads, limbs sprawled all over, and even the gun was splashed with flesh and brains sticking on metal.' They were all boys Mellican had known. An officer ordered that nobody was to leave until the mess had been cleaned up.

'We made makeshift stretchers from bits of wood, e.g. damaged furniture and doors. "Have you got an arm or a leg?" calls were made and eventually we had six figures ready. I recognised only two of

---

* The final death toll from the first day of Japanese bombing was more than 2,000.

them, "F. B." and "J. K."' Both were boys Mellican had known from his schooldays. As he helped carry a stretcher away it became tangled in a hedge. When he looked back he saw that the intestines of the dead boy had caught in the hedge and unravelled. With his hands he freed the spilling guts and placed them gently back under the blanket. That night he slept in a bunkhouse that was quiet with the shock of war.

The crisis was compounded by problems of command at every level. Brooke-Popham, the C-in-C Far East, whose responsibilities included Malaya, Singapore and Burma, succumbed to the pressure of events and was replaced. In late December a new commander, General Sir Archibald Wavell, was sent to establish the short-lived ABDACOM,* a unified allied command based in Java, which was described by the Chief of the Imperial General Staff (CIGS), General Sir Alan Brooke, as a 'wild and half-baked' scheme. In the space of a few months, responsibility for operations in Burma shifted first to India, then to ABDACOM, and finally back to India. In Rangoon there was similar confusion. The GOC Burma, Lieutenant General D. K. McLeod, who had spent much of his life as a staff officer, was replaced on 27 December by Lieutenant General T. J. Hutton, who was himself sacked two months later. An Associated Press report from London had welcomed Hutton's appointment and spoke of how 'much has been done to strengthen the land forces which Lt. Gen. Hutton now takes over'. It was the propaganda of illusion, as the defenders would soon discover.

The Japanese launched their ground offensive from Thailand on 8 January. They sent two divisions against one and half British and Indian divisions.† But it was the quality of troops and command, not the numbers, that really mattered. When General Hutton failed to

* Wavell took over the American-British-Dutch-Australian Command (ABDACOM) on 30 December 1941. It was disbanded a week after the fall of Singapore.

† This would later increase to four divisions against two British and Indian divisions and eight, inferior, Chinese divisions based in the north.

stem the advance he was replaced, on 5 March, by General Harold Alexander, a favourite of Churchill's, who acknowledged that never had he 'taken the responsibility of sending a general on a more forlorn hope'.

The official verdict on the failure to protect Burma would not emerge for another decade. But the conclusion was damning: 'The effect that the loss of Rangoon would have on the British war effort was well known to the War Cabinet, the Chiefs of Staff and to all commanders in the Far East ... Yet, despite the breathing space of six weeks between the outbreak of war and the start of the Japanese drive into southern Burma, no adequate steps were taken to build up the forces required ... Burma still remained practically defenceless.'

An Irish engineer, Professor W. H. Prendergast, working for the Indian Railways, was sent to Rangoon to see what help was needed by his counterparts on the Burma Railways, who were struggling to keep their locomotives running. 'In the streets of this great thriving city nothing was to be seen but the scurrying jeeps, the criminals, the looters and the insane. No one was left except a small band of "Last Ditchers" and garrison troops who had volunteered to remain until the end.' British troops and police shot looters. 'Others, both soldiers and civilians, were punished by caning.' The official history of the Indian Army described how 'the deserted city and oil refineries and shattered storage tanks along the river presented an awe-inspiring spectacle as huge columns of flame leapt skyward beneath a vast canopy of smoke.'

Prendergast witnessed the last train departing Rangoon steaming slowly away and noted how 'behind it pathetically followed, the spaniels, the Airedales, the terriers, all the big and little pets with their appealing eyes saying "Surely you cannot abandon US".' He travelled from one bombed station to another, helping with repair work. One morning he found the bodies of eighteen people who had died from cholera during the night. The American war correspondent Clare Boothe described the destruction by fire of part of the ancient royal capital of Mandalay in a dispatch for *Life* magazine. 'It was to me a smell not unfamiliar. I remember, one hot summer, when I was a child, a dog died under our veranda porch … It was that smell. But a thousand times magnified until it seemed, as we whirled through the streets, all creation stank of rotting flesh … Here and there on the side of the streets lay a charred and blackened form swaddled in bloody rags, all its human lineaments grotesquely foreshortened by that terrible etcher – fire.'

Japanese air raids on the cities drove people into the countryside. Gripped by panic, the large Indian population of Burma, many of them labourers who worked in the mines or in the fields, headed towards the border with India. Some of the wealthier and more influential sought a passage by air or boat, but with limited space, and with priority given to whites, money was no guarantee of a seat. Nor was it always safe to attempt escape by air, as the Japanese enjoyed command of the skies. For the majority who set out on foot the journey meant navigating a mixture of terrain that exhausted even the strongest among them. The route north to safety lay over nine hundred miles of jungle, scrub, swamps and high mountain passes. It meant trying to ford raging rivers and struggling to gain a footing on liquid mud paths over mountains that rose to more than 8,000 feet.

The refugee columns were shadowed by flocks of vultures. The carrion-feeders settled in the trees over temporary camps or waited on the fringes of small groups whose members were too exhausted to move any further. It is the sound, rather than the sight, of vultures feasting that stays in the mind, an obscene cracking and tearing, which rose from countless roadside encampments on the retreat. There were anguished scenes as the elderly, so often the first to fall sick, urged younger family members to go on without them. A British eyewitness recalled seeing children with 'distended bellies supported on sticks of legs, and all of them moved slowly, dragging along with expressionless faces, eyes on the ground and bodies wasted to the bone'. Of the more than half a million people who fled across the border to India over five months of the retreat, an estimated 80,000 died from a catalogue of diseases – cholera, dysentery, scrub typhus and malaria – and from the effects of malnutrition and exhaustion.* The dead lay all along the routes towards India. A British army officer carrying out a reconnaissance of the route north described a clearing where a band of refugees had expired: 'I found the bodies of a mother and child locked in each other's arms. In another hut were the remains of another mother who had died in childbirth, with the child only half born … A soldier had expired wearing his side cap, all his cotton clothing had rotted away, but the woollen cap sat smartly on the grinning skull. Already the ever destroying jungle had overgrown some of the older huts, covering up the skeletons and reducing them to dust or mould.' The Scotsman, George Rodger, who would become a famous war cameraman, encountered a constant stream of fleeing people and was struck by 'the incongruity of the items they had chosen to salvage from their homes … One man carried a cross-cut saw over his shoulder, another lugged along a large tom-tom, several had umbrellas, and one carried a bicycle with the back wheel missing …'

Most reports suggest the Japanese did not attack refugees. But they were preyed upon by Burmese dacoits and frequently attacked by villagers resentful of the Indian presence in Burma. As is so often the way when war causes a vacuum in authority, the meanest elements of society emerged to terrorise, pillage and resurrect old hatreds. The Burmans also attacked minorities like the Karen and the Chin, both of which had remained largely loyal to the British.

Troops frequently encountered the bodies of Indian families butchered by the Burmans. A British officer, Captain James Lunt, remembered seeing a beautiful Indian woman 'striding along like a Rajput princess, her child clasped to her left hip … her pleated dark red skirt swinging like a kilt at every stride. Bangles at her wrists and ankles tinkled as she passed, her kohl-rimmed eyes meeting mine for a brief moment.' He would see her again. One evening he was driving past a line of refugees and noticed corpses by the roadside. 'A

---

* Estimates vary between 10,000 and 100,000. The figure of 80,000 is regarded as being the most accurate. See Christopher Bailey and Tim Harper, *Forgotten Armies: The Fall of British Asia, 1941–45* (Penguin/Allen Lane, 2004), p. 167.

bright red skirt caught my eye and we stopped the jeep. She lay there, her long black hair streaming out into a pool of fast-congealing blood, her throat cut from ear to ear ... the bright red skirt had been pulled up above her waist in a final obscene gesture. The child, a little way apart, lay with its brains spilling on to the tarmac.'

The teenager Donald Mellican, of the Burma Auxilliary Force, was manning a barricade outside Rangoon when he saw the Governor come past with his entourage en route to an airfield in the north of the country. The most senior British official in Burma urged the troops to fight on, but left too quickly to hear the men shout curses after him. Governor Dorman Smith had been given strict orders by Churchill to get out of Burma before he could be captured by the Japanese. Mellican trudged out of Burma in a long procession of soldiers and civilians, keeping despair at bay by reciting times tables and nursery rhymes. At one point he saw an Indian woman and two small children standing by a steep drop on a hairpin bend. 'Before the next bend I turned to look back and only two children were to be seen.'

Mellican reached India after walking for three weeks. Only later would he find out that his mother and five siblings had died crossing the Hukwang Valley. One of them, Patrick, suffered an infected toe which quickly swarmed with maggots. They soon covered his entire body, 'which made him go off his head before he died'. His father and his youngest brother, Reggie, struggled on until they met a Gurkha family. By this time the father was too weak to care for the child. Leaving him with the Gurkhas, he trudged on towards India, where he died soon after arriving.

An American missionary doctor retreating with refugees and Chinese troops recorded the primitive conditions in which he had to operate. 'No sooner had we finished lunch than the Friends brought in another thirty-five patients,' wrote Dr Gordon Seagrave. 'One of them had his enlarged spleen shattered by a shell fragment. Insects were so numerous that they kept dropping into the wounds of the abdominal cases ... We have been burning up the bloody remnants of clothes we have had to cut off our patients and cleaning up the grounds ... My, what a stink!'

The locally recruited forces deserted the British in droves. According to one official estimate, by the end of the retreat only just over 6,000 remained out of a pre-war total of 20,000. Most were probably driven by the understandable desire to get back to their villages to protect their families, unwilling to risk a long exile in alien India or death for a cause they did not believe in. Some were also subject to political pressure from nationalists. Desertions among Indian troops in the Burmese army were prompted less by political considerations than by a desire to join their families who were fleeing the country.

The families of British officers in Burma joined the exodus. In most cases their men had already been called to duty. Mollie Birch set off with her two-and-a-half-year-old daughter for India a few weeks after her husband was sent into action. She passed from train to refugee camp and then on again before arriving at the Chittagong Social Golf Club in Bengal on the evening of its annual dinner-dance. 'They had heard evacuees were expected, had arranged for us to be taken to the club and to be given their dinner. As soon as we appeared the music stopped and everyone looked our way, we must have looked a very sorry sight, talk about chalk and cheese, here we were about thirty, dirty, smelly women and children – they were immaculate.'

Captain James Lunt, a Staff Officer with 2 Burma Brigade, was astonished by the behaviour of some of the British civilians he met along the route. 'One man, a civilian whom I had known in happier times, sat down on my stretcher weeping copiously as he estimated his chances of obtaining some priority for the air trip to India. Another, a woman whom I had met in Mandalay, beseeched me to take her fur coat with me. She was wearing it at the time. Since I could barely stand, let alone walk, a fur coat was the last thing I wanted to be encumbered with.'

With the fall of Malaya and Singapore in the preceding months, the loss of Burma in May 1942 completed the trampling of imperial prestige. Emboldened by the Japanese successes Burmese nationalists lit large fires close to British positions to help guide Japanese bombers, while small groups of British troops had to be wary of attack from guerrillas. Across the newly taken Japanese possessions the first phase was underway in one of history's epic movements: in Malaya and Burma, across French Indochina and the Dutch East Indies, putative nation states, rival political groups, competing ideologies and numerous ethnic minorities, would emerge to stake their claims to power. Writing as the retreat north was gathering pace and a fortnight before he became deputy Prime Minister the Labour Party leader, Clement Attlee, put the matter succinctly. What was taking place was a continuation of European decline in Asia that had begun with the defeat of Russia by Japan in 1905. 'The hitherto axiomatic acceptance of the innate superiority of the European over the Asiatic sustained a severe blow. The balance of prestige, always so important in the East, changed. The reverses which we and the Americans are sustaining from the Japanese at the present time will continue this process.'

Many were nervous of Japanese intentions. Sometimes they were the victims of savage Japanese repression. In Burma looters were shot on sight and their bodies publicly displayed as a warning. Drunks were tied up at traffic islands and made to stand for twenty-four hours without food or water. Ramesh S. Benegal, an Indian living in Rangoon, walked to Soortie Bara Bazaar, one of the city's main shopping areas, and was confronted by a grotesque vision. At each of the four corners of the bazaar a severed head had been mounted on a pole. A note told passers-by that this fate awaited any who transgressed the law. But whether they were nationalists who welcomed the Japanese, or were simply cowed by the new occupiers, all were conscious that the age of the white master had gone.

Some officials certainly sensed the larger historical implications of the catastrophe. 'We will never be able to hold up our heads again in Burma,' said F. H. Yarnold, a deputy commissioner in the district of Mergui. For the fighting men retreating towards India there was little time to reflect on the great sweep of history. As the Japanese advanced from the east and south, the soldiers of the British, Indian and Burmese armies fought to escape a gigantic trap.

TWO

The Longest Road

They were walking through elephant grass near the Sittang river, some 66 miles from Rangoon and the last great natural barrier before the Burmese capital. Private Bill Norman of 2nd battalion, Duke of Wellington's Regiment, heard planes approaching and thought it was Hurricanes or Tomahawks, until he heard the sergeant blow his whistle. After that, the air erupted with noise. Machine-gun bullets, the kind that could take a man's arm off, smashed into the ground beside Private Norman. He ran into a rubber plantation and dived under some trees. Looking up, he saw an Indian soldier, with thin legs resembling 'worn army leather bootlaces', standing in the open and aiming his rifle at the Japanese planes. 'I shouted at him in my very best barrack-room Hindustani to stop firing and take cover. With the greatest of smiles, with his beautiful white teeth, he held out his handspan and in the best of his barrack-room English said, "Twenty-one degrees, Sahib." Telling him how well he was doing I let him get on with a fine bit of soldiering.'

The Japanese invasion had started three weeks before and, advancing from the east, had pushed the British and Indian forces back to the bridge over the Sittang. The heat, the lack of water, and the relentless movement took a heavy toll. Men began to fall out exhausted, unable to move another yard. Norman saw a sergeant go to one man and kick him as he lay on the ground. 'Get on your feet and march or we will leave you to die,' he said. The man did not get up, and was left to his fate. As the British retreated, the Japanese would emerge to attack from the surrounding jungle and then disappear.

19

In a few short days Private Norman became accustomed to the sight of dead bodies, many of them his comrades. By night the troops shivered in shirts that had been soaked by the day's perspiration, hiding up in the jungle and hoping that the Japanese would not discover their position. Then, in the depths of the night, the calling would start, high-pitched Japanese voices that made Norman wish he could get even closer to the man beside him. Many soldiers found themselves torn between the fear of discovery by the probing Japanese and the urge to respond by firing off a few rounds. An official narrative of the battle described how the Japanese, 'using coloured tracer ammunition, uttering war cries ... succeeded in creating confusion in the darkness ... [which] led to indiscriminate firing by certain units ... the uncontrolled fire caused some casualties amongst our own troops'. Some of the troops retreating in the direction of the bridge were machine-gunned in error by the RAF. In the early hours of 23 February Private Norman heard a huge explosion in the distance. The bridge over the Sittang had been blown in order to stall the Japanese advance, but the result was that the bulk of a division, including Norman and his comrades, were trapped on the wrong side of the river. For years afterwards the timing of the demolition would be the source of bitter debate and recrimination. The troops left on the Japanese side, many of them Indian and Burmese, were both scared and furious, convinced their British commanders had abandoned them.

Silence descended over the area after the explosion, followed after a few minutes by the sound of the encircling Japanese chattering and screaming. Some of the stranded men worked frantically to make rafts from timber huts and bamboo, while hundreds threw away their guns, equipment and clothes, and plunged into the water. 'As we crossed, the river was a mass of bobbing heads. We were attacked from the air, sniped at from the opposite bank.' Many men drowned in the treacherous currents as they struggled to cross the mile-wide river. Lance Corporal Frost, 2nd battalion, King's Own Yorkshire Light Infantry (2/KOYLI), hurled himself into the water even though he could not swim. It was a measure of the terror the Japanese inspired. Strong swimmers went to the aid of men in difficulty, some even making two or three trips to drag across the wounded. A major and two corporals went to the broken span of the bridge and looped ropes across to create a lifeline which enabled around four hundred troops, mostly Gurkhas, to reach safety.

The Japanese harried the retreating army. Private Yoshizo Abe, a sapper with 33rd Engineer Regiment, was advancing through a town near the river when British armoured vehicles came racing through. 'The houses in the town were all burning and British armoured cars came bursting through the flames,' he remembered. 'We threw grenades and mines into the cars passing through the town. I did not take note of how long it lasted. I was euphoric and did not remember what I had done.' Six or so British vehicles had stalled in the road, their occupants blown apart and burned as they tried to escape. Outside the town, Abe saw Indian soldiers advancing and firing from the waist. Each time the Japanese tried to advance they were beaten back by a hail of fire. Eventually Japanese firepower drove the Indians back. The Indians could only flee into the jungle and hope to avoid being caught.

Another Japanese private, Shiro Tokita, an infantryman with 33rd Division, remembered looking down on the Sittang bridge after it had been blown. 'There were many fish floating in the water, killed by the explosion. On the river bank I saw a lot of shoes, and clothing scattered here and there.' Tokita witnessed the surrender of a small British unit at a pagoda that was being used as a field hospital. The doctor of his battalion had the extraordinary experience of meeting a British doctor with whom he had studied in Germany. They tended the wounded together. At Shwedaung, later in the retreat, a Japanese officer, Major Misao Sato, encountered a dying British soldier lying under a tree. He was young, perhaps eighteen years old, and had been sniping at the Japanese from behind a bush. 'I asked him in my broken English, "Where are your father and mother?" He said just a word, but clearly, "England", and as I asked, "Painful?", he again said a word, "No." I knew that he must be suffering great pain.' A stream of tears ran down the dying soldier's face. Sato held his hand and found himself crying. The soldier died a few minutes later.

Such moments of chivalry were rare. In the 2/KOYLI missing personnel file there are many heart-rending accounts from soldiers who saw their comrades killed at Sittang. In the middle of one close-quarter fight, Lance Corporal W. Smith saw a wounded private pick up a Tommy gun and stand up, shouting at the Japanese to come out in the open and fight. He was shot in the head. Men struggled desperately to help one another under fire. Smith and a comrade tried to rescue a Lance Corporal McDonald who was wounded in the legs: 'he told us to go and get out of it for he said there was no hope for him getting out of hear [sic] alive. And I told [him] that when we could get to the hospital we would send somebody for him, and then I felt somebody pull on my shirt and it was L/Cpl Rowley, and he said he was [dead], so with not having any spades with [us] we put him in a hole and covered him over with some wood.'

Corporal E. Rylah, despite being fully fit himself, volunteered to stay with a wounded comrade, although this meant trusting his fate to the Japanese. Private W. Hewitt was seen going in the opposite direction to his retreating company, because 'the sound of the machine guns had temporarily unhinged his mind and he did not know where he was going'. One party of men 'flatly refused to attempt the crossing and collected Tommy guns and disappeared in the direction of the Japanese lines'.

Private Bill Norman reached the river after the main crossing had taken place, finding only a handful of men still trying to get away. Like the others making the crossing, he abandoned his weapon. With a friend, he grabbed a thick bamboo pole for buoyancy, and the two of them set off across the river. With physical exhaustion setting in and the pole waterlogged, out of nowhere, it seemed, another figure joined the struggling pair, a big man and a strong swimmer who grabbed the pole and pulled them across.

The Cabinet papers for February 1942 described how 'our troops have fought well and inflicted heavy casualties', but acknowledged that the 'Japanese attack has been remarkable for the excellence of its ground to air communications and for the coordination of air with land forces'. The RAF and pilots of the American Volunteer Group challenged the Japanese but were eventually overwhelmed by superior numbers.*

Rangoon was abandoned on 7 March 1942 and occupied by the Japanese the following day. The British managed to evacuate sufficient supplies of food and petrol to maintain their forces on the retreat, saving the army from starvation as it trudged towards India. Units fought through Japanese roadblocks, battered and demoralised by the enemy's constant outflanking movements and encirclements; men with no aim but escape.

Almost a fortnight after the fall of Rangoon, General Alexander appointed a new commander to lead the forces in the field. Major General William Slim, a former officer of a Gurkha regiment, was serving in the Middle East when he was appointed to take command of the newly constituted Burma Corps on 19 March. He would become arguably the finest British general of the Second World War and a man loved by his multi-racial army. But with Rangoon gone and Japanese forces attempting the encirclement of the British and Indian forces retreating north, it was too late for Alexander or Slim to do much but try to save as many men as possible to fight another day from the two divisions and armoured brigade of Burma Corps.

Watching the rout of an army is always a salutary lesson, but Slim's gift was to be able to watch and learn. He was a rare kind of soldier: quick-witted and daring; loved by his men because they knew he would not spend their lives cheaply; and possessed of a moral courage that allowed him to acknowledge his own errors. The lessons Slim learned in those terrible months from March to June 1942 would be embedded in his consciousness forever and would be used to weld troops from the British and Indian armies into one of the finest fighting units of the war, 14th Army.

---

* The American Volunteer Group, or 'Flying Tigers', was a clandestine unit of American pilots operating in support of the Chinese Nationalists. Established in 1941, it became part of the United States Army Air Force in July 1942.

Slim had grown up in a lower-middle-class family in Birmingham, the son of a failed small businessman and a devoutly Catholic mother, whose strong personality seems to have been inherited by her son. After leaving school he went to work as a teacher among some of the poorest and toughest boys in Birmingham, an experience that later gave him an invaluable insight into the minds of the men he would lead into battle. There were other jobs, including a periodic recourse to writing stories for magazines, but a childhood passion for military history found an outlet in the Officer Training Corps at his brother's university. At the outbreak of the First World War, Slim was commissioned as a second lieutenant and was wounded at Gallipoli. During the early stages of the Second World War he was wounded again, while fighting the Italians in Eritrea. To his men he would always be 'Uncle Bill', a man of imposing physical build, with a protruding jaw that emphasised an air of resolution and command.

Slim conducted a skilful fighting retreat, buying time to allow the bulk of his army, and tens of thousands of their Chinese allies, to escape destruction or capture. When the monsoon broke in early May the principal routes of retreat became mires in which men slipped and fell as they trudged towards India. Slim watched troops shiver with fever as they lay on 'the sodden ground under the dripping trees, without even a blanket to cover them'. In May, Lance Corporal W. Long of 2/KOYLI was retreating north from the town of Kalewa when his group was joined by a private suffering from cholera. The man had been in hospital but had decided to try to escape with his comrades rather than trust his life to the advancing Japanese. The seriously ill soldier lasted for eight miles of marching and then fell out. Lance Corporal Long reported, 'We carried on marching. Two days later another party who set off marching after us caught us up and told us that they had passed Pte Powell lying dead on the side of the road.'

In one instance rough justice was meted out to a soldier accused of abandoning his post. Sergeant W. Butcher, 2/KOYLI, described how a private in his platoon deserted in the early hours. Private

Ramsden was arrested three hours later and brought before the commanding officer, Major Mike Calvert. Calvert would go on to become the most successful of the Chindit commanders and one of the founders of the SAS. In the case of Private Ramsden he showed no mercy and ordered him to be shot.* Sergeant Butcher was given the job of carrying out the execution. 'I tied him to a tree with his back to me. I placed a pistol between his shoulders and shot him at point-blank range. He was definitely dead before I left him.' Private Ramsden had fallen in love with and married a Burmese woman.† The statement by his executioner refers to her as a suspected fifth columnist who was later arrested.

Burmese found aiding the Japanese could also be subjected to summary justice. Lieutenant Colonel C. E. K. Bagot of the 1st Glosters described an encounter on 3 May 1942: 'At 1930 hrs signalling was observed on our right front and a patrol stalked 3 Burmans who were caught in the act. One man carried weapons and Japanese money. He was shot, the remainder were taken back 25 miles under escort of the Burma Frontier Force and dispersed, after they had been made to witness the execution.'

The final stage of the journey brought the troops through the Kabaw Valley. Captain Gerald Fitzpatrick and the survivors of 2/KOYLI encountered a scene of horror there that spurred them onwards. The rotting bodies of numerous refugees lay in the sun being devoured by vultures, while countless flies swarmed around the troops. 'The impact of witnessing the vulturine disposal of the unfortunates, on our sick and wounded men, was quite miraculous. It was

---

* Calvert wrote in his autobiography of being threatened with court martial because of allegations that he had shot deserters during the retreat. He vigorously denied the claims but asserted that Slim's intervention had saved him from court martial. 'I thought back to Wingate's approval of Slim and silently added mine to it.' Michael Calvert, *Fighting Mad* (Pen and Sword, 2004), p. 105. The account of Sergeant Butcher appears to contradict his denial.

† The Commonwealth War Graves Commission register of men killed in action during World War Two lists a Private Benjamin Ramsden, King's Own Yorkshire Light Infantry, as having died on 26/04/1942. He is named on the Rangoon War Memorial alongside soldiers of 2/KOYLI who died in battle.

like a Lourdes cure; the pace quickened, backs straightened, men simply dare not fall back and die in this place.' The jungle was endlessly strange. Ralph Tanner was ill with dysentery and had to briefly drop out of the column near the top of a hill. While he squatted, he saw 'swallow tail butterflies drinking the salt on someone's knees when there was a halt near the summit'. Volunteers from the Society of Friends (Quakers) were operating ambulances caring for wounded soldiers and civilians.* Doctor Handley Laycock was attached to the British forces and recalled a strange combination of cheerfulness and horror along the route to the border. 'During these days we saw many scenes of intense horror. A man dying on this path usually remains until the rapid assaults of ants and other insects have reduced him to a skeleton. In the process he blocks the path and his presence there is exceedingly unpleasant. In some camps we found the dead and dying together, the latter too feeble to crawl away from the former. On the whole the morale of the men we met was high and they usually returned our greeting with a broad grin, and expressed embarrassingly profuse gratitude for anything that we could do to help them ...'

As he tramped the last yards into India, Captain Fitzpatrick of 2/KOYLI looked up and saw two figures in uniform standing on a mound of earth just above him. One of them was General Sir Harold Alexander, GOC Burma, and the other was 'a less flashy officer', General William 'Bill' Slim.

Watching the retreating army, Slim felt a mixture of pride and anger. They looked like scarecrows dragging themselves across the border. But Slim noted that they still carried their weapons and looked like fighting units. 'They might look like scarecrows but they looked like soldiers too.' His anger arose from the reception accorded to his men by the military in India, where commanders and staff officers who had sat out the fighting in safety stood at the border hector-

---

* The Friends Ambulance Unit on the China–Burma front was staffed by Quakers from America, Britain, New Zealand, Canada and China. The FAU was originally established during the Great War as a form of service for conscientious objectors. About 170 were active on the Burma front. (Source: Anthony Reynolds, 'Society for Anglo-Chinese Understanding.)

ing the arriving troops. Sarcastic comments and parade-ground bellowing were directed at men who were on the verge of collapse. Ralph Tanner remembered being asked for his identity card by a corporal before finding his way to a train and eventually to hospital. On the way he used his penknife, sterilised with a match, to lance a wound on the arm of a soldier. 'This let the pus out and the arm got better during the trip.'

In Slim's view, his troops were received as if they were in disgrace. He acknowledged that to some extent they were paying the price for the 'rabble' of deserters, refugees and non-combatants that had crossed the border ahead of them over the previous weeks, but he could not excuse their treatment. According to official figures, 13,000 men were killed, wounded or missing on the retreat, not counting those who would die later from disease.

As the troops made their way into the main British base at Imphal, they were sent to camp on steep jungle hillsides, where there was no shelter apart from the trees and scant clothing, blankets, water or medicine. The psychological effect was devastating. Men lost the will to carry on. By Slim's estimate, as many as 8 per cent of those he watched come out of Burma died from illness. Yet when he said goodbye to them he was cheered by the men, an experience he found 'infinitely moving – and humbling'. Leaving Imphal he did not even have a jeep and it was left to his 'faithful Cameronian bodyguard' to coax back into life an abandoned refugee car that would carry them towards a small hill town called Kohima. Here the engine gave out. This town, with its small garrison of local troops and a military hospital and engineering works, was one of the furthest outposts of British power in India, an insignificant and sleepy place which had, in recent months, found itself directly in the path of a mass flow of refugees from Burma. Slim did not stay long. Together with his bodyguard he pushed the car out of Kohima until they reached a steep descent. From there they coasted downhill towards the railhead at Dimapur until a rise in the road stopped them. After that, they hitched a ride in a lorry and then found their way onto a crowded train. Slim would not see

Kohima again for more than two years, but when he did it would be in vastly changed circumstances, and the little village he had passed through without fanfare would be associated forever with the fortunes of his army.

Many of the sick from Burma Corps were sent to hospitals in Ranchi in Bihar, where Slim went to visit them and argue for better conditions. He saw officers and men dying in squalor, the wounded lying on verandas and under trees waiting for admission, while overworked medical teams laboured relentlessly with the bare minimum of supplies.

But it was also at Ranchi that Slim began what was probably the most painstaking analysis of defeat undertaken by any British general of the war. In his account of the campaign Slim wrote of the despair that can descend on a defeated general. 'In a dark hour he will turn in upon himself and question the very foundations of his leadership and his manhood. And then he must stop! For, if he is ever to command in battle again, he must shake off these regrets, and stamp on them, as they claw at his will and his self-confidence. He must beat off these attacks he delivers against himself, and cast out the doubts born of failure. Forget them, and remember only the lessons to be learnt from defeat – they are more than from victory.' Although there were many more setbacks ahead, Slim was already preparing to take the war to the Japanese.

THREE

At the Edge of the Raj

In the hottest or wettest of weather the deputy commissioner wore a jacket and tie. Tall and with a face that invited confidence, he seemed like a Victorian housemaster remoulded as a servant of the Raj on its most remote frontier. But those who stayed longer than a few hours in his company found a man whose stiffness was in fact shyness, and when his reticence faded with acquaintance Charles Pawsey was a kind companion. Advice on the Naga Hills was freely offered, once he was sure the visitor would do nothing to disrupt the calm.

By early 1942 the peace of the hills had been disrupted. Charles Pawsey was standing on the Imphal road just outside Kohima when the first refugees from Burma came trudging in. The early arrivals seemed to be in good health and had some money. But in February Pawsey began to report the arrival of destitute groups of soldiers. A camp was established at the Middle School in Kohima to provide shelter. Soon the passage of exhausted, starving people had become 'out of control'. An English volunteer who helped in the relief effort remembered these destitute thousands 'hungry, thirsty, exhausted, numbed with shock ... One's taskmaster ... is the crying need of hundreds of fellow beings displayed daily in all its nakedness.' There were separate canteens for Europeans and Indians, with sandwiches for the former and rice for the latter.

The Daily Refugee Report from the Governor of Assam to the Viceroy of India for 14 May 1942 reported large parties of refugees trying to reach the railhead at Dimapur, about forty-six miles north-west of Kohima. They were being joined by Chinese troops fleeing the front. It was in this chaotic phase that the army staff formed their grim impression of the retreat. 'Binns reports [the Chinese] Army [is] mere rabble who will reduce refugees behind them to pitiful condition … disarm and control Chinese if possible as otherwise will consume all food … including dumps and will become embroiled with hillmen whose loyalty will be seriously shaken if they are looted by our allies.' Four days later, on 18 May, the Governor was reporting that approximately 3,000 refugees a day were on their way to Dimapur, and that the maharajah of neighbouring Manipur had abandoned his administration and vanished. In the middle of this Charles Pawsey was trying to provide assistance for the multitudes arriving in Kohima, and was becoming angry about the government's failure to help him. Delhi had never planned for a retreat. Amid the stink of the refugee camps, Pawsey struggled to acquire adequate supplies of rice and to find labourers who could construct shelters or improve the tracks along which supplies would have to come. 'There was no equipment of any kind,' he wrote. 'Supplies were a nightmare. So was lack of transport.' With the help of civilian volunteers, many from tea-planting families, Pawsey was able to establish a system to feed and then transfer the refugees deeper into India.*

By July the flood of refugees had diminished to a trickle, and once the influx had come to an end Kohima and the Naga Hills settled into a nervous peace. The Japanese 15th Army was sitting on the other side of the Chindwin river, about seventy miles away at the nearest point. But they had halted for now. The Indian official history recorded that, by June 1942, 'the onset of monsoon, long lines of communication in the rear, the need for reorganising forces for a major venture and opposition [in India] to any external aggression, prevented the Japanese from extending their conquests beyond Burma.' The physical barriers to an attack were considerable.

---

* The Indian Tea Association (ITA) established a 'Refugee Organisation' to help deal with the influx of people into Assam. It was an early example of a civilian administered aid effort that would become so common in the later years of the 20th century.

Between Kohima and the Japanese lay the Chindwin river and a mountain range, whose 8,000 foot peaks and steep jungled valleys were thought to be impassable by large military formations. If there was to be an invasion of India, the British believed it would come further south, via the Imphal plain or through the Burmese province of Arakan into Bengal. For now, Charles Pawsey could concentrate on re-establishing the normal routines of colonial administration.

By the time he became deputy commissioner at Kohima, Charles Pawsey was thirty-five years old and he had already exceeded his own life expectancy by many years. He was one of those rare creatures who had enlisted in 1914 as a teenage officer and survived to see the armistice in 1918. Educated at Berkhamsted, where he was briefly a contemporary of Graham Greene, Pawsey was an enthusiastic cadet and was praised in the school magazine for his 'doggedness' on the athletics track. He went on to study classics at Oxford, but when the First World War broke out Pawsey joined the Territorial Army and was commissioned in time to join the 1/8 Worcestershire Regiment in France in April 1915. More than two decades later, at Kohima, in the midst of another terrible battle, Pawsey would remember the experience of clearing the dead from the trenches at Serre on the Somme. The rotting corpses lay everywhere and 'those trenches remained long in the memories of the officers and men, as their worst experience of the horrors of the field of a great battle'. Pawsey distinguished himself by going out repeatedly into no-man's-land in daylight to rescue wounded men, until he was caught in a German gas attack and invalided away from the front. He was awarded the Military Cross for his bravery on the Somme, before being transferred to the Italian front in 1917. There he was captured during hand-to-hand fighting on the Asiago plateau, some 4,000 feet up in the mountains above Lake Garda. Captain Pawsey was a prisoner of the Austro-Hungarian empire until the armistice in November. Then he and a few other British prisoners commandeered a train with a wood-burning engine and rode south to freedom.

Discharged from the army in 1919, he might have chosen to return to Oxford to continue his studies. But Charles Pawsey decided instead to go to India, where he had family connections. His uncle Roger had served as a government collector in east Bengal. He successfully sat the exams for the Indian Civil Service and was assigned to work as an assistant commissioner in the province of Assam in the north-east. It was a job that would involve extensive travel in remote districts, with considerable risk from malaria and the potential for encounters with hostile tribes. Yet to a young man who had survived the horrors of the First World War the journey to Assam must have held fantastic promise. With its vast tea estates, trackless jungles and tribes of headhunters, it was unimaginably far from the desolation of post-war Europe.

Pawsey rose steadily through the ranks of the Indian Civil Service, spending much of his time engaged in resolving land disputes, and eventually reaching the rank of deputy commissioner of the Naga Hills, in which role he acted as de facto ruler of more than 40,000 tribespeople in an area that covered 6,400 square miles of some of the most remote territory on the planet. On clear nights Charles Pawsey would stand on his veranda and look out over the valley to see shoals of stars splashed across the Naga Hills. To the east this silvered horizon dropped behind the mountains into Burma, and westwards it stretched towards the plains of Assam and the distant India of cities and crowds. Situated at 4,137 feet, and with no swampland nearby, Kohima was regarded as the healthiest settlement in the area. The air was clear and mountain streams provided a continuous supply of fresh water flowing into a tank in Pawsey's garden. Although temperatures could soar to 90° Fahrenheit in the middle of July, the weather was cool for most of the year. Like the rest of the region, Kohima was washed by the annual monsoon, when annual rainfall of as much as one hundred inches could bring movement along the local tracks to a halt.

The settlement was spread out along a ridge made up of a series of hills. Charles Pawsey and the local police commander had their bungalows on Summerhouse Hill at the northern end of the ridge. On the adjacent hills stretching southwards were the stores, workshops, clinics, barracks and jail of the colonial administration. Beyond these were the heights of Aradura Spur, which in turn led on to the dark and jungled form of Mount Pulebadze, towering over Kohima at 7,500 feet above sea level. On the other side of the valley, across the road linking Kohima with Dimapur to the north and Imphal to the south, lay the so-called Naga Village, where the huts of the tribespeople had gradually agglomerated to form a settlement of several hundred dwellings.

European visitors to Kohima first noticed the clear mountain air and the profusion of flowers. There was a famed local orchid called *Vanda coerulea*, its colour a striking blend of turquoise and maroon stippled with tiny squares, as well as rhododendron trees which could grow to over a hundred feet. The young English traveller Ursula Graham Bower first saw Kohima while on a visit to India in the winter of 1937. Entering Mr Pawsey's domain she was first struck by the tidy appearance of the place, with its red-roofed bungalows and official buildings stretched across the mountain ridges; gazing further afield, she saw on each ridge a 'shaggy village, its thatched roofs smoke-stained and weathered'. She was only twenty-three when she stood on the ridge and looked out over the valleys, but she felt irrevocably changed by that moment and in her writing we find a young woman faced with something that challenged her capacity for awe: 'One behind the other the hills stretched away as far as the eye could see, in an ocean of peaks, a wilderness of steep fields and untouched forest, of clefts and gulfs and razorbacks which merged at last into a grey infinity. That landscape drew me as I had never known anything do before, with a power transcending the body, a force not of this world at all.'

Charles Pawsey's bungalow stood above the road linking Kohima with Imphal. It was built of wood with a red tin roof and a spacious veranda; it was pretty and spacious, surrounded by pale pink cannas and scarlet rhododendrons, but not lavish. When a small road had to be cut to the bungalow, Pawsey, following the service rules, paid for it himself. Above the bungalow, reached via a terraced hill, was a tennis court upon which Pawsey's occasional visitors could enjoy an hour or two of civilised sport. His life there was comfortable but not luxurious, for he was a man of ascetic temperament, driven by his work and a conviction that the welfare of the Naga people was his life's mission. That he was a paternalist is beyond doubt – those who knew him remembered how he spoke of the Naga as 'my children'. But that is not to cast him as a cartoon figure, the dutiful imperialist shepherding the childlike natives. He was driven by a sense of imperial duty but also by a deep, empathetic humanity, a quality that the horror of his experiences in the First World War had only served to deepen. Sachu Angami, a Naga born and brought up in Kohima, remembered seeing Pawsey walk around his bungalow garden every morning. 'He was always calm and he would smile when he saw us children. But we were too scared to talk to this white man, of course. This was a man who, when he spoke, the words turned into orders that would be carried out.'

Pawsey rode out by mule on his visits to the villages, sometimes accompanied by an escort of police and stopping off for the night in government bungalows or huts, or at the homes of the handful of British residents. Pat Whyte was a young girl living at a coal-mining works in the hills and recalls Pawsey coming to stay with her family. She was about seven or eight years old when she walked in on him while he was reclining in the bath, causing the deputy commissioner considerable embarrassment. 'I remember him calling to "get this child out of the bathroom". He wasn't very happy!' Pawsey also acted as magistrate for the Naga Hills and would set up his court on the veranda of the Whytes' bungalow where, surrounded by magnificently adorned warriors – Pat Whyte saw one man wear an entire bird as an earring – the deputy commissioner would consider the complaints of one clan against another. There were arguments over boundaries which could easily end in a blood feud if not handled with tact. Once, when Pawsey was hearing a case of murder after a headhunting expedition, a policeman emptied out an entire sack of heads in front of him as evidence. The deputy commissioner's reaction is not recorded. It was also the magistrate's duty – although this was usually carried out by Pat Whyte's father – to disburse the opium ration to registered dealers. The supply, which smelt 'sort of sickly sweet', was meticulously weighed out before being hidden away again under lock and key.

Until the arrival of the railhead at Dimapur, about forty-six miles from Kohima, in the early 1930s, the European residents of the Naga Hills largely depended on the land to feed them. With water drawn from wells and springs, and using local labour, they grew vegetables, and what could not be grown they bought or bartered for: rice, goat meat and fruit. The cooking was European; only on Saturdays did they eat curry, and then it was a bland concoction.

The railway engineer W. H. Prendergast, who arrived in the area around the same time as Charles Pawsey, recalled nights in the government bungalows deep in the forest where a 'fiendish shriek ... made every nerve tingle, as some animal was chased to death'. Prendergast's work on the railway line near Dimapur was hindered by the effects of earthquakes and by elephants which were in the habit of tearing up the wooden sleepers. For anybody travelling in the forests the tiger was the most dangerous enemy, stalking its prey through the thick foliage, a silent springing killer that could drag a man down from the back of an elephant. One man-eating tigress killed eleven people, including a soldier, before a Kuki tribesman, armed with an ancient muzzle-loading rifle, managed to kill her. By day the hills pulsated with the noise of wildlife. Gibbons and rhesus monkeys screeched in the canopy, while brilliantly coloured birds flashed through the trees – hornbills, the symbol of the Naga people, rare Burmese peafowl, and the bar-backed pheasant.

In the monsoon months Pawsey could find himself severely restricted. The rain swamped the jungle tracks and whole hillsides would come crashing down, a wall of rock and mud blocking the paths, forcing diversions through the jungle with its abundant leeches and the danger of malaria. Pawsey's friend, the anthropologist Henry Balfour, curator of the Pitt Rivers Museum in Oxford, described a typical day travelling in the Naga Hills during the 1920s: 'The going was appallingly slippery and it was not easy to keep the horses on their legs on the narrow ledge-like track ... Most of the way it is rather "trick-riding" along a ledge track with a nearly sheer fall on one side.' Conditions had changed little twenty years later when British and Japanese troops operating in the hills would see animals and men plunge to their deaths over these sheer drops.

When the Second World War broke out few in Delhi believed they would find Japanese armies sitting on the Burmese border. Once this situation presented itself, Charles Pawsey understood that it would fall to him to ensure that the Naga people and the other tribes of the Naga Hills did not go over to the Japanese. Given their history with the British they might have been tempted.

The story of rebellion in the Naga Hills is one of the least known of the colonial wars of conquest, but, once the extent of the bloodshed and the repression meted out to the tribespeople is understood, the magnitude of Pawsey's task not only in maintaining peace but in recruiting the Naga into the formidable network of fighters, spies, scouts and porters who would help save the British at Kohima becomes all the more remarkable.

The British called them 'barbarous tribes of independent savages'. Caught as they were between the advance of British imperialism and the equally ambitious kings of neighbouring Burma, the tribes of the Naga Hills could be forgiven for employing 'savagery' in defence of their independence. British interest in the Hills dated to the first Anglo-Burmese war of 1826 but the first military expedition was not launched until 1839 to punish villages that had raided into Assam. In the fighting that followed the invaders discovered that although 'armed with only with spears, daos and a very few old muskets, [they] were a foe by no means to be despised'.

Closer in appearance to the people of Tibet and Nepal than to the Indian people of the plains, the Naga people are believed to be descended from tribes of hunter-gatherers who roamed out of the Pacific region and settled across the central Asian plateau. The Nagas encountered by early British explorers were tough warriors, divided into clans and sub-clans, which might share a village but have separate allegiances. They were led by elders who debated important issues around a ceremonial fire. The Naga martial culture, and that of other mountain tribes like the Kuki, centred around the taking of heads. A Naga male could not consider himself a true man until he had taken his first head, and the greater the number of heads taken in battle, the greater the prestige of the warrior. It was believed that in capturing the head a warrior seized the spirit and vitality of his enemy. The rotting heads would decorate the eaves of the Nagas' bamboo and thatch homes, or would be hung from ceremonial poles in the villages. When it came to warfare, men, women and children were all considered fair game. A British military observer in 1879 cited one witness: 'A party from one village attacked one of the clans of another large village in pursuance of a blood feud while the men were all away in the fields, and massacred the whole of the women and children ... One of the onlookers told me ... that he never saw such "fine sport: it was just like killing fowls".'

Miekonu Angami grew up in the powerful village of Khonoma, which contained no fewer than three stone 'khels', or forts. As a child he saw the warriors returning home with the heads of their enemies. 'They would cut close to the chin and catch the hair and carry the head that way ... sometimes they brought the ears only. They put the heads and ears at the gate and everybody would come and touch the head and then could pass into the village. It was like saying a prayer. After that they would make a party and only the men could come to that.' He could remember, too, a time between the wars when the British killed some warriors and dumped the bodies outside the village, laughing and shouting at the villagers. 'Before, the British did not control us: there were brave men and great headhunters who were our leaders.' Despite his feelings about the British, Miekonu would learn to prefer them to the Japanese.

The Nagas were gifted craftsmen and created a rich culture of visual art, exemplified in clothing, carving and body tattoos. A Naga warrior would cut his hair in a pudding-bowl shape and decorate it with the bright feathers of a forest bird and the tusks of a wild boar; he would garland his ears with shells and feathers or with the tresses of one of his victims; while around his neck he would string numerous strands of brightly coloured beads. The shawls they wore varied according to sex, age and marital status. For the warriors they could be red, or a mix of red and yellow stripes against a black background, often adorned with symbols denoting wealth and martial prowess. The warriors' shields were frequently adorned with the hair of those they had slain in battle.

Until the First Anglo-Burmese war, the Naga Hills were nominally under the control of the Burmese kings of Ava. Under the Treaty of Yandaboo the lands were ceded to the British, who, like the previous rulers, exercised nominal control, certainly for the first fifty years of their administration.* The outsider presence was restricted to groups of missionaries, occasional explorers and anthropologists, and the more intrepid traders from the Assam plains.

By the 1870s, however, a combination of Naga raids into British-administered territory and the expansionist designs of the Raj towards neighbouring Burma made a more comprehensive imperial intervention inevitable. Another factor intervened, too: the discovery of wild tea growing in the jungles of Assam had led to a massive programme of plantation along the frontiers of the Naga territory and the importation of hundreds of thousands of indentured labourers. The presence of unruly tribes who could threaten the future of this lucrative enterprise was not to be tolerated. The Lieutenant Governor of Bengal, Sir Cecil Beadon, a man of notably dubious judgment, was concerned that, 'exposed as Assam is on every side, if petty outrages are to be followed up by withdrawal of our frontier, we should very speedily find ourselves driven out of the province'.† Contemporary accounts of

---

* The Treaty of Yandaboo was signed in February 1826 and brought to an end the First Anglo-Burmese War. The treaty was a humiliation for the Burmese monarchy, which lost control over vast tracts of territory. Fifteen thousand British and Indian troops died in the war and many more on the Burmese side.

† Sir Cecil Beadon (1816–80) was criticised in an official report and in the House of Commons for his administrative failures during the Bengal famine of 1866–67 and ended his career in ignominy. He also told a House of Commons committee on the opium trade that the government was motivated solely by considerations of revenue, and that it would 'probably not' be moved by concerns about the ill effects of opium on those who bought it. Frederick Storrs Turner, *British Opium Policy and its Results to India and China* (Low, Marston, Searle & Rivington, 1876), p. 256.

the fighting that followed are full of references to 'barbarians' and 'savages'. It is the language of a particular time, when the unassimilated native, whether on the North-West Frontier or in the jungles of the Naga Hills, was viewed by the imperial warrior with a mixture of fear, bemusement and condescension.

In November 1878 the Raj extended its administrative reach to what was then the native village of Kohima, at the centre of the most troublesome of the Naga districts and lying along a mountain track that led to the plains of Manipur, a princely state whose maharajah gave his allegiance to the British.* The British appointed a political officer, G. H. Damant, to Kohima in 1878, and when he set out for some mutinous Naga villages with only a small escort, the inevitable occurred. Despite being warned by friendly villagers not to continue on his way, Damant rode at the head of the column, straight into an ambush at Khonoma. Thirty-nine men were killed, including Damant, whose headless and handless corpse was found months later by a British patrol. The official inquiry noted, with characteristic understatement, that his preparations 'had not in all respects been well judged'. A general rebellion followed the killing of Damant and the Naga advanced on the British fort at Kohima where 414 people, including women and children, had sought shelter. The first siege of Kohima began on 16 October 1879. There were just over 130 men under arms inside the stockade, but many of them were raw recruits, and the water situation was perilous. Attackers could easily cut off the spring that flowed into the fort.

Water rations were reduced to a quarter and food began to run low. A contemporary account described what a 'pitiful sight it was to see the poor little creatures [children] crowding together, holding out their cups'. The siege was eventually lifted when a British officer

---

* This loyalty lasted only until 1891 when palace intrigues deposed the maharajah and installed a regent. On arriving to punish the usurper, the British were greeted by a band playing 'God Save the Queen'. After a good dinner at the residency the British retired to bed, and were promptly attacked and their forces routed. NA, WO 32/8400, Proceedings of the Court of Inquiry assembled at Manipur on the 30th April 1891 and following days to investigate the circumstances connected with recent events in Manipur.

leading Manipuri state troops rode through the mountains and scattered the Nagas. The retribution was savage. A punishment force of 1,300 troops, all of them Indians under British officers, along with mountain artillery and rocket units, was sent into the Naga territory in November 1879. As they advanced the British burned villages and destroyed the Nagas' crops and livestock, rendering thousands of people destitute. The less militant villages were fined in rice and made to provide labour for the army. Villages that failed to supply the number of coolies demanded as forced labour were warned with the firing of shells and rockets around the settlement. 'This had the desired effect and the coolies were speedily produced,' the commanding officer reported.

In his telegram to the government of India at the end of the campaign the expedition commander, General Nation, was exultant, taking particular pride in the punishment meted out to the Khonoma Nagas, the most troublesome of the clans. 'Their lands have all been confiscated and themselves broken up as a village community forever … The occupation of the country for so long by such a large body of troops has inflicted serious punishment, as we have drawn largely on their supplies of grain and labour … their fortified village [has been] levelled with the ground, and their magnificent stone-faced, terraced rice land, the work of generations, has been confiscated.' In this manner was the Pax Britannica brought to the Naga Hills.

In Parliament the following year the Irish Home Rule MP, Frank Hugh O'Donnell, asked, with his tongue firmly in his cheek, whether 'the Nagas have asked for annexation to the British Dominions'. The British then dispatched a deputy commissioner to Kohima, as well as political officers working under his direction. Together, they acted as a mix of spy, liaison officer, magistrate and mediator, and above all they provided an early warning system to ensure that Delhi was never again surprised by an uprising. Peace of a kind settled on the hills.

In 1918, when Charles Pawsey was fighting on the Italian front, the territory was again convulsed by violence. This time it was not the Nagas but a neighbouring tribe, the Kukis, who rebelled against the British, an uprising partly motivated by fear that men were about to be forcibly recruited to serve in the Labour Corps on the Western Front. The British achieved their declared aim of 'break[ing] the Kuki spirit' by blockading their fields. 'For had they not surrendered ... they would have been too late to prepare the ground for the next harvest, and would in consequence have been faced with famine.' A total of 126 villages were burned. The official report noted that a policy of search and destroy 'energetically carried out' and 'giving them no rest at all ... has always subdued rebellious savages and semi-civilised races'.

The last uprising of any significance took place in 1931, before Charles Pawsey became deputy commissioner but at a time when he would have been working in the Naga Hills. A Naga religious visionary rose against the British and proclaimed a sixteen-year-old girl named Gaidiliu to be his priestess. She told her people to destroy their grain because the end of the British time was coming and they would inherit a new world. The priestess also promised the warriors that by sprinkling them with holy water she would protect them from the bullets of the enemy. When they charged a section of Gurkhas at Hangrum village eleven warriors were killed and many more wounded. Gaidiliu was eventually captured and imprisoned for fourteen years.*

Four years later, a statutory commission, which included Labour's Clement Attlee and the Tory MP Stuart Cadogan, visited the Naga Hills to investigate the opinions of the local tribes. Cadogan referred to the Naga as 'little headhunters' who met the British for a palaver. 'Presumably the District Commissioner had informed the tribal chieftain that my head was of no intrinsic value as he evinced no disposition to transfer it from my shoulders to his headhunter's basket which was slung over his back and was, I think, the only garment he affected.' Cadogan listened while the Nagas spoke of their fears about the future. Rumours about the protests led by Mr Gandhi and his Congress Party had reached the Naga Hills. The British

---

* Rani Gaidiliu survived the Second World War and was declared an honoured freedom fighter by the government of Jawaharlal Nehru. She went underground again in the 1960s when she led her followers against the dominant Naga political group in a brief civil war.

politicians were told that the tribespeople feared the arrival of a 'Black King' who would replace the Raj. It is a measure of the isolation in which they had been kept that they told the delegation they preferred to have Queen Victoria as their ruler. Cadogan told the House of Commons: 'they are an extremely moral people and live apparently decent lives, and ... if we leave them alone, they will leave us alone.' Clement Attlee, who as prime minister would eventually have to decide on the future of India and the Nagas, agreed with Cadogan: 'There was overwhelming evidence that these people must be protected, and that they are far more liable to exploitation.'

Another British visitor was RAF Sergeant Fred Hill who spent a week living among the Naga as part of a survival course. Hill's memories are not those of an anthropologist or a politician but of a working-class boy from Birmingham entranced by an alien world. From the Nagas he learned how water could be found in bamboo stalks and how to watch what the monkeys ate because 'whatever they eat you can eat because if it kills the monkeys then it will kill you'. But he also recorded the deaths of Nagas from food poisoning as a result of eating rotting rations abandoned by the British. 'Civilisation was no good to them, not our type of civilisation.'

Charles Pawsey saw his mission as one of protection. To achieve this he enforced the doctrine of Naga separateness laid down by the Raj. Visitors to the Naga Hills had to have a permit, and these were given out sparingly. Except in isolated cases, the planting of land for commercial purposes was forbidden. The same prohibition applied to private industry, with a handful of exceptions. Within the constraints of the imperial imagination this policy was benign and it ensured relative peace in the region, but its effect was to preserve Naga life in a political vacuum. As one Indian writer has put it, 'Any observer of the North-East Indian situation may conclude that the tribal people there were purposely kept in isolation from the Indian nationhood.' The logic of Naga separateness, codified under imperial rule, was to have devastating consequences when the Raj retreated.

Pawsey, like so many other servants of the Raj, could hardly have foreseen what war and the rising tide of nationalism would do to this

world within a very short space of time. But the Japanese conquests in 1941–42 had an electrifying effect in India. By the summer of 1942 Gandhi and his supporters in the Congress Party had launched the Quit India campaign, demanding an immediate British withdrawal.*
In the tea country of Assam next to the Naga Hills there were anti-British protests. In September 1942 thirteen people were shot dead in demonstrations at police stations. The following month Congress activists derailed a train carrying British troops into Assam, causing several deaths and widespread injuries. A militant was hanged and many others were sentenced to long prison terms. British troops arriving in India that year could find themselves confronting angry crowds. Captain Gordon Graham of the Cameron Highlanders arrived with the British 2nd Division in June 1942 and recalled asking a Sikh man for directions to the police station: 'My friend,' the Sikh told him, 'you will learn that the police in India are not here to help people. And neither are you.'

But among the Naga population, mistrustful of the Indians from the plains, there was negligible support for the Congress protests. If anything, Naga opinion had been radicalised in support of the British by the behaviour of some Indian troops retreating through the Naga Hills from Burma earlier in 1942. Rape and looting were reported from several areas as gangs of deserters moved towards Assam. To the Nagas, Charles Pawsey and his colonial administration seemed a far safer bet than the unknown quantity of an Indian liberation movement.

---

* The Quit India campaign was launched on 8 August 1942 after the failure of the mission by Sir Stafford Cripps to persuade Congress to support the war in return for a gradual devolution of power and the promise of dominion status. Gandhi called for immediate independence and was immediately arrested along with Nehru and the rest of the senior leadership of Congress, who would spend the next three years of the war in jail. There were an estimated 100,000 arrests and several hundred deaths in the rioting and crackdown that followed. By March 1943 the campaign had been suppressed, although the British had to devote fifty-seven battalions to maintaining internal security. The British official history of the war estimated that the training of a number of army formations and reinforcements was set back by up to two months and 'there was a general loss of production in all factories turning out arms, clothing and equipment'. S. Woodburn Kirby, *The War Against Japan,* vol. 2: *India's Most Dangerous Hour* (HMSO, 1958), p. 247.

Still, the world of genteel drinks parties at Pawsey's bungalow, of long treks into the interior by visiting anthropologists and botanists, of illiterate tribesmen living by the fiat of British officials, was slipping towards its twilight. Its last hurrah would be glorious and tragic, a drama of war that was both modern and inescapably Victorian, replete with outnumbered garrison, fanatical enemy, heroic last stands, and a cast of characters whose diversity and eccentricity belonged to the age of high empire.

FOUR

The King Emperor's Spear

On their way to Kohima from Burma, refugees would occasionally encounter Japanese units. They were not prevented from leaving Burma by the patrols and were usually able to carry the news of their encounters to Pawsey and the tea-planters who were organizing the relief effort. 'Some of them gave us the grim information,' wrote a planter, 'that the Japs did not intend to bomb the road too badly as they looked forward to making full use of it themselves.' The British and Indian forces were in no state to face a serious Japanese offensive. The 1st Glosters were stationed in Kohima as part of 17th Indian Division from August 1942 but were still suffering the effects of the retreat. As well as sick and wounded, a high proportion of troops were on leave. The battalion had left most of its equipment behind in Burma and supplies of food were short because of transport problems. As Captain H. L. T. Radice recalled, the road was constantly disintegrating because of heavy rain. 'As a result, the battalion was on half rations.' A Japanese reconnaissance plane came over frequently, but to the intense relief of the Kohima garrison it was never followed up by an air raid. As the refugees left, the village returned to its usual function as supply depot, a convalescent centre for sick and wounded troops, and the administrative headquarters of the Raj in the Naga Hills. Soon the officers were enjoying a social life once more. Lieutenant Dennis Dawson of the Royal Indian Army Service Corps described a bucolic existence: 'It [was] a lovely place, a sleepy place. We had parties. There were three hospitals. Plenty of nurses and we thought "well this is a lovely life up here"."

The autumn of 1942 was taken up with training exercises. The most excitement was a series of mock attacks on each other's camps. Patrols were sent out to gain knowledge of the country and its people. 'Everywhere these patrols went,' said Captain Radice of the 1st Glosters, 'the local Naga tribesmen showed themselves to be friendly and hospitable.' From his experience of the terrain, Charles Pawsey understood that the first line of defence against any potential Japanese incursion into the area, large or small, should be an 'invisible' intelligence screen. Regular formations marching in long columns could not provide this. Only the Nagas could pass through the jungle as ghosts, moving between India and Burma to spy on Japanese troop concentrations, ingratiating themselves with Japanese officers by pretending to support the overthrow of the British and hanging around Japanese camps to pick up intelligence while playing the role of simple-minded rustics. One of the more exotic snippets that later reached army intelligence came from a Naga who reported the presence of a Japanese commander 'living with two wives and a maid and … having two monkeys with him trained to hurl grenades'. The unnamed officer who wrote down this story added a coda that speaks loudly of contemporary attitudes: the information had come, he wrote, 'from a Naga who may not have known the difference between a Jap and a monkey'.

The dilemma for the planners in military intelligence was how to use the Nagas and other tribal groups in a way that imposed some kind of order on operations but allowed them the freedom to range behind enemy lines. By the standards of contemporary military thinking the answer was unusually flexible. Lieutenant Barry Bowman, commander of a Chindit reconnaissance platoon later in the war, was standing in a jungle clearing one day when he heard a clanking noise coming down the track. The platoon took cover and waited to open fire, convinced it was a Japanese unit. 'To our great relief and surprise an elephant hove into view. On its back was a crude bamboo howdah and perched half-in and half-out of it was an eccentrically clad British officer who waved to us cheerily … A quick cup of tea and he was on his way … he was a tall, biblically bearded fellow in flowing white robes, striding along at a great pace holding up a large black umbrella against the sun … His personal servant close behind him carrying a 12 bore shotgun.' Bowman had met an officer of V Force, one of the more esoteric units of the entire war, a combination of tea-planters, adventurers, regular officers, old soldiers, former headhunters and Indian troops. In the Naga Hills the local tribes would act as guides, spies and soldiers in the ranks of V Force.*

The founder of V Force was Brigadier A. Felix Williams who, at forty-seven, had already spent fifteen years learning the art of guerrilla warfare on the North-West Frontier. As commander of the Tochi Scouts,† he had pursued the Fakir of Ipi up and down the mountains and gullies of Waziristan. To establish V Force, Williams was given £100,000 and a headquarters staff, and promised a delivery of 6,000 rifles. The guns never turned up, so the brigadier embarked on an extraordinary gun-running operation. He sent his men into the bazaars of India's great cities to buy up what weapons they could. Then he turned to the most reliable suppliers in the entire subcontinent, the arms dealers of the North-West Frontier. Under the direction of local police, the gunsmiths of Peshawar turned out thousands of rifles which were shipped to Assam in a first-class carriage. Some of the money given to Williams was spent on enticements for the Naga Hill tribes: red blankets, beads, osprey feathers, opium and elephant tusks were among the cargo carried into the villages where men would be recruited into V Force. Many of the V Force officers were planters or policemen, whose local knowledge and years of experience with the hill tribes were thought to make them better

---

* Set up in 1942, the plan was for V Force to operate in six areas along the 800 mile frontier between India and Burma, with headquarters at Cinnamara in Assam. Its existence was predicated on the assumption that the Japanese would eventually attack. In the event, V Force was to remain behind and carry out hit-and-run operations. Several other clandestine groups, including Z Force and Force 136, as well as the Special Operations Executive, also operated in the frontier area.

† The Tochi Scouts were made up of around twenty white officers and 2,000 native troops. The Canadian correspondent Gordon Sinclair wrote in his book *Khyber Caravan* (re-issued by Long Riders' Guild Press, 2001) that they were 'the only branch of the service who did, and do, wheel into action on their own responsibility without the okay of politicians'.

suited to clandestine operations than regular soldiers. The truth was that it depended almost entirely on the individual: some V Force officers took to the life with gusto while others became sick and dispirited, discovering that weeks of trekking in thick jungle were a different prospect altogether from walking the hills of a tea plantation.

In its early days V Force enjoyed considerable freedom. It was supplied by the army but operated according to the instincts of its officers, many of them characters who would never have fitted into normal military routines. Operating in the Naga Hills later in the war, Lieutenant Bowman discovered that patrolling in the tribal areas could be a source of both trial and astonishment. Like almost every other officer engaged in special operations, he was impressed by the Nagas' loyalty to the British. This was the outer limit of empire and yet echoes of home could be found in the most unlikely places. Entering a village one evening, Bowman's patrol was greeted heartily by the headman. 'The Pahok headman was extremely pro-British and insisted on us having dinner in his big long hut. It was all very claustrophobic, full of smoke and very dark with just one or two primitive oil lamps. However, the chicken and rice and rice beer were extremely welcome. The headman rounded off the evening by producing a battered old HMV gramophone on which he played his only record – it was Harry Lauder singing his old music hall song "Keep right on to the end of the road". Highly appropriate.' In another village the headman saved the lives of Bowman and his colleagues by alerting them to the presence of Japanese in a nearby hut. Having sprinted into the jungle, Bowman then regrouped with his unit and worked back to cover near the hut. 'I decided not to hang around any longer and we opened fire. The Japs leapt and fell back under the hut and we raked the hut for a few rounds more and then hightailed back up the hill.'

Each of the six V Force areas was covered by at least two cells operating independently of each other, so that information could be cross-checked in case the Japanese tried to spread false intelligence. But the idea of using the V Force units as proper guerrillas gradually faded away because they could never muster enough firepower or trained men to challenge the Japanese in battle. The jungle also took a heavy toll. As one V Force commander, Colonel R. A. W. Binny, wrote, 'Experienced officers were wounded, went sick or were relieved and their places filled by young officers from units in India. Though keen enough they could not quite keep up the patrolling standards or endure the same hardships as the earlier ones.' The hardships were considerable, particularly for young men fresh from barracks in India. Lieutenant Colonel Ord, who commanded 5 V Ops Area, wrote that all the men under his command had to be able to march an average of thirty miles a day across the hills, unencumbered by heavy baggage. 'A heavily loaded man is not a guerrilla.'

There were other, more esoteric elements to their jungle education. Edward Lewis was a V Force officer operating inside Burma, where local Chin tribesmen instructed him in the traditional means of body disposal. 'When somebody died they put the body into a tree and let the ants eat the flesh. They would then go and collect the bones and put them in a hole.' An official document noted that the Chins operating with V Force were 'very fond of biting each other which is considered more satisfying than a mere brawl with knives'.

The V Force experiment was far from perfect: sectarian feuding among local tribes in the Arakan compromised its operations; and the lack of experienced officers inevitably reduced efficiency. An attempt to introduce fiercely warlike Afridi tribesmen from the arid North-West Frontier into the jungles under V Force command ended in mutiny and the disbandment of the Afridi Legion. A few senior generals viewed V Force, and all similar secret organisations, with disdain, believing they absorbed considerable resources for minimal gain. Some of this was undoubtedly based on genuine concerns, but there was also a strong element of prejudice. General Slim was more generous. 'Later, along the whole front,' he wrote, 'V Force became an important and very valuable part of the whole intelligence framework.' The Commander-in-Chief India, Sir Archibald Wavell, visited V Force headquarters at Imphal, nearly ninety miles from Kohima, where, having listened to an officer outline plans, he gave his blessing in a few brief sentences: 'Good. Remember I back you. Make and commission your own officers. If you want help let me know. Good night.'

The extraordinary range of individuals drawn into V Force and other guerrilla organisations is wonderfully described by Ranald Macdonald, who served as superintendent of the Lushai Hills during the war.

I had seen a Haka Chin rifleman on guard at the perimeter of our bivouac. What force kept him there, risking death and torture for an apparently losing cause? His home and family were now behind enemy lines; his officers were defeated and baffled; his rations were short; his companions were mostly gone; what made him stay? And that rich rancher, what had brought him from South America to share a teaspoonful of bad gin out of a bamboo cup to celebrate with us the incoming of the New Year? Or the Southern Irish doctor, joking between jerks of the dysentery that would kill him a few days later, what took him from his still peaceful country, where he could have remained usefully and comfortably and profitably earning the respect of all? And that Punjabi battalion – flame leaping Khataks from near the Afghan border, proud Rajputs from Jammu, Sikhs and Muslims welded together from between Amritsar and Lahore, every man a volunteer – what welded them under two Sikhs, a Hindu, a Muslim, a Parsi, three Englishmen, a Maltese and a Jew commanded by a Welshman, to become one brotherhood committed to the defence of a territory whose very existence had been unknown to all of them a few months before?

Macdonald's wife Daphne stayed on with her husband and their young son after the Japanese advance on the Indian frontier. Mrs Macdonald took charge of the wireless set and organised the headquarters of her husband's guerrilla band. When she became pregnant with the couple's second child, Daphne Macdonald marched one hundred miles to the nearest doctor and one hundred back.

*　*　*

At the age of twenty-four she had made her first solo journey into the jungle. 'There was a great deal of tut-tutting and a firm belief that at the end of three days I would be borne home in a fainting fit.' Instead, Ursula Graham Bower stayed out for several weeks and came back 'happy as a sandboy', clutching specimens of Naga art. Her second trip took her to the Ukhrul district, on the border with Manipur, an area where the Nagas still practised headhunting and where three unfortunate Manipuri traders had been decapitated a short time previously. Ursula Graham Bower rationalised the practice: 'If you come home with the head then you know that the rest of the gentleman is not looking for you.'

Within three years of that first jungle excursion, Ursula Graham Bower was commanding her own unit of V Force in the Naga Hills. The story of her conversion from Roedean debutante to commander of a tribal force is one of the most extraordinary of the war. The creation of V Force had led to a demand for officers who had lived among and were trusted by the Nagas. In the febrile atmosphere of 1942 this meant sweeping away the normal conventions of recruitment and opening the way for mavericks like Graham Bower.

She first visited the Naga Hills in 1937 when her ambition to study archaeology at Oxford was thwarted by a slump in the family fortunes. That summer a schoolfriend, Alexa Macdonald, invited Ursula to accompany her to India, to visit her brother who was a civil servant in Manipur. The two women went by ship, train, river steamer, train again, car, foot and bamboo river raft. Travelling by raft, they knitted to while away the hours drifting down long rivers. Stopping to explore a small island, they had to run for their lives after a guide spotted tiger prints in the mud. After her adventure Ursula would never feel at ease in London again. Back home she began to cultivate senior fellows of the Royal Geographical Society, impressing them with her knowledge of Naga life and her enthusiasm for research. She made a second visit to Naga country before returning home in April 1939 to join the London Ambulance Service as war approached. The boredom of the phoney war, 'knitting interminable jumpers and waiting for a siren that never came', and her longing for the Naga Hills got the better of her and she announced to her family that she was going back to India. They responded with shock, suspecting that she had 'gone completely off her rocker', but hoping that she might meet a nice young officer in India – somebody who might prove more capable than they had been of taming her adventurous spirit.

She reached Kohima in November 1939, only to be told that a permit to travel out into the hills could not be granted yet. For reasons that were probably to do with the outbreak of war, the Naga Hills were strictly off-limits on the orders of the political agent. Frustrated in her ambition, Ursula Graham Bower suffered a nervous breakdown. 'I hadn't realised that a shock of this sort could stun one physically,' she wrote. 'I remember almost nothing of the next twenty-four hours.' She went to see the political agent in person at Manipur, but he would not change his decision. Afterwards Ursula wandered alone in the dusk for hours. Her nervous collapse lasted a fortnight, during which time she put away or locked up anything that might be used as a suicide weapon. 'It was a giddy path. The holds were so small; one clung hand by hand, a finger.'

Eventually permission was granted and she set off for the Cachar Hills, some eighty miles, as the crow flies, from Kohima. This was a district adjoining the Naga Hills, where the sixteen-year-old priestess-cum-rebel Gaidiliu had been active against the British. Gaidiliu had told her followers that even in prison the British could not kill her spirit, and that she would return in a form that her enemies would be unable to recognise.

When Ursula Graham Bower arrived she was surrounded by adoring locals who clearly believed she was the vanished priestess. The impression was reinforced by her physical appearance: the Englishwoman was tall and statuesque. 'She [Gaidiliu] was tall and rather strongly built and one of her more lunatic followers decided I was the reincarnation ... half the population appeared to go stark staring mad ... they were rushing at me clawing at me and calling me Goddess.' Warriors who had fought under Gaidiliu came in from their villages to see the reincarnation. Privacy became impossible. At one point she was having a bath when an elderly man carrying a gift of a chicken walked into her hut. She had no towel and only a bar of soap with which to cover herself. She screamed and a bodyguard rushed in to hustle the old man out. When she reported back to the government an official told her, with the ingrained cynicism of his species, that 'if they must have a goddess they might as well have a government one'.

Ursula's parents had nurtured visions of her attending glittering balls in Delhi or taking afternoon tea in Simla, but by the middle of 1942 their debutante daughter was about to become the first female guerrilla commander in the history of British arms. Although her only experience of war thus far had been taking care of refugees and wounded soldiers coming out of Burma, the fact that she lived in the hills and was respected by the local Nagas made Ursula Graham Bower a logical choice for command.

After consulting with Charles Pawsey and other officials, the head of V Force dispatched an elderly officer to bring her the news of her appointment. The man he sent, Colonel Douglas Rawdon Wright, was an old India hand who had ridden with the Deccan Horse on the Somme in one of the last great cavalry charges of British arms. He had also spent several years as an officer with the Assam Rifles. Although badly wounded in the leg on the Western Front and forced to retire to England, he yearned to return to the India where he had soldiered as a young man. Colonel Rawdon Wright badgered the military authorities for a job. Eventually they sent him out to Assam to a desk job with V Force. Rawdon Wright soon tired of the inertia of headquarters and the nagging sense that younger men were laughing at the desk-bound old warrior with the pronounced limp. When asked to go into the Cachar Hills and give Ursula Graham Bower news of her command he seized the opportunity with enthusiasm.

Looking out of her bungalow one August lunchtime, Graham Bower saw an elderly white man limping down the narrow path to the village. She immediately sent a man with a note to invite the visitor to lunch. A reply came a few minutes later: 'So sorry but I've got a gammy leg. I'd better go straight on down to the rest-house.' Later in the after-noon she made her way down to meet the colonel and saw that he was unable to bend his leg. But when they set out to explore the district he refused all offers of help from the Nagas: he would not be carried about 'like a woman' or some effete civil servant from Delhi. And so the group traversed steep inclines over several miles while Rawdon Wright struggled along, sometimes going down on all fours to force his way upwards, and all the time chatting with Graham Bower about the quality of the fishing in the hills or about people they knew in common in Kohima and Imphal. 'He was superb,' she wrote later. 'We might have been sitting in a club veranda.' On his way back down from the hills the Naga offered to provide a litter on which he could be comfortably carried. Again he refused. Graham Bower's account of his departure can be read as an elegy not only for an old soldier, but for an ideal of imperial duty that was entering its twilight. She stood with the village headman and watched the colonel climb over the rocks and over the slippery ground, leaning on the shoulder of his guide until he reached the turn of the road that would take him out of view. He stopped and turned back to wave. 'We waved back. Then the white shirt was gone. Nobody said anything, because there was too much to say.' On his way down to the plains he fell over three times. The journey ruined his health and he was dead before the end of the year.

Ursula Graham Bower lived in the Cachar Hills among terraced rice paddies whose surfaces glistened like signalling mirrors whenever the sun broke through the monsoon clouds. The area had recently experienced severe hunger, the consequence of decades of competition over land, and the destruction of the rice crop by grasshoppers. Graham Bower believed the area, which lay outside Charles Pawsey's bailiwick, had been neglected and mismanaged by officials 'not always of the best type', men who regarded Cachar as merely a way station on the road to a better job. The government was not loved here; there was an awareness of neglect, and lingering bitterness over the suppression of the Gaidiliu rebellion, which would test Graham Bower's political skills to the utmost. Colonel Rawdon Wright had told her to recruit from all the villages of the area. Recruit first, he said, and the guns and ammunition would follow. But then what? By now the stories of what the Japanese did to anybody they captured were well known. Death from a bullet would be a highly desirable outcome for a young woman caught with a weapon in the Naga Hills. A V Force patrol that had infiltrated back into Burma at the end of the previous May had been captured by the Japanese near the Chindwin river. An Indian officer had had his eyes gouged out before being killed, while two tribal scouts had been tied to a tree and executed.

Ursula Graham Bower would never have recruited her little army, or found the confidence to lead operations, without the help of Namkiabuing, a warrior of the Zemi Naga group, who became her bodyguard and assistant. She wrote of him in terms that rose above the contemporary European discourse of the 'good native'. 'He had an intense, a vivid sense of right and wrong. They were to him a personal responsibility. He could no more compromise with wrong than he could stop breathing.' From the start Namkia made it clear that he was no pliant instrument of European rule. The two argued regularly and he submitted frequent resignations before returning to work. His granddaughter, Azwala, thought Namkia regarded Ursula more as a younger sister than as his employer: 'He was very protective to her ... because ... they do not have a sister. So Ursula Graham Bower was a very beloved sister of the family.'

It was in the villages that Namkia proved his gift for debate. There were many in the area with bad memories of recruitment during the First World War, when labour battalions were raised for the Western Front. The men who returned brought back tales of horror. Graham Bower recorded a typical argument during one of her recruitment drives:

A Hangrum man [stood] up: 'You'll take us away! It's a trap!'

Namkia [stood] up in an answer: 'No! It's an honest offer!'

'Why should we fight for the Sahibs? We didn't fight for the Kacharis, we didn't fight for the Manipuris – why should we fight for the British?'

Namkia again: 'Why shouldn't we? Did the Kacharis or the Manipuris stop the Angamis raiding? Haven't the Sahibs done that? Haven't they given us roads and salt markets? Haven't they given us protection and peace? Don't we owe them something for that?'

And so it went on. Recruits were eventually offered but they were not warriors. Graham Bower noted that the village had offered up 'the lame, the halt and blind'. Eventually, after she had sworn an oath that the men would not be taken away from the hills, the village relented and offered fitter specimens.

Next, the problem was to arm the recruits from the different villages. It was government policy to keep arms out of the hands of the Nagas and other tribes in order to stop them raiding each other or turning the weapons on the British. The arrival of the Japanese on the border removed this restraint. Graham Bower's men were issued with guns, ninety ancient muzzle-loaders, which were probably as much a danger to themselves as to the Japanese. Still, they boosted the recruits' self-esteem and their confidence in Graham Bower. They patrolled the hills with knowledge of the terrain and of concealment that no European could have matched. V Force headquarters gave orders that they were to avoid engagement with the enemy. Intelligence gathering was the priority.

A British soldier sent to learn jungle warfare skills with Graham Bower remembered her effect on both the Nagas and his British comrades. 'When she spoke she had the most beautifully cultured voice and when she spoke we were captivated. Everyone of us said later that if she said "I want you to hang yourself by the neck from the nearest tree," I am sure we would have done it. And these Nagas worshipped her.'

Closer to Kohima, Charles Pawsey had his own Naga intelligence network constantly bringing updates from the border area. In early September 1943 he received a message from a village reporting a suspicious-looking man claiming to be local but believed to be Japanese or Chinese. A fortnight later Pawsey was reporting to his deputy that 'Japanese in great numbers had entered the hills ... three villages have been bombed and burned for disobeying their orders and five people killed'. There were worrying reports, too, about some village chiefs offering their services as guides to the Japanese in return for gifts of salt. The Naga Hills were tense and expectant.

Perhaps because of wartime tension, the sense of the prevailing order being threatened, the hills experienced a brief revival of head-hunting in late 1943. The Governor's Fortnightly Report for the first half of December recorded that two villages had joined with a Burmese village in a major raid across the border. A second report to the Governor evoked the tense nature of affairs: 'In the Naga Hills Tribal Area the powerful Konyak village of Sangnyu is reported to be threatening to interfere with the carriage of supplies for us by Zangkam who are their hereditary enemies.'

There were less threatening annoyances. Ursula Graham Bower was disturbed one morning by the arrival of an officer with a large retinue of porters. He had made his way to her post by claiming that he was a V Force officer. The lieutenant was in fact attached to an engineering unit and had been sent to look at the wreckage of a crashed American aircraft. Graham Bower was suspicious of the empty litter being carried by his men. When questioned, he told her it was for a sick subordinate. But the Nagas discovered that it had been used to carry the lieutenant through the hills, 'making him the laughing stock of several villages in the process'. He told the Naga headman that because he was over forty he could not walk the difficult terrain. The headman was himself over sixty. It was an image of simpering weakness that could undermine the image of V Force among the local tribes. Remembering poor old Rawdon Wright and his brave progress across the hills, Graham Bower was furious and decided to teach the newcomer a lesson. 'We had not been so bitter or angry for years,' she wrote. Having learned that the lieutenant was also terrified of the ghosts that were reputed to stalk the hills, she arranged for two Nagas to terrorise him with fearful noises throughout the night. He left the following morning, whey-faced with exhaustion and fear.

Both Ursula Graham Bower and Charles Pawsey decided to stay on the wild frontier and take whatever the war might bring. Although as different in personality as it was possible to be – she the feisty extrovert, he the eternal reticent – they were driven by something more than duty to the empire. One could describe what they came to feel for the Nagas as loyalty, except that it was more intimate than that. By different paths they had come to love the Naga people and would stand or fall with them when the hurricane struck. It was a love that would be reciprocated at Kohima in courage and blood.

FIVE

Kentish Men

In old age it could still fill them with pride and reduce them to an agonising grief. Only in the company of those who had been with them could they hope for true understanding. That would be the nature of Kohima for the survivors of 4th battalion, Queen's Own Royal West Kent Regiment. Yet at the time they joined up not one among them could have imagined fighting a war in the jungles of north-eastern India. Germany and Italy were the only enemies then and the war was just a few miles away on the other side of the Channel.

Citizen soldiers. It is an overused phrase, but it is hard to think of another that could properly describe the men of 4th battalion, a Territorial Army formation made up of men who had joined up before the war, and others who had been transferred from local militia after limited conscription was introduced in April 1939. The formation of which they were a part traced its roots to the eighteenth century, when it was raised as a regiment of foot during the Seven Years War. In time, and with the depredations of war, the battalion would absorb fresh drafts of men from all over Britain, but at the outset it was overwhelmingly Kentish in character, and most of its officers and men amateur soldiers.

The coastline of their county, with its long sandy beaches, towering cliffs and sheltered coves, had witnessed the landing of the Roman conquerors and now beckoned to Hitler's armies a few hours' sail away in France. The officers and men of the 4th West Kents shared an attachment to this landscape, a county still dominated by green fields and hop farms with the conical towers of brewers' oast houses. According to tradition, men from the west of the county were called Kentish Men, while those from the east were Men of Kent. The division between them followed the contours of the River Medway, which bisects the county on its way to the sea. As the county boundary blurred with that of Greater London, growing numbers of city dwellers gravitated towards the ranks of the Royal West Kents. The regimental history, written in the stolid prose of a different age, describes the qualities of the West Kent soldier: 'The stubborn alertness of the Londoner is thus merged with the slower solidity of the worker in the Garden of England.' In more prosaic terms, they might have been described as an intimidating concoction of hardy yokels and urban wide-boys.

They formed their first bonds in the small drill halls of rural Kent. The shared sense of place provided essential glue in the 4th West Kents until the normal regimental allegiances could be forged through training and combat. As one recruit put it, 'the Drill Hall proved to be a great social club for the young men of the town, and I remembered how good it felt to have left the Church Choir and Boy Scouts ... to become one of the men!'

Private Ivan Daunt, from Chatham, where the naval dockyards were accelerating production to meet the German threat, was one of the battalion's notable characters. Conceived when his father was on leave from the First World War, he was one of nine children and was blessed from an early age with a gift for getting into trouble. Constantly playing truant, he eventually left school aged thirteen and became an apprentice carpenter. On the day his apprenticeship finished Daunt was called up. He resented the blow this represented to his earnings: 'I was getting one shilling sixpence ha'penny an hour as a carpenter which was good money and I was doing quite well. And then I go into the army on one shilling and sixpence per day! And then they took sixpence of that for barrack damages.' But Daunt surprised himself and took well to the army life, helped by the fact that most of his comrades were of the same age and from the same part of Kent. The private's mood was further improved on discovering that his wages would go up to two shillings on the outbreak of war.

The officers were the sons of lawyers, stockbrokers, wealthy farmers and teachers. The men of the ranks came from the same great pool that had filled the ranks of the British army for hundreds of years: factory workers, farm labourers, apprentice tradesmen, but also, now, the sons of an aspirant working class, boys who looked to white-collar jobs or even to go on to university.

John Winstanley was beginning his studies as a trainee doctor at St Thomas's Hospital in London when war broke out, 'and I was happy because I thought I'd much rather be with my army chums than studying for medical school ... and I had another two and half years before I could qualify'. He took well to military life. 'I loved the Territorial Army, and the whole way of life; we were in the outdoors and I loved the marching and the comradeship.' The First World War had been a brooding presence in the lives of many of the troops. In the town of Tonbridge an editorial in a school magazine in 1917 had included the following wry comment: 'Lack of literacy may surely be pleaded by the editors this term – the literary half of them have suddenly been called up for military service!' Fifty-three pupils and seven masters from Tonbridge School were to be killed in France.

Private Peter Goodwin saw his father descend into the torment of severe shell shock. Goodwin was born in Tonbridge two years after the end of the war, one of three brothers in a working-class family. 'There was a place outside Tonbridge ... where there was a colony of shell shock victims. Once a weekend they would bring a party in to go to the cinema and they would walk ... in all sorts of weather. It was terrible to see them, but to some extent it was also accepted as the normal order of things.' His father ended his days in a psychiatric hospital. The generation of young men who joined 4th battalion at the outbreak of the Second World War did not set out with illusions of glory. This would be important in the trials to come.

By the time the 4th West Kents made their stand at Kohima in April 1944 they were a battle-hardened outfit that had fought the Germans, Italians and Japanese, suffering exceptional losses. It was the fierce nature of what they had endured during the fall of France and later in North Africa that gave this battalion its formidable character, a self-belief that would carry them to war in Burma convinced that they could live up to their regimental motto of 'Invicta': the Unconquered.

More than half of 4th battalion were either captured or killed during the last weeks of May 1940. In battle Ivan Daunt found a courage and resourcefulness that civilian life would never have demanded of him. Retreating to Dunkirk, he was trapped behind German lines. 'Our whole bloody battalion had gone ... not a word mate, not a word,' he recalled. Daunt made a hazardous cross-country hike with a few other men to reach Dunkirk. The beaches were packed with waiting troops. Captain John Winstanley spent two to three days on the beach, with Stukas making regular bombing runs. Unless there was a direct hit on your position, he remembered, the sand tended to deflect the explosions upwards, a small mercy in the circumstances.

The men marched in an orderly line along the beach until they were directed to a point where small boats would take them to a waiting ship. 'We were like sheep ... we had to stand there and hope for the best,' recalled Ivan Daunt. On board, the decks were crowded with exhausted soldiers and their gear. Daunt eventually found a space where he, and the new silver cutlery service he had 'liberated' from an abandoned house, would be comfortable. Sadly for him, a sailor came and told the men to hand over any heavy material in their possession. Every last inch of space was needed and every ounce of excess weight had to go. His rifle and cutlery went over the side. The men on the decks could see the German aircraft screaming down to bomb the waiting ships. A hospital ship and a destroyer received direct hits while the 4th West Kents were waiting to sail.

Their first taste of war had been of defeat and chaos. Half of their comrades lay dead, dying, or on their way to German prison camps. But the rescue at Dunkirk had salvaged some self-respect. More than 300,000 men had been evacuated and the 4th West Kents shared in the pride of that achievement. Private Wally Jenner knew he would live to fight another day. On a personal level, he was proud he had managed to hold on to his rifle. It made him feel, as he put it, 'like a proper soldier'.

On 31 May 1942, the 4th West Kents, supplemented with a fresh draft of troops to replace the dead and missing, boarded a train for Liverpool where the SS *Laconia* was waiting to ship them to the desert battlefields of North Africa. The officers were wedged five and six to a cabin, and more than 3,000 men were crammed on to the lower decks. There was a blackout in force at night to ensure that no enemy aircraft or U-boats could spot the ship's lights twinkling in the darkness. The floors and walkways were awash with vomit, the air filled with the smell of sick and sweat, and all of it accompanied by the constant thrum of the engines and the groans of sick men. There were submarine alarms that produced a 'nerve-wracking uncertainty'.* Because of U-boat activity in the Mediterranean, the *Laconia* was forced to take the long way round to Egypt, down the West African coast and up the other side. There was a stop at Freetown in Sierra Leone to take on supplies and from there the ship ploughed on to Cape Town, arriving on 1 July. Here there was a four-day stop for some shore leave, bars and girls for the men, lunches in the homes of respectable locals for the officers. It was here that the West Kents received the news that the British base at Tobruk in Libya had finally fallen to Rommel's Afrika Korps, with 35,000 Allied troops marching into captivity.

One of the new officers was Lieutenant Donald Easten, from the leafy town of Chislehurst. Easten was an English countryman, the son of a solicitor, who lived for shooting and fishing whenever he found time away from his work as a clerk in the City of London. After Hitler invaded Czechoslovakia in 1938 a friend of his father's had asked if he had joined the Territorial Army yet. 'And when I said no

---

* There was a tragic postscript. On the return journey, loaded with over 3,000 people, among them many Italian prisoners of war, the *Laconia* was torpedoed off the West African coast. Over two thirds of those on board lost their lives.

he said: "Why the bloody hell aren't you?"' He joined up and was sent to the 4th West Kents in time for the journey east. On the long sea journey he thought often of his bride, Billie, who was serving with an anti-aircraft battery in London. 'We were all bloody miserable ... There was a grim silence. Everybody alone with their memories wondering, am I ever going to see her again?'

On 24 July 1942, nearly two months after they had set out from England, the 4th West Kents arrived in the Gulf of Suez and disembarked at Port Tewfik, where they prepared to join the allied counter-offensive against Rommel. The German general's aim was to break through the allied defensive line stretching from El Alamein into the desert and open the way for an assault on Cairo, the last step needed to drive the allies out of North Africa. If he moved quickly enough, and if his enemy stumbled, there was a chance the Desert Fox could steal victory before the continuing build-up of British men and armour would make his task impossible.

The 4th West Kents spent a fortnight doing 'toughening up marches', without water, conducting mock attacks and practising night manoeuvres in the desert. The war diary for this period describes a battalion rapidly preparing itself for action, but the only incident of note was the death of a soldier who was accidentally shot.

One night Private Ivan Daunt was sitting with a few friends when he heard his name called out. An officer came over carrying a telegram from home. 'I got down, put a sheet over my head and lit a match and it says: "A son is born." I wouldn't see him for another three years.' In the desert night he felt a combination of joy and unspeakable sadness.

On 20 August a distinguished visitor arrived at 8th Army head-quarters. The prime minister was on his way back from Moscow where he and President Roosevelt had met with Stalin, 'the old Bear', as Churchill described him to the welcoming party of officers. Now promoted to captain, Donald Easten was serving as a liaison officer between 132 Brigade, of which the 4th West Kents were part, and 8th Army headquarters. He suddenly found himself called upon to act as scout for the prime minister's visit to front-line positions, a journey that would involve traversing a minefield. He practised the route several times in advance. 'I was thinking I was going to meet the General and Churchill and two or three other people in vehicles. I found that I was leading something that looked like an armoured division! There were so many newspaper people, reporters and armoured cars and heaven knows what else.' Easten led the convoy through the desert, found the gap, and made his way through to the other side. There he handed over to another officer and Churchill waved him goodbye with a shout of thanks. When he got back to the division headquarters he was immediately summoned and given 'the most tremendous rocket'. He had apparently taken a fifty-yard detour off the safe route without knowing it. 'However I didn't blow the old man up,' he recalled, still with an expression of considerable relief more than fifty years later.

Orders came down for the 4th West Kents to prepare to move off and mount an operation to interdict Rommel's supply lines in the area of Alam Halfa. The troops moved out into the darkness at 2300 hours on 3 September, but German planes had spotted them forming up in the early evening and the sound of their vehicles was already attracting enemy mortar fire. Captain John Winstanley moved forward with B company on a 'wonderful moonlight night', but from the outset things went wrong. As the New Zealand official history describes it, the 4th West Kents 'became considerably disorganised, with trucks on the wrong routes and often, in losing the way, becoming stuck in the soft sand or in the minefields ... there was a confused mass of men and trucks'. Unbeknown to the battalion one of the few truly effective elements in the Italian army was waiting for them, holding fire in trenches that lay right across the line of advance.

The Folgore Division was an elite formation of paratroopers who could be depended on to stand and fight. As the advance eventually got under way, Winstanley heard the sound of men moving along on either side of him in silence. And then fury was unleashed. 'The silence was shattered by a roar of automatic fire, and showers of Italian grenades burst among the forward companies. Many of the men were hit but the leading platoons charged the enemy positions.'

Enemy mortars crashed into the battalion's vehicles and fires lit the sky, silhouetting the advancing men and making them an easier target for the machine-gunners. John Winstanley was firing his rifle lying flat on the ground when a bullet pierced his arm. He screamed in pain but maintained his position, urging his men to fight while trying to return fire himself.

Enemy aircraft now appeared and dropped parachute flares to illuminate their targets. Caught in the open desert, the majority of the 4th West Kents could only lie flat on their faces and pray. Most of their entrenching tools were in the burning vehicles and in any case it would have taken hours to dig proper foxholes in the flint-hard ground. The strafing and bombing by Stukas and the mortar and machine-gun fire from the Italians pulverised the battalion. Some men did make it into the Italian trenches and fought hand to hand with the defenders; they even managed to take some prisoners. But the battle was going badly and by 3 a.m. the order was given to withdraw. Carrying the severely wounded with them, the 4th West Kents, including an exhausted John Winstanley, eventually found some cover at a ridge several thousand yards back from the scene of the battle. Winstanley was evacuated to a military hospital, where he spent several weeks recovering from his wound. Private Ivan Daunt reflected bitterly on the experience of Alam Halfa: 'The intelligence wasn't thorough ... we weren't there long enough to know.' The battalion lost 250 men killed, wounded or missing, more than half its strength. It was an agonising reminder of the catastrophe of France in 1940.

The regimental history recorded that the 4th West Kents were 'thrown away in a suicidal attempt to cut off the retreat of the enemy'. It was, as twenty-two-year-old Peter Goodwin put it, 'a complete cock-up. That was when morale reached its lowest point in the war. Everyone knew that it was a wasted effort and we lost a lot of people.' Ivan Daunt felt changed by the desert, older and wiser, and determined that the war was something he would survive and see through to the end. Twice he had been caught up in disaster. He swore it would not happen again.

*   *   *

As had happened after France, new men and officers arrived to make up for the losses suffered at Alam Halfa. Among them was Lieutenant Tom Hogg, a transport officer who had grown up on a farm in the Yorkshire Dales. He had already survived death once by the time he joined the army: a motorcyclist had knocked him down when he was ten and left him with a fractured skull and broken leg. In those days the cost of the operations he needed ran to the price of 'ten good milk cows by my father's reckoning, and therefore a considerable loss to him'. At Giggleswick village school he was written off as a plodder and 'suffered terribly from the impatience of teachers who clearly thought me too dim to be worthy of their time'. On leaving school in 1939 he joined the Territorial Army in Yorkshire, becoming, according to the *Daily Mirror*, the youngest sergeant in the British army at the outbreak of war. He found his way to the 4th West Kents after escaping from German captivity near Tobruk. To Ivan Daunt, the new members of the battalion like Tom Hogg were a source of strength: 'A lot of them had been in other battles. They had been elsewhere. They weren't rookies … And the NCOs … we got hardened ones coming in. And that made a lot of difference. Especially at Kohima.'

Hogg remembered some of his early experiences with particular distaste. On several occasions the 4th West Kents would see a group of Italians waiting to surrender and approach them. All of a sudden there would be a shout in German and the would-be prisoners would throw themselves down, revealing a German machine-gun crew who would open up on the British. The idea was to capture the transport. 'This particular trick caused "bad blood" among our men, and I recall seeing one of our Red Caps … roll a live grenade into a trench full of prisoners who had already surrendered. I wondered how he would have felt if the roles had been reversed.'

A new commanding officer arrived at the battalion that autumn. Lieutenant Colonel H. W. Lambert was a pious man with a fascination for the holy places of the Middle East. He was liked by the men. Lambert began his command with inspections 'in detail' of all the battalion companies; drill routines, bathing procedures, battle training and leave procedures were all examined rigorously. Company commanders referred men they did not regard as physically or mentally fit to the medical officers for regrading. Lambert was restoring morale in the most sensible way possible, by ensuring that normal battalion life was resumed.

In December 1942 the 4th West Kents became part of 161 Brigade, 5th Indian Division, with which they would serve until the end of the war. As part of 161 Indian Brigade they would fight alongside two Indian battalions, the 1/1 Punjab and 4/7 Rajput. The practice of brigading two Indian battalions with one British battalion dated back to the fear-filled aftermath of the Indian Mutiny of 1857.

The West Kents were to be sent to Iraq to counter the possibility of a German thrust from the Caucasus against the Iraqi oilfields. Lieutenant Hogg found himself leading the column and navigating by the sun. 'I was supplied with a jeep with a sun-compass on the bonnet and by keeping a careful watch on the sun's relative movement we were able to arrive within sight of the bridge superstructure at Fallujah, after 700 miles of desert-driving, which was not bad!' The journey was punctuated by numerous stops ordered by the devout Colonel Lambert. Captain Donald Easten remembered, 'We had to stop and get the soldiers out of their vehicles to listen to the CO talk about the holy places. I remember hearing the sergeant major telling the lads to get out of the trucks: "Out ye get lads, more Jesus stuff."' Ivan Daunt and his comrades would mutter and dutifully dismount for another wholesome lecture.

Wintering in Baghdad, Captain Harry Smith remembered the sullenness of the locals, the dust storms that whipped grit into the most well-covered orifices, and the endless waiting for a German thrust which every man of them sensed would never come. Smith was a schoolmaster and had married on the eve of the war. The school magazine printed the usual congratulations, but with a poignant coda: 'Congratulations to Mr. H. Crispin Smith on his marriage on 13th November to Miss Iris Reaves … Though we miss him greatly, we know he is giving another kind of service, and we hope that later, in a war-free world, he will resume his normal work with us.' He had been wounded at the battle of El Alamein and spent most nights in Baghdad in a state of semi-wakefulness. Shortly after arriving he awoke to find a pack of wild dogs, the snarling and mange-ridden brutes that haunted Baghdad's alleys, rooting through his belongings. He froze and feigned sleep until the pack moved on. Not only were there dogs and jackals for the men to fear at night, but also the rifle snatchers, some of the best and most ruthless thieves in all of Iraq, 'who wouldn't think twice about using a knife if they were cornered'.

The battalion made route marches of more than twenty miles and conducted repeated mock attacks. But any danger of a German attack from the Caucasus vanished with the defeat of von Paulus's German 6th Army at Stalingrad in early February 1943. Soon after-wards a new commanding officer arrived to replace Lieutenant Colonel Lambert. The devout and steady leader was replaced by Lieutenant Colonel F. S. Saville, a man of genial nature but with no experience of battle. At the end of May the 4th West Kents were given fresh orders. They were to sail for India where a new army was being readied for war with the Japanese. For Captain John Winstanley it was exciting news, for he had strong family connections with the East. His parents had lived in the Burmese jungle, where his father had worked as an officer for the Burma Forest Service. When his mother became pregnant with John it was decided that she should return to England for the birth. Her husband stayed behind to join the Burma Sappers and Miners, and was eventually posted to the North-West Frontier. He died there of typhoid in 1919. The telegram announcing his death reached Winstanley's mother just as she prepared to rejoin her husband. She would never see India or Burma again.

The new CO, Lieutenant Colonel Saville, regaled his officers with the joys awaiting them in India. Donald Easten recalled, 'When he heard we were going to India he said, "You will all have three or four servants and you will have to play polo. The problem for some of you will be that you will only be able to afford one pony, but the rest of you should be able to afford two or three." We were all saying to one another, "Perhaps we ought to tell him we're at war!"' Before long his enthusiastic word pictures of life on the subcontinent earned the unfortunate lieutenant colonel the nickname 'Playboy of India'. Saville had not been with the battalion in the crucible of the Western Desert and it would have taken a personality of considerable force to impress the battle-hardened troops. Lieutenant Colonel Saville was not that man.

Camp was struck swiftly in Baghdad and the men boarded trucks for the start of their journey south to the port of Basra, passing on the way the walls of Kut al Amara, where thousands of British and Indian troops, among them men of the Royal West Kents, had been killed or else died in Turkish captivity in April 1916. From Basra they steamed slowly down the palm-lined fringes of the Shatt al-Arab, passing the dhows of fishermen and little inlets where women washed clothes and children swam and splashed in the muddy water. The landscape beyond the waterway was an immense plateau of reeds, braided through with little canals along which the fishermen constructed their huts of dried reeds. The children waved to the men on deck as the ship glided down towards the open sea.

Approaching Bombay on the morning of 20 June 1943, the battalion heard the sound of a brass band as they came into the harbour. The triumphal reception was being granted because of their part in the victory at El Alamein. It was, no doubt, also intended as a reminder to the more mutinous subjects of the Raj that British fortunes were improving. One officer recorded that 'there was a faint hint of comic opera about our arrival. Bombay greeted us with a brass band and grave warnings to the effect that irresponsible talk about Japanese fighting ability was liable to have a bad effect on the morale of British troops.' He also noted, almost as an afterthought, that Burma was to be their destination.

Bombay occupied a special place in the history of the Indian national liberation movement, for it was there that the Congress Party had been founded nearly sixty years before, and there that Mohandas K. Gandhi had launched the Quit India movement. By the time the 4th West Kents arrived, Gandhi, Nehru and the other main leaders of the Congress were in prison. The troops knew little of this state of affairs. What information they had came from a handful of old soldiers who had served in Bombay before the war, when the Raj had guaranteed that the humblest of white men could feel themselves among the earth's chosen. The old soldiers painted a glorious picture of life in the army camp for Private Ivan Daunt and his comrades as they crowded on the gangways to disembark. There were servants to take care of every need. Best of all, Daunt was told, were the punkah-wallahs, who fanned the soldiers while they took their nap during the hot afternoons, operating the overhead fans with their toes until they too, invariably, nodded off. Daunt was advised to keep a boot ready to throw at any punkah-wallah sleeping on duty.

Of all the cities of the eastern empire, Bombay was the most self-consciously striking in the first impressions it gave: a jumble of architectural styles which could have appeared as a grandiloquent folly but invariably inspired the admiration of visitors arriving by sea. Its buildings were not only a fusion of the impulses that drove the dream of empire but a tribute to the enduring power of its institutions, from the government secretariat to the law courts to the university, all facing towards the great bay on the Arabian Sea. Waiting at the docks to greet the West Kents, dressed in distinctive red dhotis, was an army of coolies, the carriers and bearers of the Raj, kept in order by supervisors swirling their long lathis.*

Wartime disembarkation in Bombay could be a lengthy and frustrating process. Men, weapons, vehicles and supplies had to be unloaded on to the quayside. Robert Kay, a gunner with the Royal Artillery, remembered being woken at 4.30 in the morning to start the process: 'The whole operation took place in the cramped spaces of a troopship, with on-board temperatures exceeding 95 degrees Fahrenheit, with men all dressed in battle equipment, sweating and swearing and carrying kit bags and everything else they owned.'

---

* A long bamboo rod still used by police to keep public order in India.

Others would curse the bureaucracy of the Colonel Blimps who charged a West Kents officer two shillings customs duty on his double-barrelled shotgun. Irritation and impatience were mixed with awe. An officer remembered the shock of the exotic when he looked out over the side of the ship to see a giant sea snake, twelve feet long and highly venomous.

In the streets that day the West Kents saw snake charmers and acrobats, and a man who could put a meat hook through his nose and pull it out through his mouth. They were assailed by the pungency of the great port city, the smell of spices piled high in the small shops and curried food being cooked on the footpaths, the reek of open drains and piled garbage and the constant raucous hymn of supplication: 'Baksheesh, baksheesh.' Ivan Daunt remembered that the beggars called him 'Rajah' and that he saw two men carrying a pole on which was hung a beggar-man, 'all mangled and his legs, arms all bent'.

The rise in nationalist sentiment had not inhibited the famed entrepreneurial spirit of Bombay. Taxis ferrying officers to the Taj Hotel, right next to the Gateway of India, bore the Union flag on their radiators and the drivers made the appropriate patriotic noises. The hotel had been converted into an officers' club where five- or six-course meals, followed by cabaret and dancing, could be enjoyed. Walking outside at dusk, one group of newly arrived officers saw a profusion of street sleepers. They were 'staggered to see Indian bodies lying there on the pavement, pedestrian islands and almost anywhere; they all looked quite dead, and the more so as their faces were covered with a shroud'.

The 4th West Kents marched to the railway station and set off on a 1,000 mile train journey across India to the training base at Ranchi, where General Slim's 14th Army was being readied for war. The men were loaded into third-class carriages with hard wooden seats and the officers dispatched to overcrowded sleeper compartments. Diaries of those wartime journeys recall heat, dust, discomfort, and the excitement of traversing the subcontinent. Captain Arthur Swinson, a staff captain with the British 2nd Division, who would later encounter the West Kents at Kohima, was a budding writer who kept a careful account of the sights of India. 'Every station brought its new quota of ragged half-starved children demanding "bukshees", some on their own and some egged on by their equally ragged parents. I hardened my heart against them but "Boggie" (who is to take holy orders after the war) feels he must go about doing good and so gives them annas.* This causes their wails to increase tenfold. The persistence of the Indian beggar is equalled only by his ingratitude.'

But for all his irritation with the beggars, Swinson was not immune to the magic of India, the immensity of the visions it offered, temporal and divine, or the ingenuity of its cultures. When the train stopped on the banks of the Ganges he noticed groups of Indians bathing themselves and their water buffalo. A woman among the crowd changed her dirty sari for a clean one, 'without exposing one square inch of flesh that she shouldn't'. The troops on board cheered her when she had finished, but 'she was a lady ... and made pretend she didn't hear a thing'. A friend of Swinson's, Lieutenant Keith Halnan, recalled that when they stopped for lunch, 'there would be tables laid out on the platform for the sahibs and we would sit and have lunch and the train waited until we were finished. What a life!'

For the other ranks experiencing India for the first time, the journey was a blend of chronic physical discomfort, appalling tedium and moments of wonder. Ray Street, who would become a battlefield runner for the 4th West Kents, believed he was witnessing scenes from a Bible story when he paused at some of the bigger stations and huge crowds 'swept towards the train, dressed in their white flowing garments'. A platform guard gave the signal for departure by striking a length of old railway track with a piece of wood and this precipitated a final rush of hopeful travellers, clinging to doors and windows and the roof. Wary of the onrush, the troops stored their rifles under the wooden seats, having been warned that they would fetch a price of £100 on the North-West Frontier. Street remembered

---

* A unit of currency in British-ruled India, roughly equivalent to one sixteenth of a rupee.

seeing a band of dacoits chained together and led along the platform by a policeman at one of the stations.* They were, he reckoned, the roughest-looking bunch of individuals he had ever seen. His friend, Lance Corporal Dennis Wykes, felt unnerved passing a building where vultures feasted on human corpses. The building had no windows, doors or roof. The bodies were laid out on metal bars and when the bones had been picked bare they would fall through the bars to the ground. 'It was so strange to me, coming from England like,' he remembered. What Wykes saw was a Zoroastrian 'Tower of Silence', where the body is left to be eaten by vultures so that it does not pollute the earth.

Later on he would become, if not exactly blasé about seeing corpses, then certainly less inclined to worry about them. The train crossed central India on its journey towards Ranchi, through dry scrub and forest, across great rivers and mountains, a five-day journey moving steadily eastwards towards western Bengal, where the high summer temperatures were rendered more tolerable than in the furnace of the plains by the monsoon rains. The schoolmaster Captain Harry Smith was transfixed by the world unfolding outside his carriage. He would remember the light fading to deep blue on the plains as evening came on, the sound of langur monkeys squabbling in the forest by the track, and the fires of wood and animal dung which produced a sweet acrid smell – 'for me always the smell of India' – when the train passed near villages.

In the cool of dusk the train would stop and cooks would alight to prepare the evening meal, invariably a concoction that involved bully beef or soya-link sausages and whatever else they had been able to scavenge. Tinned food was favoured, not for its flavour but because it reduced the chance of stomach upsets. Dinner was eaten on the ground in the shade of the carriages and washed down with tea made from water drawn from the engine's boiler. As Harry Smith recalled, 'it was tea made with lashings of sugar, condensed milk and water that tasted of engine oil. Delicious!'

---

* Dacoits are bandits or outlaws frequently operating in large groups.

Many who took the troop train to Ranchi that June would not come back; others would return without limbs, or brutally disfigured in other ways; some would be wounded in the spirit by the loss of friends or the memories of what they had endured and seen. As the West Kents rattled slowly across India, the generals, British and Japanese, were laying plans to change the face of the Asian war.

SIX

Fighting Back

By the middle of 1943 General Slim knew his enemy well and was certain that the fight to retake Burma would be hard and bloody. Of the Japanese soldier he wrote: 'He fought and marched till he died. If five hundred Japanese were ordered to hold a position we had to kill four hundred and ninety-five before it was ours – and then the last five killed themselves. It was this combination of obedience and ferocity that made that Japanese Army, whatever its condition, so formidable, and which would make any army formidable.' The previous November, British and Indian forces had stumbled to disaster in the Burmese province of Arakan in a vain attempt to drive the Japanese back and begin the recapture of Burma. After an initial advance, the Japanese had driven the British and Indian forces back. No ground had been gained despite a casualty toll of 5,057 killed, wounded or missing.*

The Japanese used the tactics of outflanking and encirclement that had caused Slim's troops such anguish on the retreat from Burma. The terrain on which they fought was ribboned by rivers and streams, harboured numerous swamps, and was bordered to the west by the sea and to the east by the Mayu range of hills. These rose to 2,000 feet at their highest and were covered in dense forest. It was, recalled one British officer, 'the sort of jungle country in which there could be no front line', covered in thick primary forest, full of exotic plants and animals, and providing awe-inspiring views, and one of

---

* The official breakdown of these figures is 916 killed, 2,889 wounded, and 1,252 missing, including prisoners of war. S. Woodburn Kirby, *The War Against Japan*, vol. 2: *India's Most Dangerous Hour* (HMSO, 1958).

the very last places on earth you would choose to fight a war. When the south-west monsoon arrived, rainfall could reach as much as two hundred inches. The tracks became impassable and the waterways were the only practical means of movement. Even these, swollen with new rain, became, in the words of a senior British commander, 'very formidable obstacles, all of which have to be bridged to allow passage of troops and transport ... Indeed campaigning in the monsoon in Burma may be said to be one of the most arduous operations anywhere in the world today.' A staff officer sent to investigate wrote: 'our troops were either exhausted, browned off or both, and both Indian and British troops did not have their hearts in the campaign. The former were obviously scared of the Jap and demoralised by the nature of the campaign i.e. the thick jungle and the subsequent blindness of movement, the multiple noises of the jungle at night, the terror stories of Jap brutality ... the undermining influence of fever, and the mounting list of failures.' Just as had happened on the retreat the previous year, Slim found himself dispatched to lead the ground operations when it was already too late to effect change. Yet it was here in the Arakan that Slim was now planning his first offensive against the Japanese.

The failure of the first Arakan campaign was rooted in practical and political problems. The battle readiness of the troops was paramount. Over the previous eighteen months the Indian Army had recruited massively. At one point recruits were being dispatched to training centres at a rate of 50,000 per month. There had been too little time to turn these raw recruits into soldiers ready for the challenge of the Arakan, or to prepare the British troops fighting alongside them for jungle warfare. The cream of the Indian Army was fighting overseas, where resources were being devoted overwhelmingly towards the fighting in North Africa.

Looming over it all were the politics of the Grand Alliance. Since the attack on Pearl Harbor in December 1941 and the loss of the Philippines the following April, American ships and planes had routed Japan's carrier fleet at the Battle of Midway on 4 and 5 June

1942. Four carriers, several battleships, around 275 planes, and nearly 5,000 men were lost. Yet the British were still sitting in the positions to which they had retreated after the fall of Burma. There were many in Washington only too keen to accuse London of lassitude. A song doing the rounds of senior American military figures after the fall of Malaya and Singapore that gave an indication of American attitudes to the officer class of the British empire:

> To lunch they go at half past one –
> Blast me, old chap, the day's half done.
> They lunch and talk and fight Jap,
> And now it's time to take a nap.

The British in Asia were widely caricatured as blimps and buffoons, selfish and self-satisfied, borne aloft on the suffering of millions of brown and yellow subjects. Roosevelt himself was determined that victory in the Far East would not lead to a reimposition of the colonial status quo. The Atlantic Charter, which was signed at the Arcadia conference held by Churchill and Roosevelt in December 1941–January 1942, committed the allies to ensuring 'the right of all peoples to choose the form of government under which they will live'. The Americans believed this included India and the rest of the British empire, as well as the French and Dutch colonial possessions occupied by the Japanese. Churchill emphatically did not.*

---

* What American opinion tended to ignore was the human cost of the USA's own expansion. The conquest of the West had been achieved only at the expense of the native tribes. The inhabitants of Hawaii, Puerto Rico and the Philippines, where America had fought a savage war of conquest, had been given no say over the annexation of their lands. The racist segregation within the American army, to say nothing of the discrimination practised in the Southern states of the USA, suggest a convenient myopia on the part of those who condemned Churchill for his imperial revanchism. Roosevelt could himself adopt a tone of condescension towards Asians which would have resonated with the most reactionary of British imperialists. Writing to Churchill on 16th April, 1942 he declared: 'I have never liked Burma or the Burmese and you people must have had a terrible time with them for the last fifty years. Thank the Lord you have HE-SAW, WE-SAW, YOU-SAW under lock and key. I wish you could out the whole bunch of them into a frying pan with a wall around it and let them stew in their own juice.' (PSF/BOX37/A333EE01, Franklin D.Roosevelt Presidential Library and Museum.)

An aggravated Churchill wired his deputy, Clement Attlee, in London about 'the danger of raising the constitutional issue in India at a moment when the enemy is on the frontier'. But he was a shrewd enough politician to realise that preserving the Raj in the face of American opposition demanded a serious military effort in South-East Asia. Limited resources would always make Europe the priority and would ensure that Britain was the junior partner in the Far East. But if the British possessions in South-East Asia were still in enemy hands by the time the Americans defeated Japan, as they surely would be, how could Churchill make any claims for the recovery of territory in the post-war negotiations?* Fighting and defeating the Japanese in Burma would not alter the outcome of the world war, but it would give Churchill valuable political capital.

The British and Americans also had very different strategic aims. Churchill believed British and Indian forces should aim at driving the Japanese out of Rangoon as an initial step towards the recovery of British territory in Singapore and Malaya. The Americans saw the campaign in markedly different terms. China was the priority and British resources should be used to drive the Japanese out of northern Burma in order to secure the supply route to Chiang Kai-shek.† Defeat the Japanese in China, the Americans reasoned, and they would gain a 'back door' to Tokyo, airfields from which to launch bombing raids against the home islands of Japan. For a man of ruthless political calculation in so many other regards, Roosevelt was

---

* In such circumstances, Churchill wrote, 'the United States Government would after the victory feel greatly strengthened in its view that all possessions in the East Indian Archipelago should be placed under some international body upon which the United States would exercise decisive control.' (Winston Churchill memo, 29 February 1944, cited p. 412, *Allies of A Kind*, Christopher Thorne, Oxford University Press, 1978.)

† With this aim in mind work began in late 1942 to build a 400-mile-long road across mountains and through jungles to connect the railhead at Ledo in Assam with the 717-mile road that ran from Lashio in Burma to Kunming in China. The new road would bypass the part of the old 'Burma Road' now in Japanese hands. This immense project was driven forward by the American general Joseph 'Vinegar Joe' Stilwell, chief of staff to Generalissimo Chiang Kai-shek. It involved 17,000 American engineers and around 50,000 Indian labourers and huge numbers of Chinese troops. From the outset Slim was sceptical, writing that 'if it were left to me I would have used the immense resources

obstinately myopic when it came to China. The China he imagined bore no relation to the corrupt and chaotic world of reality. In November 1943 he wrote of the 'triumph of having got the four hundred and twenty million Chinese in on the Allied side. This will be very useful twenty-five or fifty years hence, even though China cannot contribute much military or naval support at the moment.'

General Slim would wrestle with the pressures caused by high-level disagreements as he planned his campaign to retake Burma and throughout the battles to come. But his task would be made infinitely easier by the creation of a new command structure, and notably by his new superior, a charismatic and controversial aristocrat. The initial omens were not good. Lord Louis Mountbatten had planned only one military operation of note, two years before, and it had ended in disaster. As Chief of Combined Operations, he had directed the disastrous Dieppe raid of 1942 in which 3,623 Canadian troops were killed, wounded or captured. In August 1943 he was appointed to head the new South-East Asia Command (SEAC). Mountbatten was only forty-three years old, a Navy captain with the acting rank of admiral, and first cousin to the king. He was regarded by many senior military figures as a self-promoting dilettante who had won his position through Churchill's weakness for those who promised dash-ing victories, and through his royal connections. The CIGS, General Alan Brooke, wrote of being driven 'completely to desperation' by

---

required for this road, not to build a highway to China, but to bring forward the largest possible combat forces to destroy the Japanese army in Burma.' (p. 249, *Defeat Into Victory*, Field Marshal Sir William Slim, Cassell, and Company Ltd, 1956.) Completed in January 1945, the 'Ledo Road' contributed little to the defeat of Japan. The airlift on the 'Hump' route across the Himalayas delivered more than four times the amount of war materiel to the Chinese Nationalists than the 'Ledo Road'. The plan to use bases in China to attack Japan proved a failure. When American raids were launched from bases in Eastern China in May 1944 the Japanese counter-attacked furiously and by January 1945 forced the removal of the bombers to India and thence to the Mariana Islands where the major bombing effort against Japan was based. A US Army historical analysis concluded that 'the air effort in China without the protection of an efficient Chinese Army fulfilled few of the goals proclaimed for it.' ('World War II: The War Against Japan', Robert W. Coakley, American Military History, Army Historical Series, Office of the Chief of Military History, United States Army, Washington, 1989.)

Mountbatten, who was 'quite irresponsible, suffers from the most desperate illogical brain, always producing red herrings'.

But as supreme commander Mountbatten would prove a success. He brought the glamour of royalty to the forlorn front lines of South-East Asia, even if that meant shipping in a barber from London to take care of his tonsorial needs, and he infused the troops with a sense that their battles mattered. His skill in negotiating the often fractious relationship with the Americans helped Slim beyond measure. The American president addressed Mountbatten with the familiar 'Dickie', a habit formed when Mountbatten and Edwina stayed with the Roosevelts a few months before Pearl Harbor. After Mountbatten's accession to SEAC, Roosevelt had gushed to him, 'for the first time in two years I have confidence in the personality problems in the China and Burma fields – and you personally are largely responsible for this'. He added affectionately, and perhaps with a wary sense of Dickie's fondness for the limelight, 'Be a good boy.'

What emerged in South-East Asia was one of the most important partnerships of the war: in Mountbatten, an aristocratic supreme commander who navigated Anglo-American rivalry with skill; and in Slim, the down-to-earth son of a Birmingham shopkeeper, who made war according to a gospel of patience, shrewdness and relentless attention to detail.

A massive reorganisation of the supply, training and medical systems was set in motion. With half a million men under arms in the subcontinent the demands for food and equipment – everything from fresh vegetables to .303 bullets for rifles – had placed an impossible strain on the pre-war colonial infrastructure. Ports, roads and airfields were all upgraded. More than 50,000 labourers were sent to improve the main road to Burma, which passed through Kohima to Imphal.* The tea-planters of Assam provided half of the labour force. By 1943 Indian factories and farmers were producing more goods for the war effort than Australia, New Zealand and Canada put together.

---

* Eight million Indians were employed on war-related work during this period.

Rations had been a constant source of complaint from the men, with the 'staple meal … a bar of dehydrated goat meat looking like a bar of tobacco and when boiled up smelling like an ancient billy-goat'. Now Slim's head of administration, the aptly nicknamed Major General Alf 'The Grocer' Snelling, set out to revolutionise the quality and delivery of the food. He flew in some Chinese to start a duck farm which would produce eggs and he sent his men to India to procure live goats and sheep. Later Snelling would establish a jungle farm to keep up a steady supply of fresh food to the front-line forces, and he would perfect the art of dropping supplies to surrounded troops, painstakingly calculating and packing the supply needs of an entire division. When Slim was told that he could not get adequate supplies of parachutes in India he decided it was 'useless to hope for supplies from home. We were bottom of the priority list there, for parachutes as for everything else.' So he called in the ever-dependable Snelling and a few of his officers and told them that if proper silk parachutes were not available they should find a substitute. They began a search of the paper mills and jute factories of Calcutta, which ended with the development of a 'parajute', made entirely of jute, which was 85 per cent as effective as the normal parachutes. They were not about to drop men or fragile equipment from the air with them, but for food and ammunition they would be invaluable. Slim picked Colonel 'Atte' Persse, a man with a reputation for 'making himself a nuisance to all and sundry until he got what he wanted', to make sure tanks reached the Arakan in time for his offensive. Stone was shipped in from Madras to turn some of the jungle tracks into routes along which tanks could operate.

The most important change took place in the air. At the height of the retreat in 1942 the army could call on only four airfields with all-weather runways and up-to-date facilities. By the following November, thanks to a massive programme of American-sponsored construction, that number had increased tenfold.* The existing fleet

* *The Official History*, vol. 111, p. 317, gives a total of 41 for Assam, Manipur, Eastern Bengal and Calcutta.

of Mohawk fighters was reinforced with Hurricanes, Beaufighters and Spitfires. From the point of view of the fighting man on the ground, one of the fighters' most important roles was to protect the transport planes that brought him food and ammunition.

The health of 14th Army was one of Slim's gravest preoccupations. In the retreat of 1942 around 80 per cent of the British and Indian troops fell ill because of disease. British 6 Brigade lost half its strength in the Arakan, a staggering dissolution of fighting capacity. The official account stated that the 'incidence of malaria during this campaign reached unimagined proportions'.

It struck British and Indian troops with equal force. Major David Atkins commanded a transport unit travelling the road between Dimapur and Imphal and watched his Madrassi drivers falter with fever, one by one. 'The Havildar clerks and the senior NCOs were changing so frequently because of fever, that orders given to one man were not passed on before the man you had given them to went sick. If you spoke to the new man, he would be replaced the next day by the former one.'

Strict discipline on the taking of medication was enforced in 14th Army: if men started to come down with malaria their officers could be cashiered. It took the sacking of three commanders to drive the point home. Hospital admissions for disease dropped from 185 per thousand troops in 1942 to 100 per thousand in 1944.

There were also changes in surgical practice. Treating wounds sustained in jungle fighting was a different prospect from treatment in Europe or the desert. The humidity, the frequently filthy conditions, the difficulty in finding clean water supplies, all presented an immense challenge to the many young and inexperienced surgeons of 14th Army. Wounds had to be cleaned out thoroughly and quickly, the medical chiefs warned. 'The Japanese missiles have a habit of carrying not only clothing and equipment, but also jungle debris, leaves and dirt into the deeper parts of the wound.' In such conditions a man with a minor wound could die from blood poisoning within twenty-four hours. Men were drilled in the importance of field hygiene. As one West Kent put it, 'You learned to bury your crap and above all keep it away from the water source.'

Slim also recognised that the battle for men's minds would be central in the fighting to come. In 1943 the C-in-C India, Sir Archibald Wavell, agreed to appoint a psychiatrist to every division in India. Captain Paul Davis was sent to 2nd Division, which would fight at Kohima the following year. He set about weeding out unsuitable men. 'As a result of this large numbers of dullards, psychoneurotics, and a few psychopaths and psychotics were unearthed. Combatant officers proved to be extremely enthusiastic at the idea of getting rid of these men.' Davis found most of the commanders he encountered helpful. There had been a shift in military attitudes since the First World War, when shell-shock victims could be regarded as cowards, although there was one battalion commander who asked him, 'Why should I send these men to you so that they will survive the war and go home and breed like rabbits, whilst all my finest men are going to risk being killed?' During the battle of Kohima Davis set up a small psychiatric clinic just sixteen miles behind the front.

Slim was aware that neither Churchill nor the CIGS, General Sir Alan Brooke, had much faith in the British and Indian soldier ever being able to meet the Japanese on equal terms in the jungle. Churchill believed that going into the jungle to fight the Japanese was 'like going into the water to fight a shark'. But the Japanese did not come from a land of jungles and swamps. The jungle was no more a natural environment for them than it was for the British. The Japanese had trained and adapted. Slim's 14th Army would do the same. An Infantry Committee set up after the Arakan debacle reported that troops needed to be fit and to be led by officers experienced in the jungle; they needed to avoid roads and learn how to use jungle tracks, and to be trained in concealment and jungle hygiene. One of the most prescient recommendations related to leadership: 'command must be decentralised so that junior leaders will be confronted with situations in which they must make decisions and act without delay on their own responsibility'. To this, Slim added his own developing philosophy of jungle warfare. If encircled, stand fast and hold your ground, rely on air support for resupply and trust in

the reserves to come up and hit the Japanese. They would outflank
the enemy and cut *their* line of communication. Tens of thousands of
men passed through the jungle training courses, where they were
drilled in the basic dogma of encircle and outflank. Above all they
learned to live with the strangeness of the jungle.

As he planned his reconquest of Burma, Slim recognised that ultimate victory would depend on the soldiers of the Indian Army. More
than two thirds of his 14th Army were drawn from the immense
hinterlands of the empire, the majority from India itself. In the
British mythology of the Raj few figures were more warmly drawn
than that of the faithful native. In novels like Talbot Mundy's *For the
Salt He Had Eaten*, the Indian soldier risking, and often giving, his
life for the white sahib is eulogised: 'Proud as a Royal Rajput – and
there is nothing else on God's green earth that is even half as proud
– true to his salt and stout of heart.'

By the end of 1943 the Indian Army had experienced surrender in
Singapore, retreat in Burma, defeat in the Arakan, and the convul-
sions caused by the Quit India movement.* Yet it had not risen as a
body in mutiny or experienced mass desertions. There were more
than two million men serving the allied cause in North Africa and
India, the largest volunteer army in history. In spite of this, Churchill
frequently expressed his mistrust. Wavell noted in his journal in 1943

---

* Even before war broke out there had been problems. As early as August 1939 a Sikh
platoon in the Punjab Regiment deserted after a religious leader 'so lowered their spirit
that they deserted rather than face the dangers of war'. Later that year a group of Sikhs in
Egypt rebelled when asked to load lorries, believing such coolie work was beneath them.
A year after the first outbreak in the Punjab a squadron of the Central India Horse
refused to board ship in Bombay. A mutiny and hunger strike among Sikhs of the Hong
Kong and Singapore Royal Artillery in 1940 was provoked by orders that the men should
wear solar topis. The investigators sent from India blamed the 'faulty administration' and
told the regiment to back down on the helmet order. The troubles prompted one far-
seeing intelligence officer, Colonel Wren, to write in 1940: 'We have by our policies
towards India, bred a new class of [Indian] officer who may be loyal to India and perhaps
to Congress but is not necessarily loyal to us ... The army would be helped by a more
positive policy on the part of His Majesty's Government ... which will transform our
promises of independence for India into reality in the minds of the politically minded
younger generations.'

that the prime minister feared the army could rise at any moment, 'and he accused me of creating a Frankenstein by putting modern weapons in the hands of sepoys, spoke of 1857, and was really childish about it. I tried to reassure him, both verbally and by a written note, but he has a curious complex about India and is always loath to hear good of it and apt to believe the worst.'

The events that followed the fall of Singapore had done much to stoke the prime minister's paranoia. On their surrender, between 40,000 and 60,000 Indian prisoners of war had joined the new pro-Japanese Indian National Army (INA).* The INA, under the leadership of the charismatic former Congress politician Subhas Chandra Bose, would play only a minor role in the fighting to come. But Bose's promise that India would rise once his men had crossed the border encouraged the Japanese and worried the British.

One of Slim's most able commanders, General Sir Philip Christison, found himself being teased about army loyalty at the birthday party of the Maharajah of Mysore, Jayachamaraja Bahadur, in Krishnarajasagara. The general's host was one of the most sophisticated men in the East, a philosopher and musicologist who once sponsored a concert for Richard Strauss at the Royal Albert Hall. He was also regarded as a friend of the British. 'This was a great occasion,' recalled Christison, 'and not affected by any wartime restrictions.' On the night of the party the palace was lit with 30,000 light bulbs and fireworks banged and whizzed across the sky. At the top of the palace steps Christison was greeted by the genial figure of the maharajah, who was standing between two huge stuffed bison. There was a grand procession into the dining hall and after a lavish banquet the ruler decided to take the general into his confidence. 'He told me

---

* The desire to escape the hellish conditions of Japanese prisoner of war camps was a decisive factor for many. Among the officers there were undoubtedly substantial numbers who had been alienated by the racist treatment they received at the hands of colonial officials in pre-war Malaya. This could range from being forced to sit in separate compartments from Europeans on trains and excluded from clubs where a colour bar operated. The INA also drew thousands of recruits from Indian communities in South-East Asia, many of them from the rubber plantations of Malaya and drawn by Bose's promise of a new India in which the restrictions of caste would be overturned.

he had two sons. When Japan entered the war he sent one to Japan ... the other to serve in the British Army. "Who knows who will win?" he said.'

The Japanese intelligence officer Lt.-Colonel Iwaichi Fujiwara, who worked closely with Bose, learned to be circumspect about the INA's military capabilities, writing of Bose that 'the standard of his operational tactics was, it must be said with regret, low. He was inclined to be idealistic and not realistic.' However, the British were certainly alert to the political and intelligence danger posed by the INA. During the Bengal famine of 1942–43, when between one and a half and three million people died, Bose had announced that he would send Burmese rice to feed the starving, and INA broadcasts placed the blame for the catastrophe on British indifference and incompetence.* The Japanese war leader, Prime Minister Hideki Tojo, fanned the flames assiduously, declaring in the Diet on 16 June 1943: 'We are indignant about the fact that India is still under the ruthless suppression of Britain ... we are determined to extend every possible assistance to the cause of India's independence.'

Between 1942 and 1943 there had been several failed INA probes into British territory.† As 1943 drew to a close Mountbatten asked for an intelligence assessment of the INA. It was delivered to him on 13 November, with the instruction that henceforth the INA should,

---

* The famine was caused by a complex interplay of factors: a cyclone that devastated huge areas of rice cultivation; the loss of Burmese rice imports after the Japanese occupation; rumours about shortages and subsequent hoarding of food; incompetence and corruption in the regional government; and the failure of the British and Indian governments to act speedily. Food was being shipped out of Bengal to support the war effort while the population starved. As the historian of the famine, Richard Stevenson, writes: 'The famine in Bengal was caused by a lack of money, not by a lack of food. A hyperinflation was created in Bengal in 1942 as a result of the war and as a result of government policies. A part of the population, British and Indians connected with the war industries, was protected ... the other part, the cultivators and the fishermen, was not protected ... The economy of rural Bengal was too simple and impoverished to withstand the profound and prolonged disruptions applied to it by the government, a British government, in pursuit of its war goals.' Richard Stevenson, *Bengal Tiger and British Lion* (iUniverse, 2005), p. viii.

† Twenty out of twenty-four INA soldiers trained in espionage and parachuted behind allied lines were captured; two raiding parties landed by submarine were also arrested.

for 'counter propaganda purposes', be called JIFS – for 'Japanese Inspired Fifth Columnists' – an acronym designed to strip away the nationalist image of Bose's army. The British also set up 'josh', or 'enthusiasm or verve', units to boost troop morale. The 750 josh groups were intended to 'inculcate the doctrine that India must destroy the Japanese or be destroyed by them and to prepare Indian units for possible encounter with armed JIFS in the field'.

Propaganda broadcasts and leaflet drops were also stepped up, urging INA men to return to British lines where they would be treated fairly. But troops were told that if they encountered former comrades in the field they were to be shot if they did not surrender. General Slim would later say that some Indian units had to be restrained from shooting surrendering INA troops. Sepoy Gian Singh of 7th Indian Division heard Bose's passionate calls for an uprising but was unmoved. 'He promised to liberate India and said the Japanese were the friends of India. Not many truly believed him. Least of all us who saw the Japanese in their true colours. Much as we felt sorry for our brothers who had taken the salt but turned traitor even though they had an excuse. We often gave them no mercy.'

But the question of loyalty was nuanced. Soldiers of the 1st battalion, Assam Regiment were reminded of their duty of loyalty at josh sessions. Sohevu Angami, from the Naga village of Phek, listened to the propaganda about the INA and resolved to kill any of Bose's men he came across. 'We did what our officers told us to do and followed them. The Japanese and the INA were against the British and that made them our enemies. Did I really know what I was fighting for? No.' Yet he had a sneaking regard for the INA leader. 'I think his ideas were good. Even though we were opponents I came to respect him and what he was fighting for.'

In the case of many – perhaps most – soldiers, their loyalty was to their unit and not to the Viceroy or King Emperor. Indian officers did not as a rule feel that they were defending British overlordship, or that serving the Raj meant rejecting the ideals of Gandhi or Bose. A senior British civil servant at the War Department in Delhi wrote that 'even those who were most convinced they had been right to go to Sandhurst and enter the King's service saw it as a way to serve the independent India of the future ... at the end of the war when the whole truth was known, many of the loyal Indian officers who would be the backbone of India's new army felt some sympathy with those who had followed Bose.' The growing realisation among officers and men that independence must come after the war tended to act as a brake on discontent. Major Ian Lyall Grant of King George V's Own Bengal Sappers and Miners had fought alongside Indian officers since the retreat from Burma and was confident of their loyalty. 'I remember saying that Independence was inevitably coming ... I think it was generally known that we were on the way out ... which made it much more difficult for them to hazard their lives on our behalf but they gave absolutely no sign of that to me.'

The Indian Army had also embarked on a transformation of its officer corps.* Discrimination in pay between Indian and British officers had been ended and, having started the war with only a thousand Indian officers, there were more than 6,566 by 1944. Although senior command positions were still overwhelmingly the domain of British officers, there were now Indian battalion and company commanders who gave orders to white subordinates.

Slim was an influential advocate of reform. 'The fair deal meant', he wrote, 'no distinction between races or castes in treatment. The wants and needs of the Indian, African, and Gurkha soldier had to be looked after as keenly as those of his British comrade.' However, Slim acknowledged that some of the newer British officers thought that all an Indian or African required was a 'bush to lie under and a handful of rice to eat'. If paternalism had dominated the Indian Army of old, ignorance of culture and environment could be a hallmark of the younger officer class. Sepoy Gian Singh was crouching behind a small bush during a training exercise when he heard a hiss. A snake was lurking somewhere very close. Singh carefully backed away, only

---

* The transformation was directed by General Sir Claude Auchinleck who replaced Wavell as C-in-C India in 1943. Auchinleck began his career in the Punjab Regiment before rising to become one of the most senior British generals. He was immensely popular with the Indian troops.

to see a deadly krait sitting where his head had just been. The training officer came up and began to harangue Singh:

'What the hell are you up to,' shouted the Captain coming up to me. 'What's all the fuss about such a small snake!'

'That, Sir, is a krait,' I replied.

He had to be told by a Subhadar that it was just as deadly as a .303 bullet. He shook his head in disbelief. That man had a lot to learn and little time to do so.

To many young British officers arriving in India the daily routines of Indian Army barracks life could seem little changed from a century before. On his first morning with 7/2 Punjab Regiment, Lieutenant John Shipster was woken by his bearer with a mug of sweet tea and a banana, and the salutation 'Sahib, *bahadur ji jagao*' – 'Mighty Warrior, arise'. 'Servants were plentiful and one could live like a king on a pittance … For those in the army it was a sportsman's paradise,' he recalled. Shipster had arrived in India aged nineteen and fresh from Marlborough College. He was based at Meerut, headquarters of India's most prestigious pig-stickers, the Meerut Tent Club, although Lieutenant Shipster's forays on horseback were confined to the Ootacamund Foxhounds, chasing the indigenous jackal. The young officers wore tweed jackets and jodhpurs while the master and whips besported themselves in hunting pink. But Shipster was far from the stereotype of the 'pukka' young sahib. He walked the lanes of the poorer districts to practise his Urdu and on his first leave he went with his orderly, Khaddam Hussein, to stay at the man's home. The two men hired a camel to carry their bags and walked to the village. 'I wanted to see how they lived, and I liked my orderly, and I knew that there were some distinguished Indian Army officers living in the area, and I called on them and they all, without hesitation, invited us to a meal, usually a curried chicken or this or that, and I enjoyed the friendship.'

In late 1943 Shipster's 7/2 Punjab were ordered to the Arakan as part of General Sir Philip Christison's 15 Corps. By now Shipster was a captain with the temporary rank of major. Before they left, the officers were gathered together in an old cinema in Ranchi and given a rousing talk by their divisional commander. 'It was nothing short of a call to war. It was brief, with flashes of humour and full of confidence … exciting and uplifting, but … it left me feeling apprehensive about the future.'

The Commander of 15 Corps was an old colleague of Slim's, with whom he had taught at the Army Staff College between the wars. During the First World War Christison had been badly wounded at Loos and awarded the Military Cross. A keen shooting and fishing man, with a countryman's eye for landscape and fauna, Christison revelled in the fecundity of the natural world in the Arakan. 'Monkeys, gibbons, hornbills, woodpeckers and Scops owls were common and their eerie cries frightened many a Madrasi soldier and were extensively used by the Japs to communicate with each other. There were few snakes but one day a large python was brought into my headquarters. Inside was a barking deer which, contrary to belief, had been swallowed head-first.' On occasion, clouds of butterflies appeared so that the ground seemed 'as if it was shimmering'. Christison was particularly taken with the sight of wild orchids growing on rotting tree stumps. The general had a dangerous encounter with an elephant that pushed his jeep into a ravine when they met along a jungle track. Other soldiers could retell the cautionary tale of the young RAF officer who set off with a machine gun 'to bag a "Tusker"' but was found trampled to death.

Christison's immediate priority was to restore the morale of the men under his command. He decided that worms might be a factor contributing to poor morale. He set about removing men from the line, giving them a de-worming treatment and a fortnight's rest at the coast playing games on the sand. At the end of this, he reported, 'they were raring to have a go at the Japs'.

As the end of 1943 approached, Slim and Christison made final plans for an offensive in the Arakan. The main target was the island port of Akyab, 120 miles south of the Indian frontier on the Bay of Bengal.

Akyab offered strategic airfields and access to the main waterways of the Arakan. Whether the allies ultimately decided to try and retake Burma by land or by sea, or a combination of both, they were going to need air cover all the way to Rangoon. Akyab offered the best facilities. The operation would also pre-empt any Japanese attempt to use Akyab as a base to encroach into India.

There was also another, more directly political, reason for an assault towards Akyab. The airfields had been used to launch Japanese raids on Calcutta at the end of the previous year, a strike that had little military importance but had sent thousands of refugees flooding into the countryside where there had already been massive displacement due to the famine of the previous year. There were five hundred civilian casualties and only a tenth of the normal workforce remained at work on the docks. The 5 December raid also saw fear-stricken merchants close down their grain shops, forcing the government to requisition stocks in order to avoid civil unrest. 'A false alert the following day did nothing to improve morale in the city,' the official history noted. Any suggestion of Japanese strength undermined attempts to project to the Indian population the image of an unruffled Raj.

The original plan was to mount a joint sea and land operation but at the last moment the landing craft were taken away for use in Europe. General Christison's 15 Corps would have to do it the hard way, advancing overland in a three-pronged attack on Japanese positions on both sides of the Mayu range. To blast them out, Slim's artillerymen would use their 5.5 inch guns, although the armchair generals in Delhi feared they would never succeed in hauling them into the mountains. 'Stroking their "Poona" moustaches,' a young officer wrote, 'they remarked that these pieces would never get over the trails and through the jungle of Burma.' As in so much else, Slim's soldiers would prove the doubters wrong.

SEVEN

Jungle Wallahs

By the time they reached the training camp at Ranchi, the officers and men of the 4th West Kents were an exhausted mass. Stiff and sore, they climbed on to waiting trucks which took them to the base where Colonel Saville had imagined his subalterns playing polo and the old soldiers in the ranks had spoken of armies of punkah-wallahs cooling their afternoon naps. The shock of the Ranchi base was profound. It was desolate and dusty and they would live in tents; the place was generously populated with snakes and scorpions, one of the latter giving a painful sting to Ivan Daunt as he worked on repairing a storage building. Daunt recovered after a few days but found little of the Ranchi experience to his taste, although with considerable sangfroid he went on to help his company win the weekly snake-finding contest, organised to entertain the men and keep the serpent population at bay.

One of the first challenges for the West Kents was to get used to living and working with the great and unsung hero of the Burma campaign – the mule. During the misery of the retreat from Burma in 1942, General Slim had realised the imperative of creating armies that could move swiftly, unencumbered by dependence on 'the tincan of mechanical transport tied to our tail'. The immediate answer to this problem was the mule, a crossbreed of horse and donkey with greater intelligence and endurance than either. Without these beasts the armies would never have been able to fight in the trackless expanses of the jungle, where trees barred the way to jeeps and the ground became a sucking swamp in the monsoon. As John Winstanley recalled, 'The mules, of course, were with us all the time.

They were our lifeline. We were now an animal borne infantry battalion.' The search for sufficient mules for Slim's army ranged far and wide. In one instance 650 mules were transported from Bolivia by an Anglo-Argentine cattle-rancher, Robin Begg, who brought a team of Argentine gauchos with him on the ship to India. The animals were so well cared for that all but three survived the rigorous journey.

Lieutenant Tom Hogg was allocated five chargers and sixty-five mules. As the son of a farmer, he was judged the right man for converting the 4th West Kents to animal transport. There were several London bus and taxi drivers among his men and he wondered how they would make the transition. There was no need to worry. 'Many became so attached to their particular mule that they would not allow anyone else to touch them, and later on, grieved terribly when some of the animals unavoidably got wounded or killed in the fighting.' But Ivan Daunt remembered how the mules learned to regard the approach of a soldier with foreboding. 'Oh dear, oh dear ... as soon as the mule sees you coming towards him ... Cor blimey, poor buggers, I felt sorry for 'em. Some of the climbin' they had to do.' A mule could take loads of up to 80 pounds on each of its flanks, and in the case of mountain artillery mules more than twice that amount. The mules had one major disadvantage, though. In the still of the jungle, their braying carried long distances and alerted the enemy. The 14th Army solution was to cut out the vocal chords of the unfortunate beasts. A Chindit remembered one mass de-braying: 'Round came the doctor with a chloroform rag, put over the mule's mouth or it may have been an injection, I don't remember. However, one soldier had to sit on the mule's head with a thing like a dunce's hat as soon as the doctor cut into the mule's sound box! The chloroform and blood was so unbearable that the bloke on its head could only stop for a few minutes as it nearly put the soldier to sleep; so all had to take turns. It was horrible – I took my turn!! ... When the operation was completed [we were] told to undo our ropes and await the water-man ... After one or two splashes the poor animal looked up, all glass eyed, struggled to its feet and tried to use its voice ... with no sound coming out!'

Arthur Davies, a signals operator with the Royal Air Force, was assigned to work with the Chindits, where he was given responsibility for several mules. 'They seemed to delight in scaring the wits out of us by suddenly lashing out with their hind legs.' Davies saw muleteers who had incorrectly balanced the load on their animal being 'dragged along the ground for a number of yards before releasing the reins ... and sailing sky-high, only to crash with great force on the ground.'

The men learned to move silently through the jungle, and learned how to react if they made a noise or heard a noise. As one British officer remembered, 'the answer to noise was silence; this was particularly important at night – to freeze for as long as it takes and let the enemy make the mistake and make a noise – although it could have been a monkey following us through the trees.' The troops were taught how to prepare panji pits as booby traps for the Japanese: these were staves of sharpened bamboo placed in and around concealed pits. They could be smeared with dirt or excrement to ensure the wound inflicted would become poisonous. They learned, too, how to remove leeches by burning them with a cigarette: simply pulling them out with your fingers left the head embedded in the skin and caused blood poisoning. To their disgust, the leeches proved adept at finding their way into the most intimate corners of the anatomy. In return for gifts of cigarettes and salt Indian labourers showed them how to make shelters and beds from bamboo, and which plants were edible and which to avoid. Men from the pioneers, like Ivan Daunt, learned to construct bridges for fording jungle streams and small rivers. Daunt also recalled that they were introduced to American K rations, which included such treats as chopped ham and eggs, veal loaf, instant coffee, cigarettes and chewing gum. All the 4th battalion men regarded them as infinitely superior to the British diet.

Troops heading into the jungle for the first time learned how easy it was to become lost and to miss a target by a wide distance. An officer later recalled, 'It was often proved that some soldiers would nearly always move to the right around an obstacle in their path, others would always go round to the left of it. If one continued moving this way for, say, 1,000 yards the objective could be missed by a large margin. The soldier had to bear this in mind and make corresponding corrections as he moved.' Above all, no one wanted to find himself alone in hostile jungle.

They carried out mock attacks. Ivan Daunt was lying in a ditch when a senior officer appeared and said, 'bang bang bang ... I am a machine-gunner.' The men in the ditch were supposed to consider themselves dead. But one of the 4th battalion wags replied, 'Yes, sir, and I'm an anti-tank gun.' As Private Daunt recalled, 'It cracked us up.' On another occasion, during a night exercise, a patrol surrounded a group of officers sitting in the dark and talking, a habit that might cost their lives fighting the Japanese. The men captured them with a shout of 'Gotcha!'

There was a growing feeling among company commanders like John Winstanley and Donald Easten that the exercises were exposing the inadequacy of their commanding officer. After talking it over, the younger officers went in a delegation to see Lieutenant Colonel Saville. Donald Easten described what happened next. 'We went to see him and each of us told him in turn that we had no absolutely no confidence in him. So he turned to us and said: "Do you realise this is mutiny?" And we said: "It might be, we don't know. But we have no confidence in you, in putting the lives of our men in your hands in action in Burma."' The 4th West Kents were by now part of 161 Brigade, whose commander was the avuncular, if occasionally fiery, Brigadier Frederick 'Daddy' Warren. As the senior officer among the group John Winstanley was nominated to take the matter to Warren. 'He gave me absolute stick ... for this mutiny really ... to go and say that you are not going to go and work under this man! ... and I was sent packing, and the man was removed because as the brigadier said, "Well, you've made it impossible for him to command anyhow."' Lieutenant Colonel Saville was sent to a staff appointment in Delhi. The man who replaced him would make a profound mark on the 4th West Kents and the whole story of Kohima: he could inspire devotion among his men and the contempt of those he crossed, and he would carry the 4th West Kents through their darkest days.

He did not at first sight cut an intimidating figure. The new CO was about five foot nine and not heavily built. But Lieutenant Colonel John Laverty had a presence that could cow the toughest of the battalion's hard men. He was forty-four when he came to lead 4th battalion, still a comparatively young man but nearly two decades older than most of those under his command. Laverty was variously known as 'Texas Dan', because of the cowboy-style military hat he wore, or 'Colonel Lavatory', the latter nickname apparently derived from a rugby song the precise lyrics of which have been lost to history. Neither men nor officers ever dared to use the nicknames to his face. Laverty carried a long bamboo rod to use as a climbing stick; it could also give him the appearance of a prophet descending from the heavens with the judgement of God.

John Laverty did not tolerate muttering from his officers. When Lieutenant Tom Hogg went to him to complain about problems created by a soldier in his platoon, Laverty immediately asked him which rifle company he wanted to join. 'By those who understood the situation this amounted to a "slap across the face" for me,' recalled Hogg. 'In fact, that aspect of it went completely over my head at the time, and I enjoyed the prospect of doing some real fighting.'

One of the battalion medical orderlies, Lance Corporal Frank Infanti, gave a different picture of Laverty. Infanti had a troubled history with the battalion. Both his parents were Italian and this had led to his brother being interned in the opening months of the war, ironically while Frank himself was being evacuated with the West Kents from Dunkirk. When he was refused permission to visit his brother in the internment camp Infanti said he would no longer carry a rifle. In a moment of compassion the then CO decided against disciplinary action and made Infanti a medical orderly. 'I got on extremely well with Laverty because I'm a little fella. I would never have got in the army normally because I'm too short. And he sort of respected me because I kept up with everybody! On the marches and all that. He was an unusual bloke, Laverty. He used to call me "Doc" Infanti which was a great compliment to an orderly ... he spoke in a very cultivated voice ... almost as if he had had elocution lessons.'

John Laverty was born Henry Jarvis Laverty in Londonderry on 8 October 1900 to a prominent family in the building trade. His father Henry built the Protestant cathedral of St Anne's in Belfast and had a large brickyard in Carrickfergus, which one employee reckoned had 'made the mortar for half the houses in Carrick in those days'. He went to school at Foyle College, which numbered a Lord Chancellor of Ireland, numerous rugby internationals and a Viceroy of India among its alumni. A month before the end of the First World War, John Laverty applied to Sandhurst, from where he was commissioned into the Royal Inniskilling Fusiliers in 1921. These were bad years in his home country. Ireland was convulsed by war between the IRA and the forces of the crown. As a member of a prominent Protestant family who had decided to join the British army, it is safe to surmise that John Laverty would have had little sympathy with Irish rebels.

What Laverty retained of that Ulster Protestant upbringing was the flinty outward manner of a man raised among righteous but unyielding citizens. His son Patrick, who saw his father only once during the war, thought him a soldier to the core. 'Pure and simple he was a warrior. That is what he was good at ... He was pretty tough. They called him bloody-minded and I think he probably was. You didn't get anywhere. I mean once he made up his mind he couldn't be varied at all. He was absolutely pig-headed in that regard.'

After three years in the Inniskilling Fusiliers, Laverty joined the Essex Regiment, where his index card referred to him as 'Mad Jack', possibly a reflection of the bloody-minded personality described by his son and some of his junior officers. His war-fighting experience was gained in the small colonial police actions of the inter-war period, firstly in Kurdistan and later in Sudan. He was awarded a Military Cross during the suppression of the Kurds in 1932 and was later promoted to be Inspector of Signals for the British-controlled

Iraqi army. By the time the Second World War broke out John Laverty was back with the Essex Regiment, with the rank of major, and had married Renee Stagg, a doctor's daughter from Southend, whom he had met while playing golf. Within a few months of their wedding she was pregnant with the first of three children. On the outbreak of war Laverty was posted to the East End of London on 'anti-panic' duty, while Renee and her baby were sent to Shropshire to escape the Blitz. 'There was a big parting of the ways. Everybody was going through those kind of separations,' Renee recalled. John Laverty was eventually posted to serve with the Essex Regiment in India in 1942. By the following year he had been promoted from major to the temporary rank of lieutenant colonel and sent to lead 4th battalion, Queen's Own Royal West Kent Regiment, into battle.

Captain Donald Easten remembered his arrival. 'I thought to myself, "Thank God, at last we have someone who knows what he is talking about." He was not the kind of person you would say, "I would do anything for this chap," but at least he was competent. You knew his decisions would be properly thought out. I didn't love him. I don't think any of us did. We respected him.' Respect would have been enough for John Laverty.

The men were coming to the end of their training period and could properly call themselves 'jungle wallahs'. Ray Street was one of the smaller men in the battalion and weighed only eight and a half stone, but he was quick on his feet and brave, ideal material for a battlefield messenger who would have to run quickly between positions under fire. He had started the war as a soldier in the Worcester Regiment but after undergoing his jungle training in India was sent off to 4th battalion to help bring them up to full strength for the fighting ahead. Street had not seen combat yet, but had heard his father's stories of the fighting at Gallipoli and the throat wound that had nearly ended his life. His experience of war on the home front had been eventful. Having enlisted first into the Home Guard, Street was allocated to Birmingham city centre and found himself there during a German bombing raid. A stick of bombs hit the street next to where he was standing. Running to the scene he saw that a cinema had been hit and the street was full of screaming, wounded people. He rushed inside to help evacuate the survivors. A woman sat with her arms folded serenely in the seat where she had been watching the film. But her head had been sliced cleanly off by a piece of flying metal.

By now the old Kentish character of 4th battalion had changed. There was still a core of men like John Winstanley, Ivan Daunt and Donald Easten who had been through France and North Africa together, and who came from within a few miles of each other at home in England. But Ray Street was a Brummie and his mate Dennis Wykes came from Coventry; the new CO was an Irishman; and there were Welsh and Scottish voices to be heard too. The Kentish component had gradually come to accept Dennis Wykes and the other replacements, although he was still some way from being able to call any of them his friends. 'They looked at us warily as if to say "you haven't seen any action and we wonder what you're going to be like."'

The oddest of the newcomers to join them in India was the posh boy. Of all the men in the ranks of 4th battalion, John Harman was the most enigmatic, not only because of the extraordinary nature of what he would do, but also because his background was so different and his personality so resistant to easy definition. He must have been one of the most unlikely candidates to win the Victoria Cross of the whole war. John Pennington Harman, known to his friends as plain 'Jack', was the eldest son of a millionaire. His sister Diana, one of three siblings, said, 'Although he seemed to disregard society right through his life he wasn't at all insensitive. It's just that he didn't play by the same rules. He found that they led you up blank ways. He didn't find that he was pursuing the things he was interested in if he conformed.' At prep school in Bristol he was unhappy; it was not just the normal pain of a child removed to a boarding school at seven years of age, but also the sense of being forced into a straitjacket of discipline and expectation for which he had no sympathy. There was an added complication. John's dormitory was close to the Bristol Zoo in Clifton and at nights he was distressed by the sounds of animals.

They represented, according to his sister, 'unwelcome captivity and restraint'. He ran away from school twice before his parents brought him home.

He was then sent to the famous Bedales School in rural Hampshire. Founded by J. H. Badley in 1893, Bedales was a revolutionary establishment by the standards of its day. Stressing that each child needed to be treated as an individual human being, Badley saw the era after the First World War as 'a great opportunity, one of the greatest in our history, if only it can be realised and utilised to the full'. The school was a haven for nonconformists and while John never focused on his academic work, lacking 'concentration in things which did not interest him', he was allowed to indulge his love of nature in the school's ample grounds. As his sister Diana saw it, 'he seldom wanted to finish something he had embarked upon – it didn't seem quite important enough to engage him'.

John's father, Martin Coles Harman, owned Lundy Island, a craggy and beautiful piece of land off the Devon coast. Harman senior was prone to eccentricity. He liked to consider Lundy his private fiefdom, even going so far as to mint his own coins, a presumption of sovereignty that saw him prosecuted and fined. Lundy became for his son the one place where he could live according to his own designs. The cliffs and coves, the old granite quarry, were places where dreams could be fashioned without disturbance from the mundane demands of everyday life. John dreamt of finding precious metals on Lundy and engaged in a prolonged correspondence with a Spanish mineral 'diviner' who claimed extraordinary powers of underground perception. Boreholes were drilled but nothing was found. The family's retainer on Lundy, Felix Gade, wrote that John 'seemed to feel that it only needed a stroke of genius for him to be provided with a fortune, without grinding work!' The two shared an interest in the island's bees and worked together on the hives, with occasional advice from John's father. John's friends from Bedales would visit Lundy in the summer holidays and were, according to his sister, 'all oddities, people like himself, who didn't quite conform'. There was a chaste romance with a girl called Denny, one of six children who formed a large gang with the Harmans. They swam, fished and chased all over the island, and in the evenings read Dickens by lamplight. His sister remembered John's body shaking with laughter.

His diaries of life on Lundy reveal a boy who was a careful observer of weather, wildlife and landscapes, but not remotely sentimental about the harsher aspects of the natural world. Entries for February 1932 describe shooting a cock sparrow with his catapult at twenty yards and witnessing a staged fight between a ferret and a rat. 'The ferret killed the rat in about 30 seconds.' Yet a week later he was describing how he heard a thrush and a lark singing in the morning and was nursing a chaffinch with a broken leg given to him by Felix Gade. 'Thurs. 31st ... Heard Chaffinch singing in Millcombe. My chaffinch is still all right and ought to be singing soon.'

But to understand John Harman and the exceptional figure he later became at Kohima, it is necessary to examine what happened to his world at the beginning of the 1930s. His mother, Amy Ruth Harman, was a beautiful and vivacious woman who enjoyed the social whirl of London far more than the countryside but who, by the close of the 1920s, had become seriously ill with kidney failure. She was given morphine to ease the excruciating pain but died in 1931 at the age of forty-seven. John Harman was deeply distressed by the early death of his mother, in the same year that he was due to leave school. And the family's troubles were set to deepen.

Martin Coles Harman had made his fortune in corporate finance, quitting school at sixteen to join Lazard's as a clerk on £48 per year and eventually accumulating a portfolio of companies worth an estimated £12 million – a vast sum in the 1930s. The *Daily Sketch* described him as the 'pre-war City's wonder man'. 'Bushy-browed Martin Harman always did things the big way ... Veteran financiers clucked their tongues as Harman zoomed from a bank clerk's high chair to the chairman's swivel chair in a dozen different board rooms – all this between 1923 and 1933.' Yet a year after the death of his wife he was declared bankrupt, with liabilities of £550,000 and assets of just £10,000. The precise source of Harman's financial catastrophe is hard to ascertain; family members suggest he got into difficulty during the Great Depression. Worse was to follow. In 1933 Harman senior was convicted of embezzlement and sent to Wormwood Scrubs prison for eighteen months. According to Diana Keast, her brother was devastated. 'He so looked up to his father. They really were very close. I know that it hurt him a great deal to see that happen to his father. Of course he never doubted his father, never.' Throughout this grim period Lundy Island remained the beacon of stability. Martin Coles Harman had placed the island in trust so that it could not be seized by his creditors.

It was at this time, when he would have been about eighteen years of age, that John set off on his travels. His journey would take him the best part of four years, from Spain to South Africa, Australia and New Zealand. He worked on sheep farms, cut timber in forests and tried his hand at gold prospecting, always eventually moving on. The only note of any romantic involvement was with a woman in New Zealand who shared with him an interest in the paranormal. Throughout his life John Harman would seek out clairvoyants and soothsayers. After returning from his travels he went to Lundy and worked again with Felix Gade and the bees. But in November 1941, with the tide of war still running against Britain, John decided to enlist in the Household Cavalry, believing he would be working with animals. Almost immediately, and predictably, he found that military life was not to his taste. Writing to his father – now free from jail and discharged from bankruptcy – he cursed the life of the barracks. 'Life is just bloody hell, dirty, noisy, crude and inefficient. I heartily wish I had never joined up. There is no time to do anything after the set tasks are done ... how I would like to be stalking deer in NZ a free man ... I learn almost nothing each day.' In April 1942 he was thinking of running away 'to a life of solitude ... I can hardly constrain a desire to desert and damn the consequences.'

One can imagine how strange this well-spoken son of a millionaire must have appeared to his fellow soldiers, a great many of them tough working-class lads from the inner cities. There are several references in John Harman's letters to the 'crudeness' of barracks life, the boredom of being a soldier and the pain caused to his feet by marching. What is perplexing is Harman's refusal to take the commission that would have offered him a more comfortable existence. With his education and background, even allowing for the disgrace of his father's imprisonment, Jack Harman would have been a likely candidate for officer training. In a letter to his father he explained his reluctance, in spite of the fact that he considered himself to be a 'gentleman'. Self-doubt was at the root of his decision: 'I have given the matter of taking a commission a lot of thought and there is no doubt that if I was an officer I would be able to resume the life I was used to, to some extent. On the other hand I am constitutionally so unsoldierly that I am filled with doubts about the whole thing … Does the status of Gentleman entitle a man to be an officer with the King's Commission though he is not the soldier-type? I think not … well!'

By September, John was with the Worcester Regiment and having second thoughts about his status in the ranks, writing to his father that he was going to apply for a commission as soon as he could. He never did. 'I am still a private soldier after a year in the army,' he wrote to a friend. He was still interested in divining and considered putting up a proposal to the War Office to use his 'special knowledge' to help detect submarines. Nothing seems to have come of that. By the end of January 1943 he had changed regiments once more and was soldiering with 20th battalion, The Royal Fusiliers, and on his way to India. A friend, Wally Evans, who was with him on the troopship to the East saw Jack frequently gathering up 'empty beer bottles that were laying around the ship in order to recover the deposits paid on them'. He would use the money to buy equipment that was lighter and less bulky than his own. When a call went out for volunteers to join depleted regiments, John Harman and several others put their hands up to join a draft going to 4th battalion, Queen's Own Royal West Kent Regiment. 'The biggest blunder of our lives,' remembered Evans, 'for what we had to go through in Burma.' But Harman was looking forward to the possibility of fighting in Burma, or at least getting himself to the jungles of South-East Asia. In August 1943, just over a month before the 4th battalion shipped out to the front line, he wrote to his father with a romanticised view of jungle warfare: 'Four years in NZ stand me in good stead and if we ever have to fight in the Burmese Jungles it will be right down my street. Frankly, I would rather hear the noises of the jungle than the ceaseless clattering and yapping of the barrack rooms; and eating food almost entirely out of tins gets me down. In the jungle a man may "spit" a snake over a fire and eat it all himself and make a decent cup of tea.'

Harman was sent to D company, under the command of Captain Donald Easten, an assignment that was providential: he was placed under the authority of a man who wore his rank lightly but with great effect. Easten had the wisdom to look the other way at the minor indiscretions of his men, and he had the gift of showing them that he cared for their welfare. He was swift to sense the potential in John Harman. 'He was a great countryman who found his way everywhere day or night, he understood ground as well as obviously being a very solid citizen who wasn't going to bolt if something nasty happened. He was brave and of course in the end it was proved.'

In early October 1943 John Laverty was given orders to move out for Burma. The 4th battalion was to be shipped across the Bay of Bengal for General William Slim's coming offensive. What Slim did not appreciate was that the Japanese were also planning an attack in the Arakan. The operation, code-named Ha-Go (literally Operation Z), was designed to draw away British resources and attention from the frontier with India, where the commander of the Japanese 15th Army was planning an audacious surprise. Lieutenant General Renya Mutaguchi sweeps through the story of the Burma war like a force of nature, and in late 1943 he was offering his superiors a tantalising vision of victory.

EIGHT

The Master of the Mountains

Even in the middle of war the town preserved an atmosphere of grace. Forty miles east of Mandalay in central Burma, Maymyo had been the summer capital of the British administration where civil servants and soldiers escaped the enervating humidity of Rangoon among broad avenues of towering eucalyptus and pine. They enjoyed the cool air of a hill town and the fresh victuals of its abundant gardens, where around 'the spacious houses of red brick the cannas flaunted gay flags of pink and orange; trailing masses of crimson bougainvillea topped the bamboo hedges'. For a period in early 1942 it was the headquarters of the retreating Burma Corps, until the Japanese signalled their advance by bombing the poorer district, forcing its inhabitants to flee in panic towards Mandalay. Colonel Emile Foucar passed lines of retreating Chinese troops and 'several yellow-robed corpses, Buddhist monks shot by the Chinese'.

Now, where British civil servants had played polo and sipped gin in the twilight, there were new masters. Where the British other ranks might have slipped out at night to the seamier fringes of town while their officers drank in the mess, these latest occupiers brought with them their own entertainment. The geisha house of the 15th Army command was called 'The Inn of Brightness' and it was run by established brothel-keepers from Osaka. It served pure sake and tuna sushi imported from Japan, and the girls played music, recited poetry and had sex with the officers of the Imperial Army – all part of that curious blend of the aesthetic and the priapic which prevailed among the army's officer corps. These were men who could weep at the elegance of a haiku, or sit down to practise exquisite calligraphy, on the same day that they presided over the beheading of prisoners. Arguments over girls could result in unpleasant scenes. The British intelligence officer Louis Allen, who interviewed many Japanese prisoners, described how a major general had found a colonel making a pass at 'his' girl. The colonel was dragged outside and, in front of the sentry, slapped across the face for his temerity.

In this particular instance, the senior officer would have felt more than the usual degree of impunity. After all, Major General Todai Kunomura was chief of staff to the most powerful Japanese officer in northern Burma, a man with the best of political connections, a track record of success, and upon whom the destiny of the entire imperial project in Burma now rested. Kunomura was the most devoted of servants – a lickspittle if you believed his enemies – to Lieutenant General Renya Mutaguchi, commander of the Japanese 15th Army. Mutaguchi, aged fifty-five, was at the height of his powers when he set up his headquarters at Maymyo. During the invasion of Malaya in 1942 he led the 18th Division with panache and had been wounded in the shoulder by an enemy grenade at Johore on the approach to Singapore, his leadership earning him a congratulatory letter and bottle of wine from General Yamashita, the so-called 'Tiger of Malaya'. Tall and powerfully built, Renya Mutaguchi was physically brave and, like most Japanese officers of his time, a disciple of the warrior code of bushido,* though what this actually meant in practice could vary significantly between individuals.

In Renya Mutaguchi's case it meant being an exemplar of the bushido ethic of physical courage, but he was also a man whose bombast and egotism were at variance with the principles of humility and caution that informed the true spirit of bushido. That said, those virtues were hardly valued in the Japanese military hierarchy of the 1930s, and Mutaguchi was a true creature of that rash decade. Born in Saga prefecture on the southern island of Kyushu, he was the

---

* Bushido, *The Way of the Warrior*, was a code originating in the Samurai era which emphasised the virtues of discipline, sacrifice and courage. Every Japanese officer was enjoined to embrace bushido as his guiding principle.

son of the once prominent Fukuchi family, which had fallen on hard times. His father had died when Renya was young, leaving the boy and his brother to be brought up 'almost like orphans'. He was eventually adopted by the Mutaguchi family and made their heir; this was a common practice, dating from the Samurai era, when families who did not have a male heir could adopt in order to preserve the family line and name. A few years after Mutaguchi's death in the 1960s, his son Morikuni told a biographer that his father had gained his driving energy to succeed from the difficulties of his childhood. 'Where his father had drifted, he was determined to forge ahead resolutely. Where his father had faltered before opposition, he would blast it aside.' In later life Mutaguchi never spoke willingly of his father. It was as if he felt shame or anger towards him, or perhaps a mixture of both. More than anything, it seems, he was determined not to be weak. The military offered the strength and resoluteness that he craved.

The Japan in which Mutaguchi grew up regarded the military as a higher caste, in whose ranks lay the great hope of national unity. Wars had been fought and won against the Chinese and Koreans, but also against Tsarist Russia, the first European power to be defeated by Asians in the modern age. The distinguished historian of Japan, John Dower, quotes a song from the 1880s that presages the intentions of this new power:

> There is a law of the nations it is true
> but when the moment comes remember
> the strong eat up the weak.

The lives of young Japanese males were circumscribed by two core imperial rescripts. The first was a code of ethics for all the military, which was the most important document in preparing for a militarised society. 'Loyalty [is] their essential duty,' it declared, 'death is lighter than a feather.' Soldiers were told that orders should always be regarded as coming from the emperor himself.* Military training

---

* It should be pointed out that the rescript also emphasised that 'superiors should never treat their inferiors with contempt or arrogance ... making kindness their chief aim'.

was brutal and designed to instil an attitude of mercilessness towards their opponents.

Takahide Kuwaki was born in 1918, the son of a lieutenant general who had fought in China and served as a military attaché in Turkey and France. Kuwaki graduated as a doctor before being sent for military training where, to his shock, social class and educational qualifications made no difference to the way he was treated. 'I was surprised by that! They slapped me if I said something wrong.' Hiroshi Yamagami left home for an army college at the age of fourteen. At school he remembered feeling sorry for people who were not Japanese. The Chinese were referred to with contempt. 'We called them "Chankoro", which means Chinks,' he said. His parents rowed incessantly and the military life offered him an escape. There was fun sometimes but what he remembers most is a great deal of suffering. The day began with a three- or four-hour run to build up physical stamina. The slightest infraction was severely punished. 'The teacher beat you with his fist and the reason for the punishment would be something like not saluting properly, or if you were not standing properly to attention. Sometimes the whole group would be slapped because of what an individual had done. The punishment to the soldiers would be worse; we would instruct the NCOs to hit our soldiers. They would slap harder and more often. They would stick their stick into them or beat them with them. Or they would keep the man standing in the same posture for an hour. The Japanese army trained soldiers very strictly in order to make a strong army.' Violence was a matter of policy, not occasional excess.

Renya Mutaguchi emerged into manhood in a society where parliamentary democracy was still relatively new, and constantly threatened.* The Japanese military was captive to expansionist ideas, not simply as an expression of historical destiny but as an answer to the more pragmatic issue of limited national resources. Japan imported more than 80 per cent

---

* The first election with adult male suffrage in Japan did not take place until 1928. Two years later a right-winger shot the prime minister, and two years after that young naval officers killed his successor. The slide into military rule and international isolation quickened. In 1931 the army, ignoring the Cabinet, staged an incident in Manchuria that led ultimately to Japan's departure from the League of Nations.

of its oil from the USA, a humiliating and strategically crippling dependency. If Japan were to meet its destiny as a great world power, an empire in more than name, it would have to expand beyond the portions of China and Korea that it controlled and into the resource-rich nations of South-East Asia. The Japanese military constructed the 'Greater East Asia Co-Prosperity Sphere' as a cover for their new imperialist expansionism. It was a charter to loot the resources of these territories, with even more rapacity and brutality than the incumbent powers.

Renya Mutaguchi joined the army as a teenage cadet in 1908. As a young officer he served with the international expeditionary force dispatched to Russia in the wake of the Bolshevik Revolution in 1917, as military attaché in France, and on active command in China. It was a heady time for young officers like Mutaguchi, as military influence in Japanese society was growing rapidly. Cliques within the military formed secret societies, all pledging devotion to the emperor, all propagating expansionism, but divided, often murderously so, over the exact nature of the state they wished to create.

Tokyo was snowbound on the night of 25 February 1936 as the death squads fanned out across the city. One of their targets was the Lord Privy Seal, the elderly Viscount Makoto Saito, who had spent the evening at a private showing of *Naughty Marietta*, featuring Nelson Eddy and Jeanette MacDonald, in the home of the American ambassador. Within a few hours the old man was dead from an assassin's bullet. The finance minister, Korekiyo Takahashi, who had resisted a huge rise in the military budget, was lying in his bed when the killers arrived. When an army captain told him he was to receive the *Tenshu* – the 'punishment of heaven' – he told him he was an idiot. Minister Takahashi was shot, then disembowelled and his arm hacked off.*

---

* The coup might have succeeded if Emperor Hirohito, in whose name the rebels claimed to act, had chosen to support the Imperial Way. But he was appalled by the attacks on his most senior advisers and condemned the plotters; martial law was declared and the mutinous officers either committed suicide or were captured and executed. But the 26 February incident boosted the military, which used the instability that followed as an excuse to increase their grip on the levers of power. It was the critical moment after which the march to war in Asia became inevitable. John Toland, *The Rising Sun: The Decline and Fall of the Japanese Empire 1936–1945* (Pen and Sword, 2005), p. 17.

Although he is not mentioned in the contemporary accounts, Renya Mutaguchi came under suspicion as a member of the Imperial Way faction which launched the coup and he was sent away to China to command a regiment. There he made the fortuitous acquaintance of Major General Hideki Tojo, a coming force in the Japanese military, whose advocacy of expansion into China had helped set Japan on its collision course with the USA. The relationship would prove valuable in the years to come. By the time he reached his regiment in Peking, Mutaguchi had a finely developed sense of his destiny. On earth he contented himself with indulgence in women and alcohol – he was a prodigious drinker – and the admiration of sycophantic junior officers. But glory also existed for him as a posthumous ideal. He already inhabited his own glowing obituary.

Later, he would claim his place in history by asserting that he had precipitated the Sino-Japanese war of 1937 by ordering the firing of the first shots at the Chinese in the Marco Polo Bridge incident.* Whatever the precise truth of Mutaguchi's claim, he was certainly one of the central instigators of the pivotal act of Japanese aggression towards a gravely weakened Chinese state. Then came the war with the British and his triumph in Malaya. By the time he was appointed to command the 15th Army in March 1943, Renya Mutaguchi yearned for even greater glory and looked to the west, across the Burmese frontier into India, to realise his dream. He longed to exercise a 'definitive influence' on the outcome of a war that was daily slipping from Japan's grasp.

Throughout 1943 there had been steady American gains in the Pacific. There had also been an ominous growth in submarine attacks on Japanese shipping, all of it prompting the emperor to announce in October that the country's situation was 'very grave'. Imports of bauxite, the aluminium ore that was vital for building aircraft, were among the worst affected. The shortage of oil, too, had

---

* Japanese forces stationed in China under an international agreement provoked a confrontation by staging night manoeuvres on 7 July 1937. After a dispute with the Chinese over the alleged kidnapping of a Japanese soldier during the operation the Japanese opened fire on Chinese positions. The soldier was later found unharmed.

consequences beyond the restrictions it placed on war industry, for it dramatically reduced the flying time available to train pilots. The young men being rushed through training to replace dead pilots were a poor match for their allied opponents.

Japan's troops still defended stubbornly, fighting for every inch of ground, and her armies still controlled great swathes of China and the Pacific, as well as South-East Asia. But the problem for Tokyo was brutally simple: with American sea power in the ascendant, the island nation of Japan would soon be cut off from her empire, and the country lacked the industrial capacity to replace its supply aircraft and fighters as quickly as the Americans were shooting them down, or to replace the ships being lost daily to allied attacks.

The British build-up in the Arakan, and Slim's wider preparations in India, had been observed. Japanese spies in India reported the arrival of thousands of new troops and the assembling of forces in the north-eastern border areas; they reported the increase in the number and quality of allied aircraft in the region, and the road-building programme near the frontier. Three Chinese divisions under the American General Joseph Stilwell were threatening the north of Burma.

If Burma were to be lost, followed by the collapse of Malaya and Singapore, the humiliation could fatally undermine the grip of the militarists on the direction of the war. It would also remove from Japanese control supplies of Burmese oil, rubber, timber and metals, and, if the British kept marching, it could ultimately threaten the vital oil reserves in the conquered Dutch East Indies. Defeat in Burma might also free hundreds of thousands of allied and Chinese troops for action elsewhere, including China, where the Americans wanted to advance to airbases closer to the Japanese mainland. If the war had been launched in the name of expanding Japanese power into Asia and securing essential resources, how could this reverse be explained to the people of Japan? Even to a man as dismissive of the public will as prime minister Hideki Tojo it would have been a tall order.

The idea of attacking the Indian frontier was not new. In fact, the British had been expecting such an assault since they were driven out of Burma in 1942. Then the Japanese had considered a plan to march into Assam and east Bengal, with the twin aims of defeating the British land forces and severing the air link that kept Chiang Kai-shek's troops supplied in China. The so-called Plan 21 led to the issuing of an order 'to attack and secure important strategic areas in north-east Assam state and the Chittagong area and to facilitate the air operation … to cut the air supply route to Chiang Kai-shek'.

Plan 21 was allowed to slip into abeyance, however, not least because Mutaguchi, among others, believed it was impossible to send anything larger than patrol-sized groups across the mountains into India. But in February 1943 imperial headquarters, fearful of a British offensive, came up with a new proposal. Using the careful phraseology 'When the general situation permits', the plan called for a thrust into east Bengal or Assam.

In the same month Brigadier Orde Wingate led a force of more than 3,000 men, seven columns divided into two groups, with mules to carry supplies, deep behind Japanese lines, where they remained until April, carrying out ambushes and attacks on rail lines.* The Chindits, named after a lion-like creature of Burmese mythology, unsettled the imperial command, which believed that 'these operations were … a reconnaissance in force prior to a large scale counter-offensive'.

But if imperial headquarters regarded the Chindit incursion with dismay, Mutaguchi saw it as a piece of vital intelligence. Wingate had

---

* Major General Charles Orde Wingate (1903–1944) has remained as divisive a figure after his death as he was in his lifetime. His ideas for long-range penetration operations behind enemy lines, and the use of air power to deploy and supply these troops, foreshadowed the special operations forces of today. Perhaps his most important achievement was in boosting public and troop morale with his first Chindit expedition in 1943. Coming after the humiliation of the retreat from Burma and the failed first Arakan offensive, the image of the British forces surprising the Japanese behind their own lines was a morale and propaganda coup. It also inadvertently hastened the Japanese to disaster by convincing them that they could send large forces of men across the mountains into India. They did not appreciate the appalling human cost of Wingate's operations or the extent to which he increasingly depended on the diversion of huge air resources to deploy and supply his troops. Of the 3,000 Chindits who entered Burma on the first expedition, one thousand never returned and a further six hundred were too ravaged by illness to ever fight again. On the second Chindit expedition – 'Operation Thursday' – a force of some 12,000 men sustained 944 dead, 2,434 wounded and 452 missing. Wingate was killed on 24 March,1944 when his plane crashed near Imphal.

proved that the impossible – in this case the crossing of the mountains between India and Burma – could be achieved. If Wingate could do it coming east, then what was to stop Mutaguchi going west? But the Chindits had survived for as long as they had because the allies were able to drop supplies at key points on their route, and they had done this with limited opposition from Japanese aircraft. In the jungle hills of the north-east the army that could be supplied was the army that would win. As he contemplated invasion, Mutaguchi relegated this vital element of his plans.

In early May 1943 fishermen along the banks of the Chindwin encountered a Japanese patrol mounted on elephants and led by a friendly and inquisitive officer. This Japanese had none of the arrogance that was typical of his rank. He spoke to the local Burmese in a respectful tone, asking them about the movement of British troops in the area. Lieutenant Colonel Iwaichi Fujiwara was a rising star who specialised in fomenting trouble for the British by recruiting nationalist groups. Mutaguchi had dispatched him along the Chindwin in the wake of the Chindit incursion with instructions to find out what the British were up to. Were they were merely conducting a reconnaissance, or were they the advance guard of a major offensive? Along the way Fujiwara claimed to have captured more than three hundred British prisoners, most of them men who were either lost or too sick to continue and had, according to the Chindit rule, been left behind. Many Japanese officers would have tortured and executed them. But Fujiwara needed intelligence and apparently the men were well treated. Certainly no war crimes charges were later laid against him.

From the prisoners Fujiwara learned of the existence of Orde Wingate and of his epic trek across mountains and rivers. A less gifted intelligence officer might have concluded that the ragged prisoners he had interrogated were symbols of another British failure. But on the long trek back to Maymyo by elephant, mule and foot, Fujiwara reached a different conclusion. When he went to see Mutaguchi at 15th Army headquarters he told his boss that he detected a new spirit in the British army – a reading that Mutaguchi, fatefully, chose to ignore.

The following month Fujiwara was back in the field, this time accompanied by fourteen spy-school graduates with whom he reconnoitred likely crossing points for a Japanese invasion of north-eastern India. He came back with the news that a crossing was possible in the dry season and that enough food was available on the Japanese side of the Chindwin to sustain an invasion force. What he could not say was what conditions were like on the other side of the river. How much food was available? What was the attitude of the local tribes? Most crucially of all, he could not vouch for conditions in the mountains once the monsoon descended. Fujiwara nonetheless remained enthusiastic about a dry-season offensive. Even if he had entertained serious doubts he would have been given short shrift by Mutaguchi.

There was no room for troublemakers at Mutaguchi's headquarters. When his chief of staff, Major General Obata, made clear his view that the invasion could not succeed because of problems of supply, disease and topography, he was sacked and replaced by the sycophantic Major General Kunomura, the man whose jealous rage over a geisha girl would lead him to assault a fellow officer. Mutaguchi surrounded himself with men whose agreement he could count on. With no dissenting voices left on his own staff, he turned his attention to bullying those further up the chain of command into agreement.

In late June 1943 Mutaguchi addressed a conference of senior officers in Rangoon. But instead of allowing the debate on an offensive to take its course, he tried to bounce those present into swift agreement by presenting his own ready-made plan for the invasion of north-east India. It included, most controversially, proposals to move beyond establishing a new defensive line and to break through into the plains of Assam. The ever-obliging Kunomura was given the job of presenting the plan, but was quickly savaged and put in his place by a furious officer who accused him of trying to pre-empt the conference.

Mutaguchi also ran into opposition from sceptical senior officers, including a brother of the emperor, Prince Takeda, who did not believe the 15th Army could be supplied in India and reported this view to imperial headquarters when he returned to Tokyo. Mutaguchi planned for his men to survive by capturing British supplies, an idea described by another officer as trying to 'skin the racoon before you caught him'. However, Mutaguchi had the benefit of influential supporters and propitious circumstances. A nation facing defeat always runs the risk of becoming captive to desperate adventures. Japan needed a victory and Mutaguchi's strike against British India offered the best hope. His superior, Lieutenant General Mazakazu Kawabe, was an old colleague from China days and ensured that his subordinate's plans for India were not swept aside. The sceptics were told to have faith. Kawabe would keep an eye on Mutaguchi and any final decision would be his.

Kawabe is a man one might have expected to exercise restraint. He was in many respects the antithesis of his junior: cautious and famously abstemious, he was a moral puritan where Mutaguchi was a glutton. In appearance Kawabe was bespectacled, short and thin, with a twirling moustache. Perhaps he saw in Mutaguchi a virility and hunger for success that he knew to be conspicuously lacking in himself, confiding to his diary at the end of June 1943: 'I love that man's enthusiasm. You can't help admiring his almost religious fervour.' In the end, the imperative of success carried the day for Mutaguchi. With strict provisos that he was to make a detailed examination of the supply situation, and to keep to the remit of a limited operation to establish a new defensive line, Mutaguchi was told to start planning his offensive.

The bulk of his forces would be directed against Imphal, where the British 4 Corps was based and where there were several important airfields and vast supplies of fuel and ammunition. If Slim was to mount his offensive against Burma from Assam, Imphal would be the launching pad. The three divisions of 4 Corps were all separated from each other, with the majority of forces deployed close to the frontier. This made them vulnerable to being cut off and encircled. Once a siege was under way the defenders of Imphal would have to rely on the road to the base at Dimapur for food supplies. Cut this road, Mutaguchi believed, and Imphal could be starved into submission.

In August 1943 Mutaguchi held a war game at his headquarters in Maymyo during which he revealed that he planned to send an entire division to block the road to Dimapur. They would do it by seizing the best defensive position along the route: the lightly defended hill town of Kohima. With Kohima under his control, Mutaguchi would be able to march on to Dimapur and capture the biggest supply base in the region. It would doom the defenders of Imphal and devastate Slim's plans to invade northern Burma.

In an official recording only to be released three decades after his death, Renya Mutaguchi described his projected invasion of north-eastern India as the first step in turning the tide of war in Japan's favour: 'The motivation for starting this campaign is nothing but winning the Great Far Eastern War.' The Imperial headquarters and the Southern Area Army under Count Terauchi hoped for a battle that would drive the British back from the Indian frontier. Japan would then consolidate a new defensive line and sit out the monsoon. Mutaguchi and his acolytes still hoped, with a chronic absence of appreciation of the global situation, for a favourable turn in the war in Europe that might, in conjunction with a Japanese victory in India, force the British into a separate peace and out of the war with Japan.

Mutaguchi's dream of victory was encouraged by the lobbying of Subhas Chandra Bose, leader of the Indian National Army, who assured both Mutaguchi and Prime Minister Hideki Tojo that India would rise in rebellion once his men planted their flag on Indian soil. The 'March on Delhi' was bragged about on Tokyo radio and spread as a rumour by Japanese agents eager to foment instability in the Indian Army. In *Defeat into Victory* General Slim speculated that the defeat of British power in India was the ultimate aim of the invasion.

'Here was the one place where they could stage an offensive that might give them all they hoped,' he wrote. 'If it succeeded the destruction of the British forces in Burma would be the least of its results. China completely isolated would be driven into a separate peace; India, ripe as they thought for revolt against the British, would fall, a glittering prize into their hands ... it might indeed, as they proclaimed in exhortations to their troops, change the whole course of the world war.' Certainly Mutaguchi indulged himself in 'private speculations' and, according to one author, even day dreamed about riding a white horse into Delhi. But a Japanese army with a line of communication extending across high mountains over a thousand miles to the docks at Rangoon, and with virtually no air and naval cover, could never have hoped to march deep into India, even with the supplies it captured from the British along the way.* Neither Tojo, Count Terauchi or the Emperor entertained any thoughts of a 'March on Delhi' at this point in the war. By late 1943 defence was the paramount concern and Burma was the western anchor of Japan's 'Absolute Defence Sphere'. There would of course be spin-offs. Chiang Kai-shek would be isolated once more in China and the British would be humiliated in the eyes of their Indian subjects and American allies. If the resulting chaos kept the British tied down indefinitely in India so much the better.

On 22 December 1943 Mutaguchi called a conference in Maymyo attended by Lieutenant General Kawabe, who commanded the Burma Area Army, and Major General Ayabe, deputy chief of staff to the commander of Southern Army, Count Terauchi, who controlled operations across South-East Asia. By now the doubters on Mutaguchi's own staff had been silenced or banished. But he needed

---

* The Japanese plan for a 'Co-Prosperity Sphere' approved by the Cabinet in 1940 made no mention of India, nor did the Japanese officials who outlined the Empire's territorial ambitions in their discussions with Germany ever suggest such a conquest. When the British conducted an inquiry in 1948 and interviewed fourteen top ranking Japanese officers, it concluded that 'a search of all the available records failed to reveal any documents which would provide a conclusive answer to the question of whether or not the Japanese government entertained concrete plans for the invasion of India by the Japanese Army.' (Cited p. 142, *The Imperial War Museum Book of the War in Burma*, Julian Thompson, Sidgwick and Jackson, 2002.)

the final go-ahead from Tokyo. Fearful that the British would grasp the initiative and attack first, he pleaded his case with Ayabe. The deputy chief of staff agreed to make the argument for imminent action with Count Terauchi.

A veteran of the great victory over Russia in 1905, the count was well respected in the imperial hierarchy and without his support Mutaguchi might have found himself delayed indefinitely. The Japanese war leadership, focused on the Pacific and the looming threat to the home islands, was, if not reluctant to commit to the Indian offensive, certainly too distracted to give it a high priority. Count Terauchi listened to his vice-chief's account of the Maymyo war game and agreed to send him on to Tokyo to put Mutaguchi's case directly to imperial headquarters.

Ayabe was an experienced political operator. He had served in numerous senior staff positions and was posted abroad as military attaché to Poland in the early 1930s, and later as a liaison officer to the Axis powers in Berlin and Rome. Arriving in Tokyo, he found himself cast as persuader-in-chief for Mutaguchi's adventure. For three days senior staff, including the chief of operations, questioned him closely about the risks of the offensive. Ayabe felt he had made the case well but knew a final decision could only come from Tojo. The deputy chief of staff was on his way back to the airport when he received news that a colonel had been despatched to see Tojo to seek final approval.

The colonel in question was Susumu Nishiura, head of the Bureau of Military Affairs, who would later produce the first account of the war from inside the military hierarchy. His account, 'Records of Showa War History', laid bare the incompetence and decadence of the system.

Arriving at Tojo's home, he was told the prime minister was in his bath. Nishiura spoke to Tojo through a glass partition overlaid with steam. He recorded the following conversation:

Tojo: What's the matter?
  Nishiura: Sir, we urgently want a decision on the Imphal operation.

Tojo: Imphal ... yes ... How about communications? Have they been properly thought out? Eh? Eh? It's difficult country towards India you know.

Nishiura: Yes, sir. The whole plan has been gone into in great detail.

Tojo: What about Mutaguchi? Are his plans up to schedule? Eh? Has he got any problems?

Nishiura: He is anxious to go ahead, sir.

Tojo: What about air cover? We can't help him much. Does he realise that?

Nishiura: I take it he does, sir.

Tojo: Now what about the result of pushing our defensive line towards India? What problems is that going to make for us? Eh? Are you sure it will make things better rather than worse? What will happen if the Allies land on the Arakan coast? Has anyone thought of that? Eh? Eh?'

Tojo then climbed out of the bath and towelled himself before subjecting the colonel to a detailed interrogation on the strengths and weaknesses of the plan. Eventually Nishiura was told that the order would be signed. But Tojo warned that 15th Army was not to be 'too ambitious'. When the order was finally issued a week later, Tojo stressed the defensive nature of the operation. 'In order to defend Burma the Commander-in-Chief, Southern Army may occupy and secure the vital areas of north-east India in the vicinity of Imphal by defeating the enemy in that area at the opportune time.' Count Terauchi was warned to keep a tight rein on Mutaguchi. As one Japanese officer put it to Mutaguchi when the latter told him he wanted to die on the Indian frontier, 'It would no doubt satisfy you to go to Imphal and die there. But Japan might be overthrown in the process.'

Tojo had delayed in approving the operation because he recognised that it was a significant gamble. Yet he reported optimistically to the Emperor that 'we will achieve the objective before the rainy season which begins in mid-May, defeat the enemy in northern Burma and thoroughly cut the route from India to China'.

As 1943 came to an end two complementary Japanese offensives were being planned. Before Mutaguchi would launch across the Chindwin there would be the diversionary strike in the Arakan. The 55th Division would attack General Christison's 15 Corps, and would be supported by loud propaganda that they intended to march on Calcutta. While this was underway Mutaguchi's 15th Army would ready itself to cross the Chindwin and catch Slim unawares, striking the decisive blows at Imphal and Kohima. The British and Indians would be swiftly overwhelmed. On this assumption was disaster built.

NINE

The Hour of the Warrior

Across the Arakan, in the camps of the British and Indian troops of 15 Corps, and in the tunnels and bunkers of the Japanese, a sense of expectation was spreading as the two armies scouted out each other's positions, uncertain when the other would strike. The 4th West Kents arrived in early November after sailing across the Bay of Bengal and marching for seven days to reach Chota Maunghnama, a coastal fishing village on the fringe of Japanese-occupied territory. The heat on the march would suck the energy from the fittest of men after a couple of hours. Vehicles passing them on the road threw up clouds of dust, covering the troops who responded with shouts and curses. In places locals were sent out to douse the dust with gallons of water; this was intended to prevent rising clouds of dust that could betray their presence to Japanese aircraft. 'Despite their efforts,' Ray Street recalled, 'dust rose everywhere, but we weren't attacked.'

After a day of this Colonel Laverty issued an order that all marching would be done at night. Accordingly, the column swapped the dust for the attentions of the Arakan's plentiful mosquitoes, which descended in malign clouds after nightfall. The advance into Burma had its moments of comedy. In the middle of one night the column collided with a long mule train coming in the other direction. Men and animals became entangled in the darkness and the strict order of silence was quickly forgotten amid a welter of curses and slaps. From their camp near Chota Maunghnama, the troops began patrolling the surrounding territory, a mix of jungle, swamp and hillocks, or 'pimples', as the troops called them. Laverty was preoccupied with creating an an anti-infiltration force that could respond quickly to any Japanese attempt to sneak around the back of his units.

An Australian brigadier who had fought the Japanese in New Guinea was brought in to lecture on tactics. Ray Street learned to move silently through the jungle, with anything that might rattle – a water bottle, ammunition pouch, or weapon – carefully secured. The men made their bivouacs away from streams and rivers where the populations of leeches and insects were most numerous. Still, one sergeant made the mistake of falling asleep beside a stream and became covered with leeches. An officer wrote that he died from loss of blood, although septicaemia from one of the wounds is another possible explanation.

The West Kents began to use the rivers as a source of food. Lieutenant Tom Hogg of B company took his men on 'fishing' expeditions using home-made bombs. 'I used gun-cotton primers on short fuses which were dropped in the water and all nearby fish leapt out of the water half-stunned. They were easy to pick up from the surface, as the native Burmese also realised, until one of our lads dropped a primer into one of their dugout canoes to discourage their theft of "our fish". As a rule British troops did not mistreat the local Burmese, but there could be rough handling of anybody suspected of refusing to divulge important information. General Sir Philip Christison, who would lead the Arakan offensive, recalled an incident in which two men were taken from a village and questioned about what they knew of Japanese movements. They were too scared to talk. The Japanese troops might return at any time. The British interrogators told them they could either talk or be shot. Still there was no cooperation. One of the men was hauled off into the jungle. A shot rang out. The remaining man talked and gave the British vital intelligence about three Japanese battalions in the area. His friend was then produced unharmed. General Christison later wrote: 'This information was vital, and the means of getting it justifiable.' It did not tend to win Burmese hearts and minds, however.

On 5 December 1943 the 4th West Kents' war diary records that the artillery opened fire on a sampan, believing it to be a party of infiltrating Japanese. The boat was filled with Burmese. The diary does not record how many were killed or wounded. The last few days of December were spent celebrating Christmas with extra rations of beer, rum and Christmas cake, and a delivery of mail from home. Ray Street ate his Christmas lunch of roast duck and vegetables, washed down with a bottle of beer, sitting on the wall of a rice paddy. He felt lucky. The men out on patrol had to content themselves with bully beef and biscuits.

The padre, the Reverend Roy Randolph, led a Christmas Day service and was available to any men troubled by news from home, or who simply wanted to try and talk away their fears. Randolph was tall and thin, with melancholy eyes and a gentleness of manner that seemed out of place on the battlefield. He had an abiding hatred of any kind of physical violence, but he believed that men's souls were all the more needful of salvation in the places of death. The men would come to regard him as one of the bravest among them.

The new supreme commander, Lord Louis Mountbatten, came to visit. Lance Corporal Dennis Wykes was amazed at how a man who was related to the king, and 'looked like a movie star' in his spotless uniform, could be so down-to-earth, calling the lads from the battalion to gather round him in a semicircle. On the morning he set off for his visit Mountbatten had recorded the 'terrible tragedy' of the death of his pet mongoose Rikki Tikki, who had been accidentally stepped on by his steward, Moore. 'Poor Moore was quite white from the shock of having been the cause of her death.' But Mountbatten did not let his grief over the dead mongoose deter him from cheering up the men of 4th battalion. After shaking hands with the officers, Admiral Mountbatten announced that Germany would collapse by the end of 1944 and all the allied war effort would be directed towards defeating Japan. He was well aware of the resentment felt in 14th Army over the priority given to European operations. The subtext of his speech was important for the men: they would be going home sooner once Hitler was defeated. Giving Europe priority made sense when you looked at it like that. He made a joke. 'Optimism is not allowed in England because the people would stop working.' There was loud laughter. Then he told them a story from his days as a naval commander about a 'fat old Admiral coming on board my destroyer and saying "Gad, go in and fight 'em" when they knew the old b— would be back in his bed'. The battalion war diary recorded that the supreme commander 'had an enormous reception … Morale was raised as if by magic'.

On the night of 30 December, under the code name Operation Jericho, 4th battalion and their Indian comrades in 161 Brigade – the 1/1 Punjab and 4/7 Rajput – set out to attack the bunkers that covered the road in front of the major Japanese position at Razabil. This fortress blocked the only road along which troops and supplies could be moved across the Mayu range. Without securing the road, Christison's forces would be divided on either side of the mountains and vulnerable to being cut off and encircled. In the darkness men bumped each other. There were whispered curses, but no voices were raised. Laverty had drilled into them the necessity of silence. 'Success on this op is dependent … on surprise … [there will be] no imprudent talk or movement.' To make the point, the NCOs moved up and down the line of men preparing to march off. They glared at the more loquacious characters in the ranks. But the usual suspects were quiet. All knew by now that within a day or less they would face the Japanese for the first time. The men had left behind all traces of their old lives. Laverty had ordered that no pay books, letters or regimental cap badges were to be taken, nothing that could identify a man or his unit if he were killed or captured. The mules were all loaded and were fresh from their own bout of training; the handlers had been warned to make sure every animal had been made accustomed to crossing water. There would be plenty of streams and rivers ahead of them in the jungle and they could not risk the heavily laden animals delaying the column's advance.

Lance Corporal Dennis Wykes was scared of what lay ahead. In training he had been 'horrified' at the noise the rifle made when he first fired it. Hours on the range had cured him of that. Now he was waiting to march off to battle and wondering if he would be a competent killer. 'How do you know what it is to kill another man? You have never done it before. You never thought you would. I thought oh Christ this is the sharp point. This is it. We either perform or not.'

John Winstanley, now promoted to major after the depletions in North Africa, had spent several nights on reconnaissance with his company behind Japanese lines, filtering back and forth in the darkness until he and his men had an intimate feel for the ground they were to occupy once the attack started. The plan was that the West Kents would infiltrate and blockade the Japanese lines of communication, while the 4/7 Rajput launched the frontal assault and 1/1 Punjab joined the attack from the east.

The 4th West Kents marched through the night and before dawn they were in position astride the Japanese line of communications. Dennis Wykes lay crouched in the darkness waiting for first light. All around him the sounds of the jungle morning began to rise, a chorus of birds and insects. The waiting was torture. He wanted the fight to be on and then done with, but he wished he was anywhere but lying in this rice paddy with the battle-hardened Japanese a few hundred yards away. He heard the first shell come in and hugged the ground. Ray Street saw a man's face torn off by the explosion. He would always remember the look of horror on the face of another soldier as a fragment of steel sliced into his chest, killing him where he stood. Wykes looked fearfully upwards and saw one of the battalion veterans standing coolly smoking a cigarette, apparently unmoved by the thunderous explosion. It felt reassuring to the young soldier – until he thought about it later, about what the man must have already seen and heard. Three men were killed in that first shelling, among them a popular company sergeant major.

On 6 January 1944 Wykes joined a night attack on the Japanese positions. As they waited to move off he couldn't get out of his head the thought that he might be about to die. He walked at a steady pace with fixed bayonet and listened for anything that might alert him to where the machine guns were sited. The West Kents were nearly on top of the Japanese positions when they were hit by withering fire. A friend of Wykes's from Birmingham, Billy Danks, aged twenty-three, 'was shot to pieces'. Wykes kept moving forward. Afterwards he would ask himself was it his training, or not wanting to let the rest of the lads down, or some kind of trance, that kept him going forwards in spite of the bangs and screams. He couldn't remember whether he had opened fire or not. The wounded called out for stretcher-bearers, but they were shot too. The West Kents lost twenty men but kept advancing until the Japanese pulled out of the forward defences. Dennis Wykes felt the relief of all soldiers who survive. 'We knew we was all in the same boat and it could easily be one of us. You were just thankful it wasn't you. We knew somebody was going to get it.' When the battalion entered the Japanese positions they found one dugout 'literally soaked in blood', but with no bodies. Nearby they found the freshly dug grave of a Japanese corporal. His left hand had been amputated. In this way the West Kents learned how the Japanese kept their promise to their dead comrades: some part of them, be it as small as a nail clipping or a lock of hair, would be brought back to be buried in the homeland, so that the soul could enjoy eternal rest.

Much of the killing around the Razabil positions was carried out by snipers. The NCOs had warned the men not to remove their jungle kit for fear their white skin would show through the vegetation and offer a target. There was a lad named Heath – they called him 'Happy' Heath because of his easy-going nature – who made the mistake of showing too much skin. 'There was a shot from somewhere far off and this chap Heath went down.' Private T. J. Heath, aged twenty-nine, died on 1 February 1944.

Patrolling by night was hindered by the bright moonlight. It lit the rice fields and threw shadows across the jungle. Wild animals wandered into the lines, including a bear attracted by the scent of the empty bully-beef tins. Wild fowl frequently set the sentries' nerves on edge as they moved back and forth through the undergrowth. Men staring out into the night found their eyes playing tricks: a distant tree became a Japanese soldier and started a rush of adrenalin, until the sentry realised he was mistaken; what looked like the shadow of a palm tree turned out to be a Japanese, and the sentry opened fire in the nick of time. Three Japanese were killed and three wounded just ten yards from C company's position on a hilltop. They were led by a big NCO who had hacked his way steadily through the jungle until a grenade exploded on his chest. It blew off part of his head and ended the incursion. Dennis Wykes remembered the shock of his first encounter with a Japanese corpse, not so much because of the sight of a dead body but because of the size of the man: 'Before we went into Burma they had always portrayed these Japanese as little men, like monkeys climbing through the trees ... I thought it would be a piece of cake. We would knock this lot over in no time. We saw this dead Jap and he was six foot!'

Ray Street's job was to run messages between the C company position and Laverty's headquarters. Among the most important lessons was the art of crossing open spaces. Street soon learned to study the earth banks and trees for any sign of bullet marks. A pockmarked bank or shredded leaves was a sure sign that a sniper had the ground covered. 'You would run across wherever you saw a pockmarked bank. You would pretend you didn't see it and then you run across. He had an automatic but he kept firing a burst and missed me. They got him in the end.' Street did this several times each day for a month. Sheer exhaustion stopped him ruminating on the danger. 'You were always too tired to think about it. You just put your head down and you were asleep. Then they wake yer and say the two hours is up and you're up again.'

In D company John Harman had been promoted to lance corporal after showing courage under fire. His comrades could be less enamoured of his fearlessness. On patrol with his friend Wally Evans, Harman came under machine-gun fire while crossing a dried-out stream. Evans and the other members of the patrol hit the ground while the tracer flew over their heads. 'I discerned the figure of someone still standing up on the edge of the chaung. My first thought was "who is that bloody fool up there!" Not surprisingly it was John. He was trying to pinpoint where the rifle fire was coming from – the man knew no fear.'

On another occasion Harman had run out under fire with a Bren gun to help relieve Evans and some others who were pinned down by the Japanese. Or at least Evans thought that was his purpose. Harman had something different in mind. 'Soon, I imagined what was going through his mind and realised that our minds were not thinking along the same lines! He was trying to qualify me for a posthumous award by attacking the hill, whilst I was wondering how the hell we were going to get out of our present predicament. There did not seem to be any chance and John, on reflection, must have accepted that the task he was contemplating was too great. Only Errol Flynn, with the help of Burt Lancaster, could have silenced that Jap position.' As he grew into the role of warrior, John Harman might have been a little surprised at himself, but certainly gratified.

One of his skills was in supplementing the men's diet of bully beef, soya-link sausages and biscuits. Wally Evans witnessed him vanish into the jungle and return with a wild pig for the section cook to fry up. On another occasion Harman asked Easten if he could shoot one of the local cattle. Easten asked Lieutenant Colonel Laverty at headquarters but was given an earful and warned not to precipitate trouble with the locals. 'It was as if they thought India would come into the war against us if we shot a cow,' he recalled. Easten duly reported the bad news to Harman, but then added a caveat: 'I said to him that if one broke its leg or something like that you would have to put it out of its misery.' An hour later he heard a burst of Tommy-gun fire. A smiling Harman appeared. 'It's a most extraordinary coincidence, Sir,' he said. 'A cow broke its leg right in the cookhouse!' D company lived on fresh meat for the next week.

At around the same time, Harman told Easten that he believed he was destined to survive the war. D company was being shelled and Easten and Harman were cowering next to a mud bank. Harman shouted into Easten's ear. 'Don't worry, Sir, you are safe with me.' He then proceeded to tell his commander that while he was travelling in Spain he had met a fortune-teller who assured him he would live to a very old age. There had been another fortune-teller, too, in Durban, who had read his palm and predicted he would live until the age of seventy-two. 'That means anybody who is with me will be safe too,' said Harman. Easten thanked him for this information and continued to hug the ground very tightly.

John Harman wrote to his Aunt Beryl on 20 January 1944, reflecting on his post-war plans. 'I am satisfied with the way I shape up under difficulties ... the whole country grows on one in time ... India and neighbouring countries abound in opportunities for the industrious Britisher ... if I settled out here I think I could earn two or three thousand sterling without much trying (per annum).'

Further battles loomed. But the West Kents' anxieties eased as they watched British and American planes relentlessly bomb the Japanese positions. On one occasion, Dennis Wykes remembered, 'they blew the top of a hill straight off'. By 12 February the Japanese outer defences had fallen and Major John Winstanley was leading B company tentatively forwards towards Razabil itself. 'To our amazement the closer we got there wasn't a shot fired, and we actually captured the fortress. The Japs had pulled out just before we attacked, so that was a happy success without any casualties. That put our tails up thoroughly.'

When the troops entered Razabil they found a large cavern where the Japanese had treated their wounded, and, abandoned all over the position, the detritus of war – boots and uniforms and ammunition boxes and strands of barbed wire, shreds of clothing and piles of human excrement, the malodorous signature of any besieged position. Captain Antony Brett James, Indian Corps of Signals, entered the bunkers and saw 'horror mixed with ingenuity, ruin with triumph, carnage with new tenantry, in this objective named Razabil, upon which we had gazed since Christmas and hitherto failed to conquer. Now it was finished.' Except that Razabil was not the end of the matter.

While the struggle for Razabil was reaching its conclusion a decisive battle had been unfolding to the east on the other side of the Mayu hills. There the Japanese had sprung a surprise and launched a major offensive against 7th Indian Division which occupied what would become known as the Admin Box, a defensive stronghold of approximately 1,200 yards in diameter. This was the Japanese blow intended to draw Slim's attention away from Mutaguchi's army on the north-eastern frontier. There was a thick mist in the Kalapanzin valley when the Japanese troops moved out on 3 February and began to cross the rice fields. The sentries heard the sound of troops and animals moving through the gloom but assumed they were friendly forces. The falling of the morning dew from the trees was also so loud at this time of year that it helped camouflage the sound of footsteps. Such was the suddenness of the assault that the 7th Division commander, General Frank Messervy, was nearly captured. In the pre-dawn dark he heard loudly chattering voices near his tent. Summoning his Gurkha orderly, Messervy told the man to go and tell the troops to shut up. The orderly duly went and shouted at the men. As Christison recalled: 'They took no notice and so he advanced and took a rifle from the nearest man so that he could be punished in the daylight. He returned to the General and showed him the rifle: "Good Lord that's Japanese." At that moment the Japs rushed the H.Q. and after a struggle the General and his staff and a few signallers managed to escape into darkness and confusion.' So great was the rush that General Messervy had to escape in his pyjamas and without his hat. Resupply aircraft soon dropped a replacement.*

The Japanese reputation for brutality to prisoners was reinforced when infiltrators overran the main dressing station for 7th Indian Division near Sinzweya. Doctors were executed and the wounded butchered where they lay. One doctor was placed in a chair and a revolver twice fired into his ear. On each occasion the bullet exploded in the chamber. He collapsed from shock and loss of blood, but lived to tell the tale.†

---

* Seven officers, and ninety-eight other ranks, British and Indian, were either killed or posted missing in the first morning of fighting. Anthony Brett James, *Ball of Fire: The Fifth Indian Division in the Second World War* (Gale and Polden, 1951).

† The attack on the dressing station took place on the night of 7 February 1944. Soldiers who retook the position found the bodies of thirty-one patients and medical staff.

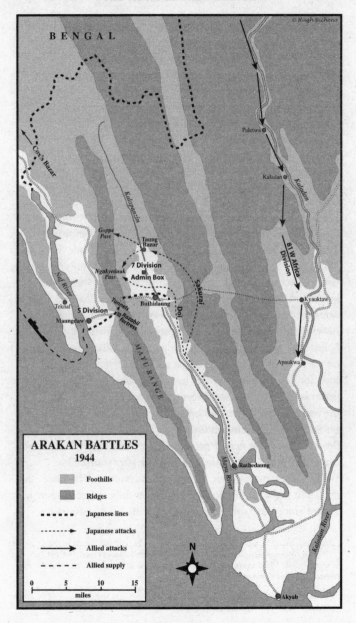

© Hugh Bicheno

BENGAL

Cox's Bazar

Paletwa

Kaladan

Kaladan

81 W Africa Division

Goppe Pass

Taung Bazar

Kalapanzin

7 Division

Ngakyedauk Pass

Admin Box

Sakurai

Buthidaung

Doi

Kyauktaw

Naf River

Teknaf

5 Division

Tunnels

Maungdaw

Razabil fortress

MAYU RANGE

Apaukwa

Mayu River

Rathedaung

Kaladan River

ARAKAN BATTLES
1944

Foothills

Ridges

Japanese lines

Japanese attacks

Allied attacks

Allied supply

N

Akyab

0   5   10   15

miles

Sepoy Gian Singh, an infantryman with the 7th Indian Division, recalled that from that moment onwards, 'we were determined not to show these small yellow men mercy. We often saw on patrols what they did to captured men ... We saw our men who, when captured, had been tied to trees with their turbans and used for bayonet practice.' It surprised Gian Singh when he found how easy it was to push a bayonet into the body of another human being and how it made him feel 'somehow good'. Every patrol was told that it would be given special leave for any prisoners captured. But Gian Singh could not remember a single instance of the men bringing in a Japanese alive. The enemy was determined never to surrender. Gian Singh learned from the Gurkhas how to fight the Japanese in hand-to-hand combat. 'Firstly, you get in close to your enemy and stab him in the lower body. When the kukri goes in, the enemy always doubles up. You then swiftly withdraw your kukri and take his head off. With a sharp blade that's easy.' Major John Shipster became accustomed to ignoring the cries of the Japanese wounded. 'In any civilised war we would have sent a stretcher bearer out,' he recalled. But this was the least civilised of wars. A wounded Japanese could still pull out a grenade or stab with a bayonet.

Yet there were occasional moments of compassion. One of John Shipster's Indian comrades, Lieutenant M. A. Gilani, found a letter on the body of one of the dead Japanese. His wife had written it on their son's first birthday. Gilani had it translated by a Japanese interpreter at the end of the war. Tears came into the man's eyes as he read the letter. 'I show your photograph to our son and he has started recognising you. I am sending you a few leaves of your favourite flower. All are fine here. I get your letters very late. When are you coming on leave? I miss you a lot ... Look after yourself.'

The Corps commander, General Christison, admitted later that the battle of the Admin Box put him under the greatest stress he had known since the battle of Passchendaele in 1917.* After a week of

---

* The two battles of Passchendaele took place between July and November 1917 on the Western Front. Allied casualties were estimated to be in the region of 310,000, while German losses were around 260,000.

fighting one of his senior staff suffered a nervous breakdown. The general wrestled with two imponderables: would the men in the Admin Box hold out, and would Slim's strategy of resupplying besieged forces from the air succeed? The former depended entirely on the latter. At first the air drop faced stiff resistance from the Japanese; not only were pilots having to evade Japanese fighters but flying as low as two hundred feet over the drop zone made them vulnerable to ground fire. Over five weeks Troop Carrier Command, responsible for air resupply, delivered almost 2,300 tons of supplies in a total of 714 sorties.

Major Michael Lowry, 1st battalion, Queen's Royal Regiment, watched the red tracer fire of the Japanese zipping past the tails of the Dakotas. 'This morning the ground is littered again with thousands of many coloured parachutes. Half closing the eye they look like confetti ... Private Wiseman, my dedicated, quick-witted cockney company clerk, leant over from his slit trench and said to me during the drop: "Sir, 'ere come our reinforcements; they're dehydrated Americans!"'

A British officer wrote: 'Later their hearts thrilled to watch, with eyes weary from lack of sleep and a night's work by the light of a flickering hurricane lamp, the first supply-dropping planes roaring over the hills, led by the American Brigadier-General Old. The Japanese might curse the spectacle, but there was not a Briton or Indian who did not heave a sigh of relief and take new courage and hope at seeing the Dakotas circling above the narrow valley ... Day after day those who defended the box turned their bloodshot eyes northwards when their ears caught the drone of approaching aircraft above the noise of tanks and bullets.' The operation worked so well it drove one exasperated Japanese commander to exclaim, 'How can one fight an enemy that not only drops food and ammunition but gin, soap, socks and even razor blades to his troops!'

The material superiority of the allies was beginning to tell. The re-equipping of the RAF and the Indian Air Force with Spitfires to augment the slower Hurricanes radically changed the battle in the skies over the Arakan. By the end of December 1943 the allies would claim twenty-two Japanese aircraft had been shot down for the loss of thirteen fighters. The Japanese later admitted they had lost 142 aircraft in the area in five months. It was a heavy loss for a country that could never hope to match the industrial capacity of the allies. The cost in men to the Japanese was also great: they lost 5,000 of the 8,000 troops who attacked the Admin Box, and the eventual victory of 14th Army had, in Slim's words, 'the greatest moral effect on our troops'.

On the other side of the Mayu Hills the 4th West Kents had pushed on, with the 1/1 Punjab and 4/7 Rajput on either side of them, towards their next objective: the Japanese positions at the old railway tunnels on the Maungdow-Buthidaung road. They moved through hot and hilly country, fighting their way past Japanese delaying positions, grabbing an hour or two's sleep when they could, always short of water and too often dependent on cold rations. It was too risky to light fires which could give away a position to the Japanese. The war diary for 11 March 1944 noted: 'Two cups of tea in the middle of an operation becomes equivalent to a meal, and in any case experience showed that normal replenishment was nigh impossible, movement with mules at night in jungle country being most undesirable.'

After a contact the troops would search the track for bloodstains or listen for the sound of moans coming from the jungle. This was how they captured their first prisoner, who was 'so well treated that he divulged valuable information without the least inhibition'. A day later the Japanese sprang an ambush, killing one West Kent and capturing some equipment. This was the war of grinding advance against an enemy who could seem like ghosts flitting through the forest. Captain Donald Easten remembered the tension of probing through thick vegetation. 'It's very difficult to see the enemy in jungle conditions. One did occasionally get a fleeting glimpse of a Japanese soldier, and sometimes when they fired at fairly close quarters you could pinpoint the position. They were probably amongst the bravest soldiers in the world ... they never gave up. The only way you could beat them was to kill them.' Easten lost three men killed and several wounded in the advance. They may have cursed every footstep forwards in that march through jungle and up on to and across razor-backed hills, but for the newer men like Dennis Wykes and Ray Street it was a journey that earned them the respect of their experienced comrades.

Because so much of the fighting was done when patrols bumped up against small groups of Japanese, the more junior officers found the brunt of immediate decision-making devolving to them. A general or colonel at headquarters was in no position to direct a close-quarter engagement in the bush. So the jungle became a place where a young man with guts and initiative could prove himself. The commanders of B and D companies, John Winstanley and Donald Easten, were making their names as brave and resourceful leaders of men.

On 15 March the West Kents were close to the western tunnel. If they could drive the Japanese out and link up with the 7th Division troops on the other side of the Mayu then the offensive would be close to success. The battalion was desperately short of water, with each man having to survive on his water bottle for more than thirty hours in the severe heat. By 16 March, Colonel Laverty had deployed the entire battalion forward, with companies sent to probe the high ground on either side of the tunnel and the main approach. The men of C company were climbing to the north of the tunnel. 'We advanced quite a way,' recalled Private Ivan Daunt. 'It was all hilly and jungle, real jungle … It was all very dense. You found a gap and went through the gap. You had to keep probing all the time to find room.' One of their officers spotted a Japanese sentry and immediately opened fire. There was a storm of return fire and the troops fell back, unable to advance through a narrow gully to the Japanese position. A soldier from Dublin, Paddy Fanning, who had tried to work his way behind the Japanese, was killed by a sniper. 'We walked into a trap,' said Private Ivan Daunt.

Major John Winstanley came up with a plan to outflank the enemy which they put to Colonel Laverty. Tom Hogg of B company said that Laverty 'was intent on winning a DSO' for capturing the tunnel and accepted the plan, 'giving us the privilege of carrying it out'. It involved B company fighting its way on to the higher ground and getting behind the Japanese forward positions. On the morning of 18 March Winstanley led his men off towards a ridge to the north of the tunnel. They marched all morning without encountering any significant opposition from the Japanese. The route was similar to that undertaken by C company two days previously. But it led them through thick undergrowth and the climb through the bamboo forest was slow and hard going.

By the middle of the day the men were in position and very tired. They had evaded detection by the Japanese. Orders were given to stop and rest. Men flopped gratefully to the ground. They drank carefully from their water bottles. Some chewed on rations while others slept.

Down at the foot of the hills, at battalion headquarters, the medical orderly Lance Corporal Frank Infanti was waiting for the sound of shelling. Whenever an attack was due to start he could feel his stomach tighten and he checked and rechecked his kit of dressings, bandages and the all-important injections of morphine, in the sure knowledge that very soon he would be trying to patch up wounded men under enemy fire.

Up on the hill Major Winstanley got on the wireless to call in the artillery which would precede his attack. As he was doing so, Tom Hogg noticed a large gash in a nearby tree trunk. It looked very like shell damage, as if a lump of shrapnel had gouged away part of the tree. Immediately Hogg thought to himself that the artillery had been firing on the point earlier to find its range and had decided that this was a Japanese position. Somebody had misread a map. Before he could warn Winstanley he heard the rumble of the guns, followed by the high scream of shells coming into B company's position. The explosions tore through the ranks, spraying the hillside with flesh and blood, a terrifying eruption of fire and steel which killed the company's signallers with the first salvo, so that the survivors were reduced to shouting down the hillside for the firing to stop. The stretcher bearers were killed too. Forty-eight rounds struck B company, a devastating concentration in a small space. Back at the starting point, Company Sergeant Major Bert Harwood and the rest of C company could hear the shells going over. 'All of a sudden I heard somebody shout "stop them bloody guns, they're only shelling B company."'

The Japanese quickly realised what was going on and added to the nightmare by firing smoke shells from their mortars and setting alight the dry jungle around B company. As the fire crept closer to the bodies of the dead and wounded, the flames ignited ammunition and grenades in the men's webbing pouches. Men wounded in the initial shelling now saw the flames sweeping towards them. Bodies exploded as grenades went up in the inferno. The screams of the dying and wounded mingled with the bangs and the static crackle of the fire.

A runner was dispatched to race through the burning jungle and fetch help. But it was nightfall before Frank Infanti and the other medics were able to reach the position and start bringing men down. 'We went to pick up the bits and pieces,' he recalled. His abiding memory is of John Winstanley, 'a very brave man, calm as a cucumber', giving orders and taking care of his men. Word came through from Lieutenant Colonel Laverty that the survivors were to dig in for the night and hold out until a relieving force could get through. As the medics made their way back down the hill with the wounded they came under Japanese sniper fire. Another Japanese group attacked the survivors, but was driven off after throwing a few grenades. Seventeen men were killed and forty-one wounded. Winstanley had lost roughly half his company strength. CSM Harwood and C company moved in to replace Winstanley's ravaged group. 'We moved through them and I've never seen anything like it. Bodies … arms hanging in the trees and what have you.' Captain Harry Smith, the schoolteacher from Suffolk, went forward with the pioneer platoon to bury the dead. They dug a communal grave and 'buried the sad, shell-torn victims' under continuing mortar fire.

That night at battalion headquarters Laverty called in the artillerymen and demanded an explanation. It turned out that the hill positions had been wrongly mapped – an ever-present danger in such thick jungle country – with the Japanese placed where B company were lying in wait to attack. It had been a devastating experience not only for B company but the entire battalion.

On the road in front of the western tunnel the battle continued for Donald Easten and D company. After reaching the western tunnel, Easten positioned a platoon on one side of the road and two platoons on the other, with company headquarters in a gully close by. The fire from the Japanese positions was intense. Two of Easten's men were killed on the road, the bodies lying there until after dark because it was too dangerous to retrieve them in daylight. Lance Corporal John Harman was close by and volunteered to creep up towards the Japanese positions. But Easten did not want to lose any more men to the machine guns.

After several failed attempts by the infantry to gain ground, the battalion called up tanks. Easten had pinpointed the Japanese firing points and volunteered to climb aboard a tank and direct the gunner. But there was insufficient room inside and he was forced to sit outside behind the turret, shouting instructions through a telephone. The Japanese fired at him constantly, the bullets zipping past as he tried to give accurate directions to the gunner. 'It was most unpleasant,' he recalled.

A few days later the West Kents were relieved and sent to the rear to clean up and, they hoped, enjoy a proper rest, the first in several months. The battalion was exhausted. The men had suffered the catastrophe of being shelled by their own artillery, and many had seen death for the first time. But they would never forget that throughout the Arakan fighting the battalion had never been forced to retreat. When they did meet the Japanese the enemy proved tough, but not superhuman. They could be beaten.

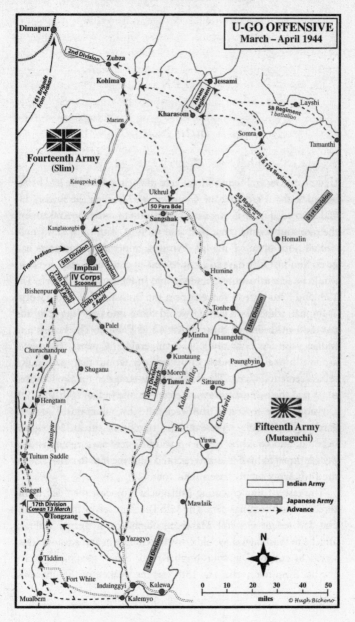

U-GO OFFENSIVE
March – April 1944

Dimapur
2nd Division
Zubza
161 Brigade from Arakan
Kohima
Jessami
Assam Regiment
Layshi
58 Regiment 1 battalion
Kharasom
Marum
Somra
Tamanthi
138 & 124 Regiments

Fourteenth Army
(Slim)

Kangpokpi
Ukhrul
50 Para Bde
31st Division
Kanglatongbi
Sangshak
58 Regiment 2 battalions
Homalin

From Arakan
5th Division
23rd Division
Imphal
IV Corps
Scoones
Humine
7th Division
Cowan 9 April
Bishenpur
20th Division
5 April
Tonhe
15th Division
Palel
Churachandpur
Mintha
Thaungdut
Shuganu
Kuntaung
Paungbyin
20th Division
13 March
Moreh
Tamu
Sittaung
Hengtam
Kabaw Valley
Chindwin

Fifteenth Army
(Mutaguchi)

Yu
Tuitum Saddle
Yuwa
Singgel
17th Division
Cowan 13 March
Tongzang
Mawlaik
Manipur

Tiddim
Yazagyo
Fort White
33rd Division
Mualbem
Indainggyi
Kalewa
Kalemyo

Indian Army
Japanese Army
Advance

N

0 10 20 30 40 50
miles
© Hugh Bicheno

TEN

Sato San

Lieutenant General Renya Mutaguchi understood that he had better be quick about crossing the Chindwin and beating the British. He had succeeded in diverting British attention towards the Arakan, but the monsoon loomed in a couple of months, with rains that would end all hope of supplying his divisions. Imperial headquarters had given him just fifty days to complete his operations. Three divisions would be sent across the Chindwin into India from early March. The 15th and 33rd were to move against the British and Indian 4 Corps at Imphal, while 31st Division would climb into the Naga Hills and cut the British line of communication at Kohima. The British and Indian positions certainly looked vulnerable on paper. The forces around Imphal were widely dispersed over terrain that made quick reinforcement difficult. The defensive line straggled for two hundred miles and the two main forward elements, the Indian 20th and 17th Divisions, were separated from each other by mountains. The small garrison at Kohima represented no significant threat, Mutaguchi believed, and could be rolled up within a few days, removing any British threat to his flanks and rear and allowing him to strike against the 14th Army supply base at Dimapur.

The task of implementing Mutaguchi's 'modest plan' fell to his three division commanders. The 15th Division, led by the old aristocrat Lieutenant General Masafumi Yamauchi, a former military attaché to Washington, would cross the Chindwin and advance westwards to cut the Dimapur–Imphal road, before turning to attack Imphal from the north. The 15th was the weakest of the divisions, with its three infantry regiments below full strength and one regiment each of field artillery and engineers. By the time the offensive began, 15th Division troops were still arriving from road-building duties in Thailand. Lieutenant General Yamauchi was chronically ill with tuberculosis and enveloped in a mood of gloom about the operation. One of the few comforts for this ageing warrior on the long road to Imphal was his 'thunderbox' – the Western-style pedestal lavatory carried in the general's baggage train.

The 33rd Division, under Lieutenant General Genzo Yanagida, was the best armed, with attached tank, engineer and medium artillery regiments. Yanagida was to make a two-pronged advance towards the Imphal plain. The main force would march up the Kabaw valley, where so many refugees had perished on the escape from Burma, and emerge to destroy the 20th Indian Division at Tamu, near the Chindwin, before seizing the airfields on the northeast of the Imphal plain. The other column would destroy 17th Indian Division before marching on Imphal from the south.

The third element, 31st Division, was led by a man whose character is central to understanding the crisis into which the Imperial Japanese Army was propelled during the spring and summer of 1944, and whose personal battle with Renya Mutaguchi would ultimately destroy the careers of both men. Lieutenant General Kotuku Sato had been an adversary of Mutaguchi's from the army's pre-war factional fighting and the mutual animosity lingered. He mistrusted Mutagushi's bluster and his belief that will alone could conquer all difficulties – the fatal conceit at the core of Japanese military thinking. The words 'moron' and 'blockhead' were liberally used by Mutaguchi's divisional commanders, but only Sato would ultimately be willing to openly confront the army commander.

In both background and character they were very different men. Kotuku Sato was born in Amarume, in Yamagata prefecture, in 1893 into a family of twelve children – five boys and seven girls – who were all encouraged to compete with each other. The general's mother, Haruyo, was the dominant figure. His grand-nephew, Shigehiko Sato, recalled her as a 'very strict woman' who pushed her children to achieve. 'They said she was strong like a man. She urged them to be the best.' Haruyo Sato also believed in the further education of women, an untypical view in the Japan of the early twentieth-century. One of her daughters became the first woman from Amarume to go to university.

The Sato family had traded in the town for over three hundred years, running a kimono factory and a pharmacy. They were well respected, and the young Kotuku was treated with deference by the townspeople. Hakuho Abe, now a revered Buddhist monk in Amarume, remembered that the family was one of the richest in the area. 'They were upper middle class. I came from the poor temple and he was from a rich family, so there was a bit of a distance. I got the impression he was a bit proud.'

Kotuku was the first in his family to join the army, after hearing Admiral Tetsutaro Sato, a much garlanded veteran of the Russo-Japanese war, speak at his school. 'That meeting really touched him and it made up his mind to be a soldier,' Sato's grand-nephew recalled. The admiral was an advocate of the expansion of Japan's naval power and one of the architects of the pre-emptive strategy that led to the attack on Pearl Harbor. The admiral took a keen inter-est in Kotuku's military career and remained a mentor until his death in 1942. His influence on Kotuku Sato's future path is best expressed in one of the admiral's favourite sayings, uttered by the military commander he most revered, the sixteenth-century Korean warrior Yi Sun-sin: 'If I pursue honour by flattering people in power, it will be a tremendous shame.'* Throughout his lifetime, and despite the devastating personal consequences, Kotuku Sato adhered to this precept.

Sato had been one of the outstanding students of his class at the military academy and by the age of forty-four he was commanding the 75th Regiment in the Japanese puppet state of Manchukuo. He

* Yi Sun-sin led the Korean navy against repeated Japanese invasions. During his career he suffered imprisonment, torture and reduction to the ranks as a result of political machinations. He was killed at the battle of Sachon Bay on 15 December 1598.

was an ardent supporter of imperial expansion and was friendly with Tojo. His son Goro Sato remembered being taken to General Tojo's house in Tokyo where the future prime minister patted him on the head while he discussed politics with his father.

Sato fought the Russians as a brigade commander at Lake Khasan on the Soviet–Korean frontier in July 1938, a battle that saw the Soviet commander, Vasily Blucher, executed afterwards by the NKVD for incompetence and where Sato led successful assaults against Soviet fortifications. He faced the Soviets again in 1941 at the battle of Nomonhan on the Mongolian border. The catastrophe there led to Japanese casualties of more than 50,000 killed, wounded or captured in the largest tank battle the world had ever seen.* At one point in the battle there was just one pontoon bridge to bring supplies to the front line, hopelessly slowing the logistical effort. An army whose supply lines were so precarious could not hope for victory. It was a lesson Sato would remember well.

General Sato was married young, to Fumiko, the daughter of a wealthy aristocratic family in Sendai, the largest city in north-eastern Japan. Her life with Kotuku, like that of any military officer's wife, was entirely subordinate to the army's demands. She moved from Japan to Korea and Manchuria with him, transferring her son through four different elementary schools and three high schools. She also endured the boorish drinking parties that were part of the ritual of barracks life. The general would dance for his men and sing. On one occasion he arrived home speechless with drink and wearing a flowerpot on his head. His son Goro remembered dinners at which his father would fall asleep drunk while his subordinates carried on carousing around him. 'He was always saying: "Come to my house and drink." My mother understood the situation. He would just tell her: "You've got to take care of them." She accepted it. I really never

---

* The Soviet commander was a then little-known lieutenant general, Georgi Zhukov, who at Khalkin Gol used the tactics that would bring him victory at Stalingrad and Kursk and all the way to Berlin. He won in Mongolia by combining massive firepower with a ruth-less disregard for casualties that the Japanese would have understood. The Soviets enjoyed total material superiority and the Japanese ran out of supplies for their artillery.

saw her complain.' At the that time Sato probably drank in the same manner as the majority of Japanese officers; it was a culture of alcohol-soaked machismo, but it was not allowed to interfere with his daily work. It was only later, after the disaster, that alcohol became the destroyer.

An officer of the 138th Infantry Regiment who served with Sato at Kohima wrote an affectionate account of his commander. 'It is evident that My Lord Sato's face is round. His nose is like rice dumpling. His eyes are slightly sharp. Due to such a facial feature, you may imagine that he laughs in such a large-hearted way but the truth is that he giggles with pipe in his mouth. It was one of his uniquenesses to giggle when he made the other person puzzle and face a predicament. When it is funny, he lets his body roll back and laughs "Ha, Ha, Ha" shaking his big belly. My Lord Sato was a funny person.'

In September 1943 General Sato and his headquarters staff flew from Bangkok to Rangoon before moving to the town of Pegu. Here 31st Division aroused the animosity of the locals. As a Japanese civilian, Shudo Akiyama bore the brunt of people's anger. They came to his language school every day to complain. The soldiers beat the population and took their food at gunpoint. Women reported being attacked after nightfall.

Akiyama had been sent to Pegu by the ministry of education in April 1942 and found it a quiet, pleasant town with a 'mild environment'. There were shady, tree-lined streets, a lake to sit by in his spare time, and the statues of the Buddha, reclining and four-faced, which were famous across Asia. The only Japanese there when he arrived were the stationmaster, four military policemen and a handful of businessmen. Now, in May 1943, the place was crammed with troublesome soldiers. 'The number of cases grew and it was so frequent it was beyond my capacity,' he wrote. Akiyama decided to go to the aide-de-camp of the divisional commander and seek a meeting with his boss. 'In those days I was a hot-blooded young man. I left with a determination to meet and have a fight with the aide if that was necessary.'

He arrived at the commander's residence and managed to get to speak with the general himself. He remembered him as heavy-set and pale, with short-cropped hair and, at first, a stern expression; his face and physique reminded Akiyama of the statue of the last of the great samurai, Saigo Takamori, in far-off Ueno Park in Tokyo. The general listened impassively to Akiyama as he listed the complaints against the division. 'Burma was not the enemy land and I appealed upfront that it is important to maintain rapport with Burmese people and respect their customs.' When he had finished the general exclaimed in a loud voice, 'Understood. I issue an order immediately today.' It is easy to imagine the general's anger. Had he not made a point of taking his officers round the villages to point out the similarities between the Burmese and Japanese? As far back as the 1930s, when he had been stationed in Korea, he had drummed into his own son the importance of winning over the local population. When Goro Sato was in his second year at elementary school, and living in barracks with his parents, he had teased a Korean woman who cut the grass in their garden. 'That woman got really mad at me and she chased me with the grass clippers. That night my father heard what happened. He said to me: "Don't tease these people. Now you go back to the woman's place and apologise to her." I was sent with my mother and a lieutenant to go and apologise. My father hated the idea of racism or the division between rich and poor. He didn't have that kind of feeling. It was the kind of thing that really made him mad.'

The day after Akiyama had made his complaint a young officer arrived at the language school to apologise for the failure to maintain discipline among the troops. Later the general himself arrived, wearing an artificial cherry blossom on his chest where his badge of rank would normally be. '"I am General Cherry," said he, bursting into laughter as soon as he saw me. "Please refer to me as so to your students to keep military secret," he said. That day I had my students sing Japanese school songs in choir. He was charmed by their singing.' Akiyama was to become Sato's friend and the chronicler of the events that unfolded in the spring of 1944.

* * *

The previous December, Lieutenant Susumu Nishida of the 58th Regiment led a scouting party into the Naga Hills to map routes to Kohima. The spies noted trails and found a sizeable track that the British had cut from the banks of the Chindwin leading to the village of Jessami, one of the advance posts of the garrison at Kohima. The British had been working on the track in preparation for their own offensive. The reconaissance showed that even if they did manage to get help from the local tribes, Sato's division would need to show extraordinary resilience until they reached the vast stocks of British food which, Mutaguchi promised, were waiting to be snatched.

The 31st Division infantry group was made up of three regiments: the 58th and 138th had both seen action in China and then spent several months on garrison duty in Malaya; the 124th had fought against the Americans at Guadalcanal in 1942–43, in fierce battles which ultimately claimed 24,000 Japanese casualties.* Supporting the infantry group was a mountain artillery regiment. The group was commanded by Sato's best officer, the diminutive and plump Major General Shigesaburo Miyazaki, another member of the league of non-flatterers, respected by the troops for his personal bravery, and a loyal subordinate to Sato. His one eccentricity was to ride into battle with a pet monkey called Chibi perched on his shoulder.

Sato lacked heavy artillery and tanks, and even if the latter had been available they could never have traversed the steep mountain tracks into the Naga Hills. The whole of 15th Army was hamstrung by chronic deficiencies in air support, weaponry and ammunition. The artillery units of the 31st Division carried only 100–150 rounds per gun, compared with 1,000 rounds per piece for the 33rd Division heading towards Imphal. This was a reflection of chronic shortages throughout the Imperial Japanese Army. One senior officer reckoned there was a 'difference of a century' between the equipment and weapons of the British and the Japanese at this point in the war.

---

* The battle of Guadalcanal in the Solomon Islands took place over seven months in 1942–43 and ended with the Americans forcing the Japanese defenders off the island. It is not possible to say how many veterans of Guadacanal fought at Kohima.

Beyond a generalised picture of a British build-up on the Imphal plain, Mutaguchi's headquarters was miserably short, too, of reliable intelligence on the enemy's capabilities. Lieutenant Colonel Iwaichi Fujiwara was furious at the low priority given to intelligence. The problem was systemic. 'In every Japanese HQ, intelligence officers are regarded as subordinate to planning and operations officers and are given poor facilities for intelligence work.' The Japanese struggled and failed to break British codes, while forward British units like V Force could operate 'without [our] ever being able to discover details of their organization and methods'.

American pressure in the Pacific had dramatically reduced the numbers of aircraft and pilots available for Burma. Aerial reconnaissance was negligible. The deficit of fighters also meant that there were no escorts for supply-dropping transports, although these aircraft, too, were in pitifully short supply. Mutaguchi ordered his supply dumps to be carefully concealed in thick forest, but estimated that up to 20 per cent of the stocks were destroyed in allied bombing raids. The great hopes of resupply for Mutaguchi's army rested with the new Thailand–Burma railway, and yet allied aircraft constantly harassed that line.

Only half of the 48,000 tons of supplies promised to Mutaguchi by Southern Area Army headquarters in Singapore had arrived in Burma by the end of January 1944, and the plan to move up to 3,000 tons per day to the front was stillborn. Throughout the period of Mutaguchi's offensive only four hundred tons per day were ever transported, and most of this would go to the divisions advancing towards Imphal.

Lieutenant Yoshiteru Hirayama of 58th Regiment experienced constant pressure from allied air raids on his journey north to the invasion launching point. Along with the problems of supply, they made him doubt the invasion plan. 'From Rangoon we went to Mandalay and from there to Sangin. That journey was my first experience of seeing bombs fall from a plane. The allied air power was very strong and this added to my doubts. But this was not the kind of thing you said openly, for two reasons: if the *Kempeitai* [military police] heard that you were saying such things you could get your head chopped off! Also it would only reduce the men's morale.' He remembered back to an incident in officer training school when a cadet who had been to university in America was asked to talk about his experiences. What was the country like? How many people were there? What kind of cars and machines did they have? The cadet stood and started to mutter his answer. 'It was like he was not speaking the full truth, as if he didn't want to tell us how powerful it was.' The young man was killed serving in New Guinea later in the war.

The 31st Division would have to cross the Chindwin river and face an obstacle course where mountains soared up to 8,000 feet and plunged into humid jungle valleys. Mutaguchi and his planners estimated it would take the division twenty days to reach Kohima. Each soldier was given twenty-five kilograms of rice and a salt ration to last until they could capture British supplies. The supply clerks carried Indian currency to buy food in the villages. Japanese problems with food supply pre-dated the invasion. A secret memorandum sent by a V Force officer in January 1944 had given early warning of the crisis that would face the Japanese, and of British plans to reduce the amount of food available to be captured. 'As the Japs are so very short of food in their forward areas, rice dumps would be one of the most valuable things for them to capture. I am therefore keeping our stocks well back and draining border villages of their stocks so that if the Japs effected a sudden advance they would obtain no additional food. I am aided in this by the fact that the villages in the S.E. corner of North Lushai have had similar crop failures to the Chin Hills. I am further reducing their stocks by borrowing rice to feed the Punjab Coy and "V" Force troops and porters. I give a receipt in return for the rice and the chief can either have payment in cash or rice returned from our near stocks within 3 months. This also relieves patrols and porters from carrying their rice rations on long trips, and rice eaters can live off the country.'

Mutaguchi could not claim ignorance of the situation. Sato and his fellow commanders all complained about the supply situation before the offensive began. The 31st Division commander recalled that they 'expressed huge concern and each division offered its opinion … and tried to spur the senior staff'. A senior air force officer, Lieutenant General Tazoe, commander of the 5th Air Division, who watched the build-up of allied air strength, and the fly-in of Wingate's Chindits, warned Mutaguchi he was facing a very different enemy. 'The Allied power to bring in transport, troops, guns, tanks, and equipment is beyond anything you have visualised.'

The army commander, however, ignored the warnings and put his faith in captured stocks. It had worked before in China and Malaya, why not in India? He clearly preferred not to think about what had just happened in the Arakan, or to dwell upon the disastrous experience of the Japanese in New Guinea in 1942, where some troops had resorted to cannibalism when supplies failed to reach them. To bolster his supplies, Mutaguchi looked to the example of Genghis Khan who fed his Golden Horde with cattle on the hoof. Orders were sent out to conduct an experiment to find out how far cattle could march in a day. Some cows were duly selected and taken on a day-long forced march. The beasts managed thirteen kilometres. What Mutaguchi had failed to take into account – or had decided to ignore – was that the cattle had been marched along roads in the Burmese staging areas and not up steep mountains like those on the Indian frontier. And they had only been tested on their endurance over a day's march, whereas they would be expected to keep moving for nearly three weeks to pass through the Naga Hills. Fifteen thousand cattle were assembled. Mutaguchi also ordered that each division be given ten thousand sheep and goats.*

The divisional supply officers were less sanguine about the prospect of living off the land. Lieutenant Masao Hirakubo was a supply officer with the 58th Regiment and arrived in Rangoon to a bleak message from the divisional accountant. 'He said to me: "We know this campaign cannot be carried out but GHQ ordered us and

---

* In a rare moment of candour he wrote later: 'the animals collapsed on their way and in the end it was not a useful idea'. Japanese National Diet Library, transcript of audio recording of talk given by Renya Mutaguchi, 1965.

we should do this. That is a soldier's destiny. I cannot expect to see you again."' With this gloomy forecast, Hirakubo learned that he was responsible for feeding a thousand men. He remembered back to the arguments he had had with his father in the lead-up to the war. Hirakubo senior had opposed the conflict and told his son that Japan would survive only by building up her trade. 'I was very young and militarised. Always I was shouting at him while he spoke of negotiations and compromise. Now I felt that my father was right. Japan had got the politics all wrong.'

Preparations were dealt a further blow when Mutaguchi was faced with having to delay his offensive. The main infantry strength of 15th Division had been held back in Thailand for a mixture of road-building and security duties, amid rising tension in the kingdom. The intelligence officer Fujiwara was sure that this made a significant difference to the invasion plan. 'When a decision was finally made to send this Division most of them moved on foot [and] the main battle strength ... was still on the way by the middle of March.' But Mutaguchi forged on, convinced that the British and Indians on the other side of the Chindwin would fold and run as their comrades had done before.

Our view of the Japanese fighting man has been conditioned by accounts of savagery and unyielding fanaticism. The massacre at Nanking, the slaughter of ethnic Chinese at Singapore, the devastation inflicted on Manila, and the merciless treatment of POWs, all earned the Japanese soldier a reputation for barbarism in modern warfare outdone only by the SS divisions in eastern Europe. Yet if the Imperial Army acted in a manner that confounded the capacity for understanding, its soldiers were no less varied as individuals than their British, Indian, Chinese and American enemies.

The men of Sato's 31st Division who prepared to advance across the Chindwin were fiercely loyal to their emperor and their unit but they grumbled to each other as much as any soldier anywhere. A barrack-room ballad found on the body of a dead Japanese at Kohima in June 1944 was written in the universal voice of the soldier.

Any man who joins the bloody army of his own free will is an
Absolute fool, but it's all in the sacred name of patriotism.
You've to forsake your parents, dedicate your body to the state.
Then do your damndest for your country.

The author was writing about army life before the battle. He listed his
complaints in detail. There was the endless guard duty, midnight
raids on barracks to check for absentees which dragged everybody
out of bed, the NCOs and officers who were 'a swell-headed lot' and
scroungers, the close arrest if you got back five minutes late on a leave
pass.

The system is so well organised that you do every blessed thing
To the bugle – get up, go to bed, attend sick parade and 'orders' –
You even eat at its bidding.
There's pay parade every ten days, but you get so little that
You can't even buy yourself fags.

Had the ballad been discovered, the man would certainly have faced
pain at the hands of the *Kempeitai*. Yet the tone of disillusionment
does not mean he would refuse his duty. It simply shows after seven
years of war, with victory no closer, he had few illusions left.

Yoshiteru Hirayama was a new lieutenant with the 58th Regiment
and was given command of a machine-gun company which had seen
combat in China. The men were clearly wary of their new officer and
tested his reactions with numerous stories of how difficult their
experience had been in China. 'All the stories had been about how
hard it had been … they didn't indicate how I should behave in
combat or what I should do. They just said how tough it was.'

Chuzaburo Tomaru, the son of a banker from Nagoya, was a
supply officer with the 138th Regiment and could trace his doubts
back to the moment he was crossing a river near Changsha in China.
'I just heard that the war against USA started. I thought Japan was in
big trouble. We were already fighting with China and then a big
country like USA became our enemy. It was massive.' Tomaru had

already gained plenty experience of 'living off the land'. It meant stealing from Chinese peasants. 'There was no food coming from behind so we went into Chinese houses. It was usually a family without men. I saw women trembling on the bed. We took their food.' His enduring memory of China was the day they brought in a suspected spy. In practice this could mean anybody arrested on the whim of a Japanese soldier. The man was terrified. One of Tomaru's comrades dug a hole and forced the suspected spy to sit in it. Then the company commander came to Tomaru and asked him if he wanted to behead the man. 'I said I did not want to. I had never done it before. So another soldier cut his head off and the man rolled over in the hole and they covered him with sand.' Such scenes were repeated with nauseating frequency in Japanese-held areas of China. After his service at Changsha, Tomaru was sent to Shanghai, where he set sail for Singapore and ended up marching five hundred miles into Thailand. On the way he met British prisoners of war constructing a bridge on the Kwai river. The men were 'miserable'-looking but he remembered how one had said to him that British forces would one day cross this bridge to defeat the Japanese. 'I thought "what are these guys saying?" They will have no chance.' But as he marched away, the image of the emaciated men haunted him. It looked to him like a possible vision of his own future.

Senior Private Manabu Wada, of the 138th Regiment, had a similar encounter. 'A British soldier came up to me and said, "Japanese master, please give me a cigarette." He was a very tall man. Owing to the hard daily work he was skinny but well shaped ... I gave him a few cigarettes from my chest pocket, and we each lit one and smoked together. He smoked with great enjoyment and blew out great puffs of smoke. Although we could not understand one another clearly we managed a dialogue with gestures.' The POW told him Japan would be defeated because it had to depend on human labour rather than machinery to build the railway. Without fail the British would win, he said. 'I was displeased with his words because he was actually smoking my cigarettes ... "Japan will win definitely," I said.'

Dr Takahide Kuwaki, an army doctor from Tokyo serving with 124th Regiment, was an ideologue, deeply influenced by the ultra-nationalist circles in which he had moved while at university. There was also a wilful streak in his nature. Against the tradition of the times, he defied his parents and married for love, with a girl he had met at university. By the time of his departure for the war, Takahide was the father of a baby boy. 'It was an extraordinary thing to do in that period when arranged marriages were the thing to do. I had a very strict upbringing and my father was really mad.' The family would acknowledge neither wife nor child. When the time came for him to leave, Takahide's wife was forbidden from accompanying him to the station. That would have involved her meeting his parents. Travelling to the forward positions of 31st Division, he was enraptured by the landscape of 'high mountains, big rivers and wild fields', and convinced by the propaganda about Asian unity. The 124th Regiment had lost nearly a third of its strength at Guadalcanal and Takahide had every expectation that they would be in the forefront of Sato's advance into India. 'I had a firm resolve to die. I believed human beings had to do something good and correct. When I was young I learned about people who gave their lives for something good and that was something I believed in. I thought the percentage chance of my surviving would be low. Even in a situation where 90 per cent of people are dying I didn't want to survive in that circumstance. To escape was a nonsensical idea.'

Sato spent the last weeks before the attack camped within easy march of the Chindwin. His infantry were based at three points along the approach to the river, waiting for the order to advance. One day Sato and his staff officers sat discussing the routes each regiment would take after crossing into India. They were debating how long it would take them to march from the Chindwin through the hills to Kohima. A soldier who was present recalled what happened. He refers to Sato throughout by the old samurai honorific, 'My Lord'. 'Most of the men, especially the young ones like us measured a map by ruler and answered the distance. My Lord got angry and said: "You cannot instruct the campaign that way. In a battle in mountainous area, the vertical level of mountains affects marching schedule. You have to think about the distance, considering this level." Just like My Lord said, I wrote the vertical level of mountains on the graph ... It means that if there is 100 km, then you actually have to march 200 km. My Lord instructed to consider the gap between regular paths and rocky paths; whether there are bridges on mountain stream or not and so on.' With his experience of battle, and his foreboding about the operation, Sato knew such details could mean the difference between life and death.

On 12 February 1944 Sato received a visit from an old friend, Lieutenant General Naka, chief of staff of the Burma Area Army. They had both attended the Sendai Military Academy and Sato felt able to press him on the question of supplies. The whole business needed to be re-examined, he said. As a parting gift Sato gave his friend a pair of peacocks and an elephant's tooth. After the meeting he reached a decision in his own mind that, if supplies were not forthcoming, the 31st Division would leave the battle. Not long afterwards, he received a second and more unwelcome visitor. Mutaguchi had sent his sycophant, the geisha-loving Major General Kunomura, with new orders. 'I have a special request to pass on from the Army Commander,' said Kunomura. 'If 31 Division sees the opportunity, he wants you to advance to Dimapur. It is his most earnest wish.'

There followed a blazing row. Sato rounded on Kunomura, saying he could not accept that he was being asked to turn a plan to consolidate the defence of Burma into an offensive on the main British supply base in north-east India. 'My orders from the 15 Army itself are to occupy Kohima. I will do my utmost to achieve that. But how can I move on to Dimapur at a moment's notice? What is the enemy strength there? What supplies will I have? Just saying "Go to Dimapur" without examining any of these factors is foolish.' In an attempt to placate Sato, Major General Kunomura committed 15th Army to delivering ten tons of supplies per day once Sato had set off. The promise would lead to bitter recrimination later on.

By 24 February, more than a fortnight before the 31st Division crossed the Chindwin, the war correspondent of the Domei News

Service, Yukihiko Imai, travelling with the 58th Regiment, noted that the men were already eating pineapple roots and wild grasses to preserve their food stocks. 'They were suffering diarrhoea, gastric ulcers and beri beri.' He also recorded that allied aircraft could be heard constantly flying above the canopy. Many of the 31st Division veterans recalled their anxiety at seeing British and American fighters overhead and an almost complete absence of Japanese planes. The Commander of 15th Army was not deterred. A visitor to his headquarters in Maymyo met him in the blooming garden where Mutaguchi told him: 'My officers do everything, I just tend my roses.'

ELEVEN

Into the Mountains

It was a job that demanded patience, stealth and strong nerves. The Chindit officer, F. H. A. Lowe, gave a vivid account of jungle patrolling. 'Visibility is practically nil – a man could creep to within five yards of a sentry without being seen – the jungle is full of small sounds – the creaking of trees, the rustling of bushes and undergrowth, the snapping of twigs and branches, the whisper of grass disturbed by a snake or small animal – or was it a man's stealthy footfall? The call of a night bird – or was it a signal to a lurking enemy? The jungle closes in on the motionless sentry, every flickering shadow seems to be a man. Let any man who has never known fear stand in such circumstances, and, if he has any imagination at all, his hair will begin to prick the back of his neck, his spine will chill, and, if he is honest, he will say "I am afraid."' The secret war was escalating. All through December reports were coming from the villages of probes by the Japanese and their INA allies. By day and night V Force was tracking the infiltrators. On occasions the war of track and skirmish developed into full-scale battles. There was hand to hand fighting between the Assam Rifles troops of V Force and the Japanese on 23 December with the attackers 'being cut up by our kukris'. As the year came to an end such encounters became numerous.

The intelligence told Slim to expect an offensive by the 15th Army in mid-March. Imphal would be the target but a smaller force, probably no larger than a regiment, would be sent to cut the road at Kohima. The conventional military response would be to strike first and gain the initiative.* In the background, but always an insistent presence, the Americans were pressing for offensive action to forestall Mutaguchi. On 23 February, 1944, Roosevelt wrote to Churchill: 'The continued build-up of Japanese strength in Burma requires us to undertake the most aggressive action within our power to retain the initiative and prevent them from launching an offensive that may carry them over the borders into India ... I most urgently hope therefore that you back to the maximum a vigorous and immediate campaign in Upper Burma.'

But Slim planned to do precisely the opposite. He would wait for Mutaguchi to come to him. In fact he would do something even riskier. Once the enemy offensive had begun, the divisions facing them on the Chindwin would be ordered to withdraw, conforming to the stereotype of previous British retreats. The Japanese would follow, their line of communication getting steadily longer and more exposed, until Slim stood and faced them on the Imphal Plain. There he had ample supplies of food, an advantage in armour and artillery and, most important of all, two all-weather airfields. Slim knew there were generals in Delhi who were petrified at the risk he was taking. Suppose the Japanese advanced too quickly and outflanked the retreating divisions? The staged retreat might easily become a chaotic rout? Timing, Slim agreed, was everything. Fatefully, he left the decision on that with his Corps Commander, Liutenant General Geoffrey Scoones.

---

* Slim's intelligence came from an eclectic variety of sources, most of which operated without coordinating their activities. There were no fewer than five organisations gathering information on the ground: the patrols of V and Z Force, the SOE (Special Operations Executive), led Force 136, the MI6-controlled ISLD (Inter-Services Liaison Department), and the Burma Intelligence Corps. In addition to this was signals intelligence gathered by the Ultra code breakers based at the Wireless Experimentation Centre (WEC) in Delhi. According to an account written by Alan Stripp, who worked on Ultra at WEC, Slim had access to 'operational and movement orders, strength returns and locations which ... gave General Slim a complete order of battle of the Japanese force.' (P. 167 *Codebreaker in the Far East*, Alan Stripp, Oxford University Press, 1989.) Stripp was quoting his superior and the man who organised the distribution of the Ultra Intelligence, Group Captain F.W. Winterbotham. Winterbotham was later criticised for overstating the importance of Ultra in some operations.

In Kohima they had been getting reports about increased Japanese activity in the Naga Hills since the beginning of the year. Infiltrators had attempted to recruit villagers as spies. Charles Pawsey's deputy, P. F. Adams, wrote on 17 January that he had entered a village that he suspected was going over to the enemy and recommended it 'should be strongly dealt with'. Another village was also suspected of entertaining the Japanese. 'I then decided to punish Sahpao by destroying one half to two thirds of their rice houses, this would also prevent the Japs buying supplies of rice. This was done and we then withdrew.' Nowhere in Adams's account is there any indication of concern about the consequences of such destruction for a people caught in the middle of a war.

It would be wrong to conclude that the British regarded these as anything more than small scale probes but they fitted with the bigger intelligence.

'The whole disposition of the Japanese forces,' wrote Lieutenant Steyn of the 1st battalion Assam Regiment, '... implied that an offensive was contemplated along a broad front.'

In early February the 1st Assam, which had large numbers of Nagas and other hill-men in its ranks, was ordered to deploy to Kohima. The 1st Assam had been raised just three years before and was part of one of the youngest regiments in the Indian Army. 'You have the prouder and more arduous task of making your own history,' the Governor of Assam had told them, '... grand as it is to carry on glorious traditions, it is even grander to make them.' The battalion contained only three Sandhurst trained officers; the rest were mostly young men on secondment from British and Indian units, or tea-planters, among them an Austrian who had fled Vienna just ahead of the Nazi takeover. In the beginning there was an air of the grand colonial adventure about the war. At the first guest night at the regimental mess a local planter presented two wild boar tusks to the regiment from his trophy collection. Among the British NCOs brought into train the recruits was a six-foot machine gun sergeant from Yorkshire who found himself being taught to hunt with a crossbow and mud pellets by a diminutive Naga. Sohevu Angami, a Naga, was twenty-five when he set out for the regimental depot at Shillong in Assam. 'When I was a child I would see soldiers playing football in our village and I thought to myself that it looked like an easy life! When they set up the Assam Regiment I think that picture was in my mind … having fun and a good time!' To a young man who had spent his childhood hunting with spears and knives, the jungle held no fear, neither did the rigours of training. Sohevu remembered that the British officers treated the Nagas well, 'because they believed we were braver than the Indian soldiers who came from the plains'. He recalled that the commander's wife even sent mufflers from London to keep the Nagas warm.

Lieutenant Colonel W. F. 'Bruno' Brown was forty-four years old when he became commander of the 1st Assam. He was a native of Cambridgeshire and an experienced colonial soldier who had served in Afghanistan, Persia, the Punjab and the Naga Hills.* Brown had fair hair and large eyes which projected a fierce intensity at the person to whom he was speaking. One account described him as 'physically extremely tough, able to march his battalion off its feet and demanding a very high standard from the young British and Indian officers who had come to him from civilian life and whom he expected, like himself, always to live rough'.

Of all Brown's officers it was the fiery-tempered Major Albert Calistan who left the strongest impression on the young recruits. Sepoy Sohevu Angami recalled that the major looked like a Punjabi, and was certain that he came from an Anglo-Indian background. When he passed by, men jumped to attention; those who failed to react to his presence immediately found themselves on punishment duty, running in full pack or tasked with extra work around the camp. 'This man was the kind of person who scared us. Yes, we were frightened of him. He gave tough orders and heaven help you if you didn't get to it. But you end up respecting a man like that because you

---

* Brown was deputy commander before taking over full command on 27 December, 1941. The 1st Assam spent the first two years of its existence on jungle training excercises, patrolling remote areas of the border and doing garrison duty at the Assam oil fields at Digboi.

159

felt he was strong. If he was tough with us then he would be tough in the battle.' At some point in the middle of Brown's tough training schedule Calistan was given leave during which he met, and subsequently married, an American military nurse. The unfortunate bride was court-martialled for breaking the army code and sent back to the USA.

There were some promising soldiers. Even before he joined the Assam Regiment, nineteen-year-old Wellington Massar showed a talent for sticking his neck out. When the British launched a campaign to eradicate kala-azar, a potentially fatal disease spread by a parasite, Massar was one of five members of his tribe to volunteer to be infected and treated. 'He had already shown courage in the public service,' recalled the Governor of Assam. 'The result of this experiment was to establish scientifically the method of transmission of this disease … and thus to provide material assistance in the campaign against it.'

On 17 February 1944, Lieutenant Colonel Brown and his staff left for Kohima just after dawn, followed an hour later by the rest of the battalion. The only exception was a Scot, Captain John Young, who was deputed to stay behind and hand over the base to the incoming unit, the 1/9th Regiment. He also attended a josh group intended to reinforce the men's morale against Indian National Army propaganda.

Young was a Glaswegian who had come to the army from a lower-middle-class family, a bank clerk who was the son and brother of bank clerks. In May 1939 he had joined the Territorial Army and after three weeks was promoted to lance corporal. John McCulloch Young was strongly built, 5 feet 11 inches and 12 stone 7 pounds. Within the next twelve months he was promoted to sergeant, indicating a talent for soldiering that saw him commissioned into the Argyll and Sutherland Highlanders in 1941. In the summer of 1942 he sailed for India, where he found himself seconded to the 1st Assam. By March 1944 he had been five years in the army.

At Kohima, the 1st Assam were welcomed by Charles Pawsey, who invited the officers to a cocktail party in his bungalow. Brown's belief that they were already in 'battle mode' led him to order his officers to attend in battle dress. Some nurses from the two Kohima hospitals, where wounded or malaria-infected troops convalesced, were invited to cheer the men up; most knew they would be heading to remote jungle outposts where there would be no socialising for months. An officer who was present remembered no sense of foreboding, 'only the laughter of good fellowship'.

The other ranks were fed and issued with new uniforms from the stores of the Assam Rifles, the police unit permanently based at Kohima. Kohima in those days was the centre of a major supply depot for units like V Force. There were bakeries, the ovens of which filled the air with the scent of fresh bread every morning, butcheries where dozens of men worked to keep the garrison supplied with fresh meat, and several engineering workshops.

The 1st Assam were to provide a screen in front of Kohima. Brown would establish defensive positions at the villages of Jessami and Kharasom, on the route any Japanese troops were likely to take through the Naga Hills. A battalion of the Burma Regiment and some V Force men established a third position at the village of Phek. None of these positions had the strength in men or weapons to do more than delay a Japanese advance. It was all entirely speculative, of course. Perhaps the Japanese would not come that way at all. The morning after the cocktail party the troops began marching the sixty miles to the village of Jessami. It took them three days. 'Although the march was strenuous,' an officer wrote, 'the fitness of the men and the wonderful scenery around them made the war seem very distant.' On 23 February Brown had sent Captain John Young ahead with an advance party to Jessami, and then onwards to Kharasom, with a force of a hundred men. Young was to establish the first blocking post in the way of any Japanese advance from the Chindwin. The main Assam base would be at Jessami. Brown would never see the young Scotsman again.

Jessami had a bad name with the other Nagas in the area, as Brown discovered when he asked why there were so few paths leading to other villages in the area. Black magic was the problem. Ursula

Graham Bower remembered it from pre-war days as a place where her Naga friends would only venture with great reluctance. 'One after another they came to me to explain why we shouldn't go.' On arrival at the village, the normally stout-hearted Nagas became panic-stricken, 'shaken to gibbering point', and pointed at an object hanging in the gateway to the village. On inspection, it proved to be a large egg in a basket. According to the scouts, this represented black magic of the most fearful kind. 'The very large cat was, of course, now out of the bag,' she wrote, 'Jessami was a nest of wizards.'

Brown ordered the building of strong defensive perimeters. Sohevu Angami, by now promoted to the rank of havildar, knew the area well. His own village of Phek was only three miles away. 'To me it was as simple as going to my home area. I spoke the same dialect and was familiar with the countryside. By this stage I was in charge of a mortar platoon so we dug our pits and got ready for whatever might happen. I don't remember being frightened at this stage. Not at all. It was still exciting for us. My concern was for my parents and my two sisters who were still in the village.' Lieutenant Colonel Brown began sending out patrols along routes the Japanese might be likely to use. It was one of these that would bring him the first news of Japanese invaders heading his way.

On the last day before crossing the Chindwin river, 15 March 1944, Susumu Nishida remembered the dew on the trees and the deep blue of the north Burma sky, and it reminded him of autumn in Japan. Lieutenant Nishida, of the 58th Regiment, had already reconnoitred the tracks towards Kohima on the other side of the Chindwin. Now he would lead a company of around 110 men across the river and into the war. They had been waiting for several days at their staging point about four kilometres from the Chindwin. On this last morning men were cleaning their weapons, checking their knapsacks, collecting rations, and some hummed songs from their homeland. Some grumbled about the weight of their packs. Even for men as used to the hardship of soldiering as the 58th Regiment, the extra weight of twenty days' rations was a painful burden. The lighter men found it difficult to stand up again with their packs once they had sat down.

Nishida checked the plan for the crossing repeatedly but was still convinced he had forgotten something. The day dragged on. He worried that the order to advance would be cancelled at the last minute. Then at last the sun, great and flaming, began to sink beneath the mountains. 'The time passed 19.00, 20.00 and 21.00. I wondered [when] was going to be the advance order. The tension turned to irritation and my brain was occupied by uneasiness and suspicion.' At 21.15 an orderly rushed in with instructions to get ready to move. All along the river bank, through the regiments of General Sato's 31st Division, there was a stirring of men and animals. To Nishida it was as if the hands on his watch were speeding up. By the time he had finished summoning his company, checking animals and equipment, it was 22.30. There were ninety minutes left to X-hour. Platoon leaders were checking their men, quietly warning them about making noise. Nishida described it poetically. 'When my slow footpath stopped at the centre of [the] line, the air was filled with complete and stuffy quietness.'

The men remembered the special order of the day from the army commander, issued when preparations were gathering pace. Lieutenant General Renya Mutaguchi had told them this operation might even lead to the conclusion of the war. 'This operation will engage the attention of the whole world and is eagerly awaited by a hundred million of our countrymen. Its success will have a profound effect on the course of the war, and may even lead to its conclusion. We must therefore expend every ounce of energy and talent to achieve our purpose.' To men who had fought in China and at Guadalcanal, bringing the war to an end was no doubt an appealing prospect.

Nishida faced his men and drew out his sword, which flashed in the light of the full moon. 'Fix bayonet,' he shouted. Then, 'Present arms!' He thought the line of bayonets flashing in the moonlight looked like the crest of a wave. Nishida noticed that the soldiers' eyes were wet with tears. He felt the blood throbbing in his veins. They pledged their lives to the fatherland:

Into the mountains
To see his bones bleached in the Battlefield,
Let's die alongside the Emperor,
We would not regret.

The troops moved off towards the river. Within an hour they were moving through head-high reeds, aware of the noises of load-carrying elephants, of a tiger roaring on the other side of the river, and the allied planes far above in the darkness. At last they emerged from the reeds and saw the Chindwin in the moonlight.

Earlier, Lieutenant General Sato had addressed his senior officers. 'I'll take the opportunity, gentlemen, of making something quite clear to you. Miracles apart, everyone is likely to lose his life in this operation. It isn't simply a question of the enemy's bullet. You must be prepared for death by starvation in these mountain fastnesses.' No one could say they set out with illusions.

From their staging points in an arc around the town of Homalin, the soldiers of Sato's three infantry regiments, his mountain artillery and support units were now converging on their designated crossing points.* The war correspondent Yukihiko Imai saw the tiny red lights of soldiers' flashlights on the other side of the river, guiding boats into the bank. The flickering lights and the sound of the engine on the sampan would remain in his memory forever.

Hiroshi Yamagami, the colour-bearer with the 58th Regiment, remembered that it was quiet on the boat. 'We didn't talk. We expected resistance. Then nothing happened. It was a relief. I felt "the time is coming." I had high spirits and the rest were the same.' The machine-gunner Yoshiteru Hirayama crossed the river twice. On the first occasion he had to carry his unit's baggage across with the engineers. The following day he crossed with the troops, telling himself as they approached the bank, 'We have got to fight, we have to go for it.'

---

* The Japanese 33 Division and some elements of 15 Division had crossed the Chindwin on 8 March.

But the Japanese were being observed from the jungle. Lieutenant Walton, seconded to V Force from the Frontier Force Regiment, was on the enemy side of the river on the night of 15 March. From his jungle hiding place he saw a large fire being lit and heard noise and hammering. Boats were being pushed together into an improvised pontoon bridge. At 2 a.m. Walton judged it was safe to go as far as the river in the direction of the noise. He reached what he took to be a stores area and found another hiding place. 'I lay up all day and considerable quantities of stores were carried up from lorries to the top of the hill where I was. In the evening they were taken down to the river bank.' Once the bridge was in place, the troops, ponies and bullocks began to cross. To infiltrate as far as he did was an enormous risk. Capture would have meant brutal torture and death. But Walton, like many of the V Force operatives, had become adept at jungle movement. He crept away and made for Imphal, evading a Japanese patrol on the way and carefully noting every unusual detail: creeping through the jungle near the road, he saw a Japanese dispatch rider and new telephone wires strung along the route of the advance. Walton does not appear to have had a wireless set with which to warn his headquarters about the scale of the advance.

A group of Chindits, flying in for 'Operation Thursday' behind Japanese lines, had crash-landed near the Japanese staging area and noted the crossing of the 31st Division.* Lance Corporal Mullen, of 82 Chindit Column, was with a group of eighteen survivors who emerged stunned but otherwise unhurt from the wreckage. The pilot was killed, the wireless smashed and all the weapons lost. The men first burned their operational maps and struck out in the direction of

---

* Operation Thursday was launched on 5 March 1944 and landed up to 10,000 men of Special Force, along with artillery and mules, at two remote jungle clearings. It was the largest airborne operation in history up to that point. On the second day the Chindit leader, Major General Orde Wingate, was killed in a plane crash. Operation Thursday caused some disruption to Mutaguchi's lines of communication and the Chindits helped the American General Joseph Stillwell and his Chinese troops in the capture of the northern Burmese city of Myitkyina in August 1944. The overall impact on the battles at Kohima and Imphal was negligible, although the Chindit 23 Brigade harried General Sato's lines of communication.

the Chindwin. On the march they were attacked by a Japanese patrol and six men went missing in the jungle. Arriving at Thangdaut on 17 March, the Chindits hid out and watched the river. 'From one hour after sunset to one hour before sunrise we watched Japanese crossing continually in collapsible boats similar to our assault boats ... our Sergeant, who was the only one who could swim, crossed the Chindwin but was never seen again.' Two days later the men found an abandoned sampan and used it to cross the river, finding a solitary Japanese asleep on the western bank. They had no weapons so they quietly stole the rice from his mule and made off into the jungle. Without a working wireless they had no means of relaying the intelligence.*

There were three Japanese columns advancing on Kohima via different routes. General Sato sent Miyazaki off with the main infantry group in the direction of the village of Ukhrul, where he would capture stores and then move to block the road at Kohima. Another battalion of 58th Regiment was sent through the wilds of the Somra tract to the north, while Sato's own column would travel the central route via Kharasom. The routes of advance were dictated by what passable tracks existed and took the advancing Japanese in the direction of three British garrisons. There was little room for improvising on the move, given the size of the army and the wildness of the terrain. Lieutenant Nishida's map-making foray would gain Sato vital time on his advance, but for the marching soldiers the journey into India was a trial.

The supply officer, Lieutenant Masao Hirakubo, felt physically weak compared to the other soldiers of 58th Regiment. He was a softly reared city boy, whose speciality was administration. The privates, who had spent more than three years in China, were mostly peasants who could walk for days without proper sleep. Hirakubo trudged along up the steep mountains. Just after crossing the Chindwin he heard the sound of massed aircraft overhead. 'What is

---

* Mullen arrived in Imphal in time to be debriefed and his intelligence was sent to 14th Army on 24 March. What he witnessed indicated something larger than a regimental sized crossing of supplies and ancillary troops, yet the information was not passed on to the garrisons in the way of the 31st Division advance. Cited in Leslie Edwards, *Kohima – The Furthest Battle* (History Press, 2009), p. 68.

it?' men called to each other. Somebody said they were gliders heading behind the Japanese lines. What Hirakubo and his comrades had heard were the Chindits heading to landing strips inside Burma. Deep in the jungle, he heard monkeys chatter and birds call, and experienced a darkness so thick that men tied ropes from wrist to wrist so as not to become lost off the path. The column was accompanied by a thousand oxen to carry baggage and provide meat on the hoof. But the animals quickly tired in the mountains. The soldiers' remedy was to light a candle and hold it to the animal's tail. But once this had been done three or four times the animals would simply refuse to get up. Then a soldier would shoot the ox and the luggage would have to be carried by the troops. Lieutenant Shosaku Kameyama of the 58th Regiment knew that Burmese oxen were used to pull carts and not to carry baggage. 'Soldiers of the company had a hard time training oxen for carrying loads on their backs, for oxen did not budge when they were tired. These ideas of top brass proved to be wishful thinking which disregarded the harsh reality.'

To the war correspondent Yukihiko Imai, the sound of human and animal cries mingling in the mist-shrouded mountains was mournful; the cold weather was the greatest shock to his system. Even in daytime, the severity of the cold made it difficult to sleep. At one point he collapsed on the peak of a mountain after forty hours' hard marching. He was woken by the sound of a tiger growling nearby and fled to catch up with his party. The terrain here, and the creatures and maladies it concealed, was utterly different to anything the men had experienced in China or on Guadalcanal. They were introduced to the hideous Naga sore, best described by an Englishman who treated refugees fleeing from Burma in 1942. It begins, he wrote, 'as a small blister usually on the leg or foot in a place where there is not much flesh. It develops rapidly for four or five days and then stops. By this time it may be five inches in diameter and half an inch deep, destroying all the upper layers of skin and often the tendons and muscles as well. Though it often has a clean appearance when washed, the under part frequently stinks to high heaven from the pus which rapidly accumulates in the cavity ... On one occasion kerosene oil was poured into a hole in a small boy's head, and three hundred and fifty half-inch maggots, of four different species, were removed.'

Men pushed up near-vertical slopes. On occasion, food and ammunition had to be abandoned because there were no means to carry them. Animals died from exhaustion or fell over the side of cliffs. 'Many, many times that happened. It was a big noise,' recalled Masao Hirakubo. Finally it happened to Hirakubo himself. Reports had come back from the front of the column of an engagement with the British. A three-day forced march followed. 'On that occasion everybody was walking and sleeping. There was no road. These mountains were 3,000 to 5,000 metres above sea level.' Hirakubo weighed seventy-five kilograms and carried a pack of more than twenty-five kilograms. Swaying in a semi-sleep, he toppled and fell over the side of the cliff, plunging a hundred metres. The lieutenant frantically grabbed at leaves and roots as he tumbled down. About two thirds of the way down he struck a large rock and was knocked unconscious. He did not know how long he had been knocked out, but on coming to he saw flashlights and heard shouting. 'I thought they were praying for my soul. I shouted. I heard them talking, saying I was still alive. A doctor and three soldiers were sent down to me. I was told to follow slowly. He said "the fact you didn't die after falling all that distance means you have been guaranteed your life for the whole operation."' Cut and bruised, he was transferred to a stretcher and then left at an improvised aid station. There was no doctor and it was bitterly cold. Hirakubo eventually decided to take his chances and make for the front with a mountain artillery unit that was passing. But for all the privations of the march, Sato's army remained in good spirits and advanced steadily on the British positions leading to Kohima.

Since at least February Slim had anticipated a thrust into the Naga Hills by a relatively small force. In *Defeat into Victory* he wrote: 'A Japanese regiment (three battalions) would, we foresaw, make for Kohima to cut the main Imphal-Dimapur road and threaten the Dimapur base.' A regiment of the Imperial Japanese Army amounted to approximately two-and-a-half thousand men. It was a small force but given Japanese fighting ability it was not inconsequential, as Slim must have known. Slim always maintained that his greatest mistake was to underestimate the Japanese ability to move a *large* force through the Naga Hills. But the failure to prepare to meet even a regimental size force, let alone the division that would materialise, would establish the mood of crisis, and exact a heavy price on the men sent to defend Kohima. By Slim's own account Dimapur had been left without a garrison at all, and Kohima only a 'scratch' force. Allied intelligence gave a date of 15 March for the start of Mutaguchi's offensive. It was not that Slim failed to appreciate the danger, but rather the speed at which the entire machine of command responded that created the crisis. With ever-stronger signs of impending attack Slim asked his superior, the Army Group Commander, General Sir George Giffard, for substantial reinforcements. On 5 March, a few days before Mutaguchi's first troops crossed the Chindwin, the Supreme Commander, Lord Mountbatten, told Giffard to expedite the movement of troops to cover Dimapur and Kohima. Mountbatten was away between 7 and 14 March, visiting the Chinese armies of General Stilwell at Ledo, when the first Japanese crossed into India. Going to see Stilwell was not one of Mountbatten's more pleasurable tasks. Like most British officers he found the American tiresome, carping and a remorseless anglophobe. Mountbatten, however, had the grace, and good sense, to rise above Stilwell's tendency to bait his British guests and established a working relationship with the American. It was the battlefield tour that the American laid on that distressed the supreme commander.

'I have never taken kindly to the few fresh battlefields I have visited, chiefly because the smell is so appalling, but this was particularly unpleasant. At one place I saw at least fifty Japanese bodies and half a dozen horses which had been killed the day before. Already the maggots were running all over their faces, which looked puffed and blown out, and it was with the greatest of difficulty that I overcame a wave of nausea and avoided being sick.' Worse was to follow. On his way back to Stilwell's base Mountbatten, sitting in an open jeep, was struck by a bamboo stick jutting out from the side of the road. He was taken to see Captain Scheie, the famous US Army ophthalmic surgeon, who ordered him to bed. The Supreme Commander spent five days with both eyes bandaged while the nurses were 'feeding me like a baby, washing me, reading to me and attending to all my other wants'.

Mountbatten was not dallying while the Japanese advanced. The eye injury was severe and he was lucky to save it. Once discharged, on 14 March, Mountbatten flew directly to see Slim and the Commander of the 3rd Tactical Airforce, Sir John Baldwin. The news from Imphal was of potential disaster. The 17 Indian Division was fighting to escape a Japanese encirclement on the road to Imphal and an urgent airlift of reinforcements was needed to protect the base. According to Slim Mountbatten 'saw the urgency at once'. That night in Delhi the Supreme Commander challenged Giffard about the delay in moving reinforcements. In fact Giffard had given orders for three brigades to move to the Dimapur front and the 5th Indian Division was to move once it could be freed from the fighting in the Arakan.* It was all taking too long, however. The British 2nd Division was available in India but Giffard told the Supreme Commander he was worried about 'getting a division to the Central front over the already crowded Assam line of communication, and of maintaining it there on arrival.'

In another time it would have been a reasonable consideration. But this was a moment to take what Giffard later called an 'administrative risk' and get 2nd Division moving. If Mutaguchi took Dimapur there would be no line of communication at all.

Mountbatten's Chief of Staff, Lieutenant General Sir Henry Pownall, by no means an uncritical servant of the supreme

---

* One was the 50th Indian Parachute Brigade and the other two were Chindit units, not designed for the defensive role the situation demanded. Writing in March 1945 Giffard said he had 'for many months been anxious to increase the strength of 4 Corps by another division; but the low capacity of the line of communication had prevented its maintenance in that area and I had to be content with one extra brigade ... with the start of the Japanese offensive, administrative risks had to be taken and General Slim decided to move 5 Indian Division from Arakan to Imphal-Kohima area ... the move was finished on the 12th of April.' (General Sir George J. Giffard, Commander-in-Chief, 11 Army Group, South-East Asia Command, 'Operations in Burma and North-East India from 16th November, 1943 to 22nd June 1944', Despatch submitted to the Secretary of State for War on 19 June 1945, supplement to the *London Gazette*, Monday 19 March 1951 (HMSO).

commander, found Giffard 'extremely cagey on the subject and distinctly complacent about the whole situation'. Giffard told Pownall that Slim had 'plenty of troops and could move them as he wanted … it was clear he didn't propose to intervene himself or give the spur to Slim and he made it plain that he would regard intervention by Mountbatten as unwelcome.'

The crisis exacerbated the already poor relationship between Mountbatten and his senior soldier. During the Great War, Giffard had chased the columns of the German Commander, Von Lettow-Vorbeck, around East and Central Africa. He was wounded and awarded a DSO. As the commander of all allied land forces in South-East Asia he had worked hard to ensure Slim was given the authority and resources to build the force that would become the 14th Army. Giffard was a decent and thoughtful soldier who struggled to take his much younger and less experienced supreme commander seriously as a military equal, let alone superior. Giffard's humour was also soured by the endless interventions of the Chindit leader, Major General Orde Wingate, who was attempting to promote his own interests directly with Mountbatten. Giffard was right that Mountbatten was no strategist, but the supreme commander did have an instinct for spotting trouble. The mess he saw enveloping 14th Army would sweep Giffard, Slim and Mountbatten away, to say nothing of tens of thousands of troops, if something wasn't done quickly. Even allowing for Mountbatten's already tainted view of Giffard, and his tendency to describe himself as essential to great events, he had a point when he wrote to Edwina of how 'desperately worried' he was about 'the way situation got out of control while I was away'.

The problem now for Mountbatten was that finding the necessary aircraft would involve diverting American planes carrying supplies into China.

Mountbatten decided to send the planes and get permission afterwards. It was the kind of imperious, and absolutely necessary, act of a man gifted with supreme self-confidence. Mountbatten took care to enlist the support of Churchill in London, who cabled Roosevelt that 'the stakes are pretty high in this battle, and victory would have far-reaching consequences'. Not to mention defeat. Within five days Mountbatten had diverted twenty C-46 'Commandos' from the 'Hump' route into China. Such a triumph could not be allowed to pass without a little self-glorification. He told his wife Edwina on 20 March that 'if the Battle of Imphal is won it will be entirely due to Dickie overriding all his Generals!'

Slim's senior general for the coming battle at Kohima would be the commander of 33 Corps, Lieutenant General Montagu George North Stopford. On the morning of 16 March, as yet unaware of his appointment, Stopford was sitting in his office in Poona, eighteen hundred miles from the Burma frontier and having a tedious time. It began with 'weighing off a young arse called Parsons who had lost his identity card'. Judging the man to be a victim of bad luck the general let him off. There were more interviews to follow, all of them 'awful'. The tone in his diary is of a soldier who is bored, aware that the action is taking place elsewhere while his forces must bide their time.

Stopford was the great-grandson of an Anglo-Irish earl and had the mien of a landed aristocrat. One journalist wrote that when 'he walks around his units he might be inspecting his barns, or noting the progress of his crops'. He entered the Rifle Brigade from Sandhurst in 1911 and was awarded the Military Cross in France during the Great War. Afterwards he was an instructor at the Staff College, a contemporary of Arthur Percival, who would go down in history as the man who surrendered Singapore, and the future Chief of the Imperial General Staff (CIGS), General Sir Alan Brooke. Stopford was tall and strongly built, an imposing physical figure, with a manner that suggested a man resolutely sure of his own judgement. A staff officer who met Stopford around the time of the Japanese invasion remembered that while 'his walk was unhurried, his mind moved very fast ... He was very ambitious; some would call him ruthless; but that he was a very professional commander, there could be no doubt whatsoever.'

On the day Slim summoned Stopford to take command of the Dimapur area the 33 Corps commander wrote in his diary, 'we are going to buy a very sticky show unless we are careful'. By 21 March

Stopford was experiencing a 'pretty thrilling day' organising his move to the front. At this point Stopford had only one division, the British 2nd, under his command. But when Stopford met the 2nd Division commander, General John Grover, he found him 'completely bewildered'. Grover was hardly to be blamed. On 16 March he had met General Giffard to discuss another issue and, aware of the growing crisis, he raised the issue of reinforcements for Dimapur and Kohima. Given that Giffard was under intense pressure from both Mountbatten and Slim to get troops moving, the scene Grover describes in his diary is decidedly unusual.

> Had personal discussion with General Giffard, who showed me latest situation on his Ops Map showing three Japanese Divisions having started to cross the Chindwin on 15th March, and indicating a threat to 4th Corps L. of C. I asked at once whether there was not now a possibility of 2 Div. being employed operationally as a formation. General Giffard replied that there was no such chance, and that in any case it would not be possible to maintain a British Division in the 14th Army area because of the shortage of British reinforcements. Arrangements for dispersal of 2 Division could continue.*

Grover was told to disperse his troops to barracks after the completion of training. Now, just four days later, he was being ordered to hurry them to the front as quickly as possible. Stopford was 'more concerned than ever that Army Group [Giffard] and S.E.A.C. have no control of the situation'.

The troops of 2nd Division had spent months training, not for warfare in the mountains and jungles, but for amphibious landings which had repeatedly been postponed because landing craft could not be spared from Europe. In fact Grover's initial orders for Burma on 18 March were to prepare to move to Chittagong as a departure point for the Arakan. There they would relieve the 5 Indian Division which would be airlifted to Dimapur. But two days later those orders

---

* Indian troops were not used as reinforcements in British regiments.

were countermanded. Grover's division was now to make for Dimapur. It would not be the last twirl in the dysfunctional gavotte of order and counter-order.

Major General John Malcolm Lawrence Grover was forty-seven years old when he was ordered to the Kohima front and had been with 2nd Division since 1941 knowing 'almost everyone in it by name regardless of rank', according to Major David Wilson, who served under Grover from 1942.* Wilson gives an impression of a Grover as a man who was liked 'but could frighten the life out of each of us with his elegantly phrased rockets of displeasure'. Wilson remembered that when he arrived at the Division, instead of being marched in front of Grover as was usual, he was asked to join him for dinner in the mess. The man he met there was 'short, lithe, very smart, very precise in his speech, and blessed with very blue piercing eyes'. According to another young officer Grover was 'highly charged with nervous energy ... correct, punctilious, and a perfectionist', the kind of general who would berate a cook with dirty fingernails. 'Wherever the General walked the air quivered with nervous excitement and apprehension'. Yet for all that he was popular with the ranks whom he made a point of visiting frequently to discuss their food and welfare. But both Grover and his division had always visualised fighting their war against the Germans and not, according to one of his officers, 'to defend a fading empire against Japanese aggressors'.† They were now being called upon to save the British empire from what could be the most humiliating defeat since the fall of Singapore.

---

* Grover was born in the Punjab, the son of an Indian Army major, and was sent to England as a boy to be educated at Winchester and Sandhurst. He was wounded three times in France during the Great War and awarded the Military Cross, before being posted to India where he spent most of the inter-war years. During 1939 and '40 he was in France as a staff officer before being appointed to command 2 Division in 1941.

† 'On the Silence of General Grover', Gordon Graham (*Dekho!*, Winter, 2009). Major Gordon Graham, MC, of the Cameron Highlanders, recalled that after being shipped to India in April 1942 the division was greeted less than wholeheartedly by the colonial authorities. 'At troop level, evidence of a cool welcome was confinement, for ten days after our arrival, to troopships, which we had now occupied for two months ... to GHQ India, the 2nd Division became a prolonged headache and it was mutual.'

General Stopford flew to Comilla to see Slim on 23 March, arriving in a torrential downpour and after a hideous flight which had made several of his staff sick. Slim's headquarters was situated in a spacious and elegant colonial home with a large garden, and after tea the two generals sat down to discuss the growing crisis. Slim must have been typically blunt about the continuing threat to Imphal and the danger posed by the Japanese coming through the Naga Hills, for the meeting unsettled Stopford. Afterwards, he confided to his diary: 'The situation in North Burma is not good and it is touch and go whether reinforcements arrive before the Japs can get to Imphal and Manipur Road.'

At Imphal a potentially disastrous sequence of events had unfolded. The order to withdraw 17th Indian Division, the key to luring Mutaguchi's main forces onto the plain where they could be destroyed, was given too late by the 4th Corps Commander, General Geoffrey Scoones.* Since 13 March the Indians had been fighting their way through Japanese attempts at encirclement. It took three major battles for 17th Indian Division to reach Imphal in early April.

Nearly three hundred miles away in the Arakan, Ray Street, the runner with C company, 4th battalion, the Royal West Kents, was making the most of his rest after the battle of the tunnels. Brigadier Warren addressed the men on parade and told them of his regret at the loss of so many lives. They were based in a deserted village and camped in the empty bashas. New men started to arrive as replacements for those killed at the tunnels. Most of the new faces were

---

* A decade after the war Slim told the Official Historian that he had been 'too optimistic about the way the Imphal battle would go.' He had been asked why he had committed six divisions to the Arakan while 4 Corps 'was left with its original three divisions to meet the enemy offensive …' It was the critical question. 'Obviously in view of what happened I ought to have done so [placed more troops in Assam], and if you say I made a mistake I will not contradict you,' Slim wrote to the historian. He explained that he was anxious for an emphatic victory in the first major test of the new army in the Arakan, that there were worries about being able to maintain extra reinforcements in Imphal due to the number of non-combatants building the base there, and that he had calculated there would be enough time to move troops to the north east to meet the expected threat there. (Cited in Ronald Lewin, *Slim, The Standard Bearer* (Wordsworth Military Library, 1999 edition), pp.159–60.

Welsh and that night, over some beers, the West Kents welcomed them with a sing-song. Street and some others found a lake and waded in, only to find that it was just a foot deep. 'We stripped off and dashed towards the lake, naked like a crowd of eager school kids … we made the most of it splashing and cooling off.' There were parcels from home. Street received cigarettes and chocolate, and there were extra rations of beer and food. The entertainers George and Beryl Formby were flown in and Street recalled how Beryl was persuaded 'to sit on the back of an elephant … the elephant sat down and she slid off. Of course everyone erupted with laughter.'

Street was resting in the shade of his basha when an NCO came and told him to tell the company commanders to report to battalion headquarters. His instinct told him it meant trouble. On 23 March the battalion was placed on two hours' notice to move. Lieutenant Colonel Laverty had been told about the Japanese offensive developing along the Chindwin but he was struggling to get information on the West Kents' exact destination. A measure of his frustration can be gleaned from an entry in the battalion war diary: 'One formation approached for information seriously suggested reference to … [military] newspapers.' Two days later, Laverty received his orders and briefed his officers and NCOs. The battalion was to move to the airstrip at Dohazari and would be flown from there to the front.

Lance Corporal Dennis Wykes remembered being told that the Japanese were threatening Dimapur and that if they got there it would cause serious trouble, 'because India at the present time was still a troubled place. I didn't think they had too much care for the British anyway and the Japanese might have had a lot of sympathy there.'

The entire 5th Indian Division of 15,000 men would be flown, along with artillery, vehicles and mules, into the battle zone over the next few days, in 748 sorties. Laverty and his headquarters staff left for Dimapur on 27 March, followed two days later by the rest of 4th battalion and their comrades in the 1/1 Punjab and 4/7 Rajput. The men were crammed on to barges for the journey to the airstrip at Taungbro. No sooner had they embarked than they were told that the troops sent to replace them in the Arakan were in trouble and that they might have to go back and help them. Everybody climbed off the barges. The rumour proved false. The men and mules were loaded once more, amid much swearing. Arriving at the village of Taungbro, they were told they would have to march the rest of the way. There were more curses and muttering. But the men were in high spirits as they marched through the forest to the airstrip. Waiting officers saw the dust from the advancing column rise above the tree tops. The men were singing:

> Japs on the hilltop
> Japs in the Chaung
> Japs on the Ngadkedauk
> Japs in the Taung
> Japs with their L. of C. far too long
> As they revel in the joys of infiltration.

On arrival they were given water and fresh food. There was time to purchase chocolate, cigarettes, soap and razors from the nearby base. Private H. F. Norman spent his waiting time at the airstrip eating a large breakfast and getting a haircut and shave from the nappi wallah. At some point he got into a conversation with an American aircrew member and told him how much he wanted to visit New York. The Yank replied that, as he came from the west, he hated the city.

Lieutenant Tom Hogg was dispatched to the airstrip early by Laverty to oversee the loading of the RAF Dakotas and the larger American C-46 Commandos. The airstrip was nothing more than a clearing hacked out of the jungle. Above it hung a thin drift of mist. Along the fringes of the forest cover there were anti-aircraft positions, manned by Sikhs who had downed a Japanese fighter three days before. It was one of the few Japanese aircraft to get past the squadrons of Spitfires dominating the skies. Hogg watched the guns being dismantled, probably for the first time since North Africa, and listened to the curses of the gunners. Next came the mules, which were loaded six to a Dakota. 'Immediately the engines roared into action,' Hogg recalled, 'the Mules urinated and the results leaked through the floor and collected in the bottom of the fuselage where it sloshed about among the electrics … The tropical humidity and high temperatures created a powerful odour of which the aircrew did not approve.'

Donald Easten of D company, now promoted to major, was amused by the technique used to get the mules on board the aircraft. On either side of the aircraft doors were two rings. A rope was tied to one of the rings and then looped past the mule's backside to the second ring to act as a pulley. 'Then as many men as were required pulled and the poor old mule went zipping up the thing.' The Americans were unsentimental about obstreperous mules that might endanger the aircraft. An animal that became unruly in the air was immediately shot. The jeeps, too, had to be loaded. This was done by bouncing them from the ramp through the plane's loading door, and then bumping them by hand into the narrow interior.

After his troops had boarded, Donald Easten remembered an American crewman sticking his head through the door and barking instructions. 'There's a guy called "Slide Rule" is gonna be comin' round here,' the American said, 'and he if tells you to move something you move it. OK?' The careful distribution of weight was essential to keep the aircraft from crashing. 'Slide Rule' duly appeared and ordered ammunition to be moved here and there. Ray Street remembers how the navigator kept telling them that if they saw any Japanese they were to shoot through the windows with their Bren guns. 'That didn't do much for our confidence.' Most of the men had never been on an aircraft before.

These Yanks were tired, scruffy and unshaven. They swore at the Indians loading the planes if they slowed down for a moment. A mobile canteen stood next to the line of aircraft and crew members would break off periodically to wolf down breakfast. The pressure of time on these men was enormous. While the aircrew slept for a few hours, the ground technicians worked through the night to prepare the aircraft.

The RAF account described, in typically understated fashion, the touch-and-go nature of the operation. 'It was, in fact, a matter for speculation whether this enemy thrust would be started before the fly-in.' The airlift shuttled men to both Dimapur and Imphal. There were, after all, two potential sieges to worry about. The Japanese 33 and 15 Divisions were still fighting towards Imphal while Sato's 31 was advancing into the Naga Hills. Crammed together in the sweaty interiors of the Dakotas and Commandos, the men heard the engines roar and felt the aircraft rattle as they took off across the jungle towards Dimapur. Private Ivan Daunt was sitting next to a cockney who asked the American aircrew why they had parachutes and the West Kents didn't. 'Because it's our plane,' came the reply. The cockney responded by leading his comrades in song:

> We are the West Kent boys.
> We are the West Kent boys.
> When we are marching down the Old Kent road,
> the doors and windows open wide,
> then you'll hear the people shout,
> put those bloody Woodbines out,
> 'cos you are the West Kent boys.

TWELVE

Flap

When the telegram came on 20 March, Colonel Hugh Richards might have wondered what fresh misfortune was about to befall him. The colonel had set his heart on fighting with Wingate's Chindits but, having completed the rigorous training, he was told that at the age of forty-nine he was too old for the jungle. Those who had served with Richards in West Africa, where he had commanded 3 West African Infantry Brigade, thought Wingate's decision 'total nonsense' and an injustice to 'an enormously popular commander'. He had spent the war until that point on the sun-withered northern border of Nigeria preparing to attack the neighbouring Vichy colonies. But when the French declined to resist the allied occupation of Timbuktu the West Africans were sent to India and given to Wingate. The Army Group Commander, General Sir George Giffard, was a fellow veteran of West Africa and had known Richards for years. He gave the unhappy colonel a job as commander of the Delhi area, an unappealing sideshow in which a man might languish indefinitely in boredom. The March telegram from General Giffard brought what appeared to be good news. Richards was to leave Delhi immediately and fly to Imphal. From there he would travel up to Kohima and take command of the garrison. There is no trace in the military records of an explanation as to why the commander of a West African brigade, recently rejected by Wingate, had been chosen for this task; Richards had no experience of commanding Indian and Burmese troops, who provided the majority of the garrison, and he had never fought the Japanese.

The appointment might have had a lot to do with the exigencies of war when the British were still scrambling to catch up with the pace of the Japanese advance. Richards's African bond with Giffard may also have helped push him to the forefront. But the appointment also had something to do with the personality of Hugh Richards himself. He had a reputation for being steady. When Giffard was told to send an officer to hold Kohima, he replied, 'I will send you someone who will do that.' Tall and strongly built, Hugh Upton Richards wore a slim moustache and an expression of calm. He was not a fire-eater or a martinet. Like the man who would become his great friend, Charles Pawsey, Richards had been tested in the fire of the Western Front, and was another of the few who had survived from 1914 through to 1918. Like Pawsey, he had also been taken prisoner.

Richards came from a middle-class family in Worcestershire and joined up as a private before being commissioned in the field in 1915. His experience in the ranks gave him a sympathy for the ordinary soldier that would prove invaluable when it came to the desperate onslaughts on the trenches at Kohima. Between the wars in Nigeria he befriended an Australian oil engineer, a man of some wealth, who helped the eternally penurious Richards with funds to educate his son. 'This man was a truly generous person. I think he admired my father who was a kind and upright person,' his son recalled. 'My father loved that life in Africa. He could live properly there and not constantly worry about money the way he had to at home.' Between the wars he also served in Palestine.

Hugh Richards's orders were clear on the issue of command: 'You will be in operational control of *all* [author's italics] the troops in KOHIMA and of 1 Assam Regiment.' This would assume great importance for Richards as the battle developed and he came to appreciate the challenge of working with a man as tough and self-contained as the CO of 4th battalion, the Royal West Kents, Lieutenant Colonel John Laverty.

On 22 March Richards flew to Imphal and the following day he boarded a two-seater plane for the short flight to Dimapur, 'touching down on a rough airstrip which seemed to be in the middle of nowhere ... nothing but jungle was visible from the airstrip'. Richards was taken to Charles Pawsey's bungalow where Pawsey immediately gave permission for him to establish a garrison head-quarters at the residence. Captain Walter Greenwood, who acted as Richards's staff captain, remembered that it was ridiculously over-crowded. At any time there could be up to fifteen staff officers work-ing in the small building, along 'with any visitor who happened to drop in'.

Richards toured the defences and was shaken. 'I had been told there were no defences, but even so, I was appalled at what I found.' Part of the problem was that the existing commander had only recently emerged from a three-week hospital stay. Those who had been charged with building defences in his absence had been tardy. Richards noted: 'Trenches had in many cases not been dug by men who had a knowledge of what was required to provide protection against high explosive. They were too wide and few had any head cover.' Hugh Richards, veteran of the Western Front, understood the necessity for strong trenches. The digging had been done by Naga labourers and not by soldiers. He also noticed that the troops were organised into small box formations, placed near the main installa-tions such as hospitals and stores. But they were too widely dispersed and could easily be picked off by the enemy. Astonishingly there was no barbed wire.*

Of equal concern was the constant change in overall garrison strength. Lorries were leaving and arriving at a dizzying rate. Some carried supplies and ammunition, others came to bring men from the hospital down to Dimapur. As an official account put it: 'The[re was] constant fluctuation of the Garrison. Many units were moved without reference to Garrison HQ, and the size of the Box and the number of troops available to man it were therefore almost impos-sible to compute.' An Indian Army officer, Lieutenant Dennis Dawson, one of the logistics officers based at Kohima, felt sorry for Richards.

---

* Barbed wire was banned in the Naga Hills due to a pre-war ordinance designed to protect local farmers.

'Nobody took any notice of him, because we came under 253 sub area administratively, and whatever he said, we said, "well you'll have to go through district." He didn't know from one day to another how many troops he had in Kohima at all. Nobody could tell him. We were in a terrible position.'

When he looked at the quality of the soldiery available to him, Richards was apprehensive. The best unit, 1st battalion, Assam Regiment, had been deployed to Jessami and Kharasom to delay any Japanese advance. Among the assortment of troops at Kohima there was a battalion from the Royal Nepalese Army, a detachment of Assam Rifles, two companies of Burmese troops, and two platoons of Mahratta Light Infantry. In addition, there were several hundred line of communications troops – signallers, construction teams, cattle controllers – and about two hundred British troops at the reinforcement camp, mostly older soldiers or men recovering from tropical illnesses. Walter Greenwood, a survivor of the fall of Singapore, arrived in Kohima to find the place full of a 'motley crew of useless mouths and hangers on' with 'no real competent soldiers in charge'. Some of the ancillary units such as canteens, rest camps and field hygiene sections were sent back to Dimapur. Greenwood estimated that by the time some 3,000 non-combatants had been evacuated, there were 2,500 men left, but more than half were ancillary troops. The total number of riflemen numbered around a thousand, pulled together from 'all sorts and services'. Richards was inclined to be generous when speaking of his eclectic band of warriors, reaching back to a memory from the First World War. 'It struck me that the composition bore some similarity to the line as it was composed in front of Hazebrouck in 1918 when the cooks and the bakers and the butchers turned to [soldiering].'

Lieutenant Pieter Steyn, a South African serving with the 1st Assam, described the mess. 'In spite of the deplorable military situation,' Steyn wrote, 'a clear plan had not been formulated for the defence of Kohima. Administrative arrangements had been completely disrupted and telephonic communication was chaotic.' There were three separate telephone exchanges in the town and nobody seemed to know which military sector each was supposed to serve. With such inadequate communications between headquarters and the other sectors, 'command therefore devolved almost entirely on local commanders, for the most part inexperienced junior officers, who were called on to exercise and assume unexpected responsibilities often beyond their rank'.

Kohima had been the responsibility of General Scoones at Imphal until 28 March but under mounting pressure himself he was incapable of preparing the defence of the ridge. As Scoones was about to be cut off at Imphal, and with Stopford still on his way, Slim ordered General R.P.L. Ranking, who commanded the rear area and line of communication, to prepare to defend both Dimapur and Kohima. Slim described the appointment as 'a sudden plunge from administrative duties in a peaceful area into the alarms and stresses of savage battle'. It was a considerable understatement. Ranking was an Indian Army man who was awarded a Military Cross on the Somme before returning to Regimental Headquarters in Uttar Pradesh, but he was not a battlefield general and with the few days left to him he could only hope that his garrison commander, Hugh Richards, could hold Kohima until reinforcements arrived.*

As late as 23 March, Richards was being told by his superiors that the narrow jungle paths could not be passed by any force larger than a regiment and that there would certainly be no artillery. The intelli-

---

* A decade after the events in question Slim wrote that *within a week* (author's italics) of the Japanese offensive ... it became clear that the situation in the Kohima area was likely to be even more dangerous than that at Imphal. Not only were the enemy columns closing in on Kohima at much greater speed than I had expected, but they were obviously in much greater strength. *Indeed it was soon evident* (author's italics) that the bulk, if not the whole, of the Japanese 31st Division, was driving for Kohima and Dimapur.' (*Defeat Into Victory*, p. 305.) This assertion deserves examination. If one takes the start of the Japanese offensive into the Naga Hills as 15 March, Slim seems to be saying he was aware by 23 March that the Japanese were in much greater strength than a regiment. Colonel Hugh Richards wrote that he only became aware of the size of the approaching Japanese force from Naga scouts on 27 March. The 11 Army Group Commander, General Sir George Giffard, wrote in his official dispatch that 'we became aware' that a division was on the way on 29 March. Slim may have been mistaken in his recollection. It is hard to imagine the defenders of the Kohima area would have been left in ignorance of the size of the attacking force if 14th Army had known earlier.

gence showed the nearest Japanese were some thirty-five miles east of Kohima. There was one shaft of light. On 24 March Richards looked down the road to see a convoy of trucks grinding up from Dimapur. They were carrying some old friends. The British troops who arrived in Kohima that afternoon were from the 2nd battalion, West Yorkshire Regiment, with whom Hugh Richards had served as second-in-command for three years in Palestine. Since then, they had fought in North Africa and Burma. With new hope, he wrote, 'I felt reasonably happy about our ability to hold the enemy.'

In the last days of March General Slim toured the defences at Dimapur with customary cheer, not betraying his unease for a second. 'As I walked around, inspecting bunkers and rifle pits, dug by non-combatant labour under the direction of storemen and clerks, and as I looked into the faces of the willing but untried garrison, I could only hope that I imparted more confidence than I felt.'

Throughout India a vast war machine was on the move. General John Grover's British 2nd Division was crammed into trains heading to Dimapur, and the entire 5th Indian Division, which included the 161 Indian Brigade of which the West Kents were part, was being airlifted. The commander of 161 Indian Brigade, D. F. W. Warren, arrived at Dimapur ahead of the main body of his troops. He was an avuncular figure, an old India hand, well liked by the men, who nicknamed him 'Daddy'. Warren was acutely conscious of the human cost of his decisions. His son was serving as a company commander in the Arakan.

At a meeting in Dimapur, Slim gave Warren and the local commander, Ranking, three tasks: prepare the defence of Dimapur and hold it; reinforce Kohima and 'hold that to the last'; and prepare to receive the large reinforcements that were coming. Slim called Warren outside and walked up and down the path with him. He outlined 'without any attempt to minimise the hazardous task he was being set, a fuller view of the situation, and especially of the time factor'. In plain language Warren was told to get his troops moving up the road fast. If there were a breakthrough at Kohima, the battle would be lost. Slim's instinct was to make a stand at Kohima. It offered the best defensive position on the approach to Dimapur. The ridge dominated the road and whoever held it had a huge tactical advantage. But everything was predicated on the defenders holding out until reinforcements arrived from the British 2nd Division.

General Grover's 2nd Division was made up entirely of troops from English, Scottish and Welsh regiments. Among the reinforcements was Captain Arthur Swinson of the 7th Worcestershire Regiment, who found his train 'packed so tight we can hardly move'. At Calcutta on 31 March he bought a copy of the *Statesman* newspaper, which reported that three Japanese columns were advancing over the frontier. The following morning his train reached the Brahmaputra river in the early mist and the troops transferred to a ferry; he saw from the deck the green hills of Assam and away to the north the mountains of Tibet. They boarded another train and moved through the wet jungle. At lunchtime the war intruded in an unexpected way. Wounded from the Imphal battles appeared. 'We were having lunch when an ambulance train passed. The tail end of it stopped opposite us for a few minutes and I looked at the rows of weary men. Some sitting up smoking, others lying quite still, but all with a glazed hollow look in their eyes. It does you no good seeing ambulance trains, not when you're on your way to the front, it doesn't.'

Swinson was attached to the staff of 5th Brigade, whose commander, Brigadier Victor Hawkins, was a tall, spare figure, explosive when annoyed and inclined to hound his younger officers into joining him in ostentatious displays of fitness. However, Hawkins was a brave and thoughtful soldier. Although Swinson suffered the lash of his tongue, he wrote, 'the whole brigade had a great affection for him', not least because 'he detested the waste of a single life'.

Hawkins's progress to the front had been frustrating and emblematic of the chaos induced by the Japanese advance. When he arrived at Stopford's headquarters as ordered he ran into a senior officer, who was puzzled by his presence. 'Hallo, what are you doing here?' he asked.

'We were told to report here,' Hawkins replied.

'Oh, we cancelled that last night,' he was told. Hawkins was to go directly to Dimapur. After a rough night's sleep in an improvised mess, he went down to the airstrip for his promised flight to Dimapur. Again, there was nobody to meet him. There followed a search of various buildings until he found the aircrew. His temper was not improved by the situation he found at Dimapur. 'The local situation was staggering. There was no appreciation of the seriousness of the situation, or even of the situation itself ... There were some 80,000 unarmed coolies in the base depots liable to stampede at the first shot. There were no immediate defence plans. There were two transit camps full of troops from IV Corps who had now been cut off from their units and could not get back. None of these were organised in any way ... discipline seemed to be conspicuous by its absence. In fact, complacency was the chief order of the day, and plans were completely lacking.'

When Stopford arrived to see the situation for himself he was challenged by Hawkins, and 'things began to alter for the better'. The first of Hawkins's troops reached Dimapur on the evening of 1 April, and Arthur Swinson had his first brush with death. A soldier clearing his rifle discharged a shot which whizzed past his ear. The Dimapur base was 'in one big flap' and what Swinson called the 'chairborne troops in the L of C area' were digging trenches and rolling out wire. Wild-eyed Indian drivers were speeding north with only six inches between the trucks, and haggard-looking porters staggered around with huge loads. Refugees were also flooding in, 'with their whole world on their heads'. Some collapsed and blocked the traffic, but nobody made an effort to assist them. Rumours were flying. There was a story that there were only 10,000 rifles for the 80,000 men in the place; one sentry was allegedly seen with a wooden gun.

Slim later wrote that he had asked the brigadier commanding the base how many men he was feeding. 'Forty-five thousand near enough,' he told the army commander. 'And how many soldiers can you scrape out of that lot?' I inquired. He smiled wryly. 'I might get five hundred who know how to fire a rifle.' This puts Slim's nervousness about facing even a regiment of Japanese at this early stage into perspective.

At dinner Swinson met a Royal Army Medical Corps officer who had been up the road to Kohima and was pessimistic. 'He didn't like the look of things and thought the lack of plans was pitiful.' Swinson went to bed soon afterwards but could not sleep. His nerves were on edge. That night he wrote in his diary: 'Lord, give us time and we'll ask nothing else.'

Lieutenant Bruce Hayllar of the Indian Armoured Corps arrived in Dimapur a day later. He had been pottering about in Secunderabad, where his regiment was training with tanks and troop-carriers, when orders came to go to Dimapur. Before he left there had been a big party. 'Very, very merry. Played tiger – tossed in the blanket – I got debagged.' He discovered his trousers up a tree, before staggering to bed at 2 a.m. On his way to Dimapur with fellow officers, Hayllar stopped in Calcutta for four days, waiting for transport to the front. Writing home to his parents on 31 March, his voice is that of the eager public schoolboy, still astonished that he has been given charge of the lives of other men. 'We had breakfast in bed at 10. We joined the Saturday Club and bathed there daily. We dined at Firpo's (price about 10/-), we ate luscious cream cakes at a Swiss Café, we sat in the best seats in the best cinemas and saw lovely films. We drank Scotch Whiskey at 2/6 the glass and Indian hooch at 1/- the glass ... Everyone there has some sort of story to tell. It was quite the most romantic place I have ever been to. And all of this was heightened because the Japs had started advancing into India and the news wasn't good.'

Boarding a train for Dimapur, Hayllar saw some Indian and West African troops squaring up to each other with knives. He put this down to persistent stories of the West Africans bullying the Indians and stealing their women. He finished his letter with an unusual apology. 'This ending is very bad, sorry, but really can't write a dramatic sob-stuff ending because I may go nowhere near the fighting. Just assume everything is allright. It always is.'

Hayllar arrived at Dimapur on 1 April. That night he wrote in his diary, 'March in circle to rest camp. The biggest shambles you ever saw ... the flap on. Raining. Air raid alarm.' A call went out for officers to volunteer to go up to Kohima and help with the defence. Bored and desperate to see action, Bruce Hayllar immediately stepped forward. 'I volunteer,' he wrote in his diary. 'Up the Hayllars!'

There were also troops pushing through Kohima to help the defence of Imphal. The journey to Kohima was a stomach-churning progress along the steep, winding road. Lieutenant John Hudson, a sapper with 91 Royal Bombay Field Company, experienced constant hold-ups as lorries overheated. His column never went more than 10 miles per hour. Men were thrown from side to side as the trucks lurched around hairpin bends. Worse, there was 'Burma Road Sickness', caused by a combination of engine fumes, dust, tobacco smoke, rising heat, a constant backward view and gut-wrenching potholes. 'Man after man vomited over the stern gate and collapsed into stupor.' Passing through Kohima, he glimpsed the village 'set like a jewel on the rim between Assam and Manipur. Whitewashed buildings gleam amongst rich foliage, the red splash of the corrugated tin roof over the Mission Chapel and the mown precision of the tennis court contrasted with the tumbled savagery of the blue-green mountain backdrop.' It would be one of the last occasions a traveller would ever have such a view of Kohima.

In the Naga Hills British and local scouts were retreating fast ahead of the Japanese advance. Ursula Graham Bower in remote Cachar was one of the last Europeans to get news of the Japanese attack. On 28 March she heard a radio announcement about the Japanese advancing on a wide front. For the previous eighteen months she had done little soldiering but a great deal of relief work dealing with victims of hunger and disease. On the same day as the broadcast her assistant Namkia announced the arrival of two British soldiers. The sergeants told her that fifty Japanese had been seen in the vicinity. 'They said "Please Miss have you seen any Japs?" … This was a little startling … Things were looking a little nasty.' Worse still, she learned that the frontier had been rolled back so that the only British-occupied areas were Imphal, Kohima and the handful of posts held by the Assam Regiment at Jessami and Kharasom. The V Force detachments nearer the Chindwin had either been overrun or had fled. 'I woke up one

morning to find out we were twenty miles behind the front line …
we had no troops at that moment and 150 Nagas armed with
muzzle-loaders who were supposed to be watching the tracks for
agents filtering through.' Her darkest moment came when Namkia
and the other leaders in the group asked for permission to go back to
their villages. 'This is it,' she thought to herself. She was alone with
the Japanese army heading towards her. Twenty-four hours later the
Nagas were back. They had gone home to make their wills, say goodbye to their families, and to dress for battle, leaving the sacred heir-
loom necklaces behind for their sons to inherit. 'After all,' Namkia
said to Graham Bower, 'which was the better thing? To desert and
live, and hear our children curse us for the shame we put on them; or
to die with you, and leave them proud of us for ever?'

A telegram was sent from V Force telling her to get out of the
Cachar district immediately. It crossed with her own cable to headquarters: 'Going forward to look for enemy. Kindly send weapons
and ammunition soonest.' Graham Bower set about posting her men
into the jungle so that they could warn of any Japanese approach.
Runners were sent into the hills to call the scouts in from their labour
and hunting, and within two days a line of sentries had been established. Graham Bower herself kept to a normal routine, staying in the
village even though she knew it would be the first target of any
advancing enemy. To sleep in the jungle would have given the
impression of panic to the locals. Code words were established. 'One
Elephant' meant ten Japanese. This had unintended consequences, as
Graham Bower later wrote: 'Somebody caused confusion left and
right by turning up on the Silchar border with forty genuine
elephants.'

As the leader of a guerrilla band, Graham Bower could have
expected no mercy if captured. A Mr Sharp of the Indian Civil
Service had been appointed to the temporary rank of major in V
Force and was captured by the Japanese five days later. He was never
heard of again. Patrolling in the thick jungle terrified Graham Bower.
She watched the faces of the experienced scouts, learned from the
way they moved and from the manner in which they listened to the

jungle. Without the skill and knowledge of those born to the forest she would not have lasted a day at war. This she always cheerfully acknowledged. She told a story of how a Naga was taking a patrol through particularly dense jungle, walking point ahead of the main group, when he walked straight into a Japanese patrol. Had he doubled back the Japanese would have caught the patrol unawares, so the man stood and fought, killing the leading Japanese before the others riddled him with bullets. Another stayed behind in his village when the Japanese approached, because 'he was a subject of the king and he was going to do his bit'. The warrior attacked with his spear, sword and shield and killed five Japanese before they shot him.

Many V Force officers fleeing from the advance owed their survival to the Nagas. Captain Tim Betts, a tea-planter in civilian life, was with a small party of Indian troops when his post was overrun. Betts was seventy miles from Kohima in a direct line but the steep mountains, thick jungles and absence of any road meant the journey was nearly three times that distance. It was Betts's initial bad fortune to have Kuki tribesmen as scouts. This was the same tribe that had experienced brutal repression at the hands of the British in the 1920 rebellion, with the loss of their harvest and livestock and the destruction of their villages. The scouts rapidly deserted to the Japanese once they arrived.

Betts kept a diary of his extraordinary escape. On 25 March he recorded: 'I can't go on with this cross-country mountaineering. My only chance is the river and the main tracks, and that is the only way we will make progress. If the men won't come with me we shall soon have to part. I was for getting down to the river again where we could at least get fish and flat going and not this appalling hillside clambering among slipping precipices and gulf-like nullahs.' He then met some Nagas who gave the group food. But it became clear to Betts that his men were losing the will to keep going. He gave the order to move and began to march himself. After half a mile he stopped and looked around. There was no sign of the troops.

On 27 March he wrote that he 'felt no compunction [about leaving]. They had a day's rice and knew where they were, and [had] the only blanket, cooking pot and kukris. I had a map and compass and a tin of bully and one of sardines and half a dozen K biscuits.' Betts kept moving through jungle and up steep ridges, bypassing a village full of Japanese, their fires blazing and torches casting beams of light across the darkness. Clambering up an 8,000 foot ridge he attempted to sleep, covering himself in grass for warmth. Weary and disorientated from thirst and hunger, he found himself wandering along a dry river bed where the sharp stones sliced through what remained of his boots. At several points along the way Nagas had given him food and pointed him in the direction of Kohima. Using dynamite he had brought with him, Betts caught fish, and in abandoned huts he found firewood, rice and sweet potatoes. Ursula Graham Bower, who would later meet the young officer in her jungle stronghold, told how Betts met an old Naga lady who burst into tears on seeing his condition. '[She] gave him her only food ... some pork ... with that he carried on for another two days.'

Tim Betts reached Kohima on 2 April, having walked across some of the most forbidding territory in the world. 'Flat out with violent diarrhoea, feet like footballs,' he wrote, 'and so weak I could hardly stand.' His normal weight was 11 stone 7 pounds. He now weighed just six stone.

Through the hills from north to south, indications were mounting that the Japanese were coming. Nagas ran to alert British outposts. The V Force officer Lieutenant Colonel E. D. 'Moke' Murray managed to send a last message on his high-powered radio transmitter before he escaped into the jungle. Murray eventually ran into an Indian patrol on 16 March and gave them a note for their headquarters warning that he believed a full-scale offensive was under way. The patrol passed the message on to headquarters, where it was somehow mislaid and never passed up the chain of command. A patrol from the 1st Assam was settling down in a V Force stockade when they heard that three hundred Japanese were heading towards them. That night the Japanese attacked the stockade and found it empty.

The only formations now standing between Sato's advance and Kohima were the 1st Assam troops at Jessami and Kharasom and elements of 50 Indian Parachute Brigade, which arrived in the mountain-top village of Sangshak on 21 March. The CO, Brigadier M. R. J. 'Tim' Hope-Thomson, was a veteran of Palestine, where he had won the Military Cross, but had spent his time in India preparing the first ever Indian Army airborne unit for battle. The 50 Indian Parachute Brigade was carrying out training and patrolling around Kohima when news came of the first Japanese crossings of the Chindwin. Sangshak was crucial because it occupied a position astride routes leading to both Kohima and Imphal.

Because much of the available transport was being used to ferry non-combatants out of Imphal, Hope-Thomson was short one company when his two battalions arrived in the area. They found themselves short of entrenching tools and barbed wire, and with a chronic lack of access to fresh water. The spiny ridges of the border area were notably short of water sources. Everything would depend on supply from the air. In the recriminations that followed the disaster, much was made of Hope-Thomson's decision to make a stand at Sangshak. It was a barren hilltop, around which the perimeter stretched 'about 600 hundred yards long and 300 yards at its widest, shaped like an hourglass'. With the exception of a small area in the middle, the ground was too rocky to be able to dig defensive positions deeper than three feet. 'It was volcanic glass, or obsidian, as immovable as granite,' recalled Lieutenant Harry Seaman, a platoon commander at Sangshak. Once the Japanese began to pour in mortar and artillery fire they could not fail to hit the defenders.

The great chronicler of the Burma war, Louis Allen, chided Hope-Thomson for choosing his perimeter 'without regard to its lack of water', a serious problem in a siege. But Hope-Thomson had not chosen the position. He came to take over from an existing force and, his defenders argue, never had the time to construct a new base. Frequent requests to headquarters for more barbed wire elicited no response.*

---

* Sangshak lay outside the Naga Hills and barbed wire was permitted.

Wire is the infantryman's first line of defence. It slows the enemy within killing range and prevents the kind of creep-and-rush tactics the Japanese used to terrifying effect in the darkness. A well-wired perimeter also allows defenders the possibility of some sleep during the day. Later, the survivors of Sanghsak would react with angry disbelief when they struggled into Imphal to find headquarters buildings surrounded by triple lines of barbed wire.

Hope-Thomson had no intelligence on the size or direction of the Japanese forces in his area. As far as he knew, the main thrust of the Japanese attack was against Imphal, along routes a long distance from Sangshak. As one of his battalion commanders, Lieutenant Colonel Hopkinson, wrote later, they knew 'nothing about any offensive towards Imphal ... and Kohima from our front'. From Hope-Thomson's point of view, the strength of his base and outposts should have been adequate to deal with a small Japanese formation. He had a thousand fighting men. There were another eight hundred or so support troops. However, a Japanese group of even regimental strength would have substantially outnumbered the defenders.

Hopkinson wrote that he had 'always been very puzzled as to how the Japanese managed to cross the Chindwin apparently entirely unobserved from the air and by ground posts'. But they had been observed. The intelligence was simply never passed on to 50 Brigade.* It meant that brigade was still adhering to a training schedule as the Japanese 58th Regiment bore down on its way to Kohima.

Hope-Thomson had sent men from his 152nd battalion to join the 4/5 Mahratta Regiment at positions about nine miles from Sangshak, at a place called Sheldon's Corner, along the route of any likely Japanese advance. Three miles further along again were the last defensive outposts at Point 7378. The CO of 152nd battalion, Lieutenant Colonel Paul Hopkinson, met V Force stragglers and

---

* The mislaid evidence of the V Force officer Colonel Murray was not the last instance of intelligence going astray. An agent of Z Force, one of the clandestine units operating inside Burma, was able to report that three Japanese battalions had crossed the river on 16 March. This was logged in the intelligence diary of 4 Corps at Imphal on the same day, but was never passed on to 50 Brigade at Sangshak.

Nagas who reported seeing parties of Japanese. But there was no suggestion that these were large groups or that they were advancing on Sangshak. However, on 18 March he received a wireless call from his outpost down the road. The officer told him that an exhausted V Force man had just stumbled into the camp with an alarming report. The Japanese were across the Chindwin in strength. As many as nine hundred had already been counted and they were heading up the track towards the forward positions. Early the following morning Hopkinson sent another message. Battle was under way.

THIRTEEN

Onslaught

It was only a week since they had left the Chindwin but to Lieutenant Yoshiteru Hirayama, machine-gun squad leader with 3rd battalion, 58th Regiment, it felt as if they had been marching forever. There was sun and clear air at the top of the mountains, and always a heavy blanket of wet air waiting at the bottom. 'It was up and down and up and down every day. I couldn't wait to get there. I had no map to see where we were or how long was left.' They were tormented by leeches. No matter how tightly a man buttoned his tunic or wrapped his puttees, the bloodsuckers found a way in. There were occasional distractions from the monotony of the march, like the watercress the men found growing at the streams in the bottom of valleys. 'We took them to our mouths as hungry locusts,' remembered the war correspondent Yukihiko Imai. Later, he saw the bright green stools of several hundred soldiers scattered all over the ground.

He also recorded how the Japanese recruited local labour. 'As soon as we reached the hamlet we caught the women and the children, and the soldiers locked them up in the cottage. It was sure their husband or parent come back to help and they got their near relative in exchange for their own labour. When we reached the next village we released them and in the same way we got labour next.' The Naga would remember this in a few months' time when the Japanese were passing in the opposite direction.

The first indications Lieutenant Hirayama had of the British presence were the machine-gun bullets zipping through the foliage around him. He found cover with the rest of his unit. The lieutenant was now able to see the British trenches, but every time a Japanese soldier moved there was a burst of fire in response. A day attack was impossible. Waiting for darkness, he understood that the China veterans around him would watch every move he made. Hirayama faced his first great test as a soldier and a leader. At school he had suffered bullying because of his class background: he was the son of a monk, well-to-do and well dressed, living apart from the peasant children whose tiny houses skirted the monastery gates. They would not accept him. Now he commanded a unit of tough peasants who were obliged to offer him respect because of his rank. He would not feel he had earned it until the men had seen him act bravely in battle.

When night came, Hirayama was given orders to mount a flanking movement to the left of the British trenches. Once in position, he settled down and waited for further orders. Suddenly he saw figures moving in front of his position. Should he shoot? He held off. 'It was actually our men and it was good I didn't shoot!' he recalled. It was his good judgement rather than physical bravery that first inclined his men to have faith in their young officer.

Hirayama and the rest of 3rd battalion had bumped up against C company, 152nd battalion of the Parachute Brigade. The first Japanese assault was beaten off. But through the night there were two subsequent attacks which gained ground. There were about 170 defenders, among them seven British officers, but with the main mortar section out of range on another hill, the company commander could only hope to slow down the Japanese. Hopkinson received a last message from Point 7378 at dawn on 20 March. The commander, three other officers and forty men were already dead. Relieving troops had become bogged down in thick jungle or found the Japanese resistance too stiff to penetrate.

The official history of the 58th Regiment described the closing stages of the fight. A party of about twenty British and Indians charged downhill, firing and shouting as they came. But between them and the Japanese was a wide ravine, into which some of the men fell. Most of the others were forced to surrender, while a few escaped. The Japanese then witnessed an extraordinary scene. 'At the very top of the position an officer appeared in sight, put a pistol to his head and shot himself in full view of everyone below. Our men fell silent, deeply impressed by such a brave act.' The suicide of an officer in full view of the enemy was not part of any British military tradition. But it was a gesture the Japanese understood perfectly and it gave them food for thought. These were different soldiers from the ones routed in Burma and Singapore.

The 58th Regiment suffered 160 casualties in the thirty-six-hour battle, during which 'the enemy had resisted with courage and skill'. In the immediate aftermath Hirayama was sent to check a nearby track. As the patrol moved along, a landmine exploded, killing his friend, Second Lieutenant Oshima. Years later, what would remain with Hirayama was not the blood and gore but the image of his friend's sandals which were packed away in his backpack. 'They were the sandals for mountain hiking which he loved. That was his personality, a man who loved the open places.'

The defenders at the main blocking position three miles further back in the direction of Sangshak now retreated. On reaching Sangshak, Lieutenant Colonel Jackie Trim, CO of the 4/5 Mahratta, was allocated an area of about fifty square yards for his entire battalion, such was the confined space of the perimeter. 'There was much confusion,' he wrote, with considerable understatement. As his men were digging in, a heavy thunderstorm descended and a company commander received a severe electric shock. To add to his woes, Trim found himself under fire from his own machine guns. Frightened soldiers were shooting at shadows. 'The men were hungry and tired and as a result became trigger happy but we managed to calm them down,' he wrote. The storm did bring one benefit: the heavy rain provided a source of water for the parched Mahrattas.

The Japanese were busy foraging for food in the nearby village of Ukhrul. Lieutenant Shosaku Kameyama of the 58th Regiment arrived to find, 'to our great disappointment', that the British had set fire to their stores before leaving. A sergeant major found a bottle of whisky which he presented to the infantry group commander, General Miyazaki, who had arrived to direct the battle. Kameyama's men were desperate for rest after a tough six-day march from the Chindwin. Miyazaki had no intention of stopping now.

By the time the Japanese encirclement was complete, Hope-Thomson had approximately 2,000 men inside his perimeter. They were well trained but facing battle together for the first time. Because of insufficient transport, the remainder of his 153 battalion was left behind in the village of Litan, between Sangshak and Imphal.

General Miyazaki was not meant to stop at Sangshak. Kohima was his objective and any attack on Sangshak was supposed to have been left to the 15th Division, which was heading this way towards Imphal. But the 15th Division was behind schedule and 50 Indian Parachute Brigade was a threat to Miyazaki's line of communications. In his view, marching past Sangshak was not an option.

At dusk on 22 March the Japanese launched the first concerted attack. It came from the west, down a hill and across the village football field. As they flitted between burning native huts, the defenders saw them as shadows and spectres, smashed backwards by the fire from mortars and mountain guns, but regrouping for a second attack – a relentless enemy whose high-pitched war cries carried across the contested ground between the blasts of high explosive. In the darkness, and with the smoke from explosions, a defending soldier might only see a Japanese as he arrived in front of him. 'With the firing, Very lights and shouting, we might have been watching a Hollywood movie,' wrote medical officer Eric Neild. Another described the effect of seeing the troops tumbling in the face of machine-gun fire as watching men die in slow motion.

A Japanese lieutenant urged his men forward screaming '*Tsukkome!*' – 'Charge!' – and, reaching the first trenches, used his sword to cut down four Indian soldiers before being felled by gunfire. Lieutenant Yoshiteru Hirayama was surprised by the amount of artillery fire. 'It felt like hundreds of shells.' His platoon was driven backwards. 'We set up our machine gun and we could see the British trenches. The British shot down at us as they had dug their trenches first.' The heavy fire gave an impression of defensive strength at variance with the reality.

The colour-bearer with the 58th Regiment, Second Lieutenant Hiroshi Yamagami, smoked a last 'Java' cigarette with his comrades before going into the attack. If he were killed, it was agreed that one of the NCOs would take up the flag. If the nominated man were killed, another would take over, and so on. The last man would burn the colours with gasoline and destroy the coat of arms with a grenade. A canteen full of gasoline was permanently on hand.

Lieutenant Kameyama of the 3rd battalion saw his company commander break down in tears because the enemy fire was too heavy for his men to recover the bodies of the dead. The CO was wounded in the neck but continued to shout instructions. 'Hearing my report, the commander finally realised that the attack could not be carried out and he broke down in tears, a man weeping in front of his subordinates, saying, "Too shameful not to recover the bones of Lieutenant Ban and soldiers of 8th Company."'

At dawn on 23 March, the defenders looked across the football field to see around one hundred dead Japanese. Only twenty men had survived from one company and they had lost their commander. One battalion would lose more than four hundred killed and wounded in repeated attempts to breach the perimeter. The sight of so many dead Japanese gave heart to the encircled troops.

The mood of optimism did not last long. An air drop of supplies that afternoon fell outside the perimeter and into Japanese hands. The Dakota pilots, with one exception, were flying too high for the accurate drop the tight perimeter demanded. Day after day the same scenario was repeated. The Dakotas flew too high, except for one which flew so low that the defenders 'could almost distinguish [the pilot's] features in his cockpit, and watch the dispatchers at work in the doorway as the aircraft passed attracting a storm of small-arms fire from the enemy on each circuit, as the brave and skilful crew delivered every last pound of its priceless cargo within the bounds of the perimeter'. Lieutenant Colonel Paul Hopkinson, 152nd parachute battalion, later discovered that this particular aircrew had taken part in training with 50 Brigade and felt a special responsibility to the men on the ground.

Hope-Thomson was starting to run short of mortar and artillery shells. Patrols scouting outside the perimeter sent back reports that elephants were hauling Japanese artillery in the direction of Sangshak. The 15th Division's artillery was arriving, along with another of Miyazaki's infantry battalions. There was heavy shelling on the night of 23 March. The medical officer, Eric Neild, remembered that 'anyone in the open was likely to become a casualty'. The machine-gunners who had wreaked such destruction on the advancing Japanese were being picked off by snipers. The attackers adopted a new tactic that night. Instead of men attacking in large formations, an officer and perhaps five or six troops would try to rush the perimeter. But concentrated firepower still stopped them every time. The 2nd battalion, 58th Regiment, lost three company commanders whose experience Miyazaki would struggle to replace.

On one of the night raids a treasure trove fell into the hands of the defenders. A full map of plans for the Japanese 31st and 15th Divisions was found on the body of a dead officer. It showed that Slim had initially guessed wrongly about the Japanese intentions. Instead of a regiment, an entire division was now heading for Kohima. Immediately realising its importance, Hope-Thomson dispatched his intelligence officer on a hazardous thirty-six-hour round trip through the Japanese lines to Imphal, where the papers were given to 4 Corps. Here the story becomes murky. The 4 Corps war diary makes no mention of receiving the documents. Lieutenant Harry Seaman concluded that 4 Corps staff either failed to understand their significance or lost the material. Either way, a vital warning was not passed on to the garrison at Kohima.

On 24 March, as the Japanese tightened their grip, a message of congratulations from headquarters was transmitted to the defenders. 'Well done indeed ... of greatest importance you hold your position. Will give you maximum air support.' To men who had spent the last few days watching precious supplies drift into Japanese hands it was a hollow promise. By night the men were ordered to stay in their fixed positions. Anybody moving around would be treated as an enemy and shot. This imposed a terrible burden when men heard their own wounded screaming. A shell landed directly on a three-man bunker, killing two and leaving another terribly injured. As Lieutenant Seaman recalled, 'the rest of the company had to endure his screams until daybreak before venturing out of their own bunkers to see if they could help'. Across the intense blackness of the jungle night they heard the Gurkha soldier calling for his mother. He died shortly before dawn, and before his comrades could reach him.

The relentless threat of attack meant sleep was impossible. Men were growing weak from lack of food and water. By the third night of the siege, the defenders found their reactions slowing and sleep overcoming them. Officers were dispatched to the sentry positions to keep the men awake. At four in the morning on 25 March the Japanese launched another sustained attack, this time on the 152nd battalion positions at the church on the north-west perimeter. A fierce fight saw the position occupied, retaken by the defenders and then lost again. The Japanese account speaks of 'how those who entered the enemy's position were annihilated and the remainder withdrew with heavy losses'.

Lieutenant Kameyama saw two grenades tumbling down the slope towards him. His battalion commander seized one and threw it back, while Kameyama kicked the one nearest him back towards the defenders. 'The one I kicked must have killed an enemy soldier. The rule of the battlefield is "If you do not kill the enemy you will be killed." That is why war is a vice.'

On the same day, Lieutenant Susuma Nishida, the intelligence officer who had made the first reconnaissance of the area the previous year, was near the British positions when he heard a voice calling out in Japanese. Crawling along, he found a corporal who had been shot the previous day. He recognised him as a tough old veteran of the China campaigns. The corporal was wounded in the stomach. 'As I pulled him into the shade, he pleaded for some water,' Nishida recalled. But they had been told in training that a man with a stomach wound cannot be given water. The wounded soldier told Nishida he knew he was not going to survive in any case, so it would make no difference. 'Just one mouthful of water,' he begged. Nishida relented and gave the man his flask. 'He looked me straight in the face and said clearly, "I never dreamed that I should have the honour to be given my last drink of water by you, Sir Commander," a bit tongue-in-cheek with a big smile.'

Nishida now had to decide what to do with the remainder of the company. There were about ten soldiers able to fight. The wounded were being hit again and were dying. He had orders not to retreat but recognised that his situation was hopeless. He made up his mind to send back the wounded and to blow himself up. 'Those who can move, withdraw. Help those who can't move!' he shouted. Nishida was in the process of taking off his medals and tearing up his documents when several subordinates ran up to him. They insisted on staying and making a last attack with him. All were now committing themselves to death, yet Nishida described himself as 'suffused with the joy of having such dedicated subordinates'. He sent one man back so that somebody would be alive to command the remains of the company. Then Nishida and three others ran into battle. He was the only survivor. 'I sob at the irony of fate,' he wrote. But Nishida's attack made a strong impression on the defenders. Captain Eric Neild remembered that the raiding party overran two of the mountain artillery gun positions.

On the West Hill another group had hauled an artillery piece up the slope so that they could fire over open sights on the British below. The position at Sangshak was untenable. Hope-Thomson's men faced annihilation. All the officers of two companies were dead or seriously wounded. The British weapons pits were, in the words of the 152nd battalion war diary, 'a shambles of dead and dying, both our own and Japanese'. Lieutenant Colonel Jackie Trim of the 4th Mahratta was making his way to brigade headquarters when he saw a fellow officer, Major Smith, 'lying by the path with his intestines spilled out'.

The Japanese were suffering equally devastating losses. Six of the eight company commanders in the attacking battalions were dead or wounded, and both formations had lost about three hundred men each. Of the 120 men Nishida led into battle, only eight survived and all were wounded. But the Japanese still had numbers, ammunition, artillery and momentum on their side. Nishida had eleven bullet wounds in his body when he was carried back to General Miyazaki's headquarters about a mile north of Sangshak.

Masao Hirakubo, the 3rd battalion supply officer, was watching the battle from headquarters and remembered Nishida as 'a typical professional Japanese soldier, not like us who were conscripted. He was a real professional.' As the battle raged on, Hirakubo and his men were foraging for food in the surrounding villages. The British had done a thorough job of burning any supplies before they retreated. It compounded the sense of unease that Hirakubo felt. The plentiful British food that Mutaguchi had promised was being burned before they could capture it. At night Hirakubo could see the artillery and tracer fire 'like a very beautiful fireworks', and he thanked heaven he was not on the receiving end of it all.

As dawn broke on 26 March, Hope-Thomson realised he was facing the final Japanese onslaught. All around him were the corpses of the dead. British, Indian and Japanese rotted and stank in the rising heat. Scores of pack mules, trapped inside the perimeter, had been killed and the decomposing carcases added to the stench. The 152nd battalion had run out of grenades, losing their best weapon for breaking up Japanese attacks at close range. 'Rations were down to a bare minimum and what little there was had to go the Field Ambulance for the wounded ... we had enough for one small mug of tea per man per day.'

Lieutenant Harry Seaman described how an 'imperturbable Gurkha cook, served up an unvarying stew made of the only items in more or less constant supply: mule in different stages of decomposition, curry powder to disguise the mule, and apple puree to soften the whole'. It was a vile mix but was eaten ravenously. At each evening conference held by Brigadier Hope-Thomson, the officers wondered who would be left alive to attend the next night. Even getting to the command post involved the risk of death. The crawl trench leading to headquarters was 150 yards long but only eighteen inches deep, pitifully shallow cover for a crawling soldier. The only other choice was to make a dash across open ground, which was invariably greeted by a burst from the Japanese machine-gunner. Luckily the gunner's reaction was slow, Hopkinson remembered, and 'one was well on one's way and the burst came behind one'.

The colonel sent a party to set fire to the church in an attempt to deny the Japanese an important position from which they could fire down on the remaining guns and the field ambulance. The 153rd battalion commander, Dick Willis, also sent his Gurkhas into the attack. A Japanese survivor, Warrant Officer Isamu Yamamoto, of 2nd battalion, 58th Regiment, testified to the ferocity of what followed. 'We had completely occupied the corner of the enemy's position … The Gurkha soldiers, famous for their courage, rushed on and on though many had fallen, screaming as they advanced despite their wounds. Hand to hand fighting was everywhere and hand grenades flew everywhere. Our comrades encouraged us, the enemy screamed at us. Thus the top of the hill turned to hell on earth.' A friend of Yamamoto's fell badly wounded by his side. When he went to help, Yamamoto heard his friend ask him which way was east. Turning the wounded man towards the east, Yamamoto held his head. 'He slowly raised both arms and whispered: "Long Live the Emperor!" Lowering his arms, he died.'

By now infantry from the 15th Division were arriving and manoeuvred through the jungle to within two hundred yards of the defenders' trenches. In order to coordinate their attack with the 58th Regiment, an officer talked to Miyazaki by field telephone. He was harangued. 'What's the matter with you?' Miyazaki shouted. 'Don't you know the meaning of "the soldier's compassion?"' This was at a point in the battle when Miyazaki was about to commit the battered remnants of his 2nd and 3rd battalions to a final and, he believed, victorious assault on Sangshak. His men had borne the brunt of the fighting and he did not want any other regiment seizing the glory. The 'soldier's compassion' was the unspoken respect one warrior should have for another. He told the young officer to inform his commander that once Sangshak had fallen, his troops would be free to take as much food and ammunition as they wanted.

As the Japanese pushed their way through a break in the perimeter Brigadier Hope-Thomson committed his only reserve, the platoon set aside for defence of brigade headquarters. They were annihilated.

As night approached on 26 March men inside the perimeter went around saying goodbye to their comrades. At 1800 hours Hope-Thomson received a message from divisional headquarters. 'Fight your way out. Go South then West. Air and Transport on the look out for you. Good luck our thoughts are with you.' The order posed a terrible dilemma. What would he do with his wounded? There were around 450, among them 150 men who could not be moved. If past experience were anything to go by, leaving them behind was an invitation to murder. A heartbreaking process of triage was carried out. Captain Eric Neild recalled 'much discussion and heart-searching' before the decision was taken to sedate heavily and leave the wounded.

Lieutenant Colonel Jackie Trim of the 4 Mahratta was reluctant to abandon any of his men and wavered. Eventually he agreed. A major was given the job of detailing men to take care of those who, it was felt, had a chance of surviving. They crawled over the corpse-strewn ground, shaking each body for signs of life. There was no moon and they were unable to use lights for fear of attracting snipers, so the officers could only feel their way in the darkness from body to body. All too often they were forced to leave wounded men behind. Those who were conscious were left in an opiate stupor. '[They] could do little to help themselves or realise what was happening,' wrote Lieutenant Colonel Hopkinson. Even among those who were unwounded, the state of exhaustion was so great that there were cases of men who were 'too worn out to realise the time had come'.

At 2200 hours Hope-Thomson ordered what was left of his artillery to fire their remaining ammunition. By 2230 the survivors of the Sangshak garrison were filtering out in small parties. With as much stealth as they could muster, and under the cover of the shelling, they found a way through the encirclement.

Lieutenant Harry Seaman looked back at Sangshak from a point about a mile distant and saw the torches of the Japanese moving into the abandoned positions. Everybody waited for the sound of shooting as the wounded were finished off. It never came. 'At this distance in time,' Seaman wrote later, 'survivors are uncertain which of two emotions were uppermost in their minds at that moment: their physical craving for water or their mental anguish for helpless friends left behind in Sangshak.' Jackie Trim of the 4 Mahratta led a party of around three hundred which reached Imphal in three days, crossing terrain that included two climbs of around 4,000 feet. On the way they encountered a lone Japanese officer who called out to them not to fire. He was immediately shot down.

Lieutenant Hiroshi Yamagami passed numerous corpses as he moved forward. Could it be that the firing was really over? The air had been full of the noise of machine-gun and small arms fire. Hundreds of bullets skimmed overhead. Shells exploded in the midst of the advancing men. Yamagami had dug frantically with his hands but the ground was too hard. After two terrifying hours the shelling ended. Suddenly an orderly appeared with news that the British were gone. Warnings about landmines were sent along the line of men. He saw a few Indian soldiers coming forward to surrender. 'The trenches looked horrible. There were dead British soldiers on their backs, lapped over dead Indians, all were comrades then with big holes in their chests and heads. The sight told everything about the terrible combat that had taken place.' Wandering through the abandoned positions, he saw a young British soldier lying across an artillery piece, facing up to the sky. 'He looked so young. It made me feel so sorry for him.' Yamagami thought it looked like what a battlefield of the Russo-Japanese war must have been like. Then he and his men set about collecting rations from what was left of the British supplies.

The machine-gunner Yoshiteru Hirayama believed the British had left because they had inflicted enough damage on the Japanese.

There were, according to his recollection, only some wounded Indians and a single white man left alive. British and Japanese sources agree that at Sangshak the wounded were well cared for. There was a good reason for this. When Miyazaki arrived on the battlefield he saw that a popular Japanese officer who had been killed in the battle had been wrapped in a blanket and given proper burial. 'Our men were all moved by this,' wrote Lieutenant Shosaku Kameyama. 'As the enemy treated our company commander respectfully, our regimental commander ordered that enemy wounded should be treated as prisoners of war [and those captured] should not be killed.' Miyazaki bowed over the corpses of his own dead and thanked them. The British badly wounded were sent to Japanese field hospitals with instructions that they were to be well treated. Those able to walk were pressed into service as porters, before being stripped of everything save their underpants and released near the British lines.

There may have been one exception to the good treatment afforded the prisoners. The war correspondent Yukihiko Imai recalled seeing a group of five or six prisoners, among whom were some English. When the men were searched, they had letters and photographs on them. Imai thought, from the photographs, that they came from a rural area. He then saw the soldiers being led away into the shadow of the mountain by some Japanese. 'The Japanese soldier only came back to our line. I noticed their shoes were changed to the new English ones.' He remembered one English soldier, 'young and tall, bending his head in the blue moon', who had now disappeared from sight. 'The persons in the photograph in his pocket whom he loved best in England, I felt that on this eastern night they would be expecting his healthy return in high spirits. I knew they would be thinking of him today.' When he spoke to the Japanese lieutenant in command about what had happened he received the simple reply: 'This is the war.'

*   *   *

Approximately six hundred defenders were killed, wounded or taken prisoner at Sangshak, out of a garrison of approximately 2,000.* The survivors staggered through the jungle, across the same kind of razor-backed mountains that the Japanese infantry had cursed on their way to Sangshak. They drank from streams on the valley floors and ate the leaves of magnolia trees to ease the pangs of hunger. There was no question of using the mountain tracks by day, when Japanese patrols were moving about. Harry Seaman remembered the 'nightmare for the wounded' as they were carried or limped along winding tracks in the darkness.

As for General Miyazaki, he had won, but at a heavy cost. Two infantry battalions had been ravaged. Of the eight hundred men of 2nd battalion only half were fit for duty; of equal concern was the loss of many of his best officers, from platoon to company commander level.† The 58th Regiment still contained formidable fighters, but it was not the same unit that had crossed the Chindwin eight days before. What was more, Hope-Thomson had delayed the Japanese advance on Kohima by six days. He had bought time for Slim to rush reinforcements up to the front. Despite warm praise from Slim later on, the 50 Brigade commander received no decoration for the defence.§ Instead, he was wrongly blamed, by malicious

---

* This is the figure given by the official history. S. Woodburn Kirby, *The War Against Japan*, vol. 3: *The Decisive Battles* (HMSO, 1961), p. 237. Harry Seaman gives a figure of 900, 'of whom 100 were made prisoners of war, later to be released … Just two British officers remained unwounded to reach Imphal and join the ninety fit men who won through it all to remuster a single company.' Seaman quotes a casualty toll of roughly 80 per cent in the 152nd battalion, with some 350 dead out of the 700 who had started the battle. The 153rd battalion lost 35 per cent of its strength; the brigade defence platoon and machine-gun company sustained losses of 75 per cent, and the machine-gun units each suffered 25 per cent casualties.

† Out of the 2,180 men in the Miyazaki column, the Japanese gave a casualty figure of 580, of whom nearly half were killed. Again Seaman differs. His figure is 1,000 men killed and wounded, based on the estimate of an officer responsible for calculating the food supplies for the 58th Regiment.

§ Slim's 'Special Order of the Day', 31 August 1944, acknowledged that 50 Indian Parachute Brigade had borne 'the first brunt of the enemy's powerful flanking attack, and by their staunchness gave the garrison of Imphal the vital time to adjust their defences'.

whispers in the staff offices at Imphal, for having made a stand in a poor position and almost getting wiped out in the process. According to Harry Seaman, Hope-Thomson suffered a knock on the head and concussion when he fell during the retreat. The gossip mills began to grind immediately. Before long it was 'common knowledge' that the brigadier had suffered a nervous breakdown. According to Lieutenant Seaman this diagnosis was placed on Hope-Thomson's file. The 50 Indian Parachute Brigade was blamed, at first by word of mouth, and then implicitly in the official report by the 4th Corps Commander, General Scoones. The bitterness at this unjust portrayal of events would remain with many veterans for the rest of their lives.

Lieutenant Shosaku Kameyama's facial wound was causing him such pain that he could hardly open his mouth or eyes. His only food was milk poured into his mouth as he tilted his head upwards. He came across his company commander, who was also wounded, and who asked him if he would go on to the next battle. 'I had to say, "I will accompany you," against my personal inclination. So both the commander and I were bandaged like monsters and went to Kohima.'

FOURTEEN

To the Last Man

They were coming. Nobody doubted it any longer. The 1st Assam patrols had already ambushed the enemy east of Kharasom, about nine miles away, and killed a 'lot of Japs with little loss to themselves'. Colonel Hugh Richards, who was visiting Brown at his base in Jessami on 26 March, found an 'atmosphere of complete confidence and eager anticipation'. Lieutenant Colonel 'Bruno' Brown's men had been busy. He had chosen the junction of two jeep tracks to make his stand. There was an outer ring of bunkers and foxholes and inside it a second line where the command, mortars, and dressing station were sited. Unlike Hope-Thomson at Sangshak, or Richards at Kohima, Brown had ample supplies of barbed wire and his perimeter was well secured, with vegetation slashed away to clear accurate fields of fire.* Any Japanese infantry appearing along the road would come straight into a withering fusillade.

Richards told Brown that if the Japanese bypassed him he was to take to the jungle and strike at the enemy from the rear. Brown reassured Richards that he expected an attack within twenty-four hours by a battalion-sized Japanese force, usually around 1,400 men, and 'could hold out indefinitely against a formation of that size'. There is an interesting coda to the meeting, indicating some unease beneath Brown's usually tough exterior. Just before Richards left, he asked him if the order he had been given to fight to the last man and the last round

---

* Jessami also lay outside the administrative reach of the Naga Hills and barbed wire was allowed.

stood. 'I said that it must,' Richards recalled. 'On my return journey I was very much worried about this order.' Richards spent the night with Charles Pawsey, who was helping refugees in a village along the road towards Kohima. He thought through the night about what was being asked of Brown. There was no proper water supply inside the perimeter at Jessami and the garrison would inevitably be cut off from outside sources. Nor was it planned to stage the main battle at Jessami. It was intended merely as a delaying post. In those circumstances it made more sense for the 1st Assam to fight but then withdraw, continuing to launch hit-and-run attacks on the Japanese as they advanced.

Back in Kohima on 27 March, Richards received two devastating pieces of information. First he was told that the West Yorkshires, his only infantry battalion, was to be withdrawn and sent to Imphal to strengthen the defences there. Later, Pawsey's Naga scouts arrived with news that the Japanese force moving up from the Chindwin was not a regiment but an entire division. True, this was intelligence coming from outside the normal military chain, and doubters might ask how a Naga tribesman could tell the difference between a division and a regiment. But the Nagas had been schooled by V Force officers in estimating the size of military formations, and they had been reliable informants up to now. Pawsey was convinced they were right.

The 1st Assam detachments numbered four hundred in total and now faced thousands of Sato's men advancing along the tracks to Kharasom and Jessami. Brigadier Warren of 161 Brigade and the area commander Ranking met Hugh Richards at Kohima on 29 March, where they discussed what to do about the 'last man, last round' order to the Assam Regiment. Given the disparity in numbers, it was far better to get the Assam men back to help defend Kohima. Richards decided to cancel the order and send troops from 161 Brigade to help the Assam Regiment fight its way out of Kharasom and Jessami.*

---

* A company of 1/1 Punjab from 161 Brigade was sent to try and relieve the Assam Regiment at Kharasom. It clashed with the Japanese and the Indians lost seven men killed and fifteen wounded and killed fifty Japanese, but were unable to break through to the beleaguered Assam troops. Another battalion from 161 Brigade, the 4/7 Rajput, also attempted unsuccessfully to break through to the defenders of Jessami.

Richards's unease about the position of 1 Assam dated to the night of 26 March. But the ultimate decision on the battalion's fate was not Richards to make. It was not until his conference with General Ranking and Brigadier Warren on 29 March that it was agreed Richards should order the withdrawal of the Assam troops.* The delay has never been explained but it made the task of transmitting new orders infinitely more difficult. Brown vanished from radio contact on the 29th, which meant the only available means for passing on orders was by couriers infiltrating through Japanese lines or by aircraft dropping a message; both were hazardous, with no guarantee of success. There were two attempts by air, both of which failed, and the messages fell into the hands of the Japanese. They were not coded, because Richards feared Brown lacked the facilities for decoding, and the result was that the Japanese now knew precisely what the defenders were going to do. Three different attempts by men from the Assam Rifles, who knew the terrain well, also failed to get through to Brown. Eventually an Assam Regiment officer managed to slip through the Japanese lines and warn Brown. The battalion adjutant, Captain Michael Williamson, heard firing and shouting on the southern perimeter as men responded to what they thought was a Japanese probe, 'but very soon we heard John Corlett [the messenger] shouting like mad at us to stop firing'. But the message was too late for the isolated detachment at Kharasom.

As the crow flies, the village of Kharasom is just nine miles south of Jessami. But to men relying on a narrow jungle track it is twice that distance. Looking down the track towards the Chindwin at daybreak on 27 March, Captain John Young of A company, 1st Assam, saw a Japanese battalion approaching fast: the elephants hauling artillery,

---

* Richards gave conflicting accounts of the dates. In a speech to an Assam Regiment dinner in London in 1962 he placed his meeting with Warren and Ranking as taking place on 28 March. In a typed draft of his account of Kohima sent to Arthur Swinson he again gives 28 March as the date. But in another typed draft he places the meeting on 29 March. The official records agree that it took place on 29 March. The discrepancy may have been due to a lapse in memory concerning events that had taken place some eighteen years earlier.

mules loaded with ammunition and supplies, and the long line of infantry with bayonets at the ready. Young ordered his mortars to open fire. Calculating the time it would take to reinforce his position, and the time it would take the Japanese to reach him, Captain John Young knew that A company would be fighting on its own. He had 120 men with him, including the mortar detachment and some signallers, and even though he had chosen a strong defensive position on top of a hill, Young, who was vastly outnumbered, understood that if he stood and fought he must eventually be overrun. But his orders were to fight to the last man and that was what he would do.

When he had arrived in Kharasom the previous month, Young had established his perimeter about three hundred yards outside the village and sent patrols out towards the border. Nothing was heard of the Japanese until the first V Force reports reached Brown at Jessami on 20 March. Four days later, Young welcomed a part of V Force and the Assam Rifles escaping the Japanese advance. At 0610 on 27 March 2nd Lieutenant D. B. Gurung heard the enemy attack. 'It was felt that the attack was coming from all sides. The enemy was charging, shouting and firing as they charged.' Young called Brown on the field telephone to tell him the shooting had started. It was the last the CO or anybody else heard from him. The line was cut just after his call. Now only a courier, or an extremely accurate message drop by the RAF, would be able to get orders to Young. Neither course was attempted. With the Japanese almost on top of his small force, it would probably have been too late.

The troops advancing towards him were from the 138th Regiment, an advance guard of the main 31st Division column making its way to Kohima. Lieutenant Chuzaburo Tomaru, a supply officer with the 138th Regiment, was hiding behind some rocks as the infantry went in. The first waves were mown down. 'I saw killed infantry troops sent from front line again and again. Looking at them, I thought that this may be it.' Tomaru had been drafted into the military in 1939 and moved from a machine-gun company to administrative work, a possible indication of his superiors' view of his soldierly skills. Tomaru dreaded the enemy machine guns but did not have to join the attack. At Kharasom the Japanese had more troops than they needed. A commander on the right flank, instead of making direct for Kohima as directed, had decided to follow the sound of the guns and join the assaults on Kharasom and Jessami. The proverbial hammer was being taken to the nut. When General Sato came forward and saw the imbalance in forces he was livid. Why were so many men being deployed against such small objectives when they could be marching to Kohima? He upbraided the major who had deflected from his course: 'Your correct course of action was to leave enough troops to contain the garrisons here and push on to Kohima.'

After Miyazaki's delay at Sangshak, Sato was losing patience with commanders who were failing to see the wood for the trees. There were three Japanese attacks on Young's positions before nightfall. All were repulsed. The defenders had laid out two lines of wire around the perimeter which made Japanese infiltration all the more difficult. Scores of Japanese were shot down in repeated assaults the following day.* Havildar Sohevu Angami, based with a mortar platoon back in Jessami, met one of the Assam survivors soon afterwards. 'The man told me that Young shouted at them to "wait, wait" until the Japanese were very close before firing. He was brave that Young. There were so many Japanese but Young refused to surrender. The Japanese were screaming at our men all the time and Young was shouting out, "I won't go, I won't go."'

Two days after the action began the Japanese managed to break into the perimeter, where the astonished defenders saw them gorging on animal feed; the shadow of hunger followed the 138th Regiment just as it had the 58th at Sangshak. By the morning of the third day the pile of bodies in front of A company's positions was swelling and stinking in the heat. Young sent men to clear the corpses away and to repair breaks in the line. They were sniped at but succeeded in fixing

---

* Interrogated after the war, Lieutenant Colonel Iwaichi Fujiwara gave a figure of only fourteen Japanese dead at Kharasom. This conflicts with British accounts of substantial numbers of corpses and, given the Japanese propensity for costly frontal assaults, seems unlikely. See NA, WO 203/6324.

the wire. Inside the perimeter Young's situation was becoming impossible. He was running out of water, food and ammunition. On the morning of 30 March he saw fresh columns of Japanese arriving, and they continued to arrive throughout the day. Japanese spirits were also raised when they drove back an attempt to relieve Kharasom by Indian troops from the newly arrived 161 Brigade.

Young did not know about the failed attempt to relieve his position. Had he done so, it would surely have confirmed the painful decision he now made. Calling together his officers and NCOs, he announced that they were to evacuate under cover of darkness. However, he would not be going with them. As one of his officers, Lieutenant D. B. Gurung recalled, the captain, 'seeing the hopelessness of the situation gave orders for the company to withdraw to Kohima'.

He told his officers he 'could not leave the wounded'. Come nightfall, they were to filter through the lines and make for Kohima. Fifty-six men reached Kohima two days later. Young was last seen stacking grenades and Tommy-gun magazines in his bunker, where a wounded Indian soldier had joined him to man the Bren gun. The Nagas reported that the Japanese attacked at dawn. There was a short and fierce exchange of fire, followed by silence. Hugh Richards described Young in fulsome terms: 'As an example of complete self-sacrifice nothing could be more magnificent. It is sad that such a gallant officer should have been lost.' Despite such praise, John Young was never awarded any medal beyond those given to all who served in the Burma theatre. Had he been a cook at Dimapur he would have received the same acknowledgement. His family never complained publicly and the failure to honour him was never explained.* Later, the local Nagas told Charles Pawsey that the Japanese had been so moved by Young's bravery that they had shaved

---

* A British campaigner, Roy McCallum, pursued the Ministry of Defence on the question as late as 2009 but was told that the case would not be reopened. Young could not have been put forward for a Victoria Cross as his final actions were not witnessed; however, it would have been possible for him to have been mentioned in dispatches. Thanks to Mr McCallum's efforts, Glasgow City Council agreed to erect a plaque to the memory of John Young at 7 Jedburgh Gardens, where he had lived before the war.

his head in the tradition of fallen heroes and buried him with full
military honours.

At Jessami Brown's force had spent their time in 'feverish preparation', expecting the Japanese to arrive at any moment. Scouts
reported columns advancing from the east and south of the village.
One of the forward positions spotted a party of about twenty-four
Japanese coming up the track. The concealed Assam troops waited
until they were almost on them and then scythed down the advancing men. Two crawled away into the undergrowth. 'Spirits soared as
the news spread through the garrison,' an officer recorded. The first
that Havildar Sohevu Angami knew of the Japanese arrival was when
he saw a comrade from the Kuki tribe being shot down. 'The
Japanese were screaming at us and we were screaming back at them.
The sound of our voices stopped us being afraid. I have to say the
Japanese were effective fighters. We could tell this straight away.' The
havildar was lightly wounded by a shell fragment which struck his
forehead. He kept fighting, exhorting the men of his platoon as they
fired mortars into the attackers. Over the next three days the
Japanese infantry threw repeated attacks against the perimeter. Some
broke through but the majority fell in tangled heaps. The Bren guns
did murderous work. Soldiers scorched the flesh on their hands as
they replaced the red hot barrels. 'Japanese grenades and cracker-
bombs were picked up and thrown clear of the trenches with all the
calmness in the world, and there did not seem to be a man in the
garrison afraid to carry out any task given to him,' the War Diary
recorded. By now the Japanese were pushing five battalions of
infantry, a mountain artillery regiment as well as 31st Division
Headquarters along the Jessami track, the bulk of ten thousand men.
Brown's position at Jessami had been under attack for three days
when Hugh Richard's messenger finally made it through. 'We were
shooting at him until we realised it was our own man,' remembered
Havildar Sohevu.

Hugh Richards's orders called for the Assam Regiment to leave at
0300 hours, but the pressure on the perimeter was so great that

Brown put off the move for twenty-four hours. Brown called a conference of his officers and told them the battalion would pull out at 0300 hours on the following day; they would travel in two large parties, one travelling east and the other west, both making for Kohima. The Japanese attacked throughout the day with concentrated artillery and mortar fire. Agonisingly for the defenders, an RAF plane came in low and dropped a message that fell directly into the hands of the Japanese. Brown now knew for certain that his plans for withdrawal were compromised. There was no question of waiting until 0300, when the enemy would be waiting for the move. Nor could the battalion move off in two large groups. Instead, smaller parties would filter out as soon as it was dark enough to do so. The withdrawal began at 1900 hours and continued until midnight, when the command post was evacuated and all documents destroyed. One of the last to leave was Sepoy Wellington Massar, the Khasi tribesman who had taken part as a human guinea pig in the fight to rid the hills of kala-azar. Massar had fought hard at Jessami, the pile of dead bodies outside his bunker attesting to his remorseless Bren-gun fire.

The Japanese did not strike during the evacuation. They had, however, prepared ambushes along the tracks leading away from Jessami. No sooner had the first troops moved off into the jungle than they faced Japanese attacks. As a result the battalion fragmented, with some troops heading towards Kohima, others reaching Dimapur, and some killed, wounded or captured by the Japanese. One British officer was beginning to go blind with shock and hunger but was saved by Naga villagers. He would later recall how they put him to sleep in a large double bed with the words 'Home Sweet Home' embroidered on the pillows. A group of sepoys and their havildar were captured by the Japanese and taken to a village where they saw a captured British officer with bleeding feet and a loose rope hung around his neck. He was kept away from the other prisoners. The group was forced to lie on the ground where the Japanese guards taunted and jabbed at them with bayonets. One of the men, Sepoy Ngulkathang, struck out in fury and used his feet to knock down a Japanese officer. It was a fateful mistake. He was forced to his knees and beheaded. That night the havildar and other sepoys managed to undo their bonds, steal some weapons and flee into the jungle. In another incident Major Albert Calistan and a large column were leaving one end of a village as the Japanese were entering at the other. 'Had the Japs caught up with us there is little doubt that most of my party would have been too weak to put up much resistance,' he wrote. On arrival at Kohima Calistan and his party of 167 men were fed, clothed and given 'a liberal issue of rum and cigarettes'. Out of an original strength of around 400 men Lieutenant Colonel Brown was able to call on 260 to help defend Kohima by the time the last of the stragglers reached the garrison on 3 April 1944.

By nightfall on 29 March, when the 1st Assam were still fighting for their lives at Jessami and Kharasom, 4th battalion, the Royal West Kents, had settled into temporary billets in Kohima. Battalion head-quarters was set up in one of the hospital buildings, from which convalescing soldiers had been evacuated to Dimapur. The troops dug in around the position and the cooks got to work. In every new position the cooks played a role beyond the merely physical; they were the great normalisers, the men who kept the customary rhythms of battalion life moving. For the evening meal they served up bully beef rissoles, potatoes, carrots, plum duff and tea. As the men settled down for the night, much of the talk was about the nature of the terrain. From Dimapur the road climbed and dropped, passing into the gorge of Nichuguard, which ran for about four miles and was, according to a local tea-planter, 'a fisherman's paradise and a motorist's nightmare. The road consisted of a ledge cut out of the almost perpendicular cliff. On the left the rock rose straight up to anything up to five hundred feet, on the right it fell sheer away to the river 200 feet below which flowed through the gorge in a series of rapids and tempting pools.' The gorge offered the best position from which to defend Dimapur should the Japanese either bypass or breakthrough at Kohima. Leaving Nichuguard, the road climbed, skirting rice fields and brushing the side of steep cliffs. At Zubza, 3,000 feet above sea level, the West Kents caught their first glimpse of

Kohima Ridge, ten miles away. The road climbed sharply once more, some 1,700 feet in a space of seven miles, before reaching Kohima, from where, looking south, they could see mountains and the ghosts of mountains, the brooding heights of Mount Pulebadze and Aradura Spur, whose jungle slopes could have concealed an army. Men felt dwarfed, crowded in by the immensity of the ranges.

That night they were struck by the quiet of the high mountain world and many found it hard to believe that thousands of Japanese troops could be out there in the darkness. The oil lamps flickering in the remaining occupied buildings were a comfort to the sentries. On the road from Dimapur they had passed Nagas; the appearance of the warriors with their cloaks and elaborate headdresses, and the stories of headhunting, compounded the sense of strangeness felt by the men. The C company runner Ray Street thought the Nagas looked like 'Red Indians ... carrying old shotguns. Others had spears and bows but all wore a Gurkha style knife on their hips.' However much the Nagas waved and smiled as the trucks rolled by, there was in those early moments at Kohima a distinctly uneasy feeling, as if they had entered a landscape whose surprises would be many.

The horrors inflicted by their own artillery at the tunnels had not broken morale; instead, these men took pride in their ability to endure. As Lance Corporal Dennis Wykes put it, 'We were up for it. The lads moaned all the time like any soldiers would, but they had great pride in the battalion. When you get the daylights hammered out of you as many times as we did you either go to pieces or you feel you are special, and we were special.'

Lieutenant Colonel Laverty had still been given no full information on the threat faced by his men. The impression at Kohima was that there was still time to prepare proper defensive positions, although an entry in the battalion war diary foreshadowed a crucial problem. 'Water situation is precarious,' it noted simply. It was only a few days later that Laverty would discover quite how precarious. Lieutenant Tom Hogg was struck by the number of line of communications troops and civilians still hanging about in Kohima. He estimated there were 'perhaps 3,000 leaderless non-combatants milling around', a dangerously high number of 'useless mouths' for a position that could soon be under attack from what was now known to be a Japanese division.

At 8.30 a.m. on 30 March, Laverty called his company commanders together and sketched out a plan for the day: they would reinforce the defences around the brigade headquarters and mount patrols along the road from Kohima towards Imphal. They spent the next two days digging and patrolling, but there was no contact with the Japanese. There was a scare on the second night in Kohima. Some Indian troops were jittery and opened fire at what they thought was a Japanese soldier. 'It turned out to be a cow and they killed it,' recorded Private Norman in his diary. At 0800 hours on 31 March he was sent to patrol the road for some twenty miles beyond Kohima. The West Kents who patrolled down the road towards the 1/1 Punjab positions had the eerie experience of travelling into clouds on the roller coaster of the mountain roads. Worse, the jeep driver's cap fell off and he took his hands off the wheel as they went round a corner. Private Norman saw to his horror that there were two crashed jeeps at the bottom of the ravine. The driver seized hold of the wheel in the nick of time. That night the rain fell and the men huddled in the cold. There was still no contact with the Japanese. On the same day, Laverty accompanied his boss, Brigadier Warren, on a visit to Mao Songsang, about twenty miles from Kohima on the road to Imphal, where the 1/1 Punjab were based. He was told that the West Kents were to remain at a half-hour's notice to move back to Dimapur.

On the morning of 1 April rumours flew around the ranks that they were to be moved back along the road to set up a new defensive position at the Nichuguard gorge, outside Dimapur. Then Private Norman heard they were to stay where they were. Finally, orders came through. 'We got a message through the rest [of the brigade] wouldn't be following us up,' remembered Major Donald Easten. 'We were to go back!' To another young officer, Lieutenant Tom Hogg, it 'smacked of confusion in high places – difficult for a young Lieutenant to explain away and/or for his men to accept with equanimity'. Men who had spent hours digging trenches in the rain at Kohima cursed the brass who seemed to change their minds at a whim. Lance Corporal Wykes could not understand what was happening. 'It was the obvious time to dig in and get ready.' Private Norman was now nursing a severe cold and felt thoroughly 'browned off'. His only consolation was a conversation with Laverty, whom he met walking around the position. Norman does not record what was discussed, but it is hard to think he did not give Laverty the full bene-fit of his views on the new orders.

For the garrison commander, Colonel Hugh Richards, and for Charles Pawsey, the order defied comprehension. They had already watched as a battalion from the West Yorkshires had been pulled in and out of Kohima, and in and out again, in the five-day period between 24 and 29 March. Now Kohima was once more being stripped of battle-hardened troops.

Captain Arthur Swinson blamed the local area commander, General Ranking, for the decision: '2,000 men left in Kohima and the area commander is quite confident they can hold it. By the tone of his voice the Brigadier [Warren] indicates he is not.' The gravest problem was that the majority of the men in Kohima were a mix of various colonial, line of communications and convalescent troops, unused to fighting together and untested in the face of a substantial Japanese force. Only the men of the 1st Assam Regiment, who were struggling to get to Kohima from Jessami, could be regarded as a solid infantry formation. The deputy commissioner, Charles Pawsey, was livid. 'With one Brigade in Kohima, and the troops already there, we should have been quite happy. To the chagrin of everybody the Brigade was taken back to the Manipur road ... this was heartbreak-ing.'

But Ranking was merely the messenger. Slim and Stopford had now decided that Dimapur was the more likely target for a Japanese attack. There was a logic to their decision. Why would the Japanese pause to give battle at Kohima when they could take the greater prize at Dimapur? Should the Japanese arrive in the next few days, the base, with its paltry defence and milling refugees, would certainly fall. Ranking called Brigadier Warren and told him that 161 Brigade would have to leave Kohima. The pressure from on high had been exacerbated by intelligence received from RAF pilots that a sizeable Japanese force was threatening the rail line near Dimapur. When Warren told Pawsey about this he thought the idea was nonsense. Any movement on a large scale would have been reported by his Naga scouts. In fact, all the indications from his informants were that the Japanese were bearing down on Kohima, and at some speed.* The West Kents claimed the Dimapur story was invented by a radio unit that fled a village having 'left their equipment behind and brought instead this story'. The inaccurate report was not of itself decisive, but it chimed fatefully with what the higher command believed.

Brigadier Warren pleaded with Ranking to visit Kohima to see the situation for himself and at least to listen to the arguments for staying in place. The general drove up and met with Richards, Pawsey and Warren. They were unanimous. The brigade must stay in Kohima. Warren argued that the Japanese would not bypass Kohima if it contained a sizeable force. The threat to Sato's rear and his line of communication would be too great for him simply to march on to Dimapur. Conversely, if Sato succeeded in taking a poorly defended Kohima Ridge, it would take a long hard fight, with many casualties, to drive him off. Why leave now, when there was a chance of stopping Sato in his tracks? Besides, argued Pawsey, the Nagas would feel they were being abandoned by the Raj. Ranking defended the orders he had been given. Richards wrote that 'It was a frightening situation for him, with his responsibility, to contemplate.' There were angry words. Warren and Pawsey offered to fly and put the case directly to Slim. Ranking rejected this and promised he would relay their fears. At midnight on 31 March, Slim went to see the 33 Corps commander, General Stopford, who would take overall control of the battle, to tell him that Ranking had been on the phone. He told him about what the 'political people' – Charles Pawsey – had said about the impact on the Nagas. 'I had to refuse to listen to these

---

* The 'Japanese force' spotted by the RAF turned out to have been a party of labourers going home.

suggestions', Stopford wrote, 'and made it clear that I had my plan and must stick to it.' In the greater scheme of things the vast supply base, railhead and airfield at Dimapur mattered more, at that point, than Kohima.* There were other 'political people' with more influence than Charles Pawsey. Stopford knew that Churchill and the Americans would create 'a hell of a row if we lose [Dimapur]'.

Hugh Richards was given another order on 1 April, but one that he decided to keep to himself. The '202 Area Operation Instruction No. 3' from Ranking said that he was to hold Kohima 'as long as possible without being destroyed yourselves'. The next part of the order filled Richards with foreboding. 'If and when it is decided to withdraw the Deputy Commissioner should be told to impress on all Nagas that such a withdrawal will be of a temporary nature only and it is the intention of the British to return and destroy all Japanese west of the Chindwin.' It concluded with a blindingly self-evident statement: 'such an announcement must NOT be made prematurely'. Nobody knew better than Richards the potential effect of such orders on his garrison or on the local population. The garrison commander stuffed them in his back pocket, mentioning them only to his second-in-command, who was sworn to secrecy. 'I regarded this [order] as highly dangerous from a morale point of view,' Richards wrote. 'Nothing could be more unfortunate or undesirable

---

* In his diary Stopford writes of Slim 'eventually accept[ing]' his argument, suggesting a prolonged debate. IWM, Swinson Papers, Diary of General Montagu North Stopford, 1 April 1944. After the war, Slim blamed Ranking for the decision that he and Stopford had taken. Acknowledging that 161 Brigade should have been kept at Kohima, where it could have delayed the Japanese advance by 'several days', Slim went on to write that 'Ranking's order to withdraw was influenced understandably by the stress I laid on his primary task – the defence of the Dimapur base … the withdrawal … was an unfortunate mistake.' Field Marshal Lord Slim, *Defeat into Victory* (Cassell, 1956), p. 310. But Ranking was not 'influenced', he was following clear orders. Nor does Slim's book make any mention of Ranking's urgent telephone call after his return from meeting Warren, Richards and Pawsey in Kohima. Stopford attempted to set the record straight later on. Writing to Arthur Swinson in 1965, nearly a decade after Slim's account had been published, he said, 'it is most unfair that Ranking should have been blamed for it … if blame is attached to anyone it should be me … probably I was overanxious about the likelihood of Japanese infiltration.' Letter of Lieutenant General Montagu Stopford to Arthur Swinson, 3 May 1965.

than that there should get abroad any idea that there was a possibility of a withdrawal from Kohima, however remote.'

It was still pouring with rain when the West Kents and the other elements of 161 Brigade in Kohima began to pull out at lunchtime on 2 April. Pawsey watched them go with a feeling of anger. For over two decades he had preached to the people of the Naga Hills the gospel of a caring and paternal Raj, and asked that in return they give their unconditional loyalty to the crown. How was he to explain this betrayal? Pawsey's answer was typical of the man. As a civil servant, there was no question of his being expected to stay in a battle zone. In fact, the idea would have been positively discouraged. The Japanese would kill or torture him as quickly as they would any soldier. He could leave on any of the numerous trucks that were evacuating non-combatants by the hour. There was still something of the warrior in Charles Pawsey. The veteran of the Somme and the Italian front had already seen the horrors of total war and, without a wife or children, he might have felt he had less cause than most to take a ride away from danger. But at the root of his decision to stay was loyalty. If he stayed with the Naga, they might see that the Raj still had honour. So he told Richards he would be staying put and helping to coordinate relief for Naga refugees, as well as doing what he could to help with the defence. Together they watched the West Kents mount their lorries in the downpour. Rain rattled violently on the roofs of the bungalow, hospital, treasury – on all the buildings of the little outpost, adding to the feeling of desolation as the last of the vehicles vanished in the direction of Dimapur.

Kohima settled into a nerve-racking wait. The young cavalry officer Lieutenant Bruce Hayllar, who had arrived the previous day, found Kohima at 'real panic stations. Everything was a bit all over the place.' He was a trained tank and troop-carrier man but found no armour in Kohima. 'The defences were poor. It was really surprising … we really were useless.' Hayllar was given a composite group of Indian troops and told to man a position on Jail Hill. Before heading up, he was introduced to Charles Pawsey at his bungalow. 'I remember saying to myself "this is going to be a proper war and they are

going to destroy this bungalow so I better go and use the loo!'"
Lieutenant Hayllar's only wish was that the fight would last long
enough for him to be shot at.

Richards's best hope now was for the arrival of Brown's men from
Jessami. The survivors of 1st Assam did not begin to appear in any
numbers until 3 April, and when they did appear they were all
exhausted and hungry, many without boots and in tattered clothing.
In all, 260 men would be available to help strengthen the defence.
The first seventy to arrive included twenty who were ill or wounded
and had to be evacuated to Dimapur. When Lieutenant Colonel
'Bruno' Brown arrived his ragged condition so moved Charles
Pawsey that he went to his bungalow and found him a polo sweater
to wear.

Kohima Ridge was about a mile long and roughly four hundred
yards in width, a series of hills and gullies that ran alongside the road.
With steep slopes along much of the road side of the perimeter, it
presented a formidable obstacle for any attackers trying to scale their
way up. But it was a narrow space from which to repel an enemy
attacking in strength and the other side of the perimeter, away from
the road, was overlooked by mountain slopes which offered enemy
artillery any number of ideal firing positions.

Across the garrison, work parties were busy digging in, frantically
trying to rectify the weaknesses. Richards had already moved to
consolidate his defence around a single box. At the southern end of
the ridge was GPT Ridge, where the Assam and Nepalese troops
watched the road to Imphal. Beside it, but on the other side of the
road, was Jail Hill. From there the defensive line swung back across
the road in front of Detail Hill, Supply Hill, Kuki Piquet and
Summerhouse Hill, soon to be renamed Garrison Hill, where
Colonel Richards had his headquarters.* Above him, on what was
known as Hospital Spur, was a series of hospital buildings; on the
lower slopes stood the district commissioner's tennis court and below

---

* On 3 April he moved his command post from Pawsey's bungalow to the less comfortable
but less exposed surroundings of a bunker roughly halfway up the slopes of Garrison Hill.

that his bungalow with its gardens tapering down to the road. From his headquarters, looking north across the road towards Dimapur, Richards could see the Treasury and the huts of the Naga Village.

The great difficulty for anybody trying to defend Kohima Ridge was water. All the water sources lay outside Richards's perimeter, at the mercy of a besieging force. There was a steel tank near Charles Pawsey's bungalow which was filled by a pipe that ran all the way south to a source on Aradura Spur; the pipe could easily be cut once it was discovered by the Japanese. Worse still, the other eight tanks, a mix of canvas and steel, had not been dug in and presented an obvious target for Japanese snipers. Soon, Richards would watch helplessly as thousands of gallons of precious liquid spilled across the ridge. He would later blame himself for the failure to conceal the water supply. Happily, Kohima's position as a major store for the area meant that there was no immediate shortage of food or ammunition. Fifteen days' rations were distributed, along with grenades, ammunition for 2 and 3 inch mortars, pistol rounds and cartridges for Very lights, the flares so important in the howling darkness of a Japanese night attack.

News of the approaching enemy crackled through Kohima. Pawsey's Nagas were invariably first with reports of sightings. Richards's outlying patrols were also bringing regular information. At 1800 on 2 April the Nepalese Shere Regiment had reported some Japanese about three miles outside Kohima. A patrol brought in three Japanese ears as proof of the enemy presence.

The following day Lieutenant Dennis Dawson of the Royal Indian Army Service Corps went with a patrol to Aradura Spur to the south. A Major N. R. Giles had asked him if he wanted to join him for a 'spot of fun'. They reached the foothills of Aradura and made camp for the night. Dawson heard digging near his position. Then there was a shot. 'Round about three or four in the morning a Japanese sentry came across our sentry and he shot my chap dead. So that gave our position away. We had just time to drag him to where I was.' A friend of the dead man took his personal papers and the patrol fled, leaving the body. The Japanese were now all around them. Another member of the patrol, Lieutenant Bruce Hayllar, was enthusiastic for the battle. 'We went to try and find the Jap and beat him up … at dusk we met the Jap and after a bit we lay in the circle in the wood, with the Major in the middle.' Then it started to rain heavily and Hayllar felt afraid. He recited Psalm 23:

> Even though I walk
> Through the valley of the shadow of death,
> I will fear no evil
> For you are with me;
> Your rod and your staff
> They comfort me.

Hayllar was astonished that Major Giles, a jungle veteran, could fall asleep when the Japanese were just twenty-five yards away. He cursed himself for a being a fool and having volunteered. Then the attack started and his fear vanished. 'I just felt very excited and concentrated on the job of keeping control of my own fire and trying to locate the Japs creeping in towards us … The men all seemed to feel the same, some sort of savage instinct comes to ones [sic] aid when logically a man should be scared stiff.' A man was shot through the heart beside him, but Hayllar was too busy to pay much attention.

Dennis Dawson remembered his men shooting and killing several Japanese. The shouting and the shelling from the Japanese side wore at the men's nerves. 'It was horrible. It just went on and on,' recalled Lieutenant Bruce Hayllar. He prayed again to overcome his fear. The men fell back to Kohima in groups of three and four. On the way they shot four or five of the encircling Japanese. Hayllar was moving from tree to tree, trying to avoid presenting a target, when he saw a Japanese standing on the track in front of him. He squeezed the trigger and the man fell. For a moment Hayllar had the sense of being caught in a dream, as if the dead man lying in front of him was merely play-acting and would rise to life again. 'It is pretty horrid to kill. But if you have seen them killing our lot then you want to repay. It's a horrible feeling.' The patrol reached Kohima later that morning with Dennis Dawson wondering if anybody would go back for the body of his sentry. Decades later he was still thinking about the dead man.

From dawn on 3 April patrols were sent out from Kohima, but there was no sign of the Japanese until 1600 hours, when some were spotted working round to the right flank of GPT Ridge. The defenders here were a mix of 1st Assam, a composite Indian infantry company, a Gurkha company and some V Force. The rain of the past few days had gone and a bright moon lit the landscape beyond the trenches; anybody attempting a frontal assault would be spotted early on.

Men did their best to sleep. The only noise came from the work parties still trying to improve the dugouts. At 2000 hours a Japanese sniper fired shots over the position. What followed appalled the 1st Assam commander, as the war diary recorded: 'The immediate result of this was that almost every L.M.G. [Light Machine Gun] and rifle in the position opened up and fired wildly in every direction for about an hour. Complete lack of fire control and discipline and troops obviously shaken.' Several soldiers were wounded by the firing of their comrades. To make matters worse, a platoon of the Shere Regiment came galloping through the position at 2045 hours, fleeing from some Japanese who, they claimed, had attacked their post. Their lack of steadiness was to cost the garrison dearly. Wild firing at real or imagined threats is known as 'starting-gun' syndrome: a man who is frightened, but not trained in fire discipline, will open fire, sparking general mayhem. To a disciplined enemy it is a gift. All they need do is carefully to spot the muzzle flashes and they will be given a clear picture of the defences. The Japanese were nothing if not diligent in this regard. Captain Walter Greenwood, a staff officer with the garrison, gave a stark assessment of the difficulties facing Richards: 'The difficulty of controlling a body of men consisting of perhaps 10 infanteers, 50 RIASC drivers, mule-drivers, a few signallers, pioneers, sappers and miners, etc., with no officer and perhaps no senior NCOs has to be experienced to be believed, and it is remarkable that there were not very many casualties through our own fire.'

The following day, 4 April, the Japanese offered something more than sniper fire. At 1600 hours they opened up with mortars and machine guns on the GPT Ridge position. It was not a heavy bombardment – most likely these early arrivals were simply probing the defence – but it drew another exasperating and, for Hugh Richards, profoundly worrying response from the defenders. 'This was answered by our own troops again [firing] wildly and in all directions for most of the night and was only stopped by B.O.s [British officers] going round positions.'

On GPT Ridge a potential disaster was unfolding. Troops were starting to abandon their positions. By 2300 hours, the 1st Assam's war diary records, a platoon of Sikhs, a mortar detachment of the Shere Regiment, a mixed infantry company, and a number of Indian officers had abandoned their trenches. 'These positions were in the centre of the defences. These officers and men were not seen again,' the diary records. In one episode a Sikh officer reported that 120 of his 140 men had bolted. This, in turn, exposed a Gurkha company to enfilading fire. When the order to send in the reserve was given, the word came back that a commander and his forty men 'could not be found'. It was later discovered that these men, too, had vanished. The panicked soldiers were making for Dimapur as fast as they could run. Further back on Supply Hill and Kuki Piquet, officers stepped forward with pistols drawn to stop the fleeing men from crowding their trenches.

The men who remained could hear Japanese and Indian voices shouting at them to surrender. The propagandists of Bose's Indian National Army were at work and Lieutenant Bruce Hayllar, commanding a composite group of Indian troops, found them frightening.* 'Sometimes they would shout to our soldiers, "Kill your officers." If it was your own men you could be sure of them. But I was

---

* One division of the Indian National Army, an estimated 7,000 men, joined Mutaguchi's advance towards Imphal. The INA soldiers encountered at Kohima probably belonged to small groups attached to 31st division for propaganda purposes. The INA suffered heavy casualties on the retreat from India and troops complained bitterly of being used as porters by the Japanese.

put in charge of people I had never seen before ... It was a horrible situation.' Hayllar threatened to shoot wavering men. They in turn threatened to shoot him. His bluff worked. There was no shooting and the majority stayed loyal. Early on 5 April, Hugh Richards was alerted to an unusual sighting on the track at the other end of the perimeter from Jail Hill. It was around 0200 hours and there were flickering lights to be seen moving towards the Naga Village across the valley. The number of lights indicated an enemy force much larger than that which was probing the defences of GPT Ridge at the other end. There was a company of the notoriously jumpy Shere Regiment on picqet duty at the Naga Village and Richards can have had few illusions about what would occur when the flickering lights materialised into enemy soldiers.

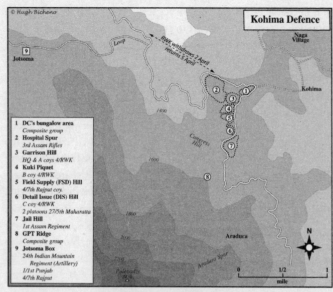

Kohima Defence

© Hugh Bicheno

Naga Village

Kohima

Jotsoma

RWK withdraws 2 April
returns 5 April

Loop

1400

Congress Hill

1600

1800

2000

2200

Palebaito
2946

Aradura

Aradura Spur

1 DC's bungalow area
  Composite group
2 Hospital Spur
  3rd Assam Rifles
3 Garrison Hill
  HQ & A coys 4/RWK
4 Kuki Piquet
  B coy 4/RWK
5 Field Supply (FSD) Hill
  4/7th Rajput coy.
6 Detail Issue (DIS) Hill
  C coy 4/RWK
  2 platoons 27/5th Maharatta
7 Jail Hill
  1st Assam Regiment
8 GPT Ridge
  Composite group
9 Jotsoma Box
  24th Indian Mountain
  Regiment (Artillery)
  1/1st Punjab
  4/7th Rajput

N

0   1/2   1
mile

KOHIMA 5 APRIL 1944

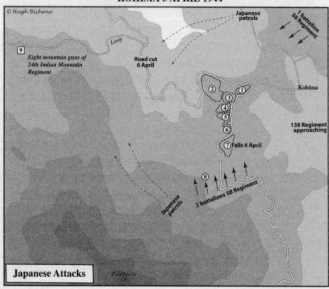

© Hugh Bicheno

Japanese patrols

1 battalion 58 Regiment

9 Eight mountain guns of
   24th Indian Mountain
   Regiment

Loop

Road cut 6 April

Kohima

138 Regiment approaching

7 Falls 6 April

8

Japanese patrols

2 battalions 58 Regiment

Palebaito

Japanese Attacks

FIFTEEN

Siege

After Sangshak, Miyazaki drove them even harder. There was time to be made up. The supply officer Lieutenant Masao Hirakubo felt tougher now. He could keep pace on the all-night marches. But he still hated the mud of the jungle tracks and the endless leeches dropping into his clothes. Now, as he emerged from the jungle, his feet were marching on asphalt. There was something beautiful about the feeling of the road underfoot. The soldiers felt lighter, listening to the sounds of their comrades scuffing along beside them. The 1st battalion had gone ahead of them and cleared the opposition away, ambushing some British who were having lunch at a hilltop village. The surprised defenders were shot at and attacked with grenades where they sat.

Hirakubo was told to stay behind with three others and gather food from the villagers. His battalion commander was terse. 'He told me that in one day we arrive at Kohima and everybody's rice will be gone.' The local chief was told to produce a large consignment of rice for purchase by four in the afternoon. The Japanese were lounging in the shade of a basha when they heard aircraft approaching; two British planes flew around the village twice and then disappeared. 'Has it ever happened in the past?' Hirakubo asked a villager. The man said no. At four, people began to pile rice in the middle of the village. Standing with his bag of Indian currency, Hirakubo paid a rupee for each bag of rice. Then suddenly the planes reappeared. This time they came straight in for the attack. There were four of them, machine-gunning and bombing. Village houses erupted in flames and people ran screaming in all directions. By nightfall the village was an empty, smouldering ruin. But the rice had not been damaged. Twenty men were recruited from a neighbouring village to carry the vital food to Kohima.

A captured notebook belonging to a Major Yamaguchi, a staff officer with the 31st Division, painted an interesting picture of relations with the local Nagas. For Miyazaki's 58th Regiment, 'the attitude of local inhabitants was favourable, because it was strictly laid down that no troops except administrative personnel specially detailed were to go into villages. Purchase of food was easy.' This is disingenuous. The Nagas had little choice when confronted with heavily armed Japanese, who would have seized the food had it not been given up. The major's notebook noted mournfully that the 'purchase of food became more and more difficult as the villages were abandoned owing to our artillery fire'. Even Charles Pawsey acknowledged that the Japanese behaved comparatively well at this stage. 'In some cases the first thing the Naga knew was their village was full of Japs when they woke up in the morning,' he wrote. 'The Japs did not treat the local population badly to start with. They wanted to win them over, to make them supply rations to help the invasion.' A twelve-year-old boy, B. K. Sachu Angami, from Kohima, met Japanese who 'did not behave like strangers. They came and talked to the villagers as brothers. They said to us "we are from the same race." Of course we were also afraid of them when they came. But they were so friendly that the fear slowly went away.' A note sent to Pawsey by 'Levi', the head clerk of Khonoma village, reported the 'behaviour of the Japs in this area was not so cruel as expected. Their dealings with women and children were fairly good.' However, villagers who protested against the taking of cattle and rice were assaulted and men at Khonoma were forced to act as labour for the Japanese. Miekonu Angami was a thirty-two-year-old farmer and hunter recruited into Japanese service at Khonoma. His recollection is of being ordered to carry ammunition and food supplies towards Aradura Spur and its bigger neighbour Mount Pulebadze, where the Japanese had first engaged Lieutenant Bruce Hayllar and his patrol. 'On the first day they gave us no food. We stayed a few days but still we got no food. The only supply we could get was from villagers there. When there was no food coming we left and came back to Khonoma.' Soon he would volunteer his services to the British.

In spite of the delay at Sangshak, the 58th Regiment was still the first to arrive at Kohima. The other 31st Division formations were also moving rapidly towards Kohima. General Sato himself arrived within a day of Miyazaki and set up his headquarters in the jungle about four miles behind the front line. It was a spartan affair, made of bamboo poles and leaves, camouflaged to blend in with the jungle and avoid the eyes of the RAF, but within earshot of a river, the soothing noise of which was like the waterway where the general fished near his home in Amarume.

For Sato's boss, Lieutenant-General Mutaguchi, Kohima offered the potential of breakthrough in an offensive that was elsewhere grinding towards attrition in the face of determined defence. The 4th Corps had recovered from the crisis caused by the late orders to withdraw towards the Imphal Plain. The 33rd Division commander, General Yanagida, cloaked in pessimism, recommended to Mutaguchi that the battle be abandoned. 'My goodness, I was troubled,' Mutaguchi wrote. 'Yanagida thought, "this is not good" and became a bit weak-kneed, saying that, "it was impossible to go all the way to Imphal with so little preparation." The momentum to progress was completely killed.'

The intelligence officer Lieutenant Colonel Iwaichi Fujiwara, who observed the crisis at 33rd Division headquarters, remembered the course of events differently. General Yanagida needed more artillery, tanks and ammunition as his men battered away at the British and Indian forces. When the required supplies were not forthcoming, there were 'exchanges of violent and angry signals ... great ill feeling between the Army commander and the Division Commander'.

The 15th Division, under its ailing commander Lieutenant General Yamauchi, fought past Sangshak and succeeded in cutting the road to Imphal on 29 March. Another column took up position in the mountains overlooking the British headquarters at Imphal.

The garrison was now cut off by land, but the same airlift that had brought the West Kents to Dimapur was also flying troops and supplies into Imphal. What surprised the Japanese was not only the material superiority of the British and Indian forces, but their fighting quality. The scared soldiers of the first Arakan campaign were gone; in their place were men whose determination to resist was as fierce as that of the Japanese themselves.

With the Imphal operation stumbling, Mutaguchi waited anxiously for good news from Kohima.

Lieutenant Naoji Kobayashi of 11 company, 58th Regiment, led the first platoon. They could see the Naga Village on the edge of Kohima, but dawn was about to break and the men were exhausted. The order was given to sleep. Kobayashi was tense and unable to rest. As the light came up, he saw figures moving on the hill opposite. 'It was the enemy all right. But they seemed to be unaware of our presence.' He roused his men. Word was sent to the other platoon commanders in the company. The whisper to get ready ran like an electric current through the dozing men. They were to prepare to attack. Only a handful of Nagas had remained behind in the village. Twelve-year-old B. K. Sachu Angami saw Kobayashi arrive. 'When he came to the gate of the village he said, "Open it, Kobayashi has come." Out of fear the old people near the gate opened it and let the Japanese enter the village. After that they started asking, "Did you see the Gurkhali?" That was all they asked, not about the Britishers.' The troops' uniforms were covered in grass camouflage and they came from all directions, he remembered. Another villager, Rushukhrie Angami, looked out of his home to see two Japanese attempting to disguise themselves in Naga shawls. They then surprised and killed two sentries from the Shere Regiment. These unknown Nepalis were the first casualties of the siege of Kohima.

Khumbo Angami, a teacher at the government high school, witnessed the same incident. 'I saw one of the Japanese shoot and kill two Gurkhas with one shot, because these two Gurkhas were standing quite close together each one facing the opposite side.' Angami was nearly shot himself because he wore khaki trousers and military-issue boots. He immediately ran to his uncle's house and changed into Naga dress. Later that morning he encountered several Indians in military dress. They were officers of the Indian National Army who had advanced with the Japanese to spread propaganda in the villages. 'But these Indian soldiers said they were fighting for the side of the Japanese, they also showed us Indian national flag and some badges. I therefore told them they must not be so "nimok haram", that is "so ungrateful", because they were wearing British uniforms and had British arms and all they have belongs to the British. When they heard these words from me one of them got angry and said, "Do you know what English people are doing for us? The English people are taking away all good things from us. The world knows that India is one [of the] richest countries" ... I told them there will never be peace if the Indians rule ... the Indians hate our hill people and Indians are always after our women folks.'

Another Shere Regiment soldier was wounded in the knee but pulled a sackcloth over himself and played dead. When night came he crawled to the house of an old Naga woman, who sheltered him. He was eventually discovered by the Japanese, who tried to bayonet him. But the old woman stood in their way, saying he was her son.

At 0900 hours a party of Shere troops came down to the village to draw rations, happily unaware of the presence of hundreds of Japanese soldiers. They were immediately set upon and taken prisoner. Panic spread as the villagers realised what was happening. A visiting Indian missionary and his daughter escaped only by dressing up as servants. Hunger was overcoming the restraint toward civilians noted at other villages. Rushukhrie Angami saw them killing pigs and fowl, 'and if the owners tried to resist they threatened to stab with their bayonets or shoot with rifles'. They moved from house to house, searching for valuables 'and snatched away whatever money, and precious jewels found on the bodies of the people'.

Some of the Kohima Nagas were forced to carry their own rice to other villages where Japanese troops were based. This amounted to humiliation in front of other tribes, something no self-respecting warrior could easily forgive. According to Rushukhrie, the marches took as long as nine days, without any food, prompting the Kohima Nagas to pronounce a curse on the Japanese. 'Under this brutal treatment every man and woman uttered in low voice the words, "We will pay you in your own coin when our British will come back."'

Masao Hirakubo's immediate preoccupation was with finding food supplies. He discovered a huge warehouse containing what he estimated was three years' supplies for the entire 31st Division. It was an unimaginable treasure trove. Men were hurriedly set to work dragging bags back to a safe storage position. Hirakubo took what was required for his own battalion and left the other supply officers to look after their men. The British across the road in Kohima were now awake to what was happening and the warehouse was promptly bombed and the rice burned to ashes. It was a small moment at the beginning of a great battle, but it would resonate through the weeks to come.

The war correspondent Yukihiko Imai was with the first troops into the Naga Village. He sent an excited message to Tokyo which was immediately flashed around the world. 'Kohima has fallen,' it declared. The report was seized on by Mutaguchi, delighted to have some good news for his anxious superiors. Henry Turner, a Royal Artillery officer, was a prisoner of war on the Burma railway and heard the news from a gleeful guard. 'I recall working on the railway one day, when a Nippon corporal, who was in charge of our party, announced that India had been captured by the mighty Nippon forces. We learned afterwards that they were at Kohima near Imphal and that technically they were on Indian soil. We were delighted with this, because it meant a break of a few minutes in our work. In order to keep the conversation going, we asked about Europe and were told that mighty Nippon had long ago conquered Europe. Apparently they had not heard of Hitler, who was the resident landlord at the time.' But a British denial was quick in coming via the Reuters news agency. Imai later gracefully acknowledged that he had been wrong.

The Naga Village lay outside the northern end of Richards's defensive perimeter and it gave the Japanese a foothold for mortars and artillery. Closer to Kohima Ridge they began building bunkers and trenches for the infantry, overlooking Hugh Richards's headquarters on Garrison Hill and Charles Pawsey's bungalow. There were also Japanese gun positions to the south on Aradura Spur, the 5,000 foot ridge where the British patrol had been scattered the previous day.

At the other end of the perimeter, on GPT Ridge, Lieutenant Donald Elwell of the 1st Assam discovered that his platoon of mule drivers was now on its own after a composite Indian company had fled. Elwell set off alone to find reinforcements and was given a platoon of the unfortunate Shere Regiment. On his way back he felt the ground heave as the Japanese started shelling. The Shere Regiment troops vanished. Fire whipped through the vegetation from garrison troops nearby. Elwell got back to find that his own troops had fled. Back he went again to get reinforcements, always one step ahead of the mortar blasts. He eventually rounded up his own men and a company of Gurkhas and went back to the ridge. As the day progressed, the Japanese increased their bombardment. That night, INA soldiers in the front line began calling out to Indian troops to change sides. Intriguingly, the Assam Regiment war diary refers to the 'defection' of some Indian troops; this, and the bombardment, 'affected the Gurkhas, some of whom withdrew during the night'. The remainder fought bravely and suffered heavy casualties. Japanese infantry were now swarming on to the ridge and outnumbered the defenders. By dawn, the remaining defenders had withdrawn from GPT Ridge to Jail Hill. The first of Richards's positions was gone.

Arriving at Jail Hill the ninety or so survivors found there were no trenches for them. Those that did exist were occupied by Assam Regiment troops and had been dug too shallow by garrison labour. Japanese shelling had already caused a large number of casualties and panicky shooting by garrison troops was getting worse. An Assam Regiment captain worried that his 'men were shaky and control by the NCOs was poor'.

* * *

The rain had only stopped just before midnight and had nearly ruined the troops' enjoyment of the Jane Wyman film *Tail Spin*, a tale of daring in the skies projected on to a screen under the slender shelter of a basha. Private Norman was aggravated by the downpour but had found yet another dietary consolation. Padre Randolph, ascetic and lean, looking as if he had never enjoyed a meal in his life, had taken over running the tuck shop. Norman enjoyed the packet of biscuits he had purchased. While he and the rest of the battalion struggled through the film, Lieutenant Colonel John Laverty was attending a conference with Brigadier Warren.

Now that the entire Japanese 31st Division seemed about to arrive in Kohima, Warren explained, the West Kents would have to go back up the road as quickly as they could. Transport would be ready to move them at dawn. At 2330 hours Laverty gave orders that the battalion was to be ready to move off at 0630 hours. The men knew that an order that late at night meant they were heading into battle. They had heard about the Japanese probes the previous day. There were curses about the incompetence of the brass. Sending them all back down to near Dimapur meant the West Kents had lost three full days when they could have been working on the defences and getting to know the lie of the ground.

The trucks arrived at 0430 hours. Inside the cabs, exhausted Indian drivers rubbed the sleep from their eyes. They ferried men and supplies, day and night, up and down the road to the British positions along the road to Kohima. Captain Donald Easten and the other company commanders were busy supervising the loading of equipment and supplies. Lance Corporal Dennis Wykes thought it was all a bit of a 'scurry around. They said "into the trucks we're going back to Kohima."' NCOs like himself and Lance Corporal John Harman moved around, hurrying the men along, making sure no important pieces of kit were left behind. Before they left, the cooks served up a breakfast of tea, porridge, fried eggs and sausage, before packing up their utensils and joining the convoy to the threatened village.

The West Kents made up the main body of the convoy. With them were supporting artillery – four guns – as well as sappers and a field ambulance platoon. The rest of 161 Brigade, including Brigadier Warren, would follow the advance group up the road. Lieutenant John Faulkner had only just joined the battalion and was posted to A company. It was his first appointment, and first experience of battle, after having been commissioned in Bangalore two months previously. Faulkner was stocky, with fair curly hair and penetrating blue eyes, and had been born in Bombay where his father worked for the Greaves Cotton Company. When his mother became ill with malaria, Faulkner was brought home to Plymouth, where his father took a job as manager of the Spillers flour mill. John was sent to Plymouth College, a private school, and groomed to follow his father into the flour business. In fact, he was working as a trainee at Spillers when war broke out. 'We think he may have lied about his age to get in early,' his daughter Margery said. 'He joined the army before being conscripted, very keen!' John Faulkner shared the Irish Protestant roots of his commanding officer, Lieutenant Colonel Laverty; his maternal grandfather, who came from Cork, had been a career soldier in the Royal Warwickshire Regiment. As the convoy moved up towards Kohima, Faulkner was 'fully expecting and prepared to meet opposition around the next bend'. But in the initial stages all was quiet. The schoolteacher Captain Harry Smith remembered being 'entirely ignorant' of what might await them until they met 'groups of frightened non-combatants fleeing down the road'.

These were some of the men Richards had ordered out of Kohima. 'There was all these bedraggled-looking troops coming down, all dispirited,' Dennis Wykes recalled. 'I thought to myself "if these are running the Japanese are not going to be far behind".' According to Ray Street, the fleeing men were shouting frantically and threw their weapons and bandoliers of bullets into the Royal West Kents' vehicles. There were trucks packed with men, some hanging on to the back and sides as they hurtled down the road. 'Others ran, trotted or walked. They all looked petrified.'

Private Ivan Daunt was staggered by the sight of so many fleeing men. 'Blimey they come down the road, hundreds of them, all pulling out of Kohima. You know, orderlies, hairdressers all that sort of thing. Can you imagine?' In addition to the 'disheartening stream of deserters and stragglers', Lieutenant Tom Hogg had by now learned that positions in Kohima were being abandoned without a shot being fired. 'Chaos and low morale reigned supreme. The prospect did not appeal.' John Laverty travelled at the head of the convoy and watched the oncoming stream with growing unease. 'Officers dispatched by the Commander of the Kohima garrison to meet the Bn ... brought news of the contact battle, painting such a picture of disorganisation and lack of spirit within the perimeter ...' At one point he ordered the convoy to stop and sent word back along the line that the fleeing men were not deserters but were being allowed back to reduce the number of 'mouths' in Kohima.

It was partially true. Richards was still trying to rid Kohima of the non-combatants, who did nothing more than consume rations and provide targets for the Japanese. Laverty had a harder time explaining why fully armed men were among the throng. He decided to disarm any of them carrying automatic weapons that would be valuable to his own men. But the West Kents' commander now faced his most difficult choice. For all he knew, Kohima might be about to fall; his signals men had tapped into the telephone line at the roadside but were unable to contact the garrison or 161 Brigade headquarters. In view of the emerging picture, was there any point in continuing? Might the better course of action be to return to a more defensible position along the road? Proceeding to Kohima, if it was already overrun, could result in the slaughter of his battalion. Laverty decided to go on, hoping 'the situation would not have deteriorated to a complete collapse' before his men were in.

Donald Easten's D company was the first to come under fire. They were leading the convoy as it came into Kohima. Easten saw at least two of his men killed as they got down from the trucks. There was no time to ponder the losses. 'We just debussed and charged into the position where we were told roughly where to go.' The lead vehicles had come to a halt on the road close to Garrison Hill where Hugh Richards had his command post. Lieutenant John Faulkner of A company was among the first to climb the hill. He saw the truck ahead of him pull into the side of the road. There was a bend here and a high bluff on one side of the road, with a steep drop on the other. He marched his platoon up a pathway 'past a very pleasant looking bungalow, round a cabbage patch, past two corrugated iron huts, across a flat stretch dotted with numerous tents and on up the main hill to the top'. The bungalow he had passed belonged to Charles Pawsey and would cease to look pleasant very shortly. As his men started to dig in, Faulkner heard bangs coming from the roadway below.

The Japanese gunners on ridge ranged the stationary convoy and began shelling. Lieutenant Hogg saw 'all hell let loose with artillery and mortars. Shell and small arms fire came in from all sides.' Private Ivan Daunt jumped off his lorry and crawled towards the steep bank for cover. The explosions set fires burning around him. 'You can imagine, bang here, and bang there, and a lorry catching fire a few yards away and all the drivers shouting and hollerin' ... don't know what to do, no one to lead them, tell 'em what to do.' Lance Corporal Dennis Wykes was convinced the Japanese had waited until the convoy was right beneath them before opening fire. 'We was staggered and shocked, but the Captain said "come on, out of the trucks," and fortunately at the side of the road was a monsoon ditch.' The men lay head to toe along the soaking ditch. Rounds cracked around their ears. Men were being wounded as they jumped out of the trucks. Wykes saw the doctors trying to treat screaming men in the shallow cover of the ditch. A pit was hastily dug for the wounded. But the mortars kept coming. 'They were the worst. With an artillery shell you can hear it coming 'cos of the trajectory, but a mortar just comes right down on top of you.' A private named Fred Worth was hit in the foot. 'He said to me: "I got hit in the foot but when I shake me shoe I can hear it rattling." I thought that was funny. When I went back later to see how he was getting on, he had died, as quick as that, from gangrene. It just galloped through his body and took him.'

The C company runner Ray Street saw lorries in flames and drivers running for their lives down the Dimapur road. Some were trapped in their blazing cabs. The next thing Dennis Wykes remembered was his captain walking up the road through the hail of fire and shouting at his men to get up and dig in. 'So we all bolted up the hill in spite of the fire and dug in.' Lieutenant John Wright, an officer of King George V's Own Bengal Sappers and Miners, was travelling further back in the convoy. Having seen what was happening to the West Kents, he stopped half a mile away from the shelling, got his men on to the road, and started climbing the slope to Garrison Hill. Once on top, they began digging in at speed. Looking back down the Dimapur road, Wright witnessed the disheartening spectacle of troops fleeing. 'We saw a large number of State Battalion [Shere Regiment] troops with their officers in front pass through our lines and shove off down the road back towards Dimapur.' An Assam Regiment officer who saw the West Kents arrive felt relief. 'There can be little doubt that had the battalion of the Royal West Kents not arrived that day, Kohima must surely have fallen before night was through. This fully equipped and fresh force, under command of Lieutenant Colonel Laverty, put new heart into the defenders.'

Laverty was met by Hugh Richards. 'Our meeting was not happy,' Richards remembered. He told Laverty how glad he was to see him and briefed him on the latest situation, as well as providing guides to the sectors where the West Kents were to deploy. Laverty was brusque. 'Where's Kuki piquet?' he demanded. Taken aback, Richards pointed the way and Laverty marched off, followed by several of his staff. To Hugh Richards, Laverty's attitude was inexplicable. It hurt and it would not be the last of rejections from the man who was technically his subordinate. It may have reflected something more than Laverty's lack of interpersonal skills. The scenes on the road with stragglers streaming away in panic, the reports of units fleeing before they had fired a shot, had profoundly affected Laverty, as had his earlier reconnaissance when the West Kents had been briefly dug in before being pulled back to cover Dimapur. The badly dug trenches and the critical water situation convinced him that Richards and his garrison staff were incompetents who could not be trusted with the lives of his men.

In an account given to a sympathetic author, Laverty claimed to have found a British officer cowering in a foxhole at the start of the siege. 'John stopped and said, "Who the hell are you?" The man replied, "I'm from the stores depot and I've got to get out of here quick. My men have all gone, the rotten bastards, and I'm no good. You must let me out I've got to get back to Calcutta."'* Appalled, Laverty left him there and walked on. Anybody who has ever spent time in the company of well-trained troops on the front line will understand that hostility towards other formations is part of a long tradition; men need to believe their unit is the best if they are going to risk their lives. That ingrained sense of superiority is multiplied dramatically when they encounter line of communications troops like many of the Kohima garrison. Added to this was the battalion's experience of successive disasters, from Dunkirk through Alam Halfa to the Tunnels.

There was a natural fear that the men holding the positions along-side them would cut and run. Given what had happened in the previous twenty-four hours it was a reasonable fear. Laverty found approximately 2,000 troops waiting in the garrison but 'no account had been paid to the quality, organisation and leadership' of these men. The Assam Regiment troops were exhausted from hard fighting and marching, and the rest of the British and Indian troops, while 'excellent material ... were not organised in proper fighting sub-units, did not know their officers and the latter did not know them'. The remaining 40 per cent of the garrison were line of communications troops or non-combatants, 'a heavy liability, unable or unwilling to fight, whose low morale was a danger in itself, and whose supply requirements, protection and disposal was an extra burden on a strained system'. The real fighting strength of the garrison now, including the West Kents, amounted to about 1,500 men. This to face a Japanese force around 15,000 strong.

The 4th battalion war diary's criticism of the garrison officers is an extraordinary combination of anger and condescension. On the

---

* This account is based on the anonymous statements of Laverty and other West Kent officers to Arthur Campbell for his book *The Siege* (Allen and Unwin, 1956). Hugh Richards was indignant and described the impression of morale collapse within the garrison as 'disgraceful'. It would later become the subject of a bitter dispute between Richards and Laverty and their respective supporters (see Chapter 26).

defensive preparations, it remarks: 'The Garrison Comd's own immediate HQ area was the only area well provided in this respect. Vital wireless sets were not dug in ... Water points themselves were in exposed positions and no effort had been made to construct other points ... no less than 5 separate uncoordinated R.A.P.s [regimental aid posts], not dug in, were operating when the Bn. Arrived.' The clear implication is that Richards had taken care to make his own bunker safe while failing to ensure others were equally well protected. A disparaging reference in the diary to staff officers at Richards's headquarters is scribbled over in thick pencil, Laverty apparently employing some restraint on re-reading the entry. Such restraint would vanish after the war, when accounts of Richards's alleged failings began to appear. At least one 4th battalion officer was horrified by Laverty's attitude. 'Laverty brushed him [Richards] aside with an "I'm in charge now" sort of attitude, which was unfortunate,' said Major Donald Easten. 'You had these two men each saying, "I'm in charge." And it was really uncalled for. He went around visiting chaps in the trenches and so on. I had great respect for him. He was an old man compared to us. But the sort of chap you had respect for. He was brave and a good soldier.' The conflict was not limited to Laverty and Richards. The CO of the 1st Assam Regiment, 'Bruno' Brown, also clashed with Laverty. As one of his officers put it: 'Friction soon arose over the exact distribution of command.' After a row with the West Kents commander Brown, a far more combative character than Hugh Richards, left the headquarters area and set up his own command post.

From their first meeting Laverty treated Richards as a man he would only do business with out of necessity. As for Richards's orders stating that he commanded *all* the troops in Kohima, Laverty ignored them. 'The position as it so transpired', wrote Richards, 'was that Laverty regarded himself as under command of Warren ... Warren so regarded Laverty. My orders were quite specific. I was placed in operational control of *all* [author's italics] troops in Kohima.' If Warren had decided to give orders directly to Laverty there was precious little Richards could do. The garrison now had two separate commands: Laverty directed the operations of his men, while Richards was left in command of the Assam Regiment and the various other detachments of local and composite troops. All Richards would say publicly was that 'my relations with the CO were strained and I found him difficult to deal with'. Laverty now believed himself to have 'virtually assumed command of the defenders of Kohima'. It was humiliating and frustrating for Richards and would take all his reserves of patience to endure.

While the exchange between Laverty and Richards was going on, the West Kents' various companies were deployed. Ray Street and his C company comrades were sent to Detail Hill, close to the centre of the defence; Major John Winstanley's B company was despatched to Kuki Piquet, adjacent to Garrison Hill; Donald Easten's D company was detailed as the reserve; the battalion headquarters company under the schoolmaster Major Harry Smith joined A company on Garrison Hill, where Laverty set up his own command post a little way from Richards's but further up the slope. Laverty's trench was about nine feet long, with room for himself, four of his officers and the all-important wireless set. He immediately ordered telephone lines to be run out to each of the company positions and to Richards's post just down the slope.

John Faulkner sent a party of men back to the road to collect their baggage, including essential bedding, from the trucks. A sergeant returned with bad news. Faulkner wrote down the exchange:

'Christ, sir! There's a hell of a mess down there.'

'What happened?'

'Japs are shelling the trucks and most of the Indian drivers have fucked off back to Dimapur.'

Faulkner raced down to the roadway and saw the trucks blazing and oil leaking everywhere. A water main had been punctured, probably the garrison lifeline from Aradura, and 'a dozen miniature fountains' were spraying the road and the boxes of mortars and grenades strewn across it. Faulkner could find no sign of his own kitbag. He made his way back up the hill and heard a voice calling out, 'Would you mind giving the doctor a hand sir.' Looking round, he saw a West

Kent soldier lying between two native bashas with blood streaming from his arm. The man spoke quietly and was waiting for the medic, who was busy dealing with another casualty. The second man was 'lying on his back in a grotesque attitude, his shoulder smashed'. Faulkner handed the doctor bandages and scissors as he needed them. Then he helped hold the 'poor chap' down as the doctor applied a tourniquet. 'What happened?' he asked the doctor. 'Jap machine gun caught them in here,' came the reply. Faulkner felt very scared. The same machine gun could easily open up again. But the medical officer kept working, quickly and quietly. When it was done, Faulkner 'pushed off, covered in someone else's blood and feeling a little sick'. His baptism by fire was not over. Heading back to his own position he heard two loud bangs. Two Sikhs with 3.7 inch Howitzers were trying to find the range of the Japanese guns. Faulkner had only gone a few steps when he was blown on to his face by a salvo of Japanese mortars. He heard a scream of agony and a yell for stretcher-bearers. Faulkner moved quickly to his own trench. The four-gun mountain artillery battery that had accompanied the West Kents was deployed in the bungalow area. The commander, Major Richard Yeo, was talking to Hugh Richards when the Japanese opened fire. Enemy observers had seen the guns being assembled and brought into position.

Richards ran for cover while Yeo tried to bring his guns into action. It was futile. The Japanese would knock them out once they had the range. Yeo hid the guns and decided he and his men would act as observers for 161 Brigade artillery outside the perimeter. It was a decision that probably did more to prolong the life of the garrison than any other.

Ray Street had a lucky escape from the Japanese guns. He and the runner from Easten's D company were in a trench behind a tree but feared it was too obvious a target. They moved further up the hill and started digging again. 'We were worn out and lay in our trench to rest.' He looked out and saw a man standing in the doorway of a basha, close to one of the water tanks. Suddenly a shell exploded on the spot and the man vanished, blown to pieces by a direct hit. Street threw himself down as more shells screamed over. When the barrage ended he looked down and saw that his old trench behind the tree had been blown up.

Private Norman was shouting to a corporal to jump into the pit he was sharing with his friends Dick Johnson, a bank messenger in civilian life, and Ernie Thrussel, a bookbinder. No sooner had the corporal arrived in the pit than a mortar exploded a yard from where he had been standing. To make matters worse, the food-conscious Norman was left unfed, there being no 'tiffin, dinner or tea', only endless firing. At about half past five he witnessed an unsettling spectacle. An Indian unit sharing the position was mortared and 'they started running away but we drove them back. We were told we were only here to stop [them] running away.'* Towards nightfall Ray Street heard that the Japanese had closed the ring around Kohima. The rest of 161 Brigade was down the road and cut off from the garrison, and in the process of being cut off from Dimapur. Sato had carried out a double encirclement. Hopes of being reinforced 'within a day or two' evaporated. As Major Donald Easten put it, 'the door was shut behind us and that was it. It was as close as that.'

At the other end of the perimeter from where the West Kents had arrived, a fierce battle was taking place on Jail Hill. Lieutenant Bruce Hayllar was told by Richards to take another hastily formed unit and go up Jail Hill to help the Assam Regiment and other defenders. His immersion in combat had been short and swift, but he had learned an important truth: 'You don't lead people in battle. You drive them!' He screamed at men who were simply holding on to their rifles to shoot at the Japanese. As he pushed the Indian soldiers up Jail Hill men fell dead around him.

---

* IWM, file no. 81/16/1, Diary of Private Harold Norman. Norman refers here to the Assam Rifles running away, but this is not consistent with the recorded facts. According to the garrison diary, Norman's C company was positioned on Detail Hill with two platoons of Mahratta Light Infantry and an Indian composite company. It is more likely that he mistook the latter for the Assam Rifles, who were actually based at Hospital Ridge and IGH Spur.

When some of his troops made to flee, Hayllar forced them back at bayonet point. At one point he turned to the sergeant and asked him who was in charge. 'You are,' he said. When Hayllar asked where the other officers were, the man pointed to a dead soldier lying on the ground. 'Now you've got to decide what to do,' he shouted. Very soon after that Hayllar was shot himself. The bullet struck him in the back and his courage vanished. 'The Japs were close and all my nerve went like a pricked balloon. I staggered up and fled flat out for safety.' Before leaving he had seen his orderly, a Muslim soldier from the Punjab named Allahadad, shot dead. The guilt over his death would live with Hayllar for years. 'He had a wife and a little son in India … I was the silly volunteer. He was just someone who was told to go.'

Jail Hill was turning into a charnel house for the defenders. By 10 a.m. on 6 April the forward positions had been lost. A petrol dump was struck by Japanese fire. Clouds of acrid black smoke now billowed into the sky, choking attackers and defenders alike. With streaming eyes and chests heaving with dry coughing, men looked frantically through the smoke for the enemy. Japanese mortars blasted groups of Indian stragglers who tried to shelter near the jail itself. With no NCOs or officers to steady them, they blundered around, screaming in panic and agony as the mixed force of British, Indian and Burmese troops was driven off Jail Hill.

The only hope of regaining the position was a counter-attack by the best infantry in the garrison. A message was sent to Laverty, who in turn summoned Donald Easten. As commander of the reserve, Major Easten could expect to be given the nasty jobs that cropped up around the perimeter. Laverty was under the impression that the position was occupied by no more than a platoon of Japanese. Accordingly, he sent only a platoon to try to dislodge them. Easten soon realised the odds were against him and the attack was called off. Hugh Richards estimated that two hundred men were killed or wounded in the fighting at GPT Ridge and Jail Hill. The Japanese were also bleeding heavily. At GPT Ridge alone they lost 110 men. Lieutenant Shosaku Kameyama, wounded in the jaw at Sangshak where he had seen his company reduced to twenty battle-fit men, was horrified at the fresh casualties. 'One hundred and ten men killed just to break through a position!' The southern perimeter now began at Detail Hill, where Ray Street and C company were entrenched. Soon the Japanese were pounding the West Kents from the newly captured positions at a range of a couple of hundred yards. The defenders had one big advantage, however. There was a high bluff on their side of the road. It would prove a formidable obstacle for the Japanese trying to cross and scale the ridge in the days ahead.

Laverty was trying to identify gaps in the core defences around Garrison Hill and Pawsey's bungalow. On his last visit to Kohima he had been quartered at the Treasury, which now lay outside the northern perimeter and was within easy sniping and mortar range of Pawsey's bungalow; it was important but had been abandoned by Richards before the siege because he lacked the troops to defend it. Laverty now saw it as a serious threat to the garrison and went to Richards's headquarters to press for a company to be sent. Richards was away visiting other positions and his second-in-command refused Laverty's request. The West Kents' CO did not let the issue drop. He eventually got Richards to send a company of the Shere Regiment out to the Treasury. By now Richards was well aware of the quality of the Shere Regiment and its capacity for bolting, but he had no other troops to turn to. The force of Laverty's personality may have decided the matter.

The company of the Shere Regiment was duly sent; rifle fire was heard coming from the Treasury, and the company ran back. They left an officer and several men behind, claiming the Treasury was held by the Japanese and their attack was a failure. But at dawn Richards had a message from the missing officer saying that he held the Treasury and needed the rest of the company. The familiar fiasco followed. 'I sent the company out again. No further communication was received from the Treasury, nor was the company seen again.' The British officer sent to command the Shere troops, Captain Jimmy Patrick, 7 Gurkha Rifles, wrote his own account of what happened. 'The troops refused to pass the field of fire of a sniper. Had to double across first before others would follow. All then crossed safely. Crossed main road in the glare of burning transport and advanced along south side of spur towards Treasury Knoll. Used shadows cast by clouds crossing moon to cross road between us and pine-clad slopes leading up to Treasury lawn ... solitary Jap threw firecracker. Discovered whole company had fled hurriedly, leaving me alone on lawn. Went down to foot of slope, and managed to re-form two platoons to try again. No firecracker this time but same chicken-heartedness. All ran away. After much effort, gathered together two platoons out of three who started out, and withdrew to Kohima. Reported failure.'

There was one shred of good news. A company of the 4/7 Rajput, who had fought alongside the West Kents in the Arakan, made it through the Japanese lines to reinforce the garrison. They would be the last British and Indian troops to do so for a fortnight. Richards called a conference at his headquarters. Word was sent to 'Bruno' Brown of the Assam Regiment, Major Keene of the Assam Rifles, and John Laverty. Laverty did not appear. 'At the time I thought nothing of it,' Richards said, 'there were plenty of reasons why he could have been elsewhere.' But Richards's attempt at establishing his leadership was being ignored. When he went to see Laverty at the West Kents' headquarters, immediately above his own position, Richards found that he seemed to resent his presence. 'I tried my best to get close to him but he remained aloof and his attitude to officers of the Garrison was quite unjustified. It should have been possible to work closely together and the fact that it was not was no fault of mine. Instead of help I got no cooperation.' When Richards sought to borrow a charger for the garrison wireless set – his own had broken down – Laverty refused him. It may well have been because Laverty wanted to protect his own communications, but it meant that all radio traffic to the outside had to pass through him. Laverty's direct line to Warren at 161 Brigade headquarters shut out Richards.

At ten o'clock that night, Laverty called Warren and gave his report. 'All quiet except for occasional shelling. Main threat from south, but skin not yet punctured. Body threatened by pin-pricks on all sides except right shoulder. Am trying to evacuate wounded and non-combatants tomorrow. That's all – off.' Shells smashed into Detail Hill as night fell. The defenders, battle-tested warriors and terrified amateurs alike, pressed themselves deep into their dugouts. Outside, the Japanese were digging, crawling into position, forming themselves into attacking formations. From now on, there would be no rest, only days and nights of screaming and death.

SIXTEEN

'Hey! Johnny, Let Me Through'

John Faulkner felt the round snap by him. The sniper had a good line on his position. Rounds had been flying since daylight. Sitting in his trench and hoping the war would pass him by was not an option. He was a novice and the veterans of A company watched his reactions continuously. They had not been touched by the panic of the deserters from some of the garrison units, but all it took was one scared officer and things might be very different. Faulkner went first to the cookhouse and ate breakfast and then headed for the road to try and recover some of the kit, including bedrolls, left during the shelling of the previous day. Many of the West Kents had spent the cold, damp night huddled up in trenches without bedding. As he moved down the hill, Faulkner met Lance Corporal John Harman. Faulkner would have found Harman a difficult person to understand – not that it was personal, it was just that he disliked people who didn't attempt to fit in. 'He was typical of his generation,' his daughter Margery recalled, 'he was a conformist, very aware of status.' When they met, Harman was scanning a track which ran along GPT Ridge. 'Snipers on that track,' he warned Faulkner. As they spoke, an Indian soldier darted along the track. A shot rang out and dust exploded at the soldier's heels. He kept running and reached the cover of a wall, where he turned to shout in joy. Survival at Kohima was based on the most slender margins.

Faulkner ran out himself. 'I heard the "thump" of a bullet as it passed over the track behind me.' Looking back, he saw Harman 'strolling unconcernedly down with one hand in his pocket'. Once more fate had smiled kindly on the soldier from Lundy Island. Faulkner himself endured a terrifying scuttle around the litter of abandoned and burned-out vehicles. The moment he stuck his head out from behind a vehicle a round cracked past. He dodged from truck to jeep to truck, but only found a few 3 inch mortar rounds. 'Every little helped,' he said. What stuck in his mind was the strange good luck of Lance Corporal Harman. Faulkner was probably too new in the battalion to have heard the stories about Harman from the Arakan; his daredevil sniping from paddy fields, how he shot a cow to get meat for his men, and the assurance he gave to Donald Easten that he would live to a ripe old age. Harman was living up to an image of himself that he had nurtured, as the immortal outsider who disdained the path of privilege. His fellow soldiers had long ago lost the habit of sneering at his posh accent and manifest eccentricity. Easten regarded him as the best infantryman in D company but was troubled by his strangeness. To stay alive in war a man must respect the instinct for self-preservation. He can never do it entirely, of course; battle is about facing the risk of death or maiming. But every soldier will recognise the sane margins of behaviour; a man with such contempt for snipers has either crossed the line from bravery to recklessness or is seeking a glory in death that has been impossible for him to find in life. Harman was ready for glory.

By the afternoon of 6 April, the road to Dimapur was finally closed to all traffic. Hopes of moving casualties out by that route vanished. Medical arrangements within the perimeter were seriously inadequate. The hospital was under fire from mortars and machine guns; there were several small regimental aid posts but no advanced dressing station for treating serious cases, and no central point where casualties could be brought and assessed – the crucial task of triage, in which men are separated into the doomed and the saveable. Nor was there a senior medical officer present who could direct operations. This left Richards and Laverty to manage large numbers of wounded men in a heavily shelled area at the same time as fighting a battle for the garrison's survival. They needed a well-protected dressing station with deep interconnected and ventilated bunkers where surgeons could work in safety and relative cleanliness. That was clearly impossible now. What they got instead was one of the most remarkable men in the history of war medicine.

On the afternoon of 6 April, an officer, 'slight and wiry of figure', arrived in Kohima, escorted by a handful of Indian soldiers. Lieutenant Colonel John Young, commanding officer of 75th Indian Field Ambulance, was by this stage an old friend of the West Kents. His surgeons and orderlies had treated the wounded and dying in the Arakan; Young himself had been present at the tunnels when the West Kents were mauled by their own artillery. He was a cosmopolitan figure, a good polo-player who had once studied art in Vienna, and a keen student of military tactics; he spoke fluent Urdu and, most importantly, his presence in a field hospital calmed men. Young had the gift of appearing unafraid, which is not to say that he felt no fear but that he had learned to master it. To a grievously wounded man, listening to shells landing close by, the face of the calm doctor was a last link with hope.

Back in the Arakan his men forded waist-high paddy fields under sniper fire to reach casualties. On the first day of Operation Jericho the previous December, they had dealt with eighty-three casualties in the first ninety minutes of combat. By the end of January, Young's men had evacuated 258 battle casualties and 299 sick, as well as carrying out a mass inoculation of 12,000 civilians against cholera. More prosaically, several gunners of the 24th Mountain Regiment were treated after consuming mushrooms that had produced unexpected effects. 'Typical symptoms not unlike those of acute alcoholic intoxication were noted. Complete inability to orientation was general. The mushrooms had been eaten fried for breakfast,' the war diary recorded. By the time the 75th Indian Field Ambulance reached Kohima there was little in the way of sickness or wounds they had not confronted.

Young's medical orderlies had been in action at Kohima from the moment the 4th West Kents arrived. When the shelling started, they jumped out of their trucks and began to tend to the wounded. Moments later one of their vehicles took a direct hit. Lieutenant Colonel Young was still at 161 Brigade headquarters when this news arrived. He felt his place was with his men at Kohima. At 0630 hours on 6 April Young was told by Warren that garrison morale was low and the situation in Kohima 'extremely serious'. Half an hour later the message was reinforced when shells began to land in Warren's own camp at Milestone 42, outside Kohima.* By 0900 hours Young was meeting Warren once more. Laverty's second-in-command, Major Peter Franklin, made the perilous journey out of Kohima to report that the medical situation was critical. It was enough for Young who set out on foot with his escort, passing through territory crawling with Japanese patrols to reach Kohima at 1430 hours.

Young arrived in Kohima with a vigour that must have impressed Hugh Richards. From the outset he treated Richards with the respect due to a garrison commander. He set to work straight away, inspecting the existing facilities, quickly formulating a plan, which Richards accepted. By 1800 hours the majority of the different aid posts were consolidated into an advanced dressing station (ADS) near Laverty's and Richards's bunkers; the medical stores were also brought together in the same area. A handful of posts remained with different companies to offer immediate treatment to smaller wounds or to comfort dying men.

When he arrived, Young found that medical personnel had been pulled away to act as infantry. They were swiftly brought back and given work treating the wounded. In three and a half hours seventy-nine casualties were brought in, given immediate treatment, and had their names recorded. This last was more than an administrative procedure. Recording a man's name reassures him that he is not going to be forgotten. Lieutenant Bruce Hayllar, wounded in the chaos of Jail Hill, was an early beneficiary of Young's actions. 'Young was a very good chap. There was this tiny little trench where we were treated and he was so good there, working non-stop to keep people alive. Also you felt relieved to be lying among men who had also been through it; you didn't feel so alone.'

---

* Warren and the remainder of 161 Indian brigade – 1/1 Punjab regiment, 4/7 Rajput and a mountain artillery battery – were unable to follow Laverty into Kohima when the Japanese closed the road. In any case there would have been no room on Kohima Ridge for them to deploy. Warren's new base was at Jotsoma, about two miles west of Kohima.

Young asked Laverty for a platoon of pioneers to build a dugout that would shelter up to a hundred casualties; he commandeered a hundred non-combatants to build trenches where more casualties could be accommodated. A team of stretcher-bearers was dispatched to bring in rations and 'medical comforts', a probable reference to whisky and rum liberated from the abandoned stores under cover of darkness. By the end of the day, Young could confidently declare to Warren over the West Kents' radio that the 'medical situation [was] ... fairly satisfactory'. It would not remain that way for long.

Major Nagaya's company was in mourning. Nagaya, who had wept for his dead soldiers and for the shame of not recovering their bodies at Sangshak, was gone. The colour-bearer of the 3rd battalion, Lieutenant Hiroshi Yamagami, was in his trench when the news came through. 'I was told that he went to observe the fighting and he ran into the British and was killed. He fought them with his sword. I felt so very sad about that.' Nagaya was struck on the head by fragments from a grenade thrown by hidden defenders. Yamagami heard that it had happened when Nagaya stumbled on a British pillbox near Detail Hill. Lieutenant Shosaku Kameyama was nearby and came running to his stricken leader. 'When I ran to him, he was dead, lying on a makeshift stretcher, a tent sheet tied between two poles.' A bundle of white wild chamomile had been laid near the major's nose as a death offering. Captain Kameyama gave orders to cut off a finger from the corpse, cremate it, and send the ashes to the dead man's family in Japan. Kameyama was heart-sore. 'Such a genuine man! I had felt that I could go with this man without a hesitation.'

Having given his orders about the body, Kameyama returned to his company and started to organise men for a frontal attack from the newly captured Jail Hill across to Detail Hill. He wondered about the strain on the younger ones, the replacements drafted in since China. To relieve the tension he formed them up and made a short speech. '"You see," I said to my soldiers, "keep your heads, keep cool. If you want to find out just how cool you are feeling put your hands inside your trousers and feel your penis – if it is hanging down it is good." I tested mine but it was shrunk up so hard I could hardly grasp it. More than thirty soldiers did the same thing, then looked at me curiously, but I kept a poker face. I said, "Well mine's down all right. If yours is shrunk up it's because you're scared." Then a young soldier said to me: "Sir, I can't find mine at all. What's happening to it?" With this everyone burst out laughing and I knew I had got the confidence of the men.'

The Japanese waited until nearly 2300 hours and began to move down Jail Hill in small groups. Perhaps because the bright moonlight made concealment impossible, the soldiers formed up without the usual orders for silence. They had won GPT Ridge and Jail Hill in just twenty-four hours and the men were confident Detail Hill would soon be theirs. Lieutenant Hiroshi Yamagami, colour-bearer of the 2nd battalion, was sure the defenders had seen the troops forming up for their attack. There was too much light for them to miss. It was harder for the attackers to spot the defenders hunkered in their trenches. Men who could speak a few words of English were sent up to shout at the defenders. 'Hey! Johnny, let me through, let me through, the Japs are after me; they're going to get me.' But this time there was no response. It was an old tactic: try to establish the defenders' exact location by getting them to make a noise. The West Kents had experienced this before in the Arakan; the voices in the darkness, shrill echoing cries that rose above the sound of the night insects, confirming that an attack was coming.

Above them, on the bluff that overlooked the roadway, the West Kents were waiting in their trenches. C company had just endured several hours of shellfire. One round exploded above the commander, Major Shaw, wounding him in the thigh; he was one of the best officers in the battalion but would play no further part in the battle. Shaw may have been a victim of his own tactics. He had ordered the removal of all overhead cover in order to improve his men's field of fire. His replacement, Captain Phillip Watts, nick-named 'Dodo' after the English film star Dorothy 'Dodo' Watts, was a classics scholar from Oxford who had won the Military Cross at Alam Halfa for moving 'continuously amongst the forward troops encouraging them to close with the enemy ... [and] showed great qualities of leadership under very dangerous and difficult conditions.' Watts spoke quietly to his men. They would wait and hold their fire until he gave the order. Wait until the enemy was very close.

The C company positions on Detail Hill and overlooking the road were about thirty yards long and twenty yards wide, on top of a hill that was itself only 160 yards long and about forty yards wide in the middle. The hill was overlooked by Japanese positions on the recently taken Jail Hill and could also be fired on from GPT Ridge. Cramped and exposed, the West Kents were also depending on untried garrison troops to hold the northern end of the perimeter. Beside them, on Supply Hill, the next of the Kohima dominoes, Captain Donald Easten's D company, was providing covering fire.

At about 2100 hours Private Norman, the devoted gourmand of C company, heard picks and shovels clanging and spotted the Japanese digging in nearby. His sergeant, Stanley 'Butch' Tacon, ran down the slope and threw grenades at the work party. His speed caught the enemy off guard. Before they could react, the little bombs were exploding among them. A corporal covering Sergeant Tacon shot several more. Between them they killed at least thirteen Japanese before the sergeant returned to his pit.

An hour and a half later the attack began. There was a shouted order and screaming. Ray Street heard the wave of sound approaching and felt a spasm of terror. 'The Japs made a hell of a racket, blowing bugles, screaming and shouting, psyching themselves up for the charge.' He saw the enemy come down Jail Hill and on to the roadway. Then they started to cross the road. The defenders waited. An observer from a mortar platoon crawled to the edge of the bluff to direct fire on the assembling mass. 'They were about thirty yards away when we let them have it,' Street recalled.

Lieutenant Yamagami felt as if the fire was coming from everywhere. Mortars were dropping among men whose screams of agony mingled with the shouts of encouragement from the officers. Yamagami followed his instincts. 'I jumped into the trench with colour in my hand. I was amazed about the fact that I could momentarily enter into such a small trench at the same time as the enemy's gunfire broke.' He was luckier than many of those around him. Scores of men were killed and wounded as successive attacks were broken up.

Ray Street saw waves of men sweep towards him. 'We cut them to ribbons but they still got through. There was that many of them.' Roy Wellings, a C company corporal, was in a forward trench and one of the first West Kents to experience being overrun. He was one of the replacement drafts who had joined the West Kents in India, but had come through the Arakan with the battalion and belonged now as much as any of the old-timers. Roy was the adopted son of parents who had lost two children in the great influenza epidemic of 1918–19. He could not bear to think of them getting a telegram announcing that the boy they had adopted was dead. He fired relentlessly but could not stop the wall of men moving towards him. They ran past, not even stopping to deal with him. At one point he was stabbing vertically with his bayonet as the Japanese ran over the trench. Wellings astonished himself by surviving. It was a short-lived feeling of relief. 'The only trouble with being an infantryman is that you survive one battle only to go on and fight the next. The feeling of invincibility begins to wear a bit thin.'

The perimeter was breached near C company headquarters. A cook and two privates were killed before the Japanese were driven back. The situation was so desperate that wounded men refused evacuation in order to stay and fight alongside their comrades. The commander, Captain Watts, was felled by a grenade fragment which struck him in the back. He was the second C company commander to be wounded in twenty-four hours. Watts was taken to join Major Shaw among the wounded and command passed to a B company officer.

The Japanese frontal assaults had failed. Now the attackers switched around to the northern edge of Detail Hill. Lieutenant Kameyama told his men to leave their knapsacks behind and follow him. The Indian garrison troops here were surprised and quickly overwhelmed. This allowed the Japanese to infiltrate between the C company positions; Kameyama's men took over some empty bashas while others infiltrated a warehouse and a bakery. From these positions they could fire on C company from behind and were 'so close in some places that they could throw hand grenades into their trenches'. But if Kameyama did not capture the hill by daybreak and get his men into cover, the West Kents of D company, entrenched on neighbouring Supply Hill, would spot them and start firing. He had two hours before light and there was still fire from C company, at the top of Detail Hill.

Lieutenant Colonel Laverty had ordered Donald Easten and D company to get across and 'restore the situation' on Detail Hill and as the sun came up Easten made his reconnaissance. But the gulley between his positions and the Japanese on Detail Hill was under enemy artillery fire. That made direct assault impossible. He sent one platoon to the north-east, avoiding the enfilading artillery fire, and another to a ridge at the foot of the hill to provide supporting fire. Easten and his headquarters followed the main assault platoon.

Dawn came and the West Kents' mortars began pounding Kameyama's men on Detail Hill. Kameyama could see that Easten's men were crawling up towards his newly taken positions. The West Kents on Supply Hill were mounting a counter-attack to relieve their brothers. 'So I had to say, "I will do the job with you. Fight with me to the death."' He threw grenades at the oncoming West Kents, watching as one of his section leaders was shot in the head, and another wounded by shell fragments. The supporting fire kept most of the Japanese heads down until Easten's main assault group reached the bashas and warehouse buildings. Grenades were thrown and Bren guns opened up; mortar rounds fell on the occupied bashas. As the flames crackled the defenders faced the agonising choice of waiting to be consumed by fire or shot by snipers. Many died in the bashas, burned alive or blasted by shellfire. One D company subaltern threw grenades into three bashas and 'shot at least 12' Japanese.

Sergeant Tacon of C company joined in the shooting. A later army account described the horror of that night as if it were a country shoot. 'His first bag came when Japs were seen scurrying like rabbits out of burning bungalows. He picked 15 off and felt he had had a

LEFT: An Indian woman flees with her child ahead of the Japanese advance into Burma, 1942.

BELOW: The Japanese advance into Burma, 1942. Japanese infantry crossing a river.

ABOVE: The Naga Hills near Kohima where British, Indian and Japanese forces fought one of the most savage battles of the war.

BELOW: Charles Ridley Pawsey (second from right), deputy commissioner of the Naga Hills, who refused to be evacuated from Kohima as the Japanese advanced. Here pictured with Naga warriors and the Commander-in-Chief, Indian Army, General Sir Claude Auchinleck.

ABOVE: Ursula Graham Bower, the Roedean debutante who fell in love with the Naga Hills and led her own guerrilla unit against the Japanese.

RIGHT: Naga warriors pictured near Kohima during the war.

BELOW: Namkiabuing, the Zemi Naga warrior, and ally of Ursula Graham Bower, on the day he was awarded the British Empire Medal. 'He had an intense, a vivid sense of right and wrong … he could no more compromise with wrong than he could stop breathing.'

ABOVE: Kohima Ridge today. Garrison Hill is circled.

LEFT: Lieutenant Colonel John Laverty, Commander of the 4th battalion, Queen's Own Royal West Kents. The 'bloody minded Irishman' commanded the best fighting troops in the garrison.

RIGHT: Laverty (seated) with his staff. Left to right: Captain J. Topham, who was killed on the day the siege was lifted, Major Peter Franklin, Laverty's second-in-command, and Captain J.K.D. Short.

BELOW: Colonel Hugh Richards. Turned down by the Chindits because of his age he was sent to Kohima at the last minute to lead the defence. 'I was appalled at what I found,' he wrote.

BELOW RIGHT: A sketch made of Richards during the siege.

TOP RIGHT: John Young heroically made a lone stand at Jessami after sending his men to safety. The Japanese buried him with full military honours.

LEFT: The Commanding Officer of the 1st Assam, Lieutenant Colonel W. F. 'Bruno' Brown who expected his officers 'like himself, always to live rough.'

BELOW: Major Albert Calistan (circled), 1st battalion, Assam Regiment, who led the defence of the tennis court in the final days of the siege.

RIGHT: John Pennington Harman. 'He didn't play by the same rules' as everybody else.

BELOW: The millionaire's son who won a Victoria Cross. John Harman (third from left) on Lundy Island before the war. His father, Martin Coles Harman, is standing beside him obscured by the dog.

An artist's impression of the action for which Lance Corporal Harman was awarded the Victoria Cross.

ABOVE: Havildar Sohevu Angami,
1st Assam Regiment, who fought at
Jessami and Kohima.

LEFT: Sepoy Wellington Massar,
1st Assam Regiment. He was awarded
a posthumous Military Cross for his
bravery at the battle of the tennis court.

ABOVE: Lance Corporal Dennis Wykes, A Company, 4th battalion, Queen's Own Royal West Kents. 'When you get the daylights hammered out of you as many times as we did you either go to pieces or you feel you are special, and we were special.'

LEFT: Ray Street, the C Company runner, who braved the gauntlet of snipers in the Arakan and Kohima.

ABOVE: Left to right: John Douglas Slim, 2nd Viscount Slim and son of the Field Marshal, Bert Harwood and Dennis Wykes at the Imperial War Museum in 2004 to mark the 60th anniversary of the turning point of the Burma campaign.

ABOVE: Donald Easten with young officers of the Assam Regiment in Delhi, 2008.

ABOVE: Major Donald Easten who held the dying Harman in his arms and fought on himself despite being wounded by shellfire.

RIGHT: Major John Shipster of 7/2 Punjab Regiment whose story inspired the writing of this book.

LEFT: Lieutenant General William 'Bill' Slim, Commander of the 14th Army and architect of victory.

BELOW: Mountbatten (left) with Slim (and General Oliver Leese) in May 1945. The war partnership of the suave aristocrat and the shopkeeper's son was an outstanding success.

ABOVE: Lieutenant General Montagu North Stopford, Commander of 33 Corps. 'His walk was unhurried, his mind moved very fast … He was very ambitious; some would call him ruthless; but he was a very professional commander'.

LEFT: Major General John Grover, Commander of the British 2nd Division, who would be removed by Stopford after leading his men to victory at Kohima. This picture was taken in 1947.

LEFT: Lieutenant General Renya Mutaguchi, architect of the disaster.

ABOVE: As a young officer: General Kotuku Sato with his wife Fumiko on the day of their wedding.

ABOVE: General Sato between the wars.

ABOVE: General Sato with his officers before 31st Division crossed the Chindwin. His infantry commander, Major General Shigesaburo Miyazaki, is on the right.

RIGHT: The mighty fallen: Lieutenant General Renya Mutaguchi salutes a British officer in Changi Jail, Singapore, where he was being questioned about war crimes.

ABOVE: The years of poverty: General Sato with his family after the war.
His son Goro is on the right.

BELOW: The funeral of General Sato. Major General Miyazaki is on the
far left. Lieutenant General Mutaguchi is standing fourth from the left.

ABOVE: Lieutenant Masao Hirakubo (standing, centre) with his family before the war. He argued bitterly with his father about Japan's actions.

RIGHT: Masao Hirakubo after receiving his OBE for promoting reconciliation with British veterans.

ABOVE: Lieutenant Takahide Kuwaki (in uniform), the zealous young nationalist on the eve of his departure for Burma.

BELOW: Dr Takahide Kuwaki in old age and still a believer in Japan's war.

ABOVE: 'Sometimes I met friends who were just dying there. Their faces said "Help me" but there was nothing we could do … I feel still that I abandoned those people.' Lieutenant Hiroshi Yamagami, the colour bearer of 58 Regiment.

RIGHT: Hiroshi Yamagami at home in Tokyo in 2009.

ABOVE: The deputy commissioner's bungalow which would become the focus of bitter hand-to-hand fighting.

BELOW: West Kent officers on Summerhouse Hill. This was probably the only photo taken during the siege. Standing, from left to right: Captain J.K.D. Short, Captain C.G. Steddy, Major Donald Eastern and Major Tommy Kenyon. Kneeling, from left to right: Captain Tom Coath, Captain J. Topham, who was killed on the day the siege was lifted, and Captain Fred Collett.

ABOVE: The desolation of Garrison Hill where the defenders prepared to make their last stand.

BELOW: The terraces of the tennis court after the battle.

ABOVE: The ruins of Kohima. An artillery officer wrote of 'the stench of festering corpses … flies swarmed everywhere and multiplied with incredible speed.'

BELOW: Searching for the sniper. Near Kohima, 1944.

RIGHT: One of the lucky ones. A Japanese soldier captured on the retreat is given tea and a cigarette by a Sikh soldier. As the scale of the disaster became known, more Japanese became willing to do the unthinkable and surrender to the advancing 14th Army.

ABOVE: At a ceremony of remembrance on the Kohima tennis court, Michael Shipster, son of the late Major John Shipster, with the families of Japanese veterans. Shipster's father never returned to Kohima, feeling that he could not face the battlefield again. His son laid a wreath in honour of his father and all of the fallen.

ABOVE: The tennis court today, still clearly marked out. Men hurled hand grenades and fought hand-to-hand across this small space.

LEFT: We were soldiers once and young: Donald Easten at the memorial to the fallen in Kohima. He made the pilgrimage when he was ninety years old.

good day. But he had only got his eye in ... Sitting cross-legged in the moonlight atop his trench the next night he killed 20 more ... the Japs made another bold rush at 11 in the morning – too bold in fact for Sgt Tacon killed another eleven. His officer told me, "The Sergeant just looked like a gamekeeper. He had a little black Naga dog as his companion to make it even more realistic."' Company Sergeant Major Harwood was sitting beside Tacon during the slaughter. 'He got 'em coming down that bank ... there was a big mound of bodies. He had a old stray dog sittin' with him, and we were knocking these Japs off, left right and centre.'

A corporal with C company was credited with killing nine men as they ran from the bashas and 'his next contribution was picking off individual Japs and in his own words "helping them downhill"'. A Japanese officer who hesitated at a small bluff was shot by the corporal, the force of the round sending him sailing 'through the air, his cloak billowing like a parachute'. In peacetime the corporal was a gamekeeper on the Kent estate of Lord Astor.

An ammunition dump exploded, adding to the apocalyptic vision that confronted Kameyama. He feared panic would set in. 'At this stage the only method to defend this place was to stand united. And what we needed was a dependable commander. As I was the only officer there, I pulled out my sword and cried, "Battalion Adjutant Kameyama will command you men here! Survivors of every unit! Come here with your wounded men."' About thirty able men and the same number of wounded gathered around him in a circle. They piled bags of soya beans and sugar around them and tried to dig defences, constantly sniped at by Easten's sharpshooters from other buildings. The trucks parked at the warehouses caught fire and sent flames on to Kameyama's makeshift sandbags. His men resorted to hurling cans of condensed milk on to the fires. Grenades thrown by D company were bouncing over the warehouse roof and on to Kameyama's group. The lieutenant told his men to hold up a tent sheet so the grenades would bounce off. But the casualties kept mounting. By the afternoon of 7 April there were only eighteen men capable of fighting. Forced to stay lying down, the Japanese struggled to find a safe angle from which to throw grenades, fearful always that they would drop back on top of them. Eventually Kameyama was ordered to retreat. The example of his dead commander, Major Nagaya, preyed on his mind. He could not leave the dead to rot and send nothing home to their families. After the wounded had been taken off the hill, Kameyama ordered the removal of the dead. He hauled a corpse on to his shoulder and made his way downhill. Kameyama would always remember the cold of the dead man's head as it pressed into his neck. Of the thirty men who had formed up at the start, nearly half were dead.

The Japanese now held only one position, a bakery, from which machine-gun fire was being directed on to C company. Some of the attackers were taking cover in the ovens. Easten decided to call on the sappers. Lieutenant John Wright of the Bengal Sappers and Miners fastened hard guncotton on to one of the bakery doors, then added a detonator and fuse to make a large bomb. He and Easten ran towards the bakery, slammed the door against the brick wall and set the fuse, before racing back to find cover. They had just dived into a trench when a huge blast demolished the building. The disorientated survivors staggered out and were cut down. Some were on fire, screaming and rolling on the ground to try and douse the flames. One came running straight at Easten, who shot him at point-blank range.

Private Norman saw Japanese bodies falling everywhere. He killed two. Searching in the ruins, the West Kents found forty-four bodies. Two badly wounded Japanese, a lieutenant and a corporal, were taken prisoner and sent back to the ADS. In spite of blood transfusions the officer died, but his corporal survived for eight days, long enough to provide valuable intelligence about the 58th Regiment's dispositions. Hugh Richards recalled that the officer's backpack contained 'excellent Survey of India half-inch maps', a welcome addition to the garrison collection.

*   *   *

Laverty calculated that the odds against the defenders were in the region of seven to one, but still believed the garrison could hold out. It was an underestimate. An officer informed him bluntly that the odds were 'heavy by any standards'. 'Thank you Douglas,' he replied tartly. 'That puts the position very clearly.'

Examining the ruined bashas, Private Norman 'found that a lot of milk tins had been opened and all the dead Japs had milk smeared on their mouths, so they were obviously hungry'. Norman slumped wearily back into his trench. That night the wind picked up and he shivered despite the bedroll he had been given by Indian soldiers. The shelling kept up all night and he slept for only two and a half hours. By morning, the snipers were working and Norman was told to fire smoke bombs to allow stretcher-bearers to bring in a sergeant hit in a forward trench. The man was dead by the time they carried him past Norman.

Back at the warehouse buildings, Donald Easten and his D company sergeant major, Bill Haines, faced a fresh problem. Despite the ferocity of the West Kents' assault, the Japanese in his northern sector were not yet beaten. 'There were quite a lot of empty trenches, because we couldn't occupy them all … In this particular case the Japanese had got into this empty bunker and they got a machine gun in there and got us pinned down.' Lance Corporal Harman was standing close by and heard Easten ask Haines how best to tackle the gun. He interrupted, 'I think I know what to do, Sir.' 'The next thing we knew he'd gone off,' recalled Easten. Racing the thirty yards towards the bunker, Harman crept under the slit from which the Japanese were firing. Easten saw him pull the pin from a grenade, then call out 'One, two …' before dropping the grenade through the slit. By waiting the few crucial seconds Harman had made sure the men inside would have no time to grab the grenade and fling it out. Easten heard 'an almighty immediate explosion' and saw Harman charge in. Seconds later he emerged triumphantly brandishing the machine gun.

All battles are marked by confusion, but at Kohima the rate at which trenches and foxholes changed hands tested the most experienced fighters. Easten was dominating the attack in his sector, but nearby, C company was fighting for its life. That evening, 8 April, the Japanese attacked C company again. They threw ladders against the bluff to try and climb up from the road but were driven back by grenades. The Bren gunners in the forward pits were changing red-hot barrels and being constantly resupplied with ammunition by Private Norman and those further back. One of the gunners, Corporal Rees, told Norman that 'he and the others in the forward trenches were enjoying themselves knocking the Japs down in "batches"'. Inside his six foot by three foot bunker with two other men, Private Tom Greatly was cramped and exhausted, thirsty and filthy, and constantly waiting for attack. Greatly was only eighteen, having lied his way into the army two years before. 'It was awful in the trench,' he said, 'we never ate a cooked meal and we all ended up with beards and long hair.' Outside his position the bluff fell about twelve feet to the roadway. Keeping guard while his mates tried to sleep, Greatly heard noises and looked out to see a Japanese raiding party trying to climb towards him. He immediately dropped grenades down and killed them. Later he spotted a Japanese officer, probably overcome with dysentery, drop his trousers and squat in the road; only the utter desperation of illness could have made him take the risk. The eighteen-year-old watching from the bunker raised his rifle and shot him dead.

Up at his ADS on Garrison Hill, the centre of the Kohima defence, Lieutenant Colonel Young was facing a crisis. His position was already overcrowded and new casualties kept arriving. The position was now being shelled and sniped at. There were nearly a hundred walking wounded cluttering the area, as well as the terrified non-combatants. Young told Laverty that an evacuation of these men was imperative. But the West Kents' commander wondered how it could be done with the Japanese circling everywhere around them. He also knew that the sight of men leaving could spark further panic among the less steady of the garrison troops.

Young suggested taking the same route out that had brought him in, past the Indian hospital at the summit of Garrison Hill and down into the valley towards the north-west. In total it was a journey of three and a half miles across country to come out on to the road beyond the Japanese positions. This was based on the hope that they would not encounter the enemy on the way. A long line of wounded men would have no chance. Young decided to put three control posts along the route, where fit troops would manage the flow of evacuees and report their safe progress. Young would go himself, along with Laverty's second-in-command, Major Peter Franklin, to ensure there was no stampede and to tend to any men who struggled.

Captain Watts of C company, recently arrived from Detail Hill, was one of those detailed for evacuation. 'Colonel Young said he would take out all the walking wounded. So he led the head of the column and I was the tail end.' At 2030 hours the word came from an advance patrol in the valley that the way was clear. Burmese troops guarding the perimeter near the hospital reported Japanese troops nearby but immobile in their trenches. Fifteen minutes later Young went with the first batch of twenty wounded through the perimeter. He saw them as far as the valley, where they struggled 'very slowly' down the slope. He then returned for the second group. There was some firing from the Japanese near the hospital, but darkness and the fact that the men remained quiet seems to have saved them from a full-scale attack. Matters suddenly became precarious when a group of about a hundred Indian soldiers was spotted following the evacuees. Young was convinced they were deserters who would draw the attention of the Japanese and risk the lives of the wounded. 'An endeavour was made to turn them back but with little success since quietness was essential.' In fact, the men had been given orders to leave by the garrison commander, Hugh Richards, who was trying to clear the area of 'useless mouths'. He wrote later that 'with the wounded went some non-combatants'. Either the information was never passed to Young or Laverty, or it was lost in the desperate circumstances of that night. Decades later Captain 'Dodo' Watts still believed the non-combatants were a planned part of the evacuation. A platoon of the Assam Rifles was sent down to the road to stop any further movement of the non-wounded. Within an hour all of the wounded had left the Kohima perimeter.

Two of Charles Pawsey's Naga guides led the way as they struggled along the valley. The term 'walking wounded' cannot do justice to the condition of many in the column. For a fit man, the steep slopes and tangled undergrowth would have been testing; for those with bullet wounds in their arms and shoulders, or with shattered knees and leaning on the shoulder of a comrade, it was hell. Wounds tore open again as men stretched or fell. The sharp edges of broken bones jarred. The men stifled their cries, aware that the Japanese were all around them in the jungle.

At midnight Young was called to the radio at Laverty's bunker. It was brigade headquarters reporting that all the casualties had arrived safely. Captain Watts was one of those taken to a field hospital in Dimapur and then to the peace of a hill station. Fifty years after the battle, the shrapnel was still in his back.

Late into his life Donald Easten would still puzzle about Corporal Harman. He had been as close as anyone could be to the man, and regarded him as the best soldier in D company. But those last minutes on Detail Hill would be replayed over and again in his mind as he struggled to understand.

In the early hours of 9 April, Private Norman heard the tell-tale sound of digging near his trench. The Japanese were about to launch another assault on C company, the third in twelve hours. A sniper was tormenting the trenches and shot 'poor Private Nobby Hall in the head'. The stretcher-bearers were pinned down, so Norman and his comrades did their best to comfort Hall. He died after a few hours. Exhaustion and overwhelming firepower were telling against the defenders. This time the Japanese swept up the bluff and captured the forward pits.

More than ever, C company needed support from Donald Easten and his men. As the sun rose Easten could see the extent of the Japanese penetration. Detail Hill was being wrenched away from the West Kents. 'I was rather thinking, "How the hell are we going to get these chaps out?"' About twenty yards away on the right, Corporal Harman was watching some Japanese firing from an old C company trench further down the slope. Easten heard him shout, 'Give me covering fire,' before leaping out of his trench and racing downhill. A machine gun peppered his route but Harman was untouched. Sergeant Tacon popped up to shoot a Japanese preparing to throw a grenade. Harman scrambled to the edge of the pit and opened fire. Four Japanese were killed instantly and a fifth bayoneted. There is dispute about what happened next. According to Corporal Norman, 'instead of running back as we were shouting for him to do, he walked back calmly, and the inevitable happened'.

It is a description that accords with the experience of John Faulkner, who had witnessed Harman's blasé attitude towards snipers. However, Donald Easten made no mention of a calm stroll back. He could see Harman coming and then collapse, smashed in the back by a machine-gun round. Risking his own life, Easten crawled out of his trench and pulled Harman back in. 'The poor chap … I called for the stretcher-bearers but he said, "Don't bother Sir … I got the lot. It was worth it."' Easten held Harman in his arms as he died.*

The action claimed two other victims. The Welshman, Corporal Rees, dubbed with the obligatory 'Taffy' by his mates, had earlier told Norman about killing Japanese in 'batches'; he stood up to observe what was happening to Harman and was shot twice in the side. 'I tried to pull him back because the Jap had fixed lines [of fire] on our pit, but he wouldn't let me,' remembered Norman. Sergeant Tacon tried to crawl out and reach him but was shot in the arm and leg. Rees was paralysed and became delirious. He screamed and cried for eight hours. He called for his wife, mother and father, and at times he prayed. It was torment for the listening men. Rees was only a few yards away but they dared not move towards him. Eventually the screaming stopped. Corporal Rees was dead.

---

* There is some confusion over the precise date of Harman's actions. The 4th battalion war diary gives it as 7/8 April, while his medal citation refers to 8/9 April. Cited in Lucas Phillips, *Springboard to Victory*, p. 168.

Norman and the men around him begged to be allowed to evacuate their post. 'It was really nerve-wracking for the 14 of us left because we couldn't defend ourselves if we were attacked ... We kept pleading to the Company Commander that our nerves were all "shot to pieces" ... what with poor Taffy shouting, poor old Nobby Hall dying in our arms, and the continuous mortaring, shelling and sniping, we also had nothing to eat or drink since breakfast the day before.' A Japanese 75 millimetre gun was firing at the trenches over open sights. One officer was saved when his dying batman fell on top of him, shielding him from flying shell fragments. Private Norman and his comrades were now under the command of Captain Coath from B company. There were emotional exchanges as they pleaded to withdraw. An NCO with Norman told the new commander that he had no idea what the men had been through. The captain promised that if they stayed he would ensure relief before nightfall. The promised relief came in the form of a B company platoon sent to drive the Japanese out of the positions in front of Norman. The attack failed and after a fifteen-minute wait the NCO gave Norman and the others the signal to withdraw. He had no permission to give the order and the commander 'went wild but could do nothing'. The ground was lost to the Japanese.

The following day, 10 April, five days after the West Kents had entered Kohima, Private Norman was ordered to go back with five others and creep up to the new Japanese positions on Detail Hill. Whether they were threatened by their officer, or felt chastened by what had happened the previous day, or simply followed the instincts drilled into them during training, Norman and the others obeyed and crept back, convinced that it was a suicide mission. 'We were surrounded on three sides by hundreds of Japanese ... If they had looked over the side of their feature they would have seen us.' The West Kent team observed strict silence. There was shooting, but none of it directed at Norman's group. Eventually a runner crawled through with news that they could withdraw. Behind them as they slipped away, Norman and his comrades heard the Japanese attack once more, racing into the abandoned positions.

Every man in the forward positions was dead. Convinced by reports from the scene that further resistance was futile, Lieutenant Colonel Laverty ordered a withdrawal from Detail Hill. Three companies from 4th battalion had fought in different stages of the battle, but only C company had been there from the beginning to the end of the four terrible days. They had ceased to exist as a company, reduced from around a hundred to just fifteen men. All now retreated to the next position, on Supply Hill, which was the second to last defensive bastion to the north of Garrison Hill where the headquarters and the wounded were situated.

For D company there was another blow. Donald Easten was trying to direct mortar fire when a shell landed between him and a sergeant. 'It blew the poor chap to bits … and I got hit in the arm.' Easten was blown backwards into a trench. The fall knocked his spine out of joint and a tiny shell fragment had paralysed one arm. He was carried back to Young's ADS. Around him on Detail Hill the trees had all been shredded. Blackened stumps poked out of the ground. There were arms and legs too, sticking up out of the shallow graves where men were stiffening into rigor mortis. The C company runner Ray Street could smell burning flesh on the breeze. Others had observed the Japanese pouring petrol and setting fire to bodies. West Kents and Japanese burned together. The smell followed the retreating men down the hill, into the afternoon.

SEVENTEEN

Over the Mountain

There was a heavy rainstorm at teatime and at his headquarters on the banks of the Brahmaputra river General Montagu Stopford found the temperature tolerably cool. It was a balm after a day of worrying news from Kohima. The 2nd Division commander, John Grover, with his men hurriedly drafted in from training exercises, had flown up from his newly established base at Dimapur. He told Stopford that Kohima's Naga Village had been taken by the Japanese, and the Shere Regiment had bolted in the face of the enemy, who were at that moment infiltrating all around Kohima. Stopford seemed unperturbed. 'I think that all shall be well now,' he wrote in his diary for 6 April. There were, after all, strong reinforcements arriving: 5 Brigade of Grover's division was already moving forward, while 6 Brigade was arriving in Dimapur. Warren's 161 Brigade, although nearly encircled, was trying to push its way through to the garrison from a position about two miles west of Kohima. Warren was being pressed to step up his efforts. 'I am not satisfied that Warren of 161 Bde. is going flat out to clear up the situation and I feel that some ginger may be required,' Stopford wrote. Driving on seemingly hesitant commanders would become a recurring theme of Stopford's view of the battle; it was a perception that failed to appreciate the difficulties of the terrain and the threat from the Japanese who would manoeuvre around and between Warren and Grover as they tried to reach Kohima. Sato had already sent a detachment towards Dimapur with the precise intention of blocking the road to Kohima.

By 10 April, the day on which the West Kents were being driven from Detail Hill, Warren was seeking permission to withdraw the garrison. Grover responded by saying the 'garrison must stay put because withdrawal might open the road for Japs'. He also warned Warren of the 'grave' political and propaganda consequences of withdrawal, a nod to likely ructions in Delhi, London and Washington. Reinforcements were coming, he promised, and any move might hamper the advance of 5 Infantry Brigade who were at that moment deploying towards Kohima.

Privately, Grover suspected the garrison might not hold. On the same day that he turned Warren down he called Stopford who in turn signalled Slim for permission to order a pull-out if the situation looked impossible. Stopford was frustrated by his physical distance from 14th Army headquarters, located six hundred miles away at Comilla, and complained to his diary that Slim's far-away staff lacked appreciation of the local realities. It was ironic that Stopford, impatient with his own commanders as they struggled with the conditions, should feel ill done-by at the hands of 14th Army.

But there is another factor which should be considered. Generals Slim, Stopford and Grover were all veterans of the attritional battles of the Great War. Each knew what it was to fight in trenches and watch the months accumulate and the casualties rise with no clear advantage gained. However subconsciously, the memory of that experience must have lingered for all three men as the armies dug in at Kohima.

Every morning the monkeys made a 'devilish row, screaming at each other among the tree tops'. Captain Swinson also heard an elephant trumpeting in the distance before breakfast. A sentry who thought he saw a Japanese crawling up on him had wounded a tiger 'that went howling away'. A signaller got into bed to find he was sharing it with a snake. 'Apart from these odd incidents we have no excitement,' Swinson reported. He walked down to the river where a prayer service was under way. 'At the "Non Sum Dignus" the sun rose from the hills and the golden light cascaded down the valley.' The men recited the Hail Mary, 'Mother of mercy, our light, our sweetness, our hope … with rather more feeling than usual'. Arthur Swinson was an aspiring writer who carried two anthologies of war poetry in his pack; for him, the close press of the jungle was not a source of terror but a repository of the exotic that helped keep the tension of war at bay.

Swinson was with the vanguard of 5 Infantry Brigade as it prepared to advance towards Kohima. The brigade was made up of three battalions – one each from the Cameron, Dorset and Worcestershire Regiments. Their first task would be to reach Warren and 161 Brigade, and then to relieve the garrison at Kohima before the Japanese could sweep through to Dimapur. Nursing a vile cold and with his brigadier, Victor Hawkins, in a bad temper, Swinson regarded the coming days with foreboding.

On 11 April, while the West Kents were regrouping after the loss of Detail Hill, Swinson was sorting out a great traffic jam on the road. Hawkins was reduced to fury by the absence of road discipline among the Indian drivers. 'They went when and how they liked. If they didn't like they just stopped – or tried to. They parked anyhow and anywhere and trying to get things done with them was like a nightmare.' The brigadier told Swinson to sort out the mess before the Japanese started shelling 'or there'd be hell to pay'. It was here that Swinson saw the first wounded men from the battles being fought up the road. These were men of the 7th battalion, Worcestershire Regiment, sent to hold the Japanese at bay while the rest of 5 Brigade deployed. Most of them were not badly wounded but in deep shock; it was their physical expressions that struck Swinson most profoundly. The men's eyes were weary and there was an uncontrollable tremor in their voices. He was told that an officer he knew well, a man named Watkins, had been the first to be killed, and remembered back to 'the wild days after Dunkirk when he joined the Regiment, a shy boy who never quite succeeded in coming to terms with life'. Watkins had been afraid of women and ill at ease with men, and lived aloof from his fellows. 'Perhaps he would have found his niche and stumbled on the happiness his rare spirit was seeking. But 25 years was not enough.'*

The following day, 12 April, Swinson was temporarily rid of his brigadier, who had gone to establish a headquarters near Zubza, about ten miles from Kohima. Before leaving, Hawkins had addressed a gloomy gathering of his officers. He was going ahead even though the brigade was not yet ready. Troops were still arriving but the need to stop the Japanese was too urgent to wait. Kohima was encircled, Warren and 161 Indian Brigade were cut off, and the Japanese were now threatening 5 Brigade on the Dimapur road. The spectre of a swift attack on Dimapur while the British were still deploying loomed over the gathering. Battalions from the Cameron Highlanders, Worcestershire and Dorsetshire regiments were coming into the line, but there was no sure answer to the question that still haunted Slim: could they do it before the Japanese took Dimapur? When Hawkins arrived at Zubza and was able to view the terrain he quickly realised that his brigade could not hope to take Kohima on its own, as Grover had ordered. 'I was a bit appalled at my original orders.' He persuaded General Grover to come and see for himself. The result was a compromise. The garrison would be relieved first and then there would be a discussion about driving the Japanese out. Through the second week of April the Camerons, Dorsets and Worcesters were all involved in fighting towards Kohima.

Lieutenant Keith Halnan, Signals Officer in the 5th Brigade of 2nd Division, had gone ahead with the troops trying to break through to Warren. Like Swinson, he tried to keep clear of Brigadier Hawkins. 'He was rather stick in the mud ... He disliked my background. I wasn't regular. He probably thought I knew too much.' Halnan was a medical student at Cambridge when the war broke out and was gifted with a precocious intelligence. It occasionally caused him trouble, and was almost certainly at the root of his problems with the brigadier. He had alienated a previous CO by producing a paper on radar and sending it off to GHQ without consulting his boss.

---

* Lieutenant Alstan Heath Watkins was killed on 11 April 1944. Commonwealth War Graves Commission.

Halnan initially felt relieved to be out of his previous camp, littered as it was with the excrement of previous occupants. Then the shelling began. Halnan was blown to the ground. When he recovered he saw that his batman, Private Gordon Ollier, had been killed. Halnan then made the frightening discovery that a piece of shrapnel had penetrated his wallet. The wallet was sitting in a pocket directly over his heart. The shelling gave Halnan his first sight of dead bodies. That evening he had to recover the possessions of his batman and write a letter to the man's family, a task he found far more difficult than looking at the dead. He found that he could remember nothing of the incident, not even the fact that Ollier had been standing beside him. Shock had wiped his memory clean. Nonetheless 'everybody dug holes much more effectively and better after that'.

Brigadier Hawkins worried about the rawness of his troops. An early attack on a Japanese position had failed because 'we had done so many exercises and always made them as real as we could that the chaps were finding it difficult to realise they were on the real thing at last'. As 5 Brigade advanced, by night the local Nagas guided a long column of men away from the road and across the hills in a flanking move. 'We went in single file down several thousand feet at night,' Halnan recalled. The men wore plimsolls to reduce noise and carried their boots around their necks. Halnan could hear some distant shellfire but not much else. Occasionally a shell whistled as it went overhead. Before setting out the men were issued with FS1 cards which, Halnan recalled, said, 'I am well. I will be writing as soon as possible. Everything is alright.' His father had been given the same card at Ypres, just before he was gassed.

CQMS Fred Weedman of C Company 7th Worcestershire Regiment was following his mules along the same precarious path. To one side there was a cliff-face and on the other a soaring drop into the darkness. The mules picked their way along expertly, 'never faltering or stumbling'. On the morning of 12 April the company took up position on a hill to the east of Zubza which offered a good view of the local countryside. Barbed wire was run around the perimeter, with tin cans attached; ledges were dug in the trenches for lining up grenades. The following night a corporal heard movements outside the perimeter at around 2330 hours. The warning was passed via ropes which had been run from the company headquarters trench to all the others around the perimeter. A tug at the end of the rope meant 'stand to'. Dozens of eyes stared out into the night, but with no moon they could see nothing. The darkness crowded on the lips of their trenches. They heard woodpeckers tapping in the jungle. Some men thought it might be the enemy signalling to each other. Fred Weedman sensed an attack was coming, and wondered if the enemy would be the snarling, bloodthirsty creatures he had been told about. There was a twanging noise, a wire being cut. Every heart inside the perimeter pounded. Orders were quickly whispered by section commanders and the 'night was split asunder with deafening explosions followed by the screams of the Japanese wounded'.

Weedman heard bullets hit the trees and others ricocheted into the darkness 'like an angry bee'. After a long exchange of fire there was silence. Nobody in the Worcesters' trenches relaxed. A second attack came at half past two in the morning. Now the Japanese made no attempt at silence. A screaming wave attacked the right flank and ran straight into a curtain of Bren and rifle fire. Weedman heard his company commander shout to the cooks, clerks and batmen to fix bayonets and be ready in case the enemy broke through. Again the attack was beaten back. In the morning the sentries found seventeen Japanese rifles strewn about the hill, all of them outside the perimeter. A body lying about twenty yards away was seen to move. A puff of smoke rose from it. It might have been a phosphorus grenade. 'He smouldered for the rest of the day and slowly burnt himself to death.' Another Japanese body was dragged inside the perimeter and searched for maps or documents. When the men had finished, the corpse was placed in a shallow grave. A private composed an 'epitaph' which was placed on the man's grave:

> Little Jap upon the hill,
> Very cold, very still,
> To the top he tried to get,
> He doesn't know what hit him yet!

The trek towards the Kohima front had its bizarre moments. Fred Weedman was leading the mules, loaded with boxes of stew, up a steep trail in the jungle and saw one Japanese carrying another on his back. Weedman threw a grenade and there was a scream, quickly followed by a burst of Japanese machine-gun fire. At this point a mule named Gladys went wild and sprayed the area with boiling-hot stew. The Japanese vanished.

Far above Weedman, in the world of the Generals, Stopford was urging Grover onwards. When the latter said he worried about being cut off from water, Stopford brushed aside his concerns. 'The relief of Kohima must be carried.'

General Slim was feeling marginally less anxious. Flying between his Comilla headquarters and the bases at Dimapur and Imphal, he was 'beginning to see light'. At Imphal the Japanese were still battering away fruitlessly; with air supply and a continuing flow of reinforcements the risk of losing 4 Corps was rapidly receding. Like Stopford, he watched the build-up of British forces at Dimapur and read the reports of enemy losses around Imphal, Sangshak and Kohima, and concluded that the tide could soon turn. By 11 April, Grover and two of his brigades were at Dimapur with a third just arriving. In addition, Brigadier Lancelot Perowne's 23 Long Range Penetration Brigade (Chindits) had been tasked to guard the railway line and then to move out to attack the Japanese lines of communication around Kohima.

The Japanese had Kohima in a stranglehold, but Slim knew their advance had been costly. 'For their gains they had paid a higher price in dead and wounded, and, above all, in time, than they had calculated on *their* plan.' Slim had an approximate parity in numbers of troops in the area, and would soon have superiority when the 7th Indian Division arrived from the Arakan; but, above all, he had the air support and supply lines essential for victory. 'As I watched the little flags representing divisions cluster round Imphal and Kohima on my situation map, I heaved a sigh of relief. As the second week of April wore on, for all its alarms and fears I felt that our original pattern for the battle was reasserting itself.'

That was the big picture, but, as Slim acknowledged, it was by no means the complete one. Hugh Richards and the Kohima garrison were in 'dire peril'. Warren was held up on the road outside Kohima. There was still time for Sato to overrun the garrison, or to sidestep it and keep moving towards Dimapur and the railway. Slim wanted to fight his battle not on the railway but at Kohima. If the Japanese took Kohima Ridge in its entirety, it would take months of fighting – as Pawsey and Richards had warned – to shift them, and would delay Slim's plans for an offensive into Burma. This strategic reality was behind Slim's original decision to make a stand at Kohima. Subsequently he had agreed with Stopford when the latter feared Dimapur would be the target. Now, after acknowledging that error, Slim resolved to make Kohima his battleground by diverting resources from Imphal; as he put it, 'at the cost of skimping Scoones I must nourish Stopford'. There had been serious mistakes in his reading of Japanese intentions – mistakes he honourably acknowledged – but Slim was right to believe that the battle was still his to win.

Defeat at Kohima would wreck everything he had worked for since the retreat of 1942. Slim had forged a new army, despite being starved of resources and facing Churchill's scepticism and, frequently, American hostility. He had instilled in the men of 14th Army the belief that they could win. The damage to morale of defeat would be catastrophic, let alone the ramifications for relations with the Americans and for the fragile political situation in India. Slim was always alert to the political as well as military dimensions of his battles, and at Kohima this filtered down to his subordinate commanders, who felt the pressure for swift advances in a landscape where they were frequently impossible.

For now, the political priority was maintaining American air support. As Mountbatten's chief of staff, Lieutenant Sir Henry Pownall, wrote: 'The hard fact is that the Americans have us by the short hairs ... We can't do anything in this theatre, amphibious or otherwise, without material assistance from them ... So if they don't approve they don't provide, and that brings the whole project automatically to an end. They will provide stuff for north Burma operations ... but they won't for anything else ... who pays the piper calls the tune.' Slim's Burma battle would have American air support for as long as it served the American interest in keeping open links to Chiang Kai-shek's Chinese army.

Recognising the reality of the threat from Mutaguchi, Churchill backed to the full Mountbatten's push for more American aircraft. At a Cabinet meeting on 11 April, Churchill told his ministers that air transport was the key to success. The dramatic airlift from the Arakan had convinced him of that. 'We should not hesitate to press the United States authorities to make still further air transport available, at the expense of transport to China, if the urgent needs of the battle justify this.' He had already signalled Roosevelt to this effect.

Slim's entire plan, and the lives of the men at Kohima and Imphal, would depend on the continuing success of the relationship. Mountbatten played the Americans with skill. They would get the offensive action they wanted to protect the supply line to China, but American planes would be needed to do it. Writing to Roosevelt at the end of March, he had stressed that 'without air transport and air supply we are tied to roads which we have to build behind us across the most wild and desolate mountain jungle I have ever seen. Without overwhelming air support it would take years to drive the Japanese out of Burma.'

Mountbatten also kept up his morale-boosting trips to the front-line areas. Sergeant Jim Campion, of 1/8 Lancashire Fusiliers, was preparing to depart from Bangalore for the Kohima front when Mountbatten arrived. 'He was given a tremendous ovation when he said (I quote) "I know the brothels have been out of bounds since you arrived, but as from now, the ban is lifted. So, in the short time you have left here, make the best of it." This order was duly complied with.'

Arriving in Imphal on 8 April, Mountbatten went to see the 4 Corps Commander Scoones, whom he found 'full of bounding enthusiasm and [who] told me that in every encounter there with the Japanese we are getting the better of them'. Mountbatten was nearly ninety miles by road from Kohima, but the road was cut and beyond the Japanese roadblocks a vision of hell was unfolding, hardly imaginable to the supreme commander. Mountbatten was introduced to a Japanese prisoner who assured him he was being treated well, 'the same as your prisoners are receiving from the Japanese'. The statement provoked a rare outburst of fury in Mountbatten's diary. 'When I think of what they have been doing to our prisoners it makes me sick,' he wrote. He had been told a few days before of an incident in which a mule train of the West Yorkshire Regiment had been captured by the Japanese. Twenty-three men were caught, tied to trees and flogged until they passed out. When they recovered consciousness, a Japanese officer killed them all, except one, with a bayonet. 'The one who did not die and eventually recovered had twenty-one bayonet thrusts in him. This is only a sample of the many atrocity stories I am beginning to collect.' Mountbatten returned to Delhi on 13 April, impressed with the 'dash and go' of everybody he had met at the front and despairing of the negative atmosphere in the capital. Soon afterwards, and at the height of the Kohima fighting, he moved his headquarters to Kandy in Ceylon.

The great struggle at Kohima existed on the war's periphery. It is important to remember the larger context of the spring of 1944. The CIGS, General Brooke, and Churchill were preoccupied with planning the greatest invasion in history: D-Day was only six weeks away, and in Italy, allied forces were engaged in a bitter struggle to break out of the Anzio beachhead. However, it was not that the Asian theatre was ignored. Rather it was a source of deep discord. Churchill provoked the most bitter dispute of the war with the Chiefs of Staff over his demand for amphibious landings in South-East Asia. The plan, codenamed 'Operation Culverin', involved a classic piece of Churchillian dash, leapfrogging from Sumatra to Singapore and Rangoon, and obviating any need for a slog through the Burmese jungles. Brooke was exasperated at plans he regarded as impractical and a distraction. After a meeting with the Chiefs of Staff on 17 March where Churchill had pressed the case for an invasion of Sumatra, Brooke wrote in his diary: 'I began to wonder whether I was in Alice in Wonderland, or whether I was really fit for a lunatic asylum! I am honestly getting very doubtful about his balance of mind and it just gives me the cold shivers. I don't know where we are or where we are going regards our strategy, and I just cannot get him to face the true facts! It is a ghastly situation.' According to Brooke's account, after another meeting five days later the Chiefs had decided 'it would be better if we all three resigned rather than accept his solution'. Yet another discussion of 'Operation Culverin' a few days later left Brooke feeling 'like a man chained to the chariot of a lunatic!! It is getting beyond my powers to control him.' The matter was settled not by Brooke or by Churchill, but by Lieutenant General Renya Mutaguchi who, as the debate raged in Whitehall, was busy changing the facts on the Indian frontier.

Kohima is mentioned in the notes of War Cabinet meetings and in the weekly summaries prepared for Churchill by the Chiefs of Staff. On 3 April, the War Cabinet was given an optimistic, if not utterly misleading, version of events. 'To the north, other Japanese forces that had cut the road between Imphal and Kohima had been driven back. Japanese forces in this area had been drawn off in order to deal with our penetration groups further to the east.' Throughout the first weeks of the siege there is no specific reference to Kohima or to Imphal in Brooke's diaries, although on 12 April the CIGS met Mountbatten's deputy chief of staff 'to discuss India and Dickie Mountbatten's problems'. A day later he met with Orde Wingate's former second-in-command, George Symes, when Burma was discussed, followed by an hour with 'Rowland from Indian Civil Service on grain sitn etc.' Brooke was not indifferent to the war in the Far East; the lack of detailed reference in his diaries simply reflects the scale of priorities he faced. But he was hostile to allocating more resources to Burma. His pragmatism rebelled against adventures that consumed scant resources for an imperial cause that he already feared was lost. Back in February 1942, when news of Singapore's fall was coming in, he had written: 'I have during the last ten years had an unpleasant feeling that the British Empire was decaying and we were on a slippery decline!'

As for the British public, the extreme peril of the Kohima garrison and the scale of the Japanese threat were unknown. This was not in any sense exceptional or suspicious. It simply reflected the nature of wartime communications and censorship, and the peripheral nature of Burma to the overall scheme of the war. But in India the political calculation was different. The suppression of information from the front led to protests from several war correspondents who were convinced that Delhi was hiding bad news. Speaking to an open session of the Indian Assembly in the first week of April, the Commander-in-Chief of the Indian Army, General Auchinleck, sounded sanguine. 'We cannot stop every Japanese threat as soon as it makes itself apparent, but it is therefore always possible that some of these may succeed in temporarily interrupting the communications ... I am convinced that the security of Assam has never been in danger, let alone the security of India.' An Indian government statement of 8 April was at utter variance with reality. 'It is obvious that the enemy's timetable has been thrown completely out of gear ... other than attacking the key towns and gaining full possession of the roads, the Japanese effort can now be of little else than nuisance value.' This statement was greeted with astonishment in Kohima. Captain Walter Greenwood heard Auchinleck state that 'Kohima was very strongly defended' while he was crouching in Hugh Richards's bunker.

The Japanese had blocked the key road and were besieging Kohima, the one strong defensive position in front of the railway and the supply base at Dimapur. This 'nuisance', as Auchinleck described it, would cost thousands of lives. Both Slim and Stopford still feared that Sato could make a flanking move towards Dimapur at any moment. The distortions in Delhi had far less to do with preserving the morale of the fighting troops, who could see the situation for themselves, than with keeping damaging news from restive Indian ears.

There was some reporting of the fighting on the BBC and in censored newspaper accounts. Captain W. P. G. MacLachlan of the Kohima garrison remembered how 'at 5.30 p.m. each day the operator on the telephone exchange would connect all the lines, and the owner of the radio would put his telephone mouthpiece against the loudspeaker. Thus the whole camp could hear the news and when Kohima eventually figured in the bulletins, derisive guffaws could be heard over the telephone system at the BBC's bald descriptions of what we had been doing two or three days before.' One officer on General Grover's staff said they depended on the BBC broadcasts because communications with headquarters were so poor.

The government in London was also reluctant to say anything while the battle still hung in the balance. Burma had been the source of too much previous humiliation. Early attempts to obtain a parliamentary statement on the fighting in the Naga Hills were rebuffed. On 4 April, the day the West Kents were told to return to Kohima, the war minister, Sir James Grigg, was asked to make a statement. 'Not at the present time,' he declared. Grigg would repeat this for some weeks to come. In time, the defenders of Kohima would come to regard themselves as part of a 'forgotten army', but in those first weeks of April 1944 they were unaware of the marginal consideration being given in London to the fighting. The men saw no further than the corpse-littered ground in front of them, while their commanders watched the middle distance, praying that Warren or Grover, or both, would break through in time to save them.

The brigadier could give the impression of nonchalance. Having bought some chickens from a local village 'Daddy' Warren ordered a run built near the officers' mess. He could be seen eating his morning eggs accompanied by wild raspberries while the guns blasted away towards Kohima; in the evenings, according to Arthur Swinson, he played numerous hands of *vingt-et-un*. Yet appearances were deceptive. Warren worried constantly about the state of the garrison; at one point, moved by the appeals for help from Laverty, he suggested to Grover that he and his men try to march up the road and into Kohima. Luckily the request was dismissed by Grover before it resulted in disaster. Warren's position was two miles along from Kohima on the way to Dimapur. From there his eight mountain guns, in constant contact with Yeo and his observers in Kohima, could devastate the Japanese as they formed up to attack.

The guns of the British 2nd Division also pounded the Japanese. Sergeant William 'Tug' Wilson, 16 Field Regiment, Royal Artillery, directed harassing fire on the Japanese positions. 'Harassing fire means you covered an area … If you hit something that's a benefit. One gun fired one round per minute. One degree left, then reverse and go the other way … We were firing over the whole area.' It was an effective method of keeping Japanese heads down and frustrating plans for attack.

At Jotsoma Warren had fought off several Japanese infantry attacks on his positions in the first week of April. By the second week he was nearly as isolated in the Jotsoma box as Laverty was at Kohima, although experiencing nothing like the same pressure from the Japanese. The 1/1 Punjab had driven the Japanese off a ridge east of Jotsoma, offering Warren a good vantage point of Kohima. His observers could now range the enemy positions with great accuracy. With some of the 2nd Division infantry already in the battle and other brigades arriving at Dimapur and pushing up the road the numerical odds were growing in favour of the British and Indians. But there was no sign of any weakening in Japanese determination. On 14 April as dawn broke a Japanese patrol broke into the 5 Brigade HQ area killing one man and wounding two. 'The Jap party then rushed through the area on to the hill above, from which they shouted "Come on up to us,"' a General's diary recorded. 'The Worcesters accepted this invitation and organised a pheasant drive with three Companies with which they cleared the Japs off the hill feature.' The following day Brigadier Hawkins received the welcome news that a jeep had arrived to collect him. It had been sent by Warren from Jotsoma. Sato's attempt to cut the link between Dimapur and Kohima had ended in failure. The road to 161 Brigade was open.

EIGHTEEN

Dreams Dying

Whenever they got ready to form up, the shells began to fall. Someone said to Lieutenant Hirayama that it looked as if the sky was vomiting fire on them. Shards of metal, dirt, stones, and lumps of flesh rained down. 'It was so very, very, loud the artillery.' The air pressure smashed the eardrums of men close to the blast. Blood ran from their ears. Hirayama saw body pieces fly into the air. They were not pieces of the living but of the dead who had been hastily buried in the previous days. Hirayama was back at Kohima after having been sent to Zubza to block the road. He was lying in a trench near Charles Pawsey's tennis court on the northern fringe of the garrison, a critical part of the steadily closing encirclement. Having driven the defenders off GPT Ridge, Jail Hill and Detail Hill, cut the roads in and out of Kohima, and placed artillery on the ridges overlooking the garrison, the Japanese felt Kohima must surely fall soon. Yet for all the ground they had made in the first week, the attackers were suffering heavy losses from the guns at Jotsoma and Zubza, and the close-quarter fighting on Detail Hill had been a savage and costly affair, as the experience of Captain Kameyama's company proved.

Every time they formed up for an attack, units were targeted by the distant guns. Lieutenant Hiroshi Yamagami lay flat on his stomach, face in the mud, as the shells landed. 'At the same time, the trench swung like an earthquake.' He and his battalion commander had been lying in the trench since the previous evening, pinned down by the guns. Yamagami poked his head up and looked with his field-glasses at the British lines. Some troops he took to be Gurkhas

286

were firing at the Japanese trenches. In that instant Yamagami felt a flash of hatred for the men trying to kill him. 'The battle of Kohima, life in a trench for forty days, had begun.'

During one night attack the company commander was looking for an enemy trench to attack. He made the mistake of firing a flare. The British spotted the light and within minutes shells were landing, gradually ranging in on the attacking group. 'It came to us step by step and subconsciously I jumped into a nearby trench. I did really well because it was so small!' Yamagami was amazed by the accuracy of the artillery and despaired of the slaughter. 'One group would attack and be targeted and be annihilated. Then another one would come up and the same thing would happen. Gradually in a single night an entire company would be gone.'

The supply officer from the 138th Regiment, Chuzaburo Tomaru, who had refused to behead a civilian during the war in China, was never the keenest of warriors; he was sure that if he moved from his trench the British would get him. Tomaru had already succeeded in obtaining a transfer out of a machine-gun company, because 'I had heard the rumour that soldiers in Machine Gun Company are easily targeted in the battle.' The artillery was like 'thunder and it felt as if one hundred of the guns were firing all at once', but Tomaru still had to deliver food to the forward trenches. At this point there was still rice to make into a ball for each man, and 'water dropwort' from the river instead of vegetables.* Tomaru felt anguish for the infantry. 'The men were so brave and patient. At one point I was hiding behind rocks with members of battalion HQ and I saw them go out in wave after wave and being killed again and again. Eventually I had no intention of fighting myself at all.'

Tomaru was an exception. Most of Lieutenant General Kotuku Sato's troops were still willing to die for their general and emperor on the slopes of Kohima. Dr Takahide Kuwaki, a medical officer with 124th Infantry Regiment, looked out across the desolate battlefield

---

* This plant is unlikely to have been 'water dropwort', which has several very poisonous species. It is more probable that Tomaru was referring to a form of watercress or wild parsley.

and felt his death would come soon. 'When I arrived there I thought "this is the place where I will do my best and I will give my life."' Unlike the 58th Regiment, which had fought a brutal battle at Sangshak, Kuwaki's 124th had had a comparatively easy progress to Kohima, although the hell of Guadalcanal was still vivid in the memories of veterans. For Kuwaki, entering battle for the first time, the regiment was the vanguard of an army dedicated to Japan's imperial expansion, a cause for which he would gladly be martyred. Yet visions of dying a glorious death for the empire were punctuated by the mundane business of pulling lice from his clothes. In quiet moments he would set the vermin to fight each other, a pastime the dark resonance of which evaded Kuwaki at the time. Expecting his death to come at any moment, the doctor wrote some death songs to be passed on to his children, imagining that his dynasty would endure forever, in prosperity.

> Children and grandchildren
> taking thousands of years
> to die in prosperity
> that is my eternal wish.

He believed that the Japanese only needed to hold on and keep the road closed between Imphal and Dimapur and the British would be starved out. The power of British air supply, and growing hunger in the Japanese lines, would eventually disabuse him of that notion.

Kawaki regarded the British as careful. There were no rash charges. 'They first fired the guns, then they sent observers, and only then did they attack.' For the men leading the attacks on the British trenches in the second week of April, the easy successes against the Nepalese Shere Regiment and other rear-section troops were forgotten in the face of fierce hand-to-hand fighting with the likes of the West Kents and the Assam Regiment. Lieutenant Togawa, a section commander with the 58th Regiment, was caught with his men in no-man's-land and decided to make a rush attack in the middle of the night. In the darkness he fell into a trench where he was set upon by several defenders. 'I hurried to draw off my sabre, but they gripped both my arms. One enemy [struck] my head, but I felt almost none for the sake of my iron hat.' Outnumbered in the trench, he thought that if he surrendered he would be made a prisoner of war. That would be far worse than death. Togawa managed to draw his sabre, which 'glittered in the moon', and all the defenders except one ran away. 'One so brave grappled with me,' he recalled. The men rolled 'up and down, again and again', with Togawa trying to drive home his blade. The Japanese proved stronger and he stabbed his opponent, who 'ceased to move and lay on his face'. The incident shocked Togawa, for he wrote of having to 'recover' his mind immediately afterwards. When he did, he realised shells were falling. One exploded nearby and sprayed him with searing metal fragments.

The man who had launched the 15th Army into India was still at his headquarters in Maymyo, replete with geishas and sake, and increasingly convinced of the uselessness of his generals on the distant battlefields. The commander of the 33rd Division, General Yanagida, would soon be sacked for his supposed faint-heartedness at Imphal; the ailing General Yamauchi, commander of 15th Division, was also bogged down outside the town and being cursed for his lack of vigour. Lieutenant Colonel Iwaichi Fujiwara, the intelligence officer who had done so much to prepare the way for the invasion, was piecing together a portrait of disunity which induced despair. 'The Army Comdr did NOT command the complete obedience of the 3 Comdrs of the Divs he had under his command.' Fujiwara had no idea how much worse things would get.

Years later, Mutaguchi would concede that his temper had been a problem. The staff officers were too afraid to speak their minds. But typically the general excused himself. 'In a long campaign when it was not working out well, a burst of my temper from time to time is inevitable.' Of his divisional commanders, Mutaguchi had scarcely a good word to say. Only the Kohima battle still held promise, but even here Mutaguchi had been stymied. The 58th Regiment had just arrived in Kohima when Mutaguchi signalled General Sato to strike on for Dimapur and capture the British supply base. In this, Mutaguchi's aggressive instincts were correct: he wanted Sato to do what Slim and Stopford feared most. 'I then gave the order to the 31st division leader by saying "Chase the withdrawing enemy immediately and move through to Dimapur." ... I thought that the necessary food for the division's soldiers and horses would be obtained by the attack of Dimapur.' But such a move would mean eventually coming into the open, where British air superiority would count. Mutaguchi signalled Lieutenant General Kawabe, commander of the Burma Area Army, for air support. Kawabe was horrified, as 'Dimapur was not within the strategic objectives of the 15 Army'. Mutaguchi was told, 'this is not good! Considering the overall situation please stop it.' Had Sato headed straight for Dimapur on 4 April he would have found the base still in a shambles with troops arriving by rail and air.*

From his office in Rangoon, the Burma Area Army chief could feel the Imphal campaign slipping away. The weather reports indicated that the monsoon might come earlier, raising the prospect of 15th Army being swamped and unable to receive supplies, even if sufficient food and ammunition could be found – a doubtful prospect, as Kawabe knew, with matters in the Pacific getting worse. Since the start of the year the Americans had dislodged the Japanese from island after island. The Marshall, Caroline, and Mariana islands had all been assaulted and the big Japanese base at Rabaul destroyed. There was no question of Kawabe persuading Tokyo to release aircraft to support the troops in India.

Kawabe had sent Mutaguchi into the mountains with instructions to get the campaign wrapped up before the monsoon. From the outset, Kawabe had always recognised the invasion as a gamble, but he counted on Mutaguchi's track record of energy, and luck and British ineptitude to see the enemy beaten before the rains. Now it was not only the weather that filled him with foreboding. The British were not fleeing, and their air superiority had astonished the Japanese infantry. Had

---

* This is the greatest of 'what ifs' of the invasion and what Stopford and Slim had feared most. An attack by 31 Division on Dimapur would have, at the least, thrown British plans into chaos.

Kawabe paid more attention to the fighting in the Arakan that had preceded the invasion of India, he would not have been so surprised.

Communications between 31st Division and 15th Army head-quarters were becoming increasingly difficult. Lieutenant General Sato's infantry commander, General Miyazaki, found that most of his wireless batteries became useless in the damp. Even without the monsoon, men were dying of disease and hunger-related illness, and 'heavy casualties – caused mostly by artillery' had depleted his ranks at Sangshak. Yet Miyazaki remained full of vim and would have struck for Dimapur had Kawabe not cancelled the orders. General Sato, however, remained convinced that he had been sent in the wrong direction from the start. Mutaguchi should have thrown all three divisions against Imphal to strike a crushing blow against 4th Corps. 'It was a huge mistake to have directed the force to Kohima.'

Still, at that early stage, on 6 April, Sato seems to have been ready to obey the order to go forward to Dimapur, in spite of his opposition in the past. Perhaps the prospect of capturing supplies for his men had changed his mind. For all his growing misgivings about the operation, Sato felt pride in his men's achievement in getting as far as Kohima, traversing a mountain wilderness the British did not believe could be crossed by a division. 'I believe that is something that is worth a special mention in the military history … Its achievement is great and gave the enemy the damage and casualties.'

After the first week of fighting at Kohima what worried Sato most was hunger. Already men were sick. Too little nourishment had reduced their resistance to disease. The doctors were treating endless cases of dysentery. As he had feared from the outset, Mutaguchi's promise of ten tons of supplies per day had not materialised. Fewer than a fifth of the cattle that crossed the Chindwin had reached the front line and mules were being consumed in their stead. This had a knock-on effect. Fewer mules meant delays in bringing ammunition and food up from supply dumps to front-line positions. Yet, by the second week of April, Sato still believed a victory at Kohima was possible. At any moment the garrison could be overrun by his troops. Once Kohima Ridge was entirely his, the British would have an almighty job pushing him off. He banked on capturing the remaining supply stores in Kohima and digging in for a long fight.

Sato could not have known the size of the British and Indian reinforcements coming up to meet him, nor could he have fully appreciated their superiority in firepower and supplies. Slim dismissed Sato as 'without exception, the most unenterprising of all the Japanese generals I encountered. His bullet head was filled with one idea only – to take Kohima ... he could by the 5th April, have struck the railway with the bulk of his division.' Slim told of how he had to dissuade some enthusiastic RAF officers from launching an air strike on Sato's headquarters. 'They were astonished when I suggested they abandon the project as I regarded their intended victim as one of my most helpful generals!' Slim was wrong. When he wrote those words after the war he could not have been aware of Kawabe's orders not to move on Dimapur. Nor did he understand the true nature of his adversary. Sato was not stupid. His reluctance to gamble was based on care for the men under his command. 'The priority is not to make impossible demands of the men,' he wrote. 'If you do ... each unit will get exhausted.' It was a fine aspiration but, as Sato himself knew by now, what was being asked of his men at Kohima was entering the realm of the impossible.

Kohima was the furious heart of the battle and on both sides men were enduring unimaginable privation. But beyond Kohima, among the hills and jungles, the war had also swept through the lives of the Naga tribespeople with the force of a monsoon storm. Several thousand had been driven from their villages and fled to refugee camps in Assam, but the flood of refugees and retreating troops from the Imphal plain posed an even greater problem. As many as 29,000 Manipuris had fled their homes in April 1944 to cross the hills and seek safety in Assam.*

---

* Official figures are imprecise. For the initial period of the invasion the Assam government recorded 8,060 people, including Nagas, Manipuris, Nepalis and Chins, uprooted from their homes. By September 1944, relief measures were still feeding approximately 12,000 Nagas and Manipuris. In addition, there were some 29,000 Manipuris listed as refugees. NA, WO 203/4504, Assam Notes, and SECRET Cable from BURON SHILLONG TO COMERL NEW DELHI.

Among them were the flotsam and jetsam of various Indian and Burmese units overrun by the Japanese. The guerrilla leader Ursula Graham Bower deployed her twenty-strong unit of Naga scouts, equipped with muzzle-loading rifles, to protect villages threatened by looters and army deserters. Villagers were being beaten, their women attacked and food stolen. 'Though the Nagas were giving every assistance, their only rewards were assaults and lootings. Villagers took to the woods, normal life came to a standstill; and as the tide spread westwards and reached us, it became increasingly hard to maintain order – the whole intelligence network was threatened.' Augmented by a patrol of Gurkhas and a V Force officer, Graham Bower set off for one village just occupied by thirty of these marauders. In less than an hour her force had successfully surrounded and captured the deserters. 'They went off under escort in a depressed file, elated Gurkhas marched ahead and behind and Zemi porters carrying the collected weapons in firewood-baskets.'

The V Force screen along the Chindwin had vanished with the Japanese advance. She had no wireless and therefore was dependent on a series of beacons that ran from the front and could be seen from different high points in her patrol area. If they were fired it meant trouble was coming. In the jungle, her scouts cut holes in the vegetation in which to sleep. 'We honey-combed the scrub with tunnels and little chambers beaten and cut out … no outsider ever knew where exactly in the wide spread of bushes we were hidden.'

In the villages close to Kohima there was a desolate atmosphere. The population was subject to shelling and the depredations of the increasingly desperate Japanese. Up to thirty people would cram into small huts in the jungle, believing they could find safety there. But even so, the Japanese followed and dragged men off to become porters. 'The Kohima men were so angry but flesh cannot fight steel,' recalled Krusischi Paschar from the Naga Village at Kohima. According to another Kohima man, Salhoutie Mechieo, who spent the siege behind British lines, there was an argument between the deputy commissioner, Charles Pawsey, and the army over the shelling of the Naga Village. 'DC kept saying not to burn down Kohima village but the army said Japanese will occupy the village and fight us. We have to burn down the houses. If we will win we will help rebuild them. So the army, although the DC tried to stop them ... burnt down our village.'

Krusischi Paschar saw people digging trenches to evade the British artillery fire. 'The Zubza cannons vomited terrible shells into Kohima, so that the people began to dig trenches to shelter them and hide their valuables in. The Zubza shells increased more and more, thus the people had to move to low sites and to take shelter in trenches ... Kohima village was burnt seven times altogether.' In the ruins of their villages, Nagas were confronted with the disaster that war had inflicted on the most vulnerable: babies trying to nurse at the bodies of their dead mothers, children made mute by the terror of explosions, and everywhere the stench of rotting bodies. When allied rations dropped behind Japanese lines, men would frantically scramble under fire to reach them. 'We fought for that,' one man remembered. 'When we go for biscuits we die. When they [Japanese] come, they also die.'

However, the Naga men continued to volunteer for service with the British. A pastor in the village of Tolloi, Phanit Phan, described how men slipped through the lines to carry maps of Japanese positions to the British. 'This was repeatedly done. Besides we used our own laid signals to the British planes (pilots) for ascertaining enemy targets ... their secret places were almost all bombed.' Rhizotta Rino from Jotsoma was one of those who carried out mapping for the British. He initially volunteered as a porter for Warren's 161 Indian brigade and led troops to water sources under cover of dark. 'I remember taking the British through the forest to where the water was and they would stay back while we went to the water's edge. They were afraid of being ambushed at the water by the Japanese. Why did we fight for the British? They were our protectors. They were here before the Japanese and they protected us. We had to help them!' The diaries of British officers refer to the courage of Naga guides and stretcher-bearers. As the fighting escalated throughout April, warriors began to arrive at British headquarters seeking weapons with which to fight the Japanese. Captain Arthur Swinson met a group who came to 5 Brigade headquarters. In his diary he marvels at their appearance, albeit in tones that can appear condescending to the modern eye. 'A fine group of men they were, with dark, smooth skinned limbs and a manly bearing ... Their dress was pretty, there's no other word for it. It consisted firstly of a short, tight fitting skirt of some rough black material, rather reminiscent of the flappers in their early hay-day [sic]. Their knees were covered by a series of bangles piled one over the other. Their torso was left quite bare though some older men wore bright red coatees ... Carmen Miranda herself was never more loaded with bangles, rings, necklaces, beads, ear-rings, charms, nick-nacks and ju ju ... to complete the picture was their jet black hair, cut pudding basin wise and decorated with flowers.' The warriors were given captured Japanese weapons. Swinson observed that as the British government would not allow them to 'scalp each other what an excellent opportunity [it was] for keeping their hand in by practising on the Japs'.

The commander of 2nd Division, General John Grover, found his own attitude to the Nagas changed by the experience of working with them. He was struck by their intelligence and their ability to read aerial photographs at first sight, as well as their good humour in frequently grim circumstances. 'They offer to take on any job, usually of an Intelligence nature, to visit some village behind Jap lines, or to provide porters or guides whenever required, and offer to do all this for nothing. We are insisting on paying them. One has been taught to regard the Nagas as savage head-hunters. Some of them are, but the great majority are extremely lovable.' Grover established a 'Naga reception centre' where tea and biscuits were given to locals arriving with intelligence about the Japanese.

In at least one infantry brigade there was a sliding scale of rewards for enemy taken dead or alive by the Nagas. Operational Instruction No. 10 for 23 Infantry Brigade (Chindits) ordered payments as follows:

Capture alive Japanese officer:	Rs1000
Captured other rank:	Rs500
Dead Jap officer:	Rs100

Dead other ranks:	Rs50
Live hostile individual other than Jap:	Rs75
Dead individual other than Jap:	Rs25

In a frank statement of military priorities, the family of a Naga killed in action would be paid just 300 rupees, less than a third of what was paid for a live Japanese officer, whose worth as an intelligence asset was highly valued.

The schoolteacher Khumbo Angami escaped from Kohima and became an interpreter with 23 Infantry Brigade, a Chindit formation that had been detailed to guard the railway and gradually to move across the Japanese line of communications. Khumbo Angami rounded up eight other Nagas, including his brother, and set off into the jungle with the Chindits. He would be gone for three months. Any suspected enemy found by this group were to be held and questioned. A Bengali prisoner, suspected of belonging to the INA, twice attempted to escape. He had no hope of evading the Naga in the jungle, and would find the quality of their mercy strained. 'They started very early in the morning and found him in the jungle at about 12 o'clock at noon. But as soon as the Nagas saw him he threw stones at them, but the Nagas went boldly on and caught him, but he bit them and tried to run away so they chopped his head into two pieces.'

The most important function of the Naga tribes was as intelligence-gatherers. Ursula Graham Bower knew of two men who had gone into Japanese service, posing as simple-minded rustics, but had managed to steal valuable maps. With all the European V Force operatives dead, captured or in hiding, and the RAF's aerial photography of limited value in jungle terrain, the Nagas provided the only reliable flow of intelligence to 2nd Division on Japanese movements around Kohima. One thread remained consistent in all of their information. The Japanese were short of food. All the villages still occupied were reporting Japanese foraging parties seeking rice and livestock. But they were also well dug in on the ridges and hills at Kohima. They did not appear as if they intended to retreat any time soon.

NINETEEN

The Black Thirteenth

They called it the morning hate and the evening hate. It came without fail. The Japanese gunners could see them clearly. The wounded lay in shallow trenches on the slope. The tree cover had been destroyed by shelling. All the artillery had to do was to fire over open sights. The wounded could not move. So they listened for the sound of the shell firing. But the distance was so close that it had often exploded among them by the time the sound arrived. The mortars, too, arrived without any warning, dropping soundless until the moment of impact. Once it started, the wounded pulled the blankets up over their faces, like children terrorised by the dark.

Men were killed or rewounded. Bits of bodies flew into the air. Frank 'Doc' Infanti, the medical orderly with the West Kents, thought the wounded were safer in their own trenches. 'If a bloke got wounded and they shouted out "stretcher-bearers" as they used to, we would go down, dress him and he was safer left in his own trench than bringing him back up.' Even there, you could not be sure. Two of Infanti's own section were killed by mortars that dropped right on the parapet. Up at the ADS he ran into Major Shaw, the former commander of C company, who had been wounded in the attack on Detail Hill. Shaw was lying in a shallow trench with a fractured femur and several shrapnel wounds. 'I marvelled at how he lay there for the whole two weeks completely helpless, but always cheerful.' In fact, Infanti's lasting memory of the wounded was of their stoicism. 'They tried so hard not to moan or to cry out even though you knew they were in agony.'

297

By 10 April, Lieutenant Colonel John Young of 75th Indian Field Ambulance had two hundred casualties at the ADS. They lay with the smell of the dead upon them. For the most part, men rotted where they had been killed. Anybody going out to collect bodies was a target for snipers. 'Oh my God, the stink of those dead bodies!' recalled the wounded Bruce Hayllar. Too many sentences use the words 'cloying' or 'sickly sweet' to describe the smell of death. Nobody who has ever walked a battlefield could believe that. The corpse is a dead animal. It reeks of the knacker's yard. If the smell sits in the air around you long enough, you start feeling the rot is part of the lining of your skin, it sticks in your nose and mouth, as if death has partly claimed you. Take a lot of corpses and stick them in a wilderness of unburied excrement, add kerosene, cordite, stagnant water, the reek of hundreds of frightened men, stick all that in one small place and you have the smell of Kohima.

Up at the ADS, Young and his surgeons knew all the variations of rot by now. The bodies that that had been killed in the previous twenty-four hours, the ones that had been out there for a week and more; they knew how the different kinds of wounds looked when the field-dressings were peeled away, how gas gangrene stank as it worked its way remorselessly through living tissue, and how men with dysentery reeked as their strength leaked away. Gas gangrene thrived in the filthy conditions of Kohima and untreated it could kill within forty-eight hours. It is so called because of the gas blisters that form around the infected area; the wound changes colour from red to a blackish green, and the stricken man sweats profusely and feels acute anxiety. He is denied the relief of unconsciousness. Often he will be fully alert until shock brings on a coma and finally his kidneys fail.

Young and his fellow surgeons saw and smelled all of this in the two pits that served as operating theatres. They worked with only the briefest of pauses for rest. The pits were roughly six feet deep. Across one of them the Indian pioneers had constructed a timber roof; the other was protected from the elements, and from Japanese fire, by nothing more substantial than a piece of canvas. Inside the pits, flickering hurricane lamps lit the faces and hands of the surgeons and orderlies as they worked. One of Young's doctors wrote in his diary of 'Shocking wounds … terrible casualties … awful nights.' Clouds of flies settled over the dead or busied themselves on the wounds of the living. The rain swamped wounded men in their trenches, leaving them shivering in sodden clothes and lying in an ooze of mud and body fluids.

Lieutenant Bruce Hayllar, wounded in the fight for Jail Hill, was an early arrival at the ADS and remained there throughout the siege. He felt relieved to be with others who had been wounded and were still alive. They drew hope from each other's presence. There were British and Indian men lying together. 'We felt very close to each other. Whether you were a Christian or a Muslim or anything we used to pray together and help each other. It didn't matter what you were.' The most extraordinary moment of Hayllar's war came when a wounded Japanese soldier was placed next to him. The man had been captured in the battle on Detail Hill. Because Hayllar was an officer he was told to look after him. 'I remember that man. He was just like us. He was just my age, about nineteen or something, and he wasn't responsible. He could not talk. He lay under my blanket with me. We knew we were trying to help each other but that was it.' The soldier died later that night. Hayllar read 'the whole of St John's Gospel' from a pocket Bible his parents had given him and passed the holy book on to the men in the pit with him.

The other wounded were an eclectic mix of imperial soldiery. There was a seventeen-year-old Naga called Isaiah who had run away from an American mission school to join the Assam Regiment; an English officer called Hammon, blinded in one eye; a Rajput who, despite his thirst, would not drink after another person had used the cup; an old havildar of eighteen years' service; and a Jemadar* of the stretcher-bearers who 'was always grinning'. The Jemadar only broke down once, when an exhausted Young rounded on him over some mishap.

The men were visited by Charles Pawsey, Hugh Richards, or the West Kents' padre, Roy Randolph. On Easter Sunday, Randolph

---

* A rank in the Indian Army, equivalent to Lieutenant.

performed a swift service, as Hayllar recalled, 'because we were constantly under fire and lots of people were dying'. Hayllar was able to receive Holy Communion. The Reverend Randolph, a man who loathed war or any kind of violence, would always be haunted by the experience of Kohima, as his son, Roy junior, remembered. 'All he would say is he did his best to comfort the wounded and the rewounded and the dying. The memories were too painful for him to be able to talk about.'

Randolph believed that too little was being done to relieve the suffering of the wounded. A writer who met the West Kents' CO Laverty afterwards wrote that he and his staff found it 'even harder to bear because the responsibility for it rested on their shoulders and they were in no way free to show their emotions; if they did they would soon succumb and the battle ... would be lost'. Randolph wanted the wounded moved to a proper hospital, but it was out of the question now. He was able to comfort Major Shaw of the West Kents by bringing him a Bible, which he read throughout the siege.

The C company runner Ray Street, who had to race between his company position and Laverty's headquarters, took comfort in his faith. He had a strip of paper with a piece of writing from St John. 'Let not your heart be troubled neither let it be afraid.' Running to deliver messages, Street prayed frantically. 'I had to leave the trench to deliver messages. I had to deliver a message where a hand just came out of the trench from under a tin sheet and grabbed the message. One said, "Come on, Streetie, don't hang about too long. Keep moving."' Battle tends to bring out the superstitious and god-fearing side in even the most sceptical of men. Mementoes of home, lucky charms, are grasped close in the fury of combat. Street met a corporal who was helping to move some wounded but was upset because he had lost a teddy bear given to him by his wife. 'She told him that while he had this bear he would be safe.' The man was killed by a Japanese shell. The eternally pragmatic Street decided he would not hold on to any 'lucky' mascots.

Fifty-six wounded men were killed outright by Japanese shelling and many more died later of their fresh wounds. By night Indian non-combatants drafted in as orderlies carried the dead to a makeshift burial ground where they were hastily interred. Frequently Japanese shelling unearthed the corpses. The events of these hours were systematically recorded by Young, or one of his orderlies, in the battalion war diary. On 12 April the diary recorded that sixty casualties had been rewounded and ten killed. Three more men died later in the day. The following morning, on what survivors would always call the 'Black Thirteenth', the ADS was 'very heavily mortared and shelled, resulting in the deaths of casualties already under treatment and in rewounding approximately 30 more'. Twenty-one men were killed where they lay. Just after dawn, a salvo had rained down on the ADS area which lasted for an hour, an unimaginably long time to lie in the open under bombardment. The operating pit took four direct hits. The doctors took what cover they could but two Indian officers, Captains M. Y. Siddiqi and Abdul Majid Chaudry, Indian Army Medical Corps, were mortally wounded and John Young was slightly hurt. When the shelling stopped, there were body parts mingled with the medical equipment and all the other detritus of the dressing station was cast among the still-living, who lay distraught with terror in their trenches. Immediately Young's deputy, Captain F. R. Glover, set about clearing up the mess with his orderlies.

By 1530 hours the ADS was back in action. But two hours after that, the shells came in again. There were thirty direct hits over the area in which the patients lay. Ten were killed and many more rewounded. Yet another doctor was killed and one seriously wounded. That night, after having listened to the screams of the wounded and dying all day, Captain Glover wrote in his diary of 'a terrible day ... the preservation of human life appears useless. Our operations very unsuccessful, most of them dying on the table or very shortly afterwards.' Three of Young's seven doctors were killed during the siege and another badly wounded. Patients were dying of post-operative shock because there were too few nurses to care for them.

The 4th West Kents' medical orderly, Frank Infanti, remembered helping Young to perform an amputation by night in a trench away from the main pit. A blanket had been placed on poles over the trench to protect the wounded man from the elements, and to ensure that the Japanese could see no light. Infanti held the torch while another West Kent held the man's leg. Young administered anaesthetic from a bottle. 'Follow the knife, follow the knife,' Infanti was told. The thin beam stayed with the blade as it cut through muscle and bone. 'It was as if we were living a hundred years ago,' said Infanti. 'I don't think anybody who had their legs amputated survived.'

Young had enough anaesthetic and dressings left, but he had no plasma and there was a constant crisis over water. Within two days of reaching Kohima, and just as Laverty had feared, the Japanese had found and quickly severed the water pipeline from Aradura Spur. A small stream of water still seeped through, but the tanks and canvas balloons that made up the emergency supply were targeted by shelling and thousands of gallons leaked away. It was six days since Hugh Richards had issued his order restricting each man to what amounted to a pint of water per day and forbidding washing and shaving.* His staff officer, Walter Greenwood, had limited the intake in the command bunker to three quarters of a mug of tea in the morning and the same in the evening. Lieutenant Colonel Young's war diary records: 'During the night enemy captured D.C.'s bungalow area, water point now under fire. Water situation serious since could only be collected & drawn at night by amb. sepoys of 75 Ind Fd Ambulance, the remaining personnel at the ADS proving unreliable under fire.'

Laverty's second-in-command, Major Peter Franklin, took control of managing the water supply. He enjoyed a better relationship with Richards than did his boss. A roster was drawn up for the different units, which worked in relays, with priority given to the ADS. The water point was six hundred yards from the headquarters area and to reach it men had to negotiate a 300 foot drop, before returning heavily laden. The most anybody could manage to carry was two gallons. The source was little more than thirty yards from the Japanese, 'and

---

* Richards refers to a pint per day, while other sources refer to a half-pint.

men had to crawl forward singly to fill containers'. A second water point was found near the spur that overlooked the road to Dimapur, but again the Japanese were nearby and supplies could only be drawn at night. Private Leslie Crouch of the West Kents' pioneer platoon spent night after night edging his way down to the water stand. 'We had rifles protecting us but carrying two cans of water you couldn't do much … others went purely for defence. You had to go two or three times a night.' The Indian non-combatants helping the wounded were restricted to drinking the juice from the ample supplies of tinned peas and fruit taken from garrison stores.

The situation in and around Richards's bunker became increasingly crowded as the siege wore on. Walter Greenwood saw the number of men he was responsible for feeding rise from around thirty to seventy in a few days. He needed fifteen gallons of water per day for this number, but could fetch only ten. The surplus was made up by the generosity of the West Kents' water teams, with a promise from Greenwood that he would repay the favour when he could. Life inside the perimeter was governed by the overriding imperative of keeping under cover: there was not a single piece of open ground that the Japanese did not overlook. The garrison was spied on by malevolent and ever-watchful eyes. The headquarters area bunkers were all approximately five feet deep, eight feet wide and the same across. On top there were timbers and about two feet of earth to absorb blasts.

Hugh Richards regularly left the comparative safety of his bunker to visit men in their trenches, as did Charles Pawsey, who made his rounds 'in a trilby hat with an umbrella and two Naga spearmen as his escort'. Major Donald Easten was struck by Richards's courage. 'He was an old man compared to us … It was great if you were in our position to see a senior officer who was willing to face the same dangers.' Every morning Richards climbed the hill to Laverty's bunker, noting with characteristic understatement that it was a 'quite unpleasant' journey, with snipers constantly active. There they discussed the overnight reports. It was an improvement from the total distance which existed between them at the start of the siege. Yet despite the fraught circumstances, the men never bonded. Laverty kept to his bunker and was not seen in the trenches, leaving the work of encouraging the exhausted troops to Richards, Major Franklin and the company commanders. This had nothing to do with lack of courage. One of Laverty's staff, Captain Douglas Short, who spent the siege cooped up with the CO, believed his strength was as a tactical commander. He had nerves of steel, but if Laverty was shot dead in the trenches he would be of little use to his men. 'He was a fine soldier and tactics were his thing. My view is that he knew the tactical side of things and Richards didn't.' The voice of a calm CO giving orders at the end of a field telephone can be just as much use to a company commander under fire as any morale-boosting appearance in the trenches.

With supplies of water and plasma running dangerously low, Hugh Richards signalled to Warren, via Laverty's radio, for an air drop. He added grenades and 3 inch mortar ammunition to the shopping list. When the drop came, the American Dakota pilots missed the target and dropped the ammunition on to the Japanese lines. The mortar shells were quickly fired back at the garrison, using captured British mortars. A second drop by the RAF brought more ammunition but it was intended for Warren's guns at Jotsoma and useless to the Kohima garrison. When a third run succeeded in dropping water, much of it caught in the trees and the metal cans were riddled by Japanese bullets. Some containers smashed to the ground in no-man's-land and the defenders watched their supplies leak into the ground; others crashed on to and killed some Indian soldiers. The staff officer, Captain Walter Greenwood, reckoned that only 50 per cent of the parachutes fell in areas controlled by the garrison. The remainder fell equally in no-man's-land and in the Japanese lines. But some of the medical supplies from the first drop did survive. After dark, Young went with a party of non-combatants and recovered enough of them to alleviate the situation at the ADS. Patients were given morphine and gas gangrene serum.

Making his inspection of the positions, Colonel Hugh Richards was worried about the men's morale. The West Kents and the Assam Regiment had both held their ground until it was impossible to do so; other units of composite troops, with the exception of the Shere Regiment, had fought better than anybody had expected. But after the events of the Black Thirteenth, Richards sensed that the moment had come for some public affirmation of the garrison. He went to see Laverty, who suggested Richards issue a special order of the day. Crouched in his bunker, Richards dictated the message to his clerk, who duly typed out a copy for each unit and gave it to the runners. Richards's voice was firm and confident: 'By your acts you have shown what you can do. Stand firm, deny him every inch of ground … put your trust in God and continue to hit the enemy hard wherever he may show himself. If you do that his defeat is sure.'

While the fierce battles for GPT Ridge, Jail Hill and Detail Hill had been taking place between 5 and 13 April, the Japanese had started an assault in the area around Charles Pawsey's bungalow. If they could break through here, the garrison and West Kent headquarters, and Young's ADS, would be next in line. Taking Garrison Hill would give Sato command of Kohima Ridge and make resistance futile. Already, the scene on the hill was becoming chaotic. In addition to the wounded, there were upwards of 1,500 scared non-combatants milling around.

From his position, Lieutenant John Faulkner could hear shooting coming from the bungalow. Between Faulkner's trench and Pawsey's bungalow was a distance of about 230 yards. The route dropped down the hill in a succession of terraces. If the bungalow went, the Japanese would have to climb about thirty-five feet to the next terrace, where trenches had been dug at the edge of the tennis court. Lieutenant Faulkner was experiencing the mental shock of battle for the first time. His body trembled 'like a leaf' as he climbed out of the trench. In just three minutes, forty mortar shells landed in his platoon area on the hill. One of them hit the lip of his dugout. Faulkner steadied himself and went around the position. Astonishingly, only two men had been wounded: one had a shell splinter in his back, another had an eye full of dust thrown up by an exploding shell. In his handwritten account of what followed,

Faulkner headlined this chapter 'Three Day Nightmare'. Down at the bungalow a composite group of British troops, about two hundred men in all, were dug in around Pawsey's garden of rhododendrons and cannas. These were mostly older soldiers, who were part of a reinforcement camp at Kohima, and some artillerymen unable to use their mountain guns. The Japanese came sweeping up from the roadway. The defenders fought hand to hand but were eventually driven up the slope by the sheer weight of numbers. There were counter-attacks by Assam and Burma Regiment platoons. The bungalow changed hands three times in the course of the day, but by its end the Japanese were ensconced. The tennis court area became the new perimeter. Here the defenders and the Japanese faced each other in trenches across a patch of ground no more than twenty yards wide. One British soldier left behind on the Japanese side played dead until dark, trampled on by enemy in his trench, until he could jump up and run to the British lines.

Now came Lieutenant Faulkner's turn to lead. A company was sent to restore the situation at the bungalow. The rain poured down as they climbed out of their trenches and crept forward. At the tennis court, one platoon occupied the clubhouse, a little shack of brick and wood on the right-hand side, while the others took up positions along the centre and left. The composite troops who had been pushed back earlier in the day immediately attached themselves to the West Kents. For Faulkner, the morning was ominously quiet. He had the sense of plans taking shape that could involve his death or maiming. At 1300 hours the ground exploded. The mortars killed several men immediately. The dead were wrapped in blankets and laid in front of the trenches, 'until we could find time to give them holes'. Any time one of A company tried to climb along the top of the ridge to Laverty's headquarters, a sniper opened up. A light machine gun fired at anything that moved along the path down to the A company positions. Three hours after the first bombardment came a second. Faulkner was lucky. He had picked an abandoned bunker for his position. It had been well made. A direct hit caused no damage. It was the sniper and machine gun that were causing most casualties.

By the end of the day, A company had abandoned the idea of running messages and a phone line was laid to Laverty at headquarters after dark. A third barrage came in after 1900 hours. Faulkner felt that the shelling was building towards something. Three hours later they came.

'A hell of a din arose from the tennis court.' The forward sections went through boxes of grenades 'like butter' and the Bren guns sizzled. After half an hour the shooting stopped. Faulkner went forward to see what had happened. He bumped into a Sergeant Bennett, 'coming back like a young bullock that had seen red'. The NCO was desperate. He shouted at Faulkner: 'For Christ's sake let me have a section quick or they'll be through us.' The lieutenant ran to his position, grabbed four men and led them back to the NCO, skirting around the line of fire of a Japanese machine gun. Within a few seconds one of the replacements had been shot in the neck. The wounded man was carried back to Faulkner's bunker but immediately got up to go back into the line. 'Where the hell are you going?' Faulkner demanded. 'Back with Ferguson. The poor kid's alone with that gun and it needs two,' he replied. Faulkner found another man to go forward.

Lance Corporal Dennis Wykes was also dug in with A company at the tennis court. In old age, his heart would still quicken as he described the Japanese attack. 'They came howling and screaming and full of go. It was terrifying but the only good thing was the screaming let you know where they were coming from and so we got our lines of fire right and mowed them down. Wave after wave we cut them down with machine guns. I didn't know if I was killing one or a dozen. I just swept the machine gun through 'em and that was it.'

Wykes shared his trench with a boy called Williams from Wales. He was one of a draft of about twenty Royal Welch Fusiliers brought in as replacements to augment the West Kents. One day, during a lull, they were talking about food. 'I said to this lad Williams, "Oh, I'm hungry. I think I know where I can get some biscuits." So he said, "Yeah, I could do with something to eat." I'd only got about ten foot away from the trench when this shell came in.' Wykes was blown on to the ground. He looked up and saw a large cloud of smoke. Scrambling back to the trench he saw Williams lying on his back. He had been hit in the stomach; it was a death wound and Williams and Wykes both knew it. The boy grabbed Wykes's arm and cried out. '"Don't let me die. Don't let me die." And I thought, "Oh god, I can't stop you from dying, mate."' Wykes kept telling him that things would be all right. He shouted for medical help, but Williams died soon after arriving at the ADS. Another Welsh soldier, Walter Williams, heard the screaming. 'I will always remember a young Welsh boy, no more than nineteen, with his tummy hanging out calling out to his mother in Welsh. "Taffy," he says, "Taffy," he says, "I want my mother. I'm very lost" … with half his tummy out.'

Another soldier, Mark Lambert, who had worked as an assistant in a gentlemen's outfitter's store before the war, kicked and punched at the men who came for him; he used his rifle as a hammer to smash in Japanese skulls. 'You don't forget that kind of thing. From both sides we were animals.' Lambert drank heavily during the siege. 'More often than not I was tanked up with rum. I was section leader and I persuaded the men that rum was not good for them.' He offered to do the dawn guard duty in return for the men's rum ration. Lambert never thought of home. He mentally disowned his family because thinking about them brought too much pain. Only later would he find out that his younger brother in the navy had been killed off the Italian coast in 1942.

At the tennis court a battle of attrition had begun. Separated by only twenty yards, defender and attacker settled into sniping and throwing grenades, punctuated by Japanese wave attacks. A Japanese soldier who stood up in the early dawn light, believing he was out of sight, was promptly killed by a batman from A company. Much of the greatest damage was done by the artillery firing from Jotsoma under the direction of Yeo and his observers. The men in the forward trenches would hear the Japanese forming up for an attack on the terrace below the tennis court. It took all of Yeo's skill to avoid disaster and bring 'fire down on call on any sector at incredibly short distances in front of our own troops'. Everybody in the battalion remembered what had happened to B company at the tunnels in the Arakan.

The Japanese replied in kind, as Faulkner recorded: 'At 6 p.m. the Jap did his damndest to blow us clean off the whole spur. To use an Americanism, he threw everything at us except the kitchen stove.' Mortar rounds and shells from the 75 millimetre guns came screaming in. Faulkner's bunker shook from near misses. He sat with one hand on the telephone, a cigarette in the other, 'smoking furiously and trying to think of my girlfriend at home'. Another officer was sobbing uncontrollably. Two others played cards, forcing their minds to concentrate on something other than the fear of dying. Suddenly a soldier dashed in and began to scream about people being killed, 'completely off his rocker'. The phone was blown to pieces by the shock waves of the next blast. Faulkner was terrified. 'No man can be brave at times like that.' His most trusted NCO, Sergeant Deacon, stumbled into the bunker. 'He looked awful. His face was white and he couldn't say anything – just looked at me.' At that moment the roof took a direct hit. Dust flooded the interior and the beams sagged. But Faulkner's luck held. The bunker did not collapse. There was a long silence, or so it seemed to Faulkner as he watched the dust float to the ground. The sergeant spoke up. 'George Mann's dead. Heaney's badly wounded. York is shell shocked, and Stuart has buggered off. His nerve went. There's only Laver left now.' Faulkner realised that there was now a gap to his right. The shell-shocked soldier got up and went over to the sergeant. Together they left the bunker and went back to the trench on the right. A wounded man who had been resting in the bunker followed them. In this way the gap was filled. Later, Laverty sent a message to A company. 'Bloody good show!' He promised they would be relieved the following day. The exhausted men fought off two more assaults before John Winstanley's B company came to relieve them. The ground around their position was littered with broken weapons. Faulkner waited until the last of his men were gone and then raced up the hill after them, imagining the snipers taking a bead on his back. 'I ran so fast up the track that I must have been within an ace of shitting my trousers.'

Lieutenant Tom Hogg was preparing to take over the positions vacated by A company. Hogg was one of only two remaining officers under Major John Winstanley. The others were dead or wounded. The positions at the tennis court were by now very precarious. The Japanese controlled not only the bungalow area but had infiltrated snipers into some cherry trees overlooking the West Kents' positions above the court. The Japanese attacked three times on the night of 12 April, showering the defenders' trenches with grenades as they came. Heavy mortar fire from B company helped drive them back. During one of the assaults Hogg had a moment of blind terror. He watched a dozen Japanese race towards his position in the centre, but when he raised his automatic rifle it jammed. A Japanese reached the edge of the trench and stabbed at him. The blade caught in Hogg's webbing belt. There was just time to recock the weapon and empty an entire magazine into the attacker. The others swept past his trench and engaged John Winstanley's position further back. B company held on, but casualties were mounting. Tom Hogg was saved when one of his NCOs sheltered him from a grenade, taking the full blast of shrapnel into his back. A Bren-gunner in one of the forward positions, right on the edge of the tennis court, survived repeated assaults by Japanese coming from just twenty yards away, before eventually being killed by a sniper.

Walter Williams was twenty-two years old, an apprentice plumber from Caernarvon, and already married. He was manning a Bren gun in a trench at the clubhouse. He and his partner fired into a dense mass of men coming from just a few yards away. The gun barrel glowed red in the darkness. Eventually it seized up and some Japanese who had crept around the clubhouse attacked. Williams's partner was bayoneted and killed. Men were jabbing and striking. Williams grabbed a spade and jumped out of the trench to confront the Japanese. A soldier stabbed him with a bayonet and the blade sliced through his cheek and out of his nose. Enraged, Williams hacked at the enemy, using his spade like an axe. 'That made me worse. Now I was very agile and tough in those days and I killed the chap that bayoneted my friend and I walloped one or two of the

310

others and they ran away.' Williams threw grenades after the fleeing men. He was taken to the ADS to have the bayonet wound treated. As he was being treated, a shell came in and killed the doctor attending him. 'I must have a cat's life really,' he said.

The ADS was again hit by shelling just after dawn on 14 April and two casualties on whom Young had performed amputations were killed. A dugout with ten casualties received a direct hit, blowing to pieces everybody in it. Again, the process of dressing the rewounded and freshly wounded began. By 0930 hours a new ADS had been built. This one was 10 feet long by 6 feet deep, with a 'splinter-proof roof', and proved its robustness by taking a direct hit with little damage. Around midday Young lost one of his doctors to what the war diary calls 'nervous exhaustion'. In the circumstances, it is extraordinary that only one man on the medical team is recorded as having succumbed.

That same day, as he waited to be relieved, Major John Winstanley looked out at the dead piled on the tennis court. 'Somehow we hung on. The stench was terrible. The [Kohima] perimeter even to begin with was only hundreds of yards rather than miles and day by day as more and more shrinkage took place the place was just littered with our own and Jap bodies.' As a regimental historian put it, 'two days in this area was thought to be long enough', and B company was pulled out and replaced by a company of the Assam Regiment. Tom Hogg counted what was left of his platoon. Himself and two other men. On 14 April, after nine days of fighting, the Royal West Kents' strength had been reduced from around 444 to fewer than three hundred men, while the garrison as a whole had lost four hundred. With the fall of GPT Ridge, Jail Hill and Detail Hill, and the infiltration of the bungalow sector, the perimeter had now been reduced to roughly 500 by 500 yards. Word came through on 15 April from Warren at Jotsoma that relief could be expected in two days. All the garrison needed to do was hold on for that dangerous interval and they would be saved.

Richards and Young began making plans for the evacuation of the wounded. Word leaked down to the men in the trenches. Something like hope began to trickle through the lines. Some of the older hands were worried about the effect of raised expectations. 'It was only snippets I heard from the Coy Commander,' recalled CSM Bert Harwood of C company. 'I didn't tell the men ... we were getting low in numbers anyway ... it was best really to keep it to yourself ... it would upset the morale ... to think you might get relieved ... You knew that they were so near and yet so far ... You were thinking to yourself, "oh god, how much longer?"' Private Leonard Brown, who faced the Japanese on the tennis court, recalled that there were messages from Colonel Laverty. 'Every day Danny Laverty, the Colonel, said, "Hang on, if you let go India is falling" and day after day ... we got the same reply coming back from the old man, "Hang on there [2nd Division] breaking through."' Major Calistan of the 1st Assam Regiment wearily noted that 'we were continually hearing of 161 Bde coming up to relieve us, then 2 Div. being only 10 miles away, then tanks could be seen and so on, but as each day went by and still no reinforcements came up, we did not think there could be any truth in all these stories'. Havildar Sohevu Angami was among the Assam troops relieving the West Kents. As he made his way down the slope to the tennis court a sniper round whipped past. It killed Major James Askew instantly. The havildar was grimly fatalistic about the death. 'I saw him being killed. He was giving us orders and going up and down and that is when they got him. I accepted it as the thing that will happen to you in the army. If your time will come it will come.' Eight other Assam soldiers were killed or wounded. An officer moving into his position at the tennis court found several men leaning on the parapet in firing positions. He ordered them to move and then he pushed one. There was no response. They were all dead.

TWENTY

A Question of Time

General Stopford was buoyed by the good news. On 14 April he received a report from the 2nd Division commander, General Grover, 'who thinks it may be possible to push on quickly tomorrow to clear up the whole situation at Kohima'. Ever mindful of the political pressure to wrap up the battle, Stopford took the news at face value. But Grover's report was a considerable overstatement and at odds with what Hawkins of 5 Brigade had told him a few days before. Was Grover attempting to placate a superior whom he knew was anxious for swift progress? It is hard to imagine that he thought a swift victory was likely in the circumstances, with 4 and 6 Brigades of 2nd Division still deploying forward from Dimapur and the Japanese invested so strongly at Kohima. All the evidence pointed to a battle of attrition.

Had Stopford spoken to the troops working their way through the thick jungle towards Kohima, he might have come to a different appreciation. Brigadier Victor Hawkins described how a column he was leading became dispersed in the mountains. 'We were now split into four parties. I was alone with ten unarmed men. It was getting on for daylight and I hadn't the faintest notion where I was or how much farther we had to go. There was only one alternative and that was to keep going and hope that other people would do the same and that eventually we should all join up again.' Hawkins was lucky. His group was reunited later that day. But the going was slow for troops who had never operated in a mountain environment before. Ron Thomas, a runner with 1 Royal Welch Fusiliers, 6 Brigade, marched for two hours through the jungle to find his unit. They were watching for Japanese trying to cut behind the advancing forces. Thomas was the son of a coal-miner from Wrexham and was working in a steel works when war broke out. He had just come from jungle training in India, but the thickness of the foliage here terrified him. 'It is very seldom that you get a clearing and when you are walking knowing that there is some enemy in front, you are looking at every tree! You're on pins.'

Lieutenant Geoffrey Page of the 1/8 Lancashire Fusiliers, 4 Brigade, led small patrols which spied on the Japanese lines of communication around Kohima. 'It was terrible. I was frightened to death most of the time. You spent your time with a platoon or just two or three chaps, miles behind the Jap lines. You get terrified. When I got back to the unit I broke down and cried. It was the mental strain and stress and the relief when you got back. Some patrols lasted a few hours ... the worst one of all lasted all day because we were several miles to the east of where we were spying on the lines of communication and on three separate occasions we were within a whisker of walking into Japanese.' Another Fusilier remembered the jungle quiet being broken by the sound of Japanese banging tins, and shouting: 'Hey! Johnny, are you there?'

For troops new to the hills there were other surprises. Keith Halnan of the Signals thought it would be a good idea if they were to bed down in some abandoned Naga huts. 'This was a great mistake. There were mosquitoes and rats and there were bloodsucking leeches.' Sitting among his comrades, Halnan found himself privately objecting to their foul smell, until he realised that he was smelling himself.

The British and Indian forces were edging closer to Kohima. With the road open to Warren at Jotsoma, General Stopford sent the newly arrived 6 Infantry Brigade up to join the relief effort. That would mean both 4 and 6 Brigades advancing to Kohima, while Hawkins and 5 Brigade held their present positions and deployed along the road to stop any Japanese attempts at encirclement. The artillery, tank and anti-tank components of 2nd Division were also

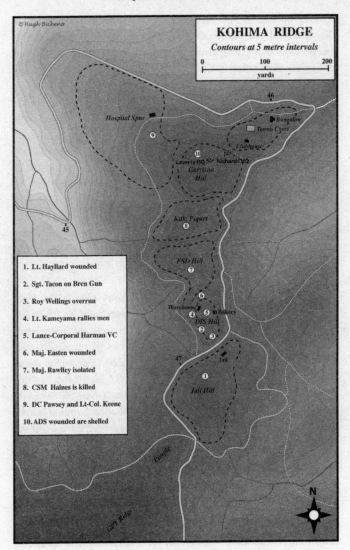

© Hugh Bicheno

KOHIMA RIDGE

Contours at 5 metre intervals

0   100   200
yards

46

Hospital Spur

Bungalow
Tennis Court

9

Clubhouse

10

Laverty HQ   Richards' HQ

*Garrison
Hill*

45

Kuki Piquet

8

FSD Hill

7

6

Warehouse   5   Bakery

4

DIS Hill

2   3

47   Jail

1

Jail Hill

1. Lt. Hayllard wounded

2. Sgt. Tacon on Bren Gun

3. Roy Wellings overrun

4. Lt. Kameyama rallies men

5. Lance-Corporal Harman VC

6. Maj. Easten wounded

7. Maj. Rawlley isolated

8. CSM Haines is killed

9. DC Pawsey and Lt.-Col. Keene

10. ADS wounded are shelled

Jungle

GPT Ridge

N

arriving to add to the pressure on the Japanese. The threat to Dimapur had been extinguished, although Stopford still feared it was possible that the Japanese general might try to cut the railway, halting supplies going to China and infuriating the Americans. The 23rd Long Range Penetration Group (Chindits) and 1st battalion of the Queen's Royal Regiment patrolled at different points along the line. Major Michael Lowry of the 1st Queen's rode with a mobile column in a specially armoured train into which were crammed eighty-four mules, the troops of the 1st Queen's and a mountain artillery battery. Passing over a series of bridges, 'nine or ten of which were unprotected', he noted how 'there was nothing to prevent a few men of an enemy fighting patrol blowing one up, or even several, or perhaps the enemy might hold a vital bridge area in strength, covered from the jungle hills'. Lowry need not have worried. The time for such an initiative had passed. Sato would not be moving anywhere.

At General Sato's jungle headquarters, about four miles from Kohima, intelligence was reporting an ominous build-up of British forces. As always, the general listened to the reports of his subordinates calmly. Inwardly he raged at Mutaguchi's plans, which were 'simply an essay written by children at their desk'. But, so far, the ill feeling towards his boss had been kept at the level of occasional comments to more trusted members of his staff. Sato listened and thought. Rising to inspect the map on the wall of his bamboo hut, he traced his finger along what his scouts believed were the lines of the British advance. He knew by now that his attempts to outflank the relieving forces had failed. The British had fought well and they had resisted the trap of encirclement. On the night of 15 April, an attempt had been made to cut the Dimapur road once more. But Hawkins's men were waiting for them. The 33 Corps account states briskly, 'they were thrown back and valuable documents captured'. At Zubza the 1st Cameron Highlanders captured an entrenched enemy position and CSM Tommy Cook, ex-Army boxing champion, seized a Japanese officer's sword and slaughtered the owner and several others with it, for which he was awarded the DCM. Tommy was later killed in Naga Village.

Now the Imphal operation was stuck in the mountains, with two divisions unable to shift the British, and he was being held at Kohima, with more British reinforcements arriving by the hour. If Sato had premonitions of defeat at this stage, like any good general he kept them from his staff. His infantry commander, Miyazaki, had started out as a believer in the operation, and still gave his staff and soldiers an impression of commitment to it. Before setting out for Kohima, Miyazaki had delivered a stirring speech to his officers. They were to have faith in one another, he said, and to see the officers and men of the Imperial Army as the divine arms and legs of the emperor. He also warned them of the challenges they would face. 'Enemy planes and firepower are, as you know, usually superior in numbers. Even in jungle fighting its progress has been quite rapidly advanced recently. When the enemy challenges us, usually they are thoroughly prepared. Therefore, never underestimate them.' But then Miyazaki lapsed into the hyper-confident rhetoric characteristic of so many Japanese generals, scorning the determination of the British and Indian forces. 'They are men without fighting spirit, a slave-like army without unity and without any noble cause. Their commander's capabilities are very limited, they lack quick decisive action, and are afraid of shock action. They have innumerable weak points … You, gentlemen, will answer the enemy's challenge, go out and meet them without fear and "bring home the bacon" … You must crush the enemy's will to oppose.'

The Royal West Kents, the Assam Regiment, and all the others who were despatched to fill gaps in the defences made a mockery of his assertions. But Miyazaki consoled himself that the perimeter was still shrinking. All it would take was for a breakthrough at the tennis court and Garrison Hill could be taken. Like Sato, he did not know the full scale of reinforcements coming up from Dimapur, although he already understood the British advantage in air supply and artillery. But that would matter less if the infantry could seize control of all of Kohima Ridge. Miyazaki knew it was a defensive position that could sap the blood and time of several enemy divisions. The orders from imperial headquarters had been to establish a line that could be held through the monsoon, until there was time to bring up reinforcements from Burma. That was still possible.

Miyazaki was impressed by his men's bravery. He did not control the individual decisions of company or platoon commanders in the heat of battle, but he did approve an overall strategy that pressed the sheer weight of numbers against the defender's guns. Against a resolute defence it guaranteed high casualties. To the Western observer there is an understandable temptation to view Japanese officers as profligate with the lives of their men, or to take the view, as Slim and his commanders did, that the Japanese were tactically unimaginative. But Miyazaki was gambling on the breakthrough that would bring the siege to a sudden end. Miyazaki had two mottos as a soldier: the first was 'Total Effort'; the second 'Get to the Objective'. They were to the forefront of his mind as the siege now entered its most decisive phase.

In a prison camp at the war's end, Miyazaki wrote a memoir of Kohima. It used a narrative device made famous by the Japanese novelist Soseki Natsume, who wrote a book in which his pet cat is the authorial voice. Quirky and subtle, it is a device popular in a culture where deep feeling is so often expressed at a remove. In Miyazaki's case the story is narrated through the voice of his pet monkey Chibi, which he carried with him throughout the war. Referring to one of the failed assaults he wrote: 'That night attack failed but I realised my master gets stronger and stronger the greater the hardship.' If the defenders thought their firepower would stop Miyazaki, they would be shown how wrong they were. He would attack while he thought there was any chance of breaking through. The 58th Regiment could be thrown back once, twice, twenty times, but as long as he thought a gap might open up they would fight on. For General Miyazaki the battle was still young; many of the men had fought long and hard in China and others at Guadalcanal and still emerged strong to fight at Kohima. Hundreds had been lost in the past fortnight. They were low on food and ammunition was growing short, but they had water and their trenches and bunkers were deep and solid. Miyazaki stressed that he wanted attacks that had a real military purpose, not glorious suicide charges for honour and the emperor. 'I feel sorry for the soldiers who committed suicide in battle. I believe it is important to live life and to bring more men home alive.'

But for Sato, who was dealing with Mutaguchi and asking for the promised food supplies, disillusionment was growing. Later he would say bitterly, 'It had been planned that 31 Div should receive supplies amounting to ten tons per week, of which seven tons were to be foodstuffs. These were to be transported to the CHINDWIN and Westwards to KOHIMA until such time as IMPHAL fell and the IMPHAL–KOHIMA road could be used to supply the division … the Division received NO rations of any kind.'

Private Manabu Wada, 3rd battalion, 138th Regiment, searched for food in burned-out buildings around Kohima's Naga Village. Such visions as their leaders had painted of supplies to be captured! Now Wada found 'not a grain of rice or a round of ammunition was left for us in the captured enemy positions'. Richards had ordered the destruction of all supplies that could not be carried into the garrison. The task of scavenging food was taking its toll on the supply officers. The majority of Naga villagers had fled into the forest and 31st Division had already consumed much of the available food in the area. Lieutenant Chuzaburo Tomaru of the 138th Regiment had experienced hunger during the war in China, but by mid-April he could tell the situation at Kohima was far more serious. Whenever rations from the allied supply drops drifted towards the Japanese lines, men would risk being shot by snipers in order to drag in the canisters of 'Churchill rations'. Tomaru remembered the 'delicious' taste of canned cheese, and the luxuries of chewing gum and cigarettes rescued from no-man's-land. He was still trying to find food for around five hundred men: rice balls, rolled in the palms of the hand, which day by day grew smaller. Tomaru would wait while his cooks boiled the rice, then, signalling to a few privates, he would divide up the ration and make the suicide run to the forward trenches. 'I thanked for my men because they were so brave and patient. When the campaign started, 15th Army promised to send food by transport aircraft, but it did not happen and there was no supply of food more than a month. I was so mad.'

The popular Lieutenant Kameyama, who had joked with his soldiers about holding their testicles before the battle of Jail Hill, consoled himself that he had not lost a battle yet. If he was going to win at Kohima it would come down to the most basic law of war. He and his troops would have to kill and keep killing until the enemy surrendered or were exterminated. 'When the enemy appeared before us ... our duty was only to bring down who ever was in front.' Kameyama consoled himself in his lonelier moments by writing a song while resting between assaults. It was gradually picked up and sung throughout the 58th Regiment, to the tune of the popular hit 'Thank you for your Trouble'. It is notable for its fatalistic acceptance of the attacker's dire predicament:

> When there is no more rice, we eat grass
> When there is no more tobacco, we smoke weeds
> When there are no more bullets, we fight with flesh
> The flag of the rising sun raised in Kohima.
> Thank you for your troubles, thank you for your troubles
> Seizing enemy pillbox
> One lights a victorious cigarette
> Another day in safety
> The crescent moon also smiling in the sky
> Thank you for your troubles, etc.
> With only three shells per mountain gun
> Even 58th Regiment soldiers
> Cannot hold Kohima.
> If only they had shells, but we can only shed blood.
> Thank you for your troubles, thank you for your troubles

The arrival of allied Hurricanes and Vultee 1 Vengeance dive-bombers in mid-April added to the pressure on the Japanese. To the supply officer Masao Hirakubo air strikes were 'fire from a long way away', which killed several men he knew. The men in the forward trenches were fortunate in only one respect: the aircraft did not risk bombing them for fear of hitting the British entrenched nearby. The planes boosted the spirits of the garrison. 'To see them roaring in low, the whole place rocking with the noise of their engines and then above this sound to hear the loud voices of the bombs, renewed our hearts every time them came,' said a soldier from the Assam Rifles.

The pilots included a large number of New Zealanders and Canadians. Jimmy Whalen, from Vancouver, had earned his status as an 'ace' fighting the Luftwaffe in France and the Japanese during the attack on Ceylon in 1942. At Kohima, Whalen flew a Hurricane fighter-bomber, or 'Hurribomber', with 34 Squadron RAF on bombing and strafing runs twice a day. The situation of the village, in a valley between high mountain ridges, meant the pilots had to pass low over well-dug-in Japanese on their approach. The small arms fire spattered upwards. Whalen's wingman, Flight Sergeant Jack Morton, witnessed his death. 'We bombed in sections of two and Jimmy and I were first in bombing with two 250 lb. bombs with 11 second delays fitted. I was slightly behind Jimmy and we dropped our bombs at about 50 feet and as we left the target area Jimmy's plane did a barrel roll and crashed. It was a very sad day on the Squadron because he was by far the most popular officer and pilot in both the Officers' and Sergeants' Mess. We carried out two more attacks that day and on both occasions we looked for his plane but there was nothing to be seen in the dense jungle.' Another pilot, a New Zealander, was forced to bail out over Kohima but had the good luck to land behind British lines. He was back flying within twenty-four hours. Another went missing and was found flying around aimlessly, possibly a victim of battle fatigue, before being escorted back to base by two comrades. 'When we landed he could not remember anything about the trip,' Morton recalled.

The Dakotas from Troop Carrier Command were now making daily supply and ammunition runs to the beleaguered garrison. Their pilots included many who had spent their pre-war lives shuttling around Asia and Africa in the service of colonial airlines, or working for oil and mining companies. In the case of Squadron Leader Alec 'Fatty' Pearson of 194 Squadron, his RAF service followed a period flying in Kenya, where he had been the pilot on Ernest Hemingway's trip to Kilimanjaro in 1937. Hemingway subsequently used Pearson as the pilot character in his short story 'The Snows of Kilimanjaro'. Joining the RAF did not cramp Alec 'Fatty' Pearson's love of the wild colonial lifestyle. Pilot Derek Thirlwell remembered Pearson pushing the plane up to above 10,000 feet to avoid turbulence, a technique perfected in the rainy seasons of East Africa. 'We carried packed lunches but first Fatty produced a bottle of sherry!! … and to my surprise it uncorked like a bottle of champagne.' On another occasion Thirlwell was sitting beside a pilot who produced a pipe and started filling it with tobacco. He then lit it and opened the pilot's window until the slipstream had the pipe glowing brightly.

'Fatty's' parties after supply drops were legendary among the aircrew. On one especially cold night he challenged each member of the returning aircrew to down three araks each, one after the other. The spirit had the taste and effect of paint-stripper. One pilot waited until 'Fatty' was looking the other way and emptied his arak into the fire. There was an explosion and coals were blown out on to the carpet. 'Fatty's' response was: 'That was bloody silly Robbie, such a waste!' He then handed him another arak and drawled, 'would somebody please put the carpet out before the mess burns down'.

The refuge sought in alcohol was understandable. The Americans reported cases of men breaking under the strain, or calming their nerves by resorting to opium, freely available at the Chinese end of the route. In a few instances, the authorities shut down officers' clubs because pilots were too hungover to report for early starts. They flew in conditions that tested nerves and skill to the utmost. Monsoon cloud formations that concealed terrifying pockets of turbulence, high winds and rain generated by powerful storms, thick mist that obscured drop zones and airfields, could all bring disaster.

One pilot with 194 Squadron recalled how he was leaving Burmese territory on a night with low visibility when he suddenly lost control of his aircraft. He found himself in a spiral dive, his stomach pushed back against his spine, the unseen earth rushing towards him. Fighting with the throttles he levelled the plane off and pushed forward into full climbing power, only just clearing the mountains. Eric Forsdyke, who flew with 117 Squadron RAF, recalled how the monsoon thunder clouds could rise up to nearly 60,000 feet from the mountain tops. If the pilots could not find a way through the cumulo-nimbus clouds they would reduce speed and put on sunglasses to protect their eyes from the flashes of lightning. Anybody who has travelled through severe turbulence in the comfort of a pressurised modern aircraft must struggle to comprehend the nightmare of battering through the monsoon in the shell of a Dakota. The squadron lost 20 men in the skies over Burma. Among them was Sergeant Forsdyke's good friend from Yorkshire, Freddie Crowther, whose aircraft was downed by turbulence. 'Almost every night in the mess he played his favourite record on the old wind-up gramophone ... That night after he and his crew failed to return we played his record in memory of him.'

The Americans who had been pulled by Mountbatten from the 'Hump' route across the Himalayas in order to help the defenders of Kohima and Imphal had flown in conditions that no peacetime pilot would have thought of attempting. A poem by an American flight lieutenant captured the daunting nature of the work:

> In the best of weather the hazards
> 'Twould take a year to tell,
> But on instruments up in the 'Soup' and ice
> The going is really hell!
> Rocky and evil and awful,
> So you're scared if you have to jump:
> Crossing the ocean is easy
> Alongside of flying the 'Hump'!

Thunderstorms could stretch for hundreds of miles. One pilot recalled: 'Knowing that the leading edge of a storm will drive you down, it is necessary to go in as high as possible to prevent being smashed into the top of a hill. However, holding absolutely to a set compass heading, this downward force suddenly ends and is replaced by such a strong upward flow that with the plane pointed down and with the engines pulling full power, we gained as much as five thousand feet in a few minutes. It took both of us using all our strength to work the controls to keep the plane from rolling over. One of the other crews did just that, plus had all their front glass broken by large hail stones, but they survived.'

As the monsoon approached there were growing risks. Flying through cloud, rain and lightning, the pilots clung to map references, scanning gaps between clouds for any sign of smoke in the shape of a letter 'L', the agreed signal for the drop zone. On one trip north of Kohima, Deryck Groocock was looking for a gap in the clouds at 8,500 feet. He was just 1,500 feet above the mountains. Groocock told his crew to prepare to drop the supplies, when he suddenly noticed the air speed dropping off. He was unable to hold the plane's nose down. It reared up and the aircraft flipped into a right-hand spin. They were suddenly plummeting at a rate of 2,000 feet per minute. Groocock's swift arithmetic told him he had forty-five seconds before the plane hit the invisible mountains. 'I took the normal spin recovery action – full opposite rudder, stick forward and thought, "This is the end." I saw the altimeter go down to 6,000 ft., 5,500 ft., and 5,000 ft. and still we had not hit. The next second we came out below the cloud at 4,500 ft. under control and in a valley with great peaks vanishing into clouds on either side of us. Trembling like a leaf, I flew down the valley.' Groocock discovered that moving the rice towards the door for dropping had pushed the centre of gravity beyond safe limits.

The pilots had rescued Slim in the first instance by flying in troops to defend Kohima and Imphal, now they were dropping supplies to keep that army fed and armed. Between January and April 1944, Troop Carrier Command delivered more than 69,000 tons of supplies, while General Sato at Kohima waited forlornly for mule trains of food and ammunition. This was the strategic advantage central to Slim's plan for victory.

Six-year-old Alan Leonard was living on the Woka tea estate, less than twenty miles from Kohima, and saw 'a virtual nose to tail stream of Dakotas and Thunderbolts heading for the hills.' On one occasion, an American Liberator bomber crash-landed in a rice field about a mile from the family bungalow. The crew survived and were spirited to safety across the Naga Hills.

Pilots engaged in bombing attacks against the Japanese were largely safe from enemy planes. The RAF enjoyed air superiority by this stage of the war. The greatest fear was what would happen if mechanical failure or bad weather forced them to bail out or ditch in the jungle. The pilots returned after each run to airstrips that were, by comparison with the conditions for the infantry, models of comfort. None had experience of living rough in the forest. The jungle below was distant and alien, a world seen through the prism of a Perspex shield.

As the fight for Kohima escalated, Ken Moses, a crewman with 'Fatty' Pearson's 194 Squadron, saw the landscape alter. The thick vegetation on Garrison Hill was gone; on the stumps of trees hung silk and jute parachutes, trenches were braided across the hills. A season of withering had swept the hills. 'I remember looking down on the devastation at Kohima while on one of these drops – it reminded me of the WWI scenes of Belgium.' A flight sergeant on another plane remembered flying in low: 'often we would end up about 250 feet over the hills, with the Japs shooting at us. All I could see was a mass of faces looking up at us. I could not see the type of weapons, only the flame from the guns.'

Across the Imphal and Kohima front, fighters and fighter-bombers from the USAAF and RAF were completing the destruction of the Japanese air force. The fledgling Indian Air Force also brought a squadron to the battle.* One squadron of American P-38s (the same type of aircraft that had killed Admiral Yamamoto of Pearl Harbor fame in 1943) claimed to have destroyed ninety-six Japanese aircraft in its first six weeks of operations. Japanese airstrips in

* Indian pilots had flown in the Battle of Britain.

northern Burma were now within easy striking range of the fighter-bombers. The commander of Third Tactical Air Force, Air Marshal Sir John Baldwin, wrote of how 'the Japanese Air Command had been forced into the humiliating position of laying on from Air Units based on comparatively secure RANGOON strips, such ineffective and fleeting support as their army – 600 miles away in the Northern mountains – received'. The intelligence officer Lieutenant Colonel Iwaichi Fujiwara thought that air superiority 'gave the enemy an overwhelming advantage … [and] had an important psychological effect on the troops'. The almost complete absence of Japanese aircraft above the Naga Hills compounded the men's growing sense of being alone in a hostile wilderness.

The Japanese Air Force made a brief appearance during the later part of the battle. Lieutenant John Paterson, 2 Division Signals, saw two Zeros wheeling into position above the main road near Kohima. Paterson and two of his men jumped into a gully as the Zeros 'swung round and made a second sortie, twice spraying the road with heavy machine gun fire.' There were no casualties and the Japanese planes left quickly, 'disappearing eastwards over the mountains.'

The Japanese still believed the ridge could be taken and that supplies could be seized from the Kohima stores. Men were also being told by their NCOs that 15th Army would make good on its promise to send fresh food and stocks of shells for the mountain artillery and mortars. Even if the men had been tempted to desert, there was nowhere they could have fled. They were told the Nagas were headhunters and even cannibals. If they did manage by some extraordinary good fortune to make it back to the Chindwin, there was the prospect of the *Kempeitai* removing their heads. Lieutenant Chuzaburo Tomaru, a man who loathed being at war, was 'fighting on because were told to. If you tried to leave you would have been heavily punished at the time. There was no such thought among us.' Machine-gun company commander Captain Keizo Moto was one of the men trying to storm the tennis court. 'How could we escape from that hole? They say the operation was so bloody and brave. But for me, I'm not brave, I was only ordered to be there.' There were plenty of others, perhaps a majority, like the military doctor Takahide Kuwaki, who still believed that laying down one's life for the emperor was the greatest possible honour. For Lieutenant Hiroshi Yamagami, who had the honour of carrying 58th Regiment's flag, it was as simple as proving he was worthy of being called a warrior. 'When I first entered the army school I thought I was fighting for my country and my family. But at Kohima it wasn't like that. I just wanted to win. Don't take it wrong, I wasn't looking for glory. I followed orders. I never thought about surviving. That was not my purpose.'

The Japanese ranks contained men of differing views and widely disparate abilities. What held them together at Kohima was a formidable mix of ruthless discipline, loyalty to their regiments, love of the emperor, and a belief that fate would somehow deliver victory. As the old Japanese proverb has it, *Un wa yusha wo tasuku* – 'Fate assists the courageous'. For General Sato, always the realist, the accumulating evidence of British strength pointed to only one conclusion: Kohima Ridge would have to be taken very quickly if defeat was to be avoided. He issued a stern warning: any man who lost or failed to maintain his rifle would be shot.

TWENTY-ONE

The Last Hill

They were red-eyed and bearded and they smelled of sweat, excrement and death. Men would light 'Victory V' cigarettes just to smell something that didn't reek of all the bad possibilities Kohima offered. 'They smelled like camel shit and tasted that way too,' one soldier said. There was barely enough water now for a mug of tea a day. Men spent most of the time parched, with their tongues swollen in their mouths and their throats raw from grit. They scratched the lice that insinuated themselves into every crevice and fold of the body; many suffered the torment of dhobi itch, angry red fungal eruptions which spread across the crotch and buttocks. Their hands and faces were black with the grime of the battlefield. For the medical orderlies the lack of personal water for washing was especially trying. Frank 'Doc' Infanti, Royal West Kents, had just finished the perilous job of treating a wounded man at the tennis court when he wandered into the HQ area. The company clerk saw him and shook his head. It was then that Infanti noticed that his hands were covered in the dried blood of the wounded man. Nobody could wash at Kohima. Those were the orders from Laverty and Richards. 'The company clerk [said], "Cor, your hands are in a bit of a state ... and he gave me a little bit of water to wash my hands."' This small act of kindness would be a cherished memory of Infanti's for the rest of his life.

In contrast to the poor relations between Laverty and the garrison staff, the West Kents got on well with the soldiers of the Assam Regiment and the other front-line troops. Lieutenant Pieter Steyn,

1st Assam, had some sympathy for Laverty's predicament. 'Laverty's relationship with Hugh Richards … was not cordial, but it must be remembered that the RWKs were the only complete unit at Kohima amidst all the confusion of order and counter order. Laverty could be excused for trying to protect his battalion in the circumstances.' But officers and men struggled to help each other. Major Franklin of the West Kents continued to keep the garrison water-carrying system running, and Captain Harry Smith was a regular visitor in Richards's bunker. A garrison officer, Captain W. P. G. MacLachlan, remembered the soothing effect of the peacetime schoolmaster's voice. '[He] regarded the Jap with the contempt of an ex member of the 8th army mingled with the didactic attitude of a house-master to an unruly fourth former. During a heavy mortar attack he could be heard muttering: "A lot of humguffery going on tonight." The word "humguffery" caught on, and his contempt of the Jap was infectious, and did much to quieten the nerves of our heterogeneous collection of soldiery, many of whom had not previously been in action.'

Captain Donald Elwell of the Assam Regiment was racing to escape Japanese mortar and sniper fire when he almost rolled in the doorway of a West Kent dugout. 'Why don't you come in, instead of cluttering up the doorway?' a voice asked. With the mortars dropping close by, Elwell crawled in and was offered a cup of tea. 'Sorry the missus isn't in, Sir,' his host declared. 'Meanwhile, here we are and here we stay. That's it, sir, isn't it?' Elwell could only nod in agreement.

If they were lucky, soldiers might catch an undisturbed hour or two of sleep. One man stayed awake, the other dozed. This was only in the daytime. Nobody risked dropping off at night. By 16 April John Winstanley and B company had moved from the tennis court and across Garrison Hill to Supply Hill, the next target for the Japanese on the southern perimeter. 'Fatigue was the greatest danger,' he recalled; 'as a company commander you had to be on your toes ready to act around the clock and the Japs never stopped and if you relaxed for a moment you would be overrun.'

Anyway, there was always too much noise. The bloody whining of the voices from Japanese loudhailers urging them to give up, the howls of the human wave as it swept across the tennis court, and then the fractured symphony of battle: Bren guns rattling vengeance, grenades and mortars, and the artillery from Jotsoma and Zubza crashing along the perimeter, the sound of weapons and fists clashing in close-quarter combat. Then came the other noises: elongated screams of pain that only a man who had been in these the trenches for days would recognise as coming from a human being. Macabre as it might sound, there was comfort of a kind in this noise. It was better than the shivering silence before a night attack.

There could be some unusual visitations. Private Ivan Daunt heard a clattering noise coming from the road. 'We heard all this noise and that coming up the road and it was a load of horses, and they drove the horses forward ... then they attacked, they come with it, and they come up the bank attacked us up the bank ... all we had to do when they come up was [throw] grenades, piece of cake that was.' Thirty Japanese fell dead among the horses. On another night, a soldier listening to the wounded crying out for water heard from the Japanese lines a voice singing the Scottish ballad 'Annie Laurie', presumably an officer who had once lived in the West.

Come the morning, men felt the adrenaline flood away to be replaced by the most unimaginable exhaustion. Soldiers found their movements slowed and would often shake uncontrollably. The effects of fatigue and shock could turn men inwards. In a few, the small details of a human death could provoke much anguish. Dennis Wykes watched the burial of a soldier in a weapons pit. There was not enough earth to cover him properly and his toes stuck out. For some reason these uncovered digits made Wykes imagine the man as he might have been when he was a boy. He turned his face away. No point in letting those feelings get a hold of you, he told himself. There was a man called Napper in Wykes's platoon who had a strange high-pitched laugh. It helped raise morale because it made everybody else laugh. One day towards the end, Napper cracked and told Wykes he was going. 'This day he said to me, with the Japs attacking, "I'm off. I can't stand for that lot. I'm going to go." So I said, "If you want to be shot in the back you better go because we will shoot you in the back." He didn't run. They're not all saints and not all good soldiers if it comes to the push. Let's face it, if it comes to the push, we were all ordinary people in ordinary life before we came here, but we had to do the best that we could.' Napper stayed put.

Ray Street of C company was under mortar fire on Garrison Hill when he saw a man called Williams climb out of his trench and start to run in panic. This was not like the man. Williams had come through Alam Halfa, and he had helped a shell-shock victim at the tunnels on the day of the friendly-fire incident. Williams had only made a few yards when a mortar landed directly in front of him. 'Although badly injured he was well aware of what was happening and we carried him back to the first aid post … his injuries were severe and three days later, he died.'

What is striking in all the accounts of survivors from the front-line rifle companies is how few men cracked. The shared imperative of killing Japanese in large numbers certainly helped keep them mentally focused. At the back of every man's mind was the knowledge of what would await anyone taken prisoner. Wykes had been up to the ADS and had seen his wounded friends lying in the open pits. He was convinced they would have been bayoneted immediately on surrender. For them, as much as for himself, he fought on. One story doing the rounds was of a West Kent who had been taken prisoner and had had his eyes gouged out with barbed wire. It may or may not have been true, but in battle with the Japanese the men were conditioned to believe the worst. Private Len Brown confronted the screaming waves night after night. 'No soldier is brave. We are all frightened. Every one of us was frightened. If we put our hands up and surrendered our battalion would have been finished … we knew that if the Japs had got us they would have shot us and tortured us.'

Captain Harry Smith felt the steady press of despair. 'Day after day our hopes were dashed … we began to walk around like zombies.' In the quieter moments officers watched their men for signs of shell shock, the dislocated stare into the distance, the lips mumbling non-stop, the trembling that was different, more intense, deeper, than the shaking they all suffered from. 'They had lived surrounded by suffering and sudden death, noise, filth, and stench and some became callous as a result,' wrote Lieutenant Pieter Steyn of the Assam Regiment. But Steyn was struck by the vagaries of human behaviour in battle. 'A man who had watched without any emotion of any kind his friends fall and die would turn and give his last drop of water to a stranger in need of it.'

Up at the ADS, Lieutenant Donald Elwell of the Assam Regiment came across some of his wounded men. He was impressed that they tried to salute him even though they were lying on stretchers. What could he do for them? They could not move and it became clear that they had lost hope of being relieved, as one told him. 'They will not be able to reach us, sahib; there are too many Japanese.' He left, promising to come and visit them again. When he did, two days later, the trench was empty but stained with clotted blood. 'Returning to my slit trench, I sat down to write to my parents and to my fiancée, but what was there to say? Censorship forbade us to say anything of the fighting. So we just wrote that we were well, we would write at length in the near future and we sent our love. It seemed a poor little letter, written with the stub of a pencil on someone else's paper and saying nothing. I folded my cap badge into Pauline's letter and thought it might be the last thing that I would ever send.' Perhaps it would be found by a Japanese soldier searching the bodies, or be blown to shreds along with himself.

Men were cautious about any movement. Soldiers were continually being picked off by snipers. CSM Bert Harwood of C company was asked by an officer to organise a party to move some boxes of ammunition on Supply Hill, the next target in line for the Japanese attacking the southern perimeter. Harwood studied the ground and saw that anybody moving towards the ammunition in daylight would be shot. 'I had an argument with him. I said, "You are asking to create more casualties by doing that at this particular time. We know it's there, the Japs must know it's there … rather than try and move it now in the daylight … it would have been much easier to do it in the dark."' Harwood believed another man was given the job and killed by a sniper.

Major Donald Easten of D company was in action again after having been wounded in the fight for Detail Hill. A shell fragment had lodged in his arm but he was keen to be away from the ADS and back with his men. He dealt with the constant tension by thinking of home. He knew that some of the men found this too painful. They lived only in the present and thought only of surviving for that day. But he found comfort in imagining himself with his new bride, Billie. His was the idealised imagery of a man who knows he may not live beyond the next hour: he saw the two of them walking in the Kent countryside in summer, or conjured visions of idling by a trout stream or riding to hounds in winter along the North Downs. That love of the country was something he had shared with poor John Harman, lying now in his shallow grave on Garrison Hill. Survival here was pure chance, he thought, nothing but chance. Could they keep holding out? As long as the Japanese kept up the human-wave tactics there was a chance. The West Kents' rifle companies had all lost up to half, in some cases more, of their numbers. But as long as there was ammunition for the Brens, and the artillery kept up its support, they could survive another few days. 'Up until that time the Japanese had it a great deal their own way – and they suddenly came up against this dogged, bloody-minded British infantry attitude; they just bashed their heads against it and didn't get anywhere. They didn't vary their tactics at all. It was just wave after wave of attacks in the same positions and places.'

For all Miyazaki's assertion that he did not want suicide attacks, to the defenders the assaults on the tennis court looked like a prolonged exercise in self-destruction. Private Leslie Crouch of the pioneer platoon saw the Japanese approach. 'They were easy targets to hit. They didn't seem to be afraid of death.' But Japanese numbers were starting to count. Private Leonard Brown saw 'literally hundreds coming at a time toward us, so much so that the manpower strength just pushed us back from one trench to a trench that was roughly ten foot behind us'. In some places the fighting see-sawed. The Japanese would gain the forward trenches and be driven back out by a counter-attack. The grappling, stabbing and hacking went on, back and forth, a murderously intimate duet in which men looked into each other's enraged and frightened eyes as they manoeuvred for the killing strike. Some of the men would remember their bayonet training at Axminster in the bitter winter of 1940, a lifetime ago; hours had been spent plunging their blades into sacks of tightly packed straw. How the instructors had yelled at them then, *Go low up and in to the hilt, use your foot if the blade gets stuck*. They had cursed the endlessness of it, the boredom and the play-acting, as their fingers froze. Now they pushed their blades home into the sinewy frames of Japanese, slicing through gut and scraping bone, or trying for a quick blow to the throat, parrying the enemy's attempt to do the same. The dead or dying Japanese lay heavy on the end of a rifle and a soldier might allow the body to topple backwards before placing his foot on the man and wrenching the blade free, making sure that he never dropped his guard but kept his eyes open, through the smoke and noise, for another enemy who might be creeping up on him. One soldier paid dearly for his attempted panache. He tried to remove a small Japanese from his bayonet by hoisting him and tossing him to one side. As he did so, a Japanese officer came up and slashed him almost in half with his sword.

Down on the tennis court the Assam troops who had replaced John Winstanley's B company found their store of rage and hurled it at the Japanese. At dusk on 16 April a party of four men, led by a local Naga corporal, jumped out of their trenches and raced down the slope and across the court. The commander, Major Albert Calistan, could sense the tension rising among his soldiers. They had survived the encirclement of Jessami and fought their way through the jungle to Kohima, but the constant shelling and the shrinking of the perimeter had shaken them. Now they could hardly move during the daytime without drawing sniper and machine-gun fire. The best way to deal with it, Calistan decided, was to take the fight across the tennis court. This would lift the feeling of impending doom. It might also, of course, result in getting every one of the raiding party slaughtered. But Calistan sensed that if he did not take a risk to boost his men's morale the chances would grow of a Japanese breakthrough at the tennis court. Calistan had two Bren guns giving suppressing fire from left and right. One of them was manned by Sepoy Wellington Massar, who had proved his courage in the fighting at Jessami.

On the night of the raid, Wellington Massar put his Bren gun on the billiard table of the ruined clubhouse on the slope above the tennis court. It gave him a good line of fire over the Japanese trenches, but once he started firing Japanese in other positions would easily spot him. The raid would have to be swift. Before they left the trenches the men would remove the pins from their grenades, giving them seconds to sprint the twenty yards to the Japanese trenches. The Japanese were taken unawares. The machine-gun team was killed and documents and an officer's sword were captured. But as the raiders raced back, Wellington Massar's gun jammed. The Japanese had time to raise their heads. He was quickly spotted and shot in the leg, rolling off the table and crashing to the floor. Despite the pain, Massar levered himself back on to the table and resumed firing until the raiding party was back. Carried out of the clubhouse under cover of darkness, he refused to be taken to the ADS, possibly deciding he was safer in his own trench than out in the open under shellfire, and that a journey uphill under the eyes of snipers would risk his comrades' life. He would linger for several more days before dying. Major Calistan sent a message to Richards saying that he would rather remain on the tennis court 'to avoid the casualties inevitable in the process of relief'. The rush attacks had stopped. Now the Assam men watched for small parties of the enemy racing up in the dark with bombs made from slabs of guncotton. One of these would have blown the occupants of a trench to pieces, but every attack was stopped by accurate fire. Calistan had been observing the Japanese tactics carefully. 'We soon came to know that the Japs worked to a timetable, for almost without fail he tried something every dusk … and again at or just before first light. All one had to do was listen acutely and if one heard the slightest movement near one, throw a grenade. In this manner all his tricks came to nought.'

The West Kents' company commanders were also asking to mount raids. Repeated requests were being sent to Laverty's bunker. He consistently refused. Laverty felt certain his men's morale would survive the constant pressure of being under attack. He told one officer, 'You know damn well that while we keep to our positions we can inflict ten times the number of casualties we suffer, but as soon as we start throwing our weight about we'll lose men in numbers we can't afford. You've only to do one of your simple sums to see how it works out. Whatever the effect on morale we must refuse them.'

By the night of 16 April the garrison had been under siege for eleven days. Advancing from the south, the Japanese had captured a succession of hills, GPT Ridge, Jail Hill, Detail Hill, and they were entrenched in the bungalow sector. They now moved against the last two positions on the ridge before Garrison Hill where Richards, Laverty and the wounded were sited. At both Supply Hill and Kuki Piquet there was a mix of West Kents, Assam Rifles, and a composite formation of Indian troops. John Laverty's skill was in the fine measurement of defence; he was constantly revising the perimeter to what he believed he could hold, and sappers were sent to booby-trap any approaches where troops were thin on the ground. Still, he was now hemmed in to an area roughly 500 by 500 yards, with around seven hundred men of the garrison still able to fight, and another 1,700 either non-combatant or wounded.

Laverty and Richards had been promised by wireless on 15 April that relief would arrive the following day. A patrol of 4/7 Rajput from Jotsoma succeeded in getting through and reinforced the message. But help did not arrive on 16 April. Richards went up to Laverty's bunker later and found the West Kents' CO talking to Warren on the radio. 'I also spoke to Warren and said that unless relief came quickly, it would be too late. He replied that he was doing his best but intended to make a proper job of it.' Some measure of Laverty's frustration can be gauged from the regiment's war diary. 'This was the fourth occasion on which, after statements by relieving forces that they hoped to make contact on the morrow, hopes of relief, reinforcement or evacuation of casualties were dashed.'

Richards, too, was becoming exasperated. Wherever he looked there were wounded men in desperate straits. 'We had many disappointments. On 10 April a message from 161 Bde that it was hoped to make a speedy relief. On 13 report from 161 Bde that effect of their advance should soon be felt. On 16 a message saying that they hoped to make contact "this morning".'

The men were briefly buoyed by an intense bombardment from Warren's 161 Brigade and 2nd Division artillery. Hugh Richards wondered how anybody could have survived the pounding given to the Japanese lines. He was sure that without the accurate fire drawn down by Major Yeo and his observers the Japanese would have long ago broken through. The RAF joined in with bombs and cannon fire.

The Japanese pressure was making life a misery for the cooks. They hunkered in covered pits trying to heat the ubiquitous bully-beef stew on open fires the constant smoke of which tormented their lungs. There was still enough food, but the problem was getting it to the men in the trenches. Ray Street saw the 6 foot 4 inch frame of Sergeant Jack Eves crawling into small trenches with tins of bully-beef stew and hot tea, apparently oblivious to the bullets whizzing past him. 'It was actions like his that lifted morale.' When the pangs of hunger hit Street he thought of Firpos restaurant in Calcutta where the men went on leave and ate duck with green peas and potatoes.

Army cooks are among the world's most highly evolved scroungers and in the early stages of the siege, when some movement was still possible, they liberated large quantities of tinned fruit and vegetables. At least one case of whisky was discovered and buried near the tennis court for distribution at the appropriate moment, presumably when the garrison was either relieved or on the verge of being overrun. The air drops helped to vary the diet, although Mark Lambert of the West Kents grew to loathe the soya-link sausages. 'They were made of soya flour and came in the shape of sausages. They tasted bloody awful!' The men at the edge of the perimeter, in places like the tennis court, could spend days without a hot meal, eating only the cold bully beef and hard-tack biscuits they had brought with them. There was another challenge, which affected them more than the rest of the garrison. With snipers constantly on the watch for movement, how were men to go to the toilet? Most waited until nightfall and crept a little way away from their position. Tom Hogg at the tennis court recalled men filling empty bully-beef tins with their excrement and then hurling it at the Japanese. 'You had to go the best place you could,' said Dennis Wykes. 'You wouldn't stand outside doing whatever. You had to keep the latrines under cover.' For men with diarrhoea or dysentery the conditions were impossible. Unable to control their bowels in the confinement of the trenches they either fouled themselves or risked a sniper's bullet.

By now the troops on Garrison Hill could see signs of fighting on the hills where 161 Brigade was trying to break through. The delay had been partly down to Sato's original roadblock, Grover's caution and the slowness of troops advancing into unfamiliar and difficult terrain. The 2nd Division commander feared being outflanked and having his line of communications cut, the perennial fear when facing the Japanese. Parties of the enemy were probing along his flanks, and captured Japanese plans showed that Sato wanted to occupy a ridge overlooking the main road. Japanese artillery could then wreak havoc on the advancing brigades. When he went forward to see Warren at Jotsoma on 16 April the latter was desperate to get his men into Kohima immediately, but Grover refused because of 'lack of security of the right flank' and because he wanted a proper reconnaissance. Rather than rush to save the garrison, he would ensure the safety of his advance; as Brigadier Hawkins had shown him, the 'country is very big and difficult and rapidly absorbs large numbers of troops. It gives great advantage to defence.'

The troops moving along the hills were facing the Naga Hills for the first time; the lack of experience slowed them. An intelligence officer with 4 Brigade wrote that it 'seemed we had not patrolled enough to gain information, that the troops were too slow to advance after the artillery concentration and that it was doubtful whether we had attacked from the right direction'. Both Stopford and Grover were planning for the battle to retake Kohima Ridge and drive the Japanese back to the Chindwin; rescuing the garrison was not incidental to this, but neither man would alter what they considered to be the best plan for the larger battle.

From his headquarters, miles away in Comilla, Slim studied the battle reports and radio messages with concern. The Japanese had caught him unawares at the beginning. He had been saved then by the ferocity of the defence at Sangshak, Jessami and Kohima, by the airlift of reinforcements from the Arakan, and by General Kawabe's fateful order to Mutaguchi not to attack Dimapur and the railway. But having got heavy reinforcements on the road towards Kohima, he now risked seeing the campaign descend into a lengthy slogging match. In his memoirs he says simply that 'progress was at times slow, as the enemy reacted with fierce local counter-attacks'. It was an understatement belying the continuing pressure on Slim. He could console himself that he was on the point of overtaking the Japanese in numbers and firepower; he was establishing a secure line of communications back to the railhead at Dimapur; and the garrison at Kohima was proving itself a match for the attackers. At Imphal the 4th Corps had stopped the advance of the Japanese 15 and 33 Divisions. But Sato was close to taking control of all of Kohima Ridge, and once in place his troops could dig in and do what the Japanese did best: defend to the last man and delay Slim's counter-strike into Burma.

The Americans were pressing Mountbatten for the return of the loaned aircraft on which Slim's massive supply operation was based; and a prolonged battle of attrition in the Naga Hills could convince the doubters in London, among them the prime minister, that the 14th Army could never defeat the Japanese in the jungle. The pressure to speed up the advance passed from London and Washington to Mountbatten, from the supreme commander to Slim and then to Stopford and Grover. On 16 April, Stopford attended a church parade in the garden of his residence and noted that there had been no startling developments at Kohima. But his expectation of imminent good news was growing. 'I expect to hear any time now that 2 Div have kicked out the Jap.' Just twenty-four hours later, Stopford erupted in frustration. Grover's plan for Kohima was 'much too slow and cumbersome', he was 'boot bound' and slow in his methods, a point Stopford intended to make forcefully when he met him.

The mist had turned to rain and across the perimeter the Japanese were attacking. They had recovered from the shock of Calistan's raid at the tennis court and put in an assault of their own. The Brens kept them out. Up at the Indian hospital buildings behind the headquarters, a raid against the Assam Rifles' trenches was beaten back with twenty-four Japanese killed. The hospital position was the 'back door' to the perimeter; situated on a steep bluff on the northern edge of Garrison Hill it was the most daunting prospect for the Japanese infantry on the road. But it did not deter them from attacking.

Up here Charles Pawsey was sharing a bunker with the Assam Rifles' CO, Buster Keene, an old friend, responsible for the policing of the Naga Hills. As the days ground on, the old soldier Pawsey was consoled by his own appreciation of the battle. He was increasingly convinced that the Japanese had thrown away the chance of a great victory. 'Had the Japs attacked with everything they had on the 5th or 6th of April they could have taken this place,' he wrote. They could have 'created panic in India', but had now lost the initiative. They might still take Kohima Ridge, though, and kill Pawsey and everybody else. He did not dwell on the prospect of imminent mortality. At the Somme, and in the high mountains of the Tyrol fighting the Austrians, he had been a whisker from death more than once. For Charles Pawsey the answer to fear was to remain occupied, to be useful to the fighting men. So whenever the shelling eased or stopped he made his rounds of the trenches and visits to the wounded. An account by an Indian officer of the Assam Rifles described how this 'unarmed civilian in the midst of all the carnage, a more unruffled man one could not imagine … a source of inspiration …'

On the southern perimeter the strain of relentless attack and declining numbers was showing. Ever since the fall of Detail Hill, where John Harman had died in Donald Easten's arms, the next position, Supply

Hill, had been the Japanese focus. The West Kents of C and D companies fell back to this larger hill with numerous small buildings. They joined the 4/7 Rajput and composite Indian troops – mule drivers, cooks, clerks, signalmen – and fought off repeated attacks before the Japanese gained a foothold. A platoon of Assam Rifles was dispatched to help and pushed the enemy back. Back and forth it went.

Donald Easten returned to the battle. With his arm in a sling he gave an outward appearance of courage. 'You mustn't let the soldiers think you are frightened. Obviously you were terrified but you didn't let anybody know that. You went out and did it.' One of the early casualties was Easten's Company Sergeant Major, Bill Haines, who was blinded by an explosion. He refused to leave the area and leaned on the arm of a private who directed him as he shouted encouragement to the men. The pressure continued to intensify. Blasted backwards by shelling, the 3 Assam Rifles and 4/7 Rajput pulled out of their positions. Laverty sent John Faulkner and his platoon from A company to try to plug the gap. Faulkner spotted a gun hidden behind a tarpaulin on the Japanese position opposite. He was about to call in a mortar attack when the Japanese opened fire. 'We kept our heads down as round after round came over onto the positions ... It was horrible to hear the solid steel shell knocking and ricocheting through the trees.' Leaves, branches, shards of wood and thick shot showered down. Private Norman of C company missed death by inches. A piece of shrapnel embedded itself in his pack. 'Luck was with us,' he wrote in his diary.

Faulkner saw the Japanese ground attack coming, the 'dimly flitted shapes outlined in the darkness', creeping towards his positions. Here the fire control of the West Kents was essential. Wait and wait, until it seems as if they are nearly on top of you. At fifteen yards the West Kents opened fire. A sergeant in one bunker shot three Japanese in quick succession as they tried to enter. The attack was beaten back. The following morning Faulkner sent a man to check whether there was any sign of the Japanese digging in around the area. It was just as well he did. 'Suddenly I heard a voice, a subdued scuffle, and he reappeared, this time with his eyes popping out of his head. "There's

Japs in a bunker 30 yards over there," he said – "and one of 'em said 'Come 'ere' to me."' Faulkner went to check. Poking head and shoulders out of his own bunker, he saw the Japanese. There were four of them sitting by the path, 'talking away as if their lives depended on it'. One of the Japanese turned around and saw Faulkner. They looked at each other 'for a long minute' and then the man spoke: 'Come here.' Faulkner was astonished. 'I thought this was a bit thick.' He returned to the cover of the bunker and sent a party out to shoot the Japanese. The Bren-gunner killed all four.

That afternoon the Japanese came again, this time under cover of mist and armed with sticks of dynamite. They blasted the trenches to Faulkner's left. Here the composite Indian troops were driven back. The Japanese were now moving between the West Kents' positions like wraiths. The Brens scythed through the smoke at unseen targets and the attack eventually fizzled out. But that night, at around 2200 hours, they were back. The trenches were silent. Only a darting shape alerted a West Kent private to the arrival of the enemy. There was the sound of guns being cocked. A tin can was kicked somewhere to the front. Then came a burst of fire. '[Private] Steele had fired at a shape that came too close.' But the silence returned. A private crept up to Faulkner and told him the Japanese had entered a basha close by. Suddenly grenades were being thrown from the basha. The West Kents opened up with a Tommy gun and grenades. The Japanese inside were still fighting. Another grenade was thrown from the basha and landed at the edge of Faulkner's trench. The West Kents now resorted to one of the simplest and most effective of all close-quarter weapons, the Molotov cocktail. After opening up with his Tommy gun Faulkner ran across to the basha and threw in the Molotov. It glowed but failed to ignite properly. Next they tried an incendiary bomb, but that failed too. Faulkner could not leave the Japanese with a foothold in his perimeter. He took a bottle of petrol and crept back to the basha. Kneeling outside he doused the walls. It was a recklessly brave thing to do. At any moment the occupants could have opened fire, or an infiltrating Japanese could have seen him. With petrol in his hand and all around him Faulkner would have been set on fire by a shot. His luck held. He ran back to his bunker and threw a grenade at the basha. It erupted in flames. 'There was more scuffling and the inmates dashed out and back down the slope. Ferguson was waiting for them with his Bren. He pulled the trigger and the gun jammed – much to his disappointment.' Another attack had been repulsed. The jamming of Brens was becoming frequent, a symptom as much of the handlers' fatigue as of wear and tear on the weapon. Exhausted men will struggle to clean a weapon properly and to make sure that it is ready to fire.

The following morning A company was pulled out of the line and sent to rest, if that were possible, near the Indian hospital at the summit of Garrison Hill. The 4th battalion had by now suffered two hundred casualties, approaching half the number that had entered Kohima; many of those with less serious wounds went back into the trenches to fight. At some point before C company was also replaced on 17 April, Private Ray Street recalled, a bottle of rum was passed round. 'I began to feel really merry and started singing aloud, "Onward Christian Soldiers". Soon the others joined in and it seemed the whole hill was singing … I don't know what the Japs made of it but we gave little thought to that. Mind you the next barrage seemed heavier.' The Assam Regiment and Assam Rifles who came in to take over the positions had earned the respect of the Royal West Kents, no mean feat given the latter's ingrained sense of superiority to any other fighting formation. The 4th battalion history recorded that both Assam units 'had proved their fighting qualities and could be relied on to hold any position given to them'.

Loyalty to comrades, as well as the terrible situation at the ADS, was decisive in the decision of wounded men refusing to leave the line. Private Norman passed through the ADS on his way from Detail Hill to get water. 'It was a most terrifying and heartbreaking experience. We kept falling over dead bodies which were black and decaying … as we passed through the hospital the smell was overpowering.' He also recorded that because of the high number of casualties C company had ceased to exist and was now part of A company. Major Donald Easten was a witness to the scene at the ADS while he was having his wounded arm dressed. 'Many of the wounded I feel sure died in the last few days because they had given up hope. Yet they were incredibly cheerful, outwardly, up to the end.'

Throughout 17 April the Japanese mounted attacks. Trenches were lost and retaken, but the positions on Supply Hill were becoming untenable. Japanese shelling, machine guns and snipers were killing and maiming the Indian troops and wearing down the reserves of faith. A young Indian officer, Major Naveen Rawlley, commanded the composite troops on the hill and led three counter-attacks under withering fire. He was an officer who found his mettle under the pressure of enemy attack; at the start of the siege he had presented himself to Richards and offered to do any job that was required. 'Are you infantry?' Richards had asked. Rawlley replied in the affirmative. '9/12th Frontier Force Regiment, Sir.' In the days that followed he welded a frequently unwilling assortment of men into a fighting unit and held on to Supply Hill, fighting alongside the West Kents and then the Assam troops, until resistance was impossible. On the night of 17 April a heavy Japanese barrage set buildings alight across Supply Hill. The defenders fled, leaving behind Rawlley, who stayed hunkered down throughout the bombardment.* He managed to escape an advancing wave of Japanese and reach the next line of defence at Kuki Piquet. This small hill was the last before Garrison Hill with its headquarters bunkers and the ADS. If the Japanese took Kuki Piquet, the garrison was as good as lost. Every remaining man, around 2,500, including all the wounded and non-combatants, would be crammed into a space barely three hundred yards in diameter. Once the Japanese were in among the defenders on Garrison Hill, the advantage of artillery support would be lost. No observer would risk bringing down fire in such a confined space.

Even the bravest man his limits, a place where courage is rendered useless by the demands of the body. After thirteen days with little or no sleep, the ever-present smell of death, the sight and sound of men dying, a chronic shortage of water, and the air filled with flying

---

* Rawlley went on to become vice chief of staff in the Indian Army after a distinguished career.

metal, the nervous system was beginning to win its struggle with the conscious mind. By the reckoning of one Assam Regiment officer, there were about forty-five battle-ready men on Kuki Piquet. They included what was left of Donald Easten's D company, the Assam troops who had survived the battle of Supply Hill, a handful of 4/7 Rajput, and the remains of Naveen Rawlley's composite force. All were physically and mentally exhausted after the flight from Supply Hill, 'infected by this panic', according to the West Kents' war diary. Preparing to attack them were at least two Japanese companies, around 360 men, with more in reserve.

Up at the Advanced Dressing Station during the day of 17 April, Lieutenant Colonel Young was making plans for evacuation. As soon as there was a breakthrough, he wanted his men ready to move. On the radio from Jotsoma, Warren told Laverty to expect a company of 1/1 Punjab, supported by tanks, which would begin the relief under cover of a massive barrage. Once the Punjab troops had deployed to cover the evacuation, the walking wounded would move off in groups of twenty; they would be followed by the stretcher cases in batches of six, at ten-minute intervals. The route would take them down to the road, past the Indian hospital, and in full view of the Japanese positions opposite. The stretcher cases would be picked up by ambulance, while the walking wounded would make their way to trucks. The tanks and artillery would keep the Japanese heads down while the evacuation took place.

Faith was slipping away from many of the wounded in spite of Padre Randolph's best efforts. He talked to men constantly and helped the orderlies clear the mess whenever a shell landed in a trench. The devout Christian Lieutenant Bruce Hayllar, shot in the opening hours of the siege, was rewounded by a shell fragment as he lay in his open trench. 'Each time they fired some of our friends were killed. It was terribly frightening. But there is always somebody worse off than yourself and you all know you are in it together. In my case I used to pray like mad. I used to say to my friends: ask for God's help. Just pray. It doesn't matter which god you pray to. You think to yourself, "If we are meant to get out, we will get out, if not it's just bad luck."' By the night of 17 April Hayllar no longer believed he would get out. 'We kept hearing we would be relieved, and it didn't happen.' Sensing that the end was near, he asked for his pistol. Other officers were doing the same. People were crying beside him, others screamed from the pain of their wounds, and he resolved to blow his own brains out rather than fall into Japanese hands. Did the idea of suicide bother his Christian conscience? 'No. In a way I think it's all right. If heaven is just around the corner and you die to get there ... We were afraid of being captured by them and being killed in a gruesome way.'

The shelling of Garrison Hill intensified and Hugh Richards believed it was the worst since the siege began. 'How my own H.Q. and R.W.K. H.Q. escaped direct hits I don't know, but they did.' Lance Corporal Dennis Wykes was nearby with some remnants of A company. Like everybody else, he heard the firing coming from Supply Hill and felt the barrage shake Garrison Hill. He began to think he might not survive. 'The officers just came round and said, "We'll fight to the last round, the last bullet and we'll stick until that happens." Our forces were so decimated one of the young lads said, "Can I put a pip on my shoulder, I'm still alive." And it was a bit of a joke, he wanted to be an officer!'

On the tennis court the Assam were still holding their own. But Calistan's troops were also being overtaken by fatigue and, for some, a conviction that they would not survive. Lieutenant Pieter Steyn wrote of how 'many were the anxious questions being asked. "Sahib, how long do you think we can hold out?" asked one man on DC Bungalow. But how could they be answered – anyhow with what certainty? Officers and men who asked such questions could only trust blindly that they were not destined to be annihilated. Many felt they were in the presence of something too big to grasp.'

On Kuki Piquet the defenders looked down the slope into the darkness and waited for the charge. Donald Easten tried to rally his men of D company. 'I was wounded but not so bad I couldn't do something. I tried to rally people. I hope to a certain extent I was able to steady things. I think I said, "Come on, chaps, it's not as bad as all that", and then I gave instructions about where they should position themselves.' Private Tom Jackson was Easten's company clerk, 'which meant general dogsbody', and was regarded by his boss as 'a wonderful fellow, a cockney and a man I became very fond of'. Jackson had delivered a signal to another trench when the Japanese opened up. 'All hell let loose: shells, rifle fire, shouting Japanese.' Company Sergeant Major Bill Haines, blind and still leaning on the arm of a helper, shouted at Jackson to withdraw to a trench further back. Jackson took off and jumped into a hole, where he met an Indian officer and the sapper Lieutenant John Wright, the man who had blasted the Japanese out of the bashas on Detail Hill an eternity ago. 'I jumped in,' Jackson recalled, 'and the lieutenant asked me what was happening. I said that if the Japanese came up the hill "we'd had our chips". He said, "Right, we'll use bayonets."'

At half past two in the morning the defenders heard screams on the slope below and the sound of men clambering towards them. This time the wave stuttered before the Bren and rifle fire but then swept onwards until the Japanese were in among the defenders. Artillery support broke up the Japanese reinforcements at the bottom of the hill for a short while, but the enemy revived and came again. CSM Haines found Jackson and told him to retreat up the hill. 'We were clearly getting a hammering and couldn't hold the position. Off we went, one of the signallers getting wounded in the leg as he jumped into a hole.' At thirty, Haines was one of the battalion's old soldiers, a veteran of France, where he had been awarded a Military Medal and, according to Easten, 'one of those chaps who never pushed himself forward but you knew if you said, "what do you think we ought to do about this?" he would come up with the right answer'.

How much could he see of what was happening around him? With his eyes badly damaged from the mortar blast, it may have been only the flaring light from the fires or shadows darting around him. But Haines would have certainly heard the noise, the screams of British and Japanese, the explosions and shooting, and his own hoarse voice urging the defenders to hold on. A few minutes after jumping into his new trench Tommy Jackson heard that Haines was dead. The men nearby quickly recovered Haines's badge, revolver and compass, and gave them to Jackson. Donald Easten had come forward to direct a Bren-gun crew when he heard the news. 'A company sergeant major in battle is your right-hand man. He was about thirty yards from me at the time. I went down to talk to some chaps about getting a Bren gun in a certain position and there was his body. It was dreadful.'

The Japanese scattered the remaining defenders before them. The men of D company, the Assam formations, the 4/7 Rajput and Rawlley's composite Indians fled from Kuki Piquet and on to Garrison Hill. This brought the Japanese to within one hundred yards of the command bunkers. In what can only have been an act of desperation, Laverty ordered Tom Hogg of B company to gather up his three survivors from 10 platoon and 'enough stray men' to retake a position captured by the Japanese. Hogg was horrified. Fortunately the conversation took place over the field telephone. 'There was no mention of any kind of support. I realised it could be only a vain suicide mission and I hesitated before replying, long enough fortunately for a shell to burst sufficiently close by to stop the conversation and I heard no more of that proposition.' John Laverty had run out of options. He did not have the numbers to make a counter-attack. The hill was crowded with fighting troops; the number of wounded had now swollen to around six hundred and added to those were the increasingly panicked non-combatants. If the Japanese were to come in strength now, he felt sure Garrison Hill would fall. Where in God's name was the relief? His mortar platoon commander, Sergeant King, struggled into the command bunker. King and his mortar team had worked relentlessly, bringing fire down on any concentration of Japanese that could be seen. He wanted permission to move his mortars so that he could fire on Kuki Piquet before the Japanese had time to form up. In an account given later, King was described as having 'half his jaw … hanging away so that he could talk, only half intelligibly, out of the side of his mouth. His right shoulder was hunched forward with the shot-away portion of the jaw resting on it. While he spoke he kept spitting out gouts of blood on to the floor of the dugout.' Laverty told King to get himself

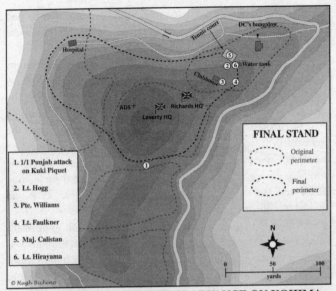

1. 1/1 Punjab attack on Kuki Piquet

2. Lt. Hogg

3. Pte. Williams

4. Lt. Faulkner

5. Maj. Calistan

6. Lt. Hirayama

FINAL STAND

Original perimeter

Final perimeter

N

0   50   100

yards

© Hugh Bicheno

FINAL STAND AND GROVER'S ADVANCE ON KOHIMA

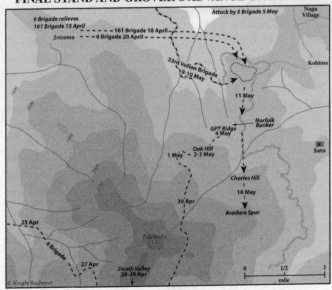

© Hugh Bicheno

treated at the ADS. The wounded man would go only after he had first been given an order to bring his mortars into action. They were soon falling on the Japanese occupiers of Kuki Piquet.

With the entire garrison in peril, 2nd Division artillery renewed its bombardment, not only on the Japanese infantry positions but on Sato's artillery as well; the British 25 pounder guns were directed by the observers inside the garrison and forward observers creeping close to Japanese positions. Captain Arthur Swinson witnessed the bombardment from the road outside Kohima. 'Stood and watched the flashes spurt and die as they fired, lighting up the camp one second to plunge it into darkness the next. What with these lighting effects and the demoniacal roar of sound, the whole scene was pitched into the over-real vividness of a nightmare.'

Somehow the Japanese guns kept up their fire, with more shells falling among the wounded throughout the night. John Faulkner was directing mortar fire and watched two men 'ramming bombs down the barrel as fast as they get 'em out again, laughing like a couple of schoolboys'. Early the following morning, Hugh Richards left his bunker and climbed towards Laverty's position. On the way he saw West Kent trenches filled with dead from the previous night's shelling. At 0600 hours Lieutenant Colonel Young and his orderlies went round the wounded telling them that they would be evacuated that morning. This time there would be no false dawn. Warren was on the radio from Jotsoma half an hour later to tell Young to expect relief by the 1/1 Punjab at any time. Once they arrived, the evacuation of the wounded could start. But this did not mean the relief of the garrison. Only a company of 1/1 Punjab was expected and an all-out Japanese assault was still likely at any moment. At 0700 hours the combined artillery of 2nd Division and 161 Brigade began pounding the Japanese once more; the shelling was to give the defenders respite and allow the relief troops to break through.

Events moved rapidly. At 0710 hours Young ordered that all patients be given morphine half an hour before being evacuated; ten minutes later the commander of the 1/1 Punjab appeared at the ADS. His men were through. The road was open. The Japanese roadblocks had been blasted away. It is hard to imagine what the troops' arrival represented to Young and the other medics. They had long passed the point at which human beings are meant to cease functioning in a logical manner. Thirteen days of siege with only snatched fragments of rest. But the newly arrived 1/1 Punjab officer found Young in complete command of the situation, punctiliously checking the arrangements for the movement of his wounded men and dispensing advice on the deployment of the fresh troops. The 1/1 Punjab had taken up positions overlooking the road from where they could help cover the evacuation. There were tanks following to give support. The combination of armour and artillery fire kept the Japanese pinned in their positions for the time being. The evacuation could begin.

At first Lieutenant Bruce Hayllar could not believe what was happening. 'It was a marvellous moment. They started saying, "If you can walk down the hill they are sending up some lorries to take you out." The walking wounded set off. Our reaction was "I don't believe it." It was wonderful when it happened. Some people were getting up and walking down to where we knew there was a road. I went with another chap. We had a stick each and walked. We met various corpses on the road. Some were ours and some were Japs.' Down at the road there were lorries and Hayllar saw the stretcher cases being loaded. He felt jealous of them because he was afraid there would be no lorries left to take the walking wounded. Hayllar made it on to a lorry, and as he was driven down towards Dimapur they met British troops marching to Kohima. 'They looked horrified when they saw us. We hadn't shaved for a fortnight and had no water. They gave us cigarettes and water. We were too ill to talk about it.' Another soldier, Mark Lambert of the West Kents, had spent the previous days at the ADS in agony from a leg wound, and from constipation. Evacuation brought sudden relief. 'I was taken down the road in an open truck. The constipation I had just stopped. The motion of the truck was like an explosion!'

Private Harold Norman was assigned to stretcher duty. He was told to check the men lying on stretchers, 'and if they were dead I had to send the Indian stretcher-bearers around the back of the feature where they put the bodies in a heap to be buried later'. At around 11a.m. he was helping carry a stretcher to the main road when shells began exploding. There was screaming from newly wounded men and from others terrorised by this last-minute assault. Corporal A. E. Judges who was helping the wounded was killed, and a West Kent captain badly wounded. He would die later. Private Norman ran for cover, passing the mutilated bodies of men who, a few moments before, had been on their way to safety. 'I saw trunks without legs and arms, and bodies with heads blown off.' The stretcher-bearers were also under pressure from Japanese machine-gun fire. Five medical orderlies, including a major, were wounded. Eventually, four tanks arrived and put the Japanese artillery out of action. Fighter-bombers again flew in and attacked the enemy trenches.

The evacuation went on throughout the day with Lieutenant Colonel Young in the thick of things. At one point he discovered that a group of casualties seemed to be missing. Young found them near the Indian hospital where the terrified stretcher-bearers had taken cover from machine-gun fire. He gathered the men together and led them down to the road to the ambulances. Among those who left on 18 April was Charles Pawsey. By staying throughout the siege he had shown the Nagas that they would not be abandoned by the British; now there was much work for him to do with the thousands of refugees who had fled their villages. Pawsey would go to Dimapur and insert himself among the officers and officials who controlled the food and medical supplies. By 1640 hours the Advanced Dressing Station, scene of so much agony, was cleared of patients. Lieutenant Colonel Young, however, stayed on. The road was open but the main relieving forces had not yet appeared.

In Laverty's bunker there was an urgent discussion about the tennis court position. The West Kents' CO wanted to know if it could be let go and the Assam troops take up new positions on the edge of Garrison Hill. 'I said it must be held,' wrote Richards, 'as if it were not the whole of Summerhouse [Garrison] Hill could be rolled up from that flank.' Laverty agreed and the 1/1 Punjab were sent to the tennis court to take over from the exhausted 1st Assam troops.

That night the Japanese artillery plastered Garrison Hill once again. Captain Harry Smith of headquarters company, 4th battalion, was struggling to get to the command post when a mortar blast knocked him over. A shell fragment lodged at the front of his skull and he lost consciousness. The 1/1 Punjab who took over the tennis court positions were heavily attacked but drove the Japanese back. There was no sign at all of an attack from Kuki Piquet. By the morning of 19 April the men in the trenches were feeling something like hope. They saw the arrival of the 1/1 Punjab as a signal of greater things to come. Later that day, Richards noted, the 'Div artillery put down a most terrific concentration on KUKI piquet for quarter of hour. Seemed nothing could live.' But enough Japanese survived to defend Kuki Piquet against the 1/1 Punjab's attempted counter-attack. John Faulkner saw them charge, 'with blood curdling yells', but they failed to gain any ground. They may, however, have given the Japanese an undue impression of the strength of the reinforcements on Garrison Hill. Sato had to draw off men from the assault in order to deal with the reinforcements arriving on the road from Dimapur, and must have realised that he would soon be forced on to the defensive. That night, the Japanese did gain some ground after the ill-fated Shere troops once more abandoned their positions, this time about forty yards from Laverty's headquarters. A counter-attack by A company of the West Kents drove the enemy out, killing over twenty of them, including a trenchful of men who were burned alive by exploding petrol and phosphorus grenades. Private Norman helped dispose of Japanese bodies on the perimeter. 'We collected all the pieces and put then in a pit and burnt them.'

The defenders held on throughout 19 April thanks to artillery support and the failure of the Japanese to launch an all-out assault from Kuki Piquet. Richards was convinced that one push was all it would take to annihilate the garrison. Perhaps it would come the following morning.

On the morning of 20 April, Captain Harry Smith, still groggy with morphine, looked up to see British troops in 'nice clean new uniforms making their way up around the top of the hill covered by a very heavy barrage of 2 Division's artillery'. The men were from 1st battalion, Royal Berkshire Regiment, 6 Brigade, and had come to take over the defence. Smith thanked God and then told the new arrivals to watch out for snipers.

Lance Corporal Dennis Wykes, A company, was in a weapons pit overlooking the tennis court that morning and came as close to death as he ever believed he would. He was staring out through an observation slit when a sniper opened fire. The bullet just missed his face and slammed into the rear of the trench. With his heart pounding, Wykes jumped back from the slit. Soon afterwards an unfamiliar soldier slid into the pit beside him. This man had shaved. He wore a clean uniform, and his eyes were clear. 'He said, "I'm taking over your position now." I said, "You're welcome to it." We shook hands. I warned him about the sniper. I said "Move quick, don't show your face." How I got off that hill I never did know.' All day the West Kent survivors staggered down the hill in twos and threes, towards waiting lorries. Private Tommy Jackson was carrying the belongings of Sergeant Major Haines as he was evacuated, knowing that the big man was lying back among the Japanese on Kuki Piquet. 'But you don't talk about that. You laugh at all the little things you got away with. It's impossible to explain,' he said.

They were shelled and sniped at again as they formed up to leave. The tanks immediately responded. Dennis Wykes felt numb with weariness. He walked for several miles until he saw an officer standing by the roadside with a large canteen full of fruit salad. 'He was ladling it out. He said "Well done lads, you done well." And I thought to myself, "You ain't done a bad job yourself here."'

The relieving forces were shocked at the survivors' appearance. Brigadier Victor Hawkins, commander of 5 Brigade, saw them coming down the road to Dimapur. 'They were a sight for the gods. Long beards of all hues and their clothes fit only for scarecrows.' The sights and smells nauseated the Royal Berkshires taking over the positions on Garrison Hill. Many doubled over and retched. An artillery officer wrote of 'the stench of festering corpses ... the earth ploughed by shell-fire ... human remains ... rotting as the battle raged over them ... flies swarmed everywhere and multiplied with incredible speed.' He came across a Japanese bunker in which about twenty men had fought and lived for several days, 'littered with their dead companions and their own excreta'. Ray Street, the C company runner, gave what advice he could to the incoming men. There was a last-minute tragedy in Ivan Daunt's trench. Daunt had just left when a sniper opened fire on Private Horace Collins, killing him and then wounding another man. Collins's brother Len had been killed a few days earlier. 'He didn't know about it,' remembered Ray Street, 'we were going to tell him about it when we'd got out.' He knew two other men who were shot by snipers as the trucks were being loaded.

Donald Easten, John Winstanley, John Faulkner and the other surviving officers of 4th battalion saw their men safely on to the trucks. Lieutenant Tom Hogg led a party of around fifteen men to the road and met an incoming patrol who offered them tea and rock buns. He could not eat. John Laverty and his headquarters staff were the last of the West Kents to leave, moving like sleepwalkers until they reached the roadway and the waiting trucks. A witness described Laverty as 'dead beat', literally sleeping on his feet as he walked to the trucks, the strain of constantly trying to fill gaps with fewer and fewer men lifted from his shoulders at last. The West Kents' CO had also lost many men whom he knew and upon whom he had depended; most of his senior officers were wounded or dead; the companies were shredded and existed only in name. The battalion had lost seventy-eight dead and nearly two hundred wounded, more than half of the men who first came into Kohima.

As the vehicles carrying the West Kents rolled down to Dimapur they were clapped and cheered by the advancing troops of 2nd Division, British and Indian alike. '*Shabash* [Well done], Royal West Kents,' they shouted. Ten miles from Kohima, Captain Arthur Swinson saw the first of the West Kents. He found it hard to believe that they were British troops. Only their rifles indicated they were not a band of ghostly tramps. He saw men with faces caked with dry blood, many covered in filthy, blood-soaked bandages. 'Some were falling fast asleep but others though palpably crazed with fatigue were buoyed with excitement and a blessed relief. Their dull, haunted eyes brightened into a smile as they waved to the troops along the roadside.'

Lieutenant Colonel 'Bruno' Brown and the Assam Regiment, who had been in battle constantly since the end of March, walked for two miles to reach the trucks. Of an estimated 400 men who had been deployed from Kohima the previous month, the 1st Assam had lost more than half in the battles of Kharasom, Jessami and Kohima. Albert Calistan described the Assam Regiment survivors 'marching and doubling some two miles down the main road to Dimapur … [where] we picked up transport'. They arrived at teatime and the battalion war diary records that the men 'although very tired indeed were in excellent spirits. They were given hot tea, and a good meal. Each man had a stretcher, sheets, blankets and pillows for the night.'

The West Kents found hot baths waiting for them, lined up in the open at Dimapur. 'They cut these drums in half,' recalled Dennis Wykes, 'so you had half a drum full of water and you jumped in, it felt really good.' They scrubbed off the grime and the smell of death, and then they shaved, using several blades to get through the tangled beards. Ray Street remembered being sprayed with disinfectant and some men having their bodies shaved because of lice. 'We slept through the next twenty-four hours, missing meals, despite being called and woken up for them.' In his waking moments, Street was disconcerted by the silence. For two weeks he had lived with the sound of shells exploding and guns firing. 'In a strange way,' he wrote, 'I missed the bombardment.'

Back up the road at Kohima, Hugh Richards watched the completion of the relief. At about four in the afternoon he got a message telling him to report to 2nd Division headquarters on the road to Dimapur. He went back to his bunker and collected his few possessions, and walked away from Garrison Hill towards the waiting trucks.

TWENTY-TWO

Attrition

True to form, Private Norman was thinking of his stomach again. On the night they reached Dimapur he took care to record what the 4th battalion was given for dinner. At 1800 hours the survivors of Kohima sat down to bully-beef rissoles, potatoes, fried tomatoes, gravy, plum duff and treacle. That was followed with 'unlimited supplies of canned fruit, jam, bars of plain chocolate, ½ packets of biscuits. Soap, chewing gum, fags, matches, playing cards.' Reading his diaries of the siege and its aftermath, one ceases to regard his obsession with the minutiae of each meal as pedantic; food, its rituals and timings, was the way for Private Norman to keep a grip on his sanity. While he could still eat, and meticulously detail the food, Harold Norman could believe that he was alive and that some part of his old self was surviving.

He was glad to see that Padre Randolph had reopened his canteen and was selling tea and half-packets of biscuits between meals. The men got mail. Norman opened five parcels, which included letters from home, a copy of the *Hotspur*, a *Hampshire Chronicle* and two crime novels. The following day he set off into Dimapur to visit Sergeant Tacon, the famous Bren gunner who had mown down the Japanese fleeing Detail Hill in the early days of the siege. Tacon had just been told that his brother had been killed in action in Europe. The sergeant was making a good recovery, but Norman's diary does not record his reaction to the loss of his brother. The schoolmaster, Captain Harry Smith, had spent an uncomfortable night, the result not of his own head wound, but of 'listening to the cries of the wounded' in the beds around him.

Private Norman was shocked by the conditions in the hospital. 'Our lads have not yet had their wounds dressed, their sheets changed or been bathed yet.' He also ran into Private Charlie Howell, who told him that a sniper had killed five West Kents with seven shots in fifteen minutes near the bungalow. For troops who had been in different sectors of the defence, cut off from each other by noise and by snipers, the first days of peace were a chance to find out what had really happened at Kohima. Some men sat in clusters and talked, others went off by themselves, and many simply slept. Those who chatted heard which of their friends had lived and which died. There was no drama. The 4th battalion had lived with sudden deaths for so long now that the men did no more than shake their heads at such news. The grief simply became part of all the other grief that they suppressed in order to survive.

John Winstanley wondered what news, if any, had reached his mother. She lived alone in a cottage in Kent and had already had 'those awful telegrams' telling her he had been wounded in the Arakan, and about the wounding of his brother in Europe. 'You don't know, is he dead or is he scratched or is he badly wounded.' She had heard no news of him since he had gone into battle in the Arakan. What would she be thinking now, this woman who had lost her husband in the last war, and who had devoted her life to her two sons' upbringing and education? He wrote immediately to tell her he was safe.

Lieutenant Bruce Hayllar was able to write to his parents from hospital in Dimapur on 20 April, two days after he had limped out of Kohima with the rest of the wounded. The experience had convinced him, he wrote, to devote his life to God. 'I have never seen, and never shall again see, such bravery and unselfishness as I saw up there.' There was in his letter a deep undercurrent of anger, not only at the war, but at some of those who had never experienced the hell of a front line. 'A man with an M.C. or D.S.O. is so far, far superior to a successful businessman or politician. Again, some people are a bit lazy about the war … content to let it run on without worrying much about it except as to how it affects themselves. They should just see what a battle involves. It is a terrific and most disgusting thing. Far worse than any slum or brothel and far bigger. As long as fighting is going on people should be conscious of this. And do all they can to help, so that it can be finished quickly.'

John Laverty was up early on the morning after their arrival at Dimapur. He called a conference of his officers for half past nine. A diminished band arrived, clean-shaven but haggard. Laverty went through the events of the previous fortnight and then read out a congratulatory message from General Grover. They discussed plans for sports for the men and for reorganising the shattered companies. Fresh drafts of troops were available in Dimapur to join the battalion. They would do what they had done after Dunkirk and after Alam Halfa. Start again with unfamiliar faces and trust the old warriors to keep the new ones alive long enough to become proper jungle fighters. Before he finished, Laverty told his officers to come back to him with recommendations for decorations among the troops. The most obvious contender was John Harman of Easten's D company, who had charged two machine-gun nests and given his life in the process. Easten decided he should be put forward for the highest medal in the armed forces, the Victoria Cross. He felt Laverty should know something of Harman's eccentric personality before he made a decision.

'He was a man who took the law into his own hands ... I went to Colonel Laverty and told him all this and he said, "There is really only one thing you can do and that is put him up for the VC."' Easten then decided to share the story Harman had told him about the old man in Spain promising he would live to old age. 'There is one thing, Sir,' he told the CO, 'I think Harman believed he was immortal.' Laverty took the news in his stride. 'Well Donald,' he replied, 'you don't judge people by that, you judge them by comparison with ordinary men and their fellow soldiers around them.' Harman would get his VC.

The following day, 22 April, Brigadier Warren, CO of 161 Brigade, arrived and spent the day with 4th battalion. The men were gathered together and Warren read out the special message of congratulations from General Grover. 'This is the first time in history that one battalion has stopped an enemy division.' It was a statement meant for the ears of the West Kents only, but it set them apart from their fellow defenders of Kohima. The war diary does not record whether the men cheered or not. Laverty told them he was being put up for the DSO for the defence of Kohima, but 'it was for all of us'. For some of those gathered listening, the time of rest and backslapping would be short.

That afternoon word went around that a composite company, made up from B and D companies, was being put together to guard a position at Milestone 32 on the road to Kohima. This was not the front line, and the job was simply to guard the line of communications up to the troops starting the fight for Kohima Ridge. But the men heard the news barely forty-eight hours after getting out of Kohima. Lance Corporal Dennis Wykes was not happy. 'We scraped out by the skin of our teeth. We weren't happy to be going back again.' The rest of the battalion would stay at Dimapur for the time being. For some of the Kohima veterans, this was an order too far. What happened next has never been mentioned in any of the written accounts of the siege, nor is it referred to in 4th battalion's war diary.

Dennis Wykes remembered it taking a week to reorganise the battalion, and during this time a corporal and ten men vanished. They walked out of the gates and into Dimapur and got on to a train. The medic, Frank 'Doc' Infanti, had sympathy with them. 'Some of them were brave men, one of them was recommended for a military medal, but they couldn't face going back up.' Dennis Wykes was called in by his company commander and told to pick three men and find the deserters. It took about a fortnight to find them. They had travelled across India and reached Bombay, where they promptly handed themselves in to the military police. There was nowhere else for them to go in India and boarding a ship home to England was out of the question. When Wykes arrived to collect them the men were lined up outside the guardroom. 'I said, "You know the score. You've all been through the siege. We've all seen that and known what you felt."' One of the men told Wykes that a bullet had parted his hair and creased his scalp at Kohima. After that he didn't worry about what the army might do to him. On the train back the corporal told Wykes that he and the other guards should get some sleep. 'It took about a week to get across India. The corporal said, "You can get yer heads down and get some sleep and we won't try to escape." So we trusted them and they didn't escape.' In the First World War such men would have been shot. But the army had moved some way in its understanding of what battle can do to the human mind. Laverty knew what the men had endured and he realised what a blot a court martial would place on the 4th battalion's achievement at Kohima. There was no court martial. According to Wykes, the men were used as ammunition-carriers for the remainder of the war.

The story of Kohima's epic defence had already reached the newspapers. As early as 18 April, a military correspondent with South-East Asia Command was quoting a West Kent private, presumably one of the evacuated wounded, praising padre Randolph, who 'used to sleep in the hospital trenches alongside the wounded and did everything to make us comfortable'. By their deeds the West Kents and the 1st Assam Regiment, and all the other defenders of Kohima, provided the army publicity machine with a boon. Within a week, public relations officers had descended on Dimapur, 'all eager to get at first hand personal stories of the doings of the battalion'. They were directed not to any of the Indian regiments but to the West Kents, where the bemused soldiery were interrogated by military correspondents.

One of them was a Captain Kitchen, described as an 'Observer with the 14th Army', who collected the first account of John Harman's death, perhaps embellishing the story in his telling of his final minutes. 'Officially he shot four and bayoneted a fifth, but it is probable he killed ten,' Kitchen announced. 'He was severely wounded by machine-gun fire, but got back to his trench. There he took off his equipment, lay back and said "It was worth it – I got them all." He refused aid from stretcher-bearers, crossed his arms, closed his eyes and, two minutes after the action, died.'

For reasons of wartime secrecy, the name of the battalion was not given. Instead, 4th battalion was referred to as 'a home counties unit'. This infuriated several of the officers, including padre Randolph, who fired off a stiff missive regretting 'the abrupt dismissal of the

work of the Royal West Kents' to *SEAC*, the newspaper of South-East
Asia Command, edited by Mountbatten's propaganda chief and
former Fleet Street editor, Frank Owen. It took until 13 June for
SEAC to name the West Kents under the headline 'First Story of a
Proud Battalion', by Reg Foster.

If the West Kents received little publicity by name, the Assam
Regiment, Assam Rifles and other garrison troops saw even less. But
the Assam soldiers were treated to a visit by the man they revered
above all others. On 2 May, General Slim came and 'walked round
and spoke to all the V.C.O.* and men in the area. He asked us to pass
on his message of congratulations to all other men in the Bn.' Within
a month the 1st battalion, Assam Regiment, was on a train to
barracks at Shillong, where the road was lined with cheering men
from the training battalion. They were given a hot meal and rum and
two days' holiday.

There was never a conspiracy to play down the achievements of
the men who had fought in the siege of Kohima; they suffered the
fate of all warriors on remote fronts. By the time the full story was
told to the press, the excitement over D-Day was inevitably dominating public attention.

Charles Pawsey had little concern for publicity. He had spent the last
twenty years of his life cut off from daily newspapers, in a place
where the happenings of the wider world were known to him only
via the crackly airwaves of the BBC, and reception was never very
good. But, the newspaper men found him. His was a story too good
to be ignored. He is described in one account as 'Pawsey Sahib' and
in another as 'The White Chief', the headline writers indulging with
abandon their fondness for the colonial stereotype. Graham Stanford
of the *Daily Mail* met Pawsey – 'tall, sinewy with graying hair' – near
Kohima at the end of April and described him as 'the type of
Englishman that I always thought lived only in the pages of Somerset

---

* Viceroy's commissioned officers were subordinate in rank to all British officers. The
rank of V.C.O. was equivalent to that of Warrant Officer in the British Army.

Maugham novels'. He recorded Pawsey's sadness at losing his collection of Naga 'craft-work' which had taken him years to accumulate.

Had Pawsey read a later dispatch of Stanford's he might have been roused from his customary good manners, for the *Mail* writer denigrated his Naga friends. 'Perched 5,000 feet up in the border mountains,' wrote Stanford, 'Kohima in peace time was a place of no importance to anyone save grinning, grunting Naga headhunters.' It was writing of its time, and little changed from the discourse of 'savages' that had informed the accounts of nineteenth-century travellers in Nagaland. Only later would the British generals and writers publicly outdo each other in their lavish praise of the Nagas.

By late April, Naga men were still heavily engaged in war work for the British, and Charles Pawsey was touring the refugee camps and villages and seeing the scale of the disaster suffered by civilians. He estimated that 7,000 Nagas needed rations immediately but warned the figure could rise to 30,000; he wanted 10,000 blankets, 12,000 earthenware pots and 3,000 mosquito nets. Some American Baptist missionaries appeared on the scene, offering to help Christians. Pawsey replied firmly that 'unless they are willing to help everybody their offer will not be accepted'. Pawsey made sure that the army chiefs knew of the Nagas' devotion to the British cause. He told a correspondent travelling with 14th Army that Nagas were supplying the army with 4,000 day-labourers, none of whom would take payment. 'They are very gentle with the wounded always carrying them at the same level no matter how steep the gradient is.'

Making his way around villages in British-occupied territory, the deputy commissioner was given messages from Naga contacts. A constable he knew well wrote to him describing how he had led troops to the capture of a government building held by the Japanese, and how he was staying on with the army in the jungle, trying to track the enemy. 'Sir I am still at Chihawa with Major Henchman collecting information from every direction and all the police within my area are employed in leading the troops in every direction. Sir I am trying to meet you soon.' Many other Nagas were crossing the Japanese lines to find Pawsey. Krusischi Pashkar, from Kohima village, saw the men marching through the jungles to the British lines, and mothers with small children being given rations at the sentry posts. Pawsey opened a temporary hospital at Dimapur and Pashkar saw him come 'every day to see the refugees and to enquire of their sufferings and to arrange their relief. Pots, clothes and tarpaulins were brought and supplied to the Kohima men.' Without the rations organised by Pawsey the refugees would have starved. Travelling from one hiding place to another, twelve-year-old B. K. Sachu Angami lived on roots foraged from the jungle. Weak with hunger the boy day dreamed about the feasts his people held before the war. A feast every month of the year with plenty of game. Now when he went into the jungle with his catapult and tried to find small birds there was silence and empty branches. 'We were taken here and there by our parents. For want of food we could hardly survive.'

By the time Kohima was relieved the threat from deserters marauding the hills had ceased. Ursula Graham Bower and her Naga scouts were continuing to patrol and gather intelligence, but the sense of imminent threat was gone. She was sent reinforcements, a half-section of Assam Rifles and their V Force officer, all of whom had survived the siege. They arrived at her hilltop headquarters and went to bed for forty-eight hours. 'When they had done that and emerged again, they cleaned everything until it glistened and then looked around for some more Japs.' Graham Bower took advantage of the relief to take herself to 14th Army headquarters at Comilla for supplies and because it was 'an excuse to let me get to Calcutta and get a perm wave'. News of her presence in Comilla reached Slim and she was sent for. Her first thought was that her command was going to be terminated; the siege was over and the days of Tommy gun-toting eccentrics, especially female ones, would be brought to an end. At headquarters she was marched by a brigadier along a long veranda with 'lots of offices going up in order of importance'. The brigadier knocked on a door and announced: 'Miss Bower, Sir!' Slim leapt up and held out his hand, a look of relief on his face. 'Oh, thank God,' he said. 'I thought you'd be a lady missionary in creaking stays.' Slim paid fulsome tribute to the Nagas and their spying work for the

British, and told her about the battles at Jessami and Kharasom where the Assam Regiment had delayed Sato's advance. After this pat on the back, Graham Bower was sent back to the hills to help train allied airmen in jungle survival techniques. For now the V Force war of stalk and ambush in the hills was in abeyance. Kohima was becoming a battle of attrition.

It had been a 'very excellent show', General Stopford agreed. The Kohima garrison had saved everybody from grievous embarrassment. The commander of 33 Corps arrived at Dimapur at eight in the morning on 18 April, as the first wounded were being brought out of Kohima. He was swiftly transferred to a jeep for the trip to meet General Grover, under whom he intended to light a small fire. Nearly two weeks had passed since Grover had assured him that the Kohima mess would be cleared up in four or five days. Instead, he was calling for more troops for what was looking increasingly like a battle of attrition. The relief of the garrison had been achieved, but the Japanese were still commanding the road to Imphal and Slim and Mountbatten wanted to know when it would be clear.

On the way General Stopford passed all the welcome trappings of an army moving forward: the lines of trucks loaded with ammunition and food, belching thick smoke on to the men following them; the mule trains which would be swinging off the road and up into the hills; the military police vainly trying to impose order on the traffic; and the picqets of Victor Hawkins's 5 Brigade protecting the line of communications. Hawkins had been the one to bring home to General Grover the difficulties of the terrain. Grover had confided in Hawkins that he was nervous about the meeting with Stopford and feared he would get a 'bowler hat' for asking for more troops. 'Don't worry sir,' Hawkins replied, 'I am quite sure you are right.'

It took Stopford nearly three hours to complete his journey and he arrived at 2nd Division headquarters to find 'John Grover ... in good form but rather strung up'. Grover went through his difficulties. He was still lacking in signals, engineers, artillery and service corps, and he feared attacks on his line of communications. To Stopford's impatient ears this may have sounded like special pleading; as he put it later, 'In view of the lack of enterprise on the part of the enemy this was over-done, and it became clear that the risk … must be accepted as normal.' Grover was told he must get moving and dominate territory.

Stopford was facing his own strains. On 20 April he confided to his diary that the Americans believed the British were in no hurry to open the road to Imphal because they could depend on American aircraft. As if that were not a problem enough, the Chinese generalissimo Chiang Kai-shek was sticking his unhelpful oar in, refusing to commit his divi-sions in northern Burma and blaming the British for 'messing up' the Assam campaign. 'Washington supports this view,' Stopford mourn-fully recorded. This information must surely have come via Slim, who was privy to Mountbatten's negotiations with the Americans.

The worsening political news translated into fresh pressure on Grover. A new memo was despatched to the commander of 2nd Division, also on 20 April, explaining 'why he must not waste time in clearing up the Kohima situation'. Grover told the officer who deliv-ered the memo to his headquarters about his difficulties – essentially a repetition of what Stopford had heard a day earlier. The Japanese were dug in on the high ground around Kohima and he feared being cut off behind. Another officer visiting 2nd Division returned to Stopford's headquarters later in the day with more baleful tidings. 'Later in the evening Steedman, who has just returned from H.Q. 2 Div, told me that he had attended John G.'s conference this morning at which the latter had painted such a picture of methodical build-up that we shall never capture Kohima.' The griping continued over the next few days. Stopford was 'disappointed', even 'horrified', and feared Kohima would not be cleared for a fortnight. If only he could have imagined how inadequate that projected timescale would be. News came on 23 April that the Durham Light Infantry, 6 Infantry Brigade, had lost two officers and ninety men wounded at Kohima, and Stopford was complaining that Grover was 'hopelessly sticky and seems to have lost his tactical sense'.

The day after receiving Stopford's letter, Grover went up to see Garrison Hill for himself. His guide was the irrepressible CO of the

75th Indian Field Ambulance, Lieutenant Colonel Young, who, after a night's sleep, was back checking the medical arrangements. Grover learned enough about the ferocity of the battle from what he saw, and from a meeting with Hugh Richards in Dimapur, to convince him that the fight ahead would be long and bloody. The chances of a swift advance were evaporating.

Stopford did not agree. On 24 April he set out for Dimapur again and had a long meeting with Grover. On this occasion the corps commander came directly to the point. He told Grover he had been very slow, 'which he did not like very much'. It is hard to pinpoint the precise moment at which John Grover's fate was sealed, for he would survive as the British commander at Kohima for some weeks yet, but by the end of April Stopford appeared to have lost faith in his ability to deliver an imminent breakthrough. Slim would later write that, while Stopford was correct to urge speed at the end of April, the terrain and type of warfare were new to the troops and 'the unavoidable arrival of the division piecemeal made the task of Grover … a difficult one'. That tolerance would evaporate over the coming weeks.

Three days after his meeting with Grover, Stopford went up to the battlefield and watched the air strikes and the infantry advancing. On the way back he stopped at a river, thinking that a spot of fishing would be nice. He proceeded to throw some grenades into the water. Water gushed up from the detonations and the surface was covered with dead catfish and carp. When weighed they amounted to twenty pounds of fish. 'Thoroughly satisfactory day,' the general noted.

General Slim followed the progress of his army from the mildewed town of Comilla, about two hundred miles to the east of Calcutta, on the banks of the Ghumti river. Since Slim had begun rebuilding the 14th Army, Comilla had become a major airbase and centre for casualties. The human consequences of the war he was directing were never far from Slim at Comilla. He disliked the place, for it had 'a sideline in melancholy all its own', presumably encouraged by the monuments to British officials murdered by Bengali rebels over the previous two decades. Still, by the end of April the first of Slim's nightmares had been put to rest. There was no question now of the Japanese seizing his Dimapur base and cutting off the line of communications. The four British and Indian brigades now invested at Kohima would soon push the Japanese aside and move down the road to break the blockade of Imphal.

There, General Scoones and 4 Corps had been holding off the Japanese 15th and 33rd Divisions since mid-March; although reinforced by elements of two Indian divisions, and well supplied and supported from the air, the defenders were not sanguine. They did not yet understand the increasingly dire state of the Japanese line of communications. Mutaguchi's divisions had been pressing on Imphal along six routes, with battles breaking out on hills and tracks as the enemy infiltrated behind the defenders and were in turn outflanked themselves. The close-quarter fighting in these encounters was every bit as vicious as at Kohima. Overlooked by the mountains, on the Imphal plain around 150,000 men were surrounded and dependent on air supply; more than 400 tons of stores per day had to be flown in by the RAF and USAAF. Delivering this essential materiel were eight Dakota squadrons, amounting to around 130 aircraft, and the twenty C-46 Commandos loaned by the Americans at Mountbatten's behest. But they were not devoted to Kohima and Imphal alone; there were still troops to be supplied in the Arakan and air drops to the Chindits on Wingate's second mission, as well as Stilwell's Chinese forces in the north of Burma. To ease the pressure on supplies, Scoones flew out nearly 30,000 non-essential personnel. But if the Americans, helped along by Chiang's drips of poison, withdrew their aircraft, Imphal's defenders would find themselves hungry before long. Adding to the problems was pressure from General Alexander for the return of the Dakotas, which had been diverted from the Italian campaign where allied forces were still struggling to break out of the Anzio beachhead.

Although it was far from a priority in the pre-D-Day months, the relief of Kohima was a welcome piece of news from an area usually distinguished by a reputation for catastrophe. The notes of the War Cabinet on 24 April recorded that 'Our stand at Kohima seems to have stayed the Japanese thrust towards Dimapur ... Generally, the outlook in the Imphal–Kohima area was hopeful.' Churchill would write later that he 'could feel the stress amid all other business', and he cabled Mountbatten on 4 May in emphatic terms: 'Let nothing go from the battle that you need for victory. I will not accept denial of this from any quarter, and will back you to the full.' Which was all very well, but the retention of the vital American aircraft was not in Churchill's gift. Nor was his CIGS, General Brooke, sympathetic to advancing any new resources to the Burma campaign.

Whatever his well-documented aversion to fighting the Japanese in the jungle, and his unrealistic schemes for seaborne landings in Sumatra, by the end of April, Churchill recognised that he was in a fight at Kohima and Imphal and that losing would inflict grievous damage on already strained relations with Washington, and leave Britain humiliated in India and the Far East. On 9 May he wrote to General 'Pug' Ismay, his military secretary and link with the Chiefs of Staff, that the aircraft gap 'must be filled at all costs ... we cannot on any account throw away this battle'. He was willing to telegraph Roosevelt and inform him of the 'disastrous consequences to his own plans for helping China which would follow the casting away of this battle'. Less than a week later he returned to the theme. Mountbatten's battle would not be ruined by the folly of sending the aircraft away. But the delay in clearing Kohima was having a negative impact in Washington. As Mountbatten's chief of staff, General Sir Henry Pownall, confided gloomily to his diary on 6 May: 'I don't think any of the Americans have any faith in the way our land operations are being conducted ...'

Slim would prove them wrong. But first he had to drive the enemy off Kohima Ridge, away from the approaches to Imphal and back across the Chindwin to disaster.

TWENTY-THREE

The Trials of Victory, and Defeat

General Sato had just come from his bath. It cannot have been an elaborate affair, the tub tucked into a basha in a thick part of the jungle close to the river bank. Emerging into the clearing outside, he met a young officer who had just arrived from Kohima. He recognised the younger man. 'You did a good job in the front line,' Sato said. 'I just finished bathing. You will take a bath now.' The muddy soldier did not know how to respond. Here was a senior general offering him the unimaginable gift of a bath, yet the young man kept picturing his men in the filthy trenches of Kohima. 'Thank you for your kindness,' he replied, 'but thinking about my men in the battle-field, I cannot take a bath.' The remark cut Sato, as he read into it a criticism of himself. He shouted at the man. 'You don't know my feeling. As a division leader, of course I would like to let all men in front line take bath if possible. Realistically, my wish does not come true, so at least I want you to take a bath on behalf of the others.' The officer took his bath and resolved not to mention it to his men.*

Sato's sensitivity had everything to do with the worsening predicament of the 31st Division and his conviction that, with Mutaguchi in charge, he was subordinate to a dangerous fool. On 17 April, Mutaguchi sent him an order to strip his division of three infantry battalions, roughly a third of its strength, and a mountain artillery

---

* Arthur Swinson asserts that the troops resented Sato's absence from the battlefield and quotes an unnamed 58th Regiment soldier who visited 31st Division Headquaters as saying: 'From this distance the battle seems like a dream … you would not know it was going on!' Arthur Swinson, *Kohima* (Arrow Books, 1996), p. 221.

battalion, and to send them to Imphal. This when the British 2nd Division was clogging the roads to Kohima with reinforcements and threatening to throttle him. Still, sitting in faraway Maymyo, Mutaguchi was working on the assumption that all of the Kohima Ridge would be in Japanese hands by 29 April. The date was no coincidence. It was the emperor's birthday and Mutaguchi intended presenting the hillside village as his personal gift. Sato initially instructed his commanders to prepare the troops for departure to Imphal at Aradura Spur, the huge ridge south of Kohima. Then he apparently thought differently and chose to ignore Mutaguchi's order. When a reminder came, Sato replied that the order was impossible. It was finally cancelled, with unconscious irony, on 29 April. Sato had signalled his future intentions by defying the 15th Army commander.

It was now well clear to the Japanese at Kohima that they were confronting a changed British and Indian enemy. Even Mutaguchi was beginning to sense that he may have underestimated them. Not only were they better armed and equipped, but they were fighting back. 'For this I could not help showing respect to the British leadership – they were once in a difficult situation, but seized the opportunity created by the delayed Japanese attack [on Kohima] and regrouped, which led them to a victory in the end.' A British correspondent's contemporary account brings home the superiority in firepower of 2nd Division. 'Across the valley ... the Japanese sit and watch the convoys roll on to Kohima. In the past few days they have seen vast lines of vehicles coming up from Dimapur to swell the British attack. Every lorry is a possible target for Japanese guns and except where the road twists behind the spurs, every mile is in shell range ... From these peaks every muzzle flash can be pinpointed and on the British side at least there is a mass of guns on call to hammer back at every Jap artilleryman who dares to fire.'

The supply officer Lieutenant Masao Hirakubo remembered the arrival of 2nd Division. 'It all changed ... every five minutes they fired. We couldn't walk in the daytime at all. Only at night we moved. I remember I said to myself "why are they making so heavy when they know we have no guns, only six shells a day for our mountain

artillery?"' At night harassing fire continued, with men never knowing where the shells would land. Aircraft attacked Hirakubo's kitchen
area. One of his cooks was shot by cannon fire and 'his stomach just
exploded'.

But it was the appearance of tanks that made the greatest impression on the new defenders of Kohima Ridge. The intelligence officer
Lieutenant Colonel Iwaichi Fujiwara thought the armour of 2nd
Division a graver threat to morale than the aircraft. Men formed
suicide squads and attacked the tanks with magnetic mines and
bombs. 'Unfortunately these tactics involved a heavy sacrifice of our
best men and could be regarded only as a temporary expedient.' The
138th Regiment supply officer Lieutenant Chuzaburo Tomaru saw a
tank shoot in his direction and thought the battle was finally lost. 'I
said to myself, "This is it!"' By Fujiwara's reckoning the pounding
from 2nd Division's artillery knocked out five Japanese guns, and
those remaining were restricted by shell shortages to firing no more
than five or six rounds each day.

For General Sato there was one more ominous portent. The river
near his divisional headquarters was a slow and sleepy jungle waterway. In early May there was a succession of downpours and the
general watched it muddy and swirl, fattening by the hour until it
swept away a small bridge and caused a mudslide on the banks. 'Its
appearance had completely changed,' he wrote. The season of mud
and disease was nearly on him.

At Kohima the men of the 1st Royal Berkshires and the 2nd
Durham Light Infantry, 6 Brigade, who had taken over the positions
on Garrison Hill, fought off the last of the Japanese attacks. Number
10 company of the Japanese 124th Regiment made little packages of
hair and nails to be sent back to their families. They were instructed to
send all correspondence back to headquarters, 'so the enemy can't say,
after you're dead, that you are unmanly and sentimental, burn all your
photographs and family letters'. The officer who gave the order,
Captain Yoshifuku, examined his own prized keepsake. It was a photograph of his eldest son in his first year at school. The boy was smiling
and thrusting his arm forward to show a badge naming him 'Top of the

Class'. He caught himself speaking to the photograph and then spotted another officer who was doing the same thing. The two men smiled at one and other. Captain Yoshifuku was killed later that night.

The familiar pattern was repeated. On the night of 22 April screaming waves of men surged from Kuki Piquet into the British trenches; the Japanese bombardment had the fortuitous effect of igniting an ammunition dump behind the defenders. In normal circumstances this might have been a disaster, but the blast set fire to the remaining tree tops on Garrison Hill and the glow illuminated the advancing Japanese, who came under a storm of Bren and rifle fire. The newly arrived British troops were thrown into hand-to-hand fighting, with ground lost and then regained, until the position was restored. The Durhams lost about one hundred men killed and wounded, while total Japanese casualties, although uncounted, were estimated to run to several hundred. Documents captured by the British showed that there had been fifteen survivors out of one company of roughly 180 men. In all, four companies were blasted and shot out of the battle. A Japanese major on Miyazaki's infantry group staff wrote of the 'hornet's nest' of defenders and how 'both Right and Left Attack Forces ... suffered many casualties without making appreciable progress ... even when he is surrounded by our forces, he will, supported by aircraft and artillery fire, resist to the bitter end'.

The tone of contempt for the British and Indian enemy was changing to one of grudging respect. The costly attacks on Garrison Hill convinced Sato to change strategy. In his own account he gives 23 April as the date he went over to the defensive, although he preferred to call it 'waiting'. He would dig in and hope that enough supplies would come soon to enable him to last out the monsoon. Sato was helped by an interlocking system of trenches and bunkers described by Slim as being 'as formidable a position as a British Army has ever faced'.

A medical orderly, George Senior, was swiftly immersed in the hell of Garrison Hill. Mortars came in about twenty yards away as the attack on the Durham Light Infantry began. Then groans and shrieks started. Terrified, the orderly started talking to himself: 'Let someone else go. Yes, someone else will go in your place, you low snivelling yellow coward … but I feel too weak to move … What would Dad say if he saw you now? … I mustn't let him down.' He jumped out and ran to the wounded. He had never seen so much blood. It was splattered everywhere. All over the wounded, the ground, the trees, and, soon, all over himself, as he went about his work. The following morning he sat by a stretcher case with a gaping wound in his shoulder. The man was being given a blood transfusion in a last attempt to save his life. 'He was restless and kept asking if he could go to sleep now but what little chance he had would have gone if he did go to sleep. So I sat there, keeping him awake and watching him slowly fall in an eternal sleep.' Nearby were the bodies of the men killed in the assault. There were not enough blankets to cover the dead and Senior saw bodies twisted grotesquely. One had a foot missing, another had half his skull blown away. Of the three Durham companies in forward positions there were only four out of fifteen officers left, while one company had shrunk from 136 men to sixty. Gordon Graham of the 1 Queen's Own Cameron Highlanders recalled how death 'was always a surprise, followed by a flash of survivor's guilt.' Ninety-three Cameron 'Jocks' were killed at Kohima but twenty-nine of the bodies were either never found or identified; the majority were killed in fighting at Naga Village.

Within a few days the Japanese soldiers in the trenches on GPT Ridge, Jail Hill, Supply and Detail Hills, and Kuki Piquet were defending against repeated British attacks. Lance Corporal Tukuo Seki fought off two attacks on his trench in the first week of May. But a heavy machine gun was blown up and the British were able to overrun the position. Seki survived and ran back, only to see a shell destroy a mortar position. At the tennis court the Japanese were mounting the last of their all-out assaults in the first week of May. The supply officer of 3rd battalion, 58th Regiment, Lieutenant Masao Hirakubo, was summoned into action for a night attack. 'Come with me to make a total attack,' the company commander screamed. Masao drew his sword and followed his commander into battle. It was pitch dark and he could barely see in front of him.

There was sudden fighting as they collided with the defenders. Men were grappling with each other and striking out. 'We dashed on them. They didn't expect us. I couldn't see his face so we hacked and stabbed.' Afterwards, still filled with adrenaline, he noticed that his sword was covered in blood. 'I killed somebody but I did not see his face. I felt nothing.'

Climbing the mound to the tennis court, Second Lieutenant Yoshiteru Hirayama, 58th Regiment, prayed that the British would not hear him coming. Hirayama did not consider himself a born warrior. He had been brought up in the calm of the Buddhist monastery in which his father and grandfather had been abbots. Now he found himself leading a ten-man section into the teeth of the British guns, fighting hand to hand with strangers and knowing death could come at any second. For weeks the same tactic had been tried. Men formed up on the mound and raced upwards to try and seize the British trenches. But so often the artillery had come down and ripped them to pieces before the attack could even begin. If that didn't do the job, they were cut down by the men in the trenches.

Hirayama's orders were to seize the first British trench on the opposite side of the tennis court. He ran with his section and jumped into an empty trench. The air around him exploded with machine-gun fire. 'One man got shot but we managed to get cover near a water supply tank on the British side. There was nothing there except bodies.' Hirayama could see that the situation was hopeless and with-drew. A few days later he was sent back and this time they managed to cross the tennis court. But again the British drove them back. As he ran, Hirayama was shot in the thigh. Blood spurted from the wound as he crouched and tried to run on. His rifle gone, he clutched a knife and hoped he would not encounter the enemy. Collapsing back into his own trench, Hirayama felt his life slipping away. 'It was very heavy blood. Another medic came with an emergency medical kit captured from the British.' The medic was Lance Corporal Tokuo Seki, who had heard a colleague shouting to him above the shooting, 'Please come and stop [the] bleeding.' Seki jumped out of his trench and raced to where Hirayama was lying. 'In his trench, there were

seven or eight injured soldiers lying in line. The trench was so smelly.'
Two younger medics were trying to stem the bleeding from his thigh
but lacked the proper experience. Seki found some pebbles and
wrapped each one in cotton wool to make a pressure compact which
he strapped into the wound. Hirayama's bleeding stopped for the
time being. He was eventually brought to a field hospital, a filthy and
overcrowded hut where he watched the flies lay eggs in his wounds.
Seki looked around at the other wounded men in the trench. None
had had their bandages changed for days. Pus was flowing out of
wounds. The medics were boiling filthy uniforms to make into dressings but could not keep up with the demand. To Japanese new to the
battlefield the sights were no less horrifying than they were to the
men of the Durham Light Infantry and the Royal Berkshires on the
other side. Sergeant Satoru Yanagi, 124th Regiment, arrived from the
rear area to Jail Hill around 5 May to reinforce the ravaged ranks of
the 58th Regiment, which had been fighting for three weeks. 'I saw all
dead soldiers, from both sides. Six hundred dead bodies I saw in that
single Jail Hill.'

Food became an obsessive preoccupation for the Japanese in the
trenches. A fortnight before, they had been able to convince themselves that supplies would come soon. But by the anniversary of their
first month at Kohima not a single grain of rice had arrived from
15th Army. Some of the supply officers were overcome with shame at
their failure to provide more than a single rice ball to each man. As
Masao Hirakubo of the 58th Regiment recalled: 'Mr Ito who worked
with the Mountain Artillery couldn't get food and was blamed by the
soldiers and he decided to kill himself. I don't know how he did it. At
least five times I met him and I said I could retain some food for two
or three days, and he had only food for tomorrow and he was so busy
trying to find it from somewhere.' A Lieutenant Nagashima of the
58th Regiment could not stand the deteriorating food and refused to
eat it, starving himself to death. Another officer who had malaria,
beri-beri and dysentery killed himself with a grenade when his
batman went to go to the toilet. The man thought he was a burden
to his servant.

According to the war correspondent Yukihiko Imai, some of the Japanese night raids were made purely to get food. He was lying on the floor of Miyazaki's headquarters, a captured barracks on GPT Ridge, when he heard the cries of the night attackers. It was about two in the morning and the darkness was filled with the sound of shooting and shells. Imai knew the men were from the 58th Regiment, 'born in snowy Niigata ... [a] tenacious and steady char-actered district'. He wrote: 'They were so hungry and sometimes they got the Churchill issue from the enemy base.'* He noted that they did not want to share their food with others in the rear. Private Manabu Wada managed to scavenge some bully beef and biscuits but was weak from hunger. 'How could he be expected to fight in these circumstances?' A perfect illustration of the supply gap between the two sides was found by the medic George Senior, who was full of praise for the quality of the bunker he occupied on Garrison Hill. It was covered with wonderfully blast-absorbent mate-rial: sacks of rice for which the British and Indians had no need.

The drivers of the 2nd Division convoys rolling up to Kohima came around the final bend before the village and saw a large white notice-board: 'From this point on you are in view of the enemy.' General Grover set out to alter that reality in early May by trying to drive the Japanese from Kohima Ridge and the positions they occupied in the valleys around it. The pressure from Stopford and Slim was unrelent-ing. They made a joint visit to 2nd Division headquarters on 2 May, with Grover noting that 'Slim was very insistent on the need for speed, very largely for political reasons. He evidently thought we had been going rather slowly, but appeared surprised at the size of the country. He was also a little sceptical as to the strength in front of us ... Later events proved that we were correct and he was wrong.' Grover was irked at the lack of understanding and was again pressed on 5 May by Stopford, who told him his projected date of 9 May for the capture of Jail Hill was too late. He pushed Grover to agree to 7

---

* The Japanese referred to captured suplies as a gift from Churchill or 'Churchill rations'.

May. As Sato had learned when he was laying siege, setting dates at Kohima was a charter for despair. The place had an awful way of destroying men's plans.

Grover's offensive against Kohima Ridge involved a three-pronged assault with 4 Brigade moving against GPT Ridge to the south, 5 Brigade swinging behind the Japanese and attacking the Naga Village and Treasury area to the north, while 6 Brigade would strike against the positions on Kohima Ridge in the centre. Each brigade would be supported by artillery and air strikes.

The 4 Brigade marched for four days across steep hills to get into position behind the Japanese at GPT Ridge, with an attacking force made up of 2nd battalion, Royal Norfolk Regiment, the 1st Royal Scots, and machine-gunners from 2nd battalion, the Manchester Regiment. Three of the Manchester's companies had not fired their guns in anger since the evacuation from Dunkirk. When they did open fire, an 'observation shoot' to see if they could flush out any hiding Japanese, the experience 'raised the men's spirits tremendously'. Before the battle of Kohima was over the Manchesters would fire a million rounds.

Private George Gordon, Royal Corps of Signals, remembered a miserable journey during which he was ravaged by fleas after having slept in abandoned Naga huts en route. The Naga porters accompanying the column suddenly disappeared. Later, it was found that they had gone to mourn comrades killed in a Japanese ambush. According to Private Gordon, the loss of the porters resulted in an exhausting trek back and forth. 'As each man had a personal load of 70 pounds, it meant that the machine guns, three inch mortars, wireless sets and batteries had to be left under guard and the machine gunners, mortar men and Signals had to make the day's march, leave their packs and return for the equipment. What a day it was! The track was wet, slippery and steep and there were places where we literally had to crawl along or pull each other up by hand.'

A Norfolks officer struggled to keep going. 'You drag your legs upward till they seem reduced to the strength of matchsticks ... Your heart pounds, so that it must burst its cage ... all you can think of is the next halt.' They climbed for nearly two miles up the steep face of Mount Pulebadze, an 8,000 foot peak, whose razor-backed ridge would bring them within striking range of the Japanese on the rear of GPT Ridge. At dawn on 4 May they came down the mountain towards the Japanese trenches. On the way they passed the corpse of a British sentry killed the previous night, with 'round staring eyes … scores of flies already buzzing around'. At 0700 hours the Japanese snipers opened up. The column was held up for around half an hour, with thirty casualties, while George Gordon reckoned 'we had hardly fired a shot ourselves!' Over the next week 4 Brigade, and the Norfolks in particular, would fire plenty as they fought from bunker to bunker to dislodge the Japanese. Captain Jack Randle, with B company of the Norfolks, was awarded Kohima's second Victoria Cross for charging a bunker despite a shrapnel wound in the knee, and silencing a machine gun that was pinning down his company. Randle was mortally wounded as he ran, but managed to throw a grenade into the bunker and then throw his own body across the slit to ensure that the Japanese could not fire out. He was twenty-six when he died and left a wife and small son in England.

Like the West Kents, the Royal Norfolks had been through the crucible of Dunkirk, where they had suffered a grievous atrocity at the hands of the SS Death's Head Division. Ninety-seven prisoners were machine-gunned at Le Paradis in the Pas-de-Calais on 27 May 1940. At Singapore three other battalions of the Norfolks were taken prisoner and badly used by the Japanese, some shot out of hand and others sent to work on the Death Railway into Burma.

In the battle for GPT Ridge the Norfolks fought with fierce zeal. 'Then the "Holy Boys" shouted their battle cries until the whole ridge rang with their challenge. The line began to move,' an officer recalled. 'The shouted orders of officers were drowned by the battle cries as the line moved forward. It was an afternoon of terror for the Japanese. Unable to fire from their bunkers because the fire slits were facing the wrong way, they came from their holes and stood in groups, petrified by the sight of the shouting British, who advanced relentlessly. Some had left their weapons in the bunkers, the weak quailed and fled, the braver ones put their weapons into the aim. Up to this point the "Boys" had held their fire, but now the Japs went down like corn before a sickle. Over 100 enemy dead were counted that day.' The Japanese were driven to the north-eastern spur of GPT Ridge, where they resisted with customary ferocity, shooting dead the 4 Brigade commander, Brigadier Willie Goschen, while he directed an attack on some bunkers. His successor was killed a week later.*

All along Grover's front the rifle companies were suffering heavy losses. Company commanders were being shot down at a fearsome rate and, according to Swinson, there were virtually no platoon commanders. In one action around the Naga Village the Camerons lost thirty-eight men killed and wounded; the Royal Welch on Garrison Hill had seven officers killed or missing, thirty-three men killed and more than a hundred wounded; the Durham Light Infantry lost 175 men and two thirds of their officers. Every unit invested at Kohima Ridge in that first fortnight of May could tell a similar story of advances halted by storms of fire. Captain Gordon Graham, Cameron Highlanders, came across the corpses of four comrades while on patrol. He found himself curiously detached from the experience. 'Looking at the corpses we found on this patrol – the first battle casualties I had seen – I felt surprisingly impersonal. Friends of mine had inhabited these bodies until a few days before, but when death is not sanitized by funeral rites you feel intiuitively that the people are still around.'

Lance Corporal Angus Taylor, 1 Royal Scots, remembered a seven-mile march that had taken eight days. On the battlefield he found the wallet of a dead Japanese soldier, in which there were photographs of the deceased man's family. One showed a woman posing shyly for the camera, alluring in her traditional dress, and standing outside the family home. The other was of a child – the couple's daughter, aged about eight – standing against a tree. There was a third photograph

---

*4 Brigade commander Jack Theobalds died on 16 May 1944. He was one of two Brigade commanders killed at Kohima; two others were wounded.

of the soldier himself, a handsome young man with his gaze fixed just to the right of the camera. The soldier would have collected these photographs before he left for war and kept them with him until the end. For sixty years they lay among another man's memories. In such a way does war bind the living and the dead.*

Arthur Swinson, the young 5 Brigade captain and an aspirant writer, wrote of how officers and men would 'look at the great ring of mountains encircling them, and wonder how on earth it could be taken, how flesh and blood could possibly stand much more'. When Grover came up to see the Dorset Regiment in the bungalow sector in early May, he recognised a scene reminscent of the First World War, where he had suffered in the trenches as a young man. All the men here had beards, he noted, although he was glad to see that the water ration was now enough to give them three pints of tea each day. Supplies of water were still being dropped by the RAF.

Victor Hawkins and 5 Brigade had set off to traverse a wide valley so that they could emerge behind the Naga Village. On 1 May he received orders to take the Naga Village quickly, 'from both a political and a military point of view'. The instruction was followed up by a personal message from Slim two days later. Hawkins pushed on and by 4 May the Camerons had captured the western tip of the position. '[There were] thousands of flies and filth of every description, including the innards of numerous pigs and cows to which the Japs had helped themselves,' wrote Hawkins. 'We not only overlooked the complete KOHIMA battlefield but right into the back of the Jap positions … we wasted no time in getting mortars on to them and disturbed them considerably.' Hawkins had the unsettling experience of shaving for the first time in several weeks and being confronted with the face of an 'old graybeard'. He looked over his shoulder before realising he was looking at himself.

* I was shown these photographs by 92-year-Angus Taylor when he attended a reading of this book in Scotland, in the summer of 2010. On hearing his account of Kohima, the audience burst into spontaneous applause.

Hawkins's 5 Brigade were making ground, and so too were 4 Brigade on GPT Ridge, but 6 Brigade were making no impression against the Japanese positions in the centre of Kohima Ridge. The Royal Welch Fusiliers briefly seized the top of Kuki Piquet before being driven off. They lost 189 men in successive attacks and their commanding officer was eventually sacked. Stopford answered Grover's plea for extra men by sending in 33 Brigade of the 7th Indian Division. An officer of the brigade, arriving at Kohima on 6 May, believed he was 'watching a dozen different battles going on in front of us'. The following day, elements of 33 Brigade attacked Jail Hill and Major Michael Lowry, Queen's Royal Regiment, witnessed the 'closest thing to a snowball fight that could be imagined'. Grenades were hurled between both sides and the Queen's 'did a fair amount of damage to these little blighters'. The rain and mist came and gave respite from the sniping. When the sun appeared again Lowry saw that a friend of his, Captain John Scott, was dead. 'In cold sweated horror I saw the contents of that clever head spread out on the ground. No grey and white matter could have been portrayed with such awful clarity.' Scott was twenty-three years old and a lawyer in civilian life. Lowry was at a loss to comprehend the wretchedness he saw around him. Like many other veterans of Kohima, he remembered the profusion of flies with particular disgust. They alighted on corpses, on latrines, on men's food, on their bodies. 'I, for one, have eaten several of the largest filthy-looking blue bottles, having settled on a bully-beef sandwich between the hand and mouth.' The attempt to retake Jail Hill was a costly failure.

Major John Shipster, seconded to 33 Brigade from the 7/2 Punjab Regiment, arrived in mid-May. Although only twenty-two, he was a veteran of the Arakan campaign where he was awarded an immediate DSO. He saw old parachutes swaying on the blackened stumps of trees and on the road he passed the body of a Japanese soldier embedded in the soft tarmac. 'As the days passed, his thin, wafer outline gradually disappeared.' At Kohima he found a vast uncovered necropolis where men learned 'to respect the dead, but did not mourn for them ... it was essential for our own mental well-being'.

The battalion padres held regular religious services in the midst of this darkness. A gunner with the 99th Royal Buckinghamshire Yeomanry, Royal Artillery, took Holy Communion to the sound of a comrade calling fire orders beside him. 'Draw near with faith, and take this Holy Sacrament to your comfort,' came the padre's solemn voice, 'accompanied by the clanging of four breeches slamming shut, the thunderous bang of our four guns, the clatter of empty cartridge cases being extracted from the breeches'. Soon afterwards the gunner had the dreadful experience of watching a Royal Armoured Corps tank knocked out on the road below him. The Japanese threw an incendiary bomb and the tank was quickly engulfed in flames. Enemy machine guns covered the road on either side. The tank crew faced a choice that was no choice at all: stay and get burned alive, or run and get cut down by the machine guns. They chose the latter and all were killed.

At the tennis court the 2nd Dorsets were gaining on the Japanese. They had been fighting their way down towards Pawsey's bungalow since their arrival on 26 April. They suffered fifteen casualties while taking over the position but gradually wore the Japanese down, advancing to Pawsey's garden by early May. Private Tom Cattle was an apprentice butcher in the beautiful Dorset village of Corfe Castle when he was called up for the army. By April 1944 he had travelled halfway around the world but had yet to hear a shot fired in anger. The Kohima tennis court would be his introduction to war. Lying in one of the pits originally dug by John Winstanley's West Kents, he watched his corporal pop his head briefly out of the trench. There was an instant crack and the man fell back on top of his comrades with a single bullet hole in the middle of his forehead. 'That shows you what you could and couldn't do.' There were three people in a trench that was no more than eight feet long and two feet wide. To sleep, they crouched on their heels. At one point of the perimeter the Dorsets were within two yards of the Japanese, prompting Grover to remark later that 'the occupants must have heard everything that went on in their post'. At one stage a Japanese soldier was digging soil from a foxhole when the dirt landed in a British trench. He was killed by the prompt dispatch of a grenade.

To drive the Japanese out of the bungalow the Dorsets needed a tank, but there was a problem. The road leading up to Pawsey's bungalow had been built at his own expense and the corners were cut rather sharply, making it slow going for a car, let alone a lumbering tank in the line of Japanese fire. The Royal Engineers came to the rescue and bulldozed a track into the garden, all the time under enemy machine-gun and sniper fire. The 2nd Dorsets' commanding officer, Lieutenant Colonel O. G. W. White, described what happened when a tank opened fire on the bungalow at point blank range. 'It got among about two dozen Japs who ran round and round wildly. They're apt to do that in a crisis. We got about a dozen of them and the tank shot some of them individually with its 75.' A mountain artillery gun fired forty-eight shells into the bungalow. Forty Japanese ran from the building. 'The gun couldn't fire at them because it had no more ammunition, but the Sikhs manning the gun fired everything they'd got at them. I'm told some of them got so excited they even threw stones.' Fighting raged from room to shattered room where Pawsey had entertained Richards and his staff to cocktails a few weeks before. A Japanese in the garden who waved a yellow and white flag from his trench had his hand shot off. Pole charges were dropped down the deeply burrowed foxholes to make sure no Japanese were left alive.

By the night of 13 May the Dorsets were in control of the bungalow sector, bringing to an end one of the most prolonged periods of close-quarter combat of the entire war. Along the rest of Kohima Ridge the sustained attacks were taking their toll on the defenders. On the same day as the tennis court was regained, the Japanese vanished from Jail and Supply Hills. They had already abandoned GPT Ridge to 6 Brigade and on 15 May they left the Treasury overlooking the road to Dimapur. General Grover appeared the following day and was there to greet Stopford, who was 'very much impressed by their tremendous morale'.

The CO of 6 Brigade, John Dee Shapland, who was responsible for the central sector that included the bungalow, thought the whole business had 'worked like a charm', but was shaken when he received the casualty list. 'I got congratulatory telegrams from my Corps commander [Monty Stopford] and John Grover – but it was no congratulations for I had lost over half my splendid men. This is one of those things we soldiers have to bear in war, but does make one feel very humble.' Shapland himself became a casualty on 28 May, as his troops advanced near Aradura Spur. Crouching in the jungle, he saw a party of Japanese moving down the slopes across the valley. 'Then I was hit, as I thought, by a cricket bat on the back of my neck [but] it was really a bullet passing through! I blacked out and saw lovely green fields …' When he came to, Shapland found his battledress soaked in blood as well as, much to his annoyance, both of the cheroots he kept in a breast pocket. 'I did manage to smoke one later on!'

It would take another three weeks of tough fighting to drive the Japanese from the positions around Kohima. On 7 June, the day after the last major position at Aradura Spur was abandoned, Stopford sent an emissary to press Grover once more to speed up his advance. Now Stopford wanted him to get on the road and break through the Japanese roadblocks between Kohima and Imphal. The message was followed up with a phone call from Stopford. The breakthrough to Imphal finally occurred on 22 June 1944, when the relieving troops of 2nd Division met soldiers of Scoones's 4 Corps fighting up from Imphal. Officers and men from both corps climbed from their vehicles and shook hands, knowing that they had broken the siege of Imphal and with it the Japanese 15th Army.

Soon afterwards General John Grover was fired. It happened, with supreme irony, on the day the three divisions of Mutaguchi's army were ordered to retreat from India. Stopford went to see Grover on 5 July. Stopford took him to one side and told him his command was being terminated. Lancashire Fusilier John McCann wrote of the puzzlement of the troops, who were 'part of a force that has inflicted on the enemy a massive defeat … [and] it is totally unjust that "the Powers That Be" have separated from each other John Grover and his men'.

Stopford's diary makes it abundantly clear that frustration with Grover had been building for several months; and it continued after the recapture of Kohima, with 33 Corps staff accusing the 2nd Division of being 'frightened of shadows' as it advanced towards Imphal in mid-June. Grover had few supporters outside of his own division. But he was also partly a victim of the military politics of the Raj in its twlight. The 2nd Division was British but was paid for by the Indian government, a source of grievance with the Congress Party and with Indian Army formations. It also cost more to maintain than an equivalent Indian division. This helped form a bedrock of resentment against Grover. More damagingly, he was perceived as having scant regard for Indian troops. One Indian Army officer set out the charges in a letter to Arthur Swinson who served under Grover in the 2nd Division. 'The impression was gained that he regarded the Indians as "coolie labour". His staff could scarcely have been unaware that this rumour was spreading, yet they appear to have done nothing to counter it ... had the General only gone around the Indian units once or twice, the pages of history might have been a little different.'

There is some anecdotal evidence from 2nd Division soldiers to lend support to this assertion. Dick Reynolds, a sapper with 208 Field Company, complained in June that 'we could get no men to reinforce us, not Englishmen anyway', and that Grover refused the offer of Indian reinforcements. According to Stopford's official account, the total British and Indian dead from 4 April to 22 June amounted to 911 with a further 266 missing and more than 3,000 wounded, the majority of those casualties incurred by the 2nd Division in its long fight to clear Kohima Ridge. When the 7th Division commander, General Frank Messervy, arrived on the scene, he is said to have been furious at Grover's use of his men. The evidence for this comes from Major David Young, an Indian Army officer, who witnessed Messervy's outburst. 'General Messervy, having visited ... 33 Brigade, went off to see, first General Stopford, then General Slim, to demand that 33 Brigade be removed from the control of 2nd Division because of the unnecessary high casualties which were occurring in consequence of what he, General Messervy, said was inept handling by General Grover. I was present when General Messervy, in a furious rage, saw Brigadier

Warren [161 Indian Brigade] and spent a few minutes in his headquarters fuming at the overall situation.'

Grover undoubtedly harmed himself at the very beginning by suggesting that he would clear up the Kohima mess in a matter of days and by continuing to promise a swift breakthrough *after* he had seen the scale of the country. The British troops moved slowly and the rate of casualties was high as they faced heavily entrenched defenders. But his men felt anger at the news. The 2nd Division had been pulled from training in central India and hurled into battle at the last minute; it was delayed reaching Kohima in full strength because Slim and Stopford feared, wrongly as it turned out, that Dimapur and the railway were threatened. As for the high rate of casualties, 2nd Division's lack of experience in fighting the Japanese was a factor, but attacks on such formidable defensive positions were inevitably going to be costly. And the Japanese were only able to gain such a foothold on Kohima Ridge because Slim and Stopford had decided to concentrate resources on the defence of Dimapur until it was almost too late to reverse the situation. Grover was sent home to become Director of Army Welfare, an inauspicious sinecure for a man still in his forties. He made no public comment except to thank his men for their sacrifice at Kohima. When the troops of 2nd Division arrived back in Britain in 1945 Grover was waiting at Southampton to meet them. As the ship came in to dock some of the men spotted Grover. The news spread quickly around the decks. A witness described how 'the Captain became concerned as all the men suddenly ran to the side near the dock, pushing all the weight over to one side'.* A chant rose up from the ranks. 'Grover, Grover, Grover.' Eventually John Grover stepped forward to cheers and made a short speech of welcome to his men. In his mind and theirs they were still *his men.* Many years later his son, Lieutenant Colonel David Grover, was asked why his father had never complained publicly about his treatment. 'He was loyal to the army,' came the brisk response.

---

* This account was given to Gordon Graham of the Cameron Highlanders by a comrade who was on board the ship.

Stopford carried out the sacking of General Grover, but it was done with Slim's full authority.*

The British drama of command at Kohima was unpleasant but it was settled in the accepted traditions of the army. Nobody complained. Nobody explained. What was about to happen between the Japanese generals would be of a different order, a story of hubris and self-deception, and a collision of powerful personalities, which foreshadowed the greatest catastrophe in the history of the Imperial Japanese Army.

---

* Slim never mentioned Grover's sacking in *Defeat into Victory*, whether out of deference to the general's feelings or a desire to bury the incident it is not possible to say. It came at the end of a period of great pressure on the 14th Army commander. Because Slim had misread Japanese intentions, Mutaguchi came close to striking a decisive blow against 14th Army. Had he started his invasion a few weeks earlier, as planned, Kohima and Imphal might well have been told as stories of British disaster. Slim was saved by his capacity to react decisively, by luck, allied superiority in planes and weapons, and the determination of his troops. 'I was saved from the gravest effects of my mistake in under-estimating the enemy's capacity to penetrate to Kohima by the stubborn valour of my troops …' he wrote in *Defeat into Victory* (Cassell, 1956), p.311. John Grover's 2nd Division suffered the majority of the 4,000 allied killed and wounded at Kohima as they fought to drive the Japanese out. For more detailed accounts of the different units involved in the second phase of the Kohima battle I refer the reader to Leslie Edwards, *Kohima, the Furthest Battle* (The History Press, 2009) and Peter Hart, *At the Sharp End – From Le Paradis To Kohima* (Pen and Sword, 1998).

TWENTY-FOUR

The Road of Bones

The hubris of the Japanese advance, the ferocity of the battle, the growing hunger and desperation, are all recorded in an anonymous Japanese doctor's diary, found by a platoon of Gurkhas lying among a hundred bodies on a hill above Imphal. At the beginning of April the doctor had noted how the enemy was defending with full force 'but it is useless against the sons of heaven'. He was proud to be on the front line but missed the season of cherry blossoms just beginning at home. Within a fortnight he was dealing with 'many cases of diarrhoea and dysentery'; a week after that, hunger was such that the men 'can barely keep going'. Lying in the jungle at night, the doctor craved sweet potatoes. A man nearby said he wanted to die with all the delicacies of Japan in his stomach. 'Even to think of what we used to eat at home makes my mouth water and my mind swim … at times you are driven to hide food from your best pal instead of sharing it with him.' The bombing was shredding his nerves. He wrote of seeing flesh fly into the air and of the ferocity of the advancing British and Indians. Only a handful of men were left in his company. On 18 May he wrote: 'Am I the only M.O. left? More than ever, then, I must try to do my utmost.' The rains descended in the last week of May and he began to pray for a night of dry weather. He had a shoulder wound which was discharging pus and was now struck by amoebic dysentery. The doctor's last entry, on 23 May, asks, 'If I weaken and fail what is going to happen?' The Gurkha major who witnessed the last hours of the doctor and his comrades told of how they were killed by a stream

389

of machine-gun fire while huddling around the flag of the rising sun. It was a scene destined to be repeated across the Imphal and Kohima battlefields.

By the middle of May, General Kotuku Sato knew that the battle of Kohima was lost. There was no food. There would be no food. The trucks that might carry food were being used to bring reinforcements to the Imphal battle, which was itself in terminal decline. In the account he wrote for 31st Division veterans, Sato gives 12 May as the day when his infantry, led by the tireless Miyazaki, realised the British could not be held off much longer. Sato ordered his troops to begin slipping away from the positions along the ridge on 13 May, moving towards the Naga Village and a series of strong defensive positions to the south of Kohima. Lieutenant Hiroshi Yamagami, the flag-man of the 58th Regiment, was told to report to Miyazaki's headquarters and prepare himself to move. 'As an officer I was expecting it … it was impossible to go on … it made no sense to stay any longer.'

Sato had been building towards his moment of truth. On 4 May he went over Mutaguchi's head and signalled the head of the Burma Area Army, Lieutenant General Kawabe, to say that 15th Army had failed to supply him with food. A furious Mutaguchi told him never to address Kawabe directly. Sato ignored him and went even higher, signalling the powerful Count Terauchi, commander of all Japanese forces in South-East Asia, as well as imperial headquarters in Tokyo. But it made no difference to his supply situation.

On 25 May, Sato signalled to Mutaguchi his intention to withdraw from Kohima. 'Retsu Division has run out of food for the soldiers and horses, and the supply of ammunition and shells is scarce. The division will withdraw by June 1 at the latest and move to a location where supplies can be received.' Predictably, Mutaguchi was livid and his reply intemperate. 'How dare you use such an excuse of difficulty of supply and renounce Kohima? I want you to maintain your position for ten days.' He asked also how Sato would explain his retreat to the 'dead heroes' and, to add a final insult, quoted the old proverb: 'Before a resolute will even the gods give way.'

Willpower could not keep hunger at bay, however, nor was it a match for Slim's army. On the evening of 26 May, the 4/1 Gurkha rifles captured one of the best-entrenched positions at the Naga Village, followed up a few days later by 1st battalion, the Queen's Royal Regiment, who chased the last Japanese away. Sato signalled to 15th Army that he would deal with the situation using his own initiative – in other words, he would ignore Mutaguchi. 'Nothing [of Mutaguchi's orders] was founded on the actual situation of the war and the Division,' he wrote.

On the night of 26 May 1944 General Kotuku Sato sent a further signal, of a kind unprecedented in the history of the Imperial Japanese Army. 'We have fought for two months with the utmost courage, and have reached the limits of human fortitude. Our swords are broken and our arrows gone. Shedding bitter tears, I now leave Kohima. The very thought is enough to break a general's heart.'

Mutaguchi told him that if he retreated he would be court-martialled. Sato's reply bristled with contempt. 'Do as you please, I will bring you down with me.' A little later he sent another signal. 'The tactical ability of the 15 Army staff lies below that of cadets.' Mutaguchi was unable to respond. Sato had turned off his wireless. Soon afterwards, the 15th Army commander issued an order of the day to his exhausted troops. Even by Mutaguchi's standards it was an extraordinary display of self-deluding bombast. 'It is my resolve', he told them, 'to reassemble the whole Army and with one great push capture Imphal ... You must realise that if decisive victory is not obtained we shall not be able to strike back again. ON THIS ONE BATTLE RESTS THE FATE OF THE EMPIRE.'

Lieutenant Chuzaburo Tomaru, the supply officer from the 138th Regiment, was foraging for food on 1 June and returned in the evening to find troops leaving their trenches. Thinking that they were deserters, he started to shout, 'What is happening here?' At battalion headquarters he met a corporal who explained, 'We got an order from division to retreat and it says, "Don't leave a single soldier alive on the battlefield."' The men packed their few belongings, collected the wounded from the trenches, and staggered away from Kohima

Ridge. The veterans do not describe a sentimental farewell, no backward glances filled with anguish for their lost comrades; there was simply relief that they were leaving hell.

For all the bad news flooding into his headquarters, Mutaguchi seemed unable to grasp the reality of impending defeat and make plans accordingly. The 15th Army commander had moved his headquarters to Indainggyi, about one hundred miles from the Imphal battle, in early May. The good life of his villa in Maymyo was gone, replaced by a simple bamboo hut. An officer remembered his increasing resort to prayer. 'Near his house he had a special place for prayer in Shinto style, a flat narrow square area covered with white sand with bamboo poles on four corners. Every morning he sat there and recited Shinto prayers loudly. As the Japanese advance was beaten back ... he spent more time there; he was praying for God's help for victory.' The war correspondent Yukihiko Imai, who had been with the 58th Regiment throughout the Kohima battle, was contemptuous of the officers he met at 15th Army headquarters. Although the battle was still a long way away, Imai found them constantly panicking and he recorded their reactions with contempt. '"Aircrafts is coming!" "The caterpillars [tanks] are near at hand!" they cried like mad in the midnight. I could not sleep with such a noisy nonsense. In the rear ... they saw the soldiers carried back to their camp wounded so awfully that it made them become more cowardly.' When the worsening picture was relayed to Tojo he put on a brave face at a staff conference in Tokyo. The meeting took place in front of the entire senior leadership of the army. Tojo chided the messenger. 'You never tell until a battle is over. Don't be so faint-hearted.' However, the Japanese writer, Ryoichi Tobe, records that at a small meeting shortly afterwards Tojo 'was perplexed, holding his head in his hands, and said, "This is an awkward situation!"' Still, the 15th Army would fight on at Imphal and Sato would be made to toe the line.

On 5 June, four days after Sato's dramatic signal of withdrawal, the commander of Burma Area Army, General Kawabe, arrived to see Mutaguchi. He noted in his diary: 'Mutaguchi was in good health but his eyes were filled with tears. "We are at the crossroads but have no fears," he greeted me. I did not touch on the situation, but postponed it until the afternoon.' Kawabe was a very sick man, ravaged by amoebic dysentery, and needed to rest before they spoke.

The following day, 6 June, as allied armies were pouring on to the beaches of Normandy, the two men held a strategy meeting that would consign the Japanese army in India to disaster. Kawabe was well aware that the British were winning on every front. The 15th and 33rd Divisions were being steadily pulverised at Imphal. With tanks advancing along the road from Kohima and blasting Japanese roadblocks, it was only a matter of time before the town would be relieved. Mutaguchi asked Kawabe for reinforcements but, astonishingly, made no mention of Sato's withdrawal. He also announced that he had just sacked the commander of the 15th Division, General Yamauchi, for his failures at Imphal. This was the second sacking of a divisional commander within a matter of weeks. Yamauchi died of tuberculosis a short time later in a field hospital.

Then came one of those moments upon which destiny turns. The two men looked at each other in silence for a few moments. After the war, Mutaguchi would claim that he almost asked Kawabe to cancel the Imphal operation. 'I guessed Kawabe's real purpose in coming was to sound out of my views on the possibility – or otherwise – of continuing the Imphal operation. The sentence, "The time has come to give up the operation as soon as possible" got as far as my throat; but I could not force it out in words. But I wanted him to get it from my expression.' According to the historian and Japanophile Louis Allen, Mutaguchi may have tried to use *hara-gei*, Japanese 'belly art', in which meanings are conveyed by subtle changes of facial expression. The intelligence officer Lieutenant Colonel Fujiwara believed that 'face' prevented either man from admitting defeat. This may be a generous interpretation. Certainly the unwillingness to confront failure was an important cultural trait; both had gambled their prestige on the success of the invasion and Kawabe had promised imperial headquarters that he could control Mutaguchi.

But equally relevant here is Mutaguchi's self-serving nature. He never lost an opportunity to divert blame for what happened on to both his subordinates and his superiors. It was Kawabe's fault, he implied, that he did not guess Mutaguchi's real wishes. As a result of the meeting, Kawabe told imperial headquarters and Southern Area Army about some of the problems facing 15th Army, but he did not seek permission to cancel the operation. 'Belly art' or no, both Kawabe and Mutaguchi showed themselves to be moral cowards. The Imphal operation was allowed to run for another disastrous month.

In the light of what had passed between them a week earlier, Mutaguchi's orders to Sato on 9 June defied belief. He was to leave a portion of his forces at Aradura Spur to block the British advance on Imphal, and go to the village of Ukhrul with the remainder to collect supplies and 'link up with ... 15 Division and *prepare to attack towards Imphal* [author's italics]'. A starving division, desperately short of ammunition, was now expected to hold the British advance on the Imphal road and join a fresh offensive against the town. Sato was to have his men in position by the following day, 10 June. He now began to suspect that Mutaguchi was losing his reason. 'I was flabbergasted ... This incredibly non-commonsensical plan simply appalled me. I could not help questioning the Army's HQ's sanity.' Kawabe learned of the plan from one of Mutaguchi's subordinates, and took no steps to countermand it. There was an unwelcome surprise for Sato on 21 June when Mutaguchi's most devoted staff officer, the newly promoted Lieutenant General Kunomura, arrived to reinforce the order. He was not a man likely to be welcomed at 31st Division. It was Kunomura who had blithely assured Sato before the advance that 31st Division would get ample supplies from 15th Army.

At first, Sato refused to see Kunomura, talking to him through a staff officer. When he did relent, the exchange between them was furious. It ended with Mutaguchi's envoy asking Sato directly, 'Do you intend to carry out Army orders or to disobey?' Sato replied, 'I have not said I will not carry out Army orders but first we must eat. Carrying out Army orders comes after that.' Mutaguchi savaged Kunomura when he returned to headquarters and threatened him with a reprimand for being too timorous with Sato. It was too much for the devoted servant, who proceeded to tell Mutaguchi the exact

state of Sato's men, who were not 'recognizable as Japanese soldiers
... never had he seen such a sight in his whole career'.

By late June, events were racing ahead of both Sato and
Mutaguchi. On 22 June the British 2nd Division swept aside the last
of the Japanese roadblocks and opened the Kohima–Imphal road.
Mutaguchi and his staff blamed the disaster on Sato's withdrawal.
The newly appointed commander of the 15th Division, Lieutenant
General Ryuichi Shibata, was furious with his 31st Division counterpart. 'I feel confident that if 31 Div had NOT begun the retreat in the
North, my own troops, weakened as they were, could still have faced
the food shortage for several weeks and, had they been given the
opportunity to attack, could have carried on indefinitely on supplies
captured from the ALLIES.' It was nonsense, the face-saving roar of
a man who has inherited defeat. The battles around Imphal had
drained the strength of the 15th and 33rd Divisions every bit as
much as the Kohima struggle had destroyed the 31st Division.
Mutaguchi would also fire the 33rd Division commander, Lieutenant
General Yanagida. The intelligence officer Lieutenant Colonel
Iwaichi Fujiwara described a collapse of trust between Mutaguchi
and his commanders. There were 'violent and angry' signals, and 'the
beginning of the breakdown of command and discipline'. Signals
staff at Mutaguchi's headquarters were reported to be horrified at the
crudity of some of the messages they were being asked to send to
subordinate commanders. 'Get your fat arse moving' was one of the
milder instructions reported.

Fujiwara was based at 33rd Division headquarters for much of this
time, but he kept his ear to the ground as regards what was happening across the divisions. Retreat and insubordination went against
the grain and he could never bring himself to accept that what Sato
did was right. But that did not make him an uncritical supporter of
Mutaguchi. As a well-trained intelligence officer, Fujiwara was always
amenable to facts. Hunger, lack of ammunition, exhaustion and the
strength of the enemy pointed to a catastrophe. Like Sato, he watched
the worsening weather and was 'surprised by its violence'.
Throughout June and into July, the storms would turn the mountain

tracks into quagmires and cut off all hope of supplying 15th Army. As it was, more than half the vehicles were out of commission due to lack of parts, and petrol was in chronically short supply. The rain came in moving walls, pummelling bodies, making pools of trenches, a rain that carried chills and fevers across the valleys, unearthing the graves of the newly dead. 'Despair became rife,' Fujiwara wrote.

As June wore on, Mutaguchi sent further messages urging Sato to send men to join the assault on Imphal, but nothing came of the scheme. The 31st Division limped on, ignoring the orders as the pleas of a madman. After the British and Indian breakthrough on the Imphal road on 22 June, Mutaguchi appeared finally to grasp the nettle. He signalled Kawabe and asked for permission to withdraw his men. Kawabe in turn asked for the approval of Terauchi in Singapore and imperial headquarters in Tokyo. While he waited for a reply – his messenger was delayed by bad weather – Kawabe persisted in sending orders for offensive action to Mutaguchi. Imaginary battalions of fit men were to be thrown against Imphal. Nothing came of the plans.

It now became a race to get what was left of 15th Army out of India and back to Burma, where they could recover to face the expected British offensive after the monsoon. What Mutaguchi did not calculate was that Slim would abandon precedent and fight through the monsoon. The 14th Army leader had the Japanese where he had always wanted them, caught at the end of a useless line of communications and facing a stronger army. It took until 3 July for the message from imperial headquarters to reach Kawabe, by now bedridden and feverish with amoebic dysentery. He signalled Mutaguchi on 5 July. The Imphal operation was over. The suffering of the defeated army, however, was about to become much worse.

* * *

By the third week of June 31st Division had lost 7,315 men killed or wounded and the dying would continue as the men moved towards the Chindwin.* They carried with them around eight hundred wounded. There was no food left save what could be scavenged on the road towards Ukhrul, the main supply base for the battle of Imphal and about fifty miles from Kohima as the crow flies. Food would be waiting here they were promised.

On the road they stopped at Kharasom, where John Young of the Assam Regiment had fought alone against Sato's advancing army at the end of March. The men had been told they would find food for four days at Kharasom, enough to keep them moving until they reached Ukhrul. But as the leading troops in the column limped into Kharasom they saw the corpses of starved Japanese lying by the roadside. Sato gave permission for the slaughter of the remaining military horses. They reached Ukhrul to find that the 15th Division still fighting near Imphal had already taken the supplies. Lieutenant Chuzaburo Tomaru of the 138th Regiment found only an empty storehouse. 'Then, I complained to high-ranking accounting officer. He offered me left-over rice in camping pot. I ate it. It was delicious for hungry stomach.' He saw men searching desperately for rice; some fought each other for small scraps and others broke into local homes. In his report on the general Japanese retreat from Kohima and Imphal, Lieutenant Colonel Fujiwara described 'a complete breakdown in morale, and the Japanese troops began to throw away their arms, quarrel and fight for food'.

Sato's column pressed on towards the village of Humine where, again, food was supposed to be stockpiled. But there they found only enough rice for two days. The scouts reported back that the landscape beyond Humine was empty of food. The procession stretched

---

* The 33 Corps account gives a figure of 3,384 Japanese killed in action, which is broadly consistent with the official Japanese count of 3,700 (Japanese Monograph No. 134, p. 164). The British figure for Japanese wounded is 3,931. A further 500 were listed as Missing in the Naga Hills by the Imperial Army. The Japanese give a figure of 6,264 men dead from 31st Division by the end of September 1944 with an estimated 2,800 hospitalised. The vast majority of those listed as still being on duty were suffering from the effects of disease and malnutrition.

back for miles along the jungle track. They moved slowly, feet squelching in the mud of the early rains, every man of them conscious of his weakening body. The lice in their armpits and crotches tormented them. A Japanese account estimated that the men marched an average of between four to eight kilometres each night. During the day they hid from aircraft and tried to forage bamboo shoots and grasses.

At some point on the route, Lieutenant Tomaru saw General Sato ride by with his staff. The men stopped and put their hands together in prayer and faced him. For a few minutes there was no noise at all among the ranks. It was, explained Chuzaburo, an expression of gratitude for taking them away from Kohima. Another soldier witnessed Sato's intervention in a fight over the attempted theft of his horse. The thief and his lieutenant, a man named Yamagauchi, were being berated by a staff officer who told them to go 'starve and die'. The witness described what happened when the general appeared. 'He heard what happened and said: "Don't say stupid things. I am fighting with Mutaguchi over food. It's not this soldier's fault but the fault of the person who sent them to fight without food."' General Sato told the soldier accused of stealing that he had fought well. He took out some dried bread from his own dwindling stock. 'Please share this dried bread with everybody,' Sato said. The soldier hesitated to accept. 'He said: "General it is way too much." But the General said to him not to be constrained ... Yamaguchi had tears in his eyes. The General said: "Now go back to your own trench and let the others eat this. Be patient and take care of yourself." ... [The men] were really touched by this. All the soldiers who got some dried bread and a piece of sugar promised they would die for General Sato.'

The unit of colour-bearer Lieutenant Hiroshi Yamagami began by marching in good order. But as food ran out men drifted off to try and scavenge in the villages. Those too sick to move were given a small supply from whatever rations were left and then abandoned on the side of the road. Yamagami would never overcome the feelings of guilt he experienced. 'Sometimes I met friends who were just dying there. Their faces said "Help me" but there was nothing we could do.

It is hard to put into words what it is like to see that. I feel still that I abandoned those people. How can I explain that emotion to you?' Yamagami told himself to be patient. At Ukhrul they would find food. But by the time he got there the meagre supplies had all been consumed. Had Mutaguchi appeared at that moment he would have been killed by the men. 'We were so angry. We had hatred of him.'

By the time Sato's column reached Humine, Dr Takahide Kuwaki, the medical officer with the 124th Regiment, was sick with amoebic dysentery and malaria. The man who had dreamed of dying gloriously for the empire was helped along by two medics who turned discreetly away when he limped into the bush to empty his bowels. To suffer amoebic dysentery is an agony even when good medical facilities are at hand. The stomach feels as if it is being slashed inside by razors, unrelieved by the repeated streams of bloody diarrhoea. The suffering is deepened by fever and headaches. There was no medicine with which to treat the men of the 31st Division and nowhere clean for them to be nursed. They died by the road in pools of their own excrement. Dr Kuwaki tried to shout encouragement to men who had given up and were waiting to die. 'Sometimes I even did it from the stretcher. But perhaps that was cynical, eh? Me on the stretcher shouting at them to keep going!'

Conditions in the military field hospitals on the retreat from Kohima and Imphal were so grim that men regarded being left there as a death sentence. In many cases they committed suicide, asked colleagues to shoot them, or were summarily shot by their own officers. A British patrol entered one hospital to find only skeletons on the beds. An account published in *The Listener* in the autumn of 1944 described the scene at a jungle camp. The British medics tried to treat the men, but most were beyond help. 'The hospital staff had deserted, leaving the sick and wounded to die without attention ... Many had acute beri-beri; they had passed the stage where the stomach swells and had become dehydrated human sticks. The skin, stretched tightly on the bone framework, was covered with sores ... on one track over 5,000 Japanese were found lying dead from exhaustion. Elsewhere the body of a high ranking Japanese officer sat in his useless staff car.'

One of the most chilling accounts was given by a Japanese Sergeant Major Tochihira of the 15th Division, retreating from Imphal. He saw about 120 men lying on the side of the road. They had been abandoned by their comrades who had heard tanks coming. Tochihira watched the scene from a hideout in the hills. An Indian soldier approached the wounded with a container of what Tochihira took to be water. He poured it over the men and then flicked his cigarette into the liquid. The wounded were engulfed in flames.

The rear-guard of the 31st Division, commanded by Miyazaki, was struggling to stay ahead of the advancing British and Indians when it reached Ukhrul at the end of June. General Miyazaki, still with his pet monkey Chibi perched on his shoulder, was an angry man. He had lost 1,700 men in the fighting around Kohima. Now, with the remaining 870 fit troops, he was trying to slow the enemy down so that the rest of the 31st Division could reach the Chindwin. Nearly half of his men would die in the process.

Looping around behind the 31st Division and across the line of communications was 23 Brigade Long Range Penetration Group (Chindits), whose commander, Brigadier Lancelot Perowne, told his men on 10 May, 'Our task remains as it was – to exterminate the Japanese vermin in our path.' Perowne was a notably aggressive commander, a veteran of the commandos in France, and wanted to make his mark on the great battle. His men experienced a gruelling slog through the jungle, killing scores of Japanese, but frustrated by terrain, weather and illness. 'We had been sodden for weeks, were covered with mud, and we stank,' one officer wrote. 'Hollow-eyed, wasted, hungry, and yet incapable of eating more than a minute meal, we talked of nothing else but food.' A column of the Essex Regiment operating with 23 Brigade took twelve hours to complete a march of twelve miles.

RAF signals operator Arthur Davies, who was deployed with the Chindits, wrote later of endless, gruelling journeys. 'Walk, walk, walk – silent columns of men meandering their way up the side of the hills rising to eight or ten thousand feet, only to drop down again to the valleys below, and always there was the fear of the enemy ambushing

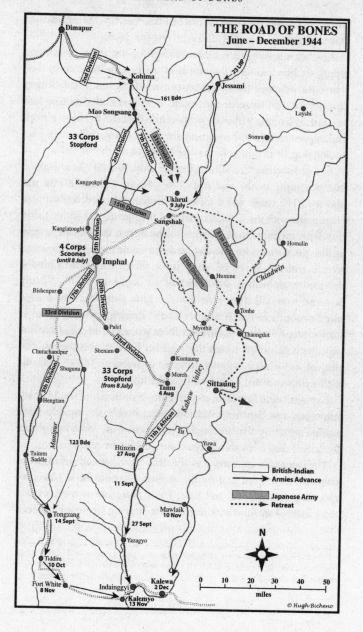

THE ROAD OF BONES
June – December 1944

Dimapur

Kohima

Jessami

2nd Division

23 LRP

161 Bde

Mao Songsang

Layshi

Somra

33 Corps
Stopford

2nd Division

7th Division

5th Division

Kangpokpi

Ukhrul
9 July

15th Division

31st Division

Kanglatongbi

Sangshak

Hornalin

5th Division

4 Corps
Scoones
(until 8 July)

Imphal

15th Division

Chindwin

Humine

Bishenpur

17th Division

20th Division

33rd Division

Palel

Churachandpur

Shenam

23rd Division

Myothit

Tonhe

Thaungdut

Shuganu

5th Division

Kuntaung

Moreh

33 Corps
Stopford
(from 8 July)

Tamu
4 Aug

Sittaung

Hengtam

Manipur

123 Bde

11th E African

Kabaw Valley

Yu

Tuitum
Saddle

Htinzin
27 Aug

Yuwa

11 Sept

British-Indian

Armies Advance

Tongzang
14 Sept

Mawlaik
10 Nov

Japanese Army

Retreat

27 Sept

Tiddim
10 Oct

Yazagyo

N

Fort White
8 Nov

Indainggyi

Kalewa
2 Dec

0   10   20   30   40   50

Kalemyo
13 Nov

miles

© Hugh Bicheno

them.' Long after the other troops had fallen asleep, the signals men stayed awake, 'transmitting and receiving messages.'

Animals were lost in mudslides. Perowne's pony broke its neck after falling six hundred feet. Two thirds of the brigade went down with diarrhoea, although there were fewer cases of the amoebic dysentery that afflicted the Japanese. Lieutenant Desmond Earley recalled how his orderly, a young Irishman, went off into the bush to relieve himself and stepped on an anti-personnel mine. 'He died soon afterwards after apologising, of all things, for having caused so much trouble.'

In late May, the Chindits had come close to Sato's headquarters but, according to the war diary, 'an attempt to stage a raid was abortive'. The result was a Japanese counter-attack, described by a Naga guide with the Chindits. 'Early in the morning at about 4 a.m. fifty Japanese came to our camp … The British troops had to fight against the enemies for two days and one whole night.' The Japanese were eventually driven off after losing fifteen men. The Chindits repeatedly ambushed small groups of Japanese so that 'many Japanese were killed by wide and energetic patrolling and a large number of prisoners and animals taken'.* Passing through Ukhrul in the footsteps of the 31st Division there was an outbreak of typhus, 'with high mortality', which the brigadier believed was the result of sleeping in bashas previously occupied by Japanese. 'This [area] was highly contaminated with dead Japs and filth.'

Captain Robin Rowland, commanding a company of the 2 Punjab Regiment, saw 'Japanese skeletons lying beside the muddy track washed white by the unrelenting monsoon rain. Most of them, I think, had died from starvation, illness, disease or suicide.'

The Japanese were harried by the British divisions advancing from Kohima and Imphal and by the revived guerrillas of V Force, re-appearing through May and June. The V Force situation reports for summer 1944 are filled with references to starving Japanese stragglers.

---

* The total number of Japanese killed, wounded and taken prisoner by 23 Long Range Penetration Brigade is given as 854, with a total of seventy-four killed and eighty-eight wounded. NA, WO 203/6388.

A note to V Force headquarters in July talks of one hundred Japanese drowned trying to cross a river; another speaks of twelve Japanese killed by Nagas. The hill tribes turned on the retreating army with a vengeance.

In some cases they lured them to their deaths with offers of food. On 20 August, three Japanese stragglers were offered rice by Nagas. As they were eating, their hosts opened fire and killed two of them. No mention is made of what happened to the other man. B. K. Sachu Angami of Kohima was hiding with other villagers in the forest when a Japanese soldier sought refuge among them. The man was given food and had his shaved so that he resembled a Naga, but he was eventually killed. 'This Naga wanted a medal and so he took him into the jungle and cut off his head.'

In another incident three INA men, offered a bed in a Naga village, were stabbed to death as they slept. 'Several noses of victims have been produced.' The reports provide a grim litany of suffering. Fifty dead Japanese found in Pyangbok village; three killed at Tuitum and an 'ear and pay book brought in'; around fifty dead on the road to Nangadeikon; a track near Thanan Nala 'littered with Jap dead … and open latrines and temporary shelters'. As the defeated men headed down the tracks towards the Chindwin, the 31st Division resembled an army of ghosts.

Yoshiteru Hirayama, the monk's son from Tokyo, managed to avoid being abandoned in a hospital. His greatest fear was that his stretcher-bearers would throw him into one of the steep ravines. It was happening with growing frequency. 'It was hell. Men would throw their friends into the valley below.' The carriers were starving and exhausted, their feet sinking into the mud, deperate men on a road without end. Hirayama was lucky. The men with him were from Niigata of the snows, 'strong men with a strong will'. When Hirayama reached the Chindwin he saw dead soldiers lining the river bank and others begging for food. They stumbled with hands outstretched and then, seeing he had nothing to give, passed listlessly on.

A recurring image in the memories of survivors is of groups of men gathering together to die. Dr Kuwaki of the 124th Regiment passed many as he was carried to the Chindwin. 'I saw the dead soldiers lying in groups under trees. It was a human thing. They didn't want to die alone. One would be dying and others would crawl towards him. I was sick as well but looking at the dead I had the will to live.' His comrade Chuzaburo Tomaru explained the clinging together as a spiritual necessity. 'I found out people goes to river side when they die. I used to hear from my father that the spirit calls spirit. It was true. One soldier approached the river side and died; then, other soldier went there and died next to him.' He saw men left behind on stretchers. He approached one sitting soldier who appeared to have his hand raised. The man was frozen in rigor mortis. In a prisoner-of-war camp at the end of the war, Tomaru heard from other survivors that the British had captured deserters and had not killed or tortured them. Such civilised treatment of prisoners would have been unimaginable to the average Japanese soldier. 'When I heard of it, I thought how kind British army was!'

At the top of every hill there were groups of men who had stopped to rest. The supply officer Masao Hirakubo found himself saying hello to men who were dead. 'Just like taking a rest. Next to him would be one already white bone. Next one would have maggots and clothes rotted. People who died earlier were existing in the same place as the ones who sat down now.' A popular soldier, a married man with children, looked up to by the others, went off on his own after telling his friends he felt much better. He would catch up with them later. They found him a short time later, dead in the middle of the road where he had placed his big toe in the trigger of his rifle, pointed the barrel at his head and blown his brains out. 'In tears some of our younger soldiers held on to him,' said Staff Sergeant Yasamusa Nishiji, 20th Independent Engineer Regiment. He saw soldiers committing suicide in pairs, one clutching a grenade to his chest and then embracing the other. Another dying man was handed a grenade with which to commit suicide by an officer who continued on his way. The dying man screamed at the departing officer: 'You've lorded it over me; what have I got in return? I'll bloody kill you.' Nishiji drew some of the scenes he witnessed. The result was a harrowing tableau: an army nurse injecting wounded men with lethal poison; men swept away in a raging river; a dying soldier raising his hand in protest after another has stolen his knapsack; another man laying out his clothes and belongings on a rock and then lying down to die.

Reaching the Chindwin was by no means a guarantee of survival. Private Manabu Wada, 138th Regiment, marched through jungle filled with corpses where 'thousands upon thousands of maggots crept out of bodies lying in streams and were carried away by the fast flowing waters'. At one stream he found the skeletons of ten or more soldiers who had, like himself, come for water. On reaching the Chindwin with three other men, Manabu helped to build a raft. They set off on their tiny bamboo craft as twilight came on, swept along by the swift rainy season currents. The water was red-brown and capped with white waves and they clung on, afraid to move for fear of capsizing. There were periodic attempts to steer towards the eastern shore. One of the men stripped to his loincloth, tied a rope to the raft and swam with the other end towards the shore. But when he clambered out of the racing waters the raft shot onwards and the rope was whipped from his hands. Manabu last saw him disappearing into the jungle. After a journey that lasted weeks – he lost count of the time – Manabu Wada was dragged to safety by his surviving comrades. At one point they beat him with a stick to wake him, knowing that if he lay down on the road he would never get up. As for the man who had sent the 15th Army into India, Lieutenant General Renya Mutaguchi, he was seen by the military correspondent Masanori Ito, sipping rice gruel while watching his men stagger towards the Chindwin. 'You want a statement,' he asked Ito. 'I have killed thousands of my men. I should not go back across the Chindwin alive … that is all I have to say.' But he did go back back across the Chindwin and continued to blame his commanders.

By the end of June, Mutaguchi had sacked the commanders of the 15th and 33rd Divisions. On 7 July he removed General Sato. The battle between the two men was about to enter a new realm of bitterness.

Mutaguchi's intention was to have Sato declared insane. That would remove the danger of a court martial at which all kinds of unpleasant facts about the supply plans for the invasion might be made public. Sato, on the other hand, wanted his day in court. He first headed to 15th Army headquarters to organise supplies for the troops he had left behind. According to his biographer, Sato succeeded in persuading a staff officer to send some relief. He then signalled 31st Division. 'General Sato is always with you.'

He followed that up with a defiant signal to General Kawabe suggesting that Mutaguchi should be examined for signs of mental illness and his staff sacked. 'They are leading the entire army's self-destruction minute by minute. The commander has lost his dignity and is shifting responsibility to the lower ranks ... This is truly unprecedented. They do not have [a] sense of responsibility; they threaten their subordinates. I have observed the truth ever since I was in Kohima.' Several days later, on 24 July, Sato sat opposite Kawabe in his Rangoon office. Here was the man whose failure to confront Mutaguchi had helped propel thousands of Sato's men to their deaths. The 31st Division leader struggled to contain himself. Kawabe nervously twiddled his extravagant moustache as he spoke.

He told Sato to prepare himself for a health check. Sato knew immediately that this was the first stage in the conspiracy to have him declared insane. 'I don't need a health examination. I am quite strong,' he snapped. Kawabe insisted. 'It has been arranged. Please take your examination.' Sato told him it was rude to force a healthy person to take a health examination, then kicked his seat away and walked out. When an officer was sent to call him for the 'health check', Sato raged again. 'How come you cannot hold a court martial openly? If I am charged for the crime of disobeying the order, then Mutaguchi and Kawabe ought to be charged for treason to massacre the Imperial army for his private gain and ambition? How dare you call me mentally ill for the fear of taking this to the court martial?' The following day four army doctors arrived at the guesthouse where Sato was staying and questioned the general. Their report is worth quoting. 'The attitude, facial expression and language of Gen Sato were completely normal and stable and no sign of anxiety and fret/impatience was seen. Speed of recall during conversations was clear with no circumlocution and idle speech. His ability to recall and memory was brilliant. There was no indication of emotional disturbance; no excitement or depression was observed. The ability to control his will was sufficient; recklessness and subservience/ meanness were not seen at all. He was a fine general.' The doctors added that Sato was mentally and physically exhausted and needed rest. Mutaguchi and Kawabe were beaten. After recuperating, Sato was sent to Java as a military adviser, where he remained until the end of the war.

Four months later, when the scale of the calamity could no longer be denied in Tokyo, a signal was dispatched removing Mutaguchi as commander of 15th Army. Kawabe was also dismissed. The two architects of the disaster lasted longer than war minister Tojo, who had clutched at the dream of victory they offered. Amid rising disquiet over war losses, he was forced from office in July.

General Sato's 31st Division had crossed the Chindwin into India approximately 15,000-strong. Nearly half never came back. A soldier came across a body where maggots were feasting on the eyes. He tried to remove the boots from the corpse and heard the man speak: 'Please ... please don't take off my shoes yet ... I will go [die] very soon.' Another soldier also recalled how dying men would cling to the legs of passing comrades and cry, 'Please bring me along.' For many of the survivors the emotional torment of hearing the dying call out for mothers, wives, children would endure for a lifetime. Some dying men asked to be cast over cliffs to spare remove the burden on exhausted stretcher bearers. Humanity and horror followed the retreating army. The remnants of the 15th Army were still being harried and killed in the corpse-littered Naga Hills well into the autumn. A British intelligence signal of 19 September 1944, reported: 'V Force patrol shot one moribund Jap straggler.' It was a poignant, if fitting, epitaph for Mutaguchi's dream of conquest.

TWENTY-FIVE

When the War Is Over

The hour of immediate trial had passed for Admiral Mountbatten. Slim was chasing the 15th Army to destruction and his line of communication was holding despite the monsoon. The American planes had been returned but the RAF was continuing to drop supplies. The supreme commander could sense a famous victory. By the time Mountbatten reached Kohima on 1 July the bodies had been buried; the British and Indians were placed in single graves, the Japanese dead piled into pits. The place was still a ruin. On Garrison Hill he was shown the bunkers where the defenders had held out for over a fortnight. 'One could not visit this pathetic little hillock without being deeply moved at the gallantry of this scratch lot of defenders,' he wrote.

Mountbatten met Charles Pawsey, back now in a makeshift office in Kohima, and heard how the Nagas had done 'everything in their power to help us and volunteered to carry our wounded back under fire, proudly refusing any pay ... These Nagas, primitive headhunters though they be, have shown themselves true friends of the British and we must do everything we can for them.' Mountbatten resolved to write to the Viceroy, Lord Wavell, to insist on the speedy rebuilding of the Naga Village. The supreme commander passed on. He would not have known, or sensed, that the hills were in a state of flux at that moment; the passage of modern armies back and forth across their lands, and the hunger and disease wrought by fighting, had traumatised traditional communities. Twelve-year-old B. K. Sachu Angami returned from the forest to Kohima at the end of June 1944.

'It was difficult to locate our plot of land because of all the destruction. Everything was gone. Everything. We saw a lot of British bodies and also Japanese … People used to go and see these dead bodies.'

Twelve thousand Nagas were still depending on food relief by the autumn of 1944; unknown thousands more had vanished into remote forests and nobody knew what their condition was. Yet in the immediate aftermath of the siege Charles Pawsey spoke with apparent confidence about returning to the old way of life. In June 1944 he told a visitor that the 'presence of war and British and Indian troops on their territory is not likely to have any profound influence on the Nagas. In the Kohima area they are very conservative and have never even been into the plains.' Cut off from the political mainstream, Pawsey was still the benevolent patriarch of a territory he knew better than any other foreigner, and he could not have been expected to imagine how swiftly the end of empire would arrive. In the vacuum left by the advance of Slim's army there was a resurgence of headhunting. Intelligence reports from late 1944 and into the following year give a vivid picture of a deteriorating situation:

August 1944: There has been some raiding between the Patkoi and the east Boundary of our Control Area and one village in our Control Area was attacked, five heads were taken.

September 1944: An outbreak of head-taking in the Southern Sangtam country is reported. The troops which were in the area till fairly recently have left and the Nagas find it difficult to understand why they cannot attack their enemies just as we attack the Japanese.

The toll in one raid in 1945 was four hundred heads of men, women and children. The war brought new weapons into the hills; for the first time Nagas were using Tommy guns and stocks of Chinese rifles sold across the border from Burma. The Governor's adviser on tribal areas, J. P. Mills, an old friend of Pawsey's and a veteran of the hills, warned officials to take armed escorts. 'While the wilder Nagas, being headhunters, are apt to kill inoffensive strangers, the tribes of the

North-East Frontier Agency only attack strangers in what they imagine to be self-defence ... precautions have to be taken against possible unfortunate results arising from an entirely unintentional shock
administered to the nerves of "jumpy" savages.'

India was still under British rule, the Congress leaders still in jail,
but the expectation of independence after the war was now palpable
among the country's educated elite. The Nagas did not belong to this
consensus. The Assam leaders of Congress regarded them as one of
many tribal groups who belonged in the united India that would
soon replace the Raj. Naga independence, or the creation of some
sort of British protectorate, was anathema to a movement faced with
the claims of numerous different ethnic groups.

The British were still too busy fighting a war to contemplate what
political future they envisaged for the hills, but in the long run, beset
by the looming crisis of partition, they would leave the Nagas to
make their way with India. A Naga minister, the Reverend L. Gatpoh,
recalled that 'most of our people were not at all aware of what was
coming into the political arena of India; they just had no idea of the
rapid developments that were taking place in the rest of the country'.
The clash of cultures between hill and plain, the separateness
entrenched under British rule, the absence of any united Naga movement, and the destabilising effect of war had left the Nagas tragically
ill-prepared for the independence that was coming. The Naga historian Sajal Nag put it well when he wrote that to the Nagas Indian
administration 'meant the rule of *babus*, a category of people they
mortally detested ... as they had found the plains people to be arro-
gant who looked down upon the Nagas as a naked and primitive
people'.

Ursula Graham Bower stayed in the hills until the war ended. She
met her husband-to-be, Major Tim Betts, when he arrived on a
butterfly-hunting expedition early in 1945. As a V Force soldier, he
had walked from the Chindwin to Kohima in the early days of the
Japanese invasion but had been evacuated just before the siege began.
On the day her guerrilla unit was disbanded, Graham Bower
presented gifts of cash, ivory, knives and guns. She handed over her

Sten gun and the Tommy gun belonging to her bodyguard Namkia. Nobody at that moment could have predicted how they might be used in the future, or what lay in store for the Nagas. Namkia scoured the countryside and found a huge pig for a feast. 'In the lengthening light the whole camp was a flurry of scarlet, of bordered Kuki clothes, of Magulong in dance-dress with huge tam-o'-shanters of wound cotton thread, and hornbills' feathers quivering in the stiff breeze. The spectators formed a ring ... they danced all night.'

Ursula became briefly famous in the British and American press. She was the subject of a comic strip, 'The Jungle Queen', and was described by *Time* magazine as 'pert, pretty ... an archaeology student who looks like a cinema actress ... [who] declared war on Japan'. The piece quoted her mother back in Wiltshire as saying, 'An extraordinary girl; she never would sit still.' With the coming of independence she and her husband returned to England in 1948. She longed for the hills. 'How could one explain that home was no longer home, that it was utterly foreign, that home was in the Assam hills and that there would never be any other, and that for the rest of our lives we should be exiles? ... We had gone, we had striven, we had tried, we had loved the tribesmen in spite of ourselves and they had loved us, and though everything else might perish – our bodies, our memories – nothing could ever wipe out and destroy that.'

The West Kents passed bodies all the way down to the Chindwin and across into Burma. On the advance 4th battalion lost Major Winstanley. First he was shot in the leg and then he went down with typhus. It was enough to see him evacuated out of the war for good. Major Donald Easten was gone too; the wound he took at Kohima became infected and he was shipped back to Britain to be reunited with his wife Billie after an absence of nearly four years. Lieutenant Tom Hogg fought on for two more months before being selected for a staff officer course. Captain Harry Smith, who had been hit by mortar fire on the last day of the siege, woke up in a hospital in Assam with a lump of metal on his bedside table. It had been removed from his skull after Kohima. Smith rejoined the battalion and crossed into Burma for Slim's advance. But the CO, John Laverty, was gone for the time being. The 14th Army sent him on a lecture tour around India to tell other battalions the story of Kohima.

His fellow commander at Kohima, Hugh Richards, spent the months after the siege at Dimapur visiting the wounded and making arrangements for their welfare. There was no fighting job for him now, but he accepted the life of the rear echelon with equanimity. At Dimapur he heard that some of the men from his old outfit, the 3 West African Brigade, were in the Poona base hospital 1,800 miles away. Back in 1943 Richards had been preparing to lead these men into Burma when Wingate had judged him to be too old. What had happened to them he wondered. Who was left alive? Lieutenant Barry Bowman, who was recovering from dysentery at Poona, recalled Richards's arrival and the West Africans' welcome. 'His was officially an inspection of the base but in practice it took the form of huge ground-nut stew lunch which he wolfed into with great relish. He departed around three hours later well watered (Ginned) and nourished. A quiet, courteous truly great man – a pivotal figure in the 14th army.'

The Chindits of Lancelot Perowne's 23 Brigade came out of the jungle in a pitiful condition. The RAF signals operator, Arthur Davies, noted how the men were only able to eat a few mouthfuls of the food that had been prepared by the cooks waiting for them at base.

> The cooks … had prepared a banquet for them, but many were sick after eating only a few mouthfuls – their stomachs just couldn't take it. Perhaps you can judge their conditions when I tell you that the mules – those strong, high-spirited animals before the campaign – were now docile, and walked, or limped, obediently behind the mule-teer as if they were old hags. Their once shiny coats shone no more, and instead the hair was matted, and deep gashes were torn in their flesh due to the wear and tear of the packs they had been carrying.

Slim went on to smash the Japanese as he had promised, driving them out of Mandalay by March 1945, and retaking Rangoon, abandoned by the Japanese as it had once been by the British, on 3 May. Privates

Ray Street and Ivan Daunt, Lance Corporal Dennis Wykes, and the other footsloggers of 4th battalion fought their way south with Slim. Often on the road they would talk about what had happened at Kohima and, remembering the men lying on the ridge, pray that they would never see anything like it again. Private Daunt was thinking of getting back to Chatham and his wife Audrey. He thought about all the days that had passed since the fall of France, when he had escaped from behind German lines. He grouched to his mates. 'What with bloody Dunkirk, with the bloody desert and now this lot, where is it going to end?' Some men contracted cholera from drinking water contaminated by Japanese bodies. Dennis Wykes contracted typhus from lice and did not wake up for a fortnight. 'As I woke up and looked around, the orderly said: "I thought you wouldn't wake up. I had a hole dug for you outside."' Wykes made up his mind to eat and continue eating; he would eat when he was hungry and when he wasn't. There was no way he was going into a hole in the ground.

The worst thing that happened to him after Kohima was not the sickness but an incident that took him into the heart of war's madness. It was around midnight, somewhere near the Sittang river, and Wykes was on the Bren gun watching A company's perimeter. He heard noise coming from the right. There were not supposed to be any British patrols in that direction. He had seconds to make a decision. If it were Japs they would be in among A company in seconds. Wykes pressed the trigger. The rounds thumped into the muggy night and he heard screams echoing back. Fuck. They were British voices. No mistaking it. He had hit a returning officer and sergeant of the West Kents coming on the wrong route to the perimeter. Dennis Wykes stood up and hurled his Bren to the ground. 'That's me finished,' he shouted, 'when I start shooting our own blokes even if they was going in the wrong place.' The company commander rushed over to calm him. '"It wasn't your fault. You did the right thing." I said, "No. I couldn't stand it." So he said, "I can see you're upset about it." I said, "Of course I'm upset about it."' The officer told Wykes he needed a few nights' rest and sent him back to the lines. On the way he passed one of the men he had wounded. It was the officer, and he thanked Wykes. The bullet had hit him in the leg and he would be going home. 'You've done me a favour,' he said. Three days later Dennis Wykes was back on duty. 'Everybody was needed. You didn't feel it was right staying away.'

It was not until they were near Rangoon that Wykes noticed a change in the Japanese. There were Hurricanes strafing the Japanese up ahead of 4th battalion and he spotted two of the enemy under a tree. They were sitting there when a Hurricane flew low and they looked up and shook their heads in resignation. They were taken prisoner soon afterwards.

Ray Street was weary of the war. On guard at night, always soaked from monsoon rain, he thought of what was happening at that moment in Birmingham. 'Dad would be getting his last pint of beer to take home … Mum would be preparing supper. Then I would perhaps sing a song to myself, or simply daydream of walking home through Birmingham.' But when he went home to Birmingham on leave he found that he wanted to get back to the front line. Street could not settle and he missed his friends. He even missed the danger.

The 1st Assam, who had held the tennis court with the West Kents, did not join the immediate pursuit of the Japanese after Kohima. They could not make up their losses as easily as the British battalions. There was no steady supply of already trained recruits from the hills. With half the battalion dead, sick or wounded, Lieutenant Colonel 'Bruno' Brown and Major Albert Calistan needed months to rebuild. By August 1944 they were still in barracks at Shillong. There was a medal ceremony that month for their dead hero Wellington Massar, with all of the survivors of Kohima drawn up on the square facing the Governor of Assam on a raised dais. It was a scene from the imperial twilight. The ranks of sepoys in starched jungle greens, the white commanding officer standing in front of them, and the King Emperor's proconsul gazing with studied benevolence upon the entire scene. 'Wellington Massar belonged to these hills,' declared the Governor, Sir Andrew Clow. Lieutenant Colonel Brown came forward and turned towards a diminutive woman in the crowd. 'His bereaved aunt, to whom we all offer our sincerest and deepest sympathy, is here

414

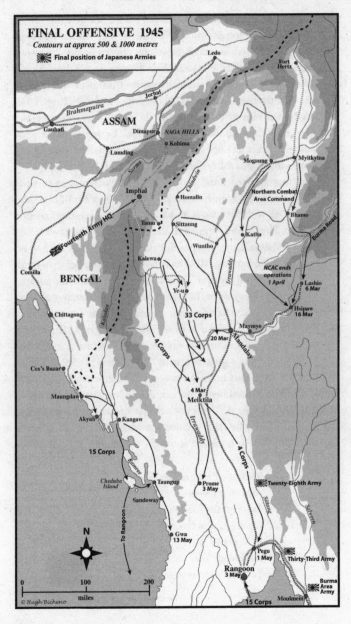

FINAL OFFENSIVE 1945
Contours at approx 500 & 1000 metres
✳ Final position of Japanese Armies

Ledo

Fort Hertz

Brahmaputra

Jorhat

ASSAM

Gauhati

Dimapura   *NAGA HILLS*

Lumding   ● Kohima

Mogaung   ● Myitkyina

Sittang   Northern Combat Area Command

Imphal   ● Honalin   ● Bhamo

Fourteenth Army HQ   Tamu   ● Sittaung   *Burma Road*

● Katha

Wuntho

Kalewa   *NCAC ends operations 1 April*   ● Lashio 6 Mar

Comilla

BENGAL   *Irrawaddy*   ● Hsipaw 16 Mar

Ye-u

Chittagong   *Kaladan*   33 Corps   Maymyo

                    20 Mar   Mandalay

Cox's Bazar   4 Corps

Maungdaw

Akyab   ● Kangaw   4 Mar
                    Meiktila

15 Corps   *Irrawaddy*

            Ramree   4 Corps

Cheduba Island   Taungup

Sandoway   ● Prome 3 May   ✳ Twenty-Eighth Army

N

To Rangoon   ● Gwa 13 May   *Sittang*   *Salween*

                    ● Pegu 1 May   ✳ Thirty-Third Army

0   100   200   **Rangoon** 3 May   ✳ Burma Area Army

miles   Moulmein

© Hugh Bicheno   15 Corps

in his stead,' he announced, 'and we can assure her that she has an undeniable right to feel as proud of her nephew as we are. Will your Excellency be pleased now to bestow this symbol of his Emperor's gratitude on Miss Florestie Massar.' Five months later 'Bruno' Brown was dead, shot in a Japanese ambush near the Chindwin, still wearing the polo sweater given to him during the siege by Charles Pawsey. His soldiers buried him in Burma, across the river from where he had helped to raise the regiment; they would have been glad to see what was written on his identity card under the designation 'nationality'. The Cambridge-born soldier had declared himself Indian.

When they reached Rangoon the West Kents were sent to what Dennis Wykes called a 'posh barracks'. After the months of mud and fleas, anything with four walls and a roof would have satisfied that description. They were supposed to start training for the amphibious invasion of Malaya. Lance Corporal Wykes could tell the men had no stomach for more fighting. 'We'd had enough of it. You began to think "you can't be lucky all the time"'. The army command and the government in London knew it too. In September 1944, as Slim was accelerating his pursuit of the Japanese into Burma, the future of 14th Army was being raised in the House of Commons. The Labour MP Aneurin Bevan wanted a delegation of members sent to Burma to assure the troops they were not 'a forgotten army'. Bevan then produced a letter from his pocket. It was in the form of a poem, short and passionate, and it came from a soldier in Burma. Bevan was mildly patronising about its literary merits. 'I will not say that he has put his ideas into the form of poetry,' he said, 'because I do not think he has achieved that level, but there is no doubt about his sentiments.' It read:

> These are the men who
> shed their blood,
> Amongst the filthy Burma mud,
> On the Arakan Front and Imphal Plain,
> In blistering heat
> and bloody rain.
> Later on, in years to come,

When you speak of battles
fought and won,
Remember these men
who fought so well,
And lived and died
in that green hell.

The Liberal MP John Loverseed, a former serviceman, said he had read letters from 14th Army men 'whose homes have been broken up, who have lost everything that was dear to them simply because of the length of time they had been required to spend outside this country'. By December, an official inquiry led by Churchill's friend the Earl of Munster, Geoffrey FitzClarence, reported to Cabinet that troops looked 'above all for a definite and firm date to which they could look forward ... I was, however, impressed with the requests made on many occasions ... that a statement on this subject should be made by the Prime Minister, in whom every man has complete confidence and trust.' It was a none-too-subtle nudge to the prime minister. The tour of duty in the Far East was reduced from four years to three years and four months, and by a further four months in June 1945.

There was medical evidence to back up anecdotal reports of disillusionment. The 2nd Division psychiatrist Captain Paul Davis worried about the rise in the number of cases being sent to him. During the fighting for Kohima the psychiatric toll had been just under 10 per cent of the total wounded. During the advance into Burma it nearly doubled, 'though the fighting was nothing as bitter and the death toll substantially lower ... the "repatriation consciousness" ... and sheer war weariness may have contributed to this'.

The British saga of command stuttered on. In May 1944 Mountbatten sacked the Army Group commander, General Sir George Giffard. 'I had the most difficult of many difficult days in this command,' he told his diary. 'I had to tell my Army Group Commander-in-Chief ... that I had lost confidence in him, and was asking for his replacement ... I suppose it really is that he is orthodox and extremely cautious, whereas I really feel that we must push on and take all the risks with the troops this monsoon.' This, as Mountbatten well knew, was only part of the truth. Giffard's fatal error had been in refusing to accept the younger man as his boss, or to take him remotely seriously as a military figure. What Mountbatten viewed as his intolerable slowness in getting troops to the front back in March confirmed Giffard's fate. But Giffard's support to Slim as he built 14th Army into a force to fight the Japanese had been immense and, as Slim commented, 'we saw him go with grief'. The man chosen to replace him, General Oliver Leese, came from 8th Army in Italy, but was destined to fail in Burma. Shut out of key decisions by Slim and Mountbatten, he was the latecomer to the party and, as Slim's biographer Robert Lyman notes, 'was never able to dominate as he wished'. He moved against Slim, with spectacularly awful timing, in early May 1945, just as 14th Army was consolidating its hold on Rangoon and pursuing the defeated Japanese southwards. Leese tried to remove Slim on 7 May, but such was the political row that followed that within six weeks Leese was himself removed and replaced by Slim. Once before, in the gloom of the first Arakan, he had been sacked and survived to see the man who gave the orders removed himself. The general seen by the troops as bluff and hearty, as close to one of them as a general could be, had proved himself not only a superb military tactician, but a doughty political survivor. He had an influential ally in Mountbatten and had won the confidence of Brooke; but it was his victory over the Japanese, and the overwhelming support of his generals and men, which made the decision to sack him seem so ludicrous and which ensured its reversal. With exasperating discretion, Slim referred in his memoirs only to 'a considerable reorganisation of the higher army command'.

One August evening, when Rangoon was at its sweltering summer worst, Dennis Wykes and a few friends heard that Japan had surrendered. 'The blokes just went mad,' Wykes recalled. The West Kents cheered in the streets. Men hugged each other and jumped on to passing cars. Japan had surrendered. Ray Street was walking in Rangoon when he heard shooting and thought some Japanese had infiltrated. Instead, he saw officers riding around in jeeps and firing pistols in the air. He was guarding Japanese prisoners at Rangoon jail, who at first refused to believe the news. 'Finally they realised it was true and became scared of what was to become of them.' Neither Street nor any other West Kent harmed the prisoners. When asked, sixty years later, if he had been tempted to abuse the hated enemy, he replied, 'Naw. You can't be like that. I felt sorry for them. They were fighting for theirselves and we were fighting for ourselves.' It has to be said that those who felt sorry for the Japanese were in a minority. Hatred of the enemy, even if it was not expressed as brutality towards prisoners, was the dominant emotion of those days.

Kohima had changed them all. It would become apparent in different ways, and in some sooner than others. The West Kent medic Frank Infanti encountered Padre Roy Randolph, the ascetic and peace-loving chaplain to the battalion, helping another officer to make a booby trap. 'I said to him, "I don't understand, you're a man of God." And he said, "Well, eh, after Kohima I had to go and look at one of our men and he had been tied up and tortured with wire. Then I decided that God had forsaken the Japanese."' Dennis Wykes was in convalescent camp after the surrender when an administrative officer called him to his tent over some minor problem. As the officer talked, a Japanese prisoner walked in. Wykes began to feel unsteady on his feet. His anger swelled. He told the British officer that he had to leave; he could not be around the prisoner. Outside he saw a group of prisoners standing chatting. 'I made them dig a trench. And I kept them digging. A bloody big trench it was!'

* * *

From the ship he should have been able to see the smoke from the big chimneys. But there was nothing at all. The men around him became quiet as the ship approached harbour. Most had wondered if they would ever see home. Now that they did, the sense of shock was profound. Masao Hirakubo landed at Otaki, one of the ports of Hiroshima, and was sent with the other repatriated men to be disinfected. They were told by the Americans to take their clothes off and were covered in powder. What a sight, these beaten men sprinkled with the cleansing dust of the conquerors. 'Hiroshima was dead. Nobody was in the street.' There was acre upon acre of smashed emptiness. So this was what the new weapons could do! He took a train to Yokohama but when he got there people told him his old neighbourhood had been destroyed in an air raid. He went into a business and asked to use the phone so that he could call his father's office. Would he be alive, and if so would he have given up hope by now of ever seeing his son again? The first call told him that his father had changed companies but that he was alive. 'I telephoned to the new company in Tokyo and spoke to my father and said, "I have come back now." He was surprised. He thought I was dead already. They had heard nothing from me in Burma except one mail. No communication for two and a half years!' They arranged to meet at Shinbashi station in downtown Tokyo. Hirakubo saw his father from the train. He was the same portly little man with a worried expression that he remembered from that other life before the war. Stepping off the train, he walked towards his father, but as he came closer it was clear that he did not recognise his son. 'I told him "It is me. I have come back." He was amazed. Japanese people never show feeling to the face but we can understand.' They went to a restaurant and ate together and then took a train to a relative's house where the family were being sheltered. When they arrived, he saw his grand-father sitting in the front room. The old man shouted for joy. Then his mother, his two sisters and his niece rushed out. 'Everybody was crying. They had been wondering about my funeral.' After a few weeks he found a job with his old trading company and tried to resume the life he had known, but his mind constantly turned to Kohima. He could not escape thoughts of death.

His 138th Regiment counterpart, Chuzaburo Tomaru, returned to find that his father had been killed in an air raid. For Chuzaburo the end of the war had been a time of madness. An officer he knew, a man who had survived the march out of India, took a pistol and blew out his own brains when he heard news of the surrender. Chuzaburo was sad at the defeat, but he had never been a committed warrior like so many of the others. The war was a hell that followed him into peace. The images flashed before him constantly. He saw himself running in torn shoes; he saw a man slip into the jungle and kill himself with a hand grenade, another shoot himself in the mouth; one time when he had amoebic dysentery he saw a wild dog slink out and eat his shit. The pictures kept coming into his old age.

In the Japan to which he and the other veterans returned, the old military was a leper caste. Men deserted in droves after the defeat and there was widespread criminality. The eminent American historian of Japan, John Dower, described how 'officers and men engaged in looting, sometimes on a grand scale, and police reports expressed that public disgust would extend upward to "grave distrust, frustration, and antipathy towards military and civilian leaders", even "hatred of the military" in general'. About 70 per cent of the military's remaining supply stocks, including machinery and vehicles, were stolen by the upper echelons and much of them sold on to the black market. By contrast, disabled veterans and war widows were abandoned to fend for themselves. Prices soared by 539 per cent in the first year after the surrender, and nearly four million people were left without housing. Destitute veterans begged in the streets of ruined cities. Hans Baerwald, an American brought up in Japan, returned to work for the Occupation administration and saw 'vast stretches of flatness, dotted with shacks made of cardboard, corrugated tin, and bits of wood for most of the way from the docks of Yokohama to downtown Tokyo'.

There were 350,000 American military personnel in the country by the end of 1945 and these new soldiers moved with their shoulders back and their chins up, as if the future belonged to them. To speak to the veterans of the 31st Division, it was as if they were barely aware of the victors' presence, certainly in the first few months after their return from Burma. Home, with all its losses and ambiguities, was still home. The machine-gunner Yoshiteru Hirayama was in hospital with cerebral malaria when he dreamt that he was on a train going home to his father's monastery in Saitama, outside Tokyo. But when the train would not stop he shouted and tried to jump off.

When he woke up, there were guards trying to stop him from jumping from the hospital window. Hirayama believed that his spirit had travelled home ahead of him. Back in Saitama, he studied for the Buddhist priesthood, eventually taking over from his father as abbot. He married and had three children, but never spoke of Kohima until his children asked. 'My children wanted to know about it but I hesitated and even then when I did talk I didn't tell them the worst. I don't really want to talk. I felt such grief.'

When General Sato came home to Amarume he was a man without a job or a home of his own. He moved with his family into his brother's home, where they occupied a few small rooms in an annexe. There was no bathroom and when he wanted to bathe the general would cross to his brother's house and ask to use the facilities there. 'I want to take a bath in my own house some day,' he told his son Goro. There was a military pension, but the family was constantly short of money. Eventually General Sato sent his son to the pawnshop with the family's valuables. 'He pawned stuff in order that we could feed ourselves,' Goro said. A cousin across the river in Sakata gave them firewood which Goro and his sisters went by boat to collect.

General Sato knew there were some in the area who regarded the retreat from Kohima as a betrayal, among them a veteran of the *Kempeitai* who ran a seed store in town and began to whisper against him. His younger brother, Kinchiko, an army colonel, was also among those who felt he had done the wrong thing. Most veterans of the 31st Division took a different view. He was invited to reunions and hailed as the man who had saved their lives. But it never removed the guilt he felt for those who had been left in the mountains. When he had finished his journey of atonement, walking the roads of Amarume to visit the families of the war dead, General Sato helped to organise a lobby group for the relatives. To his own children, though, he said almost nothing about Kohima.

Goro would go for walks with his father, or work in the family plot with him. 'I sensed it as a great loss inside him,' he recalled. The general took up calligraphy and studied with a local master, devoting hours to the delicate choreography of the brush. 'I will leave depressing days in the past,' he wrote. He went fishing with a friend but would ignore the float in the water and stare instead at the sky, a man with thoughts miles away from the river. At some point in the late 1940s, Goro noticed that his father's drinking was getting worse. He had always been a heavy drinker, but the alcohol had a grip on him now. When he became ill and went to hospital they diagnosed liver disease. 'Afterwards he asked the doctor, "How long do I have left?" and he wanted to know the name of the sickness. He pushed him to say the truth. He said: "Don't lie" ... The doctor said he had a year and a half. My impression was that he looked relieved when he knew how long he had left.' From then on, he went to more veterans' parties and meetings.

He told his son, 'Okay, from now on I live only eighteen months so I will do what I want to do.' The general's body could no longer cope with alcohol and his son watched him vomit many times, even after the smallest amount. 'It was so sad to see him like that ... just throwing up. He would ask me to massage his body because he was in so much pain.' There was a summons to the war crimes tribunal, where prosecutors questioned him and decided there was no case to answer; he was flattered when the Americans called him to Tokyo to tell their officers what it was like to fight the Russians. The drinking and his health got worse and he could be irascible with his family. His daughter, Yukiko, found him strict and chose her words carefully when answering his questions. 'I was careful of answering his question because he would consider words like "but" or "because" to be directed against him. My father would get mad saying, "you are not honest", if I forgot to do something. I tied ribbon around my finger not to forget things before I went out. If I took a rest due to a headache, my father scolded me for being "Lazy".' He lived by the codes of an older Japan in which a parent's word was law. Yet Yukiko would always revere him for making sure she had an education. By the summer of 1958 he had undergone an operation for the removal of a liver tumour. 'He was nothing but skin and bone,' his wife Fumiko recalled. The following February he went into hospital for the last time. He told his family to build an altar and then make a bonfire of his letters and documents. Only the list of the dead from

Kohima was spared. He thought of them to the end. Kotuku Sato died on 26 February 1959 on a day of heavy snow.

On the day of his funeral veterans from across the division came to the Jigan temple. There were also men who had served with him in Korea and fighting the Russians. His old infantry commander, Miyazaki, came, dressed in a grey woollen suit and looking like a prosperous businessman. He told the curious that he now made his living running a pottery shop. Goro Sato noticed a small stir at the back of the room. When he looked across he saw General Renya Mutaguchi standing among the officers. 'I didn't have a feeling of hatred. I was too busy to notice what was happening. I just said, "Well, he has come." We just accepted the fact.' What happened next astonished the general's family. Suddenly Mutaguchi got down on his knees and prostrated himself before them. 'I am sorry,' he said. The room was silent. After a few minutes General Sato's wife said something in response, but Goro Sato was so overcome that he cannot remember what it was. Word filtered out of the room to veterans in the temple corridors. Mutaguchi had apologised! The man who had never admitted he was wrong had said sorry.

If it had rested there, Mutaguchi might have seemed a larger man to them. But his post-war life was a prolonged exercise in self-justification. He was cursed by 31st Division veterans and he knew it. 'Some said, "how dare you still live?" It was a painful experience,' he told an archivist. Four years after Sato's funeral he was interviewed by a researcher from the library of the Japanese parliament, the National Diet. He began piously enough. 'General Sato passed away already. It is not right to whip the dead for his mistake,' he said. Mutaguchi then proceeded to trample over the dead man's memory. Sato had made a 'terrible error in leadership' and had disobeyed orders; he was surely mentally imbalanced. Mutaguchi even cited Slim's criticism of Sato in his list of charges, and then berated Kawabe for holding him back from Dimapur. The agreement was that the interview would not be released for thirty-three years after his death.

For a period after the war Mutaguchi had been held as a suspected war criminal. Troops under his command had taken part in the massacre of patients and staff at the Alexandra Military Hospital in Singapore. The Prosecutor General rejected the case because Mutaguchi had not been present when his troops ran riot, bayoneting and shooting the wounded. 'The massacres were committed in the heat of battle and I do not see how responsibility can be attached to a Senior Officer who was not present unless it can be shown that he had some cognizance of what took place.' He was released from Changi prison in Singapore on 5 June 1947 and sent home to Japan, where he was appointed to the staff college of the Self-Defence Force, a piece of excellent fortune for a man who had presided over the greatest battle-field defeat in his country's history, to say nothing of the disaster he had inflicted on the people of northern Burma and the Naga Hills.

The 31st Division veterans would back Sato until the end. But it took forty years to erect a memorial to him in Amarume. A monk friend of his family explained that locals wanted to forget the war. Also, Sato's actions had divided the townspeople. Abbot Hakuho Abe, over a hundred years old when we met, told me that veterans approached the family soon after Sato died. 'They asked his family for permission to construct the stone much earlier, but they could not say yes because they were blamed a lot after the war. They were made to feel ashamed.' The simple grey obelisk was erected in the spring of 1985 and after prayers the veterans posed together for a photograph. Every year they went to 31st Division reunions, and to the dinners of its component regiments. Many went back to Kohima to see the place where the bones of their comrades were buried in mass graves. As for the thousands who fell along the tracks to the Chindwin and beyond, they had a champion in the form of Hiroshi Yamagami, the colour-bearer of the 58th Regiment. I met him in his small, file-cluttered flat in Tokyo, where he has lived alone since the death of his wife. They had no children and had travelled widely together around the world. But it was Burma that kept drawing him back, and he visited the old battlefields, searching for the remains of the dead. When he found some bones he offered prayers. Some of them must have been of men he had once known. Of that he was sure.

TWENTY-SIX

The Quiet Fathers

On the train there was a bunch of Birmingham lads he got chatting with, all going home like himself, and all of them wondering how it would have changed. When he got off at Coventry they skimmed their berets across the platform through the carriage windows and cheered him on. Dennis Wykes waved goodbye, shouldered his duffel bag and walked out of the station. He was wearing his bush hat and hoped someone would notice and say, 'Hey, were you in the Fourteenth Army?' He would nod modestly if they did, even answer a few questions about how tough it had been. But nobody said anything. People looked tired and the city was in a state. Bombed to blazes. Still, the excitement kept him going for the two mile walk home. Jesus, he thought, home. How many times at Kohima had he pictured his feet quickening up Melbourne Road and then forced the thought out of his mind, because nothing is so far away as the home you might never see again.

He turned into the road and started to walk up the hill. 'I started to feel "Oh God" and then I saw they had all the flags outside and "Welcome Home". And there was a neighbour woman who was always leaning over the front gate of her house. And there she was still leaning over the front gate! She saw me coming and dashed out and rushed down the road and threw her arms around me.' Dennis walked on, up the steps, and knocked on the door. He heard feet racing through the house. The whole family was there, his mam and dad, aunts, uncles, cousins. After that it was all cheering, crying, patting him on the back and questions. He could answer them up to a point, but found himself sticking to generalisations. It was bloody hard, he told them. The Japs were savage fighters. But there was a point you could not go beyond. His parents didn't need to hear the truth of it, and he was not sure he could get the words out in any case.

There was the person who had left England and then there was him. They were so different he couldn't even start to explain. 'It was pretty hard to take ... My mother and father, I think they thought I would come home and be the same fellow. Of course I wasn't. She said, "You sit in that armchair and read your *Beano*, Dennis. It's always been your armchair, it's yours now." And I thought, "I don't want no armchair. I've been on the trot for four years in the army, at war." I never stopped moving.' Now there was time that stretched ahead forever and the habits of four years to break free from. He got up at dawn each day, put on his uniform and went out walking, looking for anybody he knew. He found himself searching the faces for dead men.

One day he was walking in Spond Street in the city centre and the loneliness was unbearable. He just wanted to sit down with an old army mate and have a drink and talk about what it had been like. For the first time in his life he went into a pub and drank himself senseless. There was another army man in there drinking who had been home for a long time and they swapped stories. 'I realised I was drunk. I said, "I can't go home and disgrace myself in front of my parents."' There was a circus on nearby and he decided to go there and try to sober up. But getting off the bus, he stumbled and was knocked out. When he came to there was a Frenchwoman sitting over him and mopping up the blood from the cut on his head. Drunk and concussed, he started pouring out his story to this foreigner, 'but I don't think she ever understood ... I was still in a foreign land really.'

The men of 4th battalion came home from the Far East to a country leached of colour by war. Winston Churchill, the leader who had sent them to India, was gone, voted from office by a nation haggard from sacrifice and eager for change. Britain had taken the first steps towards becoming a welfare state. In 1944 the Cabinet accepted the recommendation that there should be a National Health Service and by the time the men returned from India the new Labour government had introduced acts to cover pensions, national insurance and family allowances, much of this the brainchild of a man born in Bengal under the Raj, Sir William Beveridge, the most influential social reformer of modern Britain.

The war had left Britain beggared. The US$31 billion owed to the Americans in war-time loans underlined the true shift of international power. Britain could no longer afford a global empire and her imperial horizons retracted by the month, nowhere more swiftly than in the East. Burma became independent in 1948 and refused to join the Commonwealth, eventually, in 1962, becoming a military dictatorship which lasts to this day. When India left the empire the previous year she was sundered into two bitterly opposed nations whose enmity threatens the stability of the sub-continent still.

Yet if Churchill's hope of imperial redemption was forlorn, then Roosevelt's ambitions for China would prove equally misplaced. All the supplies shipped across the Hump, and up the Burma Road, all the thousands of lives lost and the millions spent could not save Chiang Kai-shek's regime from the armies of Mao Tse Tung.

Yet the returning soldiers did not tend to look backwards, or to torment themselves with questions about what the fight had been for. Very few had gone into battle imbued with a spirit of imperial glory. They had fought not for a vanishing dream but for each other and, most importantly, for their own lives. They were imbued with righteous anger by the appalling brutality of the Japanese, an anger that Slim had carefully channelled to become the great moral purpose of 14th Army. But there was a larger achievement. A Japanese victory at Kohima and Imphal might easily have propelled British India into an era of grave political instability. Remember that the battle was fought at a time when the leaders of Congress were languishing in jail, cut off from the Indian masses and watching the Japanese advance with mounting unease, as uncertain as the British about how the people would react. We are of course in the realms of speculation but a triumph for Mutaguchi in Assam could have sparked widespread unrest in the north-east and in Bengal, bringing with it communal violence and a familiar response of British repression leading to unknown consequences. Japan might only have enjoyed a short triumph; American power would ultimately have seen to that. But the humiliation of defeat would have gravely weakened the British in the post-war moves to settle the question of India. The victory over Mutaguchi did not save the Raj as Churchill had hoped. But after the humiliations of Malaya, Singapore and Burma it restored to the British the prestige needed to be able to negotiate the end of empire.

The 14th Army was made up of men of all political persuasions and it is wise to avoid generalisations about how they viewed Britain or the empire. Yet, having spoken with large numbers of veterans, the overwhelming impression is of men who returned home anxious to build, to forge ahead, and not to waste time mourning what was gone. The grief would come later and would be stirred by the memories of friends, not the loss of the eastern lands.

Dennis Wykes set up a thriving building firm and when he took his summer holidays in a caravan at Newquay he thought himself one of the luckiest men alive. He lived to get married, to have children, to see them inherit his business and go to university. When I last met him, three months before he died, he told me about a family Christmas party he had attended. He was asked to sing a song. All he could think of was one from the war. 'I got to the second verse and I just couldn't go on any more. I didn't burst into tears, I just couldn't go on any more. I was really upset. And I said afterwards: "I made a fool of myself trying to do that." But my daughter said, "No you didn't. It was a fitting thing to do."' For Dennis Wykes, there was always the voice of the Welsh boy, Williams, hit by the bomb that should have killed him, begging, 'Don't let me die,' and Dennis thinking, 'I can't stop you dying, mate.'

When the C company runner Ray Street arrived back in Birmingham he found himself missing his army friends more than he could have thought possible. His father, a veteran of Gallipoli, took him aside and told him to take his return slowly, ease himself back into English life gradually. 'Don't worry about anything,' he said. The advice was kind and was backed up by the older man's knowledge of war and its bonds. Ray married a 'very maternal' Irish girl called Anne and set up his own furniture business, working until ten o'clock every night, telling himself, 'if I can do the army I can do this. People wanted their furniture delivered and I did it every night.' The business thrived and he moved to a bigger house. When his wife died, Ray took over caring for their two children, as well as running the business. His son Bob thought him 'a kind dad, considerate and unassuming', who told stories of Kohima that 'were better than any bedtime stories, a real adventure'. Ray Street told me that Kohima had not affected him mentally, apart from one thing. 'I hate people touching me on the shoulder when I am asleep ... the shells feel like they are coming straight at you. Boom. And it might be over there.' His second wife, Valerie, learned a long time ago never to try to shake him awake. He would sit bolt upright as if somebody were attacking him.

The image of the shell-shocked soldier has become one of the stock clichés of our time. Yet war, even the horror of Kohima, does not turn every man into a shaking wreck for the remainder of his life. Many of the men, probably the majority, understandably felt emotional pain, but were not disabled by their experiences. Private Tom Greatly of C company had lied his way into the army at the age of sixteen. He was twenty-one when he came home from Burma. Several lifetimes of horror had passed before his eyes in that time. He went home to Worcestershire, married and lived a contented life; his great pleasure was to go ballroom dancing with his wife three times a week. Yet there was a shadow of the war's impact. Tom got a job working in a children's hospital, and part of his duties were in the morgue. 'It never affected me like it did some people. Maybe that had something to do with Kohima.' He was one of the men who had helped Padre Randolph collect the possessions of the dead and mark their graves so that they could be found later on.

Towards the end of his life, John Shipster of the Punjab Regiment experienced nightmares about fighting the Japanese. 'I would wake up screaming in the middle of the night, waking my wife up, and never be able to give a clear explanation of what it was. I knew it was about the war, but I never actually came to the end of it.' After the War he transferred to the British Army and went to fight in the

Korean War where he again narrowly escaped death facing the Chinese on the Yalu River. Although a professional soldier for more than thirty-five years, looking back he felt that war had been a fruitless endeavour. 'Here we were bashing each other around in a very small area, and then spending some weeks afterwards clearing up all the mess and putting people into graves, merely to move on, say, fifty to a hundred miles and do it all over again on some other plot of ground ... What did I think I was fighting for? I wasn't some crusader or anything of that sort. My country was at war and I joined up and fought in it, I never queried the individual battles, or said I'll fight in this battle but not in that. I went along with the tide. I had faith in the aims of one's particular country.'

The commander of B company, Royal West Kents, John Winstanley, survived his leg wound and typhoid and went to medical school. 'I felt I couldn't waste any more time and worked like a slave for the exams.' When his leg wound flared up, the hospital authorities told him he would have to give up his dream of being a general surgeon. So he became one of the country's most successful eye-surgeons. In peacetime he missed the intensity of friendship that war had created. There was a world of shared experience to which others, not even those closest to him, could ever be admitted. The regimental associations and the Burma Star Association became for many a kind of parallel family. 'It is just fragments, but when we get together, those who are still alive, all the old friendships and associations come out.'

Donald Easten stayed in the army and retired with the rank of colonel. On retirement he lived with Billie in the village of Wormingford where he immersed himself in the parish council, and continued to fish and shoot as he had since he was a young man. Their daughters and grandchildren were regular visitors. The residents named a street in his honour. Easten Green. When Billie died he faced the choice of moving to a smaller place but he loved the landscape and the home they had made. The River Stour is nearby, running alongside the border with Suffolk, and, now in his nineties, Donald Easten continues to walk the fields accompanied by an excitable terrier. On Remembrance Sunday he walks the couple of hundred yards to the old parish church at Wormingford to remember the boys of D company he left behind in Kohima.

I listened to the stories of the veterans over many years and was always struck by their modesty, by the way in which they resisted any temptation to exaggerate their experiences or their role in the battle. The majority had never spoken with their children about Kohima. In part, this was generational. Men of the post-war era lived by a standard of emotional restraint uncommon in modern Britain. They were the quiet fathers who made their way in a new country where interest in the Far Eastern war was always limited and where, in any case, their energies were absorbed by the imperatives of work and family. That is very different, however, from saying that the war was not present in houses across Britain.

Christine Porteus was present when her Chindit uncle came home from the war.

> I was ten and a half at the time and recall the look of horror on my father's face when his brother came to call – I was just frightened, he was shrunken and yellow, thin as a plank and with 'worried' eyes. My mother just burst into tears since she had waved off uncle when he departed for war – he was then a young man from a small village in Hertfordshire, full of life and fun. He returned a complete wreck and never really recovered. He suffered from ghastly nightmares, recurrent malaria and never really fitted in again with his family.

Margery Willis, the daughter of Lieutenant John Faulkner, remembered never being allowed to drink Rose's lime juice because it reminded her father of his time in the jungle when there was no water and only the tart lime juice to slake his thirst. 'The War was generally not to be mentioned at home at any time,' she recalled. Later, her mother told her that John had 'terrible nightmares' after he came home. To his daughter he was a controlling man, a rigid disciplinarian with a bad temper, 'a difficult man to live with'. The only glimpse she was given of what the war meant to her father was on Remembrance Sunday. The family would be told sit down and watch the service. John Faulkner would sit with them and cry. Once the service was over the war was put away again. After he died, Janet opened his diary of the siege and began to understand the man whose memory she was struggling with. Written in Dimapur a few weeks after the battle, it speaks with the voice of a young soldier astonished by his own survival. His daughter believed that settling into a normal existence after Kohima was very difficult for John Faulkner. The three years in Burma were the most important of his life. As more than one veteran put it to me: 'You can never explain it to someone who wasn't there.'

For the families whose sons and fathers never came home, the sight of demobbed soldiers could be agonising. In most cases, all they were told was that their loved one had died or was missing in action. In a war in which hundreds of thousands of British troops had died, only the extraordinary death merited more than a couple of lines. Nor did the families have graves where they could go to grieve. The dead were lying in Asian war cemeteries which the majority could never afford to visit.

The father of Victoria Cross winner Lance Corporal John Harman built a stone memorial to his son on Lundy Island where John had roamed in his childhood summers. The day of the unveiling was strikingly beautiful with a blue sky and a calm sea for the large group travelling to Lundy on the ferry MV *Lerina*. Among the party were John Laverty and several other West Kents, including Sergeant Tacon, the machine-gunner who had slaughtered the Japanese as they ran from Detail Hill. By the time they had walked from the ferry pier to the quarry, many of the group were perspiring and anxious to find shade. They clustered around the huge slab of granite on which John Harman's name and date of death were inscribed. They sang 'O God Our Help in Ages Past' and the Reverend H. C. A. S. Muller, vicar of Appledore, read from the 24th Psalm. This was followed by another hymn, 'Fight the Good Fight', and the playing of the Last Post. Martin Coles Harman told his guests that the quarry where his son had played as a child was thought to be nearly two million years old, and in 20,000 years the rocks would still look the same. Only this, he seemed to be saying, is imperishable. The island's caretaker, Felix Gade, who had taught John so much of what he knew about the natural world, told the visitors about the extraordinary thing that had happened after John had died. It was the custom in that part of the country when a beekeeper died for another to go to his hives and 'tell' the news to the inhabitants. But when Gade arrived he found all the bees had flown away.

John was the firstborn of his family and had the same wayward spirit that had carried his father through many adventures; they were alike in their romantic readiness and Harman senior had never once tried to dampen his boy's wilder ambitions. He had encouraged and helped to pay for his prospecting schemes and for the travels to Europe and New Zealand. After John's death his father never spoke of him to the other children. But he carried his son's Victoria Cross with him for years after the war and, as his daughter Diana recalled, would take it out and show it to strangers. 'Wherever he was he would say "Have you ever seen this? Well, you probably won't see another. Take a good look."'

It would be tempting to believe that the experience of Kohima gave all those who went through it a common bond. And it is true that the majority of General Slim's men – British, Indian, Nepalese and Burmese – felt that they had shared an extraordinary trial. But there was in the decades after the war an angry distance between the two men who had held together the defence of Kohima during those sixteen days in April 1944. The earlier writers on the subject, most of them former soldiers, mention the ill feeling between John Laverty and Hugh Richards, but either did not know of its scale or else decided against making it public. Given the fact that both men were still alive, their discretion is understandable. It began on the battle-field, with Laverty's curt dismissal of the senior man on the day he arrived. His refusal to engage with Richards beyond the four-word question 'Where is Kuki Piquet?' left the garrison commander feeling diminished in front of his subordinates. None of the danger the two men shared in the following fortnight altered Laverty's attitude.

It was Richards, as garrison commander, who nominated Laverty for his DSO, praising 'his personal tenacity and leadership [which] ... was responsible for the defeat of attack after attack by the Japanese ... Lt. Col Laverty was quite tireless and displayed powers of leadership and command of the highest order.' It could be said that Richards had no choice but to make the recommendation. But his post-war record was always one of public praise for the actions of the Royal West Kents. They had been magnificent, he said. So it is not hard to imagine Richards's hurt when two West Kent officers, neither of whom had served at Kohima, produced a book of 4th battalion's war experiences that undermined the garrison. Published in 1951, *From Kent to Kohima* by Major E. B. Stanley Clarke and Major A. T. Tillott declared boldly that 'The command and staff of the garrison of Kohima before the arrival of the battalion were not equal or willing to take the task of commanding the 4th Royal West Kents ... command throughout the battle was virtually operated from the Headquarters of the 4th Royal West Kents.'

There was worse to come. In 1956 another serving army officer, Lieutenant Colonel Arthur Campbell, published a fictionalized account of the siege based on the experiences of an anonymous West Kent intelligence officer. In Campbell's book Richards's bunker floor is described as being made from upturned rum and brandy bottles, while the picture of the garrison and its command is strikingly familiar to any reader of the 4th West Kents' War Diary. The impression is of a bunch of incompetents rescued by the 4th West Kents. Certainly Laverty thought Richards was out of his depth. In one of his very rare talks with his son Patrick about the war, John Laverty gave the impression that Hugh Richards was a 'complete idiot, should never have been there, and did not know what he was doing. Perhaps not the words but that was the impression. When he came in to Kohima he rated it a complete shambles, and that any junior military man worth his salt would have done better.'

* * *

This was the view communicated to Arthur Campbell by Laverty when the two met in 1956. Over a fortnight's holiday spent together in the West Country, the 4th battalion commander gave the writer his detailed account of the siege.

Hugh Richards was horrified when it was published. At first his friends, including the garrison second-in-command, Lieutenant Colonel Gordon Borrowman, demanded an apology from Campbell. In August 1956 Borrowman wrote to Campbell accusing him of doing a 'grave injustice' in a story 'that was wildly inaccurate … definitely libellous and untrue'. It was Richards and not Laverty who had been in control, and it was Richards who went to see the men in the trenches 'when the going got sticky'. There was only one issue on which Borrowman agreed with Campbell. 'What surprised me chiefly was the patience which Richards showed towards Laverty who was incredibly offensive. You have yourself given a perfect description of him as a "bloodyminded Irishman".' Campbell wrote back ten days later from his address at the Army Staff College in Camberley, Surrey. Campbell claimed that, as a serving soldier, he could not present the two sides of the story. This seems to suggest that he did not want to publicise the breach between the two commanders at Kohima. 'I therefore chose to tell the story of the battle as the RWK saw it and lived it … if anyone wants to publish the other side of the story they are at liberty to do so.' Borrowman was being given the brush-off but he refused to let it drop. In his communications with Hugh Richards he spoke of how he 'would like to rub Laverty's face in the dirt!'

Borrowman wrote to Campbell again on 24 August, with a renewed demand for an apology 'to the garrison in general and Brigadier Richards in particular', under threat of legal action. As for Campbell's assertion that as a serving soldier he could not tell both sides of the story, he wrote: '[I] would have thought that that fact should have made you even more careful not to blackguard another officer and other "serving soldiers" without even trying to learn the true facts.' Borrowman wrote to the official historian at the Cabinet Office, Brigadier M. R. Roberts, who reassured him, 'I also feel that the story is merely a glorification of Laverty.' The official version would support Richards. The row percolated to the very top of the old 14th Army command. Borrowman wrote to General Slim, who was by then serving as Governor General of Australia. The letter is intriguing, for it suggests that Slim had acted once before to redress the balance in Richards's favour. 'You will remember after the Kohima show in 1944', Borrowman wrote, 'that Laverty of the R.W.K. went about boasting that he had done everything and that Hugh Richards had done nothing – you and Sir George Gifford [sic] dealt with that at the time, but that did not stop Laverty.' Borrowman may have been referring to the lecture tour given by Laverty in the wake of the siege and the publicity accorded to the West Kents.

Giffard had written the citation for Richard's award of the DSO and described his old comrade from Africa days as 'solely responsible for this fine defence'. Slim wrote to Borrowman that he had never doubted that it was Hugh Richards who conducted the defence of Kohima, and he confirmed this in his celebrated account of the war, Defeat into Victory. 'I am sorry that Laverty has been so unjust and so unpleasant about Hugh Richards,' wrote Slim. 'I hate these public stinks but I can quite understand how Richards feels about it all.'

Eventually Richards himself put pen to paper. He was a man constitutionally averse to any kind of row, least of all a public spat with a fellow officer. But the absence of a personal apology from Campbell spurred him to action. Writing in October 1956, Richards praised his Indian troops and pointed out that it was the men of the Assam Regiment who had held the tennis court longer than any other unit. As for himself, he told Campbell that he had done him 'as grave an injury as it is possible for one man to do another'. This settled the matter for Campbell. Richards's words and the outrage of other senior officers had cut home. He wrote to Hugh Richards a fortnight later. 'I am glad to have heard from you personally on this matter. I do confirm most sincerely, that I regret the hurt I have done you personally in The Siege. I have tried to explain in my letters to

Borrowman how it came about so I won't repeat it here. I will only say that I am truly sorry.' He suggested that a film of the book was being considered and hoped it could undo the hurt that had been done. Richards had won the battle of the books. In every subsequent account, all written by former military men, he was given due credit for the defence of Kohima.

What was the truth of the matter? As this book suggests, the picture at Kohima was complicated. Richards arrived to find a garrison pitifully unprepared for war. His second-in-command, Borrowman, was only just out of hospital after a three-week stay and missed the build-up to the Japanese invasion. There was no proper planning in his absence. Five days after he arrived the Kohima area was placed under the control of an administrative officer, General Ranking, who was unqualified for such a big task. The mess could be traced to the first three months of 1944 and the failure of the Army Command to properly garrison either Dimapur or Kohima, but they in turn faced the immense challenge of planning offensives in the Arakan and the north-east with the most limited resources. Richards and his staff struggled to make the best of a messy situation, evacuating as many non-combatants as possible and desperately trying to improve the defences before the enemy arrived. What Laverty saw when he arrived was undoubtedly a sorry spectacle to an efficient soldier from a battle-hardened regiment. But his mistake was to blame Richards for the mistakes of others. In the heat of battle his assumptions might have been understandable. But not afterwards when the true facts were there to be discovered. It is equally true that without the professionalism of the Royal West Kents, and Laverty's calm leadership, and unerring ability to spot and reinforce gaps, the garrison would have collapsed within days. The 'bloody-minded Irishman' inserted steel into the backbone of every man of the 4th West Kents. What came to pass between the two commanders was tragic, not least because both were fine soldiers and decent men who in their very different styles of leadership complemented each other.

After the war Hugh Richards took up poultry farming and lived in Haywards Heath in Sussex. He was short of money and hindered by severe arthritis, but content that his reputation had been vindicated. He remained in contact with many of the old garrison staff and was an honoured guest at reunions of the Assam Regiment and his old favourites the West African Brigade, with whom he had spent the happiest days of his life. He spoke very little about Kohima to his only child, Roger, except to say that it had been 'a very close thing'. In old age he moved with his second wife to the sunshine of Malta, where he died in 1983. His son followed him into the Worcestershire Regiment and two of his grandsons joined the army as well.

John Laverty became head of the Infantry Training Centre at Colchester and then took a job in the War Office. His wife, Renee, spoke of the post-war years being 'an awful sort of let-down', in a job he hated. The War Office years were no more than a countdown to a pension, working among desk soldiers and civil servants, with whom he had nothing in common. At home he was a distant father, certainly in the memory of his son, Patrick. The war was not discussed. 'I tried to raise it with him but I got nowhere at all. You just got slapped around the choppers and told to mind your own business.' The marriage never recovered from the separation brought about by the war, and his drinking increased, though he only drank after six o'clock in the evening, his son recalled. 'We had been apart for so long. It was not easy,' his wife remembered. 'He liked a drop of whisky and it got a bit worse after the war. That's the way it went.' The couple split up some time in the late fifties. As his son Patrick put it, 'there wasn't a family to belong to after that'.

After retiring from the War Office John Laverty's life centred on the officers' club and Colchester Golf Club. A very different figure to the stern and forbidding colonel emerges in the description given by one of his golfing partners, a teenage boy. Chris Booth remembered Laverty playing regularly with his father and a retired RAF chaplain, Monsignor John Roach, an Irish catholic priest. 'Up to twenty or so golfers would turn up on a Saturday lunchtime and John, with military efficiency aided by several pink gins, would make up the four ball matches for the afternoon … John was a neat, efficient and busy type of man but had the charm of the Irish … but he had a very determined streak evident when he played golf.' Both Booth and his father had a keen interest in military history and were aware of Kohima but Laverty 'would not be drawn on the subject, at least not to me or my father'. He went to reunions of his old regiment, the Essex, but kept in touch with very few of the West Kents. In 1960 John Laverty's youngest daughter, Maureen, died of cancer. She was the child closest to him and her death left him devastated. By that time he was living alone. Patrick remembered a happy trip they made together. It was after Patrick had married and had children of his own, and was working in the west of Ireland. John Laverty travelled across to Connemara to see his son and grandchildren. It was the first time he had visited the land of his birth since he left it in 1918. Father and son played golf together and went to the pub in the village of Spiddal, overlooking the Atlantic. They talked about Ireland, about golf, about the grandchildren, but the war remained a closed book. Still, it was as close as they had ever been or would be again. When John Laverty died of cancer a year later there were many men of the West Kents among the funeral crowd.

Of all the characters who dominated the story of Kohima, only one remained with the place from the beginning to the end of the war. He knew it as a peaceful home and land of lost content. Long after the armies had moved on into Burma, Charles Ridley Pawsey was dealing with the cost of the battle. There was all his work trying to rebuild the fabric of Naga life battered by war, the business of re-establishing markets and courts; and there were the requests, coming every few days by the mail from Dimapur, for information about men whose bodies lay under the soil of Garrison Hill. On 9 September 1944, long after Grover's 2nd Division had chased the Japanese out of Kohima, Pawsey was looking for the grave of a Captain A. N. Lunn who had died on Jail Hill. 'So far the Graves Reg. Officer has not found his body,' he wrote. 'I am told he was with a V Force officer called Gould and his body has not been found. The latter's mother is continually enquiring about his grave and I've not been able to find anyone who knows where it is.'

After the war Pawsey stayed on as deputy commissioner and over-saw the construction of a new Kohima, and the creation of a war cemetery on the grounds of his old bungalow and tennis court. He set up a district council to unite the Nagas, but his dream of a peaceful future was stillborn. The Naga Hills were convulsed by the dramatic changes taking place in India. As independence approached Naga activists established a National Council to negotiate their future status. For a people so divided by clan loyalties, there was unanimity on the fundamental principle: they were not Indian and wanted independence. Jawaharlal Nehru called the independence demand 'unwise, impracticable and unacceptable'. India was divided enough along confessional lines. Pawsey, caught between his loyalty to the Nagas and the remorseless logic of history, tried to persuade the Naga National Council to accept district autonomy within India. 'Independence will mean: tribal warfare, no hospitals, no schools, no salt, no trade with the plains and general unhappiness,' he wrote. The National Council split and a more radical leader, A. Z. Phizo, from the village of Khonoma, emerged to lead the independence movement.* Mahatma Gandhi met with Naga leaders and assured them, 'I will ask them to shoot me first before one Naga is shot.' Gandhi was dead at the hands of a Hindu extremist before the promise could ever be tested. Rano Mese Shaiza, now an eighty-nine-year-old grandmother, was a niece of Phizo, and was imprisoned for her activism. She remembered Charles Pawsey with affection, but carries the sense, common among many of the older generation, of having been abandoned by Britain. 'When the British left they left us to India. But we are Nagas. We are not Indians,' she said.

By 1955 the political crisis in the Naga Hills had exploded into civil war.† Naga rebels fought the Indian army. Moderate political

---

* Khonoma had a tradition of rebellion dating to colonial times. It was here that the British political officer, G. H. Damant, met his death at the hands of Naga rebels in 1879.

† Accurate casualty figures are not available. The number of Naga dead is estimated at anything between 20,000 and 100,000. These casualties occurred as a result of insurrection and factional fighting between Naga groups and, during the 1990s, with the Kuki tribe. The Indian security forces also sustained thousands of casualties.

leaders were assassinated. Foreign journalists were banned from the area so that the scale of human rights abuses was hidden from the international community. The Nagas sent emissaries to their old friends in England. A party of four elders came to Ursula Graham Bower's home in Scotland in the early 1960s pleading with her to intercede with the British government. Would the old rulers help them to stop the persecution? Graham Bower persuaded her friend David Astor, editor of the *Observer*, to send an undercover reporter into Nagaland in April 1962 to verify the stories of atrocity. Gavin Young described a reign of terror at the hands of the Indian security forces. 'Individuals told of how they had been beaten and tied up for hours without water; how they had been bound and hung head downwards from trees to be flogged; how sons, brothers and fathers had been bayoneted to death.'

As Ursula's daughter Trina recalled: 'In the interest of *Commonwealth Relations*, which were at the time very difficult with the newly independent colonies all feeling their new freedoms and powers, and the South African debacle just beginning, nothing was done by the British Government. To Ursula's everlasting frustration she could do nothing for the people that had adopted her and done so much for the British and their interests.'

Charles Pawsey left India in 1948 and retired to Woodbridge in Suffolk where the Pawseys had lived for generations. He married the widow of an Assam sawmill owner who had also returned from India and became a gentleman farmer near the town of Woodbridge. Pawsey followed the news from the Naga Hills assiduously. His papers in the Centre for South Asian Studies in Cambridge are filled with newspaper cuttings from the period and the letters he wrote on the subject. In 1965 he was asked by the Indian government to return to the Naga Hills to try and broker a peace agreement or, as his wife Lady Jane put it, to 'knock some sense into the rebels'. He spent at least a month in the Naga Hills but it was a vain hope. Pawsey was a man from a lost age, who spoke of common sense and compromise in a place too divided and traumatised to hear him. He came home apparently appalled by the abuse of human rights in the Hills.*

When Mountbatten promised that Britain would never forget her debt to the Nagas, he was not indulging in mere rhetoric. But the supreme commander was speaking in the bright glow of victory, when nobody could have imagined a civil war in the hills. It was an easy time to make promises. Once the war was over, Britain turned to the great project of national reconstruction, and the dismantling of the rest of her empire. Relations with India were governed by the principle of British interests first. Any attempt to interfere in the new nation's handling of its domestic affairs would have been firmly rebuffed. At Kohima they had fought and won the last great battle of empire; but when it was all over, the victors found their strength sapped, their influence vastly diminished. The Nagas could plead forever, but the British had neither the power nor the political will to help them. Such is the story of empires and the small tribes caught in their fall.

The Nagas who stayed on in the Indian army after the war were posted to Bengal to police the referendum that established East Pakistan. Others were sent to the Punjab where they patrolled train stations thronged with the refugees of Partition, 'like the Burma Retreat of 1942, only worse because there was no apparent enemy'. Havildar Sohevu Angami, who had joined up after seeing soldiers playing football in his village, went home and married and resumed

---

* The era of large-scale insurgency has ended in the Naga Hills. However, India still employs the draconian Armed Forces (Special Powers) Act. Journalists are often refused permission to visit or discouraged from visiting by the simple expedient of delaying endlessly their requests for permits. On a visit to Kohima in 2009 this writer was aware of the omnipresence of Indian security forces. In neighbouring Manipur, where the battle of Imphal was fought, there are continuing attacks on the army and police and the familiar accusations of human rights abuse. The most common complaint in the Naga Hills now is of poverty. B. K. Sachu Angami was a twelve-year-old boy during the battle of Kohima and looked to the aftermath of victory with optimism. 'What we expected was that something good would come if the Britishers won. But we are lagging behind India now. We are a thousand years behind. What does independence mean in such a poor economy?' (Interviewed for this book.)

his life as a hunter. 'I had a double-barrelled shotgun after the war and I went hunting deer. I loved that.' He had twelve children who gave him more than thirty grandchildren, who have so far produced three great-grandchildren. He wrote regularly to his fellow veteran of the tennis court, Lieutenant Pieter Steyn, and would always say that he loved the British officers he fought alongside. In his village there is only one reminder of the war, the grave of a Japanese soldier killed during the retreat from India. When he visits Kohima, a rare occasion now that he is in his nineties, he dresses in his good suit and wears his board of war medals with a small badge saying *World War Two Veteran*. He is a thin, dignified figure moving slowly on his walking stick through the bustling markets, from Naga Village across the road to Kohima Ridge, and along the bottom of Pawsey's old garden where the headstones of his dead comrades shimmer white in the morning sun on that old ground where Richards and Laverty, Brown and Calistan drove them to victory, and where the words on the memorial of Naga stone remind passers-by:

> When You Go Home, Tell Them Of Us And Say
> For Your Tomorrow, We Gave Our Today.

EPILOGUE

After Hatred

It is always early when we meet. The early dog-walkers and the joggers are out and groups of children are crossing on their way to school. As we walk along the edge of the common, I constantly slow myself to keep to his pace. I have learned that it is pointless to try and talk to him when we are outside like this. My words sail over him and, although he nods and smiles, I know he has no idea what I have said. This polite man walking across Ealing Common is in his eighties now and frequently tells me that he will soon be gone. There is nothing maudlin about his statement. He is a grateful old soldier. Life after the war was good to him. He was never out of work, he lives in a comfortable house in west London, and his children are all in good jobs. They have no interest in the war. 'Perhaps it is my wife's influence. She does not like talking about the war because I am always talking about it,' he says.

At the coffee shop I take out my tape recorder and we pick up where we stopped at the end of our last meeting. From my notebook I see that he was talking about the days after the Japanese retreated. No matter how many years have elapsed, he says, there is no hiding from what happened. The faces are there as if it were today, this morning. 'I did a very wrong thing in leaving the men,' he says. I keep quiet and watch the tiny wheels of my tape machine whirr as he tells his story. He is back in the mountains. They were climbing higher and higher and had reached a small clearing when he saw the dying soldiers lying under a tree. The smell was terrible and he told himself, 'I am not with them.' So Masao Hirakubo kept on moving. When he passed through the villages he noticed that soldiers were clustered around the pagodas and calling out for rice. There were so many of them, but he did not dare to stop. He kept on going, across the Chindwin, down over the hot plains to the Irrawaddy and across to Rangoon, always marching until he left the scarecrows behind him.

It was harder to shut out the deaths of men he knew. There was an NCO who worked for him at Kohima gathering food, a man called Mr Miura, who went into the jungle and never came back. 'It hurts me still when I think of him,' he says. After the war, back in Japan, Hirakubo Masao went to Miura's family so that they would know what had happened to him. So many of those he knew and saw dying on the road of bones asked him to contact their families when he got back. *Tell them what happened,* they said.

Back home in Yokohama, Hirakubo got his old job back, working for a trading company. He still lived at home with his parents and he was glad of the time he had with his father. But the guilt dogged him constantly. Eventually, a friend suggested he visit a priest. 'I was a Buddhist and this friend was a Catholic. He said to me that I could say why I felt bad and the priest could maybe help. I wanted to know why I had escaped from death.' Hirakubo saw the priest every day for a year. By the end he believed that he was meant to be alive. There had to have been a purpose that brought him through the mountains, something to justify his survival.

The allied occupation of Japan ended in 1952 and the country was edging its way out of the grey years. His company was growing and expanding into European markets. One day the boss called him in and asked if he would like to go to England and be the representative there. This was in the early 1960s, and he wondered how a Japanese man would be regarded in London. In the popular imagination they were still the bandy-legged, buck-toothed barbarians, the slave drivers of the River Kwai. Certainly there were people in England who did not accept him. Often they were families of prisoners of war, or of men who did not come home from the East. But most were welcoming. He found the English a tolerant people. His children grew up with the English language and went to local schools. When he tried to live in Japan after a decade, both he and his wife found they could not settle there and made their way back to Ealing again. For Hirakubo there was too much to be done in England. He had found his purpose in the work of reconciliation.

The Japanese old soldier met a British veteran, Gwilym Davies, who fought with the Royal Welch Fusiliers, and together they set up a society to promote reconciliation. More British veterans became involved, among them Colonel John Shipster of the 7/2 Punjab, who travelled to Japan to meet the men he had fought against. On another occasion, the Japanese and British went back to Burma together and walked the old battlefields, and on their last night together drank beer and sang 'Home Sweet Home' in both languages.

It was not always a meeting of minds. There were vigorous arguments. Hirakubo called the dropping of atomic bombs a war crime; his close friend Philip Malins of 20th Indian Division, spoke for most of his comrades by saying the bombing had saved countless allied lives. But their friendship continued. Hirakubo was no blind nationalist, nor did he want to run from the truth of Japanese war crimes. In this he was certainly different from the men who governed his country after the war – indeed, until the present day. The culture of denial around the atrocities committed by the Imperial Japanese Army is a stain on generations of Japanese politicians.

Hirakubo never claimed to speak for the majority of Japanese veterans, except to say that they felt no hatred now towards the old enemy. That was certainly true of the dozen or so men I met in Japan. But there was a contradiction between their anguish over the experience of war and the continuing need of some to justify Japan's aggression. Dr Takahide Kuwaki, who went to Kohima determined to die for the emperor, insisted that Japan was right to make war on Britain and America. 'Did we fight a war of invasion? Did the spirits of the war dead in Yasukuni Shrine do a war of invasion? I do not think so. The spirits of the war dead did their best to protect their own country and family from foreign control.'

Perhaps nothing – no apology, no compensation – could make up for the anguish of the prisoners of war or alter the memory of

Japanese barbarism for many of the British and Indian veterans. One of the reasons they survived at Kohima was because they had learned to fear the Japanese so much that they would never surrender to them. Among the veterans of Kohima I interviewed, most had an abiding hatred for the enemy. The Cameron Highlanders' officer, Gordon Graham, attended a 2nd Division parade with his friend Masao Hirakubo and heard a veteran behind them mutter 'Japanese bastard.' According to John Laverty's son Patrick, his father would gladly have seen the Japanese veterans 'garrotted in the street'. Even the clergyman, the Reverend Bruce Hayllar, who was shelled as he lay among the wounded, refused to buy Japanese cars and struggled with himself on the few occasions when Japanese Christians came to him for Communion. He was changed by a single experience. 'I had to baptise a baby and it was half Japanese,' he recalled. 'That cured me, because I said, "Don't be so stupid. This child isn't to blame for all of this."'

Masao Hirakubo died at the age of eighty-eight and his funeral in London was a large affair. I remember the atmosphere of gentleness in the chapel, so far removed from the place that had sent Hirakubo on his long journey of reconciliation. His son, Masahiro, read from the Book of Wisdom. 'Though in the sight of men they suffered torments, their hope is full of immortality.' There were a handful of British Kohima veterans in the congregation. Many more would have come, Philip Malins told me, but they were getting too old and frail to travel far. 'We are dying out,' he said. 'Soon there will be none of us left.'

To their memory, to all the dead of Kohima, I offer this book.

ACKNOWLEDGEMENTS

During the years it has taken to research and write this book I have been helped by a wide variety of people in several continents. I am grateful to Pfelie Kezieze of the Kohima Educational Trust. The Trust was founded by veterans of the British 2nd Division in 2004 – the 60th anniversary of the battle – as an act of gratitude to the Nagas. Also in Kohima, I wish to thank Aziebu Shaiza for his hospitality and insights into Naga traditions and culture. In Delhi Shubranshu Chaudhary made some all-important inquiries, and Toby Sinclair was skilled in making the seemingly impossible happen at the last moment.

In Britain my thanks are due to: Dr Simon Robbins and Margaret Brookes of the Imperial War Museum; Michael Ball, Head of the Department of Printed Books, at the National Army Museum; the National Archives in Kew; the School of Oriental and African Studies; the Centre of South Asian Studies, Cambridge; Dr A. R. Morton, Archivist, Sandhurst Collection, Royal Military Academy Sandhurst; Bob Cook, Curator, Kohima Museum, York; the late Colonel H. B. H. 'Blick' Waring, Curator of the Queen's Own Royal West Kent Regiment museum, Maidstone; Paul Loseby and Philip Crawley of the Burma Star Association; the late John Colvin for his generous advice over a memorable lunch at the very beginning; Gordon Graham MC, Kohima veteran, for his sage observations on the manuscript and for alerting me to pitfalls; to my friend Michael Shipster for introducing me to Kohima and for being the best of travelling companions in the Naga Hills.

Mrs Diana Keast of Marlborough gave unstintingly of her time and memories of her brother Lance Corporal John Harman; I am also indebted for their assistance to Patrick Laverty, son of the late Lieutenant Colonel John Laverty, and to Roger Richards, son of the late Brigadier Hugh Richards, who allowed me access to his father's papers and correspondence. Roland Powell read the manuscript closely, highlighting errors of fact and arguing with my judgements whenever he felt I had been less than fair. His immense knowledge of Kohima and the Burma campaign, combined with a first class literary eye, helped me beyond words. Louise Byrne helped trace survivors of the battle and spoke to scores of individuals and their families, gaining their confidence with her unassuming and courteous nature. Laura Thornton, the granddaughter of a Burma veteran, researched part of the V Force story and the work of the Royal Air Force.

Seeking to chart the Japanese experience of the battle and retreat would have been impossible without the assistance of Yuki Sunada. As the granddaughter of a Burma veteran she approached the job with devotion and insight, and opened the way to a Japanese world that would otherwise have been closed to me. To her I owe an enormous debt of thanks. My thanks are also due to the late Mr Masao Hirakubo who gave me hours of his time and provided many useful contacts in Japan; Mr Shuichiro Yoshino, 31st Division Veterans Association, was most helpful in directing me to survivors of the battle; Mr Goro Sato, the son of the late Lieutenant General Kotuku Sato, gave generously of his time and memories, as well as giving me access to his family photograph album; Kyoko Murukami spent many hours translating documents for the book, including Lieutenant General Kotuku Sato's handwritten account of Kohima; thanks are also due to the staff of the National Defence Archives in Tokyo and the Amarume Museum, Yamagata Prefecture.

At Harper Collins my editor Arabella Pike was a wise, encouraging and patient presence who was always proved right in the end, and without whom much valuable time would have been spent floundering in the wood instead of seeing the trees; Michael

Upchurch at HarperCollins did much of the hard work needed to pull the manuscript the last crucial yards to completion; my agent David Godwin has the happy knack of knowing precisely when to insert his presence and when to leave well enough alone. I would, on several occasions, been lost without him. At the BBC Sarah Ward Lilley, Jon Williams and Francesca Unsworth have been the soul of understanding and support. In Ireland, where much of this book was written, I am indebted to the hospitality of my friend John King who gave up his hilltop studio overlooking Ardmore Bay to allow me space and quiet. At home in London my thanks are due to Dr Niall Campbell and Christina Garcia Llavona whose work on war trauma provided many valuable insights, and to Dr John Taylor of Toronto who answered my queries on the physical wounds of war. My friends Rob, David, Cecilia, Gordon, Paul, Fred and Ava all helped me to stay the course. Above all I am grateful to Daniel, Holly and Anne. Anne helped me to excavate the life of Charles Ridley Pawsey and was always the first to read and offer wise comments on the manuscript. The book would never have been completed without her. Nobody around me knows better what comes home from the wars.

CHRONOLOGY

1941

8 December (7 December in Hawaii)	Japanese forces simultaneously invade Malaya, Thailand and Hong Kong and attack United States bases at Pearl Harbor and in the Philippines.
10 December	HMS *Prince of Wales* and HMS *Repulse* sunk in the South China Sea.
14 December	Japanese troops cross into Burma and seize the vital airfield at Victoria Point.
25 December	Hong Kong surrenders to Japanese forces.

1942

15 January	The Japanese invasion of Burma begins.
15 February	Singapore surrenders to Japanese forces.
23 February	British blow up the bridge over the Sittang river, the last natural barrier before Rangoon.
8 March	Japanese forces occupy Rangoon.
19 March	General Slim is appointed corps commander in Burma.
1 May	Mandalay falls to the Japanese.
May–June	British, Indian, Burmese and Chinese troops complete their retreat from Burma to India, along with hundreds of thousands of civilian refugees.

8 August	Congress Party launches the Quit India campaign in response to failure of talks with British on future of India. The British respond by arresting the entire senior leadership of the party, including Mahatma Gandhi.
16 December	The British begin their first offensive in the Arakan. The operation ends in failure several months later.

1943

13 February	Wingate's first Chindit expedition begins.
13 October	Lord Louis Mountbatten appointed Supreme Commander, South-East Asia Command.
22 October	Mountbatten meets General William Slim at Dum Dum in India and offers him command of what is to become 14th Army.
30 November	The second British offensive in the Arakan begins.
31 December	The 5th Indian Division, including 4th battalion, Queen's Own Royal West Kent Regiment, begins its attack on the Razabil Fortress.

1944

4 February	Japanese launch Operation 'Ha-Go' in the Arakan.
5–29 February	Battle of the 'Admin Box'. The Japanese suffer their first major defeat in Burma.
5 March	Wingate's second expedition, Operation Thursday, begins.
8–16 March	The Japanese 15th Army begins Operation 'U Go' moving it's troops across the Chindwin river and towards its twin objectives; Imphal and Kohima.

22–26 March	Japanese forces attack 50th Indian Parachute Brigade at Sangshak. The brigade is forced to withdraw after suffering heavy casualties.
30 March–1 April	1st Assam Regiment's positions at Jessami and Kharasom are attacked. The battalion becomes divided on the retreat with some troops reaching Kohima and others Dimapur.
4 April	First Japanese attack on GPT Ridge at Kohima.
4–20 April	The defence of Kohima.
5 April	Japanese troops begin to arrive at Kohima's Naga Village. Tokyo radio erroneously reports that Kohima has fallen.
20 April	The Kohima garrison is relieved by troops of 2 British Division.
13 May	Kohima Ridge is finally cleared.
25 May	General Sato, commander of Japanese 31st Division, signals to 15th Army HQ that he is withdrawing from Kohima.
2 June	Naga Village is finally cleared.
6 June	The final Japanese positions at Kohima are abandoned.
22 June	2nd British Division advancing south from Kohima meet their counterparts advancing north from Imphal. The Imphal Road is re opened.
5 July	The Burma Area Army orders the end of the Imphal operation. The commander of 2nd British Division, Major General John Grover, is relieved of his command.
7 July	The commander of 31st Division, Lieutenant General Kotuku Sato, is relieved of his command.

1945

20 March	Mandalay is re-captured by 14th Army.
2 May	Rangoon is re-occupied by 26th Indian Division.
6 August	An atomic bomb is dropped on Hiroshima.
9 August	An atomic bomb is dropped on Nagasaki.
15 August	Japan formally surrenders.
2 September	Formal surrender ceremony held on board the *USS Missouri* in Tokyo Bay.

DRAMATIS PERSONAE

Charles Ridley Pawsey: Pawsey was the deputy commissioner of the Naga Hills, a civil servant responsible for more than 6,000 square miles of wild mountainous territory on India's north-eastern frontier. He was the de facto ruler of the territory, in charge of the administration of courts, roads, tax, labour, and security. Charles Pawsey had been living in the region for more than two decades when the Japanese invaded. Although he could have been evacuated Pawsey chose to stay in Kohima throughout the siege.

Ursula Graham Bower: Graham Bower was a Roedean debutante who grew up in the fashionable London neighbourhood of Kensington and went to the Naga Hills as an amateur anthropologist in the late 1930s. One of the local tribes became convinced she was the reincarnation of an imprisoned priestess whom they worshipped as a goddess. Bower would become the first British woman to lead a guerrilla formation and was dubbed the 'Naga Queen' by the American press.

Havildar Sohevu Angami: The havildar, roughly equivalent to sergeant, grew up in the village of Phek on the border of the Naga Hills and the state of Manipur. He was a hunter before he joined the Assam Regiment, the youngest formation in the Indian Army, shortly after the outbreak of war in the Far East. He fought in the battle of Jessami and at the deputy commissioner's tennis court where British, Indian and Japanese troops were separated by just twenty yards. He was awarded the British Empire Medal for his courage at Kohima.

Lance Corporal John Harman: Harman was the son of a millionaire and came to the army from an exclusive private school. However, he refused a commission on the grounds that he did not wish to be set above other men. Harman spent much of his childhood on Lundy Island off the Devon coast and was a lover of the natural world. He was a lance corporal in D company of the 4th Royal West Kents when he carried out the actions which earned him the Victoria Cross at Kohima.

Lieutenant General William Slim: The commander of the 14th Army was the pre-eminent allied general in South-East Asia. A decorated veteran of the Great War he served in the Gurkha Rifles and was a general in the Indian Army at the outbreak of World War Two. Slim was given the task of building a new army that would be capable of carrying the war to the Japanese after a succession of humiliating defeats. The speed and strength of the Japanese advance into the Naga Hills caught him off guard.

Lieutenant General Montagu Stopford: Stopford was born into a military family with roots in the Anglo-Irish aristocracy. On the outbreak of World War Two he commanded an infantry brigade with the British Expeditionary Force (BEF) in France. Stopford was appointed by Slim as overall commander of the Dimapur and Kohima area after the Japanese advance had already begun. He was characterised by one officer who observed him as ambitious, ruthless and extremely able.

Major General John Grover: The commander of British 2nd Division reported to Stopford and commanded the forces responsible for driving the Japanese out of Kohima and opening the road to Imphal. Grover was born in India but sent to Britain as a boy to be educated. During the Great War he served in France and was wounded three times. His relationship with Stopford would deteriorate badly as the battle of Kohima escalated.

Colonel Hugh Upton Richards: The commander of the Kohima garrison came to India after many years serving in West Africa. He was a veteran of the Somme and was wounded and taken prisoner during the Great War. He had initially hoped to serve in General Orde Wingate's Chindits but found himself transferred to command the Kohima garrison only days before the Japanese attacked.

Lieutenant Colonel John Laverty: The commander of the leading infantry unit at Kohima, 4th battalion, Queen's Own Royal West Kent Regiment, was a native of County Derry in Ireland. Laverty fought in Iraq during the suppression of the Kurdish insurgency in the 1930s and came to the West Kents after they had fought in North Africa. He was described as a 'typically bloody-minded Irishman' in one account of the siege of Kohima.

Lieutenant General Renya Mutaguchi: The commander of the Japanese 15th Army first achieved prominence during the late 1930s as a commander in the Sino-Japanese conflict. He claimed to have been behind the 1937 'Marco Polo Bridge incident' in which a Japanese provocation marked the escalation into all-out war in China. Mutaguchi yearned to play what he termed 'a decisive' role in the Far Eastern war and was the central figure behind the invasion of India by the 15th Army.

Lieutenant General Kotuku Sato: Sato led the 31st Division into battle at Kohima and was an old political enemy of Mutaguchi. A veteran of fighting against the Soviet army in Mongolia Sato understood the importance of having secure supply lines for troops operating in remote territory. He would become infamous within the Imperial Japanese Army for his handling of the battle of Kohima.

Lieutenant Masao Hirakubo: Hirakubo was the son of an accountant from Yokohama and was conscripted into the Imperial Japanese Army where he became a supply officer with the 58th Infantry Regiment. Although he set out believing in the war his experiences at

Kohima would alter his views forever. After the end of the war he would embark on an extraordinary journey to try and heal the psychological wounds of Kohima.

SELECT BIBLIOGRAPHY

Alanbrooke, Field Marshal Lord. *War Diaries, 1939–1945*. Ed. by Alex Danchev and Daniel Todman. Weidenfeld and Nicolson, 2001.

Aldrich, Richard J. *Intelligence and the War Against Japan*. Cambridge University Press, 2000.

All Burma Veterans Association, Tokyo. *A Bibliography of Japanese Books of the Burma Campaign*. 2000

Allen, Louis. *Burma: The Longest War*. J. M. Dent, 1984.

Atkins, David. *The Reluctant Major*. Toat Press (rpt.), 1986.

Bailey, Christopher, and Harper, Tim. *Forgotten Armies: The Fall of British Asia, 1941–45*. Penguin/Allen Lane, 2004.

Barker, Arthur James. *The March on Delhi*. Faber, 1963.

Barua, Pradeep. *Gentlemen of the Raj: The Indian Army Officer Corps, 1817–1949*. Praeger, 2003

Basho, Matsuo. *The Narrow Road to the Deep North and Other Travel Sketches*. Trans. by Nobuyuki Yuasa. Penguin Classics, 1966.

Benegal, Ramesh S. *Burma to Japan with Azad Hind: A War Memoir 1941–44*. Lancer InterConsult, 2009.

Bercuson, David, and Holger, G. Herwig. *One Christmas in Washington – Churchill and Roosevelt Forge the Grand Alliance*. Weidenfeld and Nicolson, 2005.

Best, Geoffrey. *Churchill: A Study in Greatness*. Hambledon Continuum, 2002.

Bond, Brian, and Tachikawa, Kyoichi, eds. *British and Japanese Military Leadership in the Far Eastern War, 1941–45*. Routledge, 2006.

Bose, Sugata. *A Hundred Horizons*. Harvard University Press, 2006.

Brandon, Piers. *Decline and Fall of the British Empire*. Cape, 2007.

Brett James, Anthony. *Ball of Fire: The Fifth Indian Division in the Second World War*. Gale and Polden, 1951.

——. *Report My Signals*. Hennel Locke in association with George G. Harrap, 1948.

Burchett, W. G. *Wingate's Phantom Army*. Thacker and Co., 1944.

Burton, F. H. *Mission to Burma: The Story of 177 Squadron*. Privately published, 1991.

Callahan, Raymond. *Burma, 1942–1945*. Books and Bookmen, 1967.

——. *Churchill and his Generals*. University Press of Kansas, 2007.

Calvert, Michael. *Fighting Mad*. Pen and Sword, 2004.

Campbell, Arthur. *The Siege*. Allen and Unwin, 1956.

Chang, Iris. *The Rape of Nanking*. Penguin, 1997.

Chaplin, H. D. *The Queen's Own Royal West Kent Regiment 1920–1950*. Michael Joseph, 1954.

Chapman Lebra, Joyce. *Women Against the Raj: The Rani of Jhansi Regiment*. Institute of South East Asian Studies, 2008.

Churchill, Sir Winston. *The Second World War*. 6 vols. Reprint Society, 1960.

Clarke, Peter. *The Last Thousand Days of Empire*. Allen Lane, 2007.

Coakley, Robert W. *World War II: The War Against Japan*. Army Historical Series, United States Army, 1989.

Colvin, John. *Not Ordinary Men*. Pen and Sword, 1994.

Cook, Haruko Taya and Theodore F. *Japan at War*. Phoenix Press, 2000.

Costello, John. *The Pacific War, 1941–45*. Harper Perennial, 2002.

Doak, Kevin. *A History of Nationalism in Modern Japan: Placing the People*. Brill, 2007.

Dower, John. *Embracing Defeat: Japan in the Aftermath of World War II*. Penguin, 1999.

Drea, J. *Japan's Imperial Army: Its Rise and Fall, 1853–1945*. University Press of Kansas, 2009.

Edwards, Leslie. *Kohima: The Furthest Battle*. History Press, 2009.

Evans, Geoffrey, and Brett James, Anthony. *Imphal: A Flower on Lofty Heights*. Macmillan, 1962.

Fay, Peter Ward. *The Forgotten Army: India's Armed Struggle for Independence 1942–1945*. University of Michigan Press, 1995.

Fergusson, Bernard. *Beyond the Chindwin*. Collins, 1945.

——. *The Wild Green Earth*. Collins, 1946.

Fitzpatrick, Gerald. *No Mandalay, No Maymyo (79 Survive)*. Book Guild, 2001.

Foucar, E. C. V. *I Lived in Burma*. Dennis Dobson, 1956.

Fujiwara, Iwaichi. *Japanese Army Intelligence Operations in Southeast Asia during World War II*. Trans. by Akashi Yoji. Heinemann, 1983.

Gin Ooi, Keat. *Southeast Asia: A Historical Encyclopedia, from Angkor Wat to East Timor*. ABC-CLIO, 2004.

Graham Bower, Ursula. *Naga Path*. John Murray, 1952.

Graham, Gordon. *The Trees Are Still Young on Garrison Hill*. Kohima Educational Trust, 2005.

——, and Cole, Frank. *Burma Campaign Memorial Library: A Collection of Books and Papers about the War in Burma 1942–1945*. SOAS, 1999.

Grant, Ian Lyall. *Burma: Turning Point*. Zampi Press, 1993.

Harrison, Mark. *Medicine and Victory*. Oxford University Press, 2008.

Hart, Peter. *At the Sharp End*. Pen and Sword, 1998.

Hastings, Max. *Finest Years: Churchill as Warlord 1940–45*. Harper Press, 2009.

——. *Nemesis: The Battle for Japan, 1944–45*. Harper Press, 2007.

Hill, John. *Slim's Burma Boys*. History Press, 2008.

Horne, Gerald. *Race War! White Supremacy and the Japanese Attack on the British Empire*. New York University Press, 2004.

Horowitz, David. *The Deadly Ethnic Riot*. University of California Press, 2001.

Jackson, Ashley. *The British Empire and the Second World War*. Hambledon Continuum, 2006.

Jowett, Philip. *The Japanese Army, 1931–45*. Osprey, 2002.

Keegan, John. *Churchill's Generals*. Cassell, 2005.

King-Clark, R. *The Battle for Kohima: The Narrative of the 2 Battalion the Manchester Regiment*. Fleur de Lys, 1995.

Kratoska, Paul H. *South East Asia, Colonial History: High Imperialism (1890s–1930s)*. Taylor and Francis, 2001.

Latimer, Jon. *Burma: The Forgotten War*. John Murray, 2004.

Leer, Martin, and Clunies Ross, Bruce. *Bodies and Voices: The Force Field Representation in Colonial and Post Colonial Studies*. Rodopi, 2007.

Lewin, Ronald. *Slim, the Standard Bearer*. Wordsworth Military History Library, 1999.

Lowry, Michael. *Fighting Through to Kohima*. Pen and Sword, 2003.

Lucas Phillips, C. E. *Springboard to Victory*. Heinemann, 1966.

Lunt, James. *A Hell of a Licking*. Collins, 1986.

Lyman, Robert. *The Generals: From Defeat to Victory, Leadership in Asia 1941–45*. Constable and Robinson, 2008.

——. *Slim: Master of War*. Constable and Robinson, 2004.

McCann, John. *Return to Kohima*. Privately published, 1993.

Marks, James Ebenezer. *Forty Years in Burma*. Hutchinson, 1917.

Marston, Daniel. *Phoenix from the Ashes: The Indian Army in the Burma Campaign*. Praeger, 2003.

Mason, Philip. *A Matter of Honour: An Account of the Indian Army, its Officers and Men*. Cape, 1975.

Masuzawa, Michiko. *A Quiet Man: About my Father, Shigesaburo Miyazaki*. Koyo Publishing, 1987.

Mercado, Stephen C. Nakano. *A History of the Imperial Japanese Army's Elite Intelligence School*. Brassey's, 2002.

'Militiaman' [anon.]. *Six for the King*. Peace Bros., 1984.

Moran, Lord. *The Anatomy of Courage*. Robinson, 2007.

Moreman, T. R. *The Jungle, the Japanese and the British Commonwealth Armies at War, 1941–45: Fighting Methods, Doctrine and Training for Jungle Warfare*. Frank Cass, 2005.

Morris, James. *Farewell the Trumpets*. Penguin, 1979.

——. *Heaven's Command*. Penguin, 1979.

——. *Pax Brittanica*. Penguin, 1979.

Mountbatten, Lord Louis. *Personal Diary of Admiral the Lord Louis Mountbatten, Supreme Allied Commander, South-East Asia, 1943–46*. Ed. by Philip Ziegler. Collins, 1988.

Murphy, Ray. *The Last Viceroy*. Jarrold's, 1949.

Nag, Sajal. *Contesting Marginality: Ethnicity, Insurgency and Subnationalism in North-East India*. Manohar, 2002.

Nisbet, John. *Burma under British Rule*. Constable, 1901 (rpt. Elibron Classics, 2005).

Orwell, George. *Orwell Diaries*. Harvill Secker, 2009.

Ottowell, Stuart. *CHHE – SAAT: Memoir of an Officer of the 6th/7th Rajput Regiment*. Manohar, 2008.

Owen, Frank. *The Campaign in Burma*. HMSO, 1946.

Parkin, Ray. *Into the Smother: A Journal of the Burma–Siam Railway*. Hogarth Press, 1963.

Peace, David. *Tokyo Year Zero*. Faber, 2007.

Pownall, Henry. *Chief of Staff: The Diaries of Lieutenant-General Sir Henry Pownall*. Ed. by Brian Bond. Leo Cooper, 1972.

Roberts, Andrew. *The Storm of War*. Allen Lane, 2009.

Rooney, David. *Burma Victory: Imphal and Kohima, March 1944 to May 1945*. Cassell, 1992

Seagrave, Gordon. *Burma Surgeon*. W. W. Norton, 1943.

Shakespear, L. W. *History of the Assam Rifles*. Naval and Military Press, 2005.

Shipster, John. *Mist over the Rice Fields*. Pen and Sword, 2000.

Shiramizu, Soichi. *The Starving Mountains*. Ashi Shobo, 1972.

Slim, Field Marshal Sir William. *Defeat into Victory*. Cassell, 1956.

Smith, Harry. *Memories of a Hostile Place: Tales of an Amateur Soldier in World War II, Major H. C. Smith, 4 Royal West Kent Regiment*. Privately published.

Spector, Ronald. *Eagle against the Sun: The American War against Japan*. Cassell, 2000.

Spencer, William. *Army Records: A Guide for Family Historians*. National Archives, 2008.

Stanley Clark, E. B., and Tillot, A. T., *From Kent to Kohima*. Gale and Polden, 1951.

Street, Robert. *A Brummie in Burma*. Barny Books, 1997.

——. *Another Brummie in Burma*. Barny Books, 2003.

——. *The Siege of Kohima: The Battle for Burma*. Barny Books, 2003.

Strip, Alan. *Codebreaker in the Far East*. Oxford University Press, 1995.

Subba, Bahadur, and G. C. Ghosh, eds. *The Anthropology of North-East India*. Longman Orient, 1999.

Swinson, Arthur. *Four Samurai*. Hutchinson, 1968.

——. *Kohima*. Arrow Books edition, 1966.

Takahide, Kuwake. *The Great East Asia War Has Not Ended*. Privately published, 2007.

Takeyama, Michio. *Harp of Burma*. Charles E. Tuttle, 1966.

Tamayama, Kazuo, and Nunneley, John. *Tales by Japanese Soldiers*. Cassell, 2002.

Tanner, R. E. S. and Tanner, D. A. *Burma 1942: Memories of a Retreat*. History Press, 2009.

Tarling, Nicholas. *The Cambridge History of Southeast Asia: The Nineteenth and Twentieth Centuries*. Cambridge University Press, 2002.

Thomas, Andrew. *Spitfire Aces of Burma and the Pacific*. Osprey, 2009.

Thompson, H. L. *The Official History of New Zealand in the Second World War 1939–1945: New Zealanders with the Royal Airforce: Air Superiority and the Arakan Battle*. Historical Publications Branch, 1959.

Thompson, Julian. *The Imperial War Museum Book of the War in Burma, 1942–45*. Sidgwick and Jackson, 2002.

Thorne, Christopher. *Allies of a Kind*. Oxford University Press, 1978.

Toland, John. *Rising Sun*. Pen and Sword, 2005.

Toshiro, Tagaki. *Mutiny*. Bungei Shunju, 1966.

Tuchman, Barbara. *The March of Folly*. Ballantine Books, 1985.

——. *The Proud Tower*. Macmillan, 1966.

Tyson, Geoffrey. *Forgotten Frontier*. W. H. Targett, 1945.

Vadeo, Vekhucho. *Mirror General Knowledge of Nagaland*. Kohima, 2009.

von Tunzelman, Alex. *Indian Summer: The Secret History of the End of an Empire*. Simon and Schuster, 2007.

Warner, Philip. *Japanese Army of World War II*. Osprey, 1973.

Webster, Donovan. *The Burma Road: The Epic Story of the China–Burma–India Theatre in World War II*. HarperCollins, 2004.

Weinberg, Gerald L. *A World at Arms: A Global History of World War II*. Cambridge University Press, 1994.

Weiner, Michael. *Race, Ethnicity and Migration in Modern Japan*. 3 vols. Routledge, 2004.

Welsh, Frank. *A History of Hong Kong*. HarperCollins, 1994.

Williams, Douglas. *194 Squadron, Royal Air Force: The Friendly Firm (Burma Campaign)*. Merlin Books, 1987.

Wilson, David. *The Sum of Things*. Spellmount, 2004.

Woodburn Kirby, S. *The War against Japan*. 5 vols. HMSO, 1957–69.

Ziegler, Philip. *Mountbatten: The Official Biography*. Collins, 1985.

NOTES AND SOURCES

A note on sources

The main documentary material sourced from archives and museums is abbreviated as follows: National Archives of the United Kingdom – NA; National Army Museum – NAM; Imperial War Museum – IWM; Royal Military Academy Archives – RMAA; National Institute for Defence Studies, Japan – NIDS; National Diet Library, Japan – NDL. The sources of all other quotations and significant points of information are to be found in the footnotes and endnotes. The classic book on the battle written by a participant is Arthur Swinson's account *Kohima* (Arrow Books, 1966), now sadly out of print. Captain Swinson kept a daily diary and after the war had access to the senior British Generals. He wrote his book while the main participants were still alive and I had the sense that there was material he felt obliged to exclude. I discovered that he had left his papers to the National Archives who had in turn given them to the Imperial War Museum, where they were presented to me with the words every writer longs to hear: 'You seem to be the first person to have asked for these.' The papers contained a wealth of material, including correspondence with senior generals and extracts from their diaries. This unpublished material helped cast an invaluable light on the extent of the pressures, political as well as military, facing the British command. I am indebted to Arthur Swinson's widow, Mrs Joy Benson, for permission to quote from his work. The papers of Brigadier Hugh Richards, who commanded the Kohima garrison, illuminated not only the conduct of the battle but the deep rift which emerged afterwards between some of the leading figures in the defence. His son Roger gave me access to this trove of letters and narrative accounts. These included different drafts of his account of the battle. They were delivered to my home in a Second World War issue brown suitcase belonging to his father. Other words which proved immensely helpful to an understanding of the battle were Brigadier C. E. Lucas Phillips *Springboard to Victory* (Heinemann, 1966), Major A. J. Barker's *March on Delhi* (Faber, 1963) and Major Anthony Brett James's *Ball of Fire – the Fifth Indian Division in the Second World War* (Aldershot, Gale and Polden, 1951). Leslie Edwards's *Kohima – the Furthest Battle* (The History Press, 2009) provides an illuminating day-by-day survey of the fighting from existing records; John Colvin's *Not Ordinary Men* (Pen and Sword, 1994) is rich in detail and suffused with nostalgia for an idea of Britain that vanished in his lifetime. On the Burma war as a whole Louis Allen's magisterial *Burma – the Longest Battle* (J. M. Dent, 1984) provided important insights into Japanese thinking about the battle. Allen was an intelligence officer who interviewed high ranking Japanese after the war. For an insight into the thinking of Lieutenant General William Slim, commander of the 14th Army, Robert Lyman's *Slim, Master of War* (Robinson, 2004) is indispensable.

Extracts from C. E. Lucas Phillips, *Springboard to Victory* appear by permission of the Random House Group Ltd. Extracts from *Mountbatten: The Official Biography* © Philip Ziegler by permission of United Agents Ltd. (www.unitedagents.co.uk) on behalf of the author. Extracts from Louis Allen, *Burma: The Longest War* by permission of J. M. Dent.

Every effort has been made to obtain copyright clearance for material quoted in this book. Any omissions brought to the attention of the publisher will be gratefully received and corrected in any future editions.

Epigraph

p. xiv 'The dreams of Empire' Corporal G. W. G. Driscol, 'To a Dead Jap',
Muse in Exile, p. 14, Burma 1944.

Introduction

p. xvi 'I had the impression that' Interviewed for this book.
p. xvi 'That is in Java' Interviewed for this book.
p. xvii 'We were being shot at' Interviewed for this book.
p. xviii 'They had murdered people' Interviewed for this book.
p. xviii 'I find Kohima appalling' Interview by Kohima Educational Trust,
Kohima.
p. xviii 'In the jungle, covered with green' Lieutenant Shosaku Kameyama,
translated by Keiko Itoh, *The Burma Campaign Society Newsletter*
(March 2005).
p. xviii 'Most were too weak' Interviewed for this book.
p. xix 'The Viceroy, Lord Linlithgow' Cited in Gerald H. Corr, *The War of
the Springing Tigers* (Osprey Publishing, 1975), p. 68.
p. xix 'there is a strong feeling' Walter Lippman to John Maynard Keynes,
April 1942, cited in Christopher Thorne, *Allies of a Kind* (Oxford
University Press, 1978), p. 149.

One: An Empire at Bay

p. 1 'bloomed with tropical profusion' James Lunt, *A Hell of A Licking*
(Collins, 1986), p. 23.
p. 2 'was entertained by dancing' Andreas Augustin, *The Strand, Yangon*
(The Most Famous Hotels in the World, 2007).
p. 2 'full of squealing pigs' Cited in Max Hastings, *Nemesis: The Battle for
Japan, 1944–45* (HarperPress, 2007), p. 220.
p. 3 'supposed to have been' NA, WO 106/3655, Report by Captain T. M.
H. Pardoe, 8 February to 8 April 1941.
p. 3 'over some of their Asiatic' *Ibid.*
p. 3 'She also owns a mine' *Ibid.*
p. 4 'A very good report' *Ibid.*
p. 5 'China had exhausted Japan' BBC People's War, Fred Millem.
p. 5 'remote contingency' NA, CAB 69/2.

p. 5 'a semi-surrender to Japan' George Orwell, *Orwell Diaries* (Harville and Secker, 2009 edition), p 268.

p. 6 'Should Burma be visited' *A Handbook for Visitors to India, Burma and Ceylon* (John Murray, 1903) <www.archive.org>.

p. 7 'ablaze with flowers' E. C. V. Foucar, *I Lived in Burma* (Dennis Dobson, 1956), p. 11.

p. 7 'insisted to the stationmaster' Foucar, *I Lived in Burma*, p. 209.

p. 7 'Things aren't what they were' *Ibid.*, p. 23.

p. 8 'a tendency among Englishmen' Sir Robert Brooke-Popham, 'Notes on Burma Operations', cited in Louis Allen, *Burma: The Longest War* (J. M. Dent, 1984), p. 90.

p. 8 'driven the more apathetic' *Annual Report on the Administration of Burma* (Rangoon: Government of Burma, 1884–85), p. 84, cited in Subir Bhaumik, 'The Returnees and the Refugees', in *Refugees and the State*, ed. by Ranabira Samaddara (SAGE, 2003), p. 187.

p. 8 'birds of passage who' Cited in Sugata Bose, *A Hundred Horizons* (Harvard University Press, 2006), p. 120.

p. 8 'The indications were plain' Foucar, *I Lived in Burma*, p. 85.

p. 8 'in the 1930s' U On Pe, 'Modern Burmese Literature', *Atlantic Monthly*, February 1958.

p. 9 'stout lady, popular with' Foucar, *I Lived in Burma*, p. 111.

p. 10 'The suspense had been snapped' BBC People's War, Fred Millem.

p. 11 'The bodies were mangled' Donald Mellican, private memoir.

p. 11 'We made makeshift' *Ibid.*

p. 12 'wild and half-baked' Cited in Arthur Bryant, *The Turn of the Tide* (Reprint Society/Collins, 1957), p. 295.

p. 12 'much has been done to strengthen' 'New Leader Appointed for Burma', *Melbourne Argus*, 29 December 1941.

p. 13 'taken the responsibility' Hans J. Van de Ven, *War and Nationalism in China, 1922–45* (Routledge, 2003), p. 29.

p. 13 'The effect that the loss' S. Woodburn Kirby, *The War Against Japan*, vol. 2: *India's Most Dangerous Hour* (HMSO, 1958), pp. 100–101.

p. 13 'In the streets of this' W. H. Prendergast, *A Galway Engineer in Assam* (Galway Library, private memoir).

p. 13 'Others, both soldiers and civilians' Bisheshwar Prasad, *Official History of the Indian Armed Forces in the Second World War* (Combined Inter-Services Historical Section, India and Pakistan, 1966), p. 208.

p. 13 'the deserted city and oil' *Ibid.*, p. 213.

p. 13 'behind it pathetically followed' Prendergast, *A Galway Engineer in Assam*.

p. 13 'It was to me a smell' Clare Boothe, 'Burma Mission', *Life*, 27 April 1942.

p. 14 'distended bellies supported on' Pat Carmichael, *Mountain Battery: Burma 1942* (Devin, 1983), pp. 212–13, cited in Jon Latimer, *Burma: The Forgotten War* (John Murray, 2004), p. 105.

p. 15 'I found the bodies of' Geoffrey Tyson, *The Forgotten Frontier* (W.H.Targett, Calcutta, 1945), p. 80.

p. 15 'the incongruity of the items' *Ibid.*, p. 19.

p. 15 'striding along like a Rajput' Lunt, *A Hell of a Licking*, p. 173.

p. 15 'A bright red skirt' *Ibid.*

p. 15 'which made him go' *Ibid.*

p. 16 'Before the next bend' Donald Mellican, private memoir.

p. 16 'No sooner had we finished lunch' Gordon S. Seagrave, *Burma Surgeon* (W. W. Norton, New York, 1943), pp. 202–203.

p. 17 According to one official estimate NA, WO 106/2677, Branch Memorandum No 6921, VCIGS to the India Office, Withdrawal of Forces from Burma to Assam.

p. 17 'They had heard evacuees' <www.burmastar.org.uk/two_families>.

p. 17 'One man, a civilian whom I had known' Lunt, *A Hell of A Licking*, p. 273.

p. 17 Emboldened by the Japanese Cited in David Horsfield, *From Semaphore to Satellite* (Privately published).

p. 18 'The hitherto axiomatic acceptance' British Library: L/PO/6/106b. *Privy Seal, Clement Attlee, for the War Cabinet on 'The Indian political situation'*, February 2 1942.

p. 18 'We will never be able to' M. Collis, *Last and First in Burma* (Faber, 1956), pp. 181–2.

Two: The Longest Road

p. 19 'worn army leather' Private W. Norman, personal account <www.euxton.com/Army-Battle-for-Sittang-16-23-February-1942>.

p. 19 'I shouted at' *Ibid.*

p. 19 'Get on your feet' *Ibid.*

p. 20 'using coloured tracer' NA, WO 203/5733, Narrative of First Burma Campaign, p. 161.

p. 20 'As we crossed' Private W. Norman, personal account.

ROAD OF BONES

p. 21 'The houses in the town' Kazuo Tamayama and John Nunneley, *Tales by Japanese Soldiers* (Cassell, 2000), p. 38.

p. 21 'There were many fish' *Ibid.*, p. 40.

p. 21 'I asked him in my' *Ibid*, p. 64.

p. 22 'he told us to go and get' NA, WO 361/206, Statement re Missing Soldiers, Ref. your MB/M/326, 22 November 1944.

p. 22 'the sound of the machine' NA, WO 361/206, Statement of No. 4690408 Pte Toplis J.

p. 22 'flatly refused to attempt' NA, WO 361/206, Resume of the Fighting by the 2/KOYLI from 20–23 Feb 42 by Capt. J. F. Laverick.

p. 22 'our troops have fought well' NA, CAB/68/9/17.

p. 24 'the sodden ground' Field Marshal Lord Slim, *Defeat into Victory* (Cassell, 1956), p. 109.

p. 24 'We carried on marching' NA, WO 361/206, Statement by no./690787 L/Cpl W. Long in respect of No.4689410 Pte W. Powell 2/KOYLI.

p. 25 'I tied him to a tree' NA, WO 361/206, Statement by 4687544 Sgt Butcher W. 2/KOYLI.

p. 25 'At 1930 hrs signalling' Lieutenant Colonel C. E. K. Bagot, MC, 'The 28th in the Concluding Phase of the Burma Campaign 1942', *Back Badge Regimental Magazine*.

p. 25 'The impact of witnessing' Gerald Fitzpatrick, *No Mandalay, No Maymyo (79 Survive)* (Book Guild, 2001), p. 255.

p. 26 'swallow tail butterflies' R. E. S. Tanner and D. A. Tanner, *Burma 1942: Memories of a Retreat* (History Press, 2009), p. 112.

p. 26 'During these days we saw' A. Tegla Davies, *Friends Ambulance Unit – the Story of the F.A.U. in the Second World War 1939–1946* (George Allen and Unwin, 1947).

p. 26 'a less flashy' Fitzpatrick, *No Mandalay, No Maymo*, p. 256.

p. 26 'They might look like' Slim, *Defeat into Victory*, p. 110.

p. 27 'This let the pus' Tanner and Tanner, *Burma 1942*, p.112.

p. 27 'infinitely moving – and humbling' Slim, *Defeat into Victory*, p. 114.

p. 27 'faithful Cameronian bodyguard' *Ibid.*

p. 28 'In a dark hour' *Ibid.*, p. 121.

Three: At the Edge of the Raj

p. 29 'out of control' RMAA, Pawsey Papers, Part 2: The Year 1942.

p. 29 'hungry, thirsty, exhausted' Ursula Graham Bower, *Naga Path* (John Murray, 1952), p. 155.

p. 30 'Binns reports [the Chinese] Army' NA, WO 208/799, From Viceroy to Secretary of State for India, New Delhi, 15 May 1942.

p. 30 'There was no equipment' Pawsey Papers, Part 2: The Year 1942.

p. 30 'the onset of monsoon' Bisheshwar Prasad, *Official History of the Indian Armed Forces in the Second World War* (Combined Inter-Services Historical Section, India and Pakistan, 1952), p. 34.

p. 31 'those trenches remained' H. Fitzmaurice Stacke, *The Worcestershire Regiment in the Great War* (Cheshire, 1926).

p. 31 Then he and a few *Firm and Forester: Journal of the Worcestershire and Sherwood Foresters Regiment* (November 1972).

p. 33 'shaggy village' Graham Bower, *Naga Path*, p. 4.

p. 33 'One behind the other' *Ibid*.

p. 34 'He was always calm' Interviewed for this book.

p. 34 'I remember him calling' IWM, Oral History Project, file no. 23088/6, interview with Pat Whyte.

p. 34 'sort of sickly sweet' *Ibid*.

p. 35 'fiendish shriek' W. H. Prendergast, *A Galway Engineer in Assam* (Galway library, privately published).

p. 35 'The going was appallingly' Henry Balfour, Diary of a tour in the Naga Hills, Assam, 1922–23. Pitt Rivers Museum Manuscript Collections, Balfour Papers, Box 3/1, entry for 19 September 1922. Reproduced courtesy Pitt Rivers Museum, University of Oxford.

p. 36 'barbarous tribes' J. McCosh, civil assistant surgeon of Goalpara, 1835, cited by Kekhriesituo Yhome in *Politics of Region: The Making of Nagas Identity during the Colonial and Post-Colonial Era*, [Borderlands e-journal, Volume 6 No. 3, 2007].

p. 36 'armed with only spears' Colonel L. W. Shakespear, *History of the Assam Rifles* (Naval and Military Press, reprint, 2005), p 19.

p. 37 'A party from one village' NA, WO 106/141, Detailed Report on the Naga Hills Expedition of 1879–80, by Captain P. J. Maitland, Deputy Assistant Quartermaster General.

p. 37 'They would cut close' Interviewed for this book.

p. 37 'Before, the British did' Interviewed for this book.

p. 39 'had not in all respects' NA, WO 106/141, Detailed Report on the Naga Hills Expedition of 1879–80.

p. 39 'pitiful sight it was' RMAA, Pawsey Papers, The Siege of Kohima.

p. 40 'This had the desired effect' NA, WO 106/141, Detailed Report on the Naga Hills Expedition of 1879–80.

p. 40 'Their lands have all been' *Ibid.*

p. 40 'the Nagas have asked' Hansard, Parl. Debs. (series 3) vol. 260, col. 364 (31 March 1881).

p. 41 'break[ing] the Kuki spirit' NA, WO 106/58, Report presented by Lieutenant General Sir H. D'U. Keary, General Officer Commanding Burma Division, Maymyo, June 1919, cited in Dispatch on the Operations against the Kuki Tribes of Assam and Burma, November 1917 to March 1919.

p. 41 'For had they not surrendered' *Ibid.*

p. 41 'energetically carried out' *Ibid.*

p. 41 'Presumably the District Commissioner' Hansard, Parl. Debs (vol 301), cc1343–54 (10 May 1935).

p. 42 'they are an extremely moral people' *Ibid.*

p. 42 'There was overwhelming evidence' *Ibid.*

p. 42 'whatever they eat' Interviewed for this book.

p. 42 'Civilisation was no good' Interviewed for this book.

p. 42 'Any observer of the' B.R.Rizvi, *J.P.Mills and the North-East,* p.76, in *The Anthropology of North-East India,* ed. by Tanka Bahadur Subba and G. C. Ghosh (Longman Orient, 2003).

p. 43 'My friend' Gordon Graham, *The Trees are All Young on Garrison Hill* (Kohima Educational Trust, 2005), p. 31.

Four: The King Emperor's Spear

p. 45 'Some of them gave us' Cited at <www.koi-hai.com>.

p. 45 'As a result, the battalion' Captain H. L. T. Radice, *The 28th in Assam, 1942–43,* Back Badge Magazine, 1950.

p. 45 'It [was] a lovely place' IWM, Oral History Project, file no. 18283, interview with Dennis Dawson.

p. 46 'Everywhere these patrols went' Radice, *The 28th in Assam, 1942–43.*

p. 46 'living with two wives' NA, WO 203/4637, Miscellaneous papers relating to the battle of Kohima.

p. 46 'from a Naga who' *Ibid.*

p. 46 'To our great relief' IWM, file no. 12438 03/23/1, diary of Lieutenant B. K. 'Barry' Bowman.

p. 48 'The Pahok headman was' *Ibid.*

p. 48 'I decided not to hang' *Ibid.*

p. 49 'Experienced officers were wounded' IWM, file no. 97/36/1, R. A. W. Binny, The Story of V Force.

p. 49 'A heavily loaded man' NA, WO 172/4585, Appendix A, Lieutenant Colonel W. A. Ord.

p. 49 'When somebody died' Interviewed for this book.

p. 49 'very fond of biting' *The Story of 'V' Force – The Phantom Army of Burma,* NAM 9412-188-27.

p. 49 'Later, along the whole front' Field Marshal Lord Slim, *Defeat into Victory* (Cassell, 1956), p. 148.

p. 50 'Good. Remember I back you' *The Story of 'V' Force – The Phantom Army of Burma,* NAM 9412-188-27.

p. 50 'I had seen a Haka Chin' Unpublished account by A. R. H. Macdonald.

p. 51 'There was a great deal' Ursula Graham Bower, interview with Professor Alan MacFarlane, Cambridge University.

p. 51 'If you come home' *Ibid.*

p. 51 'knitting interminable jumpers' *Ibid.*

p. 52 'gone completely off' *Ibid.*

p. 52 'I hadn't realised that' Ursula Graham Bower, *Naga Path* (John Murray, 1952), p. 37.

p. 52 'It was a giddy path' *Ibid.*, p. 38.

p. 52 'She [Gaidiliu] was tall' Ursula Graham Bower interview with Professor Alan MacFarlane, Cambridge University.

p. 53 'if they must have a goddess' *Ibid.*

p. 53 'So sorry but I've' Graham Bower, *Naga Path,* p. 164.

p. 54 'He was superb' *Ibid.*, p. 167.

p. 54 'We waved back' *Ibid.*, p. 168.

p. 54 'not always of the' *Ibid.*, p. 139.

p. 55 'He had an intense' Graham Bower, *Naga Path*, p. 58.

p. 55 'He was very protective' Interviewed by Mark Tully, 'Stand at East', BBC Radio 4, 11 June 2005.

p. 55 'A Hangrum man [stood] up' Graham Bower, *Naga Path*, p. 173.

p. 56 'the lame, the halt and blind' *Ibid.*

p. 56 'When she spoke' Ebenezer Jones, interviewed by Mark Tully, 'Stand at East', BBC Radio 4, 11 June 2005.

ROAD OF BONES

p. 56 'Japanese in great numbers' RMAA, Pawsey Papers, Part 2: The Year 1942.

p. 57 'In the Naga Hills' NA, WO 208/799, Assam-internal situation, official communications and reports, 1942–44.

p. 57 'making him the laughing stock' NA, WO 172/4585, V Force intelligence summaries and diaries.

p. 57 'We had not been so bitter' Graham Bower, *Naga Path*, p. 187.

Five: Kentish Men

p. 59 'The stubborn alertness' H. D. Chaplin, *The Queen's Own Royal West Kent Regiment, 1920–1950* (Michael Joseph, 1954).

p. 59 'the Drill Hall proved' Wally Jenner, 'Wally's War', private memoir.

p. 59 'I was getting one shilling' Interviewed for this book.

p. 60 'and I was happy because' Interviewed for this book.

p. 60 'Lack of literacy may' James Estlin, *What Impact Did the Great War Have on the Community of Tonbridge School*, Remembrance Day Essay, Tonbridge School, 2008, citing '*The Tonbridgian*' school magazine, 1917.

p. 60 'There was a place' Interviewed for this book.

p. 61 'Our whole bloody battalion' Interviewed for this book.

p. 61 'We were like sheep' IWM, Oral History Project, file no. 20461, interview with Ivan Daunt.

p. 62 'like a soldier' Wally Jenner, 'Wally's War', private memoir.

p. 62 'And when I said no' Interviewed for this book.

p. 63 'We were all bloody miserable' Interviewed for this book.

p. 63 'toughening up marches' NA, WO 169/5027.

p. 63 'I got down' Interviewed for this book.

p. 64 'I was thinking I was' IWM, 17537, Oral History Project, interview with Donald Easten.

p. 64 'However I didn't blow' *Ibid.*

p. 64 'wonderful moonlight night' Interviewed for this book.

p. 64 'became considerably disorganised' Ronald Walker, *The Official History of New Zealand in the Second World War 1939–1945: Alam Halfa and Alamein* (Historical Publications Branch, 1967), p. 130.

p. 64 'The silence was shattered' Chaplin, *The Queen's Own Royal West Kent Regiment, 1920–1950*.

p. 65 'The intelligence wasn't thorough' IWM 20461, interview with Ivan Daunt.

478

p. 65 'thrown away in a' Chaplin, *The Queen's Own Royal West Kent Regiment, 1920–1950*, p. 217.

p. 65 'a complete cock-up' Interviewed for this book.

p. 66 'ten good milk cows' Thomas Dinsdale Hogg, *My Life Story* (privately published, 1998).

p. 66 'suffered terribly from' *Ibid.*

p. 66 'A lot of them had' IWM, Oral History Project, file no. 20461, Ivan Daunt.

p. 66 'This particular trick' Hogg, *My Life Story*.

p. 67 'I was supplied with a jeep' Hogg, *My Life Story*.

p. 67 'We had to stop' Interviewed for this book.

p. 67 'Congratulations to Mr. H. Crispin Smith' Ballards School magazine, 1939, cited in memorial address for Harry Crispin Smith (1913–2007), by Peter Harrison, 30 April, 2007.

p. 68 'who wouldn't think twice' Harry Smith, *Memories of a Hostile Place* (privately published).

p. 68 'When he heard we were' Interviewed for this book.

p. 69 'Playboy of India' Interviewed for this book.

p. 69 'there was a faint hint' E. B. Stanley Clark and A. T. Tillot, *From Kent to Kohima* (Gale and Polden, 1951), p. 30.

p. 70 'The whole operation' Robert Kay, *Bob's Stories* (privately published).

p. 71 'all mangled and his legs' IWM Oral History Project, file no. 20461, Ivan Daunt.

p. 71 'staggered to see Indian bodies' Michael Lowry, *Fighting Through to Kohima* (Pen and Sword, 2003), p. 21.

p. 72 'Every station brought' IWM, Swinson Papers, NRA 28568, diary of Captain Arthur Swinson.

p. 72 'without exposing one square inch' *Ibid.*

p. 72 'there would be tables' Interviewed for this book.

p. 72 'swept towards the train' Robert Street, *A Brummie in Burma* (Barny Books, 1997), p. 13.

p. 73 'It was so strange' Interviewed for this book.

p. 73 'for me always the smell' Smith, *Memories of a Hostile Place*.

Six: Fighting Back

p. 75 'He fought and marched' Field Marshal Lord Slim, *Defeat into Victory* (Cassell, 1956), p. 538.

p. 75 "the sort of jungle" Michael Lowry, *Fighting Through to Kohima* (Pen and Sword, 2003), p. 71.

p. 76 'very formidable obstacles' Dispatch by General Sir George J. Giffard, Commander-in-Chief 11 Army Group, South-East Asia Command, 19 June 1945, published in the *London Gazette*, 13 March 1951.

p. 76 'our troops were either' IWM, Irwin Papers, 10516 P 139, Report on a Visit to the Maungdaw Front from 4/5/43–9/5/43.

p. 76 At one point recruits Ashley Jackson, *The British Empire and the Second World War* (Hambledon Continuum, 2006), p. 363.

p. 77 'To lunch they go' Hornbeck Papers, box 180, cited in Christopher Thorne, *Allies of a Kind* (Oxford University Press, 1978), p. 133.

p. 78 'the danger of raising' NA, CAB 120/29, cited in David Bercuson and Holger G. Herwig, *One Christmas in Washington – Churchill and Roosevelt Forge the Grand Alliance* (Weidenfeld and Nicholson, 2005), p. 220.

p. 79 'triumph of having got' President Roosevelt to Lord Mountbatten, 8/11/43. PSF/Box 36/A330NN01. Franklin D.Roosevelt Presidential Library and Museum.

p. 79 'completely to desperation' Field Marshal Lord Alanbrooke, *War Diaries, 1939–1945*, ed. by Alex Danchev and Daniel Todman (Weidenfeld and Nicholson, 2001), p. 357.

p. 80 'for the first time in two years' President Roosevelt to Lord Mountbatten, 8/11/43. PSF/Box 36/A330NN01. Franklin D. Roosevelt Presidential Library and Museum.

p. 81 'staple meal …' IWM, file no. 4370 82/15/1, private papers of Sir Philip Christison, Bt.

p. 81 'useless to hope for supplies' Slim, *Defeat into Victory*, p. 225.

p. 81 Slim picked Colonel Slim, *Defeat into Victory*, p. 224.

p. 82 'incidence of malaria' Lieutenant Colonel R. Wigglesworth, 'The Burma Campaigns, 1942–1945: A History of Casualty Evacuation', *RAMC Journal*, vol. 91 (1948), pp. 1010–24.

p. 82 'The Havildar clerks' David Atkins, *The Reluctant Major* (The Toat Press, 1986), pp. 62–63.

p. 82 'The Japanese missiles' NA, WO 222/187, Medical History of the 14th Army, November 1944–May 1945.

p. 82 'You learned to bury' Interviewed for this book.

p. 83 'As a result of this' NA, WO 222/158, Divisional Psychiatry, A Report by Captain Paul Davis, Attached to 2 British Division.

p. 83 'Why should I send' *Ibid.*

p. 83 'like going into the water' Winston Churchill to Chiefs of Staff, 8 May 1943, cited in Ronald Lewin, *Slim – The Standardbearer,* p. 123.

p. 83 'command must be decentralised' Jungle Book, Military Training Pamphlet no. 9 (India), September 1943, cited in Daniel Marston, *Phoenix from the Ashes: The Indian Army in the Burma Campaign* (Greenwood Publishing, 2003).

p. 84 'Proud as a Royal Rajput' Talbot Mundy, *For the Salt He Had Eaten* (reprint, Kessinger publishing, 2004).

p. 85 'and he accused me' Field Marshal Lord Wavell, *Wavell: The Viceroy's Journal* (Oxford University Press, 1973), p. 3, cited in Ronald Lewin, *Slim – The Standard Bearer* (Wordsworth Military Library, 1976), p. 137.

p. 85 'This was a great occasion' IWM, file no. 4370 82/15/1, *The Life and Times of General Sir Philip Christison, Bt.,* p. 120.

p. 85 'He told me had two sons' *Ibid.*

p. 86 'the standard of his' NA, WO 303/6320, Essays and Interrogations of Lieutenant Colonel Iwaichi Fujiwara.

p. 86 'We are indignant' Sisi Kumar Bose, Alexander Werth, Narayan Gopal Jog, Subbier Appadurai Ayer, *Beacon Across Asia – A Biography of Subhas Chandra Bose* (Orient Blackswan, 1996), p. 144.

p. 87 'counter propaganda purposes' NA, DMI/4746.

p. 87 'inculcate the doctrine' NA, WO 203/4756.

p. 87 'He promised to liberate' Gian Singh, *Memories of Friends and Foes* (Cwmnedd Press, 1995).

p. 87 'We did what our officers' Interviewed for this book.

p. 87 'even those who were' Philip Mason, *A Matter of Honour* (Jonathan Cape, 1974), p. 519.

p. 88 'I remember saying that' Interviewed by Mark Tully, 'Stand at East', BBC Radio 4, 11 June 2005.

p. 88 Discrimination in pay between Cited in Pradeep Barua, *Gentlemen of the Raj: The Indian Army Officer Corps, 1817–1949* (Praeger, 2003), p. 130.

p. 88 'The fair deal meant' Slim, *Defeat into Victory,* p. 195.

p. 88 'bush to lie under' *Ibid.*

p. 89 'What the hell are you' Gian Singh, *Memories of Friends and Foes.*

p. 89 'Servants were plentiful' John Shipster, *Mist on the Rice Fields* (Pen and Sword, 2000), p. 15.

p. 89 'I wanted to see how' Interviewed for this book.

p. 90 'It was nothing short' Shipster, *Mist on the Rice Fields*, p. 33.

p. 90 'Monkeys, gibbons, hornbills' IWM, file no. 4370 82/15/1, *The Life and Times of General Sir Philip Christison*, Bt., p. 124.

p. 90 'they were raring to' *Ibid*., p. 122.

p. 91 'A false alert the' S. Woodburn Kirby, *The War Against Japan*, vol. 3: *The Decisive Battles* (HMSO, 1961), p. 121.

p. 91 'Stroking their "Poona" moustaches' J. B. Knowles, 'Medium Artillery in Burma', *Field Artillery Journal* (1945).

Seven: Jungle Wallahs

p. 92 Daunt recovered after a few IWM, Oral History Archive, file no. 20461, Reminiscences of Ivan Daunt.

p. 92 'the tin-can of mechanical' Field Marshal Lord Slim, *Defeat into Victory* (Cassell, 1956), p. 33.

p. 92 'The mules, of course' Interviewed for this book.

p. 93 In one instance 650 mules <www.estancialospotrerors.com>.

p. 93 'Many became so attached' Thomas Dinsdale Hogg, *My Life Story* (privately published, 1998).

p. 93 'Oh dear, oh dear' IWM, Oral History Project, file no. 20461, interview with Ivan Daunt.

p. 93 'Round came the doctor' Private L. [Len] A. C. Reynolds, memoir published on Burma Star website, 2005.

p. 94 'They seemed to delight' Unpublished account by Arthur Davies, sent to the author by his son, Malcolm Davies.

p. 94 'the answer to noise' Michael Lowry, *Fighting Through to Kohima* (Pen and Sword, 2003), p. 66.

p. 94 'It was often proved' *Ibid*.

p. 95 'bang bang bang' IWM, Oral History Project, file no. 20461, interview with Ivan Daunt.

p. 95 'We went to see him' Interviewed for this book.

p. 95 'He gave me absolute stick' Interviewed for this book.

p. 96 'By those who understood' Hogg, *My Life Story*.

p. 96 'I got on extremely well' Interviewed for this book.

p. 97 'made the mortar for half' Interview with unnamed employee by Niamh Strudwick, granddaughter of John Laverty.

p. 97 'Pure and simple he was' Interviewed for this book.

p. 97 where his index card referred Undated correspondence between Ian Hook, Essex Regiment Museum, and Niamh Strudwick, granddaughter of John Laverty: 'I hesitate to add that his index card refers to him as "Mad Jack."'

p. 98 'There was a big parting' Interviewed for this book.

p. 98 'I thought to myself' Interviewed for this book.

p. 99 'They looked at us' Interviewed for this book.

p. 99 'Although he seemed to' Interviewed for this book.

p. 100 'unwelcome captivity and restraint' Interviewed for this book.

p. 100 'a great opportunity' J. H. Badley, *Education after the War* (George Allen and Unwin, 1917), p. 3.

p. 100 'concentration in things' Diana Keast, private papers.

p. 100 'he seldom wanted to finish' *Ibid.*

p. 100 'seemed to feel that' Felix Gade, *My Life on Lundy* (Myrtle Langham, 1978).

p. 100 'all oddities, people' Diana Keast, private papers.

p. 101 'The ferret killed the rat' John Pennington Harman, Lundy Diary. February 1932.

p. 101 'Thurs. 31st ...' *Ibid.*

p. 101 Martin Coles Harman had made *Daily Telegraph*, 7 December 1954.

p. 101'pre-war City's wonder' *Daily Sketch*, 7 December 1954.

p. 102 In 1933 Harman senior *Time*, 18 April 1937.

p. 102 'He so looked up to his father' Interviewed for this book.

p. 102 'Life is just bloody hell' Letters of John Pennington Harman to Martin Coles Harman, November–December 1941/January 1942.

p. 102 'to a life of solitude' Letter of John Pennington Harman to Martin Coles Harman, 5 and 7 April 1942.

p. 103 'I have given the matter' Letter of John Pennington Harman to Martin Coles Harman, 8 April 1942.

p. 103 'I am still a private' Letter of John Pennington Harman to Livie Noble, 22 October 1942.

p. 103 'empty beer bottles' Wally Evans, 'John Harman, VC', *20th – Newsletter of the 20th Bn, Royal Fusiliers*, May 1997.

p. 103 'The biggest blunder' *Ibid.*

p. 104 'Four years in NZ' Letter of John Pennington Harman to Martin Coles Harman, 14 August 1943.

p. 104 'He was a great countryman' Interviewed for this book.

Eight: The Master of the Mountains

p. 105 'the spacious houses' E. C. V. Foucar, *I Lived in Burma* (Dennis Dobson, 1956), p. 141.

p. 105 'several yellow-robed corpses' *Ibid.*, p. 139.

p. 105 The geisha house Cited in Louis Allen, *Burma: The Longest War* (J. M. Dent, 1984), p. 599.

p. 107 'almost like orphans' Arthur Swinson, *Four Samurai* (Hutchinson, 1968), p. 116.

p. 107 'Where his father had drifted' *Ibid.*

p. 107 'There is a law of the nations' John Dower, *Embracing Defeat: Japan in the Aftermath of World War II* (Penguin, 1999), p. 21.

p. 107 'Loyalty [is] their essential duty' Imperial Rescript, 4 January 1882.

p. 108 'I was surprised by that!' Interviewed for this book.

p. 108 'We called them "Chankoro"' Interviewed for this book.

p. 108 'The teacher beat you' Interviewed for this book.

p. 110 There had also been an Emperor Hirohito to 83rd Special Session of the National Diet, October, 1943.

p. 112 'to attack and secure' Imperial General Headquarters Army Directive no. 1237, 22 August 1942, cited in Arthur James Barker, *The March on Delhi* (Faber, 1963).

p. 112 'when the general' Directive to Commander Burma Area Army from Imperial Headquarters, 17 January 1944.

p. 112 'these operations were ...' NA, WO 303/6320, Essays and Interrogations of Lieutenant Colonel Iwaichi Fujiwara.

p. 113 When he went to see Mutaguchi Interview with Lieutenant Colonel Iwaichi Fujiwara, cited in Allen, *Burma: The Longest War*, p. 152.

p. 115 'skin the racoon' Major General Masazumi Inada, cited in *Ibid.*, p. 160.

p. 115 'I love that man's enthusiasm' Cited in *Ibid.*, p. 159.

p. 116 'The motivation for starting' NDL: transcript of interview with Lieutenant General Renya Mutaguchi, 1965.

p. 116 'Here was the one place' Field Marshal Sir William Slim, *Defeat into Victory* (Cassell, 1956), p 285.

p. 117 Certainly Mutaguchi indulged Arthur Swinson. *Four Samurai* (Hutchinson, 1968), p. 128.

p. 118 'Tojo: What's the matter?' Swinson, *Four Samurai*, pp 125–6.

p. 119 'In order to defend' Directive to Commander Burma Area Army from Imperial Headquarters, 17 January 1944.

p. 119 'It would no doubt satisfy' Cited in Allen, *Burma: The Longest War*, p. 158.

p. 119 'we will achieve the objective' Ryoichi Tobe, Edited by Brian Bond and Kyoichi Tachikawa, *Tojo Hideki As A War Leader, British and Japanese Military Leadership in the Far Eastern War, 1941–1945*. (Frank Cass, 2004), p 35.

Nine: The Hour of the Warrior

p. 121 'Despite their efforts' Robert Street, *A Brummie in Burma* (Barny Books, 1997).

p. 122 An officer wrote that Thomas Dinsdale Hogg, *My Life Story* (privately published, 1998).

p. 122 'I used gun-cotton primers' *Ibid.*

p. 122 'This information was vital' IWM, file no. 4370 82/15/1, *The Life and Times of General Sir Philip Christison, Bt*, pp 124–130.

p. 123 'Poor Moore was quite white' Lord Louis Mountbatten, *Personal Diary of Admiral the Lord Louis Mountbatten, Supreme Allied Commander South-East Asia, 1943–1946*, ed. by Philip Ziegler (Collins, 1988), p. 53.

p. 123 Optimism is not allowed' NA, WO 172/4884, War Diary, 4th battalion, Royal West Kent Regiment.

p. 124 'fat old Admiral' *Ibid.*

p. 124 'Success on this op' *Ibid.*

p. 125 'How do you know what' Interviewed for this book.

p. 126 'We knew we was all' Interviewed for this book.

p. 126 'There was a shot' Interviewed for this book.

p. 127 'Before we went into Burma' Interviewed for this book.

p. 127 'You would run across' Interviewed for this book.

p. 127 'You were always too tired' Interviewed for this book.

p. 127 'I discerned the figure' Wally Evans, 'John Harman, VC', *20th – Newsletter of the 20th Bn, Royal Fusiliers*, May 1997.

p. 128 'Soon, I imagined what' *Ibid.*

p. 128 'It was as if' Interviewed for this book.

p. 128 'Don't worry, Sir' Interviewed for this book.

p. 129 'I am satisfied with' Diana Keast, private papers, Letter of John Pennington Harman to Miss B. M. Harman, 20 January 1944.

p. 129 'To our amazement' IWM, Oral History file no. 17955/5/3, interview with John Winstanley.

p. 129 'horror mixed with ingenuity' Anthony Brett James, *Report My Signals* (Hennel Locke in association with George G. Harrap, 1948), p. 131.

p. 130 'They took no notice' IWM, file no. 4370 82/15/1, *The Life and Times of General Sir Philip Christison, Bt.,* p. 128.

p. 132 'we were determined' Gian Singh, *Memories of Friends and Foes* (Cym Nedd Press, 1998).

p. 132 'Firstly, you get in close' *Ibid.*

p. 132 'In any civilised war' John Shipster, *Mist on the Rice Fields* (Pen and Sword, 2000), p. 37.

p. 132 'I show your photograph' Cited in M. A. Gilani, *An Old Soldier Remembers* (Pakistan Defence Forums, 2005).

p. 133 Over five weeks S. Woodburn Kirby, *The War Against Japan*, vol. 3: *The Decisive Battles* (HMSO, 1961), p. 144.

p. 133 'This morning the ground' Diary of Major Michael Lowry, 13/14 February 1944, pp. 134–5.

p. 133 'Later their hearts thrilled' Anthony Brett James, *Ball of Fire – The Fifth Indian Division in the Second World War* (Aldershot, Gale and Polden, 1951).

p. 133 'How can one fight' IWM, file no. 4370 82/15/1, cited in *The Life and Times of General Sir Philip Christison, Bt.*, p. 129.

p. 133 By the end of December H. L. Thompson, *The Official History of New Zealand in the Second World War 1939–1945: New Zealanders with the Royal Airforce: Air Superiority and the Arakan Battle* (Historical Publications Branch, 1959), p. 306.

p. 134 'the greatest moral effect' Raymond Callahan, *Burma 1942–1945* (Books and Bookmen, 1967), p. 133.

p. 134 'Two cups of tea' NA, WO 172/4844, War Diary, 4th battalion, Queen's Own Royal West Kent Regiment.

p. 134 'so well treated' *Ibid.*

p. 134 'It's very difficult to see' IWM, Oral History Project, file no. 17537, interview with Donald Easten.

p. 135 'We advanced quite a way' IWM, Oral History Project, file no. 20461, interview with Ivan Daunt.

p. 135 'We walked into a trap' *Ibid.*

p. 135 'was intent on winning' Hogg, *My Life Story*.

p. 137 'All of a sudden' IWM, Oral History Project, file no. 20769, interview with Bert Harwood.

p. 137 'We went to pick up' Interviewed for this book.

p. 137 'We moved through them' Interview with Bert Harwood.

p. 137 'buried the sad' Harry Smith, *Memories of a Hostile Place* (privately published).

p. 138 'It was most unpleasant' IWM Oral History Project, file no. 17537, interview with Donald Easten.

Ten: Sato San

p. 142 'They said she was strong' Interviewed for this book.

p. 142 'They were upper middle class' Interviewed for this book.

p. 142 'That meeting really' Interviewed for this book.

p. 143 'He was always saying' Interviewed for this book.

p. 144 'It is evident that My Lord' *Dohkoku–Burma Campaign for a Newly Recruited Soldier, Retsu Division, 138 Regiment* (Amarume Museum, 1992), p. 134.

p. 144 'mild environment' Shudo Akiyama, *The Retsu Division Commander Goes Insane* (Shueisha, Tokyo, 1973).

p. 144 'The number of cases' *Ibid.*

p. 144 'In those days' *Ibid.*

p. 144 'Burma was not the' *Ibid.*

p. 145 'That woman got really mad' Interviewed for this book.

p. 145 '"I am General Cherry"' Akiyama, *The Retsu Division Commander Goes Insane.*

p. 146 One senior officer reckoned NA, WO 203/6324, Essays and Interrogations of Lieutenant Colonel Iwaichi Fujiwara.

p. 147 'In every Japanese HQ' *Ibid.*

p. 147 Mutaguchi ordered his supply NAM, Colvin Papers, file no. 9412-118-83-110, Japanese Strategy – Intelligence Bulletin No. 247.

p. 147 Throughout the period of Figure cited in Jon Latimer, *Burma: The Forgotten War* (John Murray, 2004), pp. 188–89.

p. 147 'From Rangoon we went' Interviewed for this book.

p. 148 'It was like he was' Interviewed for this book.

p. 148 'As the Japs are so' NA, WO 172/4585, V Force sitreps and diaries.

p. 149 'expressed huge concern' NIDS: General Kotuku Sato, Analysis of Retsu Division Campaign, August 1944.

p. 149 'The Allied power to' Arthur Swinson, *Four Samurai* (Hutchinson, 1968), p. 131.

p. 149 'He said to me' Interviewed for this book.

p. 150 'I was very young' Interviewed for this book.

p. 150 'When a decision was' NA, WO 303/6320.

p. 151 'Any man who joins' NAM, Colvin Papers, file no. 9412-118-83-110, Japanese Soldier's Barrack-room Ballad, Captured at Kohima, June 1944.

p. 151 'The system is so well' *Ibid.*

p. 151 'All the stories' Interviewed for this book.

p. 151 'I just heard that' Interviewed for this book.

p. 152 'There was no food' Interviewed for this book.

p. 152 'I said I did not' Interviewed for this book.

p. 152 'I thought' Interviewed for this book.

p. 152 'A British soldier came' Manabu Wada, *Drifting Down the Chindwin: A Story of Survival* (Burma Campaign Fellowship Group).

p. 152 'I was displeased' *Ibid.*

p. 153 'It was an extraordinary' Interviewed for this book.

p. 153 'I had a firm resolve' Interviewed for this book.

p. 153 'Most of the men' *Dohkoku–Burma Campaign for a Newly Recruited Soldier, Retsu Division, 138 Regiment*, p. 134.

p. 154 After the meeting Louis Allen, *Burma: The Longest War* (J. M. Dent, 1984), p. 285.

p. 154 'I have a special request' *Ibid.*

p. 154 ''My orders from 15 Army' *Ibid.*

p. 155 'They were suffering diarrhoea' IWM, Swinson Papers, NRA 28568, Recollections of Yukihiko Imai.

p. 155 'My officers do everything' Cited in Arthur James Barker, *The March on Delhi* (Faber and Faber, 1963), p. 93.

Eleven: Into the Mountains

p. 156 'Visibility is practically nil' IWM 94/26/1, diary of FHA Howe.

p. 156 'being cut up' by K. Brahma Sing, *Assam Rifles During World War II* (unpublished manuscript), p. 10.

p. 157 'The continued build-up' Cited in Winston Churchill, *The Second World War*, vol. 5: *Closing the Ring* (Reprint Society, 1960 edition), pp. 434–435.

p. 158 'should be strongly dealt with' RMAS, Pawsey papers, 'Report by Sub-Divisional Officer, P. F. Adams, for the months of January and February 1944.'

p. 158 'The whole disposition' Pieter Steyn, *History of the Assam Regiment* (Longman Orient, Calcutta, 1959), p.45.

p. 158 'You have the prouder' Address by Governor of Assam, Sir Robert Reid, on occasion of raising of 1 battalion, Assam Regiment, at Shillong on June 15 1941.

p. 159 'When I was a child' Interviewed for this book.

p. 159 'physically extremely tough' C. E. Lucas Phillips, *Springboard to Victory* (Heinemann, 1966), p. 67.

p. 159 'This man was the' Interviewed for this book.

p. 160 'He had already shown' NA, WO 172/5045, War Diary, 1st battalion, Assam Regiment, Appendix A, Speech by Sir Andrew Clow, Governor of Assam, 20 August 1944.

p. 161 'only the laughter' Steyn, *A History of the Assam Regiment*, p. 53.

p. 161 'Although the march was' *Ibid.*

p. 162 'One after another they came' Ursula Graham Bower, *Naga Path* (John Murray, 1952), p. 39.

p. 162 'The very large cat was' *Ibid.*

p. 162 'To me it was as' Interviewed for this book.

p. 163 'The time passed' NAM, Colvin Papers, file no. 9412-118-1-85, Susumu Nishida, *Taking the Field*, pp. 209–11.

p. 163 'When my slow' *Ibid.*

p. 163 'This operation will engage' 15th Army, Order of the Day, 18 February 1944.

p. 164 'Into the mountains' Nishida, *Taking the Field*, pp. 209–11.

p. 164 'I'll take the opportunity' Cited in Louis Allen, *Burma: The Longest War* (J. M. Dent, 1984), p. 232.

p. 164 'We didn't talk' Interviewed for this book.

p. 164 'We have got to fight' Interviewed for this book.

p. 165 'I lay up all day' Liddell Hart Centre for Military Archives, Gracey Papers.

p. 166 'From one hour after' *Ibid.*

p. 167 'Soldiers of the company' Kazuo Tamayama and John Nunneley, *Tales by Japanese Soldiers* (Cassell, 2000), p. 156.

p. 167 'as a small blister' Geoffrey Tyson, *Forgotten Frontier* (W. H. Targett, 1945), p. 85.

p. 168 'Many, many times' Interviewed for this book.

p. 168 'On that occasion' Interviewed for this book.

p. 168 'the fact you didn't die' Interviewed for this book.

p. 168 'A Japanese regiment' Field Marshal Lord Slim, *Defeat into Victory* (Cassell, 1956), p. 290.

p. 169 'I have never taken' Lord Louis Mountbatten, *Personal Diary of, Supreme Allied Commander South-East Asia, 1943–1946*, ed. by Philip Ziegler (Collins. London, 1988), p. 78.

p. 170 'feeding me like a baby' *Ibid.*

p. 170 'saw the urgency' Slim, *Defeat into Victory*, p. 306.

p. 170 'getting a division to' Major General S. Woodburn Kirby. *The War Against Japan*, vol. 3: *The Decisive Battles* (HMSO, 1961), p. 198.

p. 170 'extremely cagey on the subject' Lieutenant General Sir Henry Pownall, *Chief of Staff – The Diaries of Lt.-General Sir Henry Pownall – edited by Brian Bond* (Leo Cooper, 1974), p. 150.

p. 171 'plenty of troops and could' *Ibid*.

p. 171 'desperately worried' Philip Ziegler, *Mountbatten – the Official Biography*. (Collins, 1985), p. 272.

p. 171 'the stakes are pretty high' Cited, *Ibid*., p. 272.

p. 172 'if the Battle of Imphal' *Ibid*.

p. 172 'weighing off a young arse' IWM, file no. NRA 28568, Swinson Papers, diary of General Montagu North Stopford.

p. 172 'he walks around his units' Arthur Swinson, *Kohima* (Arrow Books, 1966), p. 20.

p. 172 'his walk was unhurried' *Ibid*.

p. 172 'we are going to buy' IWM, file no. NRA 28568, Swinson papers, diary of General Montagu North Stopford.

p. 173 'Had personal discussion' IWM, file no. NRA 28568, Swinson papers, diary of Major General John Grover.

p. 173 'more than concerned' IWM, file no. NRA 28568, Swinson papers, diary of General Montagu North Stopford.

p. 174 'almost everyone in it' David Wilson, *The Sum of Things* (Spellmount Publishers, 2001), p. 118.

p. 174 'but could frighten the life' NAM, Colvin papers, file no. 9412-118-1-99, Letter from Brigadier A.D.R.G Wilson CBE to John Colvin, April 30 1993.

p. 174 'short, lithe, very smart' Wilson, *The Sum of Things*, p. 90.

p. 174 'highly charged with nervous energy' Swinson, *Kohima*, p. 22.

p. 174 'Wherever the General' *Ibid*.

p. 175 'The situation in North Burma' IWM, file no. NRA 28568, diary of General Montagu North Stopford.

p. 176 'We stripped off and' Robert Street, *The Siege of Kohima: The Battle for Burma* (Barny Books, 2003), p. 42.

p. 176 'to sit on the back' *Ibid*.

p. 176 'One formation approached' NA, WO 172/4884, War Diary, 4th battalion, Royal West Kent Regiment.

p. 176 'because India at the present' Interviewed for this book.

p. 177 'Immediately the engines' Thomas Dinsdale Hogg, *My Life Story* (privately published, 1998).

p. 178 'Then as many men' Interviewed for this book.

p. 178 'There's a guy' Interviewed for this book.

p. 178 'That didn't do much' Street, *The Siege of Kohima*, p. 43.

p. 178 'It was, in fact, a matter' NA, Air 2/5665.

Twelve: Flap

p. 180 'total nonsense' IWM, diary of Lieutenant B. K. 'Barry' Bowman.

p. 181 'I will send you someone' Hugh Richards, 'How I Got to Kohima', *Firm and Forester: Journal of the Worcestershire and Sherwood Foresters Regiment*.

p. 181 'This man was a truly' Interviewed for this book.

p. 181 'You will be in operational' NA, CAB 44/190.

p. 181 'touching down on a' Richards, 'How I Got to Kohima'.

p. 182 'with any visitor' IWM, file no. 2234 92/39/1, papers of Major Walter Greenwood.

p. 182 'I had been told' Richards, 'How I Got to Kohima'.

p. 182 'Trenches had in many cases' Richards Papers, 'How I Came to Be at Kohima' (private memoir).

p. 182 'The[re was] constant fluctuation' NA, CAB 44/190.

p. 183 'Nobody took any notice' IWM, Oral History Project, file no. 18283, interview with Dennis Dawson.

p. 183 'motley crew of useless' Interviewed for this book.

p. 183 'all sorts and services' IWM, file no. 2234 92/39/1, papers of Major Walter Greenwood.

p. 183 'It struck me that' Richards Papers, 'How I Came to Be at Kohima' (private memoir).

p. 183 'In spite of the deplorable' Pieter Steyn, *History of the Assam Regiment* (Longman Orient, 1959), p. 85.

p. 184 'a sudden plunge from' Slim, *Defeat into Victory*, p. 308.

p. 185 'I felt reasonably happy' Hugh Richards, speech to Assam Regiment dinner, 29 September 1962.

p. 185 'As I walked around' Field Marshal Lord Slim, *Defeat into Victory* (Cassell, 1956), p. 309.

p. 185 'without any attempt' Slim, *Defeat into Victory*, p. 310.

p. 186 'packed so tight' IWM, Swinson Papers, file no. NRA 28568, diary of Captain Arthur Swinson.

p. 186 'We were having lunch' *Ibid*.

p. 186 'the whole brigade' Arthur Swinson, *Kohima* (Arrow Books, 1966), p. 203.

p. 186 'Hallo, what are you doing' IWM, file no. 10520 P104, Report on the activities of V Brigade, Brigadier V. S. Hawkins.

p. 187 'The local situation was staggering' *Ibid*.

p. 187 'things began to alter' *Ibid*.

p. 187 'in one big flap' IWM, file no. NRA 28568, diary of Captain Arthur Swinson.

p. 187 'with their whole world' *Ibid*.

p. 187 'Forty-five thousand' Slim, *Defeat into Victory*, p. 309.

p. 187 'He didn't like' IWM, file no. NRA 28568, diary of Captain Arthur Swinson.

p. 188 'Very, very merry' Diary of Lieutenant Bruce Hayllar.

p. 188 'We had breakfast in bed' Letter of Lieutenant Bruce Hayllar to his parents, 31 March 1944.

p. 188 'This ending is very bad' *Ibid*.

p. 188 'March in circle' Diary of Lieutenant Bruce Hayllar, 1 April 1944.

p. 189 'Man after man vomited' John Hudson, *Sunset in the East* (Pen and Sword, 2002), p. 16.

p. 189 'set like a jewel' *Ibid*.

p. 189 'They said "Please Miss' Ursula Graham Bower, interview with Professor Alan MacFarlane, Cambridge University.

p. 189 'I woke up one morning' *Ibid*.

p. 190 'After all' Ursula Graham Bower, *Naga Path* (John Murray, 1952), p. 194.

p. 190 'Going forward to' Graham Bower, interview with Professor Alan MacFarlane, Cambridge University.

p. 190 'Somebody caused confusion' Graham Bower, *Naga Path*, p. 190.

p. 190 A Mr Sharp of the NA, WO 172/4587.

p. 191 'he was a subject of the king' Graham Bower, interview with Alan MacFarlane.

p. 191 'I can't go on with' IWM, file no. 67/150/1, diary of Lieutenant Colonel F. N. Betts cited in *Imperial War Museum Book of the War in Burma*, Sidgwick and Jackson, 2002), pp. 138–140.

p. 191 'felt no compunction' *Ibid*.

p. 192 '[She] gave him her only food' Graham Bower, interview with Alan MacFarlane.

p. 192 'Flat out with violent' Betts diary, p. 140.

p. 193 'about 600 hundred yards' S. Woodburn Kirby, *The War Against Japan*, vol. 3: *The Decisive Battles* (HMSO, 1961), p. 236.

p. 193 'It was volcanic' Harry Seaman, *The Battle of Sangshak, Burma, March, 1944* (Leo Cooper, 1989), p. 72.

p. 193 'without regard to its lack' Louis Allen, *Burma: The Longest War* (J. M. Dent, 1984), p. 214.

p. 194 'nothing about any offensive' War Diary, 152nd battalion, 50th Indian Parachute Brigade, Report by Lieutenant Colonel Paul Hopkinson, Battle at Sangshak, 1944.

p. 194 'always been very puzzled' *Ibid.*

Thirteen: Onslaught

p. 196 'It was up and down' Interviewed for this book.

p. 196 'We took them to our' IWM, file no. NRA 28568, Swinson Papers, Recollections of Yukihiko Imai.

p. 196 'As soon as we reached' *Ibid.*

p. 197 'It was actually our men' Interviewed for this book.

p. 197 'At the very top of the position' Harry Seaman, *The Battle at Sangshak, Burma, March 1944* (Leo Cooper, 1989), p. 65.

p. 198 'the enemy had resisted' *Ibid.*

p. 198 'They were the sandals' Interviewed for this book.

p. 198 'There was much confusion' Diary of Lieutenant Colonel Jackie Trim cited in Lieutenant General Eustace D'Souza, *Valour to the Fore, A History of the 4th Battalion Mahratta Light Infantry 1800–2000* (ARM Publications, Mumbai, 2000).

p. 198 'The men were hungry' *Ibid.*

p. 198 'to our great disappointment' Kazuo Tameyama and John Nunneley, *Tales by Japanese Soldiers* (Cassell, 2000), p. 158.

p. 199 'With the firing' Eric Neild, 'Setting the Record Straight', *Burma Campaign Fellowship Group Journal* (October 1998).

p. 199 'It felt like hundreds' Interviewed for this book.

p. 199 'We set up our machine' Interviewed for this book.

p. 200 'Hearing my report' Kazuo Tamayama and John Nunneley, *Tales by Japanese Soldiers* (Cassell, 2000), p. 159.

p. 200 'could almost distinguish' Seaman, *The Battle at Sangshak*, p. 80.

p. 201 'anyone in the open' Eric Neald, 'Setting the Record Straight', *Burma Campaign Fellowship Group Journal* (October 1998).

p. 201 'Well done indeed' Signal from General Sir Ouvrey Roberts, 23 Division to HQ 50 Indian Parachute Brigade, 24 March 1944, cited in Seaman, *The Battle at Sangshak*, p. 85.

p. 202 'the rest of the company' Seaman, *The Battle at Sangshak*, p. 81.

p. 202 'how those who entered' *Burma Front: Reminiscences of the 58th Japanese Infantry Regiment* (58th Infantry Regimental Association, 1964).

p. 202 'The one I kicked' Tamayama and Nunneley, *Tales by Japanese Soldiers*, p. 160.

p. 202 'As I pulled him' Susumu Nishida, *A Last Drink of Water* (Burma Campaign Fellowship Group Newsletter, Issue no. 7, September 2005, trans. by Keiko Itoh).

p. 203 'Just one mouthful' *Ibid*.

p. 203 'Those who can move' *Ibid*.

p. 203 'a shambles of dead' Lieutenant Colonel Paul Hopkinson, War Diary Report, 152nd battalion, 50th Indian Parachute Brigade (Airborne Forces Archive).

p. 203 'lying by the path' Narrative of Lieutenant Colonel Jackie Trim, cited in General Eustace D'Souza, *Valour to the Fore* (ARB Publications, Mumbai, 2000).

p. 204 'a typical professional' Interviewed for this book.

p. 204 'like a very beautiful fireworks' Interviewed for this book.

p. 204 'Rations were down' Lieutenant Colonel Paul Hopkinson, War Diary Report, 152nd battalion, 50th Indian Parachute Brigade (Airborne Forces Archive).

p. 204 'imperturbable Gurkha cook' Seaman, *The Battle at Sangshak*, p. 101.

p. 205 'one was well on one's way' Lieutenant Colonel Paul Hopkinson, War Diary Report, 152nd battalion, 50th Indian Parachute Brigade (Airborne Forces Archive).

p. 205 'We had completely occupied' Seaman, *The Battle at Sangshak*, p. 96.

p. 205 'He slowly raised both' *Ibid*.

p. 205 'What's the matter' Louis Allen, *Burma: The Longest War* (J. M. Dent, 1984), p. 218.

p. 206 'Fight your way out' Lieutenant Colonel Paul Hopkinson, War Diary Report, 152nd battalion, 50th Indian Parachute Brigade (Airborne Forces Archive).

p. 206 'much discussion' Eric Neild, 'Setting the Record Straight', *Burma Campaign Fellowship Group Journal* (October 1998).

p. 206 'too worn out' *Ibid*.

p. 207 'At this distance' Seaman, *The Battle at Sangshak*, p. 104.

p. 207 'The trenches looked horrible' Lieutenant Hiroshi Yamagami's Memoir, in *Burma Front: Reminiscences of the 58th Japanese Infantry Regiment* (58th Infantry Regimental Association, 1964).

p. 207 'He looked so young' Interviewed for this book.

p. 208 'Our men were all moved' Tamayama and Nunneley, *Tales by Japanese Soldiers*, p. 162.

p. 208 'five or six of England' IWM, Swinson Papers, file no. NRA 28568, Recollections of Yukihiko Imai.

p. 208 'The Japanese soldier only' *Ibid*.

p. 209 'nightmare for the wounded' Seaman, *The Battle at Sangshak*, p. 115.

p. 210 'I had to say' Tamayama and Nunneley, *Tales by Japanese Soldiers*, p. 162.

Fourteen: To the Last Man

p. 211 'lot of Japs with' Richards Papers, 'How I Came to Be at Kohima' (private memoir).

p. 211 'atmosphere of complete' *Ibid*.

p. 211 'could hold out' *Ibid*.

p. 212 'I said that it must' *Ibid*.

p. 213 'but very soon we heard' Captain Michael Williamson, Assam Regiment, cited in Leslie Edwards, *Kohima: The Furthest Battle* (History Press, 2009), p. 97.

p. 214 'It was felt that the' NA, W0 172/5045, War Diary of 1st battalion Assam Regiment, Appendix A, Kharasom. D. B. Gurung, 2nd Lieutenant, A Company.

p. 214 'I saw killed infantry' Interviewed for this book.

p. 215 'Your correct course' Arthur Swinson, *Kohima* (Arrow Books, 1966), p. 70.

p. 215 'The man told me' Interviewed for this book.

p. 216 'seeing the hopelessness' NA, W0 172/5045, War Diary of 1st battalion Assam Regiment, Appendix A, Kharasom. D. B. Gurung, 2nd Lieutenant, A Company.

p. 216 'could not leave the wounded' Cited pp 52, 'Not Ordinary Men.' John Colvin. Pen and Sword. London 1994.

p. 216 'As an example of' Richards Papers, 'Draft of Lecture'.

p. 216 Later, the local Nagas RMAA, Pawsey Papers, Charles Pawsey narrative of the Siege.

p. 217 'feverish preparation' Pieter Steyn, *A History of the Assam Regiment* (Longman Orient,1959), p. 57.

p. 217 'Spirits soured at the news' *Ibid.*

p. 217 'The Japanese were screaming' Interviewed for this book.

p. 217 'Japanese grenades' Steyn, *A History of Assam Regiment*, p. 68.

p. 219 'We were shooting at him' Interviewed for this book.

p. 219 'Had the Japs caught' NA, W0 172/5045, War Diary of 1st battalion Assam Regiment.

p. 219 'a liberal issue of rum' *Ibid.*

p. 219 'a fisherman's paradise' 'The Indian Tea Association and the Manipur Road' <www.koi-hai.com>.

p. 220 'Red Indians ... carrying' Robert Street, *The Siege of Kohima: The Battle for Burma* (Barny Books, 2003), p. 43.

p. 220 'We were up for it' Interviewed for this book.

p. 220 'Water situation is precarious' NA, WO 172/4884, War Diary, 4th battalion, Royal West Kent Regiment, 1 April 1944.

p. 220 'perhaps 3,000 leaderless' NAM, Colvin Papers, file no. 9412-118-1-55.

p. 221 'It turned out to be a cow' IWM, file no. 4587 81/16/1, diary of Private Harold Norman.

p. 221 'We got a message through' Interviewed for this book.

p. 221 'smacked of confusion' Colvin Papers, file no. 9412-118-1-55.

p. 221 'It was the obvious time' Interviewed for this book.

p. 222 '2,000 men left in Kohima' IWM, Swinson Papers, NRA 28568, diary of Captain Arthur Swinson.

p. 222 'With one Brigade in Kohima' RMAS, Narrative of Kohima by Charles Pawsey, Pawsey Papers.

p. 223 'left their equipment' E. B. Stanley Clark and A. T. Tillot, *From Kent to Kohima* (Gale and Polden, 1951), p. 89.

p. 223 It was a frightening' Richards Papers, Speech to Assam Regiment Regimental Dinner, 29 September 1962.

p. 223 'I had to refuse to listen' IWM, Swinson Papers, Diary of Lieutenant General Montagu North Stopford.

p. 224 'a hell of a row' *Ibid.*

p. 224 '202 Area Operation' NA, CAB 44/190.

p. 224 'If and when it is' *Ibid.*

p. 224 'such an announcement' *Ibid.*

p. 224 'I regarded this [order]' Richards Papers, 'How I Came to Be at Kohima' (private memoir).

p. 225 'real panic stations' Interviewed for this book.

p. 225 'The defences were poor' Interviewed for this book.

p. 225 'I remember saying' Interviewed for this book.

p. 227 'Round about three or' IWM, Oral History Project, file no. 18283, interview with Dennis Dawson.

p. 228 'We went to try' Letter of Lieutenant Bruce Hayllar to his parents, 20 April 1944.

p. 228 'I felt very' Interviewed for this book.

p. 228 'It was horrible' Interviewed for this book.

p. 228 'It is pretty horrid to kill' Interviewed for this book.

p. 229 'The immediate result' NA, WO 172/5045, War Diary, 1st battalion, Assam Regiment, April 1944.

p. 229 'The difficulty of' IWM, file no. 2234 92/39/1, Papers of Major Walter Greenwood.

p. 230 'This was answered by' NA, WO 172/5045, War Diary, 1st battalion, Assam Regiment, April 1944.

p. 230 'These positions were' *Ibid.*

p. 230 'could not be found' *Ibid.*

p. 230 'Sometimes they would shout' Interviewed for this book.

Fifteen: Siege

p. 233 'He told me that' Interviewed for this book.

p. 234 'the attitude of local' Translation of Notebook of Major Yamaguchi, Staff Officer, 31st Division Infantry Group, found by CSM Bill Scarratt, 1/8 Lancashire Fusiliers <www.burmastar.org>.

p. 234 'In some cases the' RMAA, Pawsey Papers.

p. 234 'did not behave like' Interviewed for this book.

p. 234 'behaviour of the Japs' Interviewed for this book.

p. 234 'On the first day' Interviewed for this book.

p. 235 'My goodness' NDL transcript of audio recording of talk given by Renya Mutaguchi, 1965.

p. 235 'exchanges of violent' NA, WO 303/6230, Essays and Interrogations of Lieutenant Colonel Iwaichi Fujiwara.

p. 236 'It was the enemy' Cited in Leslie Edwards, *Kohima: The Furthest Battle* (History Press, 2009), p. 107.

p. 236 'When he came to' Interviewed for this book.

p. 236 'I saw one of the Japanese' RMAA, Pawsey Papers.

p. 237 'But these Indian soldiers' *Ibid.*

p. 237 'and if the owners' RMAA Pawsey Papers, 'Account of Fighting in Kohima Village' by Rushukhrie Angami.

p. 237 'and snatched away' *Ibid.*

p. 238 'Under this brutal' *Ibid.*

p. 238 'I recall working' Hansard, HC (series 5), vol. 487 (10 May 1951), Debate on Prisoners of War Compensation.

p. 239 'affected the Gurkhas' NA, WO 172/5045, War Diary, 1st battalion, Assam Regiment, April 1944.

p. 239 'men were shaky' *Ibid.*

p. 240 'scurry around' Interviewed for this book.

p. 241 'We think he may' Correspondence with author, 3 September 2009.

p. 241 'fully expecting' Lieutenant John Faulkner, handwritten memoir.

p. 241 'entirely ignorant' IWM, Oral History Project, file no. 19090, interview with Harry Smith.

p. 241 'There was all these' Interviewed for this book.

p. 241 'Others ran, trotted' Robert Street, *The Siege of Kohima: The Battle for Burma* (Barny Books, 2003), p. 44.

p. 241 'Blimey they come' IWM, Oral History Project, file no. 20461, interview with Ivan Daunt.

p. 242 'disheartening stream' NAM, Colvin Papers, file no. 9412-118-1-55, Lieutenant Thomas Hogg.

p. 242 'Chaos and low morale' NAM, Colvin Papers, file no. 9412-118-1-55, Letter from Thomas Hogg to John Colvin, 12 April 1993.

p. 242 'Officers dispatched' NA, WO 172/4884, War Diary, 4th battalion, Royal West Kent Regiment.

p. 242 'the situation would' *Ibid.*

p. 242 'We just debussed' Interviewed for this book.

p. 243 'past a very pleasant' John Faulkner, handwritten memoir.

p. 243 'all hell let loose' NAM, Colvin Papers, file no. 9412-118-1-55, Lieutenant Thomas Hogg.

p. 243 'You can imagine' IWM, Oral History Project, file no. 20461, interview with Ivan Daunt.

p. 243 'We was staggered' Interviewed for this book.

p. 243 'They were the worst' Interviewed for this book.

p. 243 'He said to me' Interviewed for this book.

p. 244 'So we all bolted' Interviewed for this book.

p. 244 'We saw a large' IWM, Oral History Project, file no. 22636, interview with John Wright.

p. 244 'There can be little' Pieter Steyn, *A History of the Assam Regiment*
(Longman Orient, 1959), p. 89.

p. 244 'Our meeting was' Richards Papers, draft of 'How I Got to
Kohima'.

p. 244 'Where's Kuki piquet?' *Ibid.*

p. 245 'no account had been' NA, WO 172/4884, War Diary, 4th battalion,
Royal West Kent Regiment.

p. 245 'excellent material' *Ibid.*

p. 245 'a heavy liability' *Ibid.*

p. 246 'The Garrison Comd's' *Ibid.*

p. 246 'Laverty brushed him' Interviewed for this book.

p. 246 'Friction soon arose' Pieter Steyn, *A History of the Assam Regiment*
(Longman Orient, 1959), p. 91.

p. 246 'The position as it' IWM, Swinson Papers, Letter from Hugh
Richards to Arthur Swinson, 28 April 1965.

p. 247 'my relations with' *Firm and Forester: Journal of the Worcestershire
and Sherwood Foresters Regiment* (April 1985).

p. 247 'virtually assumed command' H. D. Chaplin, *The Queen's Own
Royal West Kent Regiment, 1920–1950* (Michael Joseph, 1954), p. 396.

p. 247 'Christ, sir! John Faulkner, handwritten memoir.

p. 247 'a dozen miniature' *Ibid.*

p. 247 'Would you mind' *Ibid.*

p. 248 'lying on his back' *Ibid.*

p. 248 'What happened?' *Ibid.*

p. 248 'pushed off' *Ibid.*

p. 248 'We were worn out' Robert Street, *A Brummie in Burma* (Barny
Books, 1997), p. 46.

p. 249 'within a day or two' NA, WO 172/4884, War Diary, 4th battalion,
Royal West Kent Regiment.

p. 249 'the door was shut behind us' Interviewed for this book.

p. 249 'You don't lead' Interviewed for this book.

p. 250 'Now you've got to' Interviewed for this book.

p. 250 'The Japs were close' Letter of Lieutenant Bruce Hayllar to his
parents, 20 April 1944.

p. 250 'He had a wife' Interviewed for this book.

p. 251 'One hundred and ten' Kazuo Tamayama and John Nunneley, *Tales
by Japanese Soldiers* (Cassell, 2000), p. 162.

p. 251 'I sent the company' Richards Papers, 'How I Came to Be at
Kohima' (private memoir).

p. 251 'The troops refused to pass' J. M. P. 'Kohima Diary', *Gurkha Rifles Regimental Journal*, no. 13 (April 1958).

p. 252 'At the time I thought' Richards Papers, 'How I Came to Be at Kohima' (private memoir).

p. 252 'I tried my best' *Ibid.*

p. 252 'All quiet except for' Cited in Arthur Campbell, *The Siege* (Allen and Unwin, 1956), p. 58.

Sixteen: Hey! Jonny, Let Me Through

p. 254 'He was typical' Correspondence with Margery Willis, daughter of Lieutenant John Bruce Faulkner, 17 March 2008.

p. 254 'I heard the "thump"' Lieutenant John Faulkner, handwritten memoir.

p. 254 'strolling unconcernedly' *Ibid.*

p. 256 'slight and wiry' C. E. Phillips, *Springboard to Victory* (Heinemann, 1996), p. 133.

p. 256 'Typical symptoms' NA, WO 17/2155, War Diary of the 75th Indian Field Ambulance, December 1943.

p. 257 'Young was a very' Interviewed for this book.

p. 258 'medical situation [was]' NA, WO 17/2155, War Diary of the 75th Indian Field Ambulance, April 1944.

p. 258 'I was told that he' Interviewed for this book.

p. 258 'When I ran to' Kazuo Tamayama and John Nunneley, *Tales by Japanese Soldiers* (Cassell, 2000), p. 162.

p. 258 'Such a genuine man' *Ibid.*

p. 258 '"You see," I said' Cited in Arthur Swinson, *Kohima* (Arrow Books, 1966), p. 93.

p. 259 'Hey! Johnny, let' Arthur Campbell, *The Siege* (Allen and Unwin, 1956), p. 72.

p. 259 'continuously amongst the' NA, WO 373/22, Citation Recommending Military Cross for Lieutenant Philip Ernest Watts, 13 September 1942.

p. 260 'The Japs made a' Robert Street, *The Siege of Kohima: The Battle for Burma* (Barny Books, 2003), p. 54.

p. 260 'They were about *Ibid.*

p. 260 'I jumped into the' Interviewed for this book.

p. 261 'We cut them to' Street, *The Siege of Kohima*, p. 42.

p. 261 'The only trouble' Interviewed for this book.

p. 262 'so close in some' Lucas Phillips, *Springboard to Victory*, p. 141. Lucas Phillips is citing the "joint narrative" coordinated by several officers present at the battle as well as the war diary and a "brief narration" by Major Shaw, the wounded C company commander. Brigadier Lucas Phillips's account of these events is the most reliable.

p. 262 'So I had to say' Tamayama and Nunneley, *Tales by Japanese Soldiers*, p. 165.

p. 262 'shot at least 12' Citation Recommending Military Cross for Second Lieutenant Peter Doresa, 22 April 1944.

p. 262 'His first bag came' NA, WO 203/4637, from an account by Captain Kitchen, *Indian Army Observer* (18 April 1944).

p. 263 'He got 'em coming' IWM, Oral History Project, file no. 20769, interview with Bert Harwood.

p. 263 'his next contribution' *Ibid*.

p. 263 'At this stage the' Tamayama and Nunneley, *Tales by Japanese Soldiers*, p. 166.

p. 264 Searching in the ruins The figure of forty-four comes from the battalion war diary for 7 April. Private Norman gives a figure of seventy bodies. IWM, file no. 81/16/1, diary of Private Harold Norman.

p. 264 'excellent Survey' Richards Papers, narrative of Kohima.

p. 265 'Thank you Douglas' Cited in Campbell, *The Siege*, p. 84.

p. 265 'found that a lot' IWM, file no. 81/16/1, diary of Private Harold Norman.

p. 265 'There were quite a lot' Interviewed for this book.

p. 265 'I think I know' Interviewed for this book.

p. 265 'an almighty' Interviewed for this book.

p. 266 'he and the others' IWM, file no. 81/16/1, diary of Private Harold Norman.

p. 266 'It was awful in' Interviewed for this book.

p. 267 'Colonel Young said' Interviewed for this book.

p. 267 'An endeavour was made' NA, WO 177/2155, War Diary of the 75th Indian Field Ambulance, April 1944.

p. 267 'with the wounded' Richards Papers, 'How I Came to Be at Kohima' (private memoir).

p. 268 'poor Nobby Hall' IWM, file no. 4587 81/16/1, diary of Private Harold Norman.

p. 268 'I was rather thinking' Interviewed for this book.

p. 269 'instead of running back' IWM, file no. 4587 81/16/1, diary of Private Harold Norman.

p. 269 'The poor chap' Interviewed for this book.

p. 269 'I tried to pull' Diary of Private Harold Norman.

p. 270 'It was really nerve-wracking' *Ibid*.

p. 270 'went wild but' *Ibid*.

p. 270 'We were surrounded' *Ibid*.

p. 271 'It blew the poor' IWM, Oral History Project, file no. 17537, interview with Donald Easten.

Seventeen: Over the Mountain

p. 272 'I think that all' IWM, Swinson Papers, file no. NRA 28568, diary of General Montagu North Stopford, 6 April 1944.

p. 272 'I am not satisfied' Diary of General Montagu North Stopford, 8 April 1944.

p. 273 'garrison must stay' IWM, Swinson Papers, file no. NRA 28568, diary of Major General John Grover.

p. 273 'devilish row, screaming' IWM, Swinson Papers, file no. NRA 28568, diary of Captain Arthur Swinson, 8 April 1944.

p. 273 'that went howling' *Ibid*.

p. 273 'Apart from these' *Ibid*.

p. 273 'At the "Non Sum Dignus"' *Ibid*.

p. 274 'They went when and how' IWM, file no. 10520 P104, The Operations of the 5 Infantry Brigade, 2 Division in Assam, 30 March–12 May 1944, Brigadier V. S. F. Hawkins.

p. 274 'or there'd be hell' Swinson's account on the Worcestershire Regiment website <www.worcestershireregiment.com>. This contains slightly different accounts – sometimes edited, sometimes more copious – than Swinson's written diary at the Imperial War Museum.

p. 274 'the wild days' Diary of Captain Arthur Swinson.

p. 274 'Perhaps he would have' *Ibid*.

p. 275 'I was a bit appalled' Hawkins, The Operations of the 5 Infantry Brigade.

p. 275 'He was rather stick' Interviewed for this book.

p. 276 'everybody dug holes' Interviewed for this book.

p. 276 'we had done so' Hawkins, The Operations of the 5 Infantry Brigade.

p. 276 'We went in single file' Interviewed for this book.

p. 276 'never faltering or stumbling' RQMS Frederick J. Weedman, 7th battalion, Worcestershire Regiment, personal memoir.

p. 277 'night was split asunder' *Ibid*.

p. 277 'like an angry bee' *Ibid.*

p. 277 'He smouldered for' *Ibid.*

p. 277 'Little Jap upon' *Ibid.*

p. 278 'The relief of Kohima' IWM, Swinson Papers, file no. NRA 28568, diary of General Montagu North Stopford, April 13 1944.

p. 278 'beginning to see light' Field Marshall Lord Slim, *Defeat into Victory*, p. 314.

p. 278 'For their gains' *Ibid.*

p. 278 'As I watched the' *Ibid.*

p. 279 'at the cost of skimping' *Ibid.*

p. 279 'The hard fact is' Lieutenant General Sir Henry Pownall, *Chief of Staff, Diaries, Volume Two – 1940–44* (edited by Brian Bond, Leo Cooper, 1974.), p. 164.

p. 280 'We should not hesitate' NA, CAB/65/42/5, Meeting of War Cabinet, 11 April 1944.

p. 280 'without air transport' Library of Franklin Delano Roosevelt, Military Correspondence: 1944–45 index, box 36. Letter of Lord Mountbatten to President Roosevelt, 28 March 1944.

p. 280 'He was given' L/Sergeant Jim Campion, Jungle Hell of Kohima, personal memoir.

p. 280 'full of bounding' Lord Louis Mountbatten, *Personal Diary of Admiral the Lord Louis Mountbatten, Supreme Allied Commander South-East Asia, 1943–1946*, ed. by Philip Ziegler (Collins, 1988), p. 88.

p. 281 'the same as your' *Ibid.*

p. 281 'When I think of' *Ibid.*

p. 281 'The one who did' *Ibid.*

p. 281 'I began to wonder' Field Marshal Lord Alanbrooke, *War Diaries – 1939–1945* (Edited by Alex Danchev and Daniel Todman. Weidenfeld and Nicholson, 2001), pp. 532–534.

p. 282 'it would be better' *Ibid.*

p. 282 'like a man chained' *Ibid.*

p. 282 'To the north' NA, CAB 65/42/1, Meeting of War Cabinet, 3 April 1944.

p. 282 'to discuss India' Alanbrooke, *War Diaries, 1939–1945*, pp. 228.

p. 282 'Rowland from Indian' *Ibid.*

p. 282 'I have during the' *Ibid.*

p. 283 'We cannot stop every' Cited in Arthur James Barker, *The March on Delhi* (Faber and Faber, 1963), p. 118.

p. 283 'It is obvious that' *Ibid.*, p. 132.

p. 283 'Kohima was very' IWM, file no. 2234 92/39/1, papers of Major Walter Greenwood.

p. 283 'at 5.30 p.m. each day' RMAA, Pawsey papers, Captain WPG MacLachlan, 'Report on the Kohima Box.'

p. 284 'Not at the present' Hansard, Deb 4 April 1944, vol 398, cc1815-6W.

p. 285 'Harrassing fire means' IWM, Oral History Project, file no. 20125, interview with Sergeant William Wilson.

p. 285 'The Jap party then' stay' IWM, Swinson Papers, file no. NRA 28568, diary of Major General John Grover.

p. 285 'The Worcesters accepted' IWM, Swinson papers, General Sir John Grover, narrative of Kohima battle.

Eighteen: Dreams Dying

p. 286 'It was so very' Interviewed for this book.

p. 286 'At the same time' Lieutenant Hiroshi Yamagami's Memoir, in *Burma Front: Reminiscences of the 58th Japanese Infantry Regiment* (58th Infantry Regimental Association, 1964).

p. 287 'The battle of Kohima' *Ibid.*

p. 287 'It came to us' Interviewed for this book.

p. 287 'One group would' Interviewed for this book.

p. 287 'I had heard the' Interviewed for this book.

p. 287 'thunder and it felt' Interviewed for this book.

p. 287 'The men were so' Interviewed for this book.

p. 288 'When I arrived' Interviewed for this book.

p. 288 'Children and grandchildren' Takahide Kuwaki, *The Greater East Asia War Has Not Yet Ended: An Army Doctor's Memoir of a Trench in Burma* (Tentensha, 1997), p. 56.

p. 288 'They first fired' Interviewed for this book.

p. 289 'I hurried to draw' IWM, Swinson Papers, file no. NRA 28568, Lieutenant K. Togawa, 'Grapple with Enemy'.

p. 289 'One so brave' *Ibid.*

p. 289 'ceased to move' *Ibid.*

p. 289 'The Army Comdr' NA, WO 303/6320, Essays and Interrogations of Lieutenant Colonel Iwaichi Fujiwara.

p. 289 'In a long' NIDS, Lieutenant General Renya Mutaguchi, handwritten account.

p. 290 'I then gave the' NDL, Lieutenant General Renya Mutaguchi, interview with official historian.

p. 290 'Dimapur was not' Cited in Arthur James Barker, *The March on Delhi* (Faber and Faber, 1963), p. 247.

p. 290 'this is not good' *Ibid.*

p. 291 'heavy casualties' NA, WO 203/6324, Appendix to Bulletin no. 245, Account of Lieutenant General Shigesaburo Miyazaki, Commander of 31st Division Infantry Group.

p. 291 'I believe that' 'Memoir of Division Leader Sato.' Published by 'Retsu' Division War Veterans Association.

p. 291 Fewer than a fifth Arthur Swinson, *Four Samurai* (Hutchinson, 1968), p. 137.

p. 292 without exception' Field Marshal Lord Slim, *Defeat into Victory* (Cassell, 1956), p. 311.

p. 292 'They were astonished' *Ibid.*

p. 292 The priority is' Amrarume Museum, essay by General Kotuku Sato.

p. 293 'Though the Nagas' Ursula Graham Bower, *Naga Path* (John Murray, 1952), p. 196.

p. 293 They went off' *Ibid.*, p. 199.

p. 293 'We honey-combed' *Ibid.*, p. 193.

p. 293 'The Kohima men' RMAA, Pawsey Papers, Krusischi Paschar narrative.

p. 293 'DC kept saying' Salhoutie Mechieo, interview with Kohima Educational Trust, 2008.

p. 294 'The Zubza cannons' RMAA, Pawsey Papers, Krusischi Paschar narrative.

p. 294 'We fought for that' Anonymous villager, interview with Kohima Educational Trust, 2008.

p. 294 'This was repeatedly' NA, WO 203/6388, 'Operations of the 23rd British Infantry Brigade, Naga Hills, April–July 1944.'

p. 294 'I remember taking' Interviewed for this book.

p. 295 'A fine group of men' IWM, Swinson Papers, file no. NRA 28568, diary of Captain Arthur Swinson.

p. 295 'scalp each other' *Ibid.*

p. 295 'They offer to take' IWM, Swinson Papers, file no. NRA 28568, diary of Major General John Grover.

p. 295 'Capture alive Japanese' NA, WO 203/6388, Amdt. No. 1 to 23 Inf. Bde. Op. Instr. No. 10, dated 4 May 1944.

p. 296 'They started very early' RMAA, Pawsey Papers, Account of Column 76 of 23 Brigade against the Japanese by Khumbo Angami, Teacher, Government High School, Kohima.

Nineteen: The Black Thirteenth

p. 297 'If a bloke got' Interviewed for this book.

p. 297 'I marvelled at' Interviewed for this book.

p. 297 'They tried so hard' Interviewed for this book.

p. 298 'Oh my God' Interviewed for this book.

p. 298 Gas gangrene thrived See Gas Gangrene, Merck Manuals Online Medical Library <www.merck.com/mmhe/sec17/ch190>.

p. 299 'Shocking wounds' Cited in C. E. Lucas Phillips, *Springboard to Victory* (Heinemann, 1966), p. 137.

p. 299 'We felt very close' Interviewed for this book.

p. 299 'I remember that man' Interviewed for this book.

p. 299 'was always grinning' Letter from Bruce Hayllar to his parents, April 1944.

p. 299 'because we were' *Ibid*.

p. 300 'All he would say' Interviewed for this book.

p. 300 'even harder to bear' Arthur Campbell, *The Siege* (Allen and Unwin, 1956), p. 102.

p. 300 He had a strip of Robert Street, *The Siege of Kohima: The Battle for Burma* (Barny Books, 2003), p. 78.

p. 300 'I had to leave the trench' Interviewed for this book.

p. 300 'She told him that' Street, *The Siege of Kohima*, p. 80.

p. 301 'very heavily mortared' NA, WO 177/2155, War Diary of 75th Indian Field Ambulance, April 1944.

p. 301 'a terrible day' Cited in Lucas Phillips, *Springboard to Victory*, p. 188.

p. 302 'Follow the knife' IWM, Oral History Project, file no. 25696, interview with Frank Infanti.

p. 302 'During the night' NA, WO 177/2155, War Diary of 75th Indian Field Ambulance, April 1944.

p. 302 'and men had to crawl' NA, WO 172/4884, War Diary, 4th battalion, Royal West Kent Regiment, 8/9 April 1944.

p. 303 'We had rifles' IWM, Oral History Project, file no. 21102, interview with Leslie Crouch.

p. 303 'in a trilby hat' IWM, Oral History Project, interview with Donald Easten.

p. 303 'He was an old man' Interviewed for this book.

p. 303 'quite unpleasant' Richards Papers, Hugh Richards narrative of Kohima.

p. 304 'He was a fine soldier' Interviewed for this book.

p. 305 'By your acts' Richards Papers, Special Order of the Day, 13 April 1944.

p. 306 'until we could find' Lieutenant John Faulkner, handwritten memoir.

p. 307 'A hell of a din' Lieutenant John Faulkner, handwritten memoir.

p. 307 'Where the hell' Ibid.

p. 307 'They came howling' Interviewed for this book.

p. 307 'I said to this lad' Interviewed for this book.

p. 308 '"Don't let me die"' Interviewed for this book.

p. 308 'I will always remember' Walter Williams, personal memoir, and interviewed for this book.

p. 308 'You don't forget' Interviewed for this book.

p. 308 'More often than not' Ibid.

p. 308 'fire down on call' Richards Papers, 'How I Came to Be at Kohima' (private memoir).

p. 309 'At 6 p.m. the Jap' Lieutenant John Faulkner, handwritten memoir.

p. 309 'smoking furiously' Ibid.

p. 309 'completely off his rocker' Ibid.

p. 309 'No man can be brave' Ibid.

p. 309 'He looked awful' Ibid.

p. 309 'George Mann's dead' Ibid.

p. 309 'I ran so fast' Ibid.

p. 310 That made me worse' Interviewed for this book.

p. 311 'I must have a cat's' Interviewed for this book.

p. 311 'splinter proof roof' NA, WO 177/2155, War Diary of 75th Indian Field Ambulance, April 1944.

p. 311 'nervous exhaustion' Ibid.

p. 311 'Somehow we hung on' Interviewed for this book.

p. 311 'two days in this area' H. D. Chaplin, The Queen's Own Royal West Kent Regiment, 1920–1950 (Michael Joseph, 1954).

p. 312 'It was only snippets' IWM, Oral History Project, file no. 20769, interview with Bert Harwood.

p. 312 'Every day Danny Laverty' IWM, Oral History Project, file no. 2927, interview with Leonard Brown.

p. 312 '"we were continually hearing' NA, WO 172/5045, War Diary of the 1st Assam Regiment.

p. 312 '"I saw him being killed' Interviewed for this book.

Twenty: A Question of Time

p. 313 'who thinks it may' IWM, Swinson Papers, file no. NRA 28568, diary of General Montagu North Stopford, 15 April 1944.

p. 313 'We were now split' IWM, file no. 10520, The Operations of the 5 Infantry Brigade, 2 Division in Assam, 30 March–12 May 1944, Brigadier V. S. F. Hawkins.

p. 314 'It is very seldom' Interviewed for this book.

p. 314 'It was terrible' Interviewed for this book.

p. 314 'Hey! Johnny, are you there?' Fusilier Garry Noel, interviewed for this book.

p. 314 'This was a great mistake' Interviewed for this book.

p. 316 'nine or ten of which' Michael Lowry, *Fighting Through to Kohima* (Pen and Sword, 2003), p. 201.

p. 316 'simply an essay' NIDS, General Kotuku Sato, handwritten memoir.

p. 316 'they were thrown back' Richards Papers, 33 Indian Corps Account of Operations, vol. 1, 1 April–22 June 1944.

p. 317 'Enemy planes and firepower' NAM, 9412-118-83-110. The name of the General making this statement is not given in the file but his declaration that, 'Our group's responsibility will be to sweep down into Kohima and cut off the enemy's line of retreat' indicates that it almost certainly comes from the commander of the Infantry Group, Major General Shigesaburo Miyazaki. This was precisely his allotted task.

p. 317 'They are men without' *Ibid.*

p. 318 'That night attack' Cited in Michiko Masuzawa, *A Quiet Man: About My Father Shigesaburo Miyazaki* (Koyo Publishing, 1987).

p. 319 'I feel sorry for' *Ibid.*

p. 319 'It had been planned' NAM, Colvin Papers, file no. 9412-118-83-110,'Interrogation of General Kotuku Sato', citing IWM file no. 5009/7.

p. 319 'not a grain of rice' Manabu Wada, *Drifting Down the Chindwin: A Story of Survival* (Burma Campaign Fellowship Group, [n.d.]).

p. 319 'I thanked for my' Interviewed for this book.

p. 320 'When the enemy appeared' Lieutenant Shosaku Kameyama, personal memoir.

p. 320 'When there is no more rice' Lieutenant Shosaku Kameyama, in 'The Kohima War Record', trans. by Keiko Itoh, cited in Newsletter of the Burma Campaign Society, Issue no.6, March 2005.

p. 320 'fire from a long' Interviewed for this book.

p. 321 'To see them roaring' H. L. Thompson, *The Official History of New Zealand in the Second World War 1939–1945: New Zealanders with the Royal Airforce: Air Superiority and the Arakan Battle* (Historical Publications Branch, 1959), ch. 15 'Operation Thursday and the Victory at Imphal'.

p. 321 'We bombed in sections' Jack Morton, 'Sojourn in the Royal Airforce' <www.rcaf.com/whalen>.

p. 321 'When we landed' *Ibid*.

p. 322 'We carried packed lunches' IWM, file no. 02/49, Derek Thirlwell, 'The Early Days of 194 Squadron Royal Air Force'.

p. 322 'Fatty's' parties after' *Ibid*.

p. 322 'would somebody please *Ibid*.

p. 323 'Almost every night' BBC People's War, Eric Forsdyke.

p. 323 'In the best of weather' Second Lieutenant J. D. Broughel, 1st Transport Group, 13th Transport Squadron US Army, 'Over the Hump' <www.centercomp/cgi-bin>.

p. 323 'Knowing that the leading' Into the Wildest Blue Yonder: Memoirs of 1st Lt. John Walker Russell, US Army Air Corps', CBI Theatre of World War II.

p. 324 'I took the normal spin' IWM, file no. 02/49, Deryck Groockock, 'Supply Dropping', cited in Derek Thirlwell, 'The Early Days of 194 Squadron Royal Air Force'.

p. 325 'a virtual nose to tail' Correspondence with author.

p. 325 'remember looking down' Thirlwell, 'The Early Days of 194 Squadron Royal Air Force'.

p. 325 'often we would end up' Flight Sergeant J. V. Bell, 31 Squadron, cited in Jon Latimer, *Burma: The Forgotten War* (John Murray, 2004), p. 268.

p. 326 'the Japanese Air Command' NA, AIR 2/5665. Operations of Bengal Command, 15 November–17 December 1943 and Third Tactical Air Force, 18 December–1 June 1944.

p. 326 'gave the enemy' NA, WO 203/6324, Interrogation of Lieutenant Colonel Iwaichi Fujiwara.

p. 326 'swung round and made' Document sent to author, 29 April 2010.

p. 326 'fighting on because' Interviewed for this book.

p. 326 'How could we escape' IWM, Swinson Papers, file no. NRA 28568, letter from Keizo Moto to Arthur Swinson, 15 March 1967 [approximate date].

p. 327 'When I first entered' Interviewed for this book.

Twenty-one: The Last Hill

p. 328 'They smelled like' Private Mark Lambert, Royal Welch Fusiliers, interviewed for this book.

p. 328 'The company clerk' IWM, Oral History Project, file no. 25696, interview with Frank Infanti.

p. 329 'Laverty's relationship with' NAM, Colvin Papers, file no. 9412-118-1-91, Letter from Captain Peter Steyn, Assam Regiment, to John Colvin, 20 November 1992.

p. 329 '[He] regarded the Jap' RMAA, Pawsey Papers, Captain McLachlan, 'The Kohima Box.'

p. 329 'Why don't you come' Cited in C. E. Lucas Phillips, *Springboard to Victory* (Heinemann, 1966), p. 189.

p. 329 'Sorry the missus isn't' *Ibid.*

p. 329 'Fatigue was the greatest' Interviewed for this book.

p. 330 'We heard all this' IWM, Oral History Project, file no. 20461, interview with Ivan Daunt.

p. 330 On another night BBC People's War, Charlie West.

p. 330 'This day he said' Interviewed for this book.

p. 331 'Although badly injured' Robert Street, *The Siege of Kohima: The Battle for Burma* (Barny Books, 2006), p. 99.

p. 331 'No soldier is brave' IWM, Oral History Project, file no. 2927, interview with Len Brown.

p. 331 'Day after day' IWM, Oral History Project, file no. 19090, interview with Harry Smith.

p. 331 'They had lived' Peter Steyn, *History of the Assam Regiment, vol. 1: 1941–47* (Orient Longmans, 1959), p. 100.

p. 332 'A man who had watched' *Ibid.*

p. 332 'They will not be' Cited in Lucas Phillips, *Springboard to Victory*, p. 200.

p. 332 'Returning to my slit' *Ibid.*, p. 201.

p. 332 'I had an argument' IWM, Oral History Project, file no. 20769, interview with Bert Harwood.

p. 333 'Up until that time' Interviewed for this book.

p. 333 'They were easy targets' IWM, Oral History Project, file no. 21102, interview with Leslie Crouch.

p. 335 'to avoid the casualties' Richards Papers, 'Kohima Siege', typed memorandum.

p. 335 'We soon came to' NA, WO 172/5045, Major Albert Calistan, Kohima, April 1944.

p. 336 'You know damn well' Cited in Arthur Campbell, *The Siege* (Allen and Unwin, 1956), p. 165.

p. 336 'I also spoke to' Hugh Richards, 'Kohima Siege', typed memorandum.

p. 336 'This was the fourth' NA, WO 172/4884, War Diary, 4th battalion, Royal West Kent Regiment.

p. 337 'We had many disappointments' Richards Papers, Speech to Assam Regiment Regimental Dinner, 29 September 1962.

p. 337 'It was actions like' Street, *The Siege of Kohima*, p. 80.

p. 337 'They were made of' Interviewed for this book.

p. 338 'You had to go' Interviewed for this book.

p. 338 'lack of security' IWM, Swinson Papers, file no. NRA 28568, diary of Major General John Grover.

p. 338 'country is very big' IWM, Swinson Papers, file no. NRA 28568, letter of General Sir John Grover to Arthur Swinson.

p. 338 'seemed we had not' IWM, file no. 8092 99/21/1, Captain John Howard.

p. 339 'progress was at times' Field Marshal Lord Slim, *Defeat into Victory* (Cassell, 1956), p. 317.

p. 339 'I expect to hear' IWM, Swinson Papers, file no. NRA 28568, diary of Lieutenant General Montangu North Stopford.

p. 340 'Had the Japs attacked' RMAA, Pawsey Papers, Charles Pawesey, narrative of siege.

p. 340 'created panic' *Ibid.*

p. 340 'unarmed civilian in the' K. Brahma Singh, *The Assam Rifles in World War II* (unpublished manuscript.), p. 15.

p. 341 'You mustn't let' Interviewed for this book.

p. 341 'We kept our heads' Lieutenant John Faulkner, handwritten memoir.

p. 341 'Luck was with us' IWM, file no. 4587 81/16/1, diary of Private Harold Norman.

p. 341 'dimly flitted shapes' *Ibid.*

p. 341 'Suddenly I heard' *Ibid.*

p. 342 'talking away as if' *Ibid.*

p. 342 '[Private] Steel had fired' *Ibid.*

p. 343 'There was more scuffling' *Ibid.*

p. 343 'I began to feel' Street, *The Siege of Kohima*, p. 99.

p. 343 'had proved their' E. B. Stanley Clark and A. T. Tillot, *From Kent to Kohima* (Gale and Polden, 1951), p. 124.

p. 343 'It was a most terrifying' IWM, file no. 4587 81/16/1, diary of Private Harold Norman.

p. 344 'Many of the wounded' IWM, Oral History Project, file no. 17537, interview with Donald Easten.

p. 344 'Are you infantry?' Cited in Lucas Phillips, *Springboard to Victory*, p. 101.

p. 345 'Each time they fired' Interviewed for this book.

p. 345 'We kept hearing' Interviewed for this book.

p. 346 'No. In a way' Interviewed for this book.

p. 346 'How my own H.Q.' Hugh Richards, 'Kohima Siege', typed memorandum.

p. 346 'The officers just came' Interviewed for this book.

p. 346 'many were the anxious' Steyn, *History of the Assam Regiment, vol. 1: 1941–47*, p. 100.

p. 346 'I was wounded but' Interviewed for this book.

p. 346 'which meant general dogsbody' IWM, Oral History Project, file no. 25449, interview with Thomas Jackson.

p. 347 'I jumped in' *Ibid*.

p. 347 'We were clearly getting' *Ibid*.

p. 347 'one of those chaps' Interviewed for this book.

p. 348 'A company sergeant' Interviewed for this book.

p. 348 'enough stray men' NAM, Colvin Papers, file no. 9412-118-1-55, narrative of Captain Tom Hogg.

p. 348 'There was no mention' NAM, Colvin Papers, file no. 9412-118-1-55, Letter from Thomas Hogg to John Colvin, 12 April 1993.

p. 348 'half his jaw' Campbell, *The Siege*, p. 201.

p. 350 'Stood and watched' IWM, Swinson Papers, file no. NRA28568, diary of Captain Arthur Swinson.

p. 350 'ramming bombs down' Lieutenant John Faulkner, handwritten memoir.

p. 351 'It was a marvellous' Interviewed for this book.

p. 351 They looked horrified' *Ibid*.

p. 351 'I was taken down' Interviewed for this book.

p. 351 'and if they were' Diary of Private Harold Norman.

p. 352 'I saw trunks without' *Ibid*.

p. 352 'I said it must be held' Hugh Richards, 'Kohima Siege', typed memorandum.

p. 353 'Div artillery put down' *Ibid*.

p. 353 'with blood curdling yells' Lieutenant John Faulkner, handwritten memoir.

p. 353 'We collected all' Diary of Private Harold Norman.

p. 353 'nice clean new uniforms' Interview with Harry Smith.

p. 354 'He said, "I'm taking over"' Interviewed for this book.

p. 354 'But you don't talk' Interviewed for this book.

p. 354 'He was ladling it' Interviewed for this book.

p. 354 'They were a sight' IWM, 10520 P 104, The Operations of the 5 Infantry Brigade, 2 Division in Assam, 30 March–12 May 1944, Brigadier V. S. F. Hawkins.

p. 354 'the stench of festering' IWM, Swinson Papers, NRA 28568, Major John Nettlefield, Memorandum to Arthur Swinson.

p. 355 'littered with their dead' *Ibid*.

p. 355 'He didn't know' Street, *The Siege of Kohima*, p. 107.

p. 355 'dead beat' Lieutenant Colonel Harold Grimshaw, CO 1/1 Punjab Regiment cited in Lucas Phillips, *Springboard to Victory*, p. 216.

p. 355 'Some were falling' IWM, Swinson Papers, file no. NRA 28568, diary of Captain Arthur Swinson.

p. 356 'marching and doubling' NA, WO 172/5045, Major Albert Calistan, Kohima, April 1944.

p. 356 'although very tired' *Ibid*.

p. 356 'They cut these drums' Interviewed for this book.

p. 356 'We slept through the' Street, *The Siege of Kohima*, p. 110.

p. 356 'In a strange way' *Ibid*.

Twenty-two: Attrition

p. 357 'unlimited supplies' IWM, file no. 4587 81/16/1, diary of Private Harold Norman.

p. 357 'listening to the cries' Harry Smith, *Memories of a Hostile Place* (privately published).

p. 358 'Our lads have not' *Ibid*.

p. 358 'You don't know' Interviewed for this book.

p. 358 I have never seen' Letter of Lieutenant Bruce Hayllar to his parents, Dimapur, 20 April 1944.

p. 358 'A man with an' *Ibid*.

p. 359 'He was a man who' Interviewed for this book.

p. 359 'There is one thing' Interviewed for this book.

p. 359 'This is the first' NA, WO 172/5045, War Diary of the 1st Assam Regiment.

p. 360 'it was for all' Robert Street, *A Brummie in Burma* (Barny Books, 1997), p. 58.

p. 360 'We scraped out' Interviewed for this book.

p. 360 'Some of them were' Interviewed for this book.

p. 360 'I said, "You know"' Interviewed for this book.

p. 361 'It took about a' Interviewed for this book.

p. 361 'used to sleep in' NA, WO 203/4637, 'Personal narratives of Kohima and Imphal Battles.'

p. 361 'all eager to get' E. B. Stanley Clark and A. T. Tillot, *From Kent to Kohima* (Gale and Polden, 1951), pp. 130–131.

p. 361 'Officially he shot four' NA, WO 203/4637.

p. 361 'the abrupt dismissal' NA, WO 203/4637, 'Personal narratives of Kohima and Imphal Battles.'

p. 362 'walked round and' NA, WO 172/5045, War Diary of the 1st Assam Regiment. April 1944.

p. 362 'tall, sinewy with' *Daily Mail*, 1 May 1944.

p. 363 'Perched 5,000 feet up' *Ibid*.

p. 363 'unless they are willing' RMAA, Pawsey Papers, Charles Pawsey, miscellaneous correspondence.

p. 363 'They are very gentle' NA, WO 203/4637, interview with Charles Pawsey, 'Observer with 14th Army.'

p. 363 'Sir I am still' *Ibid*.

p. 364 'every day to see' RMAA, Pawsey Papers, Narrative of Krusischi Pashkar, Kohima Village.

p. 364 'We were taken' Interviewed for this book.

p. 364 'When they had done' Ursula Graham Bower, *Naga Path* (John Murray, 1952), p. 200.

p. 364 'an excuse to let' Ursula Graham Bower, interview with Professor Alan MacFarlane, Cambridge University.

p. 364 'lots of offices going' *Ibid*.

p. 365 'Don't worry sir' IWM, file no. 10520 P104, Account of the Operations of 5 Brigade, April–May 1944, Brigadier V. S. F. Hawkins.

p. 365 'John Grover' IWM, Swinson Papers, file no. NRA 28568, diary of General Montagu North Stopford, 18 May 1944.

p. 366 'In view of the lack' 33 Indian Corps Account of Operations, vol. 1, 1 April–22 June 1944, p. 14.

p. 366 'messing up' IWM, Swinson Papers, file no. NRA 28568, diary of Lieutenant General Montagu North Stopford.

p.366 ' Washington supports' *Ibid*.

p. 366 'why he must not' *Ibid*.

p. 366 'Later in the evening' *Ibid*.

p. 366 'hopelessly sticky and seems' *Ibid*.

p. 367 'which he did not' IWM, Swinson Papers, file no. NRA 28568, diary of Lieutenant General Montagu North Stopford.

p. 367 'the unavoidable arrival' Field Marshal Lord Slim, *Defeat into Victory* (Cassell, 1956), p. 318.

p. 367 'Thoroughly satisfactory' *Ibid*.

p. 367 'a sideline in melancholy' Slim, *Defeat into Victory*, p. 200.

p. 378 'Our stand at Kohima' NA, CAB 65/42/14, Meeting of War Cabinet, 24 April 1944.

p. 369 'could feel the stress' Winston Churchill, *The Second World War,* vol. 5: *Closing The Ring* (The Reprint Society, 1960 edition), p. 440.

p. 369 'Let nothing go' Cited in *ibid*.

p. 369 'must be filled' *Ibid*.

p. 369 'I don't think any' Lieutenant General Sir Henry Pownall, *Chief of Staff – The Diaries of Lt.-General Sir Henry Pownall – edited by Brian Bond* (Leo Cooper, 1974), p 165.

Twenty-three: The Trials of Victory and Defeat

p. 370 'You did a good job' Anonymous soldier quoted in *Dohkoku–Burma Campaign for a Newly Recruited Soldier, Retsu Division, 138 Regiment* (Amarume Museum, 1992).

p. 370 'Thank you for your' *Ibid*.

p. 370 'You don't know my' *Ibid*.

p. 371 'For this I could' NDL, interview with official historian, February 1964.

p. 371 'Across the valley' NA, WO 203/4637, account of 14th Army Observer, Kohima, 24 April 1944.

p. 371 'It all changed' Interviewed for this book.

p. 372 'Unfortunately these tactics' NA, WO 203/6324, Lieutenant Colonel Iwaichi Fujiwara, '15th Army Impressions of Allied tactics and equipment.'

p. 372 'I said to myself' Interviewed for this book.

p. 372 'Its appearance had' Lieutenant General Kotuku Sato, handwritten memoir, for Retsu Division War Veterans Association.

p. 372 'so the enemy can't' 'Biruma Sensen' (Recollections of 58th Infantry Regiment), cited in Louis Allen, *Burma: The Longest War* (J. M. Dent, 1984), p. 405.

p. 373 'both Right and Left' Notebook of Major Yamaguchi, Discovered at Milestone 87, HQ of 31 Division Infantry Group, May 1944. <www.burmastar.org.uk>.

p. 373 'as formidable a position' Field Marshal Lord Slim, *Defeat into Victory* (Cassell, 1956), p. 317.

p. 373 'Let someone else go' George L. Senior, Royal Army Medical Corps, personal memoir.

p. 374 'He was restless' *Ibid*.

p. 374 'was always a surprise' Gordon Graham. *The Trees are All Young on Garrison Hill* (Kohima Educational Trust, 2005), p. 51.

p. 374 'Come with me' Interviewed for this book.

p. 375 'We dashed on them' Interviewed for this book.

p. 375 'I killed somebody' Interviewed for this book.

p. 375 'One man got shot' Interviewed for this book.

p. 375 'It was very heavy' Interviewed for this book.

p. 375 'Please come and stop' Tokuo Seki, *Burma War Chronicle* (1991), pp. 88–9.

p. 375 'In his trench' *Ibid*.

p. 376 'I saw all dead' IWM, Oral History Project, file no. 19596, interview with Yanagi Satoru.

p. 376 'Mr Ito who worked' Interviewed for this book.

p. 377 'born in snowy Niigata' IWM, Swinson papers, file no. NRA 28568, Yukihiko Imai, *To and From Kohima* (1953).

p. 377 'They were so hungry' *Ibid*.

p. 377 'How could he be' Manabu Wada, *Drifting Down the Chindwin: A Story of Survival* (Burma Campaign Fellowship Group).

p. 377 'From this point on' NA, WO 203/4637, 'Personal Narratives of Kohima and Imphal Battles.'

p. 377 'Slim was very insistent' IWM, Swinson Papers, file no. NRA 28568, memorandum of General John Grover.

p. 378 'raised the men's spirits' R. King-Clark, *The Battle of Kohima 1944 – The Narrative of the 2nd Battalion The Manchester Regiment* (Fleur de Lys Publishing, Cheshire, 1995), p. 36.

p. 378 'As each man had' George Gordon, Royal Corps of Signals, personal memoir.

p. 378 'You drag your legs' Captain Horner, cited in John Colvin, *Not Ordinary Men* (Pen and Sword, 1994), p. 174.

p. 379 'round staring eyes' George Gordon, personal memoir.

p. 379 'we had hardly fired' *Ibid*.

p. 379 'Then the "Holy Boys" shouted' NA, WO 203/4637, 'Personal Narratives of Kohima and Imphal Battles.'

p. 379 'The shouted orders' *Ibid*.

p. 380 In one action around Figures as of 6 May cited in Leslie Edwards, *Kohima: The Furthest Battle* (History Press, 2009), p. 301.

p. 380 'Looking at the corpses' Gordon Graham. *The Trees are All Young on Garrison Hill* (Kohima Educational Trust, 2005), p. 47.

p. 381 'look at the great' Arthur Swinson, *Kohima* (Arrow Books, 1966), p. 218.

p. 381 'from both a political' IWM, file no. 10520 P104, Account of the Operations of 5 Brigade, British 2nd Division, April–June 1944, Brigadier V. S. F. Hawkins.

p. 381 '[There were] thousands' *Ibid*.

p. 381 'We not only overlooked' *Ibid*.

p. 382 'watching a dozen' Michael Lowry, *Fighting Through to Kohima* (Pen and Sword, 2003), p. 211.

p. 381 'closest thing to a snowball' *Ibid*., p. 226.

p. 381 'did a fair amount' *Ibid*., p. 228.

p. 381 'In cold sweated' *Ibid*.

p. 382 'I, for one' *Ibid*., p. 238.

p. 382 'As the days passed' John Shipster, *Mist on the Rice Fields* (Pen and Sword, 2000), p. 55.

p. 382 'to respect the dead' *Ibid*.

p. 383 'Draw near with faith' 'Militiaman' [anon.], *Six for the King* (Peace Brothers, 1984), p. 197.

p. 383 'That shows you what' Interviewed for this book.

p. 383 'the occupants must' Memorandum of General John Grover.

p. 384 'It got among about' NA, WO 203/4637, interview with BBC correspondent Richard Sharpe in 'Personal Narratives of the Kohima and Imphal battles.'

p. 384 'The gun couldn't fire' *Ibid*.

p. 384 'very much impressed' IWM, Swinson Papers, file no. NRA 28568, diary of Major General John Grover.

p. 385 'I got congratulatory telegrams' Unpublished memoir by Brigadier J. D. Shapland, sent to author by his family.

p. 385 'Then I was hit' *Ibid*.

p. 385 'part of a force' John McCann, *Return to Kohima* (privately published, 1993), pp. 410–12.

p. 386 'frightened of shadows' Swinson, *Kohima*, p. 278.

p. 386 'The impression was gained' IWM, Swinson Papers, file no. NRA 28568, letter from David Young, second-in-command Signals, 161 Indian Brigade, to Arthur Swinson, 26 September 1966.

p. 386 'we could get no men' BBC People's War, Deryck 'Dick' Reynolds.

p. 386 'General Messervy' David Young letter to Arthur Swinson.

p. 387 the Captain became Captain Bob Allen, Cameron Highlanders.

p. 387 'He was loyal to' 'On the Silence of General Grover.' Gordon Graham. 'Dekho!' Winter 2009.

Twenty-four: The Road of Bones

p. 389 'but it is useless' NAM, Major R. B. Houston, 'The Imphal Campaign', cited in file no. 1994-12-118-20, Colvin papers.

p. 389 'many cases of diarrhoea' *Ibid*.

p. 389 'can barely keep going' *Ibid*.

p. 389 'Even to think of' *Ibid*.

p. 390 'As an officer' Interviewed for this book.

p. 390 'Retsu Division has run' Cited in Shudo Akiyama, *The Retsu Division Commander Goes Insane* (Sheuisha, Tokyo 1973).

p. 390 'How dare you use' *Ibid*.

p. 391 'Nothing [of Mutaguchi's orders]' NIDS, General Kotuku Sato, Opinion about Imphal Campaign, August 1944.

p. 391 'We have fought for' Lieutenant General Kotuku Sato to 15th Army Headquarters, 26 May 1944.

p. 391 'Do as you please' Cited in Arthur Swinson, *Four Samurai* (Hutchinson, 1968), p. 143.

p. 391 'The tactical ability' *Ibid*.

p. 391 'It is my resolve' Lieutenant General Renya Mutaguchi, Special Order of the Day, cited in Arthur Swinson, *Four Samurai* (Hutchinson, 1968), pp. 143–4.

p. 391 'We got an order' Interviewed for this book.

p. 392 'Near his house' Captain Seiryo Yamashita, cited in Kazuo Tamayama and John Nunneley, *Tales by Japanese Soldiers* (Cassell, 2000), p. 191.

p. 392 '"Aircrafts is coming!"' IWM Swinson papers, file no. NRA 28568, Yukihiko Imai, *To and From Kohima* (1953).

p. 392 'You never tell until' Ryoichi Tobe, Edited by Brian Bond and Kyoichi Tachikawa, *Tojo Hideki As A War Leader, British and Japanese Military Leadership in the Far Eastern War, 1941–1945*. (Frank Cass, 2004), p. 35.

p. 392 'was perplexed, holding' *Ibid*.

p. 392 'Mutaguchi was in' Kawabe Nikki, cited in Louis Allen, *Burma: The Longest War* (J. M. Dent, 1984), p. 265.

p. 393 'I guessed Kawabe's' Cited in Allen, *Burma: The Longest War*, p. 266.

p. 394 'link up with' 15th Army signal to 31st Division, 9 June 1944, cited in Allen, *Burma, The Longest War*, p. 289.

p. 394 'I was flabbergasted' Lieutenant General Kotuku Sato, handwritten memoir, for Retsu Division War Veterans Association.

p. 394 'Do you intend to' Allen, *Burma: The Longest War*, p. 292.

p. 395 'recognizable as Japanese' Cited in Swinson, *Four Samurai*, p. 145.

p. 395 'I feel confident that' NAM, Colvin Papers, Intelligence Bulletin no. 247.

p. 395 'violent and angry' NA, WO 303/6320, Essays and Interrogations of Lieutenant Colonel Iwaichi Fujiwara.

p. 395 'Get your fat arse' Cited in Swinson, *Four Samurai*, p. 142.

p. 395 'Surprised by its' NA, WO 303/6320. Essays and Interrogations of Lieutenant Colonel Iwaichi Fujiwara.

p. 396 'Despair became rife' *Ibid*.

p. 397 'Then, I complained' Interviewed for this book.

p. 397 'a complete breakdown' NA, WO 303/6320. Essays and Interrogations of Lieutenant Colonel Iwaichi Fujiwara.

p. 398 'He heard what happened' Soichi Shiramizu, *The Starving Mountains* (Ashi Shobo, 1972), pp. 123–4.

p. 398 'Please share this' *Ibid*.

p. 398 'He said: "General"' *Ibid*.

p. 398 'Sometimes I met' Interviewed for this book.

p. 399 'We were so angry' Interviewed for this book.

p. 399 'Sometimes I even' Interviewed for this book.

p. 399 'The hospital staff' *The Listener*, 21 September 1944.

p. 400 One of the most chilling Hamachi Toshio, *Inparu sai-zensen*, pp. 243–4, cited in Allen, *Burma: The Longest War*, p. 296.

p. 400 'Our task remains' NA, WO 203/6388, Order of the Day, 10 May 1944.

p. 400 'We had been sodden' Captain P. P. S. Brownless, *Undercover in the Jungle*, p. 104, cited in Jon Latimer, *Burma: The Forgotten War* (John Murray, 2004), p. 321.

p. 400 'Walk, walk, walk' Unpublished account by Arthur Davies.

p. 402 'He died soon afterwards' Second World War Experience Centre <www.war-experience.org/collections>. Narrative of Lieutenant Desmond F. Earley, Essex Regiment, 23 Long Range Penetration Brigade.

p. 402 'an attempt to stage' NA, WO 203/6388, 'Operations of the 23rd British Infantry Brigade Naga Hills, April–July 1944.'

p. 402 'Early in the morning' RMAA, Pawsey Papers, Kumbho Angami, 'Account of Column 76, 23 Brigade Against the Japs.'

p. 402 'This [area] was' *Ibid.*

p. 402 'Japanese skeletons lying beside' Letter to author, 20 August 2010.

p. 403 'This Naga wanted' Interviewed for this book.

p. 403 'Several noses of' NA, WO 172/4587, 'V Force Sitrep No. I 2911 OF 12th Aug, 1944.'

p. 403 'ear and pay book' *Ibid.*

p. 403 'littered with Jap' *Ibid.*

p. 403 'It was hell' Interviewed for this book.

p. 404 'I saw the dead' Interviewed for this book.

p. 404 'I found out people' Interviewed for this book.

p. 404 'When I heard of it' Interviewed for this book.

p. 404 'Just like taking' Interviewed for this book.

p. 404 'In tears some of' Kazou Tamayama and John Nunneley, *Tales by Japanese Soldiers* (Cassell, 2000), p. 201.

p. 404 'You've lorded it' *Ibid.*

p. 405 'thousands upon thousands' Manabu Wada, *Drifting Down the Chindwin: A Story of Survival* (Burma Campaign Fellowship Group).

p. 405 'You want a statement' Swinson, *Four Samurai*, p 148.

p. 406 'General Sato is always' Shudo Akiyama, *The Retsu Division Commander Goes Insane* (Shueisha, Tokyo, 1973).

p. 406 'They are leading the' Signal from Lieutenant General Kotuku Sato to Staff Officer Mori, 15 July 1944, cited in Akiyama, *The Retsu Division Commander Goes Insane.*

p. 406 'I don't need a health' *Ibid.*

p. 406 'How come you cannot' *Ibid.*

p. 406 'The attitude, facial expression' 'Mental Health Examination of the Retsu Division Leader in Imphal Campaign by Dr Yamashita', *Kyushu Neuropsychiatry Journal* (1978).

p. 407 'Please … please don't' Cited in *War Chronicle of a Home Military Unit* (Military Unit Publication Society, Fukuoka, 1962).

p. 407 **Some dying men** Cited in Kozo Sugita, *Military Officer of Rebellion* (Kosaida publishing, Tokyo, 1995), pp. 171–4.

p. 407 **'V Force patrol shot'** NA, WO 172/4587, 'V Force Situation reports.

Twenty-five: When the War Is Over

p. 408 **'One could not visit'** Lord Louis Mountbatten, *Personal Diary of Admiral the Lord Louis Mountbatten, Supreme Allied Commander South-East Asia, 1943–1946*, ed. by Philip Ziegler (Collins, 1988), p. 116.

p. 408 **'everything in their'** *Ibid.*

p. 409 **'It was difficult to'** Interviewed for this book.

p. 409 **'presence of war'** NA, WO 203/4637, 'Personal Narratives of the Kohima and Imphal Battles.'

p. 409 **August 1944: There has** NA, WO 208/799, Governor's Reports on the Assam Tribal Areas, August and September 1944.

p. 409 **'While the wilder'** *Ibid.*, citing 'Report on the Assam Tribal Areas for the month ending June 30th 1945, by J. P. Mills, Esqr, C.I.E., I.C.S., Advisor to the Governor of Assam For Tribal Areas'.

p. 410 **'most of our people'** Sajal Nag, *Contesting Marginality: Ethnicity, Insurgency and Subnationalism in North-East India* (Manohar, 2002), p. 89.

p. 410 **'meant the rule'** *Ibid.*, p. 91.

p. 411 **'In the lengthening light'** Ursula Graham Bower, *Naga Path* (John Murray, 1952), p. 211.

p. 411 **'pert, pretty'** 'India: Ursula and the Naked Nagas', *Time*, 1 January 1945.

p. 411 **'An extraordinary girl'** *Ibid.*

p. 411 **'How could one explain'** Ursula Graham Bower, *The Hidden Land* (John Murray, 1953), p. 238.

p. 412 **'His was officially'** IWM, file no. 12438 03/23/1, diary of Lieutenant B. K. 'Barry' Bowman.

p. 412 **'The cooks ... had prepared'** Unpublished account by Arthur Davies.

p. 413 **'What with bloody Dunkirk'** IWM, Oral History Project, file no. 20461, interview with Private Ivan Daunt.

p. 413 **'As I woke up'** Interviewed for this book.

p. 413 **'That's me finished'** Interviewed for this book.

p. 414 **'You've done me'** Interviewed for this book.

p. 414 **'Everybody was needed'** Interviewed for this book.

p. 414 'Dad would be' Robert Street, *A Brummie in Burma* (Barny Books, 1997), p. 62.

p. 414 'Wellington Massar belonged' *Ibid*.

p. 414 'His bereaved aunt' NA, WO 172/5045, War Diary of the 1st Assam Regiment, Appendix A, 'Citation and Speeches made on 20th August 1944 at investiture of the I.D.S.M. won posthumously by No.1778 Sepoy Wellington Massar.'

p. 416 'We'd had enough' Interviewed for this book.

p. 416 'I will not say that' Hansard, HC Deb (series 5) (29 September 1944) vol. 403 cc 605–707.

p. 416 'These are the men' *Ibid*.

p. 417 'whose homes have' *Ibid*.

p. 417 'above all for a' NA, CAB 66/59/22.

p. 417 'though the fighting' NA, WO 222/158, 'Divisional Psychiatry', Captain Paul Davis.

p. 417 'I had the most' Mountbatten, *Personal Diary of Admiral the Lord Louis Mountbatten*, p. 116.

p. 418 'we saw him go' Field Marshal Lord Slim, *Defeat into Victory* (Cassell, 1956), p. 385.

p. 418 'was never able' Robert Lyman, *Slim: Master of War* (Constable and Robinson, 2004), p. 237.

p. 418 With exasperating discretion Slim, *Defeat into Victory*, p. 523.

p. 418 'The blokes just went mad' Interviewed for this book.

p. 419 'Finally they realised' Robert Street, *The Siege of Kohima: The Battle for Burma* (Barny Books, 2003), p. 147.

p. 419 'Naw. You can't be like' Interviewed for this book.

p. 419 'I said to him' IWM, Oral History Project, file no. 25696, interview with Frank Infanti.

p. 419 'I made them dig' Interviewed for this book.

p. 420 'Hiroshima was dead' Interviewed for this book.

p. 420 'I telephoned to' Interviewed for this book.

p. 420 'I told him' Interviewed for this book.

p. 420 'Everybody was crying' Interviewed for this book.

p. 421 'officers and men engaged' John Dower, *Embracing Defeat: Japan in the Aftermath of World War II* (Penguin, 1999), p. 59.

p. 421 'vast stretches of' Hans H. Baerwald, *Postwar Japan: A Reminiscence* (Japan Policy Research Institute, 2002).

p. 422 'My children wanted' Interviewed for this book.

p. 422 'I want to take' Interviewed for this book.

p. 422 'He pawned stuff' Interviewed for this book.

p. 422 'I sensed it as a' Interviewed for this book.

p. 422 'I will leave' Interviewed for this book.

p. 423 'Afterwards he asked' Interviewed for this book.

p. 423 'It was so sad' Interviewed for this book.

p. 423 'I was careful of' Memories of Kotuku Sato by his Daughter Yukiko Matsumura.

p. 423 'He was nothing but' Essay by Fumiko Sato, cited in 'Burma Campaign Memoir', Retsu 10708 Unit Veterans Group.

p. 424 'I didn't have a' Interviewed for this book.

p. 424 'Some said' NDL, Interview with Lieutenant General Renya Mutaguchi, 1965.

p. 424 'General Sato passed away' *Ibid.*

p. 425 'The massacres were' Robin Rowland, *Sugamo and The River Kwai*, paper presented to 'Encounters at Sugamo Prison, Tokyo 1945–52, The American Occupation of Japan and Memories of the Asia-Pacific War, Princeton University, 9 May 2003.

p. 425 'They asked his family' Interviewed for this book.

Twenty-six: The Quiet Fathers

p. 426 'I started to feel' Interviewed for this book.

p. 427 'It was pretty hard to' Interviewed for this book.

p. 427 'I realised I was' Interviewed for this book.

p. 427 'but I don't think' Interviewed for this book.

p. 429 'I got to the second' Interviewed for this book.

p. 430 'if I can do the army' Interviewed for this book.

p. 430 'a kind dad' Interviewed for this book.

p. 430 'I hate people' Interviewed for this book.

p. 430 'It never affected me' Interviewed for this book.

p. 430 'I would wake up' Interviewed for this book.

p. 431 'Here we were bashing' Interviewed for this book.

p. 431 'I felt I couldn't' Interviewed for this book.

p. 431 'It is just fragments' Interviewed for this book.

p. 432 'I was ten' Letter to author from Mrs Christine Porteus, 28 June 2010.

p. 432 'The War was generally' Margery Willis, correspondence with author, March 2008.

p. 434 'Wherever he was' Interviewed for this book.

p. 435 'his personal tenacity' NA, WO/373/32, 'Recommendation for the award of D.S.O. to Lieutenant Colonel Henry Jarvis Laverty.'

p. 435 'The command and staff' E. B. Stanley Clark and A. T. Tillot, *From Kent to Kohima* (Gale and Polden, 1951), pp. 123–6.

p. 435 'complete idiot, should' Interviewed for this book.

p. 436 'grave injustice' Richards Papers, Letter of Lieutenant Colonel G. Borrowman to Lieutenant Colonel A. Campbell, 2 August 1956.

p. 436 'What surprised me' *Ibid*.

p. 436 'I therefore chose to' Richards Papers, Letter of Lieutenant Colonel Arthur Campbell to Lieutenant Colonel G. Borrowman, 13 August 1956.

p. 436 'would like to rub' Richards Papers, Letter of Lieutenant Colonel G. Borrowman to Brigadier Hugh Richards, 9 March 1956.

p. 436 'to the garrison' Richards Papers, Letter of Lieutenant Colonel G. Borrowman to Lieutenant Colonel A. Campbell, 24 August 1956.

p. 436 '[I] would have thought' *Ibid*.

p. 436 'I also feel that' Richards Papers, Letter of Brigadier M. R. Roberts, to Lieutenant Colonel G. Borrowman, 15 March 1956.

p. 437 'You will remember' Richards Papers, Letter of Lieutenant Colonel G. Borrowman to Field Marshal Lord Slim, 25 July 1956.

p. 437 'solely responsible for' NA, WO 373/35, 'Citation for the award of D.S.O. to Colonel Hugh Upton Richards, 22 September 1944.'

p. 437 'I am sorry that Laverty' Richards Papers, Letter of Field Marshal Lord Slim to Lieutenant Colonel G. Borrowman, 27 August 1956.

p. 437 'as grave an injury' Richards Papers, Letter of Brigadier Hugh Richards to Lieutenant Colonel Arthur Campbell, October 19 1956.

p. 437 'I am glad to' Richards Papers, Letter of Lieutenant Colonel Arthur Campbell to Brigadier Hugh Richards, 30 October 1956.

p. 439 'I tried to raise it' Interviewed for this book.

p. 439 'We had been apart' Interviewed for this book.

p. 439 'there wasn't a family' Interviewed for this book.

p. 439 'Up to twenty or so' Letter to the author from C. Booth, 11 May 2009.

p. 440 'So far the Graves' Letter of Charles Pawsey to Lieutenant Colonel G. Borrowman, 30 September 1944.

p. 441 'Independence will mean' Ramachandra Guha, *India After Gandhi* (Pan Macmillan Ltd, 2007), pp. 269–278.

p. 441 I will ask them to' Anne Yates and Lewis Chester, *The Troublemaker – Michael Scott and his Lonely Struggle Against Injustice* (Aurum Press, 2006), p. 242.

p. 441 'When the British left' Interviewed for this book.

p. 442 'Individuals told of' *The Nagas, an unknown war*, Gavin Young (*Observer*, London 30 April, 7 May and 14 May 1962), cited Anne Yates and Lewis Chester, *The Troublemaker – Michael Scott and his Lonely Struggle Against Injustice* (Aurum books, 2006), pp. 244–245.

p. 442 'In the interest of' 'Naga Queen' article by Trina Betts.

p. 442 'knock some sense' IWM, file no. NRA 28568, letter from Lady Pawsey to Arthur Swinson, 15 February 1965, Swinson.

p. 443 'like the Burma Retreat' Pieter Steyn, *A History of the Assam Regiment* (Longman Orient, 1959), p. 245.

p. 444 'I had a double-barreled' Interviewed for this book.

Epilogue: After Hatred

p. 445 'Perhaps it is my' Interviewed for this book.

p. 445 'I did a very wrong' Interviewed for this book.

p. 446 'It hurts me still' Interviewed for this book.

p. 446 'I was a Buddhist' Interviewed for this book.

p. 447 'Did we fight a war' Interviewed for this book.

p. 448 'garrotted in the street' Interviewed for this book.

p. 449 'I had to baptise' Interviewed for this book.

INDEX

291, 316–17, 319, 370, 371, 390–2,
393, 394–5, 396; Japanese plan to
attack 115–20, 140–1, 156, 157;
Kohima road 29, 33, 80, 80n, 221,
226, 235, 282, 288, 365, 366, 385,
395, 455; non-combatants in 198;
order to withdraw from mistimed,
British 157, 175, 235, 388n;
reinforcements arrive at, British
Army 278, 390; siege/blockade
broken 368, 385, 388n; supply
problems 236, 278, 368; V Force
in 49, 165, 189

Imphal Plain xx, 31, 141, 147, 157, 175,
235, 292, 368, 416

India: battles in *see under individual
area, battle, campaign or place name*;
British Empire in (Raj) xix, xx, 5,
77, 174, 282, 409, 428–9, 443, 444,
448; British use of nationals in
intelligence gathering 36, 46–50,
53–7, 184n, 189–91, 212, 223, 293,
295–6, 364–5; effect of Kohima
upon xix, 428–9; independence 410,
411, 429,443; Japanese advance into
111–20, 140, 148, 163–6, 173, 176,
193, 194, 195, 196, 209, 291;
Japanese attempts to turn people
against British xix, xx, 85–7, 85n,
116, 156, 158, 160, 230, 237, 239,
296; Japanese spies in 111, 146, 156,
157, 158; Japanese withdrawal from
xvii, 390–2, 397, 411–18; Naga
people and *see* Naga people;
nationalism 41, 43, 43n, 69, 70, 72,
84, 85n, 85, 87–8, 386, 410, 428–9;
partition 443; retreating British
troops arrive from Burma in 26–8,
29–30 *see also under individual area
or place name*

Indian Air Force 133

Indian Army xvii, 184, 386; barracks
life 89; battle readiness 76; battles

*see under individual area, battle,
campaign or nation name*; in Burma
5, 9, 12, 12n, 13, 17, 18, 19;
Churchill's mistrust of 84–5;
importance to British Army of
84–5; INA and xx, 85–7, 85n, 116,
156, 160, 230, 237, 239, 296, 403;
Indian nationalism and xx, 85–7,
85n, 116, 156, 160, 230, 237, 239,
296, 403; 'josh' groups 87, 160;
loyalty/desertion of troops 17, 84–8,
84n, 85n, 87, 90, 116, 160, 230, 237,
239, 267, 353, 360–1; morale 76, 87,
160; officer corps, transformation of
88; pay 88; proportion of 14th
Army 84; recruitment 76; reform of
88–9; refugees from units overrun
by Japanese 292; retreat from
Burma into India 14–17, 18, 21, 23,
29, 30–1; Singapore, fall of and 84,
85; units *see* British/Burmese/
Indian/Nepalese Army units *see also*
British Army

Indian Civil Service 32, 190, 282

Indian National Army (INA)
(Japanese) xx, 85–7, 85n, 116, 156,
160, 230, 237, 239, 296, 403

Infanti, Lance Corporal Frank 96–7,
136, 137, 297, 301–2, 328, 360, 419

intelligence: Allies xx, 1–5, 25, 36,
46–50, 53–7, 93, 112–13, 156, 157,
157n, 158, 165–6, 169, 184n,
189–92, 212, 223, 293, 295–6,
364–5; Burma Intelligence Corps
157n; Chindits xx, 25, 46, 93,
112–13, 112n, 114, 149, 156, 165–6,
165n, 170n, 171, 180, 278, 316, 368,
400, 402, 412, 459; Force 131 47n;
Force 136 157n; goes astray 194,
194n, 201; INA, Japanese use of
86–7; ISLD (Inter-Services Liasion
Department) 157n; Japanese Army
3, 4, 9, 86–7, 111, 112–14, 146, 147,

156, 157, 158, 316, 325–6; Japanese
plans 156, 157n, 166, 169, 184–5,
194; Japanese spies in Burma 3, 4, 9;
Japanese spies in India 111, 146,
156, 157, 158; Japanese troop
strength 194, 194n, 201, 212, 223;
Japanese use of Chindits 112–14;
Naga gathering of 36, 46–50, 53–7,
158, 184n, 189–91, 212, 223, 293,
295–6, 364–5; Special Operations
Executive (SOE) 47n, 157n; ULTRA
code breakers 157n; V Force 47–50,
47n, 53, 55, 56, 57, 147, 148, 156,
157n, 161, 164, 165, 189, 190, 191,
192, 194, 194n, 195, 212, 214, 229,
293, 296, 364, 365, 402–3, 407, 410;
Z Force 47n, 157n, 194n
Ismay, General 'Pug' 369
Ito, Masanori 405

Jackson, Private Tom 347–8, 354
Japan: 'Absolute Defence Sphere' 117;
atomic bomb, US attack with
419–20; China, war with 4, 5, 109,
110, 110n, 111, 150, 151, 152, 287,
318; coup attempt, 1936 109–10,
109; Hiroshima 419–20; military
ethics and training 106, 107–8,
107n; Pacific war 110, 111, 147, 151,
290; post-war 419–25, 446; US
Occupation of 421–2
Japanese, Air Force 5, 10–12, 14, 22–3,
91, 105, 121, 132, 133, 146, 147, 149,
325–6
Japanese Army, Imperial xv–xvi; air
support 5, 10–12, 14, 22–3, 91, 105,
121, 132, 133, 146, 147, 149, 326;
artillery xvii, 125, 146, 164, 168,
193, 199, 201, 204, 214, 217, 218,
226, 235, 239, 243, 262, 286, 325–6,
338, 350, 352, 353, 370, 371, 376;
battles see under individual area,
battle, campaign, operation or nation

name; Burma, invasion and
occupation of 3, 10–13, 14, 15,
17–23; casualty numbers xvii,
126–7, 134, 136, 198, 200, 202–4,
209n, 215n, 250–1, 260, 278, 286,
291, 373, 399–400, 402, 402, 403,
405, 407; character of men
xvii–xviii, 20–1, 22, 76, 85n, 130,
131, 134, 138, 149–53, 208, 277, 281,
287–8, 318, 326–7, 389; in China 4,
5, 109, 110, 110n, 111, 150, 151, 152,
287, 318; Chindwin, crossing of 120,
140, 163–5; coup attempt, 1936
109–10, 109; disease and illness in
xvii, 14, 114, 155, 167, 291, 297, 389,
396, 397, 399, 400, 402, 421–2;
Greater East Asia Co-Prosperity
Sphere and 109; intelligence 3, 4, 9,
86–7, 111, 112–14, 146, 147, 156,
157, 158, 316, 325–6; *Kempeitai*
147–8, 151, 326, 422; locals peoples,
treatment of 15, 18, 144, 145, 196,
233–5, 293; 'March on Delhi' 116,
117; military ethics and training
106, 107–8, 107n; morale 147–8,
150–1, 258–9, 317, 319, 372, 397;
Pacific war 110, 111, 147, 151, 290;
Plan 21 112; plan to attack Indian
frontier 111–20; power of army over
government 108, 109–10, 109;
prisoners, treatment of xvii–xviii,
20–1, 85n, 130, 131, 150, 208, 281;
Russia, war with 4, 18, 109, 107,
109, 143, 424, 424; snipers 126, 135,
201, 206, 216, 229, 230, 251, 254,
255, 256, 262, 263, 268, 269, 298,
303, 306, 309, 310, 312, 319, 329,
334, 338, 344, 354, 355, 358, 379;
suicide attacks 319, 333, 372; supply
problems xvii, xviii, 112–13, 114,
115, 116, 117, 134, 140, 143, 146,
147–50, 151, 152, 154, 155, 157, 158,
162–3, 166–8, 198–9, 204, 209n,